‹§ VOLUME 1 §›

THE PAPERS OF JOSEPH HENRY

December 1797–October 1832

The Albany Years

Joseph Henry (1797–1878), miniature circa 1829, attributed to Julius Rubens Ames (1801–1850). This reproduction is from a nineteenth-century copy in the Albany Academy. Original is in the Smithsonian Institution.

The Papers of
JOSEPH HENRY

Editor: NATHAN REINGOLD
Assistant Editors: Stuart Pierson and Arthur P. Molella
with the assistance of James M. Hobbins
and John R. Kerwood

VOLUME 1

December 1797 – October 1832
The Albany Years

SMITHSONIAN INSTITUTION PRESS
CITY OF WASHINGTON
1972

Published in the United States by the Smithsonian Institution Press.
Distributed in the United States and Canada by George Braziller, Inc.;
in the United Kingdom, the traditional British market, and Europe by
David & Charles, Ltd.; and in all other countries by Feffer and Simons, Inc.

Designed by Crimilda Pontes.
Produced in the United States by Connecticut Printers.

ENDPAPERS: *The original Albany Academy building as it appears today.*
The statue is of Joseph Henry. Photograph by Alfred K. Sabisch.

Library of Congress Cataloging in Publication Data

Henry, Joseph, 1797–1878.
The papers of Joseph Henry.

Includes bibliographical references.

CONTENTS: *v. 1. December 1797–October 1832: the Albany years.*

1. Science—Addresses, essays, lectures.
2. Science—History—United States—Addresses, essays, lectures.
3. Smithsonian Institution—Addresses, essays, lectures.
  I. Reingold, Nathan, ed.
Q143.H6A2 1972   537'.0924   72–2005
ISBN 0–87474–123–8

To the memory of Joseph Henry and his friends,
the founders of the American scientific community

❧ CONTENTS ❧

Contents

⸭ ILLUSTRATIONS ⸭

Frontispiece: Joseph Henry

Following page 248:

Ann Alexander Henry, Joseph Henry's mother

View of Albany, 1828

Map of the City of Albany

Lewis Caleb Beck

Theodric Romeyn Beck

Stephen Van Rensselaer

Simeon DeWitt

Letter from Joseph Henry to
Benjamin Silliman, Sr.,
December 10, 1830

The large electromagnet
constructed by Henry in early 1831

✦ INTRODUCTION ✦

The common belief that we gain "historical perspective" with increasing distance seems to me utterly to misrepresent the actual situation. What we gain is merely confidence in generalization which we would never dare to make if we had access to the real wealth of contemporary evidence.
—O. Neugebauer, *The Exact Sciences in Antiquity*, viii.

Making the past come alive is popularly regarded as the task of history. Few practitioners of the discipline have the literary skills necessary to do this, and most content themselves with a more modest task—grappling with the historiographic problems bequeathed by their predecessors. Fortunately or not, there is little secondary literature on Joseph Henry. Nor are the editors of the Henry Papers afflicted with a massive, symbolic Henry, an icon embedded in both the lay and the professional minds, as in the case of the Founding Fathers and such popular heroes as Abraham Lincoln. Though hundreds of people on any summer day on the Mall in Washington, D.C., pause before the statue of Henry, which stands in front of the old Smithsonian Building, or glance at his paean to the civilizing power of science inscribed on the National Museum of History and Technology, it is unlikely that many recognize him, or carry away a firm impression of who he was and what he did. From this obscurity, we propose to rescue him.

There have been honors and recognitions, to be sure. His fellow scientists bestowed on him a measure of immortality by designating the "henry" as the unit of inductance, an honor Joseph Henry undoubtedly would have cherished greatly. Above all, he was a physical scientist, and, yet, the eponymic blessing is no substitute for the historic or real Henry, his struggles, achievements, and failures. Another symbolic Henry exists, but few lift their eyes from printed pages to see him. Under the dome of the Main Reading Room of the Library of Congress are sixteen bronze portrait statues, "representative of human development and civilization."[1] And there is Joseph Henry, along with Moses, Newton, Saint Paul, Columbus, Fulton, Gibbon, Herodotus, James Kent, Michelangelo, Solon, Plato, Bacon,

---

[1] H. Small, *Handbook of the New Library of Congress* (Boston, 1901), p. 64.

xvii

Shakespeare, Homer, and Beethoven. The editors do not pretend to fathom the rationale behind these choices nor do we necessarily rank Henry with any of the others. The bronze Henry is symbolic, we feel, of two facts, albeit little-appreciated facts. The first is local—Joseph Henry was a founder of the Library of Congress. More important is the second— Joseph Henry was a founder of the American scientific community. That is, something was being said at the turn of the nineteenth century about Americans and science.

What follows in these volumes is a documentary history of how a poor boy from upstate New York, early in the last century, generated both symbols—the physical unit and the bronze image. By going in great depth beyond the phrases denoted by the symbols, the editors hope to merge the two into a real, credible human being whose intellectual and administrative careers were of one piece.

The inaugural volume of our series documents the formative years of Henry's career in Albany, where he studied, worked, and carried on research until leaving for Princeton at the end of October 1832. For the first twenty-five years of Henry's life, documentation is scarce; an oral tradition familiar to Henry biographers and memorialists has preserved some of the flavor of the early years. This tradition has it that Henry, the son of William and Ann Alexander Henry, descended from Scottish Presbyterians who immigrated to the Albany region in 1775.[2] His father died when the son was young, leaving the family in very modest circumstances. Additional details about Joseph Henry's origins and youth—his years with his uncle in nearby Galway, his apprenticeship to an Albany watchmaker and silversmith, his flirtation with the theater—can be found in Thomas Coulson's biography of Henry and elsewhere.[3] Contemporary documentation on Henry essentially begins with his appearance in Albany's scientific and educational community in the mid-1820s.

Aside from documenting Henry's personal career, a major task of this volume is to describe the Albany milieu as an influence on Henry's scientific growth. Our episodic description will encompass the Albany environment for science, in particular, and for culture, in its broad definition. With variations, what happened in Albany was repeated in American metropolitan centers, as well as in lesser sites. We may even suspect related developments in European provincial centers.

---

[2] Among the Henry Papers in the Smithsonian Institution Archives is a brief family history as told by Henry's aunt, Elizabeth Selkirk. Following his notes on Elizabeth's account, Henry wrote that, according to his grandfather, his name originally was spelled Hendry or Hendrie.

[3] *Joseph Henry, His Life and Work* (Princeton, 1950), pp. 3–15.

Early nineteenth-century Albany was not the American frontier town one might expect but a fair-sized, wealthy, and vigorous city. In 1820, Albany was the ninth largest city in the United States; by 1830 it ranked eighth.[4] It was the seat of state government and a trading and manufacturing center at the junction of the Hudson River and Erie Canal (after its opening in 1825). Albany's leading citizens—local and state politicians, lawyers and merchants, the old Dutch families, and the newcomers from New England—actively participated in the city's progress and growth. In many respects, Henry's Albany experience foreshadowed his life and future role in Washington as Secretary of the Smithsonian Institution. The two capitals were approximately the same size (Albany, in fact, was slightly larger in 1846), and Henry learned to move as freely among Washington's politicians as he had among Albany's. He may also have acquired here his later antipathy to intermingling science and politics.

The political life, economic activity, and the availability of transportation fostered a varied and vigorous provincial culture in Albany. Newspapers, books, museums, and public lectures were readily available. Popular establishments such as the New York State Museum and Henry Trowbridge's Museum were advertised in local newspapers during the 1810s and 1820s.[5] Although both museums catered to public tastes, offering freak shows, "natural curiosities," and pseudoscientific entertainment, they also advertised modest scientific exhibits. In February 1828, the State Museum promised "Amusement and Science Combined," featuring, among other things, a mechanical model of the solar system. (The eventual decline of the museum into little better than a sideshow perhaps contributed to Henry's lifelong reluctance to treat science as mere entertainment.)

Albany had libraries, reading rooms, book shops, and book auctions. The New York State Library, established in 1818 for the use of the Legislature and today one of the nation's foremost libraries, had by Henry's young manhood amassed an impressive collection, including considerable scientific holdings. Books were obtainable by other citizens in subscription libraries and reading rooms, such as John Cook's, which, in February 1810, advertised "1200 volumes, useful and entertaining."[6] In 1820, wealthy citizens founded an apprentices' library, a forerunner of Albany's public library. Containing over 1500 books in 1821,[7] the library was just the place

---

[4] *American Almanac and Repository of Useful Knowledge for the Year 1848* (Boston, 1847), p. 213.

[5] *The Daily Advertiser,* February 29, 1828, p. 1, and *The Albany Register,* February 13, 1810, p. 1.

[6] *The Albany Register,* February 13, 1810, p. 1.

[7] William Esmond Rowley, "Albany: A Tale of Two Cities, 1820–1880" (Ph.D. dissertation, Harvard University, 1967), p. 83. Rowley surveys Albany's book and newspaper resources on pp. 82–83, 86–88.

that an ambitious boy like Henry might frequent to further his self-education. The book trade was flourishing, and local newspapers regularly advertised book sales and auctions. There were undoubtedly a number of large personal libraries. An avid reader and book collector, Henry had probably collected a respectable library before leaving the city. (Although the acquisition dates for most books in the surviving Henry library are unknown, we have been able to assign a substantial number of volumes to his Albany period.) Scientific books considered rare today apparently were obtainable in Henry's Albany. An examination of the catalogs and holdings of the libraries of the Albany Institute and the Albany Academy reveals that Henry donated first or early editions of treatises by Boyle, Descartes, and the Abbé Nollet.[8]

Public lectures on the sciences were commonplace in Albany, as they were throughout much of nineteenth-century America. On February 13, 1810, for example, the *Albany Register* announced a series of biweekly "Lectures on Chemistry and the Auxiliary branches of science," by an unnamed speaker.[9] Henry may have attended such lectures as a young man. As a teacher and physicist, we know he delivered public lectures on chemistry and natural philosophy.

Two institutions, established as Joseph Henry approached maturity, were the special pride of Albany's cultured citizens. The Albany Academy, where Henry studied and taught, and the Albany Institute, the forum for his early scientific work, were kindred institutions, founded upon similar ideologies by many of the same people. In the absence of direct evidence about Henry, the initial years, covered by the present volume, focus upon the origins and early growth of these two learned institutions. Their establishment involved a wide spectrum of the Albany elite—members of the Board of Regents of the University of the State of New York, political figures, landowners, and businessmen. Since the founders were concerned not only with formalities of organization but with details of scientific work at the Institute and the subjects taught at the Academy, the records of their deliberations provide a useful view of scientific and cultural attitudes in the Albany of Henry's day.

Despite the developing environment for learning and science, Henry's first inclinations were toward the theater. In later life, he had vague recollections of boyhood acting interests and even of writing his own play, "The

---

[8] Robert Boyle's *New Experiments, Physico-Mechanical, Touching the Air,* 2d ed. (Oxford, 1662) and *Certain Physiological Essays* (London, 1661), bound together. René Descartes, *Lettres de M. Descartes* (Paris, 1657); Jean-Antoine Nollet, *Leçons de physique expérimentale,* 6 volumes in 12 (Paris, 1759–1764).

[9] Page 3.

Fisherman of Bagdad."[10] A few days after Henry's death, the politician and publisher Thurlow Weed, a close friend from Henry's Albany days, described the seriousness of these theatrical aspirations in a letter to the editors of the *New York Daily Tribune:*[11]

> During the war with England, which had just closed, the Green Street Theatre, with a strong company, liberally patronized by the officers of the army stationed in Greenbush, awakened much enthusiasm among the young gentlemen of Albany, several of whom formed themselves into an amateur theatrical company. They fitted up a hall formerly used for dramatic representations, then known as the Thespian Hotel, on the corner of North Pearl and Patroon Sts. They attracted large audiences. Joseph Henry became a "bright particular star." His young *Norval, Damon* and even *Hamlet,* were pronounced equal in conception and execution to the personations of experienced and popular actors. His friends, charmed with his talents and genius, urged him to adopt the stage as a profession. His own thoughts and inclination rendered him a willing listener. Soon the manager of the Green Street Theatre offered him a permanent engagement with a liberal salary. With that the young aspirant for dramatic honors was greatly delighted.

Weed then recounted a decisive incident which "gave to the practical sciences one of their most distinguished ornaments." The intervention of T. Romeyn Beck, Henry's future mentor, induced him to forego a promising theatrical career for further schooling:

> But Dr. T. Romeyn Beck, principal of the Albany Academy, believed that there was a way opened to the young man promising greater usefulness and more enduring honors than the drama could confer. After consultation with the trustees, Dr. Beck invited young Henry to enter upon and complete a gratuitous academic course. While anxiously considering these conflicting offers three of his intimate friends, James Dexter, a law student, James Hunter, a printer, and myself, were called into consultation. Hunter and myself saw for our friend in a dramatic career assured fame and fortune. Dexter, less enthusiastic, preferred academic honors to those of the "sock" and "buskin." He urged, calmly but forcibly, that if the stage was to be ultimately

---

[10] Told to William Jones Rhees, his chief clerk at the Smithsonian Institution; Rhees's notes on the "Life of Prof. Henry" are dated June 15, 1868, and preserved in the Rhees Papers, Henry E. Huntington Library.

[11] May 22, 1878, p. 5. For a description of the theater in early nineteenth-century Albany, see Rowley, "Albany: A Tale of Two Cities," p. 84. We cannot vouch for Weed's account of how Henry entered the Academy.

adopted as a profession, an academic education would increase our friend's chances for enduring success, and that after completing his education he would be quite young enough to become an actor. This argument, after a long and anxious mental struggle, proved effectual. The following day "Joe Henry" rejected Manager Bernard's dramatic offer, and took his seat in the Albany Academy.

We have no further evidence, direct or indirect, on the circumstances of Henry's enrollment at the Academy, but his quest for learning was evidently long in gestation. According to later recollection, the young Henry "accidentally picked up in the house a book of a scientific character which he read with attention & it led to a new epoch in his life. His thirst for knowledge now became intense."[12] The crucial volume was very likely the *Lectures on Experimental Philosophy, Astronomy, and Chemistry* (London, 1808) by the British divine and author George Gregory. Henry's copy of the Gregory book, preserved among his memorabilia at the National Museum of History and Technology, bears the following inscription, written when Henry presented the book to his son William in 1837:

> This book although by no means a profound work has under Providence exerted a remarkable influence on my life. It accidentally fell into my hands when I was about 16 years old and was the first book I ever read with attention.
>
> It opened to me a new world of thought and enjoyment, invested things before almost unnoticed with the highest interest fixed my mind on the study of nature and caused me to resolve at the time of reading it that I would immediately commence to devote my life to the acquisition of knowledge.

As for Henry's formal schooling, various retrospective accounts indicate that his education was sparse prior to his entrance into the Academy. There are mentions of elementary schooling in Galway and of night classes attended in Albany; possibly he followed public lectures given locally on various subjects. We know that Henry attended the Albany Academy from 1819 to 1822, with an undetermined time off to earn money, probably teaching in country schools and perhaps tutoring the children of the "Great Patroon" Stephen Van Rensselaer. Virtually no contemporary evidence has survived about Henry's studies at the Academy nor do we know what provisions were made for an over-age student. Three Henry mathematical exercise notebooks (summarized in our text)[13] date from this pe-

---

[12] Rhees, "Life of Prof. Henry."
[13] "Exercises from Keith's Trigonometry," September 1, 1821, and November 22, 1821; "Student Exercise Book," [June 27, 1822].

riod, but they consist chiefly of rote exercises revealing little about the development of Henry's thinking. Contemporary descriptions of curricula and textbooks disclose that the Academy offered Henry a good mathematical and scientific education, perhaps comparable to a college curriculum of the day. T. R. Beck later reported that Henry performed so well at his studies that he employed him as his assistant in a chemistry lecture series given in the winter of 1823–1824.[14]

Whatever Henry's education at the Academy and elsewhere, it is significant that he always considered himself "principally self educated."[15] Although an avid reader and assiduous note taker, uncertain spelling and grammar attest to his lack of early formal instruction. As he grew in knowledge and as he matured, his writing skills gradually improved. To convey a feeling for this maturation, we have conscientiously retained Henry's original wordings and spellings, however awkward, except where his meaning becomes unclear.

Shortly after completing his studies, Henry began to participate in the Albany Institute and, later, the Albany Academy. He appeared initially as one of the curators of the Albany Lyceum of Natural History, a predecessor of the Albany Institute. After the Lyceum merged in 1824 with the local Society for the Promotion of Useful Arts to form the Institute, Henry was appointed one of the curators of the Institute's Second Department, its natural history component. Contemporary records unfortunately do not reveal what interests Henry may have had in natural history or what his curatorial duties entailed. In March 1829, Henry resigned as curator and became librarian of the Institute. Meanwhile, he participated actively in the scientific life of the newly established scientific society. Minutes of the meetings of the Albany Institute record frequent Henry donations, demonstrations, and lectures. In 1824, he delivered before the Institute his first public scientific lecture, a discussion of the properties of steam (printed below).[16]

During this period, the Albany Institute was housed in the Albany Academy, a second focus of Henry's professional interests. In September 1826, upon the forced resignation of his predecessor, Henry was appointed Professor of Mathematics and Natural Philosophy at the Academy where he remained until leaving for Princeton. Shortly after coming to the Academy he became its librarian. According to surviving catalogs, the Academy and Institute libraries, both housed in the Academy building, had respectable

[14] T. R. Beck to Martin Van Buren, March 10, 1826, printed below.
[15] See below, Henry's letter to John Maclean, June 28, 1832.
[16] "On the Chemical and Mechanical Effects of Steam," October 30, 1824.

collections for their day. Henry donated numerous volumes to both libraries and no doubt took full advantage of the available resources for his continuing self-education.

An unmistakable self-confidence and purposefulness accompanied Henry's emergence in Albany's learned community. A surviving draft of his
inaugural speech at the Albany Academy reveals that, as early as 1826,
Henry had formed strong opinions about the scientific enterprise and
about his own role as teacher and professional scientist. His dedication and
professionalism were evident even in the earliest stages of his career, especially in his persistent efforts to differentiate himself and all men of science
from the plethora of scientific amateurs and charlatans. Henry's self-assurance and decisiveness were facets of a developing scientific sensibility;
though a latecomer to science, Henry seemed almost born to his scientific
role. His early manuscripts disclose a certain shrewdness and hardheaded-
ness, a penchant for precise, unembellished discourse. A passing remark in
one of his early journals provides a glimpse of the typical Henry, austerely
ironical: "May 19th 1826 . . . When I visited the falls [i.e., Niagara] in Oct
1825 they did not answer my expectations. Perhaps I did not view them
with propper poetical feelings, but in this visit I have been more fortunate."[17]

A further measure of Henry's self-assurance and independence was his
decision to work in experimental physics, an unusual choice of specialty
since most Americans with scientific inclinations in that period gravitated
toward medicine, natural history, or engineering. Astronomy was the favored physical science for the few so disposed. In his research on electricity
and magnetism, Henry necessarily relied primarily on foreign literature
and looked abroad for his scientific models. Yet, Henry also responded to
scientific trends and practices within his immediate milieu.

Although no direct evidence of his deliberations has survived, it is clear
that Henry might have considered several alternatives to a career in experimental physics. A natural history tradition, broadly defined, was widely
followed in America. Henry's friends and colleagues in Albany, the brothers T. Romeyn Beck and Lewis C. Beck, were superb specimens of this tradition. Both Becks were physicians with collateral interests in various
branches of natural history, including botany and even chemistry as they
related to materia medica and mineralogy. Most chemistry in the United
States prior to this period was associated with medicine and natural history.
Similar relations in Europe were, perhaps, counterbalanced by a stronger
autonomous chemical tradition. Henry's curatorship at the Albany Ly-

---

[17] "Henry's Canal Tour Journal," printed below.

ceum and Institute suggests a possible early leaning toward natural history as does his assisting T. R. Beck's chemistry lectures at the Albany Academy. In 1832, Henry also collaborated with L. C. Beck in a series of public lectures on chemistry. Additionally, Henry's electromagnetic research probably derived in part from his chemical interests. Because acid solutions were used to generate the electric current, electromagnetic effects quite often were regarded as a subspecies of chemical phenomena. Furthermore, following the Becks to medical practice for a source of income may very well have occurred to Joseph Henry.

Henry might have considered a career in geology, another branch of the natural history tradition popular in nineteenth-century America. In 1826 he participated in a geological field trip on the Erie Canal conducted by Amos Eaton, founder of Troy's Rensselaer Polytechnic Institute and a leading American geologist. Henry's notes on the canal tour, reproduced in this volume, reveal an obvious facility and a serious interest in the subject. His interests persisted, for Henry later delivered lectures on geology at Princeton, a matter to be considered in a subsequent volume.

Conceivably, Joseph Henry could have become a physician, mineralogical chemist, or natural historian, but leavening came from another direction. Henry's friend and associate Simeon DeWitt, mapmaker and Surveyor-General of New York, represented a different constellation of interests. DeWitt, a skilled surveyor with a wide range of interests in matters physical, is an American instance of the tradition of the "mathematical practitioners."[18] One of Henry's first jobs was to head a state road survey along New York's southern tier, and there is evidence that, if offered the opportunity, he would have pursued a career in civil engineering. Surveying led both DeWitt and Henry to a series of interconnected physical problems. To check the accuracy of their land measurements, they reckoned the positions of celestial bodies and studied deviations in terrestrial magnetism. Explaining terrestrial magnetic phenomena became an end in itself and one of Henry's abiding scientific interests. This is not to say his investigation of such phenomena derived solely from surveying; rather the physical research and surveying were closely interrelated and mutually reinforcing. In turn, his research in terrestrial magnetism was linked directly and analogically with his work in electromagnetism. It also stimulated a concern with meteorology, since, in Henry's day, the earth's magnetism was thought to depend upon atmospheric phenomena (the precise interrelations are explained in annotations to relevant documents in our text). In taking meas-

---

[18] As defined in E. G. R. Taylor's *Mathematical Practitioners of Tudor and Stuart England* (Cambridge, 1954).

urements of magnetic deviations and intensity, Henry and others would routinely record temperature, wind direction, and general weather conditions. In 1825, Simeon DeWitt introduced a resolution to the State Board of Regents requiring each academy in the state to send the Regents annual meteorological reports. The resolution carried and, subsequently, Henry cooperated with T. R. Beck in compiling the data for the annual reports.

Another important Henry trait was implicit in the DeWitt surveying tradition: an interest in applying mathematics to nature. Although the standard trigonometric manipulations used in surveying were relatively unsophisticated mathematics, they instilled in Henry a respectful feeling for mathematical application. Henry's own physical research was overwhelmingly experimental, but he was clearly at ease with mathematical thinking. His reading notes contain extensive references to European literature in mathematical physics, and his early lectures reflect a high regard for mathematics itself, as well as for its scientific and technological application. At the Albany Academy, Henry taught mathematics through the calculus. Such preoccupations, we believe, immediately set Henry apart from an experimental physicist such as Michael Faraday, who was basically antipathetic to mathematical physics. We believe that Henry's amenability to mathematics not only says a great deal about his scientific development in Albany but had significant implications for his future physical research and his general scientific orientation.

Still another feature of his Albany milieu molded Henry's scientific outlook. The founders of Albany's scientific and educational institutions assumed the utility of scientific knowledge, and they strove continually for a merger of theory and practice. Conveying the essence of this ideology, Stephen Van Rensselaer told the Albany County Agricultural Society that:

> Farmers are prejudiced in favor of their own ideas of agricultural subjects, and are unwilling to allow that much improvement can be made in the present mode of pursuing the art. This is a mistaken idea; much may be learned from those who are not practical men, but who make experiments for their amusement; and still more from scientific individuals, who have attended to the nature of soils. . . .[19]

Similar beliefs in the relevance of science to practice appear frequently in the records of the New York State Board of Regents, and such beliefs were implicit in the establishment of the Albany Academy. Although personally devoted to pure scientific research, Henry was not antagonistic to using theory for utilitarian ends. On the contrary, his Albany lectures and corre-

---

[19] Quoted in the *Albany Register,* October 22, 1819, pp. 2–3.

spondence reveal a concern for the proper application of science to technology, a concern which stands out as a major theme in the present volume and will reappear significantly in later volumes. His views are not merely local but stem from attitudes widely diffused in both the United States and Europe.

*   *   *   *   *

The launching of this documentary publication was made possible by a generous grant from the National Science Foundation. The sponsoring institutions—American Philosophical Society, National Academy of Sciences, and Smithsonian Institution—have warmly supported the Henry Papers, and we are grateful for the help of their officers and staffs. Past presidents of the Society and the Academy, Henry Allen Moe and Frederick Seitz, deserve much credit for early support of the Henry Papers. The late Richard H. Shryock, then Librarian of the American Philosophical Society, called a meeting in 1964 which started the train of events leading to this series. The National Historical Publications Commission has aided in too many respects for enumeration. We are particularly grateful to the members of the Joint Committee of the sponsors for their understanding and encouragement. Two former members of the Joint Committee, Paul Oehser and Samuel T. Suratt, were most helpful in early stages.

Within the Smithsonian Institution we are indebted to many, but must single out Jack Marquardt and James Spohn of the Library for cheerfully coping with a torrent of interlibrary loan requests and bibliographic queries. The Information Systems Division was a model of enlightened cooperation in devising and implementing our computer control system. Colleagues in the National Museum of History and Technology helped us over a number of hurdles. The contribution of the Smithsonian Press is self-evident to any reader.

Our editorial tasks for this volume were lightened and the results greatly enriched by the presence of Joseph Henry's library. Later volumes will also benefit from the generous action of Melville Bell Grosvenor and his family, the heirs of Alexander Graham Bell, in depositing this library with the Henry Papers.

In the preparation of this volume we wrote, visited, and called on too many institutions and individuals for enumeration here. In almost every instance we encountered courteous cooperation. The Smithsonian Archives, the holder of the largest body of Henry manuscripts, aided us considerably. Of particular importance were the extra efforts on our behalf by John McClintock, then on the faculty of the Albany Academy, and Juliet Wolohan, formerly with the New York State Library. We acknowledge particularly our appreciation of those institutions outside the Smithsonian whose documents are reproduced here:

Albany Academy
Albany Institute of History and Art
Albany County Surrogate's Court
Burndy Library
Eisenhower Library, Johns Hopkins University
First Presbyterian Church of Albany
Historical Society of Pennsylvania
Huntington Library and Art Gallery
Institution of Electrical Engineers, London
Library of Congress
National Archives
New-York Historical Society
New York Public Library
New York State Library
Princeton University Archives
Rutgers University Library
Sterling Library, Yale University
University of Pennsylvania Library

We have benefited also from the comments of many colleagues in addition to those on the Smithsonian staff or on our Editorial Advisory Board. Any errors of commission and omission, however, remain our responsibility.

Behind-the-scene efforts have made this volume possible. We particularly want to acknowledge the contributions of Beverly Jo Lepley, the Henry Papers' Administrative Officer, and the various skilled efforts of our Research Assistant, Kathleen Waldenfels. From time to time we have had part-time workers transcribing documents, an essential step in reducing handwritten text to print. A large number of volunteers from the Smithsonian Associates have transcribed many manuscripts. Both our office staff and the volunteer transcribers have earned our gratitude and admiration for their patient skill in performing a tedious but necessary step in the editorial process.

Car rien ne supplée aux documents: pas de documents, pas d'histoire . . .
—Langlois and Seignobos,
Introduction aux études historiques,
2d ed. (Paris, 1899), p. 2.

Complete disclosure of working assumptions and operating techniques is not feasible, even with the best of intentions. The literature of history is strewn with examples of later disclosures of assumptions hidden not only from readers but even from their originators. And a detailed accounting of rationales, procedures, and techniques would soon weary even the most ardent lover of historical shop talk. What follows is an overview of our intentions and a succinct guide to necessary particulars of our practice.

Objectivity is widely ascribed to editing of documents by fellow historians and laymen alike. With the coming of the modern editorial projects associated with the program of the National Historical Publications Commission, this belief was undoubtedly reinforced. The sheer quality and quantity of the historical record thus made available has had considerable impact. We are most aware and appreciative of our great predecessors and contemporaries in historical editing. Writing footnotes on the shoulders of giants is not comfortable. While emulation animates us, so too does the consciousness of differences. And these differences, subtle and gross, arise partly from the three elements from which the objectivity of historical editing supposedly derives: the inclusiveness of the edited texts; their accuracy; and the impartial reliability of annotations.

Providing authentic historical source material is the ultimate justification for historical editing. Historical editors are predisposed to complete coverage of relevant documentation. After all, if presenting documentation is good, the more presented, the better. The importance of the subjects (e.g., Founding Fathers) often endows every scrap with an appreciable measure of value. Beyond these factors is the memory of a long, sad history of editions flawed by omissions due to incomplete research and arbitrary excisions. While the comprehensiveness of volumes in the National Historical Publications Commission's program has had most beneficial consequences, the implied goal of literal completeness has raised real problems.

In practice, of course, literal completeness is not attained, but rather inclusiveness within a carefully delimited domain. Even so, the size of the documentation plus the bulk of the editorial apparatus has generated editorial projects beyond a lifetime's capacity, perhaps even requiring several generations. If this is so for major figures of the eighteenth and early nineteenth centuries, the problems for the editors of the papers of later worthies are many times multiplied—in fact, multiplied in proportion to the increase in the numbers of surviving manuscripts.

One way out is simply to microfilm the originals, without annotations, avoiding not only the cost of printing but the burden of financing an editorial staff over a long time period. But only a few fellow specialists will look at manuscripts, filmed or original. Another strategy calls for selected editions in letterpress. Our solution is to combine the letterpress and the microfilm editions—but with one essential modification. Our printed volumes will constitute an interpretive select edition. The existence of the microfilm edition will amply discharge our obligation to present an exhaustive body of source materials, enabling the printed work to stand or fall on its merits as a history of a special kind. To aid our research and to produce a guide for the microfilm edition, we are describing and indexing the Henry documentation by means of a computer system.

Specifying fixed standards of selection is impossible for that implies foreknowledge of both the contents of all the manuscripts, even those yet ungathered, as well as complete assurance of what topics are preeminently important. Even with extensive preparation, this first volume is filled with surprising documents entailing unpredictable research. Rather than fixed standards, we operate by working resolutions. The first is to document Henry's research and professional career for an understanding of both science and the growth of the national scientific community. The second is to use the life of Joseph Henry as an occasion to present a broad documentary history of a period and a place, not merely a narrow recital of events in a career. The life becomes the thread upon which the beads of history are strung. We are impelled in this regard by the belief that science is not a foreign body embedded in the national culture but integrally part of it. Our aim is to merge imperceptibly the scientific work and the general background, to present few sharp edges between the "internal" life of science and the "external" milieu. Sharp edges occur more frequently in the literature than they do in reality. Third, we will make a deliberate attempt to include evidences of the routine of daily activities which define the texture of the past as much as, if not more than, the grand themes of the professional literature.

Still another viewpoint has influenced our editorial attitudes toward comprehensiveness and selectivity. Justifications for the letterpress editions of eminent Americans rightly and understandably stress the value of the evidence for the study of the lives and works of their subjects. All too often the richness of information beyond the obvious is overlooked. Excluding cases where time destroyed most sources, the more interesting the personage, the wider the range of topics occurring in his papers. Merely to select for known, obvious themes would deprive readers of much knowledge while presenting a distorted view of the man. Our solution deliberately strives to exploit the unexpected subject-diversity of the sources. Science, education, and institutional histories will occur in these volumes; so too will economics, politics, and religion.

To these resolutions we must add a caveat. Our treatment is limited by the nature of the surviving evidence. Topics absent or nearly so get short shrift, no matter their importance. In this volume we have very little to say about Henry before his twenty-fifth year because so few manuscripts survive. His Albany work on electromagnetic induction is barely touched upon for the same reason. In our coverage of the years in Princeton, Henry's scientific work will receive incomparably better documentation. This caveat is not a sign of weakness. On the contrary, if our documentation did not disclose much that is fresh and valuable, we might have no other choice than to ruminate endlessly over the absent topics.

The second source of the belief in objectivity in historical editing is textual accuracy. Modern editions shine by comparison with the standard of most past efforts. The obvious care for detail in converting a manuscript to print here complements inclusiveness of the sources and the density of annotations. Some details of our practice are given in the next section. Our intention is to give the text as close to the original as print permits with only a few modifications required for the understanding of modern readers. And these few modifications are explained in footnotes, if not covered explicitly by our general remarks on style. Although undoubtedly the most objective aspect of historical editing, the process is hardly mechanical. Some manuscripts are physically messy; even very legible manuscripts may contain pen strokes which no longer communicate. Errors can occur despite great care. Legitimate differences of opinion are possible. While striving for perfection, the editors have recognized that goal as other-worldly and welcome any improved readings from friends and colleagues.

Perhaps the least objective aspect of editions of historical documents are the annotations. If editors blandly limit footnotes to matter-of-fact identifications of names and the like, the impression of objectivity is further strengthened. Two different problems are involved: what is selected for footnoting and the depths to which one probes in a footnote. There is no example of historical editing which does not silently omit footnotes others might regard as desirable. (Or conversely, the edition is vulnerable for singling out minor points.) There is no example of historical editing others cannot fault for too little (or too much) annotation of particular points. Even a decision simply to give the original texts with the barest of annotations says much about an editor. Inevitably, historical editing has an appreciable element of human art. A footnote is not an occasion for mere display of erudition, but an exercise in conveying meaningful content.

We are not squeamish about stating opinions frankly. If circumstances seem appropriate, we will expand the detail given in annotations, as well as in our commentary. Readers of this volume also will occasionally encounter fairly detailed explanations of our procedures, involving both successes and failures in research. Historians have an obligation to indicate the degree of certainty of facts and interpretations. More important, we feel that the steps in historical research and reasoning should remain visible to professionals and laymen alike in order to elucidate the nature of history as a research process.

This volume (and its successors) is best understood in cinematic terms. A time succession of documents passes before the eyes of the reader. The editors, conscientious drones assembling the frames of the film, want to help the viewer of the documents. Deliberately, they insert related film clips, sometimes before the document but usually in the course of the document. These take the form of footnotes. Sometimes, the editors simply scrap a document and appear on film themselves, explaining points in the plot. What must strike the eye of the intelligent reader is the role of time. If the manuscripts are the main story line—the time-present of the plot— then the editorial apparatus is not simply about that particular moment. Past and future times are mingled in the editors' inserted film clips. Rarely are they solely about the moment of the events penned by our cast of characters.

Unlike the author of a screenplay, the editor of historical documents does not create his cast and he cannot manipulate his characters in devising his plot. Footnotes reflect imperfect comprehensions of what preceded and incomplete apprehensions of what will follow. Neither reader nor editor will really know the plot until the end. Until then, surprise and, perhaps, pleasure should draw us forward to the next volume.

❧ NOTES ON STYLE ❧

Our practices are generally similar to those of other editorial projects, particularly to those of the Adams Papers. The nature of our documents and our personal inclinations have resulted in a few departures from the style of that great project, and these are noted below. In preparing the volume we largely followed the strategy of a style manual prepared before the actual editing. On the basis of our experiences we are expanding and revising the manual. Copies of the revised manual are available to scholars interested in the editing of historical documents. Here a few points necessary for the reader's understanding are presented.

Organization

Documents are given in chronological order. If a specific date is not given or is not ascribable, the document is placed at the end of the dated documents from the nearest unit of time to which it can be tied. For example, if only the year can be determined, the document will appear at the end of all the items of that year. If the month and year are available but not the day, the document will appear after the fully dated documents of that month and year. Where the year is in doubt, the item will normally appear in an appendix, as in the case with the lecture outline printed in this volume.

Preliminaries to the Documents

Preliminaries to the documents are title, provenance note, and (sometimes) an introductory headnote.

The title briefly signals what is to come. In the case of correspondence, if Henry is the author of the letter, we simply indicate to whom he is writing:

TO BENJAMIN SILLIMAN, SR.

or we note the name of the person writing to Joseph Henry:

FROM BENJAMIN SILLIMAN, SR.

if Henry is neither the author nor the recipient, both parties are specified:

BENJAMIN SILLIMAN, SR., TO ROBERT HARE

In the case of noncorrespondence items, we prefer using the titles given on the originals. If the title is lacking or if the given title is noncommunicative, the editors will devise a suitable title, usually with an explanatory footnote.

The provenance note, immediately following the title, briefly gives the location of the original and, if necessary, the nature of the document being published (i.e., "draft," "retained copy," "notebook entry," etc.). If these matters are too complicated for the provenance note, we normally provide additional pertinent details in a footnote. The use of such traditional abbreviations as "ALS" and the like are avoided. When the particulars of authorship or handwriting are historically significant, these are elaborated in a footnote if not clear from the title and provenance note.

In a few instances an explanatory headnote, immediately after the provenance note, will introduce a document. Where important items are not suitable for publication in a work of this nature, the headnote, often expanded in size, stands in their stead.

Date and Place

Date and place are usually placed at the top, right-hand side preceding the body of the text, regardless of location in the original. Missing dates are supplied in brackets as an editorial insertion. If the place is lacking, it is only supplied or discussed in a footnote if of some historical significance. Where the dating is not obvious or hinges on a matter of moment, this too becomes the subject of a footnote.

Texts

Our general practice is to hew as close to the original as possible, so long as the meaning is reasonably clear to a modern reader. A few revisions, mostly specified below, are made silently in the interest of clarity. We prefer to retain the original and to aid the modern reader in this respect by means of our annotations; only rarely do we make changes or insertions indicated by using square brackets, [ ]. "Sic" does not appear in our texts; barring human error, a reader must assume that any strange usage in print is a faithful transcription of the original.

Hewing close to the original has a particular point in this volume. Henry had very little formal schooling when he entered the Academy in 1819. Quite clearly, he became proficient in science and mathematics while still lacking polish in the usage of the English language. The image we get is of a bright young man self-consciously engaged in a program of self-improvement, perhaps a bit sensitive about his deficiencies in this respect. While it is true that matters of usage were not firmly standardized even at this period, Henry clearly differs from the practices of many of the scientists whose good opinions he sought.

Mary Henry, our subject's daughter, bequeathed a nasty problem to this project. Shortly after her father's death Mary Henry began working toward the preparation of a biography. In her possession were most of Joseph Henry's personal papers. To this she added items gathered from friends and relatives, as well as documents culled from the official archives of the Smithsonian Institution. Mary Henry's efforts eventually progressed to the point where she had prepared a partial text which included original documents and transcriptions done by herself and her cohorts. Her text and its associated materials were largely the basis upon which Coulson based his biography of Joseph Henry. Although posterity owes Mary Henry thanks for efforts to preserve her father's literary remains, many of her actions resulted in irreparable damage to many Joseph Henry manuscripts. For example, in a number of cases she removed part of a book or transcribed a few pages, carelessly losing the entire volume. In this 1797–1832 period we have a fragment marked "copied from the Record Book of 1830" which no longer exists. A neat trick of Mary's was to remove items from groups of documents and, in the process, to lose some and hopelessly disorder and scatter the remainder. The transcriptions she prepared for the contemplated biography are another vexation she inflicted on posterity. Almost invariably they omit an undisclosed amount of text, frequently passages of great interest. The transcribing is inaccurate at times and often corrects the language to conform with later standards, sometimes changing meanings. Unfortunately, many of the originals were lost, because, we think, of careless handling by Mary Henry and her aides. Many of these faulty, unique copies are quite important. We have decided to use them in our edition, signaling their nature by the expression "Mary Henry Copy" in the provenance note. From the numerous instances where both the copy and the original survive, we are convinced these are not fabrications, that the omissions were short-sighted but not acts of suppression, and that the surviving texts are reliable enough for use. Here and here alone, in the absence of any evidence to the contrary, we resolve textual uncertainties by opting for modern usage. There seems little point in trying to recapture Henry's archaisms.

Only in the few cases where the original paragraphing causes confusion in modern print have we made changes. Grammatical usage, punctuation, and spelling are usually faithfully preserved. The biggest exception is our decision to start each sentence with a capital letter and to end with appropriate punctuation. Punctuation that is obviously intrusive is removed; ubiquitous dashes are converted to modern commas and periods, and a few commas and periods are inserted silently where absolutely necessary for clear understanding. Only in a few egregious cases do we silently correct slips of the pen. Where the reading is doubtful or where meaning is otherwise unclear, we give an editorial insertion in square brackets, [ ]. Where these insertions are offered tentatively, we indicate our uncertainty by placing a question mark within the bracket. If the entire insertion is tentative, the question mark is placed immediately after the opening bracket, [? March 6, 1832]; if only one element is uncertain, the question mark is placed immediately afterward to indicate our doubt, [March 6?, 1832]. When the insertions arise from matters of moment, they will receive amplification in footnotes.

In a number of documents there are interlineations, canceled matter, variant texts, marginalia, and even footnotes by the original author. The first are silently brought into line unless there is some point in their position. In that event we generally use a footnote to elucidate the significance, retaining the original position only in exceptional cases. If canceled matter or variant versions of expressions have historical, psychological, or stylistic significance, we place them immediately preceding the text in question in italics within angled brackets:

celebrated <*mathematical*> philosophical school at Alexandria.

Marginalia of significance are inserted into the text at the proper points with suitable comments in footnotes. Author's footnotes are given symbols other than arabic numerals which are reserved for editorial annotations.

Where one or two words are illegible or missing, we have so indicated by inserting suspension points enclosed in square brackets, [. . .]; if more than two words, we will, in addition, give an explanatory footnote, estimating, where possible, the number missing. Where a reasonable reconstruction is possible, we do so as an editorial insertion within square brackets.

Abbreviations occur frequently in the documents. If clear to the modern reader, they are retained. Otherwise the term is spelled out. The ampersand is used in place of the many variant forms occurring during Henry's lifetime. A particular problem to many readers unfamiliar with past usages is abbreviations involving raised letters, a practice quite common in Henry's generation and at least as far back as the seventeenth century. The writer would retain the first letter or letters of a word, giving the last letter or letters of the word in a raised position with or without a marking underneath:

Jany or Jan^{ry} for January.

A reader aware of this practice should have no trouble understanding such abbreviations which we leave unchanged. Some raised letter abbreviations are likely to cause trouble. Sch^{dy} for Schenectady is not exactly obvious. In such cases we simply spell out the word without comment.

Signatures or initials at the close are given as in the original, usually without any commentary. Draft or retained copies generally lack these, as will our printed versions without any further notice. Where the recipient's name appears at the bottom left of the last page of an original letter, this is silently omitted as repeating information already given in the title. Dates at the end are also suppressed as redundant unless we silently shift their position to supply the missing dating at the start. We have retained closing matter of this nature only where meaning is conveyed. In the love letters exchanged by Joseph Henry and his wife Harriet, the closing salutations tell us something about the sentiments of the correspondents and are, therefore, given.

Editorial footnotes are numbered consecutively within each entry. We follow the citation form of the 12th edition of the *Manual of Style* of the University of Chicago Press with one important exception. We prefer the ISIS form in citing the periodical literature. Of less moment, perhaps, are two other preferences. The Editor does not relish the current tendency to suppress capitalization and to use the lower case in titles of officials, names of institutions, and publications. We capitalize. There is also an antipathy here against the tendency to run abbreviation-wild. We think readers should not have to approach each footnote as an exercise in decoding. Except for a few standard usages (e.g., n.d., ibid., etc.), everything is given in full or nearly so. The principal exceptions are the items below for which we consistently use short titles or standard abbreviations.

Academy Seventy-fifth Anniversary	*The Celebration of the Seventy-fifth Anniversary of the Founding of the Albany Academy, October 25, 1888* (Albany, 1889).
Reynolds, *Alb. Chron.*	Cuyler Reynolds, compiler, *Albany Chronicles: A History of the City Arranged Chronologically* (Albany, 1906).
Allibone	S. Austin Allibone, *A Critical Dictionary of English Literature and British and American Authors, from the Earliest Accounts to the Middle of the Nineteenth Century,* 3 vols. (Philadelphia, 1859–1871).
Munsell, *Ann. Alb.*	Joel Munsell, compiler, *Annals of Albany,* 10 vols. (Albany, 1850–1859).
Sprague, *Annals*	William Buell Sprague, *Annals of the American Pulpit,* 9 vols. (New York, 1857–1869).
Biographical Directory of the American Congress	*Biographical Directory of the American Congress, 1774–1949* (Washington, 1950).
Munsell, *Coll. Alb.*	Joel Munsell, compiler, *Collections on the History of Albany, from Its Discovery to the Present Time, with Notices of Its Public Institutions and Biographical Sketches of Citizens Deceased,* 4 vols. (Albany, 1865–1871).
Columbia Alumni	M. Halsey Thomas, compiler, *Columbia University Officers and Alumni, 1754–1857* (New York, 1936).
Coulson	Thomas Coulson, *Joseph Henry: His Life and Work* (Princeton, 1950).
DAB	*Dictionary of American Biography*
DNB	*Dictionary of National Biography*
DSB	*Dictionary of Scientific Biography*
Herringshaw	Thomas William Herringshaw, *Encyclopedia of American Biography of the Nineteenth Century* (Chicago, 1905).

Howell and Tenney	George Rogers Howell and Jonathan Tenney, editors, *History of the County of Albany, N.Y., from 1609 to 1886* (New York, 1886).
Nason	Henry B. Nason, editor, *Biographical Record of the Officers and Graduates of the Rensselaer Polytechnic Institute, 1824–1886* (Troy, 1887).
Phil. Trans.	*Philosophical Transactions of the Royal Society of London.*
Poggendorff	J. C. Poggendorff, compiler, *Biographisch-Literarisches Handworterbuch Zur Geschichte Der Exacten Wissenschaften.*
Princeton Catalogue	*General Catalogue of Princeton University, 1746–1906* (Princeton, 1908).
Silliman's Journal	Benjamin Silliman, editor, *American Journal of Science and Arts* (New Haven, 1818–).
Union Catalog	*Union University: Centennial Catalog, 1795–1895, of the Officers and Alumni of Union College in . . . Schenectady, N.Y.* (Troy, 1895).

THE PAPERS OF JOSEPH HENRY

HENRY'S BAPTISMAL RECORD
Register of Baptisms, First Presbyterian Church, Albany, New York

The determination of Henry's date of birth was for many years in a state of confusion. The advocate of an erroneous date was none other than Henry himself, who believed he had been born in 1799. After Henry's death, his cousin and scientific comrade, Stephen Alexander, insisted in a letter to Asa Gray (December 4, 1878, now in the Gray Herbarium) that Henry had been born in December of 1799, but the following church record of Henry's baptism makes clear that Henry was born in 1797.

1798
Jan.ʸ 21. | Joseph son of William Henry[1] and Ann Alexander[2] born Dec.ʳ 17, 1797

[1] William Henry was born in January 1764, and lived until October 20, 1811. *Proceedings of the Common Council and the Various Religious Organizations of the City of Albany Relative to the State Street Burial Grounds* (Albany, 1867), p. 44. Additional information on William Henry may be found below, John H. Wendell to Ann Alexander Henry, June 6, 1814, especially footnote 2.

[2] Ann Alexander Henry was born December 15, 1760, and lived until April 4, 1835. Ibid.

TO PARENTS[1]
Henry Papers, Smithsonian Archives

Galway [New York]
July 26, 1808

Honoured father & Mother

I embrace this Oppertunity to write to you to inform you that I am well at this period Like wise Granmother and all the rest of my Relatives, and

[1] This is believed to be the earliest extant Joseph Henry holograph. Henry was ten and one-half years old at the time of writing, living in Galway, New York, some thirty-six miles from his parents in Albany. Though the grammar and spelling are Henry's own, a characteristic he would only partially overcome with practical experience, the stilted language of the text came from the standard letter he followed. Apparently written by Nancy Henry (d. 1856), Joseph's sister, two notations on the verso of the letter confirm that Henry copied his teacher's prose. One reads, "The first letter ever written by Jos. Henry and an exact copy of one written by the *learned* pedagogue who had then the care of

3

I flatter my self that these few Lines will find you enjoy-ing your healths, and my brother & sister it is a general time of health here. I endeavour to Make the best improvement in my Learning that I possibly can though at the first it seemed a Little irksome and hard, and I hope to gain the point at Last——pray Dear parents accept of my most humble duty to your selves and kind Love to my Brother & sister. I subscribe myself hoping You will look over the blots from your son.

Joseph Henry

---

his education." Another notes, "The first scrawl of Jos. Henry being an exact copy of a letter written by Israel Phelps Schoolmaster Galway Saratoga Co." We believe that the letter had remained in the family papers and was transferred to the Henry Papers in Mary Henry's flurry of collecting activities.

We know little about the teacher, Israel Phelps. Thomas Coulson, Henry's biographer, stresses that Phelps had little or no effect in awakening young Henry's "dormant powers." Phelps has eluded our efforts to identify him;

we know only that he was appointed on February 2, 1808, as a member of the original governing committee of the First Associated Presbyterian Church, one of the earliest churches in Galway. See George Baker Anderson, comp., *Our County and Its People, A Descriptive and Biographical Record of Saratoga County, New York* ([Boston], 1899), p. 152; Thomas Coulson, *Joseph Henry: His Life and Work* (Princeton, 1950), p. 8 (hereafter cited as *Coulson*).

◆❧ 1812 ❧◆

T. ROMEYN BECK[1] TO JOHN W. FRANCIS[2]
John W. Francis Collection, New York State Library

Feb[y] 26th 1812
Alban[y]

Dear Sir.

I received your welcome epistle of the 27th Ult. and have been prevented from answering it sooner by a multiplicity of circumstances, any one of

---

[1] Theodric Romeyn Beck (1781–1855), physician, principal of the Albany Academy from 1817 until 1848. Born in Schenectady, he was educated at the Schenectady Grammar School and at Union College (1803–1807). He read medicine with Dr. Low and Dr. McClelland (for whom see below, footnotes 22 and 14) at Albany, then entered the College of Physicians and Surgeons in New York, from which he graduated in 1811. At the time of this letter he was practicing medicine at Albany;

he continued in this practice only until 1817, though he lectured on medicine at the Western College of Physicians and Surgeons in Fairfield, Herkimer County, between 1815 and 1840, and at Albany Medical College between 1840 and 1843. It was chiefly as principal of the Albany Academy, however, that he figured in Joseph Henry's career. Beck guided the Academy through difficult years, raising it to a flourishing state. During Henry's tenure at the Academy he and Beck cooperated in mak-

which you will I suspect, allow to be a sufficient excuse. Among the most important are, the loss of health, and incessant round of pleasure & business, visiting, and staying at home, reading & writing, eating & sleeping, and last, though not least, *thinking* or as Knickerbocker[3] would style it *Pondering.* Albany has been a busy place for the last 4 weeks. The Meeting of the Legislature, the unusual concourse of strangers, [from] every part of the state, & the consequent activity perceivable in the majority of the citizens, is sufficient to interest one like me, who has never been witness to a similar scene. "I have not been myself" for sometime. I have felt bewildered, and unable to apply myself seriously to any particular Study. During the above time however, I have commenced & completed a Tabular System of Mineralogy extracted from Thomson,[4] Murray,[5] Accum[6] &c. Comprising all the Genera & Species their Synonimes, Chemical Analysis & Localities. It fills about 18 or 20 sheets of Letter Paper. It is after all nothing but a work of sheer industry, for which I claim no praise, since it has become a habit. I have presented it to the Society of Arts, to be hung up in their Mineralogical Cabinet.[7] I have accidentally discovered that D[r] Bard has published his

---

ing meteorological observations which they reported annually to Regents of the University of the State of New York (see below, excerpts of Academy Trustees' Minutes, September 9, 1825, and January 27, 1832, especially footnotes 7 and 11, respectively). *DAB*, and Dr. Hamilton, "Obituary of Theodric Romeyn Beck," in Joel Munsell, *Annals of Albany*, 10 vols. (Albany, 1850–1859), *8*:1–27 (hereafter cited as Munsell, *Ann. Alb.*).

[2] John Wakefield Francis (1789–1861), physician, classmate of Beck's at the College of Physicians and Surgeons (both graduated in 1811). Upon graduation, Francis entered a partnership with David Hosack (see below, footnotes 16 and 23) and accepted a lectureship in medicine and materia medica at the College. He later attained fame, and no little fortune, as an obstetrician. Another, with Beck, in the tradition of the gentleman natural historian, Francis was active in literary, charitable, and antiquarian pursuits. *DAB.*

[3] Diedrich Knickerbocker, the pretended author of Washington Irving's immediately successful *A History of New York, from the Beginning of the World to the End of the Dutch Dynasty,* 2 vols. (New York [etc.], 1809); its subtitle was *Containing among Many Surprising and Curious Matters, the Unutterable Ponderings of Walter the Doubter, the Disastrous Projects of William the Testy, and the Chivalric Achievements of Peter the Head-*strong, the Three Dutch Governors of New Amsterdam; being the Only Authentic History of the Times That Ever Hath Been, or Ever Will Be Published.*

[4] Thomas Thomson (1773–1852), Scottish chemist, whose textbook, *A System of Chemistry,* was very widely used. *DNB.* The fourth edition (5 vols., Edinburgh, 1810) would have been available to Beck.

[5] John Murray (d. 1820), chemist, lecturer at Edinburgh in chemistry, pharmacy, and materia medica. *DNB.* His *Elements of Chemistry,* 2 vols. (Edinburgh, 1801), went through numerous editions, as did his *A System of Chemistry,* 4 vols. (Edinburgh, 1806–1807). Beck, in his *Annual Address . . . before the Society for the Promotion of Useful Arts . . . on the 3d of February, 1813* (Albany, 1813), p. 26, cites the second edition of Murray's *System* (1807).

[6] Friedrich Christian Accum (1769–1838), German chemist, whose most productive years were spent in England. *DNB* and R. J. Cole, "Friedrich Accum (1769–1838), A Biographical Study," *Annals of Science,* 1951, *7*:128–143. Accum's *System of Theoretical and Practical Chemistry,* 2 vols. (London, 1803), went through a second edition, 1807, and there was a Philadelphia edition of the latter in 1808.

[7] This cabinet no longer exists, to the best of our knowledge.

Introductory Lecture.[8] Are they for Sale? Let me know. If not can you procure me one? I was surprised to learn by Bogarts[9] letter, that Barclay[10] was refused a Degree. It must be a very mortifying circumstance. As to the case of the bad effects of Mercury, I am so delicately situated, that I should dislike any publication of it. Besides affecting the character of my lately deceased Preceptor,[11] it would agonize the feelings of its surviving parents, whose only & beloved child it was, and who is a man of considerable reading, and would probably not be among the last to discover the circumstances. Besides, I never could give the history of the case, without some severe remarks on the impropriety of the practice, which might still farther aggravate his feelings. The statement of the case is this. A child about 12 years old, was seized with Remittent Fever. After a Cathartic had been given, Diaphoretic Powders with Calomel G[r] i;[12] to the Dose was administered, one every three or four hours. After a few days use, the mouth became affected, the strength gradually sunk, until it became so alarming, that stimulants were necessarily to be given. The Mouth inflamed, sphacelated, through the cheeks Blisters (according to Physick's[13] Plan) were applied, to no purpose—& he Died. For the last 3 or 4 Days, The Patient had no Disease, but the Mercurial Fever as described in books. This is a brief outline of the case, as far as I can recollect. The Books from which I expected to obtain the minutiae, are beyond my reach, since the Death of D[r] McClelland.[14]

[8] Samuel Bard (1742–1821), physician, had studied in London and Edinburgh and was active in New York medical circles. He was elected President of the College of Physicians and Surgeons in 1811. *DAB.* The lecture to which Beck refers is *A Discourse on the Importance of Medical Education: Delivered on the Fourth of November, 1811, at the Opening of the Present Session of the Medical School of the College of Physicians and Surgeons* (New York, 1812); also printed in *The American Medical and Philosophical Register,* 1812, *2:*369–382.

[9] Henry Bogart (?–1817), of Albany, graduated from Union College in 1810 and received his M.D. from the New York College of Physicians and Surgeons in 1813. His thesis on angina pectoris was published in New York that year. *The American Medical and Philosophical Register,* 1813, *4:*153; M. Halsey Thomas, comp., *Columbia University Officers and Alumni, 1754–1857* (New York, 1936), pp. 38, 51, 194 (hereafter cited as *Columbia Alumni*).

[10] A Robert M. Barclay received his degree from the College of Physicians and Surgeons

in 1812 (ibid., p. 193), but presumably another Barclay, who has eluded our search, is referred to here.

[11] McClelland. See below, footnote 14.

[12] One grain.

[13] Philip Syng Physick (1768–1837), surgeon. Born in Philadelphia and educated in the University of Pennsylvania Medical School, in London and in Edinburgh, he became one of the most eminent American surgeons of his time. He was on the staff of the Pennsylvania Hospital from 1794 to 1816, also giving clinical instruction there, and lectured on surgery at the University. His "Plan" called for the local application of a blistering agent (usually cantharides); see "Of the Use of Blisters in Checking the Progress of Mortification," *The Philadelphia Medical Museum,* 1805, *1:*189–194.

[14] William McClelland (1769–1812), born in Galloway, Scotland, and educated in Edinburgh, came to this country "at an early age," and set up practice in Albany. He was president of the Albany county and state medical societies at different times. Munsell, *Ann. Alb.,* 5:31; 9:93.

You will not, I hope, call it vanity, when I tell you, that I was pleased with the Review of my dissertation,[15] and with the discriminative applause the Reviewer has given to it. He has my sincere thanks. As to the communication I promised you, I hope you will excuse me for this N⁰[16] I have not been able to collect facts of sufficient importance for an introductory attempt at the plan I have projected. I pledge myself however for one for the July N⁰ Since I wrote you, I have become a Member of the Society of Arts.[17] I send you a list of their Officers elected for the ensuing year which has not yet been published & may be proper for the Register.[18]

R. R. Livingston[19] President
Simeon De Witt.[20] 1st V President
John Tayler[21] 2ⁿᵈ Vice Pres.

---

[15] Beck's thesis for the M.D. degree, *An Inaugural Dissertation on Insanity* (New York, 1811), was reviewed anonymously in the *Register* (see next note), January 1812, 2:347–352.

[16] Francis was co-editor with David Hosack of *The American Medical and Philosophical Register*. This journal, which the editors considered to be unique among American publications of its kind because of its emphasis on original papers (*1*:iii; *4*:vii), was issued quarterly beginning in July 1810. Four volumes appeared before the journal failed (1814) for want of funds. The editors were at first not named ("a Society of Gentlemen"), but in 1814 all four volumes were reissued under Francis's and Hosack's names.

[17] The Society for the Promotion of Useful Arts was founded in New York City in 1791 as the Society for the Promotion of Agriculture, Arts and Manufactures. Its laws stated that it was to meet where the legislature met, and accordingly it moved to Albany in 1796. In 1804 it received a charter from the State and at that time its name was changed to the Society for the Promotion of Useful Arts. In 1824 the Society merged with the Albany Lyceum of Natural History (founded 1821, chartered 1823) to form the Albany Institute. Joseph Henry was apparently a member of the Lyceum and a charter member of the Institute. The Institute still exists. In 1900 it absorbed the Historical and Arts Society (founded 1886) and became the Albany Institute and Historical and Arts Society, and in 1926 changed its name to the Albany Institute of History and Art, its present title. A brief history with the charters of the two parent bodies of 1824 is given as an Appendix to the first volume of the *Transactions*, Albany

Institute (1830); see also John Davis Hatch, Jr., "The Albany Institute of History and Art: A Sketch of Its Early Forerunners," *New York History*, 1946, 25:311–325, and below, Minutes of the Albany Institute, [May 5, 1824].

[18] A slightly different list of the officers of the Society was published in *The American Medical and Philosophical Register*, 1812, 3:248.

[19] Robert R. Livingston (1746–1813), lawyer, statesman, amateur scientist, was a very active and influential figure in the early history of the United States. He was the first President of the Society for the Promotion of Useful Arts and held that position until his death in 1813. Hatch, op. cit.; *DAB*.

[20] Simeon DeWitt (1756–1834), surveyor, was educated at Queen's College, New Jersey (Rutgers), and served in the Revolutionary Army. In the latter years of the war he was head of the army's geographical department. Soon after the war he was appointed to the office of Surveyor-General of New York, a post he held until his death. He was an active promoter of science in Albany and Joseph Henry's friend; his name will appear many times in the course of this volume. *DAB*, and Walter W. Ristow, "Simeon DeWitt, Pioneer American Cartographer," in *Kartengeschichte und Kartenbearbeitung*, ed. Karl-Heinz Meine (Bad Godesburg, 1968), pp. 103–114.

[21] John Tayler (1742–1829), merchant, was prominent in state and city affairs. He was Lieutenant-Governor of New York from 1813 to 1822 and President of the New York State Bank (1803). Munsell, *Ann. Alb.*, 4:306–307; Cuyler Reynolds, comp., *Albany Chronicles: A History of the City Arranged Chronologi-

James Low[22] Recording Secretary

David Hosack.[23] Southern District

James Geddes[24] Western District

} Corresponding Secretaries

Charles D. Cooper[25] Treasurer

Stephen Van Rensalaer[26] Senior Counsellor

G. W. V. Schaick[27]

P. S. V. Rensalaer[28]

I. Hutton[29]

Benjamin DeWitt[30]

Timothy Clowes[31]

E. C. Genet[32]

Dewitt Clinton[33]

John Woodworth[34]

} Counsellors

---

cally (Albany, 1906), p. 475 (hereafter cited as Reynolds, *Alb. Chron.*); Thomas William Herringshaw, *Encyclopedia of American Biography of the Nineteenth Century* (Chicago, 1905), p. 915 (hereafter cited as *Herringshaw*).

[22] James Low (1781–1822), physician, went to school in Schenectady, became an apprentice to Dr. John McClelland, and completed his education in Edinburgh. Returning to Albany in 1808, he entered McClelland's office, where he practiced for several years. He had been a student of the chemist John Murray at Edinburgh, and drew on this training to give public subscription lectures in Albany on chemistry and materia medica. Sylvester D. Willard, "Biographical Memoirs of Physicians in Albany County," in Munsell, *Ann. Alb.*, 9:90–115; see p. 99.

[23] David Hosack (1769–1835), physician, author, professor at Columbia College, at the College of Physicians and Surgeons, and at the short-lived Rutgers Medical College. A graduate of the College of New Jersey, he had studied in Edinburgh and London, and became one of the foremost American physicians of his day. *DAB*.

[24] James Geddes (1763–1838), civil engineer, began his career as a lawyer, then became interested, through his association with Simeon DeWitt (above, footnote 20), in canal building. He was one of the four "principal engineers" on the Erie Canal project. *DAB*.

[25] Charles Dekay Cooper (1769–1831) was trained as a physician at first under his father, Dr. Ananias Cooper, then under Dr. Crosby of New York City. He went to Albany in 1792 and was for a time health officer to the port. He did not, however, practice medi-

cine long into the new century, but entered politics, occupying a number of county and state offices. Sylvester D. Willard, op. cit. (above, note 22), pp. 104–105.

[26] So spelled. Stephen Van Rensselaer (1764–1839), soldier, statesman, philanthropist, benefactor of Rensselaer Polytechnic Institute at Troy, was deeply convinced of the social utility of scientific education and work. He was chosen as the first President of the Albany Institute upon its formation in 1824, and re-elected annually to that post until his death. He served as Senior Trustee of the Albany Academy from 1813 until 1819. *DAB*. Daniel Barnard, "Life and Services of Stephen Van Rensselaer," Munsell, *Ann. Alb.*, 3:202–245. See below, Academy Trustees' Minutes of March 4, 1813, and *The Celebration of the Seventy-fifth Anniversary of the Founding of the Albany Academy, October 25th 1888* (Albany, 1889), pp. 65, 67 (hereafter cited as *Academy Seventy-fifth Anniversary*).

[27] Gerrit W. Van Schaick (1757–1816) had fought in the Revolutionary War. He was first cashier at the Bank of Albany from 1792 to 1814. Reynolds, *Alb. Chron.*, p. 426.

[28] So spelled. Philip Schuyler Van Rensselaer (1766–1824), brother of Stephen Van Rensselaer (note 26), was President of the Bank of Albany. He served as Mayor of the city, 1799–1816, and 1819–1821. Ibid., p. [390].

[29] Isaac Hutton (ca. 1767–1855), silversmith, was first treasurer of the Albany Mechanics' Society (1793), sat from 1813 on the Board of Directors of the Mechanics' and Farmers' Bank, and was in general active in the affairs of the city. Munsell, *Ann. Alb.*, 1:203, 294; 3:97; 4:310; 7:240, 335.

They have also appointed a standing Committee of Mineralogy, of which I have the honour to be one. Any Mineral that you may have in your power to send to us, will be gratefully acknowledged. We intend to confine ourselves to forming as large a collection as possible of the Minerals of the State together with their localities & the geognosy of the Country. Be so kind as to request Garrison's[35] aid in sending us some which he can spare. We shall probably in a short time send Circulars to our friends. Since I wrote you last My Preceptor D^r McClelland has gone the way of all the living. His latter days were a mournful example of *"human nature in Ruins."* My Best Respects to the Doctor[36] and all enquiring friends. Believe me ever affectionately yours. I remain

T R B[37]

[30] Benjamin DeWitt (1774–1819), physician, scientist, taught materia medica and natural philosophy in the New York College of Physicians and Surgeons, of which he was also Vice President from 1813. *Herringshaw*, p. 299; "University of the State of New York. College of Physicians and Surgeons," *American Medical and Philosophical Register*, 1811–1812, 2:210; ibid., 1813–1814, 4:282–284.

[31] The Reverend Timothy Clowes (1787–1847) was educated at Columbia College, where he graduated in 1808. He became Rector of St. Peter's (Episcopal) Church, Albany, in 1810; in 1817 he left Albany and returned to his native Hempstead, New York, to teach in a classical seminary there. Among the first Board of Trustees of the Albany Academy in 1813, his trusteeship was terminated in 1818. For the rest of his years, he taught at, and presided over, various institutions of secondary and higher education. Munsell, *Ann. Alb.*, 6:56–57; *Academy Seventy-fifth Anniversary*, p. 65.

[32] Edmond Charles Genet (1763–1834), first minister of the French revolutionary government to the United States, 1792–1794, was recalled for his overly zealous attempts to get the United States to aid France in her wars with the monarchies. He later became a farmer in Rensselaer County, New York, and dabbled in science and invention. *DAB*.

[33] DeWitt Clinton (1769–1828), lawyer, statesman, and yet another amateur scientist, had studied under Samuel Latham Mitchill and David Hosack at Columbia College. He was Mayor of New York 1803 to 1815 (except 1807–1808 and 1810–1811) and later (1817–1822, 1824–1828) Governor of the State. He is best remembered, however, for his effective promotion of the Erie Canal project; it was his plan for the project which the New York legislature adopted in 1816. *DAB*. Clinton's interest in science and its potential service to the economy made a deep impression on the young Joseph Henry; the latter's library contains no fewer than sixteen pamphlets by or about Clinton.

[34] John Woodworth (ca. 1770–1858), lawyer, went to Albany from Troy in 1806. He practiced law and held various public offices until his appointment to the State Supreme Court in 1819. He was retired in 1828. Munsell, *Ann. Alb.*, *10*:418–419.

[35] A James C. Garrison received the A.B. degree from Columbia College in 1810 and the A.M. in 1816, and was enrolled in the College of Physicians and Surgeons, from 1810 to 1813. He did not receive an M.D. degree. *Columbia Alumni*, pp. 126, 189, 229.

[36] Hosack.

[37] The letter is addressed to "Dr John W. Francis. At Dr Hosacks. No 43 Broadway. New York."

❧ 1813 ❧

MINUTES, ACADEMY TRUSTEES[1]
Trustees' Minutes, 1:unpaged, Albany Academy Archives

[March 4, 1813]

The Regents of the University of the State of New York[2] To all to whom these presents shall or may come Greeting Whereas the Mayor Aldermen and commonalty of the City of Albany by an instrument[3] in writing under their Seal bearing date the first day of February in the year one thousand and Eight hundred and thirteen after stating that they had contributed in land and Money equal to thirty thousand Dollars for the use and benefit of An Academy to be erected in the City of Albany did make application to us the said Regents that the said Academy might be incorporated and become subject to the Visitation of us and our Successors and that Stephen Van Rensselaer, John Lansing Junior,[4] Archibald McIntyre,[5] Smith Thomp-

---

[1] On the page opposite these minutes there is the following notice in a later hand:

Incorporated under Sections 10, 11, 12, 13, 14, 15, 16, 17 of Chap LIX of Laws of 1813. passed April 5, 1813. Extending the provisions of Chap LXXXII of Laws of 1787 passed April 18, 1787 and Chap LI Laws of 1784, passed May 1, 1784.

See the footnote following.

[2] The University of the State of New York was established by laws of May 1, 1784 (amended November 26, 1784) and of April 18, 1787. It was not a university in the usual sense, as it had neither faculty, nor students, nor physical plant, and offered no instruction of its own. Rather it consisted of a Board of Regents with powers to charter, oversee, and aid institutions of secondary and higher learning throughout the state. Thus the Albany Academy, though governed by its own board of trustees, was legally the creation and ward of the Regents of the University. The history of the University and the acts of its establishment will be found in Franklin B. Hough, *Historical and Statistical Record of the University of the State of New York during the Century from 1784 to 1884* (Albany, 1885), chaps. 1 and 2. Additional documentation is provided in Daniel J. Pratt, "Annals of Public Education in the State of New York," *Proceedings of the Twelfth Anniversary of the University Convocation of the State of New*

York (Albany, 1875), pp. 197–274; *Proceedings of the Twentieth Meeting of the University Convocation of the State of New York* (Albany, 1883), pp. 161–180.

[3] This petition is apparently no longer extant.

[4] John Lansing, Jr. (1754–1829), lawyer, was active in the politics of the city, state, and nation. He had been Mayor of Albany from 1786 to 1790 and served on the New York Supreme Court from 1790 to 1801. He was Chancellor of the state from 1801 to 1814. His supposed murder in New York City has remained a mystery to this day. *DAB*. He was at first a Trustee of the Academy for less than one year, then served later from 1815 until 1817. See *Academy Seventy-fifth Anniversary*, p. 65.

[5] Archibald McIntyre (1772–1858) came with his parents to this country from Scotland at an early age. He was Assemblyman from Montgomery County, 1798–1802, state comptroller from 1806 to 1821, and state Senator from 1821 to 1827. Thereafter he managed the state lotteries for a number of years, and in his last years became a farmer in the northern part of the state. He served as a Trustee until 1817. See *Academy Seventy-fifth Anniversary*, p. 65; Munsell, *Ann. Alb.*, 7:157; 10:415; and Robert Harry McIntire, *The MacIntyre, McIntyre and McIntire Clan of Scotland, Ireland, Canada and New England* (n.p., 1949), pp. 12–13.

son,[6] Abraham Van Vechten,[7] John V. Henry,[8] Henry Walton,[9] William Neill,[10] John M. Bradford,[11] John McDonald,[12] Timothy Clowes, John McJimpsey,[13] Frederick G. Mayer,[14] Samuel Merwin[15] and the Mayor[16] and

[6] Smith Thompson (1768–1843), lawyer, graduate of the College of New Jersey (Princeton), Chief Justice of the Supreme Court of New York (1814–1818), Secretary of the Navy under Monroe (1819–1823) and Associate Justice of the Supreme Court from 1823 until his death. He resigned from his trusteeship of the Albany Academy later in 1813. *DAB*, and *Academy Seventy-fifth Anniversary*, p. 65.

[7] Abraham Van Vechten (1762–1837), lawyer, politician, held many offices in the city and state governments until his retirement from public life in 1821. *DAB*. He served as a Trustee only during 1813. *Academy Seventy-fifth Anniversary*, p. 65.

[8] John Vernon Henry (1767–1829), graduated from the College of New Jersey (Princeton) in 1785, then read law in Albany. Henry was prominent in community affairs; he was elected to the State Assembly in 1799, and appointed State Comptroller in 1800. Middlebury College granted him an honorary LL.D. in 1823, the year in which he retired from the Academy's Board of Trustees. See *Academy Seventy-fifth Anniversary*, p. 65; Munsell, *Ann. Alb.*, *4*:293; *8*:93; Reynolds, *Alb. Chron.*, pp. 393, 482; William Henry Eldridge, *Henry Genealogy: The Descendants of Samuel Henry . . . and Lurana (Cady) Henry . . .* (Boston, 1915), p. 104. J. V. Henry was not related to Joseph Henry.

[9] Henry Walton is listed as a counsellor in Albany City Directories for 1813 and 1814. He served as a Trustee until 1815; see *Academy Seventy-fifth Anniversary*, p. 65.

[10] William Neill (1778 or 1779–1860), clergyman, graduate of the College of New Jersey (Princeton), was Pastor of the First Presbyterian Church of Albany from 1809 to 1816. Resigning his position on the Academy's Board of Trustees, he moved to Philadelphia in 1816 to become Pastor of the Sixth Presbyterian Church there and later (1824) accepted the Presidency of Dickinson College in Carlisle, Pennsylvania. *DAB;* J. H. Jones, *Autobiography of William Neill, D.D. with a Selection from his Sermons* (Philadelphia, 1861), pp. 25, 35, 47; *Academy Seventy-fifth Anniversary*, p. 65.

[11] John Melanchthon Bradford (1781–1826), clergyman, was born in Connecticut. He graduated from Brown University in 1800, and was ordained in 1805. He was Pastor of the First Reformed Protestant Dutch Church in Albany from 1805 until 1820. He continued to serve as a Trustee until 1826. Munsell, *Ann. Alb.*, *1*:85–88; *4*:319; *8*:146; *10*:207; and Jonathan Tenney, *New England in Albany* (Boston, 1883), p. 70; *Academy Seventy-fifth Anniversary*, p. 65.

[12] John McDonald (?–1821), clergyman, ordained in 1785, was Pastor of the First Presbyterian Church, 1785–1795, and later clerk of the Presbytery of Albany. He was a Trustee of the Academy from 1813 until 1821. Munsell, *Ann. Alb.*, *1*:170, 245; *2*:294, 303; *7*:161; *Academy Seventy-fifth Anniversary*, p. 65.

[13] So spelled. John McJimsey (1772–1854) graduated from Dickinson College in 1792, was licensed to preach by the First Associate Reformed Presbytery of Pennsylvania in 1794, and ordained in 1796. He preached in Nellytown in Orange County, New York, from 1796 to 1809, when he went to Albany to become Pastor of the Associate Reformed Church there. He resigned in 1813 owing to lack of support. After maintaining a private school in Albany for two years, a school which he discontinued when he saw that the Academy would diminish its usefulness, McJimsey became principal of Dutchess County Academy in Poughkeepsie (1815–1819), principal of the Academy at Montgomery for a few years, and finally Pastor of a church in Montgomery where he remained until his death. He was a Trustee of the Academy for only two years, 1813–1815; see *Academy Seventy-fifth Anniversary*, p. 65; William Buell Sprague, *Annals of the American Pulpit*, 9 vols. (New York, 1857–1869), *9*:82–92 (hereafter cited as Sprague, *Annals*).

[14] Frederick George Mayer (?–1842 or 1843), clergyman, was Pastor of the Evangelical Lutheran Ebenezer Church, Charter Manager (1811) of the Albany County Bible Society, and a Trustee of the Academy, 1813–1818. Munsell, *Ann. Alb.*, *1*:155, 255; *10*:336; *Academy Seventy-fifth Anniversary*, p. 65.

[15] Samuel Merwin (1777–1839), Methodist minister, was educated privately, and in 1800 became an itinerant preacher. He was seldom more than a year or two in one place; he preached in the Albany vicinity in 1810, 1812–1813, 1820–1821. He resigned from the Trustees in 1814. See Sprague, *Annals*, 7:333–337; *Academy Seventy-fifth Anniversary*, p. 65.

Recorder[17] of the said City *ex officio* might be Trustees of the said Academy by the Name of "The Trustees of the Albany Academy" *Now Know Ye* that we the said Regents having inquired into the allegations contained in the instrument aforesaid and found the same to be true and conceiving the said academy calculated for the promotion of literature *do* by these *presents* pursuant to the Statute[18] in such case made and provided, signify our approbation to the incorporation of the said Stephen Van Rensselaer, John Lansing Junior, Archibald McIntyre, Smith Thompson, Abraham Van Vechten, John V. Henry, Henry Walton, William Neill, John M. Bradford, John McDonald, Timothy Clowes, John McJimpsey, Frederick G. Mayer, Samuel Merwin and the Mayor and Recorder of the said City *ex officio* by the name of "The Trustees of the Albany Academy" being the name mentioned in and by the said request in Writing *On Condition* that a part of the principal or estate before mentioned sufficient to produce one hundred Dollars annual income at least shall be set apart and shall not be diminished or otherwise appropriated and that the said Income thereof be applied solely to the Maintenance or Salary of the Professors or Tutors of said Academy. The testimony whereof we have caused our common Seal to be thereunto affixed the fourth day of March in the year of our Lord one thousand Eight hundred and Thirteen   Francis Bloodgood[19] Secretary. Daniel D. Tompkins.[20] Ch.

---

[16] Philip Schuyler Van Rensselaer, who served as Mayor from 1799 to 1816 and from 1819 to 1821. See above, T. R. Beck to J. W. Francis, February 26, 1812, especially footnote 28. He served as a Trustee of the Academy, 1821–1824; *Academy Seventy-fifth Anniversary*, p. 66.

[17] John Van Ness Yates was Recorder at this time. *Proceedings of the Common Council [of Albany]*, vol. 2, *Message of the Mayor and Reports of City Officers, 1935* (Albany, 1936), pp. xxvii–xxxvii, has a list of Mayors and Recorders of the city. Yates (1779–1839), a lawyer, was a lifelong resident of Albany and played a prominent part in the affairs of the city. He served one term in the State Assembly (1819) and was Secretary of State of New York, 1818–1826. *DAB.*

[18] The law of April 18, 1787, provided for incorporation under the Regents in Sections XII–XXI. See Pratt, op. cit. (above, footnote 2), 1875, pp. 267–270.

[19] Francis Bloodgood (1768–1840), lawyer, had graduated from Yale; he served as clerk to the New York Supreme Court and was later President of the New York State Bank. He was Mayor of Albany, 1831–1833. Reynolds, *Alb. Chron.*, p. 496.

[20] Daniel D. Tompkins (1774–1825), lawyer, graduated from Columbia College in 1795. He occupied several political offices, and was elected Governor of the state four consecutive times from 1807. His last term as Governor was cut short by his election in 1816 to the Vice Presidency of the United States, to which office he was reelected in 1820. *DAB.*

MINUTES, ACADEMY TRUSTEES
Trustees' Minutes, 1:2, Albany Academy Archives

At a Meeting of the Trustees of the Albany Academy held at the Capitol on the 24th March 1813.

Present Stephen Van Rensselaer Sen[r] trustee

Archibald M[c]Intyre	John M[c] Jimpsey
John V. Henry	John M Bradford
William Niell	Frederick G. Mayer
Timothy Clowes	Samuel Merwin
John M[c]Donald	Theodore Sedgwick[1]

Resolved that the Committee appointed to solicit Subscriptions to our Funds may leave it discretionary with the subscribers either to pay the Subscription Money or to give satisfactory security for the payment thereof at such time as each subscriber shall think proper with lawful Interest payable yearly. And the committee may further leave it discretionary with each subscriber in case the whole amount of Subscriptions shall not exceed thirty thousand Dollars to reduce or withdraw his Subscription.

Resolved that M[r] Clowes M[r] Walton and M[r] Mayer be a Committee to report a plan for a building for the Academy.

Resolved that M[r] Sedgwick be a Committee to apply for an Alteration in the Statute respecting the adjournment of this Board so that an adjournment may be made for one Month.

Resolved that this Board accept the offer made by the Mayor in behalf of this Corporation of the City of Albany of the use of the Common Council Room for the Meetings of this Board.

Resolved that M[r] Sedgwick be added to the Committee to solicit Subscriptions.

---

[1] Theodore Sedgwick (1780–1839), lawyer, author, legislator, reformer. Born in Sheffield, Massachusetts, Sedgwick graduated from Yale in 1798 and began studying law. In 1803 he began a partnership with Harmanus Bleecker in Albany (for whom see below, Minutes, Academy Trustees, March 8, 1815, footnote 1). In 1821 ill health forced Sedgwick to retire and join his family, in Stockbridge, Massachusetts. He maintained his connection with Albany by means of a membership in the Albany Institute, as a corresponding member of the first department. Sedgwick had an active retirement, involving himself in literary endeavors and various reform movements. He wrote and spoke against slavery, for free trade and temperance, for state-supervised education, and for the construction of the Boston & Albany Railroad by the state. Although an unsuccessful Democratic candidate for Lieutenant-Governor of Massachusetts, he was elected to serve in the state legislature in 1824, 1825, and 1827. He served as a Trustee of the Academy from March 23, 1813, until 1823; *Academy Seventy-fifth Anniversary*, p. 65; *DAB*; *Transactions*, Albany Institute, *1*, Part 2, Appendix:69.

The Board then adjourned to meet on the 31ˢᵗ March Instant at the Capitol at 10 o'Clock in the forenoon.

⊰{ 1814 }⊱

JOHN H. WENDELL[1] TO ANN ALEXANDER HENRY
Letters of Administration, 3:102, Albany County Surrogate's Court

[June 6, 1814]

The People of the State of New-York, by the
Grace of GOD, Free and Independent;
TO Ann Henry Widow & Relict of William
Henry[2] late of the City of Albany cartman deceased.

Send Greeting:

WHEREAS the said William Henry
at the time of his death was an inhabitant of this county, and, as is alleged, lately died intestate, having whilst living, and at the time of his death, goods, chattels or credits, within this state, by means whereof the ordering and granting administration of all and singular the said goods, chattels and credits, and also the settling, allowing and final discharging the account thereof doth appertain unto us; and we being desirous that the goods, chattels and credits of the said deceased may be well and faithfully administered, applied and disposed of, do grant unto you the said

Ann Henry
full power by these presents, to administer and faithfully dispose of all and singular the said goods, chattels and credits; to ask, demand, recover

---

[1] John H. Wendell (1752–1832), lawyer and Surrogate of Albany County. (Gorham A. Worth, *Random Recollections of Albany from 1800–1808*, 3d ed. [Albany, 1866], p. 42.) The original of this document is a standard printed letter with only the names of the deceased, the administratrix, the witness and Surrogate, the date, and other specifics written in Wendell's hand, including three of his signatures.

[2] We can determine little about William Henry's educational or vocational background, but some slight clues have surfaced. In this document William Henry's occupation is verified as "cartman"; the fact that the City's Common Council sanctioned this occupation through licensing and regulation of the teamsters' rates implies that William Henry may have been somewhat more established in the community than might be inferred from Coulson's claim that he was a "day laborer." (*Coulson*, p. 8.) It may be improper, too, to think of Joseph Henry's father as an intellectual void. We have found at least one book in the Henry library that was clearly owned by William, Montesquieu's *Reflections on the Causes of the Rise and Fall of the Roman Empire* (Edinburgh, 1775). We have been unable to determine any other attributes of Joseph Henry's father.

and receive the debts, which unto the said deceased, whilst living, and at the time of his death, did belong: and to pay the debts which the said deceased did owe, so far as such goods, chattels and credits will thereto extend, and the law require: Hereby requiring you to make or cause to be made a true and perfect inventory of all and singular the goods, chattels and credits of the said deceased, which have or shall come to your hands, possession or knowledge, and the same so made to exhibit, or cause to be exhibited, into the office of the Surrogate of the said county of Albany, at or before the expiration of six calendar months from the date hereof; and also to tender a just and true account of administration when thereunto required. And we do by these presents depute, constitute and appoint you the said———Ann Henry———administratrix of all and singular the goods, chattels and credits which were of the said William Henry.

IN TESTIMONY whereof, we have caused the seal of the office of our said Surrogate to be hereunto affixed:

WITNESS John H. Wendell Esquire, Surrogate of the said county, at the city of Albany, the sixth day of June in the year of our Lord one thousand eight hundred and Fourteen and of our independence the thirty eight.

J. H. Wendell

⊰{ 1815 }⊱

MINUTES, ACADEMY TRUSTEES

Trustees' Minutes, 1:16–18, Albany Academy Archives

March 8. 1815.

The board of Trustees of the Albany Academy met this day at noon in the Common Council Chamber of the Capitol.

Present. Stephen Vⁿ. Rensselaer, Senior Trustee

Henry Walton	The Mayor of the City;
John M. Bradford	Archᵈ McIntyre
Harmanus Bleecker[1]	John McDonald
William Niell	Chˢ D. Cooper
Timothy Clowes.	

[1] Harmanus Bleecker (1779–1849), lawyer, read law in the office of John Vernon Henry and subsequently entered into partnership in Albany with Theodore Sedgwick, Jr. Bleecker held many offices, including that of U.S. Congressman (1811–1813) and U.S. Chargé d'Affaires in the Netherlands (1839–1842). Harriet Langdon Pruyn Rice, *Harmanus Bleecker: An Albany Dutchman* (Albany, 1924).

The following extract from the Minutes of the Common Council of the City of Albany was received and ordered to be copied into the Minutes of this board.

At a Common Council holden at the Capitol Feb: 28, 1815.

Resolved, that Messrs Vⁿ. Rensselaer,[2] Brinkerhoof,[3] Humphrey[4] and Brown[5] be a Committee to confer with a Committee of the Trustees of the Albany Academy on the subject of a suitable plan or plans for an Academy in this City and that the said committee report such plan or plans together with the estimates of the expense thereof to this board, as soon as the same may be practicable.

A true extract from the minutes this 28th Feb. 1815

(Signed) J. E. Lovett[6] D[eput]y Clerk.

Resolved, that the committee[7] of this board heretofore appointed on the same subject procure a meeting with the Committee of the Common Council as soon as may be.

The Committee appointed at the last Meeting on the subject of teachers & their salaries, report—

That in their opinion the system of instruction in the Academy cannot go into beneficial operation without at least three teachers, one for the Mathematical, and two for the literary department, a principal & a subordinate.

The duties of the Mathematical & the Principal literary teacher are explained by their designations; it is expected that the subordinate literary teacher besides attending to the lower forms in the Classical School, will

[2] Killian Van Rensselaer (1763–1845), lawyer, was a member of the U.S. Congress for five terms, 1801–1811, and afterward practiced law in Albany. He served many years on the Common Council. Munsell, *Ann. Alb.*, *10*:363–364. Stephen Van Rensselaer (1764–1839) was his second cousin one generation removed. Florence Van Rensselaer, *The Van Rensselaers in Holland and in America* (New York, 1956), pp. 8–16, 22–25, 36–38, 54–55.

[3] So spelled. John Brinckerhoff (1773–1835) ran a hardware store in Albany. Joel Munsell, *Collections on the History of Albany, from Its Discovery to the Present Time with Notices of Its Public Institutions and Biographical Sketches of Citizens Deceased*, 4 vols. (Albany, 1865–1871), *2*:29, *4*:104 (hereafter cited as Munsell, *Coll. Alb.*).

[4] Chauncey Humphrey (?–1852?) was prominent in the affairs of Albany. He was canal collector for a number of years (post 1833) and a member of the Board of Directors, Albany City Bank, incorporated in 1834, Munsell, *Ann. Alb.*, *1*:296; *4*:358. He is listed in Albany City Directories from 1813 to 1851.

[5] Edward Brown (ca. 1771–1846) was a merchant who came to Albany from Connecticut. He became Dockmaster for the city in 1820, and held this post until his retirement in 1841. He served a number of terms as Assistant in the Fourth Ward of the city (six Assistants and six Aldermen were elected each year; any three Assistants and any three Aldermen, along with the Mayor, made up the Common Council). Munsell, *Ann. Alb.*, *10*: 372–373; Reynolds, *Alb. Chron.*, pp. 89–108 (City Charter).

[6] John Erskine Lovett (1794 or 1795–1847), lawyer, graduated from Yale College in 1814; he was later city attorney and an active member of the Common Council. Munsell, *Ann. Alb.*, *10*:381.

[7] Clowes, Mayer, and Walton. See above, Academy Trustees' Minutes of March 24, 1813.

also have charge of the English School, & will assist the Mathematical teacher in instructing the younger Scholars in Arithmetic, writing &c.

On the subject of salaries: the Committee propose that until further provision be made, that 1500 dollars per annum be offered to the Mathematical, & an equal sum to the Principal literary teacher; & that 1250 dollars be the salary of the subordinate teacher; making in the whole 4250 dollars per annum, expense of teachers. This sum, it is calculated may be raised in the following manner;

The Old goal[8] & lot sold for	$16.900
Grant of the Corporation[9]	5.000
Interest of which sums for 18 months at least, amounts to	2.300
Amount of subscriptions from the citizens; at least	5.100

Making the present monied funds of the Albany Academy $29.300	
The Annual interest of $29.300 is	$2.051
110 Scholars at an average of $5 per quarter	2.200
Making a yearly income of	$4.251

The Committee has had, as yet little opportunity of making enquiry for suitable teachers for the institution: the following gentlemen have however been spoken of & highly recommended—

For the Mathematical department   Benjamin Allen[10] L. L. D. & Henry Vethake.[11]

---

[8] The old jail and its lot on State Street were donated to the Academy by the City. The property (not the eventual site of the Academy building) was leased, after two purchasers in succession defaulted on payment, to various parties until 1832. On August 11 of that year the property was sold to the Mohawk Rail Road Co. for $15,500. *Academy Seventy-fifth Anniversary*, pp. 9–12, 145–146; Minutes, Academy Trustees, 2:56–59 (Meetings of August 1 and September 14, 1832).

[9] The Corporation of the City of Albany.

[10] Benjamin Allen (1770 or 1771–1836) was appointed as Mathematical Professor and Principal of the Academy (see below, Academy Trustees' Minutes of May 31, 1815), where he stayed for two years. He resigned when for reasons of economy the Trustees found it necessary to reduce his salary (see below, Academy Trustees' Minutes of May 16, 1817).

Allen graduated from Brown University in 1797 and tutored there 1797–1798; from 1800 to 1809 he was Professor of Mathematics and Natural Philosophy at Union College. Nothing is known of his later career. *Historical Catalogue of Brown University 1764–1904* (Providence, 1905), p. 84; *Academy Seventy-fifth Anniversary*, p. 69.

[11] Henry Vethake (1792–1866), mathematics teacher, political economist, was educated at Columbia, and taught mathematics and geography there for a time. In 1813 he began a long trek from college to college, teaching various subjects in seven institutions before he died. Having just missed becoming Joseph Henry's predecessor at the Albany Academy, he went on to become his predecessor at the College of New Jersey, where he was Professor of Natural Philosophy from 1829 to 1832. *DAB*.

For the literary department, principal & subordinate; Virgil H. Barber[12]
Stephen Munsell[13] James
Carnahan[14] Augustus
Wackerhagon[15] John Mc Jimpsey
James Aitcheson.[16] Joseph Shaw[17]

All which is respectfully submitted.

On Motion, *Resolved,* that this board will elect three teachers, agreeably to the opinion of their Committee above expressed; & that they will give 1500 dollars per annum to the Mathematical, & 1500 dollars per annum to the principal literary, teacher; & that the salary of the subordinate literary teacher shall be 1250 dollars, per annum. On Motion, *Resolved,* that this board will immediately proceed to choose by ballot a Mathematical teacher for the Academy.

The board proceeded to ballot accordingly, and on counting the ballots it appeared that Benjamin Allen L. L. D. was duly elected the Mathematical professor or teacher of this institution.

Ordered, that the Secretary inform Dr Benjamin Allen, of his election together with the annual salary the board will give; & desire his answer as soon as may be.

Resolved that the election of a principal & subordinate literary teacher be postponed to some future day.

On Motion, *Resolved,* that this board will now proceed to choose by ballot two trustees, to supply the vacancies occasioned by the resignation of the Revd Samuel Merwin & the Revd John McJimpsey. The board pro-

---

[12] Virgil H. Barber (1782–1847), Episcopalian minister, was for a time Principal of Fairfield Academy near Utica, New York. He later converted to Catholicism and became a Jesuit. After years of missionary work he taught at Georgetown University. John J. Delaney and James Edward Tobin, eds., *Dictionary of Catholic Biography* (New York, 1961), p. 98.

[13] Frank Munsell, *A Genealogy of the Munsell Family (Munsell, Monsell, Maunsell) in America* (Albany, 1884), unpaged, no. 501, lists a Stephen Munsill born June 12, 1796, in Winchester, Connecticut, who may be the candidate here. He was distantly related to Joel Munsell, the historian of Albany. We have been unable to trace him further.

[14] James Carnahan (1775–1859), a graduate of the College of New Jersey (Princeton), was a teacher and a Presbyterian minister. In 1823 he became President of the College of New Jersey, from which position he retired in 1854. His tenure includes the years (1832–

1846) when Joseph Henry taught there, and he will figure importantly in subsequent volumes of this work. *DAB.*

[15] Augustus Wackerhagen (1774–1865), born in Germany, was a Lutheran clergyman. He had a parish in Columbia County, New York, and died in Clermont. *Herringshaw,* p. 966.

[16] Not identified.

[17] Joseph Shaw (1778–1824) was born in Scotland. He became a minister in the Associate Presbyterian Church of North America, had a pastorate in Philadelphia, 1805–1810, and taught languages at Dickinson College from 1813 until he moved to Albany in 1815. His appointment as Professor of Languages at the Academy ended with his death in 1824. S. Austin Allibone, *A Critical Dictionary of English Literature and British and American Authors, from the Earliest Accounts to the Middle of the Nineteenth Century,* 3 vols. (Philadelphia, 1859–1871), 2:2061 (hereafter cited as *Allibone*).

ceeded to ballot accordingly & on counting the votes it appeared that John Lansing J͏ʳ & William James[18] were duly elected Trustees of the Albany Academy.

Ordered, that the Secretary notify John Lansing J͏ʳ & William James of their election

Adjourned.

---

[18] William James (1771–1832), the grandfather of a better-known William James (1842–1910) and of Henry James (1843–1916), had come from County Cavan, Ireland, at age seventeen, settled in Albany, and made a fortune in real estate. He was a staunch Presbyterian, and greatly interested in education. He served as a Trustee of the Albany Academy until his death in 1832. F. O. Matthiessen, *The James Family* (New York, 1947), pp. 3–4; *Academy Seventy-fifth Anniversary,* p. 65. His son, Henry James, Sr. (1811–1882), whose education at the Albany Academy was interrupted for several years as a result of injuries received in an accident, was, according to the *DAB* and *Coulson* (p. 23), tutored by Joseph Henry during his recovery. However, we have found no contemporary account substantiating this tale, now become traditional. It must be noted, however, that Henry and Henry James became close friends, and their exchanges will appear in subsequent volumes of the Henry Papers.

MINUTES, ACADEMY TRUSTEES
Trustees' Minutes, 1:24–26, Albany Academy Archives

May 31, 1815. The Trustees of the Albany Academy met this day in the Common Council Chamber of the Capitol: Present S. V͏ⁿ Rensselaer, John M. Bradford, Charles D. Cooper, John Lansing J͏ʳ John V. Henry, William James, John M͏ᶜ Donald, T. Clowes.

M͏ʳ Lansing from the Committee appointed for that purpose reported, that the Committee have communicated to M͏ʳ Allen his appointment as Principal of the Academy & Professor of Mathematics, and that M͏ʳ Allen had accepted of the said appointment on the terms proposed; and that he would be ready to open the Academy for the tuition of students on the 10ᵗʰ of September next.

The following Resolutions of the Corporation of this City having been this day presented to this board; ordered, that the same be filed and entered on the Minutes

"*Resolved,* provided the Trustees of the Albany Academy engage or call a competent Professor to teach the languages, if the funds of the Academy (at the end of the year) will not admit of paying the full salary to such professor, that this board will pay such deficiency of salary to the Trustees of the said Academy.

Resolved, that the Trustees of the Albany Academy be, and they are hereby requested to make an annual report to this board of the amount of their annual income from their funds and tuition, the number of Professors & teachers employed in the Academy, the salary paid to each annually, and the number of students taught and instructed in the Academy.

   In Com: Council

      May 29, 1815   Passed.

         (signed.)   H. Merchant[1]   Dep^y Clk."

Resolved, that in consequence of the foregoing provision of the Corporation of this City to make good any deficiency that there may be, in the funds of this board at the end of any year, to pay the salary of a Professor of the languages, that this board will proceed to the choice of a Professor of the languages.

Resolved, that in compliance with the foregoing request of the Corporation of this City, by whose wisdom & liberality this institution has been founded & endowed, a report shall be made to the Corporation yearly, of the amount of the annual income from our funds & tuition; the number of Professors & teachers employed in the Academy; the salary paid to each annually, and the number of students.

Resolved that a certified copy of the preceding resolutions, be delivered to the Corporation of this City.

Resolved, that at their next meeting, this board will proceed to the election of a Trustee to fill the vacancy occasioned by the resignation of Henry Walton Esqr

                                             Adjourned.

---

[1] Horatio Merchant, cited variously as justice of the peace, attorney, and deputy clerk in Albany City Directories of 1815 through 1824.

EXCERPT,[1] MINUTES, ACADEMY TRUSTEES
Trustees' Minutes, 1:29–30, Albany Academy Archives

September 15. 1815. The board of Trustees of the Albany Academy met this day at noon at the Common Council Chamber in the Capitol. Present Stephen Vⁿ Rensselaer, Theodore Sedgwick, John M. Bradford, Charles D. Cooper, William Niell, Harmanus Bleecker, John Mᶜ Donald, Archᵈ McIntyre, T. Romeyn Beck, Timothy Clowes.

The Committee appointed at a late meeting of this board to report on the qualifications proper to be required for the admission of scholars into the Albany Academy, as also, on the prices of tuition, reported the following resolutions which were adopted by the board.

Resolved that, None shall be admitted into the English School under the age of ten years, and who have not been taught to read and spell English correctly and to write a legible hand. In this school they shall be taught to read English with propriety, and to construe the language grammatically; they shall be taught English grammar and grammatical exercises, delivery of select pieces, Geography and History, the first five rules of Arithmetic, Book keeping and the principles of English composition. The price of tuition in this school shall be six dollars per quarter. A teacher shall be procured, and the school opened, whenever a sufficient number of scholars shall apply for admission.

Resolved, that the fees in the Classical and Mathematical schools shall for the present be eight dollars per quarter for every scholar. The fees in each school to be paid one quarter in advance into the hands of such person as the Trustees shall appoint to receive the same on the first day of every quarter.

Resolved that those who apply for admission shall undergo an examination respecting their qualifications by the teacher under whom they enter and when convenient and necessary in the presence of one of the other Preceptors or of one of the Trustees.

Resolved, that from the small number of Mathematical scholars which from present applications will for some months probably offer, it is judged expedient to commit them with the English School to the care of the Principal, who will have an opportunity of organizing and putting both in operation on the best plan and giving harmony and system to these schools so intimately connected with each other.

Resolved, that the Professors of the Academy be requested as soon as pos-

---

[1] A few lines from the end of these minutes, relating to routine business, have been omitted.

sible to confer together and to digest and report to this board a detailed system (agreeably to a report now before the board) of the plan of education which they may judge most proper for the institution in its present state, and also to determine and arrange the best method and the hours proper to be devoted to Classical & Mathematical studies, by those who incline to conduct these branches in concert.[2]

Adjourned.

[2] Apparently, the Trustees assumed an intimate connection between the English and Mathematical Schools but also the possibility of combining a classical and mathematical curriculum. The latter was, of course, the norm in collegiate liberal arts education in America at that time and for decades after, roughly until the triumph of the elective system. The report referred to is in the Trustees' Minutes of March 8, 1815, above.

❖{ 1816 }❖

MINUTES, ACADEMY TRUSTEES
Trustees' Minutes, 1:37–39, Albany Academy Archives

January 24th 1816 The board of Trustees of the Albany Academy met this day at 6 P.M. in the School Room of Professor Shaw in the Academy. Present—A. M[c] Intyre, Sen[r] Trustee; Mess[rs] M[c]Donald, Henry, Mayer, Bradford, Niell, James, Cooper, Bleecker.

In the absence of the Clerk,[1] M[r] Bleecker was appointed Clerk, pro tempore.

An Account of M[r] John Boardman amounting to £. 23.5.3 was reported to the board by the Committee of Accounts, and allowed to be paid.

The Report made by the Principal on the 29th day of November last, and the report of the Committee to whom the same was referred having been considered,—It was thereupon *Resolved,* that the following temporary regulations be adopted.

1. That it shall be the Office and duty of the Principal to see that the Regulations of this board as to discipline and education be duly executed; in his discretion from time to time as he may deem it necessary to attend in the school of the classical professor & the teachers, for the purpose of examining the different classes in their studies; after which examination he shall have power with the advice of the professor or teachers to remove the stu-

[1] The Reverend Timothy Clowes.

dents from lower to higher classes or vice versa, according to their standing in their respective classes.

2. That the Principal shall have power to make such regulations as he may deem necessary for the maintenance of good order in the several schools of the Academy & if any student shall be guilty of gross disobedience or disrespectful conduct to any of the teachers, his offence shall be reported to the principal who shall with the advice and consent of the professors and teachers or a majority of them have power to suspend such student until he make a written acknowledgment of his fault, and a promise of future good behavior;—that upon a second offence the Principal shall report his conduct to the Trustees, who may either suspend or expel him.

3. That the course of Latin Studies shall embrace the following authors; Cornelios Nepos, Caesar, Ovid, Virgil, Sallust, Livy, Terence, Horace, Ciceronis Orationes, de Officiis, et de Oratore; Quinctilianus, Juvenal, Persius, Tacitus &c & that the Greek Course shall consist of the New Testament Collectanea majora & minora, & Homer's Iliad, &c.

4. That the tuition in the Academy be so arranged as to admit of all the students being instructed in one or more of the following branches, to wit, Modern & Ancient Geography, Arithmetic, Algebra, Geometry, English Grammar & Penmanship, during the half of every day or the whole of every other day.

5 That the Academic Year shall commence on the first day of September; that the four quarter days be the first days of September, December, March & June, and that there be three vacations in each year; a winter Vacation from the 24th of December to the third day of January in the next year; a summer Vacation from the last day of July till the first day of September; and a spring Vacation of eight days to be appointed by the principal.

6. That the students entering during a quarter, (the present excepted) shall pay in advance, a proportionate part of the tuition money according to the time they respectively enter; that the principal shall receive the tuition money & pay the same to the Treasurer within eight days after each quarter day, that he shall keep an account of all monies expended during each quarter, in furnishing the Academy with Fuel & in repairing injuries done to the Academy, which shall be assessed by him on the students, and collected by him at the end of each quarter.

7. That every student on admission shall be registered in a book, kept for that purpose by the Clerk, and upon paying the requisite advance shall receive a certificate of membership in the following words, subscribed by the Principal

"Albany Academy
This certifies that A. B. is admitted a member of the Albany Academy
Principal"

and that every student shall be considered as a member of the Academy till he has obtained a regular dismission from the Principal which shall not be granted till he has paid his dues to the Academy.

8. That the business of every day be opened & closed with prayer.

9. That the Junior English Tutor shall officiate as Clerk of the Principal in the discharge of his official duties, and shall within five days of the Commencement of each quarter furnish the Treasurer with a list of the Students and an account of the amount of such assessment for fuel & repairs as shall be collected by the Principal, in the preceding quarter.

10. That there shall be two public examinations in every year, to commence on the third day preceeding the summer & winter vacations; such examinations to be conducted in the presence of the Trustees, by the Principal, Professor & tutors & shall embrace all the courses of Tuition in the Academy.

11. That the Trustees & Teachers shall give a token of approbation to such scholars as shall distinguish themselves by their scholarship & good conduct.

12. That a Committee of the Trustees be appointed every month to visit the Academy, and that they make a monthly report to this board.

Resolved, that Dr Niell, Mr Mc Donald & Dr Bradford, be the first Visiting Committee.

Resolved that the Monthly Meetings of this board be held on the second Tuesday of each Month at 6 O Clock. P.M.

Adjourned.

MINUTES, ACADEMY TRUSTEES
Trustees' Minutes, 1:40, Albany Academy Archives

27 February 1816. The board of Trustees of the Albany Academy met this day at 12 O Clock, at the room of Professor Shaw in the Academy: Present Arch^d Mc Intyre; John Lansing J^r; The Hon. the Mayor;[1] William James; T. R. Beck; H. Bleecker; T. Sedgwick; J. Mc Donald; J. M. Bradford; William Niell; Timothy Clowes.

[1] Philip Schuyler Van Rensselaer.

M.[r] Lansing from the Committee appointed to draft a petition to the Legislature for the establishment of a State Professorship of Chemistry and Mineralogy in the Albany Academy, reported the same; which was read by paragraphs; received some amendments; and approved.

Ordered, that it be fairly copied; that it be signed by all the members of this board now in this City; and that it be presented to the Hon. the Legislature by a Committee of this board consisting of Mess.[rs] M.[c] Intyre, Beck & Bleecker; who are also a Committee to attend the said application in its progress through the Legislature and to promote its success.[2]

Adjourned.

[2] This proposal was first formally raised in the Trustees' meeting of February 20, 1816. The legislative journals bear no trace of the petition. This was not to be the last attempt to get support from the Legislature for a chemical and mineralogical lectureship. The Trustees resolved to submit new bids on March 11, 1817, October 27, 1818 (see below), December 6, 1819 (see below), and December 5, 1820. All were unsuccessful. Only the last received any official recognition. It is the petition of December 5, 1820, which is presumably mentioned in the New York *Assembly Journal* for the 44th Session, 1820–1821, p. 92. It was referred to committee from which it apparently never emerged. Minutes, Academy Trustees, *1*:39, 76–77, 151–152, 166–167.

The repeated requests of the Trustees and similar efforts by others undoubtedly had some effect on the later willingness of the Board of Regents and the Legislature to support the distribution of scientific books and apparatus. See below, *The Statutes of the Albany Academy*, October 9, 1829, footnote 8.

MINUTES, ACADEMY TRUSTEES

Trustees' Minutes, 1:41–42, Albany Academy Archives

April 23.rd 1816. The Board of Trustees of the Albany Academy met this day at the Academy. Present. John V. Henry. Senior Trustee at this meeting. W.[m] Niell, the Mayor,[1] C. D. Cooper. T. R. Beck. F. J. Mayer. J. M. Bradford. Theod. Sedgwick, John M.[c] Donald, John Lansing, Timothy Clowes, H. Bleecker.

The Visiting Committee for February 1816. Report That they have attended to the duty assigned them, & that though the plan of education[2] & the manner of conducting it are susceptible of great improvement, yet in the opinion of the Committee, they are the best that the present circumstances of the institution will admit of, excepting in so far as they relate to the English School. The design of that school is in a great measure de-

[1] Philip Schuyler Van Rensselaer.

[2] This plan was submitted to the Trustees by the Principal, Benjamin Allen, and the Faculty on January 24, 1816; see above, the Trustees' Minutes of that date.

feated, & its teachers subjected to serious inconvenience, by the intrusion of Scholars from the classical & mathematical departments. This evil might be corrected by requiring every boy that wishes to learn penmanship, & other principles of English Grammar, to be wholly occupied with the studies of that school for, at least, one quarter.

The examination, upon the whole gave your Committee satisfactory evidence, as well of the diligence & proficiency of the pupils, as of the capacity & fidelity of the instructors. Would it not be well for the Principal & other teachers to form themselves into a Faculty with a view to carry into effect, a uniform system of discipline?

The importance of taking measures to procure a philosophical apparatus & library is respectfully recommended to the early attention of the Board. Globes & Maps are indispensable, & ought to be had without delay.[3]

(Signed) William Niell

John M. Bradford

The Revd Mr Clowes requested the board to accept his resignation as Clerk of the Board, which on motion was agreed to. *Resolved* that T Romeyn Beck be appointed Clerk in his place.

Messrs Sedgwick, Bleecker & Beck were appointed the Visiting Committee for the present month & they were instructed to enquire particularly into the state of the English School.

Resolved that Messrs Henry, Lansing & Sedgwick be a Committee to confer with the Comptroller & Corporation concerning the loan of such monies as may be necessary for the erection of the Academy, & also that they be allowed to loan any monies in the Treasury of this board not otherwise appropriated, for the above purpose to the Corporation.

Adjourned.

---

[3] For documentation on later purchases of apparatus, see below, Henry's Descriptive Catalogue of Philosophical Apparatus Purchased for the Albany Academy, [December 18, 1830].

MINUTES, ACADEMY TRUSTEES
Trustees' Minutes, 1:42–45, Albany Academy Archives

June 11th 1816.

The Trustees of the Albany Academy met this day at 12 O Clock, in D^r. Allen's room.

Present

A. McIntyre Senior Trustee at this Meeting

Wm Niell.	Timothy Clowes	J. McDonald
John V. Henry	John Lansing jun.	Wm James
John M. Bradford	T. Sedgwick	Chas. D. Cooper
Fred. J. Mayer.	H. Bleecker	T Romeyn Beck

Mr Lansing from the committee appointed for that purpose reported that they have purchased a pair of celestial & terrestial globes of Messr's Websters & Skinners,[1] for the sum of $40, which globes have by their order been delivered to the Principal, whereupon

Resolved that the Treasurer pay the said sum of forty dollars to Messr's Websters & Skinners.

An Account of Messr's Websters & Skinners & also one from John-Spencer & Co,[2] were presented, & referred to the Committee of Accounts.

The Visiting Committee for April 1816

Report

That shortly after their appointment, they attended to the duties assigned to them, & devoted the principal part of two days to an examination of the students, & also investigated the manner in which the course of instruction is pursued. They found that D^r. Allen was engaged in teaching Euclid, Algebra & different authors in Latin to several classes; that Mr Shaw was instructing in the Latin & Greek Languages; & that Mr Chapin[3] had numerous classes in arithmetic, geography, writing & english grammar, besides some scholars in Latin grammar.[4] With the proficiency of some of the

---

[1] Websters & Skinners, prominent printing house in Albany. Charles R. Webster (1762–1834) began business in 1782 as a newspaper publisher; in 1784 he started the *Albany Gazette* (which lasted until 1845). By 1788 his brother George Webster (1762–1823) was associated in the business, and in 1806 the two Websters took their nephew Elisha W. Skinner (1776 or 1777–1863) into the partnership, and the firm became Websters & Skinner. By this time, Websters and Skinner was publishing both newspapers and books. In succeeding years, two brothers of Elisha W. Skinner, Charles Skinner (1783 or 1784–1863) and Hezekiah Skinner (1784 or 1785–1833) joined the business; it was thus Websters & Skinners. After numerous vicissitudes the firm expired in 1845. Munsell, *Ann. Alb.,* 2:14, 176, 285–286, 298; 3:195; 5:10, 230–240; 8:89; 9:225, 267, 282; and Munsell, *Coll. Alb.,* 2:176; 3:244, 250.

[2] John Spencer (ca. 1780–1824), originally from New England, started a hardware business in Albany around 1808, and became in the course of the next decade one of the more prosperous merchants in the city. Munsell, *Coll. Alb.,* 3:295, 448; Munsell, *Ann. Alb.,* 8:106–107; *10:200.*

[3] Moses Chapin (1791–1865) graduated from Yale College in 1811, taught in Leesburg, Virginia, where he also read law for a time, before accepting the position as tutor in the Albany Academy (September 9, 1815). Chapin was let go after a year owing to the financial crisis which developed in 1816. (See below, Academy Trustees' Minutes, May 16, 1817.) He had, meanwhile, received his license to practice law, and he moved to Rochester to take up that profession late in 1816. In later life he held a number of judgeships in Rochester and Munroe County. F. B. Dexter, *Biographical Sketches of the Graduates of Yale College with Annals of the College History,* 6 vols. (New Haven, 1885–1912), 6:376–378.

[4] The texts used in this program are specified in *The Statutes of the Albany Academy Passed 5th December 1816* (Albany, 1816), pp. 9–14. Copy in the Albany Academy Archives.

classes they were gratified, but the result of their visit has been a serious & decided conviction that the present system is hardly calculated to answer the ends proposed, & that some important improvements have become extremely necessary. An additional teacher is much wanted in order to give more regularity to the instruction in particular branches which is now divided among all the officers of the academy. The Committee are not however prepared at present to present their views on this subject to the board, in consequence of the absence of one of their members[5] & also from their wish to consult the principal as to his ideas concerning it. The Committee therefore report *in part,* that the following circumstances are worthy of immediate attention.

1. The only system of Geography now taught is one called "Willets,"[6] a volume hardly exceeding the size of a toy book, & in the opinion of the Committee totally unfit as a text book for that important Science. They, therefore propose that Morse,[7] or some others be immediately introduced & that the Principal be request to instruct the students in that part of astronomy which is connected with Geography, as soon as he shall see fit and proper.

2. By the Regulations of this board adopted in January last, it is ordained that there shall be an examination of the students in the Academy, on the 29th day of July next, in the presence of the Trustees, & that the Trustees & Teachers shall give tokens of approbation to such of the scholars as shall distinguish themselves by their scholarship & good conduct. The Committee therefore propose that the Principal be requested to inform the scholars of the same & also that public notice be given for a week previous, inviting the attendance of parents & friends at said examination.

> (Signed) T. Sedgwick
> T. Romeyn Beck } C

June 3rd 1816.—

Resolved, that the above report be accepted & the following resolutions be adopted,

1. *Resolved* that Messrs. Henry, Bradford & Niell be a committee to con-

---

[5] Harmanus Bleecker; see above, Academy Trustees' Minutes of April 23, 1816.

[6] Jacob Willetts, *An Easy Grammar of Geography, for the Use of Schools, upon Goldsmith's Much Approved Plan* (Poughkeepsie, 1814); many editions thereafter.

[7] Jedediah Morse, *The American Geography; or, A View of the Present Situation of the United States of America . . .* (Elizabethtown, 1789) and many later editions; by at least the fifth edition (2 vols., Boston, 1805) the title had become *The American Universal Geography; or, A View of the Present State of All the Empires, Kingdoms, States, and Republicks in the Known World, and of the United States of America in Particular.* There were many subsequent editions. Morse (1761–1826) was the father of Samuel F. B. Morse, who figures significantly later on in Joseph Henry's career.

fer with the Teachers & to report to this board, what books shall be studied in the various departments, in addition to those already prescribed & also that they report a plan of education.

2. *Resolved* that the Clerk request the Principal to inform the students, that there will be a public examination on the 29th of July next & also that he give notice of the same for one week previous & invite the attendance of parents & friends at said examination.

3. *Resolved* that such tokens of approbation will be given by the Trustees at the ensuing public examination, as shall then be determined upon & that the Principals be requested to inform the students that tokens of scholarship & good conduct will then be presented.

Resolved that from & after the first day of September next, the price of tuition for such of the scholars in the English School, as may be studying Algebra, Euclid, or any of the higher mathematical studies with the principal, shall be eight dollars a quarter—

Messr's Henry, Mayer & Clowes were appointed the Visiting Committee for the present month.

Resolved that the Treasurer pay to M[r] Joseph Fry,[8] the sum of thirty four Dollars for his services in waiting on those individuals who owe subscriptions to the Trustees of the Albany Academy.

Resolved that Messr's Cooper & James be a committee to enquire into the state of the funds & that they report at the next meeting of this board.

Adjourned.

---

[8] Joseph Fry (1774–1856), printer, businessman, and for many years city gager, was born in East Greenwich, Rhode Island, and came to Albany in 1796. Fry compiled the first Albany City Directory in 1813. Munsell, *Ann. Alb.,* 5:40; 8:142, 334–335.

EXCERPT,[1] MINUTES, ACADEMY TRUSTEES
Trustees' Minutes, 1:60–65, Albany Academy Archives

Albany. Nov[r] 12th 1816.

The Trustees met, pursuant to notice

Present.

H. Bleecker.	J. Lansing jun[r]
T. Sedgwick.	J. M[c]Donald.

---

[1] Routine matters at the end of these minutes have been omitted.

J. M. Bradford Sr Tr present.	T. Clowes.
The Mayor.[2]	Wm James
T Romeyn Beck.	The Recorder.[3]
C. D. Cooper.	A. McIntyre.

Chancellor Lansing,[4] appointed to prepare a Report to the Common Council concerning the State of the Academy, during the last academic year, presented the following.

"In compliance with the resolution of the Hon, the Mayor, Alderman & Commonalty of the City of Albany, dated the 29th of May, 1815, The Trustees of the Albany Academy respectfully Report

That during the year preceeding the 31st day of August last past, at which period, the tuition in their Academy commenced, the Faculty consisted of Dr Allen, as Principal, with a salary of $2500 per annum & a House, the rent of which amounted to $200, of Mr Shaw, as Classical Professor with a salary of $2000 & of Mr Chapin, as English Teacher, with a salary of $1000—that during the year at an average eighty five students have been taught in the Academy—that the income arising from the funds of the Academy & from the tuition money amounted to $4074.54, & the amount of the disbursements relating to the establishment to $6,656.50 from which it appears that there is an excess of expenditure during the year, beyond the amount of the permanent & contingent Revenue, of $2581.96, leaving a deficit of Revenue to meet the disbursements of the year, after the $2000 for the salary of the Classical Professor shall have been satisfied by the City Corporation, of $581.96.—

The Trustees beg leave to suggest that an essential part of the Revenue of the Academy was intended to be derived from the interest of the Bond of the City Corporation for $5000—that on the 15th of March last there was due for interest on it $1050—& that with every aid which their munificence has extended to the infant Seminary they have so liberally patronized, its permanent Revenue will scarcely prove ade-

[2] Elisha Jenkins (ca. 1771–1851), merchant, was active in state politics and served as a colonel in the War of 1812. He was Mayor from 1816 until 1819 when he resigned. Reynolds, *Alb. Chron.*, p. 424. George Rogers Howell and Jonathan Tenney, eds., *History of the County of Albany, N.Y., From 1609 to 1886* (New York, 1886), p. 662 (hereafter cited as *Howell and Tenney*).
[3] Philip S. Parker (1775 or 1776–1831), lawyer in Albany for many years, was Recorder from 1816 to 1821. Munsell, *Ann. Alb.*, 7:118; *Proceedings of the Common Council* [of Albany], vol. 2, *Message of the Mayor and Reports of City Officers, 1935* (Albany, 1936), p. xxx.
[4] John Lansing, Jr., Chancellor of the State Court of Chancery, for whom see above, Academy Trustees' Minutes, March 4, 1813, footnote 4.

quate to ripen it to that state of maturity & usefulness which has been so anxiously anticipated.—They have however the pleasure to observe that the Funds of the Academy will be considerably releived in future, by the diminution of the amount of house rent, whenever the building destined for the Academy shall have been completed, which house rent during the past year was near $700."

Resolved that the above be adopted as the Report of this Board & that the Clerk present a copy of the same to the Common Council.

Mr Bleecker from the Committee appointed to enquire into the present state of the Academy presented the following Report

The Committee appointed to enquire into the present state of the Academy report, that from a statement made by the Principal it appears that on the 1st day of Octr last, the number of students was as follows,

In the 1st Class.	9	thirteen less than there were
2nd	21	in the month of August. That the
3rd	13.	income of the Academy from tuit-
4th	8.	ion money is now $970 more
5th	6	than it was the last year. With the
	57.	present number of scholars & the present
In the English School	18.	price of tuition, the whole amount
Total	75.	of tuition money will be $3,030.[5]

Add to this $1890, the interest of the permanent fund as stated in a late report[6] made to the Board & the whole annual income of the Academy will be $4,920. The annual expenses with four instructors exclusive of contingencies $6,300, being $1,300 more than the annual income. Of this last sum $800 will be saved in house rent, when the building[7] now erecting for an academy shall be finished. The annual deficiency then will be but $500, with a small sum for contingent expenses.

For the present course of instruction in the Academy, the Committee refer to a letter of the Principal accompanying this Report.

[5] These figures are apparently approximate, or else have been adjusted in unspecified ways. According to the Academy Minutes for August 5, 1816, there were 90 students. At that time, tuition was $8 per quarter for classical students, $6 for English students. In the course of September, tuition was raised to $12.50 and $10, respectively (see Minutes for August 5 and for September 14, *1*:48–57 and 58–59).

[6] See Academy Minutes for August 5, 1816, *1*:48–57.

[7] The Academy building was begun in 1815; the cornerstone was laid by Mayor Philip Schuyler Van Rensselaer on July 29 "with great ceremony before a vast concourse." Reynolds, *Alb. Chron.*, p. 416. The architect was Philip Hooker (1766–1836), for whom see *DAB* and William Lawrence Lassiter, *Philip Hooker and the Old Albany Academy* ([Albany], n.d.); Edward W. Root, *Philip Hooker* (New York, 1929). Classes opened in the new building in September 1817. Munsell, *Ann. Alb.*, *1*:200. The building still stands, but having been outgrown in this century, it passed into the hands of the City, when the Academy moved to larger quarters in 1931.

(Letter) "Dear Sir

The following is the present arrangement of studies and recitations in the Academy.

The *First* or highest class studies Mathematics, Belles Lettres, Latin & Greek Languages & recite as follows. Once a day to Proff. Shaw in Greek & Horace, once to the Principal in Euclid & once in Blair's[8] Lectures. The *Second* Class study Mathematics, Latin & Greek Languages. Recite once a day in Virgil & Livy alternately & once a day in Greca Minora to Proff. Shaw; spend the afternoon with the Principal in Algebra, will begin next week with Principal in Geography. They recite on friday in the afternoon to Prof. Shaw in Adam's Roman Antiquities.

The *Third* Class study Latin, Greek & Arithmetic. Recite once a day to the Principal in Arithmetic, once a day to M[r] Ferris[9] in Virgil & Sallust alternately & once in Greek to Prof. Shaw.

The *Fourth* Class study Latin. Recite once a day in Vici Romae to M[r] Ferris, & once to the same in Cornelius Nepos—Write once a day & recite a lesson in the grammar daily.

The *Fifth* Class study Latin. Recite twice a day to M[r] Ferris in Liber Primus—once a day in Latin Grammar. Write once a day.—

Two beginning Latin Grammar recite to M[r] Ferris, & one in Caesar, who will soon be able to join the 3rd Class in Virgil & Sallust

The English School write one hour a day—two hours in English Grammar—attend to reading & spelling. The rest of the time in Arithmetic. Three of the English School attend with the 2nd Class to the Principal in Algebra in the afternoon & two with the first class in Euclid & Blair

I am &c

H. Bleecker Esq[r]

Benj. Allen."

Ordered that the above report & letter be filed.
A letter from the Principal, dated Oct[r] 12th 1816, recommending John D. Crocker of Newyork as an English & Mathematical Tutor was read whereupon

---

[8] Probably one of the many American abridgements of Hugh Blair's *Lectures on Rhetoric and Belles Lettres* (London, 1783) which was reprinted in Philadelphia in 1802. Between 1807 and 1824, nine editions of the complete work appeared in America.

[9] Isaac Ferris (1798–1873), Reformed Dutch clergyman, graduated from Columbia College, and after teaching Latin for one year at the Albany Academy entered the New Brunswick Theological Seminary. He graduated in 1820, and went on to become an influential missionary and teacher. *DAB*.

Resolved that John D. Crocker[10] be & he is hereby appointed a Tutor in the English & Mathematical Department of this Academy, at an annual Salary of $500 to commence from the day on which he commenced instructing in the Academy & that the Clerk give him notice of the same.

---

[10] Probably John Dimmick Crocker (1793–1839) who graduated from Harvard College in 1815. He was a resident of New York when the appointment to the Academy was made, and apparently returned there after teaching for a year at the Academy and reading law in Harmanus Bleecker's office. He was practicing law in New York by 1820, and afterward moved to New Orleans. He died in Missouri. Information from MS alumni biography, Harvard University Archives; Munsell, *Ann. Alb.*, 1:300.

⚜ 1817 ⚜

MINUTES, ACADEMY TRUSTEES
Trustees' Minutes, 1:69–72, Albany Academy Archives

Albany. Jany 31st 1817.

The Trustees met, pursuant to notice

Present

John Lansing jun^r,	T. Romeyn Beck,	John Chester,[1]
John V. Henry,	J. McDonald,	S. Van Rensselaer, S.T.[2]
A. McIntyre,	H. Bleecker,	J. M. Bradford,
T. Sedgewick,	C. D. Cooper,	

Chancellor Lansing from the Visiting Committee Reported

That they have visited & examined the Academy & the various classes in it, that the numbers of each class & a description of the studies in which they are engaged are contained in the report of the Principal accompany-

---

[1] The Rev. John Chester, D.D. (1785–1829), was a Trustee of the Academy from 1816 until 1822. He was born at Wethersfield, Connecticut, and he graduated from Yale College in 1804. A student of Dr. Joseph Lyman of Hatfield, Massachusetts, he was licensed to preach by the Hartford Association College in 1807. Before moving to Albany in 1815, Chester preached in Marblehead and Springfield, Massachusetts, then Cooperstown and Hudson, New York. He quickly became devoted to the people of Albany and was a founder and president of the Albany Female Academy. He was appointed President of the Rensselaer Polytechnic Institute in June of 1828, which position he held until his death in the following January. He was most noted for his learned and eloquent preaching, his belief in the connection and interdependence of science and religion, and his devotion to the cause of education. *Academy Seventy-fifth Anniversary*, p. 65, and Henry B. Nason, ed., *Biographical Record of the Officers and Graduates of the Rensselaer Polytechnic Institute, 1824–1886* (Troy, N.Y., 1887), pp. 28–29 (hereafter cited as *Nason*).

[2] Stephen Van Rensselaer was Senior Trustee, or Presiding Officer of the Board, from 1813 until 1819.

ing this Report, that a conformity to the Statutes of the Academy appears to have been attended to as far as its circumstances will admit, but that the Books heretofore in use are in most instances still continued to be used from motives of economy, as diminishing the expense of Tuition & in some instances from the local impracticability of procuring the editions required, that these considerations appear to your Committee sufficient to warrant the delay of enforcing the recent statutes in that respect, that the Principal & Teachers unite in representing the conduct of the students as generally attentive & orderly & that there was nothing of a nature requiring the particular attention or animadversion of the Trustees.

(Signed) John Lansing jun^r

T. Sedgewick

Jany 31st 1817.   John Chester.

Ordered that the Report be accepted & that it be filed, together with the Report of the Principal (No. of Students. 73)

Resolved that Mess'rs Lansing, Cooper, & McIntyre be a Committee to enquire whether the building now erecting for an Academy, will be fitted on the first of May next, for the reception of the Students & of Dr Allen's Family & in case, it will not be, that they be authorized to procure suitable Buildings for the ensuing year, for the above purposes.

A Report was received from the Principal in pursuance of a resolution passed Novr 12th 1816, stating the number of Students admitted during each quarter since the opening of the Academy & the sums received from each for tuition money & incidental expenses.

The Committee of Accounts reported that they had examined the Accounts of Dr Allen, Principal of the Academy, with the vouchers accompanying them, & that it appears he received

For tuition for the several quarters from
the 18th of Septr 1815 to the 1st Decr 1816. $3387.01 1/2
For Contingencies charged to the Students   259.25
And for an Advance made to him by the Treasurer,[3]
by order, of the Board to defray
contingent expenses _____   100.

Making the whole amount rec^d by him to Decr 1. 1816 $3746.26 1/2
And it also appears that he has paid to the Treasurer $3291.12
And that his a/c of Contingent Expenses to the 31st

---

[3] John W. Yates (1769 or 1770–1828) was Treasurer of the Academy from 1813 until his death. He had graduated from Columbia College and read for the bar, then become clerk in the Albany Bank. Upon the incorporation of the New York State Bank in 1803 he was made cashier, which office he held for twenty-four years. Munsell, *Ann. Alb.*, 9:165.

of Dec[r] 1816, the changes in which are all supported by
vouchers, except in a few cases, where vouchers
ought not to be expected, amounts to—   455.14 1/2
                                                       ———————
                                                       $3746.26 1/2
And thus Accounts for all the Money rec[d] by him for tuition &c to the
1st of Dec[r] 1816.
Albany. Jan[y]. 31. 1817   (Signed)

A. M[c]Intyre
Charles D. Cooper

The Committee reported that they had audited the Account of Daniel I.
Winne[4] at $6.25. which was ordered to be paid.
An Account of S. Southwick[5] for printing was presented, which, on motion,
was allowed at $20; & ordered to be paid.

A letter in the following words was read

To the Trustees of the Albany Academy
    Gentlemen
        We are instructed by the Common Council of the City to confer
with you (or with a Committee to be appointed by You) on the propriety of uniting in a petition to the Honourable the Legislature to purchase the Academy, for the State, for a Governor's House.
        Be pleased to inform us, when & where we shall have the honour of
discharging the trust reposed in us by the Common Council.
                                        &c. Nich. Bleecker[6]
                                (signed) Peter D. Beekman[7]
                                        J. V. N. Yates

Whereupon
Resolved, that Messrs Lansing, Henry & Bleecker be a Committee of Conference on the part of this Board.[8]

---

[4] At least since 1813 Daniel I. Winne had acted as Albany's Marshal and Deputy Excise Officer. Albany City Directories, 1813–1817.

[5] Solomon Southwick (1773–1839), journalist, printer, postmaster, and an active Republican in New York State and Albany politics. *DAB*.

[6] Nicholas Bleecker, merchant and by 1824 clerk in the Albany Bank, was elected and reelected Supervisor and Alderman of the Third Ward in Albany from 1820 to 1832. Munsell, *Ann. Alb.,* 8:148; 9:167, 185, and Albany City Directories, 1813–1824.

[7] Peter D. Beekman (1762–1835), an Albany justice of the peace. His name was spelled Beeckman in the City Directories prior to 1821, and thereafter Beekman. Albany City Directories, 1813–1824, and Munsell, *Ann. Alb., 10:*239.

[8] Officialdom's jealous eyes must have been cast upon the Academy's nearly completed magnificent structure, but apparently no such purchase was to result from the Council's proposal. At the February 17, 1817, meeting of the Board of Trustees, the Academy's Committee of Conference was authorized to entertain specific proposals on the sale price and a substitute for the Academy building; however, no further mention is made of this transaction in the Board's minutes, and the Albany Academy occupied the building as of September 1817. Minutes, Academy Trustees, February 17, 1817.

Messrs. Bradford, McDonald & Cooper were appointed the Visiting Committee for the ensuing month.

Adjourned.

EXCERPT,[1] MINUTES, ACADEMY TRUSTEES
Trustees' Minutes, 1:83–91, Albany Academy Archives

May. 16th 1817

The Trustees met, pursuant to notice,

Present.

John V. Henry.	Theod. Sedgewick,
Arch.^d McIntyre, Senior Trustee. P.	The Recorder,[2]
John W. Yates,	T. Romeyn Beck,
Harmanus Bleecker,	William James,
Jno. McDonald,	

The Committee[3] appointed to consider of the present state of the Academy & to report to the Board what would be proper to be done
Report
    That they have investigated the state of the funds, and are fully convinced that it will be impracticable to continue the Academy upon its present establishment. . . .[4] The Corporation cannot comply with their engagements, nor is there a prospect of their doing so for some years to come. Under these circumstances, it is evident that an annual expenditure of $6000 cannot be continued, nor will a diminution of it from the dismission of subordinate teachers, tend to improve the condition of the funds. Since that in justice, should be founded on a diminution of students. However painful therefore it may be to the feelings of the Committee to propose a reduction of salaries yet such is the situation of the institution at present from various causes, but principally from the inability of the Corporation to fulfill their engagements, as to render this step indispensably necessary. On the part of the Trustees, every effort has been made, which the circumstances would admit, to obviate, if possible the necessity of resorting to this disagreeable measure. A Representation has been presented to the Com-

---

[1] We have omitted from these minutes certain financial details at places specified below.
[2] Philip S. Parker.
[3] This committee, appointed at the meeting of May 14, 1817 (Minutes, Academy Trustees, 1:80–83), consisted of Yates and Sedgwick.
[4] There follows an account of the financial state of the Academy, omitted here.

mon Council, in which the annual deficiency was stated to be such as to entitle the Academy to the aid promised by their resolution of the 29th of May 1815, but without success. An Experiment has also been made to supply the deficiency, by raising the price of tuition; this also has proved unsuccessful. The number of students has gradually decreased from 93 to about 60. A Reduction of salaries therefore is now become unavoidable. At what time, it should commence, is a subject of considerable difficulty for the Committee to determine. In justice to the present Professors, it should not be sudden, nor immediate, while a regard to the interests of the Academy will not admit of delay beyond the end of the ensuing quarter.

The Salaries paid at present amount to $5,500 per annum. The funds of the Academy in the opinion of the Committee do not admit of an expenditure exceeding $3,200 per annum. In fixing upon this sum, they estimate the Income arising from Tuition at about $1900 per annum, & the revenue from the permanent fund at about $1300. This estimate is founded on the supposition, that the Number of students, in consequence of the reduced price of tuition, will not be less than 70 or 75. It is presumed that they will exceed that number before the end of the summer session in Augst next. The teachers necessary to take charge of them, cannot be less than three, probably not less than four. But it will be safest & most adviseable to commence with the smallest number. They propose therefore that the Officers of the Academy after the   day of   next,[5] shall consist of

A Classical Professor at a Salary of	$1250
A Mathematical Professor at the same sum	$1250
An English Teacher, at a Salary of	$500
	$3000

The Duty of the Classical Professor shall be to teach the Latin & Greek Languages, according to the course prescribed in the Statutes That of the Mathematical Professor shall be to teach the several branches assigned to the Professor of Mathematics & Natural Philosophy.

The English Teacher shall teach English Grammar, Penmanship, Arithmetic, Book-Keeping & Geography.

Upon the establishment proposed, there is however reason to apprehend that the province of the Classical Teacher will be subjected to greater embarassment than that of the two others. The number of Classical students, which the low rate of tuition may bring to the Academy, may be so great as to render it extremely difficult for one teacher to instruct them. To obviate this, it has been suggested, that the mode of teaching by monitors ought be

---

[5] The effective date, here blank, was stated in the resolutions below.

adopted by way of experiment and as a temporary expedient. If however it should be found necessary to procure an assistant to the Classical Professor, it is hoped that the increased receipts from tuition, together with the annual Sum granted by the Regents, will be adequate to defray the additional expense.

With respect to the Mathematical Department, the Committee are particularly solicitous that this branch of education should form a prominent part in the Academical course. Institutions where the Ancient Languages are taught are becoming very common, but schools in which the different branches of Mathematics may be learned are comparatively few. A School in which young men can be taught Navigation, Surveying, Astronomy and the preliminary Mathematical studies is much needed & would be a great acquisition to this quarter of the states & it was hoped that before this time our own Academy would have become a place of resort for that purpose. The Committee are convinced that if it could acquire a reputation in this respect, it would immediately give the Seminary a distinction above others & secure to itself public patronage.

The Committee also propose by way of additional compensation to the Professors, that the two wings of the new Building shall be appropriated to their private use, as soon as they shall be in a fit state to be occupied.

In offering the preceeding plan, the Committee acknowledge the doubts which they themselves feel whether it will be attended with the hoped for success.

The first difficulty will be in procuring suitable persons for Professors. It cannot be concealed that the Board is placed in a very delicate situation with respect to those gentlemen, whom we brought here on the promise of munificent Salaries. They however are apprised that this institution owed its existence to the Corporation was dependent on it for support & has now suffered in common with every public body & individual, who possess real property & above all, they must be aware, that if the present establishment be continued twelve months longer, there will hardly be sufficient left to pay them one half of their present salaries. If however under present circumstances, they should think proper to resign, it will be important to take immediate steps for procuring competent teachers in their places.

Another circumstance that cannot be passed over, is the apprehension entertained by the Committee, that there may be a permanent diminution in the number of students, particularly those of an advanced age. Parents may be unwilling to place their children in this school, at least for some time, until those gentlemen, who may be procured, shall have established Some degree of reputation. It cannot be expected that their standing will be equal to those whom we have at present.

Under these circumstances, the Committee regret that they cannot present a favourable prospect of the affairs of the Academy being placed in a prosperous State for some time. They offer the above plan as the one that appears most feasible.

Other plans have however been suggested, one of which it may be proper to notice. It is well known, that in some foreign Institutions, of great reputation, the emoluments of the instructors depend entirely on the tuition fees. If the Board should be unwilling to hazard any further responsibility in employing teachers, whom they may be unable to compensate, it might perhaps be adviseable to divide the income of the permanent fund in a proper ratio among the teachers, & let similar division be made of sums received for tuition. As the emoluments would depend in great degree upon the reputation of the teachers, a great stimulus would undoubtedly be given to ardent & zealous men. There are however some difficulties attending such an arrangement—and among these, that of procuring competent individuals on such terms—the still greater difficulty, after having obtained them, of their consenting to be subordinate to a Board of Sixteen men, who are frequently changing, & who may differ in opinion on various points in the system of education, from those parents who afford emolument directly to the Teachers—& lastly, the difficulty of properly enforcing discipline.

In order to ascertain the sense of the Board on this preceeding remark, the Committe beg leave to propose the following resolutions,

1. *Resolved* that a Communication be addressed to the Principal[6] & Professor[7] informing them of the present state of the Academy, & also that it will be impracticable to continue the Institution on its present establishment after the end of the Academic year.

2. *Resolved* that the officers of the Academy shall after the first day of September next, consist of a Classical Professor, at a salary of $1250 per annum, a Mathematical Professor, at the same & an English Teacher at a salary of $500.

3. *Resolved* that the Clerk inform the Tutors[8] now engaged in the Academy, that it will not be in the power of the Board to avail themselves of their services after the present academic year.

4. *Resolved* that the above Professorships be offered to the present Principal & Professor, together with a house for each in the new building whenever the same shall be completed.

5. *Resolved* that a representation be made to the Corporation, concern-

---

[6] Benjamin Allen.   [7] Joseph Shaw.   [8] The Reverend Isaac Ferris and John B. Crocker.

ing the present State of the Academy & the plan that it is intended hereafter to adopt.

J. W. Yates Chⁿ

On Motion

Resolved that the Above Report be accepted.

Resolved unanimously that the first Resolution be adopted

Resolved that the second resolution be amended by altering the word "English" to "Assistant" & that, as thus amended, it be adopted.

Resolved unanimously that the third, fourth & fifth Resolutions be adopted.

Resolved that a Copy of the Above Report be the Communication to be addressed to the Principal & Professor.

Resolved that a Copy of the above report be the Representation to be addressed to the Corporation[9]. . . .

Adjourned.

[9] There follows the treasurer's report, here omitted.

MINUTES, ACADEMY TRUSTEES

Trustees' Minutes, 1:109, Albany Academy Archives

Albany. Augˢᵗ 14. 1817

The Trustees met, pursuant to notice

Present

Mʳ Mᶜ Intyre	Mʳ Henry	Mʳ Bleecker
Mʳ Stansbury[1]	Mʳ Mayer	Mʳ Mᶜ Donald
Mʳ Chester	Mʳ Van Rensselaer	Mʳ Sedgewick
Mʳ Clowes,	Mʳ Mayor[2]	Mʳ Yates
Mʳ Bradford	Mʳ Recorder[3]	

Mʳ Recorder, was appointed Clerk *pro temp.*

Resolved that T. R. Beck be & he is hereby appointed Professor of Mathematics in the Albany Academy.[4]

[1] Arthur J. Stansbury (1781–ca. 1845), Columbia graduate, clergyman, was Pastor of the First Presbyterian Church of Albany from 1817 to 1821. *Appleton's Cyclopaedia of American Biography.* Munsell, *Ann. Alb., 1:176; 6:125.*

[2] Elisha Jenkins.

[3] Philip S. Parker.

[4] Benjamin Allen resigned July 16, 1817 (Minutes, Academy Trustees, *1:96–99*). Beck was Principal until 1848.

Resolved that T R Beck be & he is hereby appointed Principal of the Albany Academy, & that he is invested with all the powers, & required to perform all the duties granted & enjoined by the Statutes of the Board of Trustees.

Adjourned.

EXCERPT,[1] MINUTES, ACADEMY TRUSTEES
Trustees' Minutes, 1:112–113, Albany Academy Archives

Albany. Nov.ᵣ 6. 1817

The Trustees met pursuant to notice

Present

The Mayor[2]	J. McDonald	H. Bleecker
The Recorder[3]	Theod. Sedgwick	Fred. G. Mayer
J. M. Bradford	J. W. Yates	Wᵐ James
Jnᵒ Chester	T. Romeyn Beck	

A Letter for A. McIntyre Esqʳ. was read resigning his seat as a trustee, *Resolved* that his resignation be accepted.

The Board then proceeded to nominate & ballot for a Trustee to supply the above vacancy & it appeared that William A. Duer[4] was elected, whereupon

Resolved that William A. Duer be and he is hereby appointed a trustee of the Albany Academy. . . .

The Principal reported that William H. Jephson[5] had made a present to the Academy of Cary's Atlas,[6] in imperial folio, containing sixty maps.

Resolved that the thanks of this Board be presented to William H. Jephson for his valuable donation.

---

[1] Portions of these minutes, indicated by ellipsis points, have been omitted.

[2] Elisha Jenkins.

[3] Philip S. Parker.

[4] William Alexander Duer (1780–1858), lawyer and educator, practiced in New York City, in New Orleans, and in Rhinebeck, New York. He sat in the New York Assembly from 1814 to 1820, became Judge of the State Supreme Court in 1822, and in 1829 resigned the latter post to accept the Presidency of Columbia College. In 1842 he retired and devoted the rest of his life to writing and public speaking. *DAB.*

[5] William Henry Jephson (ca. 1782–1862), merchant, is listed in Albany City Directories, 1813–1825; he apparently moved to New York City in 1825 or 1826. Munsell, *Coll. Alb.,* 3:351 notices his death in New York.

[6] John Cary, *Cary's New Universal Atlas, Containing Distinct Maps of All the Principal States and Kingdoms Throughout the World, from the Latest and Best Authorities Extant* (London, 1808) and later editions. A copy of the 1808 edition was listed in a catalogue of the Academy Library drawn up in 1839. Minutes, Academy Trustees, 2:499.

A Communication was received from the Faculty in the following words. "At a meeting held Novr 4. 1817, it was

Resolved that as a Class in the Academy has been for some time past prevented from engaging in the study of Ancient Geography, from its being considered inexpedient to require them to go to the expense of purchasing D'Anville,[7] which is very considerable, the Trustees be requested at their first meeting to grant permission to make use of *Holland's* Ancient Geography,[8] which it is presumed will answer every useful purpose & is not a tenth of the expense of D'Anville.

The present faculty on entering on their duties, found that Bonnycastle's Algebra[9] was used by the Students, instead of the system in Webbers Mathematics[10] as directed by the Statutes. They considering however Bonnycastle's the best elementary work on that Science, respectfully recommend that it be made the text Book in this institution"

A Copy

M. O' Shannessy.[11] Clerk.

Whereupon *Resolved* that Holland's Ancient Geography be for the present used as the text book on that subject & also that Bonnycastle's Algebra be & it hereby made the text book on that science in the Academy.

Adjourned.

---

[7] Jean Baptiste Bourguignon d'Anville (1697–1782), *Géographie ancienne abrégé*, 3 vols. (Paris, 1768) and later editions, translated as *Compendium of Ancient Geography*, by Monsieur d'Anville, 2 vols. (London, 1810). There were also earlier editions.

[8] John Holland, *A System of Geography* (Manchester, 1802) and many later editions. There was an American adaptation: *A Sketch of Ancient Geography, for the Use of Schools* (Boston, 1814).

[9] John Bonnycastle, *An Introduction to Algebra; with Notes and Observations; Designed for the Use of Schools and Places of Public Education. . .* , first, American edition, Philadelphia, 1806; second 1811. There were two editions published in New York, 1818, and many subsequent editions. See L. C. Karpinski, *Bibliography of Mathematical Works Printed in America Through 1850* (Ann Arbor, 1940), pp. 160–162.

[10] Samuel Webber, *Mathematics, Compiled from the Best Authors and Intended to be the Text-book of the Course of Private Lectures on These Sciences at the University of Cambridge* [Harvard], 2 vols. (Boston, 1801). Karpinski, op. cit., pp. 11, 140–141, 194.

[11] Michael O'Shannessy, teacher of mathematics at Albany Academy, 1817–1826, presumably had a hand in Joseph Henry's scientific education (Henry was enrolled in the Academy in 1819), but we know very little about him. He contributed problems and solutions to the "Mathematical Lucubrations" department of *The American Monthly Magazine and Critical Review*, 1817, *1*:477–478, 1818, *1*:237, 317; wrote a treatise on analytic geometry; and edited (sparsely) James R. Young's *The Elements of the Differential Calculus* (New York, 1833), and *The Elements of the Integral Calculus* (Philadelphia, 1833). He seems to have been a competent, if an uncreative, mathematician. The circumstances of his resignation from the Academy are related below; see the Academy Trustees' Minutes of April 14 and April 24, 1826. We do not know what his activities were after leaving the Academy; he attempted, however, to secure a teaching position at the Columbia Grammar School in New York City in 1828 (see Michael O'Shannessy to William Harris, February 7, 1828, in the William Harris Collection, Special Collections, Butler Library, Columbia University). For additional bibliographical details, see Karpinski, op. cit., pp. 294, 354–356, 585.

❧ 1818 ❧

EXCERPT,[1] MINUTES, ACADEMY TRUSTEES
Trustees' Minutes, 1:132, 134–136, Albany Academy Archives

Albany. Oct[r] 27. 1818

The Trustees met, pursuant to notice

Present

J. M. Bradford	H. Bleecker	William James
J. W. Yates	T. Sedgwick	T R Beck
A. J. Stansbury	John Chester	The Mayor[3] . . .
The Recorder[2]		

The Committee[4] on the Chemical Lectureship reported as follows

The Committee on the Chemical Lectureship begs leave to report that they consider this a proper & the most proper time for vigorous exertion. They esteem the object in itself interesting to the institution & they fully believe that it is now attainable. They therefore respectfully move the following resolutions

1. That a Chemical Lecturer be immediately appointed.

2. That a Committee be appointed to solicit subscriptions of the citizens of this place, & occupy the whole ground, that the operations of the board be not interfered with by persons without its control.

3. That a Committee be appointed to present a memorial to the Legislature of this State praying their patronage; That they endeavour to engage the friends of this institution to assist the petition; That said Committee may pledge this board that the Lectures during the session of the Legislature shall be practical & if the Legislature shall patronize them, they shall be free to the members of that body & to the officers of the State Government.

On Motion *Resolved* that the above Report be accepted.

---

[1] Portions of these minutes dealing with routine matters have been omitted.

[2] Philip S. Parker.

[3] Elisha Jenkins.

[4] This committee, composed originally of Arthur J. Stansbury, William A. Duer, and Theodore Sedgwick, had been appointed on January 13, 1818 (Minutes, Academy Trustees, *1*:114–115). They first proposed to have James Low give a course in chemistry and mineralogy, but the Board could not accept Low's terms, though it was willing to let him use a room in the Academy for a course to last only through "the present season" and to be offered by subscription. (Minutes, Academy Trustees, *1*:117–119, February 3 and 9, 1818.) Wyndham Miles discusses James Low briefly in "Public Lectures on Chemistry in the United States," *Ambix*, 1968, *15*:149. On September 8, 1818, John Chester was added to the committee which reports here. (Minutes, Academy Trustees, *1*:130–131).

Resolved that D[r] T R Beck be & he is hereby appointed Lecturer on Chemistry.

Resolved that the Mayor & Messrs Chester & Stansbury be a Committee to solicit subscriptions to arrange the terms on which they shall be received & also to make all disbursements on account of said Lectureship. *Resolved* that if it shall be deemed necessary by the above Committee, the Treasurer is hereby authorized to borrow a sum not exceeding five hundred dollars for defraying the expenses of said Lectureship, to be reimbursed from the subscription monies.[5]

Resolved that the Mayor, Messr's Bleecker & Bradford be a Committee to present a Memorial to the Legislature, requesting their patronage to the above Lectureship.[6]

Adjourned

---

[5] The committee managed to raise $180 or so, with promises from some persons for more. These sums helped to bear the cost of an initial purchase of apparatus and reagents, but the continuing expenses of the course were met by selling tickets of admission. Minutes, Academy Trustees, November 16, 1819, *1*:149–151; December 6, 1819, *1*:151–152; January 8, 1821, *1*:167.

[6] See above, Academy Trustees' Minutes, February 27, 1816, footnote 2.

⋘ 1819 ⋙

THE STATUTES OF THE ALBANY ACADEMY[1]
Albany Academy Archives

September 14, 1819

On this date the Trustees approved a revision of the *Statutes* originally passed on December 5, 1816.[2] With the exception of a few points to be noted shortly, the revisions were minor. The policies, organization, and procedures laid down in this small pamphlet governed Henry's education; they also were operative during his service as a faculty member. The next revision of October 9, 1829 (for which see below) represents a development of the initial *Statutes* with much of the text literally or essentially unchanged. In view of the importance of the Academy for an understanding of Henry's education and later professional career, issuance of the *Statutes* to Henry (chap. 2, section 8 specified that every student was to receive a copy) provides a suitable occasion for a review of the his-

---

[1] Printed, 21 pages.

[2] Printed, 18 pages.

tory of the *Statutes* and of the issues behind key sections. Prior entries from the Trustees' Minutes have given a few of the steps in this story, as well as specific examples of conditions in the Academy.

The Academy was granted a charter by the Board of Regents of the University of the State of New York on March 4, 1813. Instruction began on September 11, 1815. At a meeting of the Trustees on March 31, 1813, a committee presented a two-page description of the proposed institution;[3] this description was clearly the predecessor of the later *Statutes*. Although this text recognized that initially the Academy would have only a limited number of teachers and students, it proposed a goal "of five departments, or distinct Schools of literature and science": ancient languages, mathematics (including calculus), natural philosophy, "belles lettres," and natural history. Only the first two were formed at the opening of the Academy. The Academy admitted "any youth of competant age, who can read English tolerably, and of decent deportment . . . without examination into the Mathematical School, and into the first Latin Class."

Immediately after the school opened, the Trustees met on September 15, 1815, and resolved to ask the faculty to draw up "a detailed system . . . of the plan of education which they may judge most proper for the institution in its present state." The Board also requested that the faculty "determine and arrange the best method and the hours proper to be devoted to Classical and Mathematical Studies."[4] The Board waited two weeks, and, not receiving a report, resolved to nudge the faculty a little by appointing a committee to confer with them. The faculty at this time consisted of Benjamin Allen, Principal; Joseph Shaw, Professor of Classical Languages; and Moses Chapin, Tutor in English. The committee members were John Bradford, John McDonald, and William Neill.[5] On the 29th the faculty finally submitted its report, which, however, was not complete; they observed "that, having just commenced this arrangement, they are not at present able to give the Board of Trustees that particular detail, which they believe it will soon be in their power to give."[6] The matter rested there until the next year.

Meanwhile, however, Joseph Shaw (the Classical Professor) put in a report of his own of November 11, 1815, apparently unsolicited by the Board. Shaw did not present in his report a detailed plan, but he did discuss the relations of the classics and the sciences. Shaw put his finger on an ambiguity in educational policy as previously stated by the Trustees. It had not been decided whether the Academy was to be a preparatory school, from which students would move on into college, or whether it was to provide instruction at a college level. If the former, "then let a system corresponding to this inferior object be adopted." But if the founders of the Academy "designed it to combine a school and a college

---

[3] Copy in Albany Academy Archives.
[4] Minutes, Academy Trustees, September 15, 1815, *1*:29–31.

[5] Ibid., November 1, 1815, *1*:31–32.
[6] Benjamin Allen, "Plan of Education," November 29, 1815, Albany Academy Archives.

education, . . . then let it be distinctly understood. . . ."[7] This was the issue over which the Board and the faculty quarreled in 1816.

The Board took no action on these various documents until the following summer, when they again called for a complete "plan of education" from the faculty.[8] The faculty replied June 20 with a cursory report on the number of students in the school, a recommendation that the English School be abolished, and a statement that the faculty was unwilling to draw up a detailed plan, as the "System would materially vary, as the Academy is considered merely an elementary Institution, to prepare scholars for our colleges, or as calculated to give a course of instruction which shall complete the education of those who wish to attend it."[9] A committee (John V. Henry, Bradford, Neill) appointed to confer with the faculty rejected the faculty report as unsatisfactory, and requested that the faculty consult its "learning, science and experience" and prepare plans for the institution according to *both* conceptions of the Academy, that is, as an "elementary school," and as "a school, to give in itself a complete course of education."[10]

Several months elapsed, and the Board, having heard nothing from the faculty, resolved on November 12 to remind them that the Board was awaiting action on their part.[11] Allen replied on the 13th with a sketch for a plan in which the Academy would be divided into two parts, an elementary and an advanced department. Allen also, in separate documents, listed the classes and specified the texts.[12] In sum, Allen had submitted a curriculum, when it was evident that what the Trustees wanted was more like a constitution, in which not only curricular, but also disciplinary and procedural aspects of operating the school would be defined.

Accordingly, when the Board met on December 4, it expressed regret that "the documents received from the Principal [on November 13], are totally defective in many points, concerning which information was asked in the letter of the 24th of June last."[13]

Meanwhile, once again the indefatigable Shaw had written a plan of his own, this time at the request of the committee, by then unable to disguise its exasperation with Dr. Benjamin Allen. (Shaw's report, preserved in the Academy Archives, is enclosed by a cover which states that it was "prepared at the request of the Committee.") Once in possession of Shaw's plan, the committee sat down and drafted the *Statutes,* which, along with its report on the difficulties it had had with the faculty (i.e., Allen), was submitted to the Trustees.[14]

---

[7] Joseph Shaw, "Report . . . ," Albany Academy Archives.

[8] Minutes, Academy Trustees, June 11, 1816, *1*:42–45 (above).

[9] The report is signed only by Allen. Albany Academy Archives.

[10] John V. Henry to Faculty, June 24, 1816, Albany Academy Archives.

[11] Minutes, Academy Trustees, November 12, 1816, *1*:60–65.

[12] There are actually four documents from Allen constituting (in his words) a "system."

[13] Minutes, Academy Trustees, *1*:66–68.

[14] Shaw's plan is dated November 15, 1816. The committee report, with many of the pertinent documents attached, is dated December 4, 1816; Albany Academy Archives.

The committee recommended immediate action: "On the necessity of some plan, it is needless . . . to enter. The ill-defined powers and provinces of the teachers, the vacillating mode of instruction proved by the documents in the possession of the board, and the apathy which seems to pervade the proceedings of the faculty, are circumstances that render immediate and decisive steps by the Board, a work of imperious necessity." The Board accordingly considered the *Statutes* at the December 4 meeting, and passed them the following day, December 5, 1816.[15]

The ambiguous status of the school was not resolved by the 1816 *Statutes*. The Academy was more than an elementary school and less than a college. Eight years were required for the complete course, but no degree was given even though the level of work at the end compared favorably with the instruction in contemporary American colleges.[16] In the 1816 *Statutes,* admission to the Classical Department required simply a facility in reading English. Students were required to be ten years of age for admission to the English School, the elementary part of the Mathematical Department, in addition to being able to read and write English. The 1819 *Statutes* retained the admission requirement of the Classical Department but dropped the entering age for the English School to eight and simply asked for the ability to read English.[17] In view of the limited resources of the Academy, the requirement to educate eight and ten year olds was a severe challenge, one which detracted from the feasibility of developing the higher courses. From the Minutes of November 12, 1816, above, we can sense the reaction of Allen to this ambiguity. In the 1829 revision (see below, et passim), the problem of the elementary school loomed large.

The 1816 and 1819 *Statutes* provided for the Classical and Mathematical Departments, the English School being attached to the latter. Latin, Greek, Mathematics, and Natural Philosophy (part of the Mathematical Department) constituted the proper, standard educational curriculum of the day. Chapter 3, section 2 of both the 1816 and 1819 *Statutes* provided for the possibility that subsequently appointed professors of ancient languages might teach other sciences in which they were competent. In his report of November 11, 1815 (see above), Professor Shaw puts mathematics and natural philosophy in their proper place, at least in his opinion:

---

[15] Minutes, Academy Trustees, *1*:68.

[16] Other academies (i.e., Union, City College of New York, Hamilton) did become colleges. The act of April 13, 1787 reorganizing the University of the State of New York specifically recognized the possibility of academies becoming colleges. See George Frederick Miller, *The Academy System of the State of New York* (New York, 1969), p. 22 on this point and for a general overview of the academies. The comparison is based on S. M. Guralnick's dissertation, "Science and the

American College, 1828–1860," University of Pennsylvania, 1969. Even decades after Henry's departure, Academy graduates were often admitted to college with advanced standing. To this day the Academy has an elementary school program. Only in 1870 was it restricted to a college preparatory program. *The Celebration of the Centennial Anniversary of the Founding of the Albany Academy, May 24, 1913* (Albany, 1914), p. 29.

[17] Chapter 2 of the *Statutes* of 1816 and 1819.

But the reading of the classics should divide the time with Mathematics and the Physical sciences. For are there not many in Albany who, though they have neither time nor taste for literary pursuits, may yet wish to acquire the knowledge of Accounts, of Algebra, Geometry, Navigation, Mechanics, Astronomy, the commercial, political, and geographical relations of their own country and of Europe? And shall not the means of such knowledge be here furnished? Unless they are, many of the most promising boys in the Academy must be expected soon to quit it and seek for that instruction elsewhere, which they do not here obtain.

Although mathematics and natural philosophy were as much a part of a proper education as the classics by the standards of 1816, a modern reader senses an assumption here, which persisted, that the classics were designed to form gentlemen (i.e., those who did have the time and taste "for literary pursuits") while the sciences would do, in Gideon Hawley's words a decade later, "to prepare the greatest number of pupils for the useful pursuits of active life."[18] In other words, mathematics and the physical sciences were necessarily utilitarian. A modern reader might also wonder if Professor Shaw and others of like mind even conceived of *pure* mathematics and *pure* science. Was that a concept alien to the time? And if the lure of mathematics and science was needed to keep the classically oriented Academy afloat, was this the root of a future conflict?

The evidence we have examined does not indicate any conflict, certainly nothing of any serious dimensions. The classical curriculum and the mathematical curriculum coexisted. At the seventy-fifth anniversary celebration of the Academy the featured oration flatly declared, after granting the scientific attainments of faculty members like Henry, that the Academy was preeminently a classical school.[19] At the centennial celebration the Principal, Henry P. Warren, took up the matter at greater length:

Fathers believed that some children were ordained to gain intellectual power from books, while others, and by far the larger number, acquired their education by association, by attrition—we call it business, and they spent on book learning little time or thought after they had mastered the three R's and simple commercial forms. There was no fierce democratic spirit preaching the right of all to share in a kind of education fitted for the few, the wide training that comes from the mastery of books. The academy never attempted to popularize education. The classics were the basis of study, and it was true, as in the days of Augustus, that all roads led to Rome, and the next stadium brought the child to Athens. The only relief to him who was indifferent to the story of man, but thought naturally in symbols and revelled in things, lay in mathematics and science. It was largely through these schools [i.e. the classical academies] that mathematics came to

[18] See footnote 3 of the Minutes, Academy Trustees, September 11, 1826, below.

[19] *Academy Seventy-fifth Anniversary*, p. 41.

48

have a place in education in the United States disproportionate to that given them in Europe. We were an insular people, far removed from Europe; we spoke but a single language and the study of Latin and Greek was distasteful to many pupils; perforce they turned to mathematics. . . .[20]

Dr. Warren was a historian; he was probably giving voice to a traditional belief in his school—that it was both classical and mathematical.[21]

What was not said at the centennial celebration in 1913 was that the outstanding feature of the development of the curriculum between the *Statutes* of 1819 and 1829 was the growth of a nonelementary, nonmathematical, nonclassical curriculum in English, largely due to T. R. Beck. This included natural history and chemistry as well as courses in the humanities. The term "English School" in the early days of the Academy was applied to the most elementary instruction in reading, writing, and ciphering. The 1819 version added a few words to section 8 of chapter 3 allowing parents of children in the Classical Department to have them spend half time in English studies. By 1826, when Henry joined the faculty, the English School was on a par with both classics and mathematics. (For the English curriculum, see the entry of October 9, 1829, below.)

While the formal rules governing Henry's education at the Albany Academy survive, there is very little evidence about what actually happened to him at the Academy during his student years there. He was over-age but no surviving record indicates that he entered under a special dispensation or that any kind of scholarship aid was given to him. We know Henry was at the Academy from 1819 to 1822 with a period off for teaching in country schools.[22] There is no contemporary evidence that, for example, Henry took Latin or Greek while at the Academy, but the presence of a Greek grammar in his library and a few annotations in his books indicate at least that he had an acquaintance with the classics, perhaps a little Latin and somewhat less Greek. For examples of his mathematical training and a discussion of the science texts he used, see the entries of September 1, 1821, and June 27, 1822, below.

---

[20] Op. cit., p. 16.

[21] Dr. Warren's facts and interpretations are open to some questioning. We can only speculate about his meaning when he postulates a "disproportionate" emphasis on mathematics in America relative to Europe. One explanation is that Warren is not talking about pure or higher mathematics (in which Americans did not compare with the leading European nations in 1913) but that *more* Americans studied mathematics (of whatever level) relative to the classics than did Europeans.

[22] See below, T. R. Beck to Martin Van Buren, March 10, 1826.

MINUTES, ACADEMY TRUSTEES

Trustees' Minutes, 1:151–152, Albany Academy Archives

Albany Decr 6. 1819.

The Trustees met, pursuant to notice

Present

The Recorder,[1]	W. B. Lacey,[2]	John M. Bradford,
J. V. Henry,	John Chester,	T Romeyn Beck,
A. J. Stansbury,	Gideon Hawley,[3]	
W. James,	William A. Duer,	

Dr Beck reported that he had purchased the apparatus of Drs Low & Wing[4] on the following terms, viz A Deduction of 10 per Cent on the Valuation agreed up, leaving the balance due $218.76. Of the above, $90. to be paid immediately & the remainder to be paid out of the proceeds of the Lectures.

The Committee appointed on the Chemical Lectures beg leave respectfully to report the following plan

1. Tickets of admission to the Lectures for the season shall be sold for $5. Any person shall have for his own family, two tickets for $6, & three for

---

[1] Philip S. Parker.

[2] William Brittingham Lacey (1781–1866) was Rector of St. Peter's Church in Albany from 1818 to 1832 and subsequently a teacher and author of books on rhetoric and moral philosophy for schools and colleges. *Herringshaw*, p. 566.

[3] Gideon Hawley (1785–1870), like so many figures in the intellectual life of Albany, was a graduate of Union College. He was elected a Trustee of the Albany Academy in 1818. A lawyer by profession and active in railroad development, he was a pioneer in the expansion of public education in New York State. At this date Hawley was Secretary of the Board of Regents and State Superintendent of Public Instruction and was active, therefore, in the affairs of both the academies and the common schools. From 1842 to 1870 he was one of the Regents. *DAB*.

[4] Joel A. Wing (1788–1852), a physician, was taught medicine under the apprentice system. He came to Albany in 1814, and practiced for thirty-eight years there. Holder of an honorary M.D. degree from Williams College (1825), Wing was a highly regarded practitioner. Out-

side of this involvement with Low's proposed lectures (for which see above, Minutes, Academy Trustees, October 27, 1818, footnote 4), he had little other known scientific activity, although he was a resident member of the First Department of the Albany Institute. On February 9, 1818 (Minutes, Academy Trustees, *1*:119–120), he submitted a testimonial on Low's behalf. Since he and Low shared ownership in the purchased items, one can speculate that Dr. Wing had an interest in chemistry and, perhaps, even an interest in the possible profits from the chemical lecture series. The Minutes for November 16, 1819 (Minutes, Academy Trustees, *1*:149–151) give the estimated value of the articles as $243.06, of which chemical apparatus accounted for $156.31 and books for $50.00, the remainder being for "stove & pipe & benches." For Low, see above, T. R. Beck to J. W. Francis, February 26, 1812, footnote 22. For Wing, see Sylvester D. Willard, *Historical Address Delivered Before the Medical Society of the County of Albany in the State of New-York, November 11, 1856* (Albany, 1857), pp. 19–20, 25–27.

$10, & any number of tickets for his own family, above that number for $2, each.

2. All the expenses of the Laboratory shall be paid by the Professor,[5] except the just proportion of the attending class, of students belonging to the Academy, which shall be charged with the contingencies of the institution.

3. The Class in the Academy who study chemistry shall attend the Lectures gratis. All other students shall pay $1 each for a ticket.

4. *Resolved* that Messrs Kent,[6] Hawley, Henry, Duer, Yates,[7] Sedgewick, Bleecker[8] & the Recorder be a Committee to draw & present a petition to the Legislature of this state, praying for an annual appropriation to support a lecture which shall be open to its members & the officers of government.[9]

5. *Resolved* that the members of the Legislature & the officers of the State Government be invited to attend the first season gratis.

John Chester Chairman.

On Motion

Resolved that the report be accepted.

Resolved that the Lecturer on Chemistry shall receive for his own use all the monies that shall arise from the sale of tickets.

Resolved that the Study of Chemistry be introduced into the Academy & that *Parke's Chemical Cathecism*[10] be the text book.

---

[5] T. R. Beck.

[6] James Kent (1763–1847) served as a Trustee from 1819 to 1823. He was the first professor of law at Columbia College (1793–1798) and subsequently had various posts in the state judiciary. At this date Kent was Chancellor of the New York Court of Chancery. In 1823 he returned to Columbia. Kent's *Commentaries . . .* greatly influenced American jurisprudence. *DAB*.

[7] John Y. Yates.

[8] Harmanus Bleecker.

[9] For earlier attempts by the Trustees to win state support for the chemical lectureship, see above, Academy Trustees' Minutes, February 27, 1816.

[10] Samuel Parkes, *Chemical Catechism, with Notes, Illustrations, and Experiments* (New York, 1816). This is from the sixth English edition of 1814 "with emendations and considerable additions." Joseph Henry's copy survives and presumably was purchased when he came to the Academy. The title page bears the name of a prior owner, Horatio Lansbury (?), not identified. The contents of Beck's public lecture series and the course in the Academy are not known from any surviving documents. A reasonable presumption is that Beck followed Parkes to some undetermined extent and that the course was Henry's first in science.

Parkes (1761–1825) was a manufacturing chemist. *DNB*. The main body of the text consists of a catechetical section across the tops of the pages with a commentary at the bottom. The author specifically eschews mere memorization for understanding. Preceding the main body of the text is "An Essay on the Utility of Chemistry to the Arts and Manufactures Addressed to Parents in the Higher and Middle Ranks of Life" in which theoretical knowledge is justified by its practical advantages. The notes are a rambling commentary drawn from a wide variety of sources, some quite up to date, others quite unlike the sources cited by professional chemists even at that date. No one particular source predominates, but a modern reader might note the favorable mentions of Erasmus Darwin and Sir Humphry Davy. In addition to a glossary,

December 6, 1820

Resolved that the Study of Chemistry be commenced immediately after the study of History.

Adjourned.

---

tables, and index, the end matter has a section on experiments (pp. 475–511), including a number provided by Davy. The section closes with the admonition (pp. 511–512) not to practice the experiments merely for amusement but for instruction as "no effect, however extraordinary, or even trivial, it may appear to us, can ever happen but in consequence of some previously established law of unerring nature." Penciled scorings in the margin of this section may be Henry's and indicate which experiments he observed or even performed himself.

❧ 1820 ❧

SAMUEL LATHAM MITCHILL[1] TO T. ROMEYN BECK
T. Romeyn Beck Papers, New York Public Library

New York Dec.ʳ 6. 1820

My dear sir

I have perused with close attention the geological survey of Albany County made for the Agricultural society by yourself and Mʳ Eaton.[2] I

[1] Samuel Latham Mitchill (1764–1831) was a physician, United States Representative and Senator, and a promoter of science. A student of Dr. Samuel Bard (see *DAB* and T. R. Beck to John Wakefield Francis, February 26, 1812, footnote 8, above) and a graduate (M.D. degree) of the University of Edinburgh, he further studied law and acted as representative in the New York State Legislature. From 1792 to 1801 he occupied the chair of natural history, chemistry, and agriculture at Columbia College. He served in Congress until 1804, in the Senate from 1804 to 1809, and in the House again until 1813. In 1807, upon the founding of the College of Physicians and Surgeons in New York, he was chosen professor of chemistry, then of natural history, and finally of botany and materia medica; T. Romeyn Beck had studied there, graduating in 1811. Mitchill helped form the Rutgers Medical College in 1826, he was physician to the New York Hospital for two decades, and he participated in the founding of several literary and scientific societies. At the time of writing

this letter, Mitchill was Vice President of the New York County Society for the Promotion of Agriculture and Internal Improvements, a society comparable to the Albany County Agricultural Society (see next footnote). He published prolifically on medicine and natural history, but he distinguished himself most as a promoter both of science and of the practical application of scientific principles to life. See the *DAB* and Courtney R. Hall, *A Scientist of the Early Republic: Samuel Latham Mitchill, 1764–1831* (New York, 1934).

[2] Amos Eaton (1776–1842); see *DAB* and, below, Eaton to Stephen Van Rensselaer, March 25, 1826, footnote 1, as well as Ethel M. McAllister, *Amos Eaton* (Philadelphia, 1941). The Albany County Agricultural Society, founded in 1818, had its counterparts in practically every other county of New York; the State Assembly, through the Board of Agriculture during its short life beginning in 1819, allocated public funds to these societies for the encouragement of scientific agriculture. This geological survey of Albany County,

consider it a very valuable and highly respectable performance. The facts it contains [contribute][3] to Science and to Agriculture. They are so arranged and digested as to lead to useful and practical conclusions. The description of the rocks, and of the formation of soil by their disintegration and crumbling, appears to have been executed with fidelity as well as labour and skill.

As Mr Gibbon observed of Volney, on reading his Travels through Egypt and Syria, he wished the author would visit and describe the whole inhabited globe in the same able manner,[4] so I observe, after examining the report made by yourself and colleague, I wish you might explore every county of the State, in a like satisfactory and circumstantial way.

Your publication is a great model for imitation; and I hope it will prompt other persons to engage in similar pursuits. I utter this sentiment with a knowledge that few possess the high qualifications requisite for the task; but with the expectation, that among our young men, some will be found, and in sufficient number too, for such arduous undertakings.

I rejoice that the time has arrived when the public taste and feeling concur in promoting these inquiries. The best results may be anticipated from their further prosecution. What can be more interesting than such deductions as you have made from the analysis of arable soil, on the modes of culture and the crops to be raised?

Your notices of the organic Remains, and your sketch of the Helderberg, are particularly agreable to me.

As you have addressed me in the double capacity of a friend and Pupil, I seize gladly the opportunity of remarking that I cordially reciprocate

---

though published by the Agricultural Society, was sponsored almost exclusively by the Society's President who was also the President of the Board of Agriculture, Stephen Van Rensselaer. The highly successful survey, requiring about six weeks' time from early August until mid-September 1820 was acclaimed as "the first attempt yet made in this country to collect and arrange geological fact with a direct view to the improvement of agriculture." The survey results were communicated to the Society by Beck in October, and Beck and Eaton coauthored the publication, *A Geological Survey of the County of Albany*, before the end of 1820; the survey was printed in the *Memoirs of the Board of Agriculture of the State of New York*, Volume 1 (1821). See Amos Eaton and T. Romeyn Beck, *A Geological Survey of the County of Albany* (Albany, 1820); *The Plough Boy*, Volume 1, Number 15 (September 11, 1819), p. 119, Vol-

ume 2, Number 16 (September 16, 1820), p. 125, and Number 20 (October 11, 1820), pp. 158–159; Comptroller's Report of the Assembly, New York *Assembly Journal*, 44th Session, January 20, 1821, pp. 154–156; Munsell, *Ann. Alb.*, 3:234–235; McAllister, *Amos Eaton*, pp. 298–299.

[3] Mitchill inadvertently omitted here a word of approximately this meaning.

[4] Mitchill is paraphrasing Gibbon's exact statement: ". . . in two recent voyages into Egypt, we are amused by Savary and instructed by Volney. I wish the latter could travel over the globe." Edward Gibbon, *History of the Decline and Fall of the Roman Empire*, ed. William Smith (New York, 1911), 5:364. Gibbon was referring to Constantin François Chasseboeuf Volney, *Travels Through Syria and Egypt, in the Years 1783, 1784, and 1785* (London, 1787).

your amicable Sentiments, and that I feel proud in owning so excellent a disciple. Go on and prosper. You are doing much good. May your health and strength hold out to achieve a great deal more!

From yours sincerely
Sam¹ L. Mitchill

※{ 1821 }※

EXCERPT,[1] MINUTES, ACADEMY TRUSTEES

Trustees' Minutes, 1:175, Albany Academy Archives

July 9, 1821

The Committee appointed to rent the house belonging to the Academy reported that Mr Wilkes,[2] one of the tenants was indebted, for a considerable amount & also that he was a mechanic, able to make philosophical apparatus, whereupon

Resolved that the Principal be authorized to procure an Air pump & such parts of an Electrical machine as he may deem necessary from Mr Wilkes, provided however that the expense of the same do not exceed the rent now due.

[1] Routine business from the beginning and end of this meeting has been omitted.

[2] John Wilkes (1762–1829), letter cutter and gunsmith. Munsell, *Ann. Alb.*, 9:196, and Albany City Directories, 1813–1831.

EXERCISES FROM KEITH'S *TRIGONOMETRY*,[1] SEPTEMBER 1, 1821, AND NOVEMBER 22, 1821

Two notebooks, respectively 45 and 51 pages,
Henry Papers, Smithsonian Archives

In these two small books Joseph Henry copied texts, illustrative problems, and figures given in Keith, in addition to solving problems from that work. But for Henry's signature ("Jos Henry") and the dates on the inside of the front covers, these exercises might easily escape recognition as holographs. The handwriting

[1] Probably Thomas Keith's *An Introduction to the Theory and Practice of Plane and Spherical Trigonometry and the Stereographic Projection of the Sphere; Including the Theory of Navigation*, 4th ed. (London, 1820), since examples given in the notebooks refer to 1817 events. The only known copy of the 1820 edition in America is in the West Point Library and was not available for loan or copying because of fragility. The 1816 edition, however, was examined and seems from the relevant sections to be identical in most respects to its successor, or to deviate only slightly from it.

is neat and regular, unlike Henry's usual scrawl. Only at a few points does the writing assume characteristics approximating the more common hand of Joseph Henry.

The two notebooks are quite similar in nature to writings Henry would produce throughout the course of his life. He would carefully copy something from a printed source—a bibliographical identification, a portion of text, or sometimes a cursory précis. To these, Henry might add brief comments, references to related publications, or (if aroused by the text) an extended discussion. In these early examples Henry was studying spherical trigonometry and its application to navigation. He carefully copied portions of the textbook containing explanations and illustrative examples, independently worked out problems, and made a few references to related works. The first notebook is on "Stereographic projection of the Sphere" and contains nothing beyond the copied texts and worked-out problems. The second notebook contains "Astronomical Problems Solved by Oblique Spherics. . . ." At one point in this notebook Henry referred to "Vince's Astronomy;"[2] at another point, he cited "McKay's Navigation page 200"[3] for an azimuth projection and noted that further examples are in "Bowditch's Navigation."[4] These exercises are describable as modestly respectable but not advanced. The mathematics involved was widely appreciated in the America of 1821 because of its applicability in navigation and surveying, activities of great economic importance.

It is possible that these notebooks were school exercise-books. Henry was at the Albany Academy in the autumn of 1821. Although both Bowditch and Vince appear on the 1819 list of texts in the Academy's Mathematical Department, Keith does not. Related works are on the list, notably "Wallace on the use of the Globes" and "Lacroix's Spherical Trigonometry."[5] The Academy staff, however,

---

[2] Samuel Vince, *The Elements of Astronomy Designed for the Use of Students in the University*, first American edition (Philadelphia, 1811). Henry's copy of this survives and contains a later undated note by him that "This work appears to be an abridgement from the large astronomy of the author in 3 vols Quarto." Henry is referring to the first edition of Vince's *A Complete System of Astronomy*, 3 vols. (Cambridge, 1797–1805).

[3] Andrew MacKay, *The Complete Navigator; or, an Easy and Familiar Guide to the Theory and Practice of Navigation* (Philadelphia, 1807).

[4] Nathaniel Bowditch, *New American Practical Navigator*, probably the fourth edition (New York, 1817).

[5] *Statutes of the Albany Academy, 1819*, p. 13 (copy in Albany Academy Archives). In addition to Vince and Bowditch, the list of texts of the Mathematical Department of the Academy included the following:

John Bonnycastle, *An Introduction to Mensuration and Practical Geometry . . .* , second American edition from tenth London edition of 1807 (Philadelphia, 1818).

———, *An Introduction to Algebra . . .* , first New York edition from the tenth London edition of 1815 (New York, 1818). For the adoption of this text by the Albany Academy Trustees, see above, Minutes, Academy Trustees, November 6, 1817.

Tiberius Cavallo, *The Elements of Natural or Experimental Philosophy*, 2 vols., second American edition from the London edition of 1803 (Philadelphia, 1819). Henry's copy of volume 2 survives in his library.

Robert Gibson, *The Theory and Practice of Surveying . . .* (New York, 1814); the relatively scarce edition prepared by D. P. Adams.

"La Croix's Plane Trigonometry"

informally added and removed works from the approved list before obtaining the imprimatur of the Academy Trustees. In all probability, these notebooks were produced as class assignments, their neatness indicating they were meant for the eyes of the faculty.

Judging from the list of texts and the few surviving examples of Henry's course work, we can say that Henry received a sound education in mathematics and natural philosophy. The former culminated in the calculus. Although the calculus used the English, rather than the Continental notation, Henry's education was quite comparable in this area to the training given at that date in a French lycée in preparation for the university or one of the *grandes écoles*. It is certainly comparable to training given American students now; indeed, it may very well surpass what most actually receive. With the exception of the geography texts by Morse and Wallace, the works are all American editions, presumably pirated, of standard or at least reputable British texts with the exception of the trigonometry texts by Lacroix, the leading French mathematical textbook writer of the day.

In his extensive bibliography of mathematical publications in the Americas to 1850, L. C. Karpinski records a total of 2,998 titles and editions. He comments on this statistic:

"La Croix's Spherical Trigonometry" A minor bibliographical mystery. S. F. Lacroix's *Traité Élémentaire de Trigonometrie Rectiligne et Spherique* . . . (Paris, 1813) first appeared in an English translation by John Farrar as an 1820 edition published in Cambridge, Massachusetts, as *An Elementary Treatise on Plane and Spherical Trigonometry* . . . with an additional section on the application of algebra to geometry. Both works survive in the Henry Library and are clearly from the Albany period. Neither the *National Union Catalog*, the *British Museum Catalog*, nor L. C. Karpinski's *Bibliography of Mathematical Works Printed in America Through 1850* (Ann Arbor, 1940) lists English renditions of Lacroix as separate plane and spherical trigonometry texts. We know that such works existed in 1819 because of the notation in the Academy *Statutes*. By the time Henry's education had advanced to trigonometry, the Farrar edition had appeared. Henry's copy of the Farrar text is interleaved with blank sheets, many of which contain examples of Henry's work. Many of the pages bear scribblings by Henry.

"Morse's American Geography." See above, Minutes, Academy Trustees, June 11, 1816, especially footnote 7.

John Playfair, *Elements of Geometry*. . . .

Either the New York edition of 1819 based on the second London edition of 1814 or the Boston edition of 1814. In addition to plane geometry, Playfair covered solid geometry, plane trigonometry, and spherical trigonometry.

Robert Simson, *Elements of the Conic Sections* (New York, 1804) translated from the Latin original (Edinburgh, 1775). Henry's copy from the Academy period is in the Henry Library.

S. Vince, *The Principles of Fluxions* . . . , first American edition from the third English edition of 1805 (Philadelphia, 1812).

J. Wallace, *A New Treatise on the Use of the Globes* . . . (New York, 1812). Henry's copy was at one time owned by a Robert Johnson, according to a flyleaf inscription dated August 11, 1820. The Academy roster lists a Robert Johnson as having been enrolled in 1820–1821. *Academy Seventy-fifth Anniversary*, p. 81. Henry presumably acquired the book sometime after August 1820. Penciled check marks in the opening section of definitions may very well be Henry's, indicating this work was used in conjunction with Keith and with Vince's *Astronomy* in 1821.

Robert Woodhouse, *An Elementary Treatise on Astronomy* (Cambridge, 1812). Vince and Woodhouse are listed as alternatives.

No reasonable person should expect that in the period before 1850 America would have produced mathematicians to rank with Newton and the foremost European scientists. It was too much occupied with settlement, exploration, and expansion. The wonder is that at this time the population could furnish a body of readers of so much mathematical literature that was really valuable. *Upon the work of these years America built,* and the comparatively rapid progress after 1850 is due in no small measure to the broad and solid foundation laid in the earlier period.[6]

In the light of the education in mathematics of one American scientist as represented by these modest school exercises and by the entire mathematical curriculum to which he was exposed, Karpinski's conclusion seems quite reasonable. "The wonder" is that this interest escaped the attention of historians both before and after Karpinski's work appeared. The origins and significance of this body of mathematical publications is an important historical problem.

[6] Karpinski, op. cit., p. 17.

MINUTES, ACADEMY TRUSTEES
Trustees' Minutes, 1:188–190, Albany Academy Archives

April 8. 1822.

The Trustees met, pursuant to notice

Present

John Chester	Philip S. Parker.
John W. Yates	Eben. Baldwin[1]
T. R. BECK	Theod. Sedgwick,
	Gid. Hawley

On motion

Resolved that the 18th Sect. of the 4th Chapter of the Statutes[2] be so modified, as to allow the public speaking to be held on Friday Afternoon of each week.

[1] Ebenezer Baldwin (?1790–1837), lawyer, who had read law with Harmanus Bleecker. He was active in city affairs, and held the office of Recorder in 1825. Munsell, *Ann. Alb.*, *1*:299; *8*:122; *10*:267.

[2] Chapter 4, section 18, reads: "The Principal shall, on every Wednesday afternoon, instruct, or cause the Students to be instructed, in the correct reading of English prose, and Verse, and in the proper delivery of select pieces of Oratory." *Statutes of the Albany Academy* (Albany, 1819), pp. 14–15.

On motion, *Resolved* that the compass & chain, now in the possession of the Academy be purchased & that the Treasurer be authorized to pay Messr's Webster & Skinners the Sum of fifty nine dollars & fifty cents for the same.

The Committee to whom was referred the application of the Trustees of the Lancaster School[3] in this city
Report

That they have taken the subject into consideration & are of opinion, that it would not be productive of any material inconvenience, to admit a small number of pupils from the Lancaster School, into the Academy, to be instructed gratuitously.

They therefore recommend

1. That the number be limited to four & that none be admitted under the age of twelve years.

2. That the pupils be selected with great care & that none be admitted but such as are of a good moral character & have exhibited satisfactory evidence of talents & industry.

3. That as often as application shall be made by the Trustees of the Lancaster School Society for the admission of a pupil into the Academy, it shall be accompanied with a certificate from the teacher, setting forth particularly the qualifications of the person recommended & that the Principal of the Academy be authorized, if he shall deem it necessary, to make a strict examination into the merits of the candidate & to admit or reject him, as he shall think proper.

4. That the Principal shall have power to prescribe the course of study to be pursued by each, while in the Academy, having a view to their several qualifications & destinations in life.

5. That, if at any time after the admission of a pupil into the Academy, it shall appear to the principal, from a want of talents or industry in said pupil, or by reason of his improper conduct, that his further continuance in the Academy, would be useless or inexpedient, he shall have power to dismiss him & he shall make report thereof to the Trustees of the Lancaster School.

---

[3] The Albany Lancaster School was founded in 1810 on the Lancastrian monitorial plan, in which advanced students shared in the responsibility of teaching the younger ones. As a free school, it was intended to meet the need for public education; in its first six years alone, 1,149 students had attended the school. Apparently eclipsed by the growth of the Albany schools established as a part of the state's common school system, the Lancaster School's services diminished in the 1830s. The school's last recorded activity was in 1841. Munsell, *Ann. Alb.*, 2:304–307; see also John T. McClintock's "Albany and Its Early Nineteenth Century Schools," an unpublished paper written for the Harvard Graduate School of Education, Summer, 1967, pp. 13–20, and Appendices C through E. For a discussion of Joseph Henry's activities as a Trustee of the Lancaster School, see below, February 16, 1828.

6. That the term during which a pupil from the Lancaster School shall remain in the Academy, shall be two years, but that it may be prolonged, at the pleasure of the Principal, if, in his opinion, the extraordinary merits & proficiency of the pupil shall justify departure from the rule.

Provided always & it is understood, that all the books required by the said pupils during their continuance in the Academy, shall be furnished by the Trustees of the Lancaster School.

On Motion,

Resolved unanimously that the above report be accepted.

Resolved that a Copy of it be forwarded to the Trustees of the Lancaster School.

Adjourned.

JOHN McVICKAR[1] TO T. ROMEYN BECK

T. Romeyn Beck Papers, New York Public Library

Columbia College. 18th April 1822

Dear Sir,

Since the receipt of your letter I have made it my business to make such enquiries as would enable me to answer your enquiries satisfactorily.

The Bearer of this M[r] A B Quinby[2] comes recommended to me thro such Channels as that in case of his success, you may calculate upon a respectable Teacher and an excellent and worthy man. He satisfies also your patriotic requisite of a Native American. His other testimonials are confirmed to me by M[r] Renwick's[3] opinion of the exercises he has submitted to him. His letter from Gummere[4] of Burlington is very respectable. D[r] Adrain[5] has recommended to me and requested me to mention to you an

---

[1] John McVickar (1787–1868) was originally trained for the ministry. He taught political economy at Columbia College in New York City from 1817 to 1864. *DAB.*

[2] Very little is known about Quinby. George Daniels identifies him as one of the "Fifty-five Leading American Scientists of the Period 1815–1845" from his publications in the *American Journal of Science and Arts*, 1824–1827, on mechanical power conversions and steam engines but could not locate further information. *American Science in the Age of Jackson* (New York, 1968), p. 201.

[3] James Renwick, Sr. (1792–1863), of the Columbia faculty. He was well known for his work in engineering. As Professor of Natural Philosophy and Experimental Chemistry, his interests coincided with Henry's, especially in the work on terrestrial magnetism; Renwick will appear subsequently in this volume. *DAB.*

[4] John Gummere (1784–1845) was a schoolmaster in Burlington, New Jersey, known for his interest in mathematics. Henry may have learned surveying from his *Treatise on Surveying* (Philadelphia, 1814), as a printed set of solutions to the miscellaneous questions in this work is in Henry's pamphlet collection. *DAB.*

[5] Robert Adrain (1785–1843), a mathematician then at Columbia who independently of Gauss discovered the exponential law of error. *DAB.*

Irish Teacher[6] of this City, who will transmit to you his Certificate. In him I presume you would have the ablest Mathematician, in Mr Quinby the best Teacher and the most agreable Associate, and as your Institution now stands, I think I would prefer the latter. With the best wishes for the prosperity of the Institution over which you preside.

I remain
Respect^y Yours
John McVickar

[6] Not identified. The reference above to the preference for a native American may mean that Beck was dissatisfied with the incumbent, Michael O'Shannessy, who had served as tutor from 1817 to 1819 and thereafter as Professor of Mathematics and Natural Philosophy. O'Shannessy's departure in 1826 (see below, Academy Trustees' Minutes of April 14 and April 24, 1826) provided Henry with the opportunity for the career in science he was apparently seeking. The preference for a "Native American" of course reflects pervasive attitudes which became inflamed as the numbers of immigrants mounted in later decades. For the Albany aspects of this story, see William E. Rowley, "Albany: A Tale of Two Cities, 1820–1880" (Ph.D. dissertation, Harvard University, 1967).

STUDENT EXERCISE BOOK

Notebook, 51 pages, Henry Papers, Smithsonian Archives

[June 27, 1822]

This leather-bound notebook gives reason to speculate that much of Henry's formal education was commonly by rote. The notebook contains a few pages of work in English. The bulk of the volume is mathematical and reveals that Henry was supposed to learn mathematics by copying theorems, problems, and solutions verbatim from journals and texts available to him. Appearing at the bottom of one of the completed solutions (on page 20) is the date June 27, 1822, so we conjecture that this notebook was used at about that time, for assignments at the Albany Academy.[1]

On the first page of the notebook Henry copied a short statement, source unknown, about the virtues of studying mathematics; the neat handwriting and smooth grammatical style indicate that this text was probably part of a recitation. The point of the statement is well summed up by the conclusion: "But of all the sciences which serve to call forth the spirit of enterprise and enquiry, there are none more eminently useful than the Mathematics."

[1] On page 46 of the notebook appears, not in Joseph Henry's handwriting, a "List of Eclipses Solar and Lunar Calculated for the Meridian of Albany." Here the dates and times of lunar and solar eclipses for 1791 have been recorded, and from them the eclipses of 1793 have been calculated. As the handwriting and subject matter depart from the rest of the notebook, and as the date of the calculations is probably prior to the 1793 eclipses, the notebook was probably used by someone before Henry.

The first major section of the notebook suggests that Henry used the notebook for at least one of his English exercises. Some eight pages are devoted to "Synonymic Elucidation" in which Henry wrote out the meanings and sometimes the etymology of nine sets of common synonyms; the neatness of hand and the proper grammar suggest that this too was a copying exercise.

There follow three pages in which Henry copied three mathematical problems from James Adams's "On the Finite Value of Circulating Decimals," *Annals of Philosophy*, n.s., 2 (July–December 1821). Henry's notebook then has one page devoted to "the investigation of a rule given at page 136, Boneycastle Mensuration" and an exercise in finding "the solidity of a frustum of a cone," the organization and neatness of which indicate that it was copied from some unidentified source.

Next the notebook is filled, for twelve pages, with fifteen problems and solutions, in algebra, plane and solid geometry, and mechanics. These problems and solutions appeared in 1820 in the *New York Literary Journal and Belles-Lettres Repository*.[2] Comparison of the text with the publication confirms that Henry copied the exercises precisely, perhaps as a rote learning procedure.

The final section of the notebook, from page 33 to the end, consists of "Diophantine Problems." A three-part "statement of general principles" is followed by eighteen problems and accompanying solutions.[3] Again, grammatically and stylistically the text appears to be a copying exercise, although the original mathematical publication has not been identified.

[2] From volume 3, nos. 1 (May 1820) through 6 (October 15, 1820). The problems were supposedly posed by readers, and the solutions followed in subsequent issues. William Marrat (1772–1852, *DNB*) and Robert Adrain (1775–1843, see above, John McVickar to T. R. Beck, April 18, 1822, especially footnote 5), both mathematics teachers in New York City at the time, contributed most of the problems as well as the solutions.

[3] The final leaf of the notebook (pages 50 and 51) is physically fragmentary, there being four pieces stored separately from the notebook. They can be pieced together and made legible enough to determine that the Diophantine Problems continued at least as far as problem number 18, but enough of the bottom is missing to make it uncertain if other pages are still missing.

 1823

"LICENCE FOR BEGGING FOR THE LYCEUM"[1]
Correspondence, Albany Institute Archives

Albany Feb 24th 1823

To the Honourable Common Council of the City of Albany

[1] So entitled on the verso of the document above the Mayor's permission printed at the end of the petition to the Common Council of Albany. This is simply one example of the

The undersigned respectfully represent, That the trustees of the Albany Academy have granted to the Albany Lyceum of Natural History, the use of an unfinished room in the Albany Academy upon the condition that the Lyceum shall finish the said room at its own expense. That for the purpose of raising the necessary funds, to accomplish this object & also to procure cases &c for the minerals & plants, it has been thought expedient to circulate a subscription paper among the Citizens of this place. Your memorialists therefore representing the Albany Lyceum, respectfully request from your Honourable Body permission to raise by subscription such sums as may be necessary to accomplish the object which they have in view.

Rich Varick DeWitt[2]
M. Henry Webster[3]
Henry J Linn[4]
P. Anderson.[5]

Permission allowed for thirty days
Chas E Dudley[6]
Mayor

---

many instances of fund raising by the Albany Institute and its predecessors. A modern reader might wonder at the connotations of the word "begging."

[2] Richard Varick DeWitt (1800–1868) was a son of Simeon DeWitt. A graduate of Union College, DeWitt read law with Harmanus Bleecker. He had land holdings in Ithaca, New York, owned a steamboat line on Lake Cayuga, and established the Ithaca and Oswego Railroad, which failed in the panic of 1837. A paper of his on a steam safety valve (January 1, 1832, Albany Institute Archives) was sent to Henry for review, but no report of Henry's survives. See Munsell, *Coll. Alb.*, 4:5–7 and Cuyler Reynolds, ed., *Hudson-Mohawk Genealogy and Family Memoirs*, 4 vols. (New York, 1911), *1*:366.

[3] Matthew Henry Webster (1803 or 1804–1846) was interested in natural history and particularly active in the Lyceum and its successor, the Albany Institute. Not much is known about him. A lawyer and author, Webster attended the Albany Academy from 1815 to 1819 and received a B.A. (1822) and an M.A. from Union. Henry Hun, "A Survey of the Activity of the Albany Academy" (unpublished manuscript, 1922–1935, Manuscript Division, New York State Library and Archives of the Albany Academy); *Union University: Centennial Catalog, 1795–1895, of the Officers and Alumni of Union College in . . . Schenectady, N.Y.* (Troy, 1895; hereafter cited as *Union Catalog*). Munsell reports that he and Lewis C. Beck were partners in the business of enameling hollow ware. The elder Henry James sent an account of Webster's life to his novelist son suggesting it was "a regular Tourgenieff subject." F. O. Matthiessen, *The James Family* (New York, 1947), pp. 123–125. Munsell, *Ann. Alb.*, 10: 241, 248, 372.

[4] Henry J. Linn was an attorney (see Albany City Directories, 1825–1828). He was not an active worker in natural history so far as surviving records indicate, nor did he play any discernible role in the successor Institute.

[5] Peter Anderson was an attorney, not otherwise active in the Lyceum. He probably died in 1824 (Albany City Directories, 1823–1825).

[6] Charles Edward Dudley (1780–1841) was a merchant and a Democrat who was five times elected Mayor of Albany. Many years later his widow, Blandina Bleecker Dudley, endowed the Dudley Observatory. Reynolds, *Alb. Chron.*, p. 432.

❦{ 1824 }❦

FROM ROBERT L. WILLIAMS[1]
Henry Papers, Smithsonian Archives

Dear Friend   New York Jany 10th [1824].[2]

I take advantage of a private opportunity to [write] to you but on account of shortness of the notice [I have] merely time to write a few words.

Our residence is now faced at the corner of Vandam & Greenwich s^ts to which place you can consequently direct your favors.

I am now following the advice of sad experience which has shown me that "he who in studying the public good sacrifices his own livelyhood defeats his own intentions and is like a brave soldier who indiscreetly rushes into danger and thereby robs his country of a valuable member." All things cannot be done in a moment. It may be years before that is known which was not known and that is venerated which was passed needlessly by by the few that saw it or rather *did not see it*. Every day fixes my sentiments (in relation to affecting good in a certain way) more firmly. [My] mind is sometimes wraught up to a degree of enthusi[asm w]hich can scarcely endure to wait for anything—[But] deliberation enshures success & the demonstration that [?time] effects is irresistable. It is contrary to the nature of things for men to reject a thing which promotes that which good and bad men desire ie *their happiness*. As for impediments those we must expect as they always goe before useful things & we do not want for examples of the *sceptical opposition* that useful things have met with even in our day. I speak enigmatically but you will understand what I speak of.

Enclosed with this you will find a few copies of a song that I have just published.[3] As a copy may be interesting to my friends you will please leave a copy with Mr Meads[4] (Cabinetmaker North Market S^t) with my respects when business leads you that way.

---

[1] Robert L. Williams is listed in the Albany City Directories for 1824 and 1825 as a teacher of piano. He then moved to New York, as this letter says, and is listed in City Directories there until 1832 (except 1827 and 1831), finally as "professor of music." His last published piece apparently was "President Harrison's Inauguration March, " New York, 1841.

[2] Joseph Henry wrote at the side of the first page of this letter: "a letter from Mr. Williams 1824." The upper left corner of the first sheet of this letter is torn.

[3] This was "Kind Robin Loves Me." Williams published another piece, "Angelina Waltz," in 1835. This information and the biographical data in footnote 1 were furnished by Richard Jackson of the Library and Museum of the Performing Arts, The New York Public Library, Lincoln Center, New York, and by William Lichtenwanger, Music Division, Library of Congress.

[4] John Meads was born in England. He was a cabinetmaker in Albany for many years, active in the Mechanics' Society and prominent

When you have a convenient opportunity give a couple of copies to M[rs] Van Renssellaer[5] or what I should prefer (in speaking to any of the family about me) your mentioning that you have a piece of mine in immitation of the Scotch which I have lately published and promised to show them a copy but bring them a couple and show them. I should like to have a copy come to the hands of some of my musical friends but if a present comes directly from me others will take exceptions. Neither should I like to do any thing that would look like soliciting future favor. As "straws sometimes show which way the wind blows." Persons are too apt to judge by straws.

I feel interested to know whether things are going on according to your wishes whether you have any propositions for instructing in other families.[6] My intercourse & knowledge of families may enable me as a friend to give you some hints in such things. I shall be happy to reciprocate with you by letter as far as time and business will permit.

The circumstances you mentioned the last evening I conversed with you aught not to remain unnoticed untill it is to late. Uncertain circumstances leave a fine field for scandal with her thousand tongues and a bud that is niped can never blossom again.

Remember me to all enquiring friends & accept my sincere wishes for your prosperity & happiness. While I remain

> Your devoted Friend
> R. L. Williams

If you should like to be acquainted with M[r] Durham[7] & M[r] Flint[8] (who between you and I is Flint by nature) you can call to mention my residence or give my respects or what you please. These particularly M[r] Durham you can converse with as you would with me on *Society subjects* as *I have communicated my mind to them.*

---

enough in the affairs of the city to run twice for Alderman on the Republican ticket (1831 and 1833: he was defeated both times). He died in Albany in 1859 at the age of 82. Munsell, *Ann. Alb.*, *1*:436; *8*:111; *9*:151–152, 232, 244, 273; *10*:476.

[5] Probably either Cornelia Paterson Van Rensselaer (1780–1844), second wife of Stephen Van Rensselaer (1764–1839), or Harriet Elizabeth Bayard Van Rensselaer (1799–1875), wife of Stephen Van Rensselaer (1789–1868); more likely the former, for reasons stated in the next note. Florence Van Rensselaer, *The Van Rensselaers in Holland and America* (New York, 1956) is a good guide to this prolific family.

[6] This is one of the few contemporary references to Joseph Henry's having been a private tutor. He is said to have taught the children of Stephen Van Rensselaer (1764–1839) for two years, ca. 1820–1822, but we have some reservations about these dates. Thus it is more likely that he would have been closely acquainted with Cornelia Van Rensselaer than with Harriet E. Van Rensselaer, though of course he might have known both. See *Coulson,* pp. 16–17. It seems more probable that Henry tutored the Van Rensselaers after leaving the Academy, let us say 1822–1823 or 1824.

[7] Possibly James H. Durham, listed in Albany City Directories, 1823–1835, as teacher and proprietor of a boardinghouse.

[8] Not identified.

Please enquire of Mr Meyall[9] whether the musical society meets and if so who plays on their organ.

I shall be anxious to hear from you soon. You will not forget to notice what winds blow in Albany & minute down all the bad winds as the faults that others find behind our backs are vary acceptable to those who wish to correct themselves. If you have any commands here I shall be happy to attend to them in turn.[10]

I have another favor to request which is that when you are at the Post Office you will inquire whether there are any letters for me, and if there are, direct them or get the people in the Post Office to direct them to the corner of Greenwich & Vandam S^{ts}. In the bustle of moving I forgot to request this favor of any one.

[9] Probably William Mayell, who came from London in 1795 and set up shop as a hatter. "He was the most extensive manufacturer of hats in the city; and besides being a good mechanic, made some pretensions to science." He was active in the Mechanics' Society and in the Albany Institute, where, in 1824, he delivered a paper on the mechanical and chemical processes used in hatmaking. (*Transactions*, Albany Institute, 1830, *1*, Part 2, Appendix: 28–29.) Mayell died at Albany in 1855. Munsell, *Ann. Alb.*, 3:129; 7:148–149, 327–328.

[10] The paragraph immediately following was written over the last lines on the last page of the letter and perpendicular to them.

MINUTES, ALBANY INSTITUTE
Institute Minutes, 1:1–6, Albany Institute Archives

[May 5, 1824]

Whereas, The Society for the Promotion of Useful Arts did on the [eighteenth][1] day of February A D. 1824 send to the Albany Lyceum of Natural History a communication presenting for the consideration of the Lyceum, sundry resolutions relative to the formation of an Institute for the promotion of Science & Literature. *And whereas* after mature consideration thereof, the said Resolutions were modified and amended by the Albany Lyceum on the Fifteenth of March and having been returned to the Society for the Promotion of Useful Arts, the said Amendments were agreed to by that Society on the [?] day of March.[2] Which said Resolutions so amended and passed are in the words following:

[1] The day is not given in the original; it has been supplied here from a copy of the communication which the Society sent to the Lyceum. This may be consulted in the manuscript correspondence in the Archives of the Albany Institute of History and Art. For the Society for the Promotion of Useful Arts, see above, Beck to Francis, February 26, 1812, footnote 17.

[2] This account of what took place is slightly euphemistic. On February 18, 1824, the Society for the Promotion of Useful Arts sent to the

Resolved, That an Institution for the Promotion of Science & Literature, be formed by the name of the *Albany Institute,* to consist of Three Departments, viz.

1. The Department of Physical Sciences and the Arts:
2. The Department of Natural History; And
3. The Department of History and General Literature.[3]

Resolved, That the Society for the Promotion of Useful Arts as at present constituted be the first Department.

Resolved, That the Albany Lyceum of Natural History as at present constituted, be the Second Department.

Resolved, That Individuals be invited to form a Society for the Promotion of History and General Literature and when such Society shall be organized it shall be the Third Department of the Institute.[4]

Resolved, That the Officers of the Institute be a President, Three Vice Presidents, Three Corresponding and Three Recording Secretaries, a Treasurer, Librarian, and as many Curators as the Second Department may direct.[5]

Resolved, That the President be chosen by a plurality of the votes of the Members of the Institute.[6]

Resolved, That the Presidents of the Departments be the Vice Presidents of the Institute.

Albany Lyceum a slate of resolutions proposing a State Institute (Albany Institute Archives, Correspondence, 1795–1830); the Lyceum replied on March 8 that its members did not "consider it expedient that a State Institute should be established as recommended by the resolutions," and did not "consider an union of the Societies advisable" (ibid.). There must then have been some conferring, for by the following week, as reported by the above text of May 5, the Society made a new proposal, which was apparently accepted by the Lyceum (though we do not have documentation of the meeting at which they approved the Society's proposals) and on March 31 appointed a committee, on which members of the Lyceum also apparently sat, "to make arrangements to carry into effect the articles of Union adopted between this Society and the Albany Lyceum" (ibid.). There were significant differences between the resolutions sent by the Society to the Lyceum on February 18, 1824, and the resolutions in the minute of May 5 here under consideration. These are noted in footnotes below. In general, the changes gave greater control to the Lyceum

and guaranteed preservation of the integrity of each of the component societies within the Institute. These resolutions of May 5 were written into the Constitution of the Institute, practically without change. See below.

[3] This resolution includes the first two among those sent by the Society to the Lyceum on February 18, 1824 (hereafter referred to as the February resolutions). The second resolution there calls for "an institution to be formed by the name of the New York State Institute."

[4] This department was formed the following year; see Institute Minutes for February 2, 1825, below.

[5] The February resolutions stated that there would be "as many curators, as may hereafter be determined to be annually elected."

[6] The February resolutions stipulated that each of the three departments would nominate one person for the office of president, and if any two departments agreed in their choice, the man they named would be president. If all three nominees were different, an election would be held, a plurality deciding the contest.

Resolved, That the Corresponding and Recording Secretaries of the Departments, be the Corresponding and Recording Secretaries of the Institute.

Resolved, That the Librarian of the First department be the Librarian of the Institute.

Resolved, That the Curators of the Second department be the Curators of the Institute.

Resolved, That the Treasurer be chosen by a plurality of the votes of the Members of the Institute.[7]

Resolved, That the first Election of the Officers of the Institute be on the first Wednesday of May & that the Annual Election thereafter shall be on such days as shall be ordained by the By-Laws of the Institute which shall be so regulated as to be as soon as may be after the Annual Election of the Departments.

Resolved, That those persons who are at the formation of the Institute, the Members of the Societies constituting the Departments shall be considered the Members of the Institute.

Resolved; That the Meetings of the Institute be held every fortnight during the first four months of the year for receiving Communications from the several departments for the reading of Original Communications and for such other business as may relate to the objects of the Institute.

Resolved, That the meetings of the Institute be alternately held at the Room of the Society for the Promotion of Useful Arts and in the Apartment of the Lyceum in the Academy until otherwise directed by concurrent Resolutions of those Societies.

Resolved, That the Books now belonging to, or hereafter coming into possession of the Lyceum be deposited in the Library of the Institute, and that the Specimens of Natural History now belonging to or hereafter coming into the possession of the Society for the Promotion of Useful Arts be deposited in the Museum of the Institute.[8]

Resolved, That those persons who may be Elected Members of either Department after the formation of the Institute shall become Members of

---

[7] The three resolutions here which concern the choice of Librarian, Curators, and Treasurer comprised the twelfth of the February resolutions. It specified that they were to be elected eventually, but that at the start the Librarian of the Society was to be the Librarian of the Institute and the Curators of the Lyceum were to be the Curators of the Institute.

[8] The resolutions of February 18 required that lists be drawn up of books and specimens then in possession of the Society and the Lyceum. Books and specimens added after the formation of the Institute became the Institute's property, whereas here it was agreed that the Lyceum's books would be on deposit only in the Society Library and similarly the Society's specimens would be on deposit with the Lyceum.

the Institute on the payment of Three Dollars as an Initiation fee, and the further sum of One Dollar annually to the Treasurer of the Institute.[9]

Resolved, That if it be found impracticable to organize the Third Department as above proposed: the Institute shall be formed of the First and Second Departments as above constituted and that Every thing in these Resolutions contained in relation to those Departments shall be considered as the Articles of Union or the Constitution of the Institute.[10]

Whereupon a Joint Committee[11] was appointed by the Society for the Promotion of Useful Arts and the Albany Lyceum of Natural History to carry the above Resolutions into effect. Which Committee afterwards on the third of May caused public Notice to be given to the Members of the Society for the Promotion of Useful Arts; & of the Albany Lyceum of Natural History, that a meeting of the Institute would be held at the Room of the Society for the Promotion of Useful Arts in the Capital, on Wednesday the fifth day of May One thousand Eight hundred and twenty four.

At which meeting the following Gentlemen having appeared Viz.

Simeon DeWitt	Elisha W. Skinner	Richard Varick DeWitt
Jonathan Eights[12]	James G. Tracy[14]	S. V. R. Bleecker[17]
Charles R. Webster	M. H. Webster	Joseph **Henry**
Henry W. Snyder[13]	Lewis C. Beck[15]	William Cooper[18]
William Mayell	James Eights[16]	Fred^k Matthews[19]

---

[9] The fees suggested in the resolutions of February 18 were five dollars initial fee and two dollars a year thereafter, these sums never to change.

[10] The resolutions of February 18 made several provisions which were dropped from the slate agreed to in March. They asked that persons who were members of both the Society and the Lyceum choose in which department they would vote; that a list be drawn up of members belonging to each department and that a report on changing membership be made at each meeting; and that the debts of each society be ascertained and discharged by the Institute in a manner to be agreed upon.

[11] This is presumably the committee appointed March 31 (see above, footnote 2), consisting of Simeon DeWitt, Elisha Jenkins, T. R. Beck, Jonathan Eights (for whom see below, footnote 12), William Mayell, and unnamed members of the Lyceum.

[12] Jonathan Eights (1773–1848), physician, studied medicine with several doctors in Albany and surgery for one year in Philadelphia. He practiced in upstate New York for a number of years before settling in Albany in 1810,

where he remained for the rest of his life. He was physician to the poor of the city in various years, associate contributor to the *New York Medical and Physical Journal* (which ran from 1822 to 1830), and President of the New York State Medical Society in 1830 and 1831. Munsell, *Ann. Alb.,* 5:48; 7:143; 9:99–100.

[13] Henry W. Snyder, engraver, reported as being active in New York City, 1797–1805, and having had work published in books printed in Boston, 1807–1816, arrived in Albany ca. 1813. From 1820 to 1830 he was Chamberlain (i.e., treasurer) of Albany. His name appears in Albany City Directories until 1832. G. C. Groce and D. H. Wallace, *The New York Historical Society's Dictionary of Artists in America, 1564–1860* (New Haven, 1957), p. 592; Munsell, *Ann. Alb.,* 7:152; 8:108, 132, 158, 162–164; 9:175, 192, 201.

[14] James G. Tracy appears in Albany City Directories, 1831–1839. He was the author of two memoirs in the *Transactions,* Albany Institute, "On the Uvularia Grandiflora, as a Remedy for the Bite of the Rattlesnake," 1830, *1*:32–34 (read February 29, 1828) and, with

Lewis C. Beck, "Note Respecting the Ranunculus Lacustris," ibid., 148–149 (read June 7, 1830).

[15] Lewis Caleb Beck (1798–1853), brother of T. R. Beck, was graduated from Union College in 1817 and licensed to practice medicine in 1818. He practiced medicine in Schenectady, St. Louis, and Albany before beginning his career as a teacher. His first appointment in the latter profession came in 1824 when he was named teacher of botany at the Berkshire Medical Institution; in the same year he became Professor of Botany, Mineralogy and Zoology at Rensselaer Polytechnic Institute. In 1826 he joined the faculty of the Vermont Academy of Medicine to teach botany and chemistry; he was Professor of Chemistry and Natural History at Rutgers; lecturer on chemistry at the Albany Academy, 1831–1834; professor in New York University, 1836; Professor of Chemistry and Pharmacy in the Albany Medical College in 1840. *DAB* and *Academy Seventy-fifth Anniversary*, p. 69. Beck was a competent and well-read chemist. His published papers are of the analytical variety, and he devoted some study to mineralogy and geology. Beck also submitted a paper on magnetism to the Institute, but it was not published (Institute Minutes, February 14, 1827). In 1827, Beck and Joseph Henry collaborated in producing a scale of chemical equivalents, for which see below, Beck to Henry, April 15, 1827, and related documents. Beck wrote a chemical textbook, *A Manual of Chemistry* (Albany, 1831) based primarily on Edward Turner's *Elements of Chemistry* (London, 1827, and many subsequent editions). Beck's *Manual* is an able summary of contemporary knowledge and has the added virtue of exact and complete references to the literature on which the author drew.

[16] James Eights (1798–1882), topographical and scientific draftsman, naturalist, physician, and explorer, was the son of Jonathan Eights. He became "Dr. Eights," but apparently never practiced medicine. In 1829, he sailed with the exploring expedition to the Antarctic under Captain Nathaniel B. Palmer, who was probably the discoverer of Antarctica (in 1820), and Captain Benjamin Pendleton. Eights went along as naturalist, and reported his observations on the natural history of the South Shetland Islands and the southern seas in papers in the *Transactions*, Albany Institute, 1833–1852, *2*:53–69, 331–334, in the *Boston Journal of Natural History*, 1837, *1*:203–206, the *American Journal of Agriculture and Science*, 1846, *3*, part 2:219–223, 1846, *4*, part 1:20–24, 1847, 5, part 5:248–259, and *Niles Weekly Register*, 1834, *46*, part 1:180. After the expedition, Eights seems to have settled into a life of "rather idle and impecunious ease" (Clarke, p. 200: see below), contributing anonymous articles (1835–1840) on natural history to the Albany *Zodiac*, studying the geology of the Albany region (see *Transactions*, Albany Institute, 1833–1852, *2*:335) and reconstructing the look of the city in 1805, in a series of paintings which have become justly famous. G. C. Groce and D. H. Wallace, *The New York Historical Society's Dictionary of Artists in America, 1564–1860* (New Haven, 1957), p. 209.

Eights was chosen to go on the United States Exploring Expedition (the Wilkes Expedition) in 1837, but for unknown reasons was later dropped from the scientific corps of that venture. Little is known of his later life. Clarke believes he helped Ebenezer Emmons prepare his reports on the agriculture of New York. Eights spent his last years at the home of a sister in Baltimore, where he died. See John M. Clarke, "The Reincarnation of James Eights," *Scientific Monthly*, 1916, *2*, part 2:189–202, and W. T. Calman, "James Eights, a Pioneer Antarctic Naturalist," Linnean Society of London, *Proceedings*, 1937, Session 149, part 4:171–184. Calman's article relies on Clarke for biographical information, but provides a full bibliography.

[17] Stephen Van Rensselaer Bleecker (1803–1826) studied law in the office of Harmanus Bleecker (to whom he was not, or only distantly, related). His mother was the sister of Stephen Van Rensselaer (1764–1839). Munsell, *Coll. Alb.*, *4*:98; Munsell, *Ann. Alb.*, *1*:300; Florence Van Rensselaer, *The Van Rensselaers in Holland and America* (New York, 1956), pp. 24–25, 38–39.

[18] A William Cooper is listed in the Albany City Directory for 1829 as a grocer; later Directories (1832–1835, 1843–1853) list him without occupation, though he has an "office" address. Munsell, *Ann. Alb.*, *8*:344 noted that one William Cooper, "late of Albany," died on September 1, 1856, in Philadelphia, aged 56.

[19] Frederick Matthews (1793–1830), graduated from Harvard in 1816. He read law in the office of Harmanus Bleecker and taught, for several years after 1818, in the Albany Female Academy, of which he was also Principal (1824), but only for a short time. At the time of his death, he was with the firm of A. W. Kinsley, stereotype founder. Munsell, *Ann. Alb.*, *1*:205, 300; *7*:115; *9*:209.

Winslow C. Watson[20]   Duncan McKercher[22]   George W. Bush[24]

Richard Brinckerhoff[21]   Freeman Rawdon Jr.[23]

Jonathan Eights was appointed Chairman.[25]

Simeon DeWitt Esquire Chairman of the Joint Committee of the Society for the Promotion of Useful Arts, and the Albany Lyceum of Natural History, made the following Report

The Joint Committee from the Society for the Promotion of Useful Arts & the Albany Lyceum of Natural History beg leave to submit the following draft as the Constitution of the Albany Institute.[26]

Article 1st. The Institute shall consist of Three Departments to wit: 1st. The Department of Physical Science and the Arts: 2nd. The Department of Natural History: & 3rd: The Department of History and General Literature.

Article 2nd: The Society for the Promotion of Useful Arts as at present

---

[20] Winslow Cossoul Watson (1803–1884), son of Elkanah Watson, the promoter of scientific agriculture (see *DAB*). Winslow Watson followed in his father's footsteps as author, gentleman farmer, and amateur scientist. He was the author of *A General View and Agricultural Survey of the County of Essex . . .* (Albany, 1852) and other descriptive, topographical and historical works on northern New York. *Allibone, 3:2609.*

[21] Richard Brinckerhoff ran a hardware store in Albany for many years. He is listed in Albany City Directories, 1817–1818, 1821–1834.

[22] Duncan McKercher was an Albany businessman. He is listed in Albany City Directories from 1815 to 1819 (as a grocer), from 1830 to 1841 (as a bookseller), from 1842 to 1849 (no occupation given), from 1850 to 1862 (as a coal dealer) and from 1863 to 1868 (no occupation given).

[23] Freeman Rawdon (ca. 1801–1859), engraver, left Albany around 1833 and settled in New York City, where he worked until his death in 1859. Groce and Wallace, op. cit. (above, footnote 13), p. 525.

[24] The only George Bush of whom we have been able to find any record was a Dartmouth graduate who attended Princeton Theological Seminary, was ordained, and then tutored at the Seminary before going, under the auspices of the Home Missionary Society, to Indiana in 1824. His dates are 1796–1859. His biographer does not record that he lived in Albany, but it is possible that he passed through there on his way west. No George Bush is listed in the Albany City Directories for this period. See Woodbury M. Fernald, *Memoirs and Reminiscences of the Late Professor George Bush . . .* (Boston, 1860).

[25] Of the men appearing for this first joint meeting, Simeon DeWitt, Jonathan Eights, Charles R. Webster, Henry W. Snyder, and William Mayell were members of the Society for the Promotion of Useful Arts; we have been unable to determine the affiliation of S. V. R. Bleecker, Winslow Watson, Richard Brinckerhoff, Freeman Rawdon, and George W. Bush; the rest were members of the Lyceum. It is reasonable to surmise that all those listed after Mayell were members of the Lyceum or "Second Department." The latter group was younger. Stephen Van Rensselaer (1764–1839) wrote to the Lyceum on February 7, 1823, that he was pleased to see "the rising generation taking a higher stand in the literary & scientific world than their fathers." Albany Institute Archives, Correspondence, 1795–1830.

[26] This draft constitution does not differ essentially from the resolutions at the beginning of these minutes. There are some additional details of procedure. Article 4 adds to the provisions for electing the President and Treasurer that public notice be given of the meeting for that purpose; Article 7 adds a provision for meetings besides those called for during the first quarter of the year; and Article 10 specifies that dissolution of one of the Departments shall not dissolve the Institute. After numerous postponements, the Constitution was finally approved, October 13, 1824 (see the next document).

constituted shall be the First department of the Institute. The Albany Lyceum of Natural History as at present constituted shall be the Second department of the Institute. And the Society contemplated to be formed in Albany for the Promotion of History and General Literature, when duly organized and its accession declared shall be the Third department of the Institute.

Article 3rd: The Officers of the Institute shall be a President, Three Vice Presidents, three Corresponding, and three Recording Secretaries, a Treasurer, a Librarian, and as many Curators as the Lyceum may direct and appoint.

Article 4th. The President and Treasurer, shall be annually Elected by a plurality of the votes of the Members attending a meeting for that purpose to be duly notified in at least one of the Newspapers published in the City of Albany. The first Election to be on the first Wednesday of May next and thereafter at such times and places, as shall be directed by the By-Laws[27] of the Institute.

Article 5th. The Presidents of the Societies constituting the Departments of the Institute, shall in the order stated in the Second Article be the Vice Presidents of the Institute. The Corresponding and Recording Secretaries of said Societies, shall respectively be the Corresponding and Recording Secretaries of the Institute. The Librarian of the Society for the Promotion of Useful Arts shall be the Librarian, and the Curators of the Albany Lyceum of Natural History, shall be the Curators of the Institute.

Article 6th: Those persons who are now members of the Societies constituting the Departments, shall be Members of the Institute, and those who shall hereafter become Members of either of said Departments, shall become Members of the Institute, on paying each Three Dollars as an Initiation fee and each Member shall in addition thereto pay One dollar annually to the Treasurer of the Institute.

Article 7th: The regular meetings of the Institute shall be once every fortnight, during the first four months of the year, for receiving Communications from the several Departments for the reading of Original communications, and for other necessary transactions, and at such other times as may be ordained by its By Laws or fixed by adjournment.

Article 8th: The meetings of the Institute shall be held alternately at the Room of the Society for the Promotion of Useful Arts in the Capitol, and in the Apartment of the Lyceum in the Academy until otherwise directed by concurrent resolutions of those Societies.

Article 9th: The Books now belonging to, or coming into the possession

---

[27] The Institute did not adopt bylaws until March 1829.

of the Lyceum, shall be deposited in the Library of the Institute; and the specimens of Natural History now belonging or hereafter coming into the possession of the Society for the Promotion of Useful Arts, shall be deposited in the Museum of the Institute.

Article 10th. In case any one of the Societies hereby declared as constituting the Institute, shall be or become unorganized the Institute shall during the continuance of such case, be considered as constituted by the two other Societies.

Ordered that the consideration of the Report &c. be postponed until the next meeting.

The Institute then proceed to choose its Officers for the Ensuing: the votes of the Members present having been received and counted it appeared that the Hon. Stephen Van Rensselaer was chosen President and William Mayell Treasurer.

Messrs. S. De Witt, T. R Beck & Tracy were appointed a committee to inform the Hon. Stephen Van Rensselaer of his Election as President of the Institute and request his acceptance thereof.

On motion of S. DeWitt

Resolved. That a Committee be appointed to draft By-Laws for the government of the Institute, and that they report at the next meeting of the Institute.

Whereupon Messrs. S. DeWitt, L. C. Beck, & Mayell were appointed such committee.

> And the Institute adjourned to
> meet again on the 2ᵈ of June.
> Matthew Henry Webster Recᵍ. Secʸ.

MINUTES, ALBANY INSTITUTE
Institute Minutes, 1:10–13, Albany Institute Archives

Wednesday 13ᵗʰ October 1824.
The Institute met pursuant to adjournment in the Room of the Department of Natural History. The President and Vice Presidents being absent Simeon DeWitt Esq. was appointed Chairman and the Minutes of the preceding Meeting were read and approved.

The Constitution[1] as reported by the Joint Committee on the fifth of

---

[1] See above, Minutes of the Albany Institute, [May 5, 1824].

May, (and entered upon the Minutes of that meeting) was taken up, & having been again read was adopted.

The following donations and deposits were laid upon the Table viz: 4 Silver coins (dep^d); Venus mercenaria,[2] Rockaway L.I.[3] Impression of Ferns in Slate, Harrisburgh Penn; 9 Petrifactions; Coral; from *M. H. Webster* for the Institute.

Testudo 2 species *from the same*   [For the Institute]

Stalactite (polished) Mitchills Cave Montg[omer]y Co[unty]; 3 Geological specimens; Testudo (young); species[4] of Insects; Nitrate of Soda, South America; 2 Bottles Salt water, Salina; 4 bottles cont^g. Salt made by different processes at Salina;[5]

from Dr T. R. Beck for the Institute.

One Russian Silver coin deposited by *Richard Webster.*[6]

Brazilian Copper Coin 1802; Egg shell of the Ostrich (dep^d)

11 silver Coins (dep^d) *H. W. Snyder* for the Institute.

Coral, West Indies from *Barent S. Boyd*[7] [for the Institute].

Coral, South America, from *A. S. Webster*[8] for the Institute.

Echinus, Chalk fossil England *Mr. John Finch*[9] [for the Institute].

---

[2] The common clam or quahog, from which the Indians of the East Coast made wampum. A. H. Cooke, "Molluscs," *Cambridge Natural History*, eds. S. F. Harmer and A. E. Shipley, 10 vols. (New York, 1895–1909), *3*:97.

[3] That is, Long Island.

[4] There is a blank space in the manuscript before this word, evidently meant to be filled in by a number.

[5] For a description of the saltworks at Salina, "the most extensive in the United States," see Stephen Smith, "Notice of the Salt Springs and Manufacture of Salt at Salina, Syracuse, &c. N.Y. . . . ," *American Journal of Science and Arts*, ed. by Benjamin Silliman (hereafter cited as *Silliman's Journal*), 1829, *15*:6–12. Lewis C. Beck made a thorough analysis of the water from the Salina salt springs, "An account of the Salt Springs at Salina," *New York Medical and Physical Journal*, 1826, *5*:176–199, which he followed up in "Note on the Presence of Iron in the Salt Springs of Salina, N.Y.," *Silliman's Journal*, 1826, *16*:187–188. Beck subsequently described these springs in his "Report . . . on the Mineralogical and Chemical Department of the [New York State Geological] Survey," New York State *Assembly Document* no. 200, February 20, 1838, pp. 24–36.

[6] Richard Webster (1811–1856), the evidently precocious son of Charles R. Webster, printer.

Richard Webster attended Union College and the Princeton Theological Seminary; he was ordained in 1835 and became Pastor of the Mauch Chunk, Pennsylvania, Presbyterian Church, where he remained until his death. He was the author of *History of the Presbyterian Church in America until 1760 with a Memoir of the Author by C. Van Rensselaer and Historical Introduction by W. Blackwood* (Philadelphia, 1857). *Herringshaw*, p. 989.

[7] Barent S. Boyd is listed in Albany City Directories from 1832 to 1857 as a waterman.

[8] Ashbel Steele Webster (1796–1840), physician, attended Union College (A.B. 1815) and the New York College of Physicians and Surgeons (M.D. 1819). He practiced in Albany and in Jamaica Plains, Long Island, New York; he retired several years before his death, in 1840, in Albany. His father was the publisher Charles R. Webster (see above, Minutes of the Academy Trustees, June 11, 1816, footnote 1). *Columbia Alumni*, p. 198; Sylvester D. Willard, *Annals of the Medical Society of the County of Albany, 1806–1851* (Albany, 1864), pp. 49, 278–279.

[9] John Finch, chemist, originally from Birmingham, England, where he was a member of the Philosophical Society. In this country he seems to have made his living as an itinerant lecturer in chemistry. See Finch to T. R.

4 Shells of Mother of Pearl; Panama S.A. *E. Baldwin*[10] [for the Institute].

Pectinites in limestone, Amsterdam Montg[omer]y Co[unty] *Peter S. Henry*[11] [for the Institute].

Adhesive Clay Greenbush, 2 Specimens[12] _____ [for the Institute].

Barystrontianite? Clinton Oneida Co[unty] *George Clinton*[13] [for the Institute].

Specimen of lithographic printing on Satin[14] *Joseph Henry* [for the Institute].

Stalagmite, Mitchills Cave Montg[omer]y Co[unty]; Trilobites; & Petrifactions in Limestone Canajoharie. *James Eights* for the Institute.

Sixteen specimens of Petrifactions from the Helderbergh. *Beck, Eights & Webster*[15] for the Institute.

Two bills (Continental money) *Charles R. Webster* [for the Institute].

Calculus from the bladder of a horse *Mr. Kelly*[16] [for the Institute].

Collection dried plants, Malone Franklin Co[unty] *P. Gansevoort Esq.*[17] [for the Institute].

Beck, December 14, 1824, Beck Papers, New York Public Library and Wyndham Miles, "Public Lectures on Chemistry in the United States," *Ambix*, 1968, *15*:129–153, especially p. 150.

[10] Probably Ebenezer Baldwin, for whom see above, Minutes, Academy Trustees, April 8, 1822, footnote 1.

[11] Peter Seton Henry, attorney, no relation to Joseph Henry; he may have been the nephew of John V. Henry (see above, Minutes of the Academy Trustees, [March 4, 1813], footnote 8), whose partner he eventually became. He was born, according to Eldridge, before 1799. He graduated from the College of New Jersey (Princeton) in 1821 and by 1824 had begun practice in Albany. The Albany City Directories list him through 1839. Munsell, *Ann. Alb.*, *9*:150; William Henry Eldridge, *Henry Genealogy* (Boston, 1915), pp. 104–105; *General Catalogue of Princeton University, 1746–1906* (Princeton, 1908), p. 133 (hereafter cited as *Princeton Catalogue*).

[12] There follows in the text a straight line, probably to indicate that these specimens were also presented by Peter S. Henry.

[13] George W. Clinton (1806–1885), son of DeWitt Clinton, graduated from Hamilton College in 1825 and began studying medicine under T. R. Beck. In the late spring of 1826, Clinton, who was an enthusiast for natural history, joined the group Amos Eaton took by canal boat from Troy to Niagara to study the geology and biology of the district. Joseph Henry was also a member of this party (see below, Asa Fitch's Canal Tour Journal of May [2], 1826, related documents, and Clinton's Journal of the trip in *Publications of the Buffalo Historical Society*, 1910, *14*:273–305). Clinton later abandoned medicine for the law, becoming a judge in the western part of the state. From 1835 to his death he lived in Buffalo. David F. Day, "An Address Commemorative of George W. Clinton," *Publications of the Buffalo Historical Society*, 1896, *4*:203–225.

[14] We have found no additional evidence of Joseph Henry's interest in lithography. The process had only recently been invented, and a firm had been established in New York a few years before. See Benjamin Silliman's "Notice of the Lithographic Art," *Silliman's Journal*, 1822, *4*:169–171. All the drawings in that volume were lithographs.

[15] Probably Lewis Beck, James Eights, and Matthew Henry Webster.

[16] Not identified; there were a number of Kellys in Albany at the time, none of whom are known to have had close connections with the Institute.

[17] Peter Gansevoort (1788–1876), attorney, graduated from the College of New Jersey (Princeton) in 1808, attended Litchfield Law School and read law with Harmanus Bleecker. He was DeWitt Clinton's private secretary and on his military staff as Judge Advocate Gen-

3 Specimens containing petrifactions, St. Louis Miss[ouri]

Petrifactions (box) Rome Oneida Co[unty] 7 Petrifactions Rochester Munroe Co[unt]y from *Lewis C. Beck M.D.* for the Institute.

A notice of the Testudo ferox, genus Trionyx of Cuvier,[18] by Dr. James E. Dekay[19] of New York was read.

Dr. T. R. Beck read a notice of the Nitrate of Soda, of S. America a specimen of which was presented by him to the Institute.

Dr. T. R. Beck made the following Report,

The Committee[20] appointed to report on the Expediency & practicability of publishing the proceedings of the Albany Institute beg leave to offer the following observations to the notice of the Society.

The utility of periodical publications under the auspices of an active & intelligent Society is unquestionable, both as it respects the Members & the Public. It incites and awakens investigation among the former, & it attracts the favorable notice of the latter. The Committee do not therefore deem it necessary to enlarge on this point. There cannot be any doubt but that a well conducted publication would subserve the interests of Science & Literature in this place. The important & most difficult point to be decided is, whether the Institute is at present competent to furnish proper materials for it. The credit and reputation of the Society imperiously requires that no articles be admitted except those of real merit; & a certain degree of originality, either in the subject itself, or in its application should be demanded. If therefore it be determined, to publish the Transactions of the Society a Committee of Publications is necessary, similar to that appointed by all Societies, whose duty it must be to pass upon all articles read before the meetings.

There is another point which deserves notice. The subjects of investigation embraced by the Institute are very numerous. And it is probable that Literature may in distinction to Science furnish the subject of several pa-

---

eral, 1812–1821. He was sent in 1830 to the New York State Assembly for a term and in 1833 elected State Senator. He sat on the Albany Academy Board of Trustees for fifty years. Cuyler Reynolds, *Hudson-Mohawk Genealogy and Family Memoirs . . . ,* 4 vols. (New York, 1911), *1*:68–69.

[18] Georges Cuvier, *Le règne animal,* 4 vols. (Paris, 1817), 2:14–15: the soft-shelled turtle of the southeastern United States.

[19] James Ellsworth DeKay (1792–1851), physician and naturalist, studied medicine and biology as a young man, and took his M.D. at Edinburgh after a year spent there, 1818–1819. Returning to New York, he was asso-

ciated with the New York Lyceum of Natural History, and edited the first two volumes of its transactions. He was commissioned in 1836 to prepare the zoological part of the New York State Geological Survey; the result of this work, his *Zoology of New York,* appeared 1842–1844 in five volumes. *DAB.*

[20] Jonathan Eights and Frederick Matthews were the other members of this committee. Their manuscript report is found in the Institute Archives, Correspondence, 1795–1830. It differs from the report as recorded in the minutes in one minor respect, noted below, footnote 24.

pers.[21] Whether the diversity which would thus appear, is calculated to increase the character of the publication or its interest, is a question admitting of some doubt, but it is probable that both would be affected.

Selections from foreign Journals judiciously made should also form a part of these publications but of course only a small part.[22]

The committee recommend that if the publication be determined on, it be issued in numbers, similar to the Societies in Philadelphia and New York.[23] The expense is materially lightened & the returns are more immediate.

Should these ideas meet the view of the Institute the Committee would propose the consideration of the following Resolutions as deduced from the foregoing remarks.

Resolved, That it would be expedient to commence a publication under the auspices of the Albany Institute to be Entitled "The Albany Scientific & Literary Journal published under the direction of the Albany Institute."

Resolved, That a Committee of 5 be appointed who shall be the Committee of Publication & Selection.

Resolved, That the publication be in Pamphlets of 32 or 48 pages each, at such intervals as the materials will permit.[24]

Resolved, That a Committee be appointed to ascertain what number of Subscribers can be procured for the above Journal, & that they report at the next meeting.

Whereupon the Report was accepted, and the Resolutions proposed by the Committee having been adopted, Messrs. L. C. Beck R. V. DeWitt, & [Frederick] Matthews were appointed the Committee of Subscription.

On motion of R V DeWitt

Resolved, That the Election of the Committee of Publication & Selection be postponed until the further order of the Institute.[25]

---

[21] As it happened, there were few nonscientific papers in the early volumes of the *Transactions,* Albany Institute.

[22] The early volumes of the *Transactions* contained no translations of foreign articles.

[23] The American Philosophical Society, founded in Philadelphia in 1743 or 1744, had published its *Transactions* since 1771; the Academy of Natural Sciences of Philadelphia, founded in 1812, began publishing its *Journal* in 1817; the Columbian Chemical Society of Philadelphia, founded in 1811, had published one volume of *Memoirs* in 1813; the Lyceum of Natural History in New York, founded in 1817, began publishing its *Annals* in 1823. Ralph S. Bates, *Scientific Societies in the United States,* 3d ed. (Cambridge, Massachu-

setts, 1965), pp. 5–9, 24, 41, 43–44, 52–53.

[24] In the report as submitted by Beck, Eights, and Matthews (see above, footnote 20), there followed here a resolution that the committee on publication "ascertain & report the expence of 250 Copies of a journal of 32 pages each, & also that they report the price at which engravings in natural history &c. can be procured." This passage is crossed over in the manuscript.

[25] On February 2, 1825, the Institute elected T. Romeyn Beck, Jonathan Eights, Simeon DeWitt, Alfred Conkling, and John W. Yates to be this Committee. Institute Minutes, *1:* 16. The Committee as listed in volume 1 of the *Transactions,* Albany Institute, was Beck, DeWitt, and James Tracy.

October 30, 1824

The Recording Secretary read "Extracts from a Report on the diseases of the Elm tree in St. James' Park" by Prof. Macleay published 21 Edin⁹ Phil. Journal. 123.[26]

> And the Institute Adjourned to meet again on the 2ᵈ Wednesday of Novʳ at the Room of the Second Department.
> Matthew Henry Webster Recᵍ. Secʸ.

[26] William Sharp Macleay (1792–1865), "Abstract of a Report on the State of the Elm Trees in St. James' and Hyde Parks," *Edinburgh Philosophical Journal,* 1824, *11*:123–128.

MINUTES, ALBANY INSTITUTE
Institute Minutes, 1:13, Albany Institute Archives

Special Meeting.   Saturday 30ᵗʰ October 1824.

Pursuant to public notice a quorum of the Institute assembled in the Chemical Lecture Room of the Albany Academy, the President and Vice Presidents being absent. Simeon DeWitt Esq. was appointed Chairman.

Mr. Joseph Henry read a Communication[1] on the Chemical & Mechanical effects of Steam, which he illustrated by Experiments.

Mr. R. V. DeWitt, read a Communication[2] on the History of Steam Engines, & Exhibited drawings of different models.

The working Model of a Steam Engine, borrowed of Mr. Birbeck[3] of New York was then Exhibited, & the different parts of the Machine Explained.

On motion of Dr. T. R. Beck

Resolved, That the thanks of the Institute be presented to Mr. Birbeck for his kindness in loaning to the Society his working Model of a Steam Engine.

> And the Institute Adjourned.
> Matthew Henry Webster Recᵍ. Secʸ.

[1] See next document.
[2] This paper was apparently never published.
[3] George Birbeck is listed in New York City Directories, 1816–1825 as a smith and founder.

"ON THE CHEMICAL AND MECHANICAL EFFECTS OF STEAM."[1] ADDRESS BY JOSEPH HENRY DELIVERED AT THE ALBANY INSTITUTE, OCTOBER 30, 1824

Steam Lectures File, Henry Papers, Smithsonian Archives

Steam is the name given in common language to the visible vapour which arises from all bodies that contain moisture easily expelled from them by heat; thus we say the steam of boiling water, of sperits. &c

As the chief design of this lecture is to consider steam as a mechanical agent for the production of motion I shall confine my observations principally to the vapour of water—which is known in mechanics by the name of steam only.

In order to have a just idea of the properties of steam and of its formation we must consider the different forms under which the substance of water exists in nature. These are three viz *solid, liquid* and aerformed or *ice water* and steam.

If we place a quantity of ice in a tea-kettle over a fire the ice gradually melts into water after which the water increases in temperatur untill it boils. If the boiling continue the water will all be disipated in steam. From an observation of this fact it is reasonable to suppose that these different forms of the same substance are caused by it being combined with different quantities of the matter of heat.

---

[1] This is the title given in the Albany Institute Minutes (see preceding document) and in the *Proceedings*, which appeared as part 2 of the *Transactions* of the Albany Institute, 1830, *1*; see page 30 of part 2 (separately paginated). The abstract given in the *Proceedings* was reprinted in *Scientific Writings of Joseph Henry*, 2 vols. (Washington, 1886), *1*:1. The paper was never published though Henry made emendations at some time after its composition as if perhaps he intended to publish it. It would have required considerable work to get it into publishable shape. As it stands, it is an interesting piece of juvenalia, and shows how Henry worked before he became a professional scientist. He read everything he could get his hands on, then presented it rather in a rush, without critical thought. But it must be said that the science of heat was in a transitional state during the 1820s, and there were few known, reliable guidelines for a relatively untutored young man growing up in Albany to follow. See Robert Fox, "The Background to the Discovery of Dulong and Petit's Law," *British Journal for the History*

of Science, 1968, *4*:1–22, and Stephen G. Brush, "The Wave Theory of Heat . . . ," *British Journal for the History of Science,* 1970, *5*: 145–167.

Henry's manuscript consists of a number of sheets folded double to form a sort of booklet. Except for the first few and the last few pages, Henry wrote the body of the text on the right-hand pages only, and added corrections and additions on the left-hand page. His main authorities for the lecture were Joseph Black, *Lectures on the Elements of Chemistry,* 2 vols. (Edinburgh, 1803; there was also an American edition, 3 vols., Philadelphia, 1806); William Thomas Brande, *A Manual of Chemistry,* of which the first American from the second London edition (New York, 1821) is in Henry's Library; John Robison, *A System of Mechanical Philosophy,* 4 vols. (Edinburgh, 1822), of which Henry owned a copy; and Thomas Thomson, *A System of Chemistry,* 4 vols., of which Henry possessed the Philadelphia edition of 1818 (from the fifth London edition).

And if so we should expect the privation of this heat would leave it again in the form of water and ice. Accordingly this is fully verified by experiment for if a thin metalic tube be fixed to the spout of the tea-kettle and surrounded by ice or cold water no steam will isue, but water will constantly trickle from it in drops and if the proces be continued with proper attention the water thus obtained from the tube will be found equal in quantity to that which disappeared from the teakettle.

But there are other circumstancs attending the liquifaction of ice and the evaporation of water which are not so obvious although very nessary to be known.

If we place a thermometer in ice or snow so cooled down as to sink the thermometer to the cypher and submit it to a gentle uniform heat the thermometer will rise until it comes to the freezing point, and there remain stationary until all the ice or snow is melted; the thermometer will then begin to rise again and will continue to rise nearly uniformly to 212 or the boiling point. At this point it will remain stationary a second time and no heat that we can add to the water will made it one degree hotter.

If the fire we apply be of sufficient intensity to just *raise* the temperature of the ice one degree in a second then the thermometer will be 32 seconds in rising from zero to the freezing point or through 32°. At this point it will remain stationary 135 seconds before all the ice is melted—if we suppose that the heat has entered uniformly during the liquifaction of the ice 135 degrees of heat must have entered it which are not indicated by the thermometer, [Note added later by Henry:] 140 more correctly.[2]

The same thing can be prooved by a very simple experiment which any person may perform. Take a pound of ice and a pound of [water][3] both at 32 as indicated by a thermometer. Place them before a fire so that each may receive equal quantities of heat in the same time; at the instant the ice is all melted observe the temperature of the water and it will be found to have increased 135° while the water produced from the ice remains at the same temperature of 32°.

Therefore *ice*, at 32 and water, at 32 differ from each other, by the latter containing 135 degrees of heat more than the former: this heat appears

---

[2] Black's "139 or 140" degrees (*Lectures, 1:* 117, 136) had become 140 in a number of texts, e.g., Brande, op. cit., p. 28 and Thomson, *System, 1:*89. It was common practice at the time to express latent heats of fusion and of vaporization in degrees. No confusion need result if it be borne in mind that in this case a "degree" was actually a unit of heat since there was an implicit appeal to the specific heat of water. A "degree" meant the amount of heat necessary to raise unit mass of water one thermometric degree. But see below, footnote 52.

[3] Henry's manuscript says "snow" in what is obviously a slip.

nessary to its fluidity, and was called by Dr. Black,[4] the discoverer of this important fact, latent, or consealed heat; to distinguish it from free or sensible heat.

In order to discover the quantity of latent heat which enters into steam and causes the thermometer to remain stationary during the boiling of water let us <*observe*> note the number of seconds the water is boiling before it is all converted into vapour. This with the same uniform heat will be about 990 secconds[5] if we suppose as before that one degree enter every seccond. Steam then contains about 900 degrees of latent heat.

Therefore steam at 212 differs from water at 212 by the one containing 990 degrees of heat more than the other.

If we reverse those changes and condense the vapour into water and the water into ice all this latent heat will re-appear entirely in the form of free or thermometrical heat.

For this purpose if we suffer the steam from the spout of a tea-kettle to flow into 9 oz of water at the temperature of 106 the steam will condense and the water will rise quickly to the boiling point or 212; if at this moment we stop the condensation, we shall find that one ounce of steam has been condensed. The latent heat therefore of one ounce of steam *has raised* the temperature of 9 ozs of water 106 degrees. This would be sufficient to raise one oz. above 990 degrees.*[6]

Many experiments have been made by the most celebrated chemests to determine the latent heat of steam—the mean of all their experiments[7] gives about 900.

It is this great quantity of heat contained in steam that makes it so powerful and effectual in the business of cookery <*by steam.*> Dr Black observes that it is the most <*effectual*> fatheful carrier of heat that can be

* If water could be raised to that temperature without changing into vapour.

[4] Joseph Black (1728–1799), chemist, Professor of Medicine at Glasgow (1756–1766) and of Medicine and Chemistry at Edinburgh (1766–1799). His work on heat, dating from 1756 to 1762, is treated in Douglas McKie and Niels H. de V. Heathcote, *The Discovery of Specific and Latent Heats* (London, 1935), chaps. 1 and 2. *DSB*.

[5] The figures given in the literature for the latent heat of vaporization of water varied more widely than those for the latent heat of fusion. Black, *Lectures*, 1:167, after giving various values, reported that James Watt had informed him that the "heat obtainable from steam" was at least 900° and not more than 950°. Watt added a long note to Robison's text (2:5–10) in which he discussed experiments made in 1765, 1781, and 1783 which yielded a determination of 960° for the latent heat. Henry at first wrote "900" and at some later time corrected it to "990," though in two places in the text he left it at "900." The figure 990 seems to have come from Dionysius Lardner, *The Steam Engine*, of which Henry owned the third American, from the fifth London edition (Philadelphia, 1838); see page 32.

[6] This would make sense if Henry had left the figure at 900. See preceding note.

[7] Henry wrote the word "observation" directly under the word "experiments," in what appears to be a later emendation.

conceived, and will deposit it on such bodies only as are colder than boiling water. Hence if in a range of covered vessels communicating by tubes; whenever the first is made to boil but no sooner, the steam will go onwards to the second and raise it to the boiling point and then to the third, and so on in succession, any number of pots may be made to boil. Thus the heat that in the common process of boiling is suffered to escape up the chimney in steam is made to boil several vessels without any addition of fuel. This is the principle of the new method of distilation by steam in which all the vessels except the one to which the fire is applied are made of wood. This is cheaper and will retain the heat much better than metal.

The application of steam to heat apartements is an other valuable fruit of our knowledge of the great quantity of heat <*contained in steam*> it contains. In this method Safty cleanliness and comfort combine in giving a genial warmth sufficient for every purpose of private accommodation or public manufactory. It has been acertained that one *cubic foot* of boiler will heat about two thousand feet of space from 70 to 80 degrees of Farhenheit; so that the steam which escapes from a high pressur engine by means of pipes may be made to heat the whole factory whoes machenry it puts in motion.

Steam is also used in heating large quantities of water for baths and vats for taning with hot liquid; in this maner it is of universal application since one gallon of water in the form of steam will heat 6 gallons at 50 up to the boiling point or 1 gallon of the former will be adiquate to heat 18 of the latter up to 100 making a liberal allowance for waste of heat in the conducting pipes.[8]

<*Water and*> every <*other*> liquid under the *same atmospherical presure* has one peculiar point of temperature at which <*they*> it invariably boils.

Thus water under the ordinary pressure of the atmosphere allways boils at 212 alcohol at 176 and ether 98[9] and when brought to the boiling point these cannot be made hotter in the open air however long the application of heat be continued—for each increment of heat merely converts a new portion of the liquid into vapour.

But the boiling point of the same fluid varies greatly under <*the same*> different degrees of atmospherical pressure. According to the experiments of Dr Black even the ordinary variations in the weight of the atmospher as

---

[8] This passage indicates that Henry probably took to be accurate the larger of the two figures (900, 990) mentioned above (footnote 5). In the examples given here he assumed that about 900 "degrees of heat" would heat the water, but he also allowed for an additional quantity which would be wasted.

[9] The figures are from Brande's text, p. 523 (alcohol) and p. 532 (ether).

measured by the barrometer are sufficient to make a difference of about 5 degrees in the boiling of water—in general liquids boil *in vacuo* with 140 degrees less of heat than under the mean pressure of the atmosphere.[10]

This may be shown by means of an air pump.

On ascending to the tops of mountans as the atmosphere becomes lighter, the boiling point of water gradually falls on the scale of the thermometer. Thus on the sumit of mount blanc water is found to boil at 178, or [34][11] degrees below its ordinary boiling point at the surface of the earth. On this principle The Rev. Mr. Wollaston[12] has lately constructed a thermometric barometer for measuring heights. He finds that a difference of one degree in the boiling point of water corresponds to nearly 520 feet of difference of elivation. By following his directions as given in the annals of Philosophy[13] the height of a place may be thus rigerously determined with great convenience. His whole aparatus is simple and very portable being packed in a cylindrical tin case 2 inches in diameter and 10 long.[14]

The fact, of water and other liquors boiling at a low temperature in a *vacuum* led Mr. Watt[15] to suppose that distilation might be performed with a small degree of heat by remooving the pressure of the atmosphere and surrounding the refrigerator with cold water or ice.

He accordingly made the experiment and it succeeded perfectly well—* this is a drawing of his apparatus.[16] But he soon found by the quantity of

* Exhibit a drawing of the apparatus.

[10] The variation of the boiling point of water with atmospheric pressure was discussed by Black, *Lectures*, *1*:143–145 and by Robison, op. cit., 2:22. Black, in his *Lectures*, *1*:145 stated that liquids boil in vacuo at 120° less than under atmospheric pressure; Robison added a footnote to the text at that point to the effect that this figure is probably too low by 22 to 25°.

[11] The manuscript gives 44, an obvious arithmetic error.

[12] Francis John Hyde Wollaston (1762–1823), British natural philosopher and clergyman, was the brother of William Hyde Wollaston. The *DNB* has an article on each.

[13] "Description of a Thermometrical Barometer for Measuring Altitudes," *Phil. Trans.*, 1817, *107*, part 2:183–195; an abstract appeared in *Annals of Philosophy*, 1818, *11*:53–54.

[14] On the page of the manuscript opposite this paragraph Henry has written "Exhibit Mr Dalton's apparatus." We have not found that John Dalton, the well-known British chemist (*DSB*), constructed a barometer of

this sort; perhaps this was a lapse of memory on Henry's part when he meant to write "Wollaston."

[15] James Watt (1736–1819), the engineer famous for his improvements on the steam engine. Watt stated that "the latent heat of steam is less when it is produced under a greater pressure or in a more dense state; and greater when it is produced under a less pressure or in a less dense state." Henry probably read this in Black (see next footnote) or in Andrew Ure, "New Experimental Researches on Some of the Leading Doctrines of Caloric; Particularly on the Relation between the Elasticity, Temperature, and Latent Heat of Different Vapours; and on Thermometric Admeasurement and Capacity," *Phil. Trans.*, 1818, *108*, part 2:338–394, p. 392. Ure was quoting from Watt's "Thoughts on the Constituent Parts of Water and of Dephlogisticated Air; with an Account of Some Experiments on That Subject," *Phil. Trans.*, 1784, *74*, part 2:329–353, p. 335.

[16] The drawing has not survived, but Black's description of it is clear:

cold water warmed by the condensation of the vapour that there was no saving of fuel by this elegant process: for although the water distilled at 70 he discovered the important fact that the latent heat of the vapour thus produced was nearly 1300.[17] It has since been prooved by repeated experiments that the latent heat of steam generated under a small pressure and at a low temperature is greater than steam of a greater density formed under a great pressure.[18]

The boiling of fluids at a low temperature is shown by the philosophical toy called a pulse glass the ingenious contrivanc of Dr Franklin.[19]

The difference of the boiling point of fluids by a change of pressure is farther prooved by heating water in a strong covered vessel call a Papin's digester.[20] Water in a vessel of this kind provided it be made strong enough may be heated red hot. <*Mr Perkin's steam generator[21] is a vessel of this kind kept full of water by a forcing-pump and placed in an air furnance. On opening a valve a quantity of water is forced out which flashes into steam.*>

Water thus heated is used to desolve boan—and other substances which cannot be dessolved by water heated in the open air.

Pressure seams essentially nessary to the existance of <*bodies*> substances in a liquid form. If it were not for atmospheric pressure it is prob-

---

He [Watt] accordingly made the experiment, and it succeeded perfectly well. A very small still was half filled with water, and then closely united with the vessel which was to receive the distilled water. A very small hole was made in the bottom of the receiver, and a plug was fitted to it. The water being made to boil violently, sent the steam through the whole apparatus, (there being no water in the refrigeratory to condense it) forcing the air out by the hole. While the whole was boiling hot, and the steam blowing through the hole, this was suddenly stopped up by the plug, and the bottom of the still was set on ice. This soon cooled its contents; and the steam, which occupied the rest of the apparatus, collapsed into a few drops of water. A lamp was now set under the still, and in a few minutes the whole apparatus grew warm; a proof that steam was now produced from the water, and passed over into the receiver. Cold water was put into the refrigeratory, and the distillation went on . . . .
Lectures, 1:181–182. Note that Henry borrowed the opening sentence of this passage.

[17] This sentence is a paraphrase of Black's account of Watt's results, ibid.

[18] Cf. Ure, op. cit., pp. 391–392.
[19] Benjamin Franklin (1706–1790), American statesman, author, and scientist, did not invent the pulse-glass, but rather introduced it to scientific London from Germany, where it had been shown to him in the autumn of 1767. His description of it may be found in his letter to John Winthrop, July 2, 1768, *The Writings of Benjamin Franklin*, ed. Albert Henry Smyth, 10 vols. (New York, 1905), 5: 139–142.
[20] The digester, or what we now call the pressure-cooker, was invented by Denis Papin (1647–?), who published an account of it in 1681. *DNB*.
[21] Jacob Perkins (1766–1849), inventor, was concerned first with improvements in banknote engraving, then after about 1822 with developments in high-pressure steam engines. He was at that time working in England, where he took out several patents for improvements in engine and boiler construction. To exhibit his inventions he later established the Adelaide Gallery in London which will figure in later volumes of the Henry Papers. *DAB*, and Greville Bathe, *Jacob Perkins* (Philadelphia, 1943).

able that there would be no intermediate state but solids would immediatly pass into vapour.

This is certainly the case with respect to water for if a piece of ice be placed above the column of mercury in a barometer it affords an elastic vapour even at 50 degrees below the *zero* of Fahrenheit. If this vapour be remooved a new quantity will arise and so on till the ice is all evaporated without producing any water.

Steam over water heated to a high temperature exerts a great force of pressure on the sides of the vessel in which it is confined; this force may be increased by heat and pressure untill it exceeds that of gunpowder. From this property arises its application to the steam engine as a mooving force; for this pressure of confined steam may be employed either to expell water from a vessel or to give motion to a piston fitted to a cylender.[22]

Another source of the power of steam is the facility with which steam of a great expansive force can be condensed into the small quantity of water from which it was originally produced. Steam at 212 is 1800 times greater in bulk than the water from which it was formed[23] this by being condensed in a vessel produces nerely a vacuum and may be applyed in drawing up water into the vessel, in the same manner as a common sucking-pump. The rapidity with which this condensation is made is truly wonderful.

According to Mr. Watt two gallons of ice cold water dashed in drops through the capasity of a vessel holding three hogsheads will condense the vapour which fills it, in less than one fourth of a seccond.[24]

There is something very singular in that partial condensation of steam when it comes in contact with the atmospher and which causes the cloudy apperance which we observe. From the refraction of which the ray of light suffer in passing through a cloud of steam it is know that this steam is not condensed in drops but in vesicles.[25]

Since steam has been employed as a mooving principle it has become an object of peculiar interest. Accordingly chemests of the first talents have instituted experiments to discover the laws that govern its expansion by

---

[22] On the page opposite this paragraph Henry wrote the single word "Eolopile," correctly spelled "Aeolipile."

[23] This is Watt's figure, and it was widely quoted. Robison, op. cit., 2:67, 115n.; Thomson, *System*, 1:91, etc.

[24] Black, *Lectures*, 1:170.

[25] "We explained the opaque and cloudy appearance of steam, by saying that the vapour is condensed by coming into contact with the cooler air. There is something in the form of this cloud which is very inexplicable. The particles of it are sometimes very distinguishable by the eye; but they have not the smart star-like brilliancy of very small drops of water, but give the fainter reflection of a very thin film or vesicle like a soap bubble." Robison, op. cit., 2:13n. For the history of the "vesicle theory," see W. E. K. Middleton, *A History of the Theories of Rain and Other Forms of Precipitation* (New York, 1966), pp. 45–52.

heat. Dr Black, Mr Watt, Mr Dalton, and lately Dr Ure[26] have all studied the subject with great attention.

The object of Mr Daltons principle experiment was to determine the utmost force that vapour from water can exert at different temperatures. The apparatus he used was very simple and the experiment may be <*performed by almost any person*> repeated at pleasure.[27]

Mr Dalton in this way found the fource of vapour at different temperatures in parts and inches of mercury from 40 degrees below zero to 155 above, but for higher temperatures than this he used an apparatus similar to Dr Ure's.[28]

After repeated experiments by this method and a careful comparison of them, the result of all the <*experiments*> observations from 40 degrees below to 325 above the zero of Fahrenheit were placed in a table which may be seen under the article steam in Rees Encyclopedia.[29]

By refering to this table it will be seen that the vapour of water at 40 degrees below zero or 72 degrees below the freezing point will support a column of mercury .043 of an inch in height; at 32 or the freezing point it will support .2 of an inch; at 106° 2 inches and a 1/4, and at 212, 30 inches or is then just equal in elasticity to the atmosphere; if we increase the temperature 40 degrees above 212 the elasticity is doubled or it will support 60 inches of mercury and if the temperature raised 55 degrees still hgher, or to 307 the steam will then support 4 atmospheres or 120 inches of mercury which will press with 60 pounds to the square inch on a boiler or piston.

We see by this that the force of elasticity of vapour increases very rapidly with an increase of temperature. The force of vapour at 212 as has been observed is equal to 30 inches of mercury or one atmosphere. If this heat be doubled the elasticity will be fifty times as great or it will supporte 750 inches.[30] The great increase of the elasticity of steam by small increments

---

[26] Andrew Ure (1778–1857), op. cit., pp. 338–394. *DNB*.

[27] Dalton's apparatus consisted essentially of a barometer tube into which the liquid to be tested was introduced above the mercury. Various means were then used to heat the tube and its contents to the desired temperatures. See John Dalton, "Experimental Essays on the Constitution of Mixed Gases; on the Force of Steam or Vapour from Water and Other Liquids in Different Temperatures, both in a Torricellian Vacuum and in Air; on Evaporation; and on the Expansion of Gases by Heat," *Memoirs of the Literary and Philosophical Society of Manchester*, 1802, 5, part 2:535–602, pp. 552–555.

[28] Op. cit. (see footnote 15), pp. 344–346 and Plate XIX.

[29] Abraham Rees, *The New Cyclopaedia or Universal Dictionary of Arts and Sciences*, 30 vols. (London, 1802); 41 vols., Philadelphia, n.d. The volumes are unpaginated. The article "Steam" is in volume 35 of the Philadelphia edition.

[30] We have not found how Henry arrived at this figure. Dalton (op. cit.), extrapolating from a number of experiments he had made on the expansion of steam at lower temperatures, calculated that the force of steam over water at temperatures above 212°F. would double for every increase in temperature of about 30°, as Henry said. But this would result in a 128-fold increase in pressure from 212° to 424° (assuming that Henry meant

of heat as indicated by the thermometer has led to the invention of engines that work by steam of great elasticity or high pressure.

The engines of Mr. Trevethick of england and those of Oliver Evans in this country are of this kind.[31]

The common steam engines of Bolton[32] and Watt work with steam of but litle greater elasticity than the atmosphere and are therefore called low pressure engines. These will be fully explained by Mr. De Wit in his lecture on the steam engine.[33]

Chemists and Engineers are divided in oppinions whether steam of a high pressure is more economical as it regards fuel than that of a low <*temperature* . . .>[34] pressure.

Mr Dalton and many others[35] suppose that the elasticity of steam is in direct proportion to its density and that each increment of heat increases its elasticity not by combining with the steam already formed but by generating a new quantity which being forced into the same space increases its density and consequently its elasticity. Acording to this oppinion steam of dowble the fource contains twice as much vapour condensed into the same space; This will requires <*twice as*> double the quantity of heat for its formation. The diseption arises from the thermometer which indicates the free not the latent heat contained in the steam.

As this is a subject of considerable interest I will enumerate some of the facts which have been descovered concerning steam which may throw some light on the laws which govern its elasticity and <*serve to*> enable us to <*draw*> form a conclusion.

1st *steam of high pressure is more dense or contains mor water in the same space than steam of a low pressure:* this is prooved by the experiments of Mr Sharp as may be seen by his paper published in the *Repertory of arts.*[36] He found that the higher the pressure the more water came over by distilation in a given time.

"212 × 2" when he spoke of "doubling the heat"). Also a 50-fold increase in pressure would be 750 pounds psi rather than 750 inches of mercury.

[31] Richard Trevithick (1771–1833), English engineer and entrepreneur, played a large role in the application of steam power to locomotion. *DNB.* Oliver Evans (1755–1819), American engineer and entrepreneur, spent his life in designing, improving, and manufacturing various kinds of heavy machinery. *DAB.*

[32] So spelled. Matthew Boulton (1728–1809), engineer, was James Watt's partner from 1775 to 1800 in Birmingham. *DNB.* The engine was primarily Watt's, but for the business end, "Boulton supplied the energy, optimism, tact, and perseverance which Watt lacked." A. Wolf, *A History of Science, Technology, and Philosophy in the Eighteenth Century,* 2d ed. rev. by D. McKie (London, 1952), p. 620.

[33] R. V. DeWitt. His address on the history of the steam engine followed Henry's. De-Witt's remarks were not published.

[34] Three canceled words, illegible.

[35] Cf. Robison, op. cit., 2:17.

[36] John Sharpe, "An Account of Some Experiments, to Ascertain Whether the Force of Steam be in Proportion to the Generating Heat," *The Repertory of Arts, Manufactures, and Agriculture,* 2d series, 1813, 22:351–360;

The same thing has been lately shown by M. Le Baron[37] in a manner if possible more conclusive. He heated alcohol in a glass tube until it was converted into a vapour which occupied only twice the spac of the liquid from which it was formed.

2[d] *The latent heat of low pressure steam is greater than that of high.* This was prooved by Mr Watt as has be[en] mentioned in his experiment on distilation. It might also be infered for annalogy for steam of low pressure is more attenuated than high and consequently would yield more heat by compressure. It is probable although it cannot be prooved directly by experiment that the same weight of steam contains, what ever may be its density, the same quantity of heat; its latent being increased in exact proportion as its sensible heat is diminished; and the reverse.

Another important fact which is given by Mr Sharp is that the temperature of steam over water encreases equally in equal times with a uniform heat. <*This was proovd by heating water over a sperit lamp which gives a uniform heat. This experiment*> Water was heated in a closed vessel by a sperit lamp from 140° to 280° in the space of 45 minutes and the time in rising through every 10° was noted. It rose the first 10° in 3 minutes and 50 seconds and the last 10° in 3 minutes and 52 seconds making but 2 seconds difference. This experiment is of its self sufficient to proove that steam does not contain heat in proportion to its elasticity. Mr Dalton acounts for it by saying that the common thermometric scale is incorrect the degrees being progressively too small.[38] But M M Dulong and Petit who have made acurate experiments on the expansion of mercury find the common division of the scal nerely correct.[39] The expansion of the glass bulb makes up for the unequal expantion of the mercury.

---

the paper originally appeared in the *Memoirs of the Manchester Literary and Philosophical Society*, 2d series, 1813, 2:1–14. Sharpe (d. 1834), F.R.S., was a solicitor. William E. A. Axon, *The Annals of Manchester* (Manchester and London, 1886), p. 190.

[37] That is, the Baron Charles Cagniard de la Tour (1771–1859), French engineer (see *Dictionnaire de Biographie Française*, 7:col. 1824), "Exposé de quelques résultats obtenus par l'action combinée de la chaleur et de la compression sur certains liquides, tels que l'eau, l'alcool, l'éther sulfurique et l'essence de pétrole rectifiée," *Annales de Chimie et de Physique*, 2d series, 1822, 21:127–132, 178–182; 1823, 22:410–415; 1823, 23:267–269. This work was translated and appeared in several English journals; see *Royal Society Catalogue of Scientific Papers*.

[38] See Dalton's *A New System of Chemical Philosophy*, part 1 (Manchester, 1808), pp. 3–22 and, for a discussion of Dalton's concepts of temperature and heat, Robert Fox, "Dalton's Caloric Theory," in *John Dalton and the Progress of Science*, ed. D. S. L. Cardwell (Manchester, 1968), pp. 187–202.

[39] Pierre-Louis Dulong (1785–1838), Professor of Chemistry at the Veterinary School at Alfort and Alexis-Thérèse Petit (1791–1820), Professor of Physics at the École polytechnique, "Recherches sur les lois de dilatation des solides, des liquides et des fluides élastiques, et sur la mesure exacte des températures," *Annales de Chimie et de Physique*, 2d series, 1816, 2:240–263; and "Recherches sur la mesure des températures et sur les lois de la communication de la chaleur," ibid., 1817, 7:113–154, 225–264, 337–367. Biographical accounts of Dulong and Petit may be found in Michaud, *Biographie Universelle*.

To connect these three facts in one view let us consider in what manner steam of a high pressure is formed in a boiler partly filled with water and void of air with a thermometer in the steam to indicate its temperature. The water at the lowest temperature will fill the boiler with a vapour of small elastisity. By <*continuing*> raising the heat the water sends off a new quantity of vapour which is forced into the same space; <*in this maner the density of the steam is increased and consequently its elasticity*> in this manner the density and consequtly the elasticity of the steam is continually increased with the temperature;[40] but as the density of vapour is increasd its capacity for heat is diminished. A quantity of latent heat is therefor made sensible which causes the thermometer to rise.

The whole phenomenon is similar to what takes place in the condensation of air <*by a forcing pump*> in a vessel with a forcing-pump. As the air is condensed the vessel grows warm by the latent heat which is forced from the air. This tends to increase its elasticity as well as <*its density*> the increase of density.*[41]

In the same manner steam owes its great increase of elasticity to the increase of thermometrical heat <*added to*> combined with the increas of density.

That there is <*therefore*> a saving of fuel by using steam of a high pressure appears first from <*its heat*> elastisity being not in proportion to its <*elasticity*> [its heat] 2^d from the testimony of persons using steam of this kind and third from the laws which obtains in causing its elasticity.[42]

There is another fact concerning steam which at first sight appears rather paradoxical but which merely tends to illustrate some of the principles which I have mentioned.

When steam of a very considerable density from pressure and heat is

* This view of the formation of steam was adopted after carefully investigating the phenominon <*and*> by reading all the papers on the subject that were accessible to me at the time. Five years after a paper was published in one of the nos. of the Annals of Philosophy giving the same explanation.

But the same explanation had many years before 1816 been given by Biot in his large work on Natural Philosophy.

[40] The clause beginning "in this manner ...," is written on the opposing, or left-hand page.

[41] This note, added in February 1833, is written on the left-hand page. The reference is to Peter Ewart, "Experiments and Observations on ... the Sudden Expansion of Compressed Elastic Fluids," *The Philosophical Magazine ...*, n.s. 1829, 5:247–254. The *Annals* had merged with the *Philosophical Magazine* in 1827.

Jean-Baptiste Biot (1774–1862), physicist, held many posts in the Parisian scientific establishment. See *Dictionnaire de Biographie Française*, 6:col. 506. His *Traité de physique expérimentale et mathématique*, 4 vols. (Paris, 1816) contains a short discussion of latent heat and the steam engine in volume 4.

[42] Another version of the preceding paragraph follows which varies only in that the second and third reasons are interchanged.

made to isue from an orifice in a boiler a person may place his finger close to the aperture without feeling any unpleasant effects from the heat.

I had an opertunity of trying this experiment with the boiler of Mr Thares[43] Engine. The safty valve was loaded with upwards of 60 lb to the square inch but the steam which escaped by a leek was below the temperature of the blood and even gave a sensation of cold to the hand.[44]

This is very easily explained for if steam of high pressure contains less latent heat than stem of low pressure the suden expansion of the steam will causes all the sensible heat to be absorbed or converted into latent heat <*therefore the steem appears cold*>.

Or in other words the sensible heat of the stem is rendered latent by the change of capasity for heat which steam undergows in <*changing*> passing from a dense to a rarer state.[45]

I am happy to have it in my power to illustrat this experiment by a similar one on air which was discovered by Dr Megs[46] of this city.

This fountain[47] is filled with air condensed by means of forcing pump: it probabilly contains four or five atmospheres. A tube passes from this cock nearly to the bottom in which there is a small quantity of water. On turning this cock the air will expand so much as to absorb all the sensible heat and turn what water addhears to the tube into ice.*[48]

Mr Perkins supposes he could heat water so hot in his generator <*as that the steam would*> as to [have] it flash out in the form of snow insted of steam but this is evidently a misconception of the <*subject*> fact for the

* This paragraph was written before the fountain was filled with compressed air for the exhibition on the evening of lecture. If I recollect aright the fountain contained about 9 atmospheres. It was forced into by means of a force pump of about 2 inches in diameter until the elasticity became so great as to cause the piston to rise with my weight bearing on the end of a lever having a power of 6.

---

[43] Probably a reference to Amos Thayer, Jr., who received a patent in 1821 for a steam wheel as an Albany resident and a steam engine patent in 1823 as a resident of New York City.

[44] This paragraph was written on the left-hand page, but the handwriting and orthography suggest that it was contemporary with the main text and was intended to be a part of it.

[45] This paragraph was written on the left-hand page, and the remarks in the preceding note apply to it.

[46] Probably Richard M. Meigs, a member of the Albany Institute.

[47] See below, Albany Institute Minutes for March 2, 1825.

[48] This note was written on the left-hand

page in a hand similar to that of the author's note above which is dated February 1833. At the upper left-hand corner of the page is a computation as follows:

$$\begin{array}{r} 130 \\ 6 \\ \hline 4)780 \\ \hline 15)145(\end{array}$$

From this we learn that (1) Henry was thin in 1824, and (2) he sometimes made mistakes in arithmetic. If he weighed 130 pounds and the lever gave him a sixfold advantage, the pressure would be 780 pounds, but 780 ÷ 4 = 195, or closer to 13 atmospheres. If instead of 4 for the area the value 3.14 is used the pressure may have reached 16.5 atmospheres.

steam after it <*leaves*> escapes from the boiler contains as much absolute heat if not more than when in its confined state <*in the boiler*>. It is therefore at a point fartherest removed from snow.[49] It is probable that ice may be produced by its exp[ansion].

Having taken a brief scetch of the chemicle principles of steam and of its mechanicle properties it now only remains to describe the different methods for producing it from water with the least expenditure of fuel.

Whoever attends to the manner in which heat is applied in kitchens to boil water will be convinced that not less than three fourth of the fuel is wasted in the production of heat <*which finds its way up the chimney*> which is disipated in air.

In this process a boiler is set on the open fire in the midle of a copious stream of heated air which is incessantly rushing up the chimney. Only a very small part of this comes in contact with the boiler. The bottom is indeed heated by the fuel on which it rests but the greater part of all the heat producd is runing to waste.

Instead of this when steam is <*produced*> formed for mechanical purposes the boiler is placed in a well constructed furnace where the heated air is forced to come in contact with a greater part of the surface of the whole boiler and is thus made [to] deposit nearly all its heat in the water. Some of these furnaces as constructed by Mr Watt consume the smoke by making it pass over and through the red hot coals: thereby converting the carbon and carburetted hydrogen of the smoke into fuel; and preventing at the same time the bottom of the boiler from being covered with soot which is a non conductor of heat.[50]

A great variety of plans have been tried to make the same quantity of fuel produce greater effects by some particular formation of the boiler. Amoung all these none is more celebrated than Mr Perkin's steam generator which constitutes the most essential characteristic of his machine.[51]

This generator which supplies the place of the boiler in ordinary steam engines is a cylinder made of gun metal. The metal is about three inches

---

[49] Jacob Perkins (see above, footnote 21) patented an innovative high-pressure boiler and engine. See *DAB*. Perkins does not appear to have said this. Perhaps Henry was thinking of a passage in the account of Perkins' boiler given by the editors of the *Edinburgh Philosophical Journal*, 1823, 9:172–179, where they say that some have supposed "that the portion of water which escapes, must necessarily carry off a quantity of heat from the adjoining stratum (the temperature of which may be thus reduced below the freezing

point)." See ibid., p. 175.

[50] Watt's furnaces are described in Rees' *Encyclopedia,* article "Steam-engine."

[51] Perkins' improvements in the steam engine were described in the *Edinburgh Philosophical Journal,* loc. cit. and in the *London Journal of Arts and Sciences,* 1823, 5:36–37, 150–151, 201–204, 261–262, 305–306; 1823, 6:1–8, 202–204; 1824, 7:1–6, 262–266, 307–311. Notices also appeared in the *Albany Argus,* June 20 and September 9, 1823.

thick and the vessel, containing eight gallons of water, is closed at both ends (except the orifises for leting out and forcing in water) and placed vertically in a cylindrical furnace in which a heat of from 400 to 450 degrees of Fahrenheit is applied to the generator, which is kept interely filled with water. The steam is produced by a smal quantity of cold water being driven into the generator which forces an equal quantity of the heated and compressed water contained in <*the steam*> that vessel to pass through a valve <*after which*> when it instantly flashes into steam.

There are some things so inexplicable in several parts of this machine that the most credulous may reasonable entertain douts of the correctness of its principles.

Steam contains at least 1000 degrees of heat more than water at the common temperature of the atmosphere that is adding its latent and thermametrical heat together. Therefore before water can flash into steam its temperature must be raised 1000 degrees. But the heated water that is forced from Mr Perkin's generator is said to all flash into steam at from 400 to 450 degrees.[52]

This I do not hesitate to declair is incompatible with every principle of latent heat.

Mr Perkin's proposes to apply his generator to the boiler of the common low pressure engine. By this means he says as much low pressure steam of 4 lbs. on the square inch may be generated by one bushel of coals as could be producd in the old way by nine bushels.

Steam of 4 pounds pressure contains a certain quantity of water combined with a definite quantity of heat which heat it must receive from the fuel, a bushel of coal. The question then is how this heat can be applied in the most advantageous manner.

In the common boiler in the fore part of the boiler which serves for a furnace and the flues are made to pass and to repass through the water before they entre the chimney.

The fire is thus entirely surrounded with water so than very little heat can escape even by eradiation.

On the contrary Mr Perkins heats his generator in a open air furnace to a considerable temperature. Such heat must therefore be disapatd by eradiation. But by this method only Mr Perkins is able to make a saving of fuel as 9 to 1. This appears to be <*more*> as paradoxical <*than*> as that power may be gained without a loss of time.

---

[52] Henry here confused heat and temperature. It was not necessary, in the terms of the physics of the day, to heat the small amount of water which was released at the generator end of Perkins' boiler *to* 1000°, only to provide it with an amount of heat which *would* raise it to 1000° if it did not vaporize. The additional heat came from the surroundings.

The only circumstance that gives it an air of probibility is that a small quantiy of water is heated to the boiling point whereas in the common method several hogsheads are made to boil. But the only gain of heat by this is the first raising the water to the boling point after which every addition of heat produces a new quantity of steam and very little heat is required to keep the water at the boiling point.

If eight gallons of water be flashed into steam of sufficient rarity to fill the boiler of the James Kent[53] it would probably reduce the <*boiler*> generator temperature below [to] the freezing point as is shown by the experiment with the fountain.

Gentlemen I will trespass no longer on your time for I have already detourd you too long from the mor interesting subject of the steam engine.

---

[53] The *James Kent* was built in 1823 for the Fulton monopoly. See Fred Erving Dayton and John Wolcott Adams, *Steamboat Days* (New York, 1925), p. 37.

❧ 1825 ☙

MINUTES, ALBANY INSTITUTE
Institute Minutes, 1:16–18, Albany Institute Archives

Wednesday 2ᵈ February 1825.

The Institute met at the Room of the 2ᵈ Department, the Second Vice President having taken the chair the minutes of the preceding Meeting were read and approved.*

On motion of R V DeWitt The Institute proceeded to choose Officers for the Ensuing year, when on counting the Ballots of the Members present it appeared, that

The Hon. Stephen Van Rensselaer was Elected President

William Mayell Treasurer, &

T. Romeyn Beck
Johnathan Eights
Simeon DeWitt ⎬ Committee of Publication
Alfred Conkling[1] &
John W. Yates

* The Reports of the Recording Secretaries of the Departments should follow immediately after the first paragraph.

---

[1] Alfred Conkling (1789–1874), lawyer, judge, congressman, and author, was educated at Union College, and read law in Daniel Cady's office. In 1818 he was elected District Attorney

The Recording Secretary of the Department of Physical Sciences & Arts Reported that at the Annual Election held at the Chamber of the Department on the ____ January,[2] the following Gentlemen were Elected Officers for the ensuing year

Viz. Simeon DeWitt	President
Johnathan Eights	1st. Vice President
Joel A. Wing	2nd Do.
William Mayell	Treasurer
Peter Gansevoort	Corresponding Secretary
Henry W. Snyder	Recording [Secretary]
T. Romeyn Beck	
John Meads	
Charles R. Webster	
James Stevenson[3]	
John Taylor[4]	Counsellors
Elisha Jenkins	
W. A. Tweed Dale[5]	
Philip Hooker[6]	

The Recording Secretary of the Department of Natural History Re-

---

for Montgomery County; in 1820 he was elected to Congress, where he served one term, after which he began practicing law in Albany. In 1825 he was appointed Federal Judge for the Northern District of New York, and held this office for twenty-seven years. He was minister to, Mexico in 1852–1853. *DAB.* There are two pamphlets and one book by Conkling in Joseph Henry's Library. The pamphlets are (1) *A Discourse . . . of the Late DeWitt Clinton* (Albany, 1828) and (2) *Legal Reform, An Address to the Graduating Class of the Law School of the University of Albany* (Albany, 1856). The book, inscribed "To Professor Henry from his friend the Author Washington May 17, 1868," is *The Powers of the Executive Department of the Government of the United States* (Albany, 1866).

[2] The day does not appear in the manuscript.

[3] James Stevenson (1788–1852) was graduated from Williams College in 1807 and given an *ad eundem gradum* degree at Yale College the same year. An attorney, he was prominent in Albany affairs and served as Mayor, 1826–1828. He was also a member of the Board of Trustees of the Albany Academy, 1823–1826 and 1828–1852. Reynolds, *Alb. Chron.*, p.

460; *Academy Seventy-fifth Anniversary*, p. 66.

[4] John Taylor (1790–1863), brewer, was born in England. Though he had little formal education, he loved learning and amassed a considerable private library. He was Mayor of Albany, 1848–1849. Reynolds, *Alb. Chron.*, p. 592.

[5] William A. Tweed Dale (though the name is not hyphenated, he was always referred to as Mr. Tweed Dale), teacher, came from England. He was preceptor in the Albany Lancastrian School from its inception ca. 1811 until 1834. He died in Albany in 1854, aged 79. Munsell, *Ann. Alb.*, 2:305–306; *10*:231, 342; Reynolds, *Alb. Chron.*, p. 583.

[6] Philip Hooker (1766–1836), architect, held a number of city offices including that of city surveyor from 1819 to 1832. It was he who designed the Albany Academy building (for which see above, Minutes of the Academy Trustees, November 12, 1816, especially footnote 7), and many other public buildings in the city. "When Hooker began to design buildings," E. W. Root has written, "Albany was a Dutch frontier village; at his death it had been reconstructed, largely through his own efforts, into the semblance of a thriving, New England city." *DAB.*

ported, that at the Annual Election held at the Room of the Department on the   January,[7] the following Gentlemen were Elected Officers for the ensuing year Viz.

    Elisha Jenkins   President
    T. Romeyn Beck   1st. Vice President
    Stephen Van Rensselaer Jun.[8]   2[d] [Vice President]
    Matthew Henry Webster   Corresponding Secretary
    Joseph P. Mott[9]   Recording [Secretary]
    Duncan M[c]Kercher   Treasurer.
    Richard Varick DeWitt   Draftsman.
    Lewis C. Beck
    M. H. Webster
    R. V. DeWitt   } Curators
    William Cooper &
    Joseph Henry

The Recording Secretary of the Department of History and General Literature Reported, That the same had been duly organized, and that at an Election held for that purpose on the[10]   the following Gentlemen were Elected Officers for the Ensuing year Viz.

    Rev. John Chester   President
    John W. Yates   1st. Vice President
    Alfred Conkling   2nd   Do.
    Frederick Matthews   Corresponding Secretary
    Richard Varick DeWitt   Recording   Do.
    James Edwards[11]   Treasurer.

    M. H. Webster read a Translation of the II Chapter of Brongniart's Work on Trilobites; being an Essay on the relation Existing between Trilobites & those animals which are known to Exist at the present day.[12]

---

[7] A blank, not subsequently filled in, was left for the day.

[8] Stephen Van Rensselaer (1789–1868), son of Stephen Van Rensselaer, was the last of the patroons of central New York. Apart from serving in the state militia, he seems not to have participated actively in public life. *National Cyclopaedia of American Biography*, 2: 483–484.

[9] Joseph P. Mott, brother of Isaac Mott (for whom see below, Mott to Henry, May 10, 1829), is listed in Albany City Directories as a teacher from 1825 to 1828 and thereafter as a dealer in cider and vinegar. He died in Albany in 1846, aged 49. Munsell, *Ann. Alb.*, 10:372.

[10] The date is blank in the document.

[11] James Edwards, an attorney, was active in city affairs. He died in 1836. Munsell, *Ann. Alb.*, 4:280.

[12] Alexandre Brongniart (1770–1847), *Histoire Naturelle des crustacés fossiles, sous les rapports zoologiques et géologiques . . .* (Paris, 1822), ch. 2: "Rapports des Trilobites avec les animaux connus," pp. 40–45.

Dr. T. Romeyn Beck, read a communication on the nature and properties of Potassium;[13] he exhibited a specimen of that Metal, & performed several experiments upon it.

> And the Institute Adjourned to
> meet at Chamber of the 1st. Department
> on the 16th. Instant.
> R V DeWitt   Rec^g Sec^y

[13] This was never published.

MINUTES, ALBANY INSTITUTE

Institute Minutes, 1:19, Albany Institute Archives

March 2. 1825.

The Institute met at the Chamber of the Department of Natural History.

The President of the 1st Department in the Chair. The Minutes of the last meeting were read & approved.

Mr S. DeWitt read a paper on the "Functions of the Moon as deduced from the total Eclipse of the sun on the 16th of June 1806."[1]

Mr S. DeWitt also presented a drawing illustrative of the appearance of the Moon during the above Eclipse.[2]

Mr M. H. Webster presented specimens of fossil Pectinites[3] from the Eastern shore of the Chesapeake (Maryland) also fossil Turritella from Fort Washington on the Potomac, & also two Specimens of the Tertiary formation of the Southern States—from Fort Washington.

Genl Solomon Van Rensselaer[4] presented specimens of Iron pyrite, bituminous shale found about three miles south of Albany on the West bank of the river.

[1] Published in *Transactions*, Albany Institute, 1833–1852, 2:70–83.

[2] Ibid., plate III and figure 3.

[3] Probably molluscs of the family termed *Pectinides* by Lamarck and still referred to as Pectinidae. See, e.g., G. B. Sowerby, *A Conchological Manual*, 4th ed. (London, 1852), p. 233 and Paul Pelseneer, "Mollusca," part 5 of *A Treatise on Zoology*, ed. E. Ray Lankester (London, 1906), pp. 204–205.

[4] Solomon Van Rensselaer (1774–1852), soldier, congressman, served under General Anthony Wayne in the campaigns against the Indians in the 1790s, and in the War of 1812. He was elected to the House of Representatives in 1818 and 1820, and thereafter appointed to the office of postmaster at Albany, where he served from 1822 to 1839 and from 1841 to 1843. He was the author of *A Narrative of the Affair at Queenstown in the War of 1812* . . . (New York, 1836). *DAB*. He was a nephew of Killian Van Rensselaer (1763–1845) and a second cousin, one generation removed, of Stephen Van Rensselaer (1764–1839).

M^r McKercher to whom was referred a specimen of the black oxide of manganese, read an account of that mineral, with its application in the Arts.[5]

Mr Joseph Henry read a paper on the production of cold by the rarefaction of air, accompanied with experiments.[6]

Dr Lewis C. Beck read an analysis of the salt manufactured at Salina & Syracuse, with specimens of the same.

Adjourned.

---

[5] McKercher's paper was apparently never published. Black oxide of manganese is MnO_2.

[6] This paper was not published, nor does the text survive in manuscript. An abstract was published, however, in the *Transactions,* Albany Institute, 1830, *1,* part 2:36 and was reprinted in *Scientific Writings of Joseph Henry,* 2 vols. (Washington, 1886), *1*:1–2. The "experiment" consisted of condensing air in a vessel which contained a small amount of water. The vessel was fitted with a tube, one end of which opened under the water, the other, fitted with a stopcock, opened to the outside. The lower part of the tube had a number of small holes pierced in it just above the surface of the water, so that when the vessel contained compressed air, a mingled jet of air and water was released upon opening the stopcock. Under these conditions, the water showering forth was almost immediately frozen to snow. The principles involved were familiar, but it was a dramatic demonstration. For a treatment of contemporary theory relating to the phenomena see T. S. Kuhn, "The Caloric Theory of Adiabatic Compression," *Isis,* 1958, *49*:132–140.

EXCERPT,[1] MINUTES, ALBANY INSTITUTE

Institute Minutes, 1:21–23, Albany Institute Archives

April 27. 1825.

The Institute met, pursuant to adjournment.

The 1st VPres^t in the Chair . . . .

Mr S. DeWitt presented Tables of the Variation of the Magnetic needle at Boston, Falmouth & Penobscot, from the year 1672 to 1800 drawn up by Jno Winthrop[2] Hollis Professor of Mathematics at Harvard University,— and accompanied these with remarks on the variations observed by himself.

---

[1] A list of donations to the Institute at the opening of the minutes has been omitted; this list was printed in the *Transactions,* Albany Institute, 1830, *1,* part 2:41–42. We also have omitted two paragraphs concerning routine business at the end of the document, just before the notice of adjournment.

[2] John Winthrop (1714–1779), astronomer, mathematician, physicist, Hollis Professor of Mathematics and Natural Philosophy at Harvard, 1738–1779, one of the most distinguished of the Colonial scientists. *DAB.* It is not known who continued the magnetic observations, after Winthrop's death, to 1800, but it might have been his successors in the Hollis chair, one of whom at least, Samuel Williams (1743–1817), had a keen interest in the subject. See Brooke Hindle, *The Pursuit of Science in Revolutionary America, 1735–1789* (Chapel Hill, 1956), pp. 180–181, 349–351. According to DeWitt in the account published in the *Transactions,* Albany Institute, 1830, *1*:4–7, the tables were submitted to him by General Schuyler, presumably Philip John Schuyler (1733–1804), Major-General in the Revolutionary War. At one point in the paper,

L. C. Beck read an account of the Salt Springs in the County of Onondago, with an analysis of the Salt produced by various processes & the residua left.

The same gentleman exhibited experiments illustrative of the nature & properties of pure alcohol, when deprived of all the water that usually accompanies it.[3]

Joseph Henry read an analysis of the foetid Sulphate of Barytes found at Little Falls (N.Y.)[4]

The same gentleman also exhibited Prof. Dobereiner's Experiments of the ignition of Platina Sponge by a jet of hydrogen Gas. . . .[5]

Resolved that when the Institute adjourns it adjourn to hold a special meeting on the 2nd Wednesday in June.

Adjourned.

DeWitt mentions that Joseph Henry "surveyed a farm in the town of Coeyman's, not many days ago . . . and the variation [since 1798] was found to be one degree . . . from the north to the west . . . " (*Transactions*, Albany Institute, loc. cit., p. 5). From this it appears that Henry did private surveying before embarking on the State Road Survey starting on July 19, 1825 (see below, Henry's Books of Levels from the State Road Survey, July 19–December [15], 1825).

[3] The quest for "absolute alcohol" was perennial from nearly the beginning of chemistry. Pure alcohol was in this period considered to have a specific gravity of .796 (water = 1) at 60°F. Johann Tobias Lowitz (1757–1804) was the authority for this determination (very close, incidentally, to the modern value), but it is likely that Beck, who repeated it in his *A Manual of Chemistry* (Albany, 1831), p. 413, got it from one of the textbooks of the day, e.g., William Thomas Brande, *A Manual*

of Chemistry (1819); we have consulted Joseph Henry's copy, first American from the second London edition, New York, 1821, p. 530.

[4] Barium sulfate is itself odorless, but is sometimes found with sedimentary sulfides, which on exposure to air and water give off hydrogen sulfide, foetid indeed.

[5] Johann Wolfgang Döbereiner (1780–1849), Professor of Chemistry at Jena, had discovered, in 1823, that hydrogen and oxygen combine spontaneously in the presence of spongy platinum. "Neu entdeckte merkwürdige Eigenschaften des Platin-suboxyds des oxydirten Schwefel-Platins, und des metallischen Platin-staubes," (Schweigger's) *Journal für Chemie und Physik*, 1823, *38*:321–326. Though not the first to discover catalysis, Döbereiner, with this work, started a flood of investigations into the phenomena. His paper was picked up by the major French and English journals, and it is likely that Henry saw it in one of these.

HENRY'S BOOKS OF LEVELS FROM THE STATE ROAD SURVEY, JULY 19–DECEMBER [15] 1825
Henry Papers, Smithsonian Archives

Having left Albany on July 19, 1825, Joseph Henry participated in a survey party which started in Kingston, New York, on the next day. The object of the survey was to determine the most level and useful route for the proposed Great State Road across the middle or southern counties of the state, connecting the

Hudson River and Lake Erie. Specifically, Henry's group was concerned with leveling, that is developing a profile of the elevations and depressions which would be encountered on the proposed route. Little beyond Henry's manuscript books of levels has survived in the Henry Papers. These documents, as well as several other related documents cited below, shed light upon Henry's activities, although they are not suitable for publication in the present volume.

The books of levels consist of thirteen pocket notebooks, roughly four inches by six inches in size, averaging about forty-five pages each. Eleven of the books are lightly annotated, being comprised almost exclusively of Henry's leveling calculations; two books, on the other hand, served as repositories for Henry's memoranda and give more sidelights into the activities of Henry and his fellow surveyors.

The formal proposal for the construction of a state road across the southern tier of counties first came to the state legislature through Governor DeWitt Clinton's[1] annual message of January 4, 1825. By the end of February of that year enough public pressure had developed in the southern counties that the legislature passed a bill authorizing the Governor and Senate to appoint three road Commissioners to survey possible routes and to make recommendations to the legislature. Nathaniel Pitcher,[2] Jabez D. Hammond,[3] and George Morell[4] se-

---

[1] DeWitt Clinton (1769–1828), for whom see above, T. R. Beck to J. W. Francis, February 26, 1812, especially footnote 33, and below, Minutes, Albany Institute, February 13, 1828. The proposal was undoubtedly made with an eye toward developing the economic activity of the southern section of the state, ameliorating sectional grievances arising from the building of the Erie Canal across the northern counties.

[2] Nathaniel Pitcher (1777–1836), lawyer and politician, was born in Litchfield, Connecticut. Having moved to Sandy Hill, New York (now Hudson Falls), he apparently began his political career as Supervisor of Sandy Hill, 1804–1810. He served on the state level as a member of the New York Assembly in 1806, 1814–1815, and 1816–1817, as a delegate to the New York Constitutional Convention of 1821, as Lieutenant Governor in 1826, and as Acting Governor following the death of DeWitt Clinton in February 1828. On the national level, Pitcher served as a U.S. Representative, 1819–1821, 1821–1823, and 1831–1833. For general information on Pitcher, see F. B. Hough, *American Biographical Notes* (Albany, 1875), p. 326; *Biographical Directory of the American Congress*; E. A. Werner, *Civil List and Constitutional History of the Colony and State of New York* (Albany, 1889), pp. 127, 166,

169, 420, 425, 503, 604–605. For comments on Pitcher's political activities in New York, see Jabez D. Hammond, *The History of Political Parties in the State of New-York*, 4th ed., 2 vols. (Cooperstown, New York, 1846), 2:233, 235, 277, 288. This edition will be cited in notes to follow.

[3] Jabez Delano Hammond (1778–1855), doctor, lawyer, politician, and author. Born in New Bedford, Massachusetts, Hammond studied medicine and established a practice in Reading, Vermont, in 1799. Hammond apparently abandoned medicine to study and subsequently practice law, commencing practice in Cherry Valley, New York, in 1805. Leading an active political life, Hammond served a term in Congress, 1815–1817, and four terms as Senator in the New York Assembly, 1818–1821. Active in Albany affairs for the next fifteen years or more, he practiced law there and followed literary pursuits. He was author of *The History of Political Parties in the State of New-York*, 2 vols. (Albany, 1842) and *Life and Times of Silas Wright, 1795–1847, Late Governor of New York State* (Syracuse, 1848). Hammond served for five years, 1838–1843, as a judge of Otsego County. Having been the Superintendent of Schools in the county, he was elected to the Board of Regents of the University of the

cured the appointments on April 20, 1825. The Commissioners in turn explored and then directed to be surveyed several possible routes across the state, ordering their principal surveyors

> that they should observe and note the quality of the soil, and the face of the country with reference to its adaptation to a road; the bridges it might be necessary to construct on their routes respectively, that the convenience of solid materials for the road and facility of construction should constantly be kept in view; that the vallies and ravines should be pursued where practicable, rather than to encounter them transversely, although the effect might be to increase the distance; and that the angle of ascent and descent should in no case exceed three degrees from a horizontal line.[5]

The major routes were surveyed for the Commissioners by William H. Morel,[6] Andrew Williams,[7] William J. Nelson,[8] Jacob Trumpbour,[9] David H. Burr,[10]

State of New York in 1845, on which he remained until his death.

While a resident of Cherry Valley, Hammond was a friend and neighbor of James O. Morse, cousin of Samuel F. B. Morse whom he often entertained as a guest while Morse was conducting experiments with his telegraph.

Due to Hammond's participation on the Board of Commissioners for the Great State Road, his *History of Political Parties . . .* provides us with the most complete analysis of the beginnings, developments, and termination of activities in the state for the construction of the road. Additional information about Hammond may be found in *DAB;* see also *Biographical Directory of the American Congress;* Werner, *Civil List,* pp. 247, 367, 377, 491, 604; Records of the Cherry Valley Historical Association.

Hammond subsequently became friendly with Joseph Henry who later sent him reprints of scientific publications.

[4] George Morell (1786–1845), lawyer, jurist, and legislator. Born in Lenox, Massachusetts, he practiced law in Cooperstown, New York, and was appointed the first judge of the Otsego County Court in 1827. He was a member of the Assembly in 1829, and was reappointed judge in 1832. From late in 1832 until his death he served in various judicial capacities in Michigan. We feel that we have identified the appropriate George Morell, though at times the name appears as Morrell. See *Herringshaw,* p. 674; Werner, *Civil List,* pp. 539, 628; *DAB* entry for George Webb Morell (1815–1883), the son of George Morell.

[5] This quotation is taken from the "Report of the Commissioners of the Great State Road

Made to the Assembly, March 29, 1826," New York *Assembly Journal,* 1826, Appendix K, p. 2. The general information about the progress of the proposal and appointments is based on Hammond, *History of Political Parties . . . ,* 4th ed., 2:185, 201–203, 219.

[6] Unidentified.

[7] Possibly Andrew J. Williams (d. 1876), who received his A.M. degree from Union College in 1819, having entered college from Cherry Valley, New York. Williams later practiced law. See *Union Catalog,* p. 18.

[8] A William J. Nelson is listed in Werner's *Civil List,* p. 451, as a member of the New York Assembly in 1851 from Great Valley, Cattaraugus County. We have been unable to identify him further except to note that he began his work in the survey as Henry's assistant; see below in this text and Henry's Book of Levels No. 1, "Levels from Kingston . . . ," [p. 1], in Henry Papers, Smithsonian Archives.

[9] We have not been able to locate much information on Jacob Trumpbour. Although sometimes referred to as Judge Trumpbour, he was a surveyor by profession. J. Wilson Poucher, M.D., and Byron J. Terwillinger, eds., *Old Gravestones of Ulster County, New York,* Collections of the Ulster County Historical Society, [Kingston, New York], 1931, *1*:51, lists a Jacob Trumpbour (1779–1843). Trumpbour appears in Werner's *Civil List* as a member of the Assembly from Kingston in 1827. Henry became indirectly involved with Trumpbour when he was called as an expert witness to testify in behalf of Holmes Hutchinson (for whom see below, Joseph Henry's Deposition, May 19, 1832, footnote 4), a sur-

and Joseph Henry, while a number of additional alternative routes were surveyed by at least eight other surveyors. Dr. William Campbell[11] acted for the Commissioners as Chief Engineer of the survey, coordinating the surveying teams, compiling their findings, and rendering the report of the Commission.

How Joseph Henry was selected for the survey can only be guessed at. Through his activities at the Albany Institute, Henry became a colleague of Simeon DeWitt,[12] then Surveyor-General of the state, who may well have had some influence in the selection of surveyors. Henry would also have become known to Dr. William Campbell, a corresponding member of the Institute. We know of no other immediate connections which Henry might have had with the Road Survey Commission. Correspondence printed below indicates that T. Romeyn Beck recommended Henry for the position and that Henry was grateful for Beck's support.[13] Henry's own preparation for the survey appears to have been largely through his studies at the Albany Academy and perhaps through some learning on his own. It is possible that Henry read Gummere's *Treatise on Surveying,* which discusses the process of leveling, Henry's major assignment in the survey.[14] Henry had some practical experience in cadastral surveying.

Undoubtedly because the intention of the Commissioners was to seek a route which was most level, even at the expense of distance, the route which Henry was assigned to follow consisted largely of roads already established. Often the

---

veyor involved in a dispute with Trumpbour over a contract with the Canal Commissioners to survey lands along the canals.

[10] After serving in the road survey, Burr combined his data with the findings of others in the survey and solicited more information through circulars to produce his *Atlas of the State of New York* (Albany, 1829). For more information on Burr and the role of Henry in the writing of the *Atlas,* see below, Burr to Henry, November 25, 1829, especially footnote 1.

[11] Dr. William Campbell (1767 or 1768–1844), physician and surveyor of Cherry Valley, New York, was long active in New York State government. After practicing medicine in Cherry Valley, he became involved in surveying operations for the Great Western Turnpike about 1800. John Sawyer, in his *History of Cherry Valley* (Cherry Valley, 1898), claims that Campbell was "more celebrated as a civil engineer and surveyor than as a physician. He surveyed several of the state roads, including the Second Great Western Turnpike, of which he was for many years one of the directors." Campbell was a member of the Assembly in 1816, 1817, and 1827. In 1835 he became Surveyor-General of the State, a post which he held for three years. In 1833 he was appointed a Regent of the University,

continuing in this capacity until his death. Campbell was also active as a corresponding member of the Albany Institute. See Franklin B. Hough, *American Biographical Notes* (Albany, 1875), p. 61; Werner, *Civil List,* pp. 178, 247, 426, 429, 433; *Transactions,* Albany Institute, 1830, *1,* Part 2: Appendix, p. 70.

There appeared to be little question about Campbell's qualifications for the job. According to the report of the Commissioners to the legislature, at the Commissioners' first meeting, "they appointed William Campbell, Esq. of the county of Otsego, their principal surveyor and engineer, in order to avail themselves in their earliest operations, of his practical knowledge and professional skill." See Appendix K, p. 2. Henry corresponded with Campbell at several points during the survey, but he also retained Campbell as a scientific friend and correspondent afterward. See below, Henry to Campbell of September 25, 1829, and Campbell to Henry of September 5, 1831.

[12] For whom see T. R. Beck to J. W. Francis, February 26, 1812, especially footnote 20.

[13] See Henry's letter to Beck, November 28, 1825, and Beck's letter to Martin Van Buren, March 10, 1826.

[14] See below, Henry to Campbell, October 31, 1825, footnote 7.

party surveyed turnpike roads, sometimes less developed roads, and in a few instances they departed from established roads altogether for longer but more level alternative routes.[15] The roads already existing were a far cry, apparently, from the proposed McAdamized Great State Road; as Henry noted on September 24 or 25, just before the group reached the eastern limit of the town of Binghamton, "We here met the first carriage on springs since we left the Hudson. Any road we have passed would be fatal to them."[16]

The procedures which the survey party followed were discussed by Henry in his letter to William Campbell of October 31, 1825, for which see below. Within the survey party's assignment, it was Henry's responsibility to do the leveling; thus, the notes which survive are Henry's "levels." Through the use of a conventional level, a tripod-based instrument which would be made level and through which one could then sight horizontally both into the hillside as well as away from it, Henry would direct his target men to raise or lower the leveling staffs placed in front and behind to the height at which the vanes were pierced by the horizontal sight. The heights of the vanes were then noted, and figures were recorded for heights both backward and forward. Henry thus kept two columns of figures, "B" or "back-sight" measurements and "F" or "fore-sight" measurements. All measurements were given in feet, and at certain intervals the net difference between the "B" and "F" figures was calculated, thus rendering a figure for the subtotal elevations (if the "B" total was greater than the "F" total) or depressions (if, conversely, the "F" total was greater than the "B" total). Henry annotated his figures occasionally, pointing out, for instance, where cuts would have to be made in high passes, where the route deviated from or coincided with established routes, rivers, or valleys, or where the quality of the soil might lend

[15] Several sources have been helpful in determining the exact route followed by Henry's survey team. At the conclusion of the survey expedition, Henry handed over to Campbell his field notes, from which an atlas was compiled, being comprised of about forty detailed maps of Henry's survey from Kingston to Bath (similar procedures were followed for the notes of other returning surveyors, and it was undoubtedly these notes and atlases which Burr found so handy in compiling his *Atlas*). The atlas which depicts Henry's route has survived in the New York State Department of Waterways, along with the others. Although it is clear that the atlas was drawn up by obviously experienced cartographers, a notation on the title page, "by J Henry Eng.," appears to be in Henry's distinctive early hand, quite similar to the style of handwriting which Henry used in marking the books from the Albany period surviving in the Henry library. The atlas shows in detail the topographical features as well as such items as roads already present, bridges, houses, town lines, property lines, etc. In addition, it demonstrates the profile of elevations and depressions encountered in the survey. This atlas accompanied Henry's written report of his survey from Kingston to Bath, which included a description of the course followed, explanations of the advantages and disadvantages of the route, and a cost estimate of building the road along that route. Both the atlas and the accompanying written report were made a part of the Commissioners' report to the legislature (Appendix K), and the written report was printed in the Commissioners' report as Statement D. In determining the exact route followed by Henry and his men, reference was also made to the county maps contained in Burr's *Atlas;* in nearly all instances it was clear that Henry found the existing roads, however rough, had been established along the most level route.

[16] See Book of Levels No. 7, "Levels from the Susquehanna at Hotchkiss' Mills Windsor to Within 10 Miles of Owego, Tioga Co.," [p. 28].

itself to paving the road. Of course, throughout the survey Henry kept account of his "levels" by stations, that is the surveying stations which his group established for each new compass direction of the route.

In addition to the leveling, it was Henry's responsibility to act as head of his surveying party. As director he was called the "Engineer" and clearly had full administrative responsibility for his group. There survives in the Smithsonian Archives a copy of the final account sheet which Henry submitted to the state at the conclusion of his surveying duties.[17] The account shows that Henry had been advanced $1,120 and that he had expended a sum of $1,197.90 in wages and contingent expenses. The account thus confirms what Henry wrote to Dr. Campbell on November 16, 1825 (see below), that he had run short of money in the midst of the survey and had sustained the operation by borrowing from willing residents along the route. Henry himself had earned $885.50 at the rate of $3.50 per day for 253 days, including the time he spent compiling the data for the report to the Commissioners. What seems most significant about these figures is that Henry, by some time in March 1826, probably received nearly $900 in addition to the money owed to the lenders on the route. Henry's work on the survey had been lucrative, by the standards of the day, and may have made theoretical science seem a less attractive pursuit than engineering.

Comparing the account sheet, which lists the wages paid to each worker, with the first page of Henry's first book of levels, which lists the staff of the survey party at the outset on July 20, 1825, not every participant in Henry's group worked throughout the entire survey. In fact, Colonel Nathan Beckwith,[18] who began the survey as Henry's "surveyor" but who was not paid from Henry's account at all, stayed with Henry's group only until it reached the "village of Windsor" on September 22, 1825.[19] William J. Nelson,[20] who started out as Henry's assistant but worked for only thirty-eight days with Henry, himself headed a survey and leveling party in exploring one of the alternative routes. Benjamin Atkins[21] and William Cooper[22] appear to have worked throughout

---

[17] This account sheet, dated February 28, 1826, is filed in the "Albany Academy, Accounts for Philosophical Apparatus, 1827–1831" in the Henry Papers, Smithsonian Archives.

[18] Nathan Beckwith (1778–1865). Born in Stamford, New York, he moved to a farm in Red Hook, New York, and lived there until his death. Active in local politics, he was Town Supervisor for many years. As a lieutenant in the War of 1812 he was awarded a large land grant in Herkimer County. In 1820 he was commissioned Colonel of the cavalry by the Governor. A local notable, he served as Marshal of the Day during General Lafayette's visit to Dutchess County in 1824. He had been a classmate of Martin Van Buren at the Kinderhook Academy, where he graduated as a civil engineer. A life member of the American Bible Society and the Foreign Bible Society, he helped in organizing the First Baptist Church of Red Hook. *Commemorative Biographical Record of Dutchess County, New York, Containing Biographical Sketches of Prominent and Representative Citizens and of Many of the Early Settled Families* (Chicago, 1897), p. 767.

[19] See Book of Levels No. 7, "Levels from the Susquehanna at Hotchkiss' Mills Windsor to Within 10 Miles of Owego, Tioga Co.," [p. 2].

[20] See footnote 8.

[21] Benjamin Atkins (1795 or 1796–1840) is listed in the Albany City Directories as a teacher (1829–1830) and an accountant (1828–

the survey, at first as target men and later as assistants. Murdow McPherson[23] worked for the first 101 days as target man, and Nathan Stone[24] served apparently for the duration as axeman and commissary. But Henry's most loyal worker must have been his own younger brother. James Henry[25] worked as a target man throughout most of the survey, though he acted as Joseph's assistant by the end of the journey and well afterward as the brothers probably worked together to prepare from the field notes the data for the atlas, maps, and profiles of the route surveyed, as well as the written report to the Commission.

Henry's group began its survey at Kingston, New York, on July 20, 1825, and surveyed a route of 232.5 miles in ninety-seven days, arriving in Bath on October 24. Theirs was the proposed "southern route" to Bath from the Hudson, in that it passed to the south of the major topographical obstacle, the Catskill Mountains. The route they surveyed resembled roughly that outlined today by U.S. 209 south to Napanoch; N.Y. 55 to Liberty; N.Y. 17 to Painted Post; and N.Y. 15 to Bath. From Bath the group traveled in a week's time to Portland Harbor on Lake Erie, a town near the present Portland, New York, though a few miles to the south and on the lake's edge. Starting at the water on November 1, the group surveyed eastward to Angelica by November 29. The purpose of this twenty-nine-day tour was to survey and do the levels of a route being explored by Jacob Trumpbour, who was only a few days ahead of Henry's party.[26] The route taken by Henry resembles that today of N.Y. 17 from Westfield to Hartfield, thence eastward by various county roads to Sinclairville, Conewango Valley, Conewango, Little Valley, Ellicottville, Ischua, Cuba, and finally Angelica. From Angelica the group returned to Albany; the homebound trip, free of surveying responsibilities, consumed about two weeks.

Most of the route surveyed by Henry's group coincided with existing roads

---

1829, 1830–1841). In the Directories of 1838–1839 he is listed under B. Atkins & Co., auction and commission merchants.

[22] Perhaps the William Cooper identified above, Albany Institute Minutes, May 5, 1824, footnote 18. However, in Franklin Ellis's *History of Cattaraugus County, New York* (Philadelphia, 1879), p. 246, there is an interesting account of a William Cooper (1793–1872) who "watched, with unceasing care, the construction of all the public highways for miles around him . . . and wrought with untiring energy till they were all susceptible of travel."

[23] Murdow McPherson (1796–1841), who also worked on the survey as a chain man, later became a printer in Albany. In 1830 McPherson began publishing *The Farmers', Mechanics', and Workingmen's Advocate* (subsequently known as *The Daily Freeman's Advocate and Farmers', Mechanics', and Workingmen's Champion*), a daily newspaper. In Albany City Directories of 1833–1835 Mc-

Pherson is listed as an overseer of the poor. Later Directories list him as a printer until his death.

[24] Unidentified.

[25] James Henry (1803–1851). His books of levels from the survey are being kept along with Joseph's in the Smithsonian Archives. Surprisingly little is known of his life. He seems to have lived with his mother until her death in 1835; Albany City Directories list him as a bookseller from 1837 until his death. We know of no other instance in which the two brothers worked together in a scientific enterprise. James Henry's correspondence with his brother Joseph will appear below (August 29, 1832) and in subsequent volumes of the Henry Papers.

[26] For Henry's instructions, see below, William Campbell to Henry, October 3, 1825. For his experiences on this segment, see below, Henry to Campbell, November 16, 1825.

and thus enabled the party to work without the constant interference of nature and to pass through a number of substantial communities en route. One of the consequences was that the survey party was in frequent contact with interested citizens throughout the survey, citizens who were naturally enthusiastic about the prospect of the Great State Road passing through their communities. Just west of Deposit, New York, on September 10 Henry noted in surveying a slight variation of a route taken by Trumpbour that "The inhabitants on both routes are very anxious to have the road pass directly past their own door."[27] Through these cordial receptions, Henry had the opportunity to establish acquaintances with many of the towns' most outstanding or interested citizens, and he returned to Albany with two notebooks containing, among other miscellaneous notes, names to remember and requests for certain favors which he would perform in Albany for them. Henry had occasion to make geological and topographical notes both while surveying and while traveling homeward, and many of these observations undoubtedly contributed to the paper he later delivered at the Albany Institute[28] and published in Burr's *Atlas*. At times, too, Henry noted in his books of levels observations on natural history which were of special interest to him. In visiting towns, Henry often noted the major economic activities of the area, the state of economic development, the population, numbers of taverns and churches, and the transportation facilities available to the inhabitants. In the western section of the state Henry saw remnants of Indian culture and noted at least some ethnological folklore in his books. Nonetheless, a thorough reading of Henry's notes suggests that he never lost sight of the fact that, in order to be built, the road must serve an undeniable economic need.[29]

Interestingly, however, the route surveyed was never selected as the route for the proposed Great State Road. An alternative one, to the north of the Catskills and serving the town of Catskill instead of Kingston, was thought to be more economical, but even that route, as such, was proposed for building only in part. The Commission recommended to the legislature that "instead of constructing one continuous line of road from the Hudson River to Lake Erie, a road be constructed from the head of the west branch of the Delaware, in Delaware county, through Unadilla, Ithaca, and the head of Seneca lake to Bath, and from Bath through Angelica and Ellicottville, to the town of Gerry, in the county of Chautauque." The Commissioners hastened to point out that roads and turnpikes at either end "can and will, no doubt, be made by private enterprise" and that the state would therefore have promoted, at reasonable expense, the construction of a thoroughly modern and economical road from the Hudson to Lake Erie.

---

[27] Book of Levels No. 5, "Levels from the bench at Hawk Hill to between the Delawar and the Susquehanna," [p. 40].

[28] On October 28, 1829, Henry read "Topographical Sketch of the State of New-York, Designed Chiefly to Show the General Elevations and Depressions of its Surface," which was published in *Transactions*, Albany Institute, 1830, *1*:87–112.

[29] The arguments for the construction of the Great State Road were, after all, almost wholly economic. See, for instance, [Nicholas F. Beck], *Considerations in Favour of the Construction of a Great State Road from Lake Erie to the Hudson River* (Albany, 1827).

Nonetheless, the legislature proceeded to defeat the Commissioners' recommendation, such defeat possibly being attributable to the efforts of the Erie Canal interests which felt somewhat aggrieved at the prospect of such competition for their Erie-to-Hudson transportation facility.[30]

The fact that the Great State Road as such was never built detracted not one bit from the survey's accomplishments for both the state and Henry personally. As Henry noted at one point in the survey, "If no state road be constructed this survey will be of great advantage to the country in teaching the inhabitants to explore and awaken their attention to the subject."[31] Undoubtedly the survey was a stimulus, as the canal engineering had been, for greater geological, topographical, and economic thirst for understanding. In fact, all the survey notes made for the Great State Road study were the basis for the detailed and quite popular edition of Burr's *Atlas*. For Henry the experience was indispensable training and background for the possible pursuit of engineering. Henry had been given a chance to demonstrate his ability to direct a group and his engineering skill and promise. The immediate result was the establishment of a close working relationship with some of the older and more established surveyors and politicians; a recommendation was soon to follow, based on his survey work as well as other accomplishments, that Henry be appointed to the Army's topographical engineers.[32] Henry had participated in an interesting, enlightening, and lucrative enterprise.

---

[30] See Hammond, *Political Parties*, pp. 218–225. The defeat of the measure was not the end of the interest in developing the transportation facilities of that section of the state. It appears likely that the route which Henry surveyed was used in part for the early projection of the Erie Railroad. See Oliver W. Holmes, "The Turnpike Era," in *History of the State of New York*, Alexander C. Flick, ed., 10 vols. (New York, 1934), 5:260–267. The usefulness of roads and details about the construction of McAdam-type roads, which was the type of surfacing proposed for the Great State Road, are discussed in Simeon DeWitt Bloodgood, *A Treatise on Roads, Their History, Character and Utility* (Albany, 1838).

[31] Miscellaneous Notebook No. 1, [p. 11], no date.

[32] See below, T. R. Beck to Martin Van Buren, March 10, 1826, and related documents.

EXCERPT,[1] MINUTES, ACADEMY TRUSTEES
Trustees' Minutes, 1:251–252, Albany Academy Archives

Albany. Sept[r] 9. 1825

The Trustees met, pursuant to notice

Present

Isaac Ferris,   Jn° M. Bradford

---

[1] Routine matters from the end of these minutes have been omitted.

Henry R. Weed,[2]	The Recorder
Jnᵒ W. Yates,	Gid. Hawley,
Wᵐ James	C. R. Webster,
Jnᵒ Chester,	P. Gansevoort,
Jnᵒ Ludlow[3]	T. Romeyn Beck

The following Communication from the Secretary of the Regents was read,

At a meeting of the Regents of the University held pursuant to adjournment, in the Senate Chamber, March 1. 1825.

It was *Resolved,* that each of the Academies incorporated by this board, be furnished with a thermometer & pluviameter or rain gage, the expense of which shall be paid out of the funds of the Regents, & that the Vice Chancellor,[4] Mʳ Lansing,[5] and Mʳ Greig[6] be a Committee to provide those instruments & to prescribe the rules for making observations by them, & the manner in which the accounts of them shall be kept. Reports of which shall be annually made to this Board.

At a subsequent meeting of said Regents held on the 12ᵗʰ day of April 1825,

It was further *Resolved,* that in addition to the existing regulations to entitle the Academies to their dividends of the public fund, it will be considered necessary that they keep an exact register of observations made with the thermometer & rain gages, with which they shall be furnished, according to the Instructions that may be given them by the committee appointed for that purpose, & that, with their annual reports, they shall give

---

[2] A Phi Beta Kappa graduate of Union College (1812) and one of the first four graduates of the Princeton Theological Seminary (1815), Henry Rowland Weed (1789–1870) was Pastor of the First Presbyterian Church in Albany from 1822 to 1829 and served as an Academy Trustee from 1822 to 1831. See *Union Catalog,* p. 10; *Academy Seventy-fifth Anniversary,* p. 66; and Rev. Edward Howell Roberts, comp., *Biographical Catalogue of the Princeton Theological Seminary, 1815–1932* (Princeton, 1933), p. 1.

[3] John R. Ludlow (1793–1857) was the minister of the First Reformed Dutch Church in Albany from 1823 to 1834 and a Trustee of the Academy during those same years. From 1834 to 1852 Ludlow was Provost of the University of Pennsylvania. *National Cyclopedia of American Biography,* 1:343.

[4] Simeon DeWitt. DeWitt's interest in meteorology and its instruments was perennial. In 1827, he read to the Institute a description of a rain guage (*Transactions,* Albany Institute,

1830, *1,* part 2: Appendix, pp. 60–62) and gave an account of a simpler and cheaper form of it in 1832 (*Silliman's Journal,* 1832, 22:321–324). Among the Miscellaneous Henry Papers, Smithsonian Archives, there is an undated three-page description by Henry of the Albany Academy rain guage. He wrote that "for facility of observation and general accuracy in the result I consider this superior to any I have seen described." According to a note at the beginning of the document, the description was to be submitted to DeWitt.

[5] John Lansing, Jr. See above, Minutes of the Academy Trustees, [March 4, 1813], footnote 4.

[6] John Greig (1779–1858), a Regent from 1825 to 1858. He was a lawyer and banker from Canandaigua, Ontario County, and, from his long service as a Regent and in promoting schools locally, interested in education. He briefly served in Congress. *Herringshaw,* p. 423.

correct register of such observations & that the secretary furnish each of the Academies with a Copy of this resolution.

A True extract from the Minutes of the Regents[7]

G. Hawley. Sec[r]

Whereupon

Resolved that the Principal be appointed to carry the above resolutions into affect.

[7] For an account of the Regents' interest in meteorology, see Franklin B. Hough, *Historical and Statistical Record of the University of the State of New York During the Century From 1784 to 1884* (Albany, 1885), pp. 766–774. DeWitt introduced the resolution. Henry and Beck would eventually publish data derived from these observations. The first five *Abstracts of Meteorological Records of the State of New York, 1828–1832*, appeared in the Regents' *Annual Reports* for 1829–1833.

FROM T. ROMEYN BECK

Henry Papers, Smithsonian Archives

Albany, Oct[r] 1. 1825,

Dear Sir,[1]

By a gentleman who called some days since, I learnt that a letter addressed to you at Bath, Chenango County would reach you. I have understood with great pleasure, that everything is going on well with you. I propose lecturing on Chemistry this winter & if your engagements will allow, should be glad again to have your assistance.[2] I commence as usual on the 3rd of January. If you do not think you will be home, or cannot assist me, can you recommend me to some one who is competent. You know my engagments & how necessary it is to have some one who will take most of the business in hand. Let me hear from you, & beleive me Yours

very sincerely & truly

T. Romeyn Beck

[1] This letter is undoubtedly to Henry as the date and the address to which it was sent correlate with Henry's activities in the State Road Survey. See Henry's retained copy of his reply of November 28, 1825, below.

[2] The implication here is clear that Henry had assisted Beck in his public lecture series at least once prior to this invitation. *Coulson*, p. 18, is incorrect in saying "In October 1825 [Henry] also began to assist Dr. Beck in preparing his chemical lessons and demonstrations." In recommending Henry to Martin Van Buren in a letter dated March 10, 1826 (for which see below), Beck mentions that Henry assisted him in 1823–1824 but curiously omits any mention of Henry's assistance during early 1826.

FROM WILLIAM CAMPBELL

Mary Henry Copy,[1] Henry Papers, Smithsonian Archives

Oct 3 rd 1825

Dear Sir:

We arrived at the village of [?][2] last Saturday and are about to return to Cherry Valley. You proceed as advised on to Bath—then to Portland in Chautauqua Co. from the Harbour[3] you will follow the traverse of Judge Trumpbour[4] to Mayville—then in his southern route near St. Clairsville[5] to Elicottville to Angelica, where your levels will intersect those of Mr. Morrell,[6] who calculates to carry a line northerly of yours to Dunkirk. . . .[7]

I remain yrs &c.

William Campbell

[1] Joseph Henry's daughter Mary made or had made copies of various documents of her father's. Where an original survives, the Henry Papers will, of course, use it, not the copy by Mary Henry. In this case and in a number of others to appear subsequently, only the copy (or copies) survives. There is no reason to doubt the existence of the original at the time the copy was made. There is every reason to doubt the completeness and textual accuracy of many of the copies made by Mary Henry. Nevertheless, they will appear in this edition because they are often unique and important sources. The phrase "Mary Henry Copy" will indicate to readers the nature of the source document. In editing these items the Henry Papers will silently correct obvious errors of transcription. In the following text for example, "Judge Thompson" appears in the original instead of "Judge Trumpbour."

Not having an original to adhere to, the Henry Papers will generally follow modern stylistic usages when the transcription is ambiguous. For a more detailed discussion of problems concerning Mary Henry's transcriptions, see page xxxv.

[2] The name of the place apparently was omitted inadvertently from the copy.

[3] That is, Portland Harbor.

[4] For Trumpbour, see above description of Henry's books of levels, July 19–December [15] 1825, footnote 9.

[5] Sinclairville today.

[6] Presumably William H. Morel, who was Henry's counterpart on another survey team and who has eluded positive identification.

[7] Mary Henry's ellipses indicate that she omitted a goodly portion of the end of the letter.

TO JABEZ D. HAMMOND

Retained Copy, Henry Papers, Smithsonian Archives

New Town [ca. October 15, 1825][1]

Dear Sir,

As you directed we surveyed the route to Windsor and also took the elevation of the highest point of land passed over by the north route between

[1] The date on the original has been torn off. The date assigned is based on when it appears likely that Henry's survey party passed through New Town, in the Elmira vicinity. Henry's Book of Levels No. 9, "Levels from a point where the survey left the Susquehanna to near the Big Flat," [p. 36].

the two places. At Windsor we met Dr. Campbell who as he had not seen the commissioners could give us no general directions but ordered us to follow Judge Trumpour's survey to Owego and there if we received no other instructions to explore the route to Bath by chaining and setting monuments. Judge Trumpour's survey ended at a station 3½ miles East of Owego; in going over that space we found that to chain and set monuments would be attended with nearly as much labour and expense as to complete the survey by taking the angles of the course. I therefore hired two more hands, procured a compass and have carried the survey and level to this place.

I hope the course I have taken will meet the approbation of the commissioners and Dr. Campbell as I thought myself justifyable in adopting it not only from a consideration of the time and expense it will save but also from the conversation I had with General Pitcher[2] and yourself [near][3] Deposit. I delayed writing [until after we] have tested the practicability of [conducting] the survey with two instruments but [the] experiment has so far proved successful. [Beg] the commissioners to be assured that the survey will be as accurate and extensive as the nature of it and our time will admit. We are now running at the rate of about 5 miles a day and will probably be at Bath in seven or eight days where I hope to receive from Dr Campbell particular instructions concerning our future survey.

The inhabitants along the route treat us with the greatest kindness and respect. Mr Pumpelly[4] of Owego loaned me his best compass and offered

---

[2] Nathaniel Pitcher, for whom see above, description of Henry's books of levels, July 19–December [15] 1825, especially footnote 2.

[3] We have made this insertion, as well as the next four insertions, because the corner of the original sheet has been torn away. We feel that Henry intended approximately these expressions.

[4] Harmon Pumpelly (1795–1882), uncle of Raphael Pumpelly (1837–1923, noted American geologist and explorer, for whom see *DAB*). Born in Salisbury, Connecticut, Harmon Pumpelly moved at the age of twenty to Owego, New York, where he and his family distinguished themselves in lumbering, mercantile enterprises, and landholding. Lacking in education, Pumpelly and his older brother James had taught themselves surveying and had surveyed much of the Owego area. Harmon Pumpelly was a member of the first board of village trustees in Owego, a post to which he was reelected four times. Pumpelly had also been an officer in the state

militia. In 1841 he moved to Albany where he became President of the Albany Savings Bank, the Albany Gaslight Company, and the Albany Insurance Company. Upon his death, his estate was valued at somewhat over $1,000,000.

Just prior to this contact with Henry, Pumpelly, along with Eleazar Dana, surveyed and appraised the properties in Tioga County belonging to the estate of Alexander Alexander, reporting some 1734 acres to be worth $3,633.50. Their report, along with other correspondence on this matter, survives in the Henry Papers, Smithsonian Archives (see below, Henry to Stephen Alexander, December 19, 1825, especially footnote 5).

Pumpelly eventually did lend Henry $50.00, apparently as the survey crew passed through Owego on the return trip. Henry made notation of this debt in his pocket notebook of miscellanies, stored along with the eleven books of levels in the Smithsonian Archives.

For more information on Pumpelly, see Le-

to furnish whatever funds we might want in completing the survey to Bath; I had however received from Dr Campbell enough to carry us to Bath where a new supply will be necessary.

I have seen several gentlemen living on the Canisteo who are very anxious to have us return and survey that route from Painted Post to Hornellsville, and we will be pleased to survey as the commissioners shall direct.

> With considerations of respect
> I have the honor to be
> Sir Your obt. servant
> Joseph Henry

Roy Wilson Kingman, *Owego* (Owego, New York, 1907), pp. 138, 163–165; William B. Gay, ed., *Historical Gazetteer of Tioga County,* *New York, 1785–1888* (Syracuse, [1906]), part one (of two parts), p. 328; *Howell and Tenney,* p. 549.

TO WILLIAM CAMPBELL

Mary Henry Copy, Henry Papers, Smithsonian Archives

Portland Oct 31st 1825

Dear Sir:

We arrived at Bath last Monday where I received your letter of Oct. 3^{rd1} directing us to proceed to Portland. We accordingly left Bath on Tuesday and commenced our labor at this place to day. Not knowing your address I directed a letter from New town to Mr. Hammond at Albany informing him that I had procured a compass and was completing the survey from Owego to Bath by taking the angles of the course.[2] We proceed with both instruments with nearly as much rapidity as with the level alone for we surveyed and leveled from Newtown to Bath a distance of 36 miles in six days. The method adopted in conducting the survey was this. I went before with the leveling instrument, explored the route and directed the stations. Mr. Stone[3] carried the flag and assisted in locating. The chain man meas-

[1] See above.

[2] Prior to the acquisition of the compass, Henry's party was solely engaged in leveling. From Owego on, Henry was both surveying (i.e., using the surveyor's compass or circumferentor) and leveling. See above, Henry's let-

ter to Hammond, [ca. October 15, 1825].

[3] Nathan Stone was among the survey party as it departed Kingston, acting as axeman and commissary. See above description of Henry's books of levels, July 19–December [15] 1825.

ured from sheet to sheet.[4] Mr. Cooper followed with a compass and took the bearings of the course.[5]

To be assured of Mr. Cooper's accuracy in recording the angles of the course I inspected every angle taken during the first three days of the survey and then directed him in every case to sight back to his last station. The hind chain man (a Mr. Nichols[6] who had read surveying) also kept minutes of the course and compared them with Mr. Cooper's. Angles were also taken at different stations to mountains and other prominent objects and the distance at about every third station was measured to the river in order to collect materials for making as correct a map of the route as our survey would permit.[7]

I hope you will be pleased with this course. It saved time and expense and the difficulty a surveyor would have had in following our level by monuments was avoided. Will it not be well to inform Judge Trumpbour of this survey and direct him on some other route?

I will inform you of the particulars of the survey from Portland harbour in my next.

With respect I have the honour to be

> Your obedient servant
> Joseph Henry

[4] Presumably the front chain man who is unnamed. From the expense account we can speculate that this person was either James Henry, Ben Atkins, or Murdow McPherson. As Henry went along he established stations, or fixed points in the survey. The chain men, who probably carried a chain of half the standard length of sixty-six feet ("Gunter's Chain") used in surveying the public lands in the United States because of the hilly terrain, would measure out the distances. These would be recorded on sheets containing the preliminary sketches and data from which the final products of the survey would be produced by William Campbell. None are known to have survived.

[5] Undoubtedly the William Cooper who was among the survey party at the outset. See above description of Henry's books of levels, July 19–December [15] 1825, especially footnote 22.

[6] Given as Eli Nicols in the expense account. It is not clear here whether Nicols had another compass or used Cooper's. The latter is quite conceivable from Henry's given order of march.

[7] Surveying was both implicit and explicit in the education Henry had received at the Albany Academy. There is circumstantial evidence that he used a fairly popular work on the subject, John Gummere's *A Treatise on Surveying* . . . (Philadelphia, 1814). Among the pamphlets in his library is *Solutions to the Miscellaneous Questions in Gummere's Surveying* (Philadelphia, 1814), just what a young man learning a new area might relish.

Henry is describing a method of making a roughly accurate survey without going through the necessity of erecting monuments, certainly not going through the precise measurements of a base and the location of the base end points as in first order triangulation. For a later description of the surveying method and a defense of it by Henry, see the next document.

TO WILLIAM CAMPBELL

Mary Henry Copy, Henry Papers, Smithsonian Archives

Ellicottville 16 November 1825

According to your direction, that the surveyors and Engineers should report themselves, every week, I take the opportunity of the first post office, since we left Mayville, to inform you of our progress to this place.

We began at the Harbour[1] on the first day of November and leveled to height of land between Lake Erie and the Chautauqua Lake, as the height of this Lake above Lake Erie is known to be 723 feet. We passed over about three miles and began at the [high point][2] about three quarters of a mile East of Mayville. Then followed Judge Trumpbour's[3] route, the height of land between Chautauqua Lake and the Conewango creek which is about three miles east of Sinclairville. We have passed over ten miles and commenced at the head of a mill pond on the Conewango creek, which was passed by the Judges survey and, of which, the height is known above Wanen,[4] on the Allegany, and consequently above Lake Erie, from the levels of Dr. Whippo.[5] By taking advantage of these points, we save time and still gain sufficient data for making a sectional map of the grand features of the country. From the mill pond on the Conewango, we have travelled to Ellicottville and will, by taking advantage of some other points, probably reach Bath in two weeks. The season is so far advanced and the country is

[1] That is, Portland Harbor.

[2] Mary Henry left blank the designation of this point, but from Henry's books of levels it appears to be a significantly high point east of Mayville, probably in the vicinity of the present town of Hartfield. See Henry's Book of Levels No. 1 in the survey from Lake Erie to Angelica, "Lake Erie to the Height of the Land between Casdanga and Conewango Creeks," [p. 20].

[3] Jacob Trumpbour, for whom see above description of Henry's books of levels, July 19–December [15] 1825, especially footnote 9.

[4] Possibly Warren, Pennsylvania, allowing for Mary Henry's poor transcribing.

[5] Charles Tillotson Whippo (1793–1858) was born in Washington County, New York. After studying medicine and while practicing in Cayuga County and Monroe County, Whippo pursued his avid interests in the higher branches of mathematics as well as in astronomy, geology, and botany; interested in electricity, he purchased quantities of electrical apparatus. Clearly more interested in civil engineering than medicine, he gave up his practice to work on the Erie Canal. He left his farm in Holly, New York, in 1831 to take charge as Engineer of the Beaver and Erie extension of the Pennsylvania Canal, moving to New Castle, Pennsylvania. Later in New Castle, Whippo became a community leader, acting as Associate Judge of the county, as President of the Bank of New Castle, and as an organizer and director of the first seminary there. Whippo retired wealthy and devoted his later years to literary pursuits. See Aaron L. Hazen, ed., *20th Century History of New Castle and Lawrence County, Pennsylvania, and Representative Citizens* (Chicago, 1908), pp. 530–531; *Book of Biographies: The Volume Contains Biographical Sketches of Leading Citizens of Lawrence County, Pennsylvania* (Buffalo, 1897), pp. 353–354; Daniel H. Calhoun, *The American Civil Engineer, Origins and Conflict* (Cambridge, Massachusetts, 1960), pp. 29, 37, 114, 217.

so hilly that leveling is very tedious. The ground has been covered with a slight snow for some time which makes our labour in the woods rather disagreeable. We are all however in good spirits and determined to go through. I think our level will present some interesting facts. We have passed over ground more than 2000 feet above tide water which is perhaps the highest table of land in the United States East of the Mississippi.

I have experienced great inconvenience from want of funds and have been under the disagreeable necessity of borrowing from strangers. . . .[6] I have now about fifteen dollars which I fear will not carry us to Angelica, as we are in a country where provisions are very high and the inhabitants much in want of money.

I have heard nothing of Mr Morel.[7] Judge Trumpbour is about three miles ahead of us and is now probably between Angelica and Bath.

> I have the honour to be Sir
> Your obedient servant
> Joseph Henry

[6] Mary Henry's ellipses indicate she omitted something from the original. Note, however, that Henry's comment confirms what was revealed on the expense sheet, that he was forced to borrow. See above, in the description of Henry's books of levels, July 19–December [15] 1825, a discussion of the finances and footnote 17 therein.

[7] Undoubtedly the William H. Morel, another "Engineer" of the road survey, whom we have been unable to identify further. Morel must have been surveying alternative routes from Lake Erie to Angelica.

TO T. ROMEYN BECK

Retained Copy, Henry Papers, Smithsonian Archives

Bath Nov 28th 1825

Dear Sir[1]

We have just completed the survey to the point directed.[2] Mr Cooper starts tomorrow morning directly for Albany but in order to make some additional notes I intend to return by way of the route we have surveyed and will probably be in Albany in about two weeks. My present engagements will occupy some time but I think I will be able to attend to the

[1] The endorsement on the reverse of the last sheet in Henry's hand identifies Beck as the recipient of this letter. It is a reply to Beck's letter to Henry of October 1, 1825, printed above.

[2] Angelica. See Campbell to Henry, October 3, 1825, above.

Lectures or at all events to take charge of them with the help of an assistant.[3] We have passed through a new but interesting country and although we had little time to make other observations than belonged to the survey yet we visited the burning spring at Portland and the Oil spring in Allegany. Mr Cooper and myself collected four bottles of the gas which we sent to you directed to the care of Mr Tracey of Bufalo.[4]

The last summer has been to me a season of peculiar interest although one of labour and trial. I have devoted myself exclusively to the duties of my office and if my labours should not prove as important as I wish they may, still I hope I have conducted myself so as to merit in some degree the approbation of the commissioners and not to disappoint the moderate expectations of my friends.

I cannot suffer this opportunity to pass without expressing by letter what I should never have confidence to communicate by words, the sentiments of gratitude I entertain for the many favours Your Kindness has bestowed on me. To you sir alone I owe what little reputation I may possess and though I may appear to want feeling I shal allways remembered that your countenance gave me support when I had no friends and was almost an isolated being labouring under the disadvantages of at least a doubt.

With considerations of gratitude and respect I am Sir your

Devoted humble serv.

Joseph Henry

[3] A reference to the semi-public lectures given by Beck. From the text it is unclear if Henry will simply assist Beck or actually give the lectures himself with some unnamed third person as assistant. What Henry actually did for and with Beck in the lectures, starting with his schoolboy days, is still somewhat obscure.

[4] Perhaps Albert Haller Tracy (1793–1858), an attorney in Buffalo who served in the House of Representatives in the Sixteenth, Seventeenth, and Eighteenth Congresses. Before turning to law, Haller studied medicine and may have met Beck. *Biographical Direc-* *tory of the American Congress.*

As Beck never published an analysis, the identification of the gas is uncertain. In the Book of Levels No. 1, in the survey from Lake Erie to Angelica, Henry mentions "a burning spring emits an inflammable air which appears to be carburetted hydrogen it burns with a bright flame and smells like hydrogen procured from water by sulfuric acid & iron" three-fourths of a mile from Portland. From the description this is probably methane with an admixture of other hydrocarbons.

FROM WILLIAM CAMPBELL[1]
Henry Papers, Smithsonian Archives

Cherry Valley 12th Dec[r] 1825

Dear Sir

I expect my letters to you at Angelica & Bath have not been received.[2] They contain a request that you return by the way of Cherry Valley, for special purposes not immediately connected with our Road Survey. We wish a level carid[3] from the head of Otsego Lake to the Erie Canale in Canajoharie or Mindir a distance of about 15 or 10 miles. On the business of the Road. I wish you to come to this place, bring with all your Field notes for explanation and arrangement. When you come bring with you all our leveling apparatus, as we wish to use them on the said level from Otsego Lake. If you can attend to it you will have the refusal of it.[4] I hope you will not fail to arrive here as soon as possible. If you cannot attend immediately send up the Instruments by the first safe conveyance.

I remain yours &c
William Campbell

[1] This letter bears the address on the verso as follows: "Mr. Joseph Henry/ Engineer on State Road/ Albany."

[2] The only other Campbell correspondence which seems to have survived from this period is a letter to Henry earlier than the letters mentioned here by Campbell. See above, Campbell to Henry, October 3, 1825.

[3] i.e., carried.

[4] Henry apparently did not accept this commission. See his letter to Stephen Alexander, December 19, 1825, below.

TO STEPHEN ALEXANDER[1]
Family Correspondence, Henry Papers, Smithsonian Archives[2]

Schenectaday Dec. 19th 1825

Dear Stephen

I arrived at Albany from my long tour on the 15th ins. and left that place

[1] Stephen Alexander (1806–1883), Henry's first cousin and future brother-in-law. At this date Alexander was at the Yates Polytechny in Chittenango, Madison County, New York (for which see note 8, below) as Professor of Natural Philosophy and Mathematics. A Union College graduate, Alexander was primarily interested in astronomy. From 1830 to 1832 he worked with Joseph Henry and followed

Henry to Princeton. From 1834 to 1877 Alexander was at Princeton. He will reappear in this and later volumes as a close friend, professional colleague, and relative of Joseph Henry. *DAB*.

[2] This letter is part of a group of manuscripts containing correspondence between Henry and his relatives and between relatives. Although most, like this letter, are original

for Cherryvalley[3] on the 16th. On returning I have stopped at Schenectaday where I am much pleased to hear by your letter that your are so well employed in making observations and tracing a noon mark that you cannot but be pleased with your new vocation.

The last summer has been to me a season of peculiar interest, although one of labour and trial but I hope my conduct has been such as to deserve in some degree the approbation of the commissioners and not to disappoint the moderate expectations of my friends. Although I had to devote myself almost exclusively to the duties of my office yet I found time to visit the burning springs at Fredonia & Portland on Lake Erie and the oil spring in Allegany. I have made some minutes of these springs and will send a particular account in my next letter: as I intend when I receive an answer to this scrall to trouble you with a long letter.[4] At Owego I met with Mr. Dana[5] who informed me that he had received an almanack from you. He sends his respect &c.

Your Mother informes me that you have not settled with Mr. Webster for your Almanack. I called at Mr Websters store[6] when I came from Albany but he was not within.

I have been in Rochester this season and was agreeably surprised to meet A. S. Alexander.[7] He has opened a school with a prospect of doing well. I promised to write him when I returned to Albany.

I am expecting the stage every minute for I leave here for Albany this afternoon therefore My Dear *little man* I have only time to say that with sentiments of Respect and Affection,

I remain your Friend & cous.
Joseph Henry[8]

---

outgoing letters, many are copies retained by Henry or his relations. Not all family letters are in this location; others are found in the general run of Henry personal correspondence including both incoming letters and some retained copies.

[3] To stop and see William Campbell.

[4] Not found.

[5] Eleazar Dana who was engaged in disposing of lands in the estate of Alexander's mother, Maria Alexander (later Henry's mother-in-law). Letters of Dana to Maria Alexander on this matter are in the Henry Papers, Smithsonian Archives.

[6] See above, the note on Websters and Skinners bookstore, footnote 1 to the Minutes of the Academy Trustees, June 11, 1816.

[7] Probably Alexander Stephenson Alexander (1800–1837), the son of Joseph Henry's Uncle

John (his mother's twin). Henry grew up in John Alexander's household at Galway, New York, after his father's death. For the Alexander family, see the genealogy compiled by an Alexander descendent, Robert Gaylord Lester, in the Henry Papers files.

[8] Henry addressed this letter to Chittenango, indicating it was being conveyed through the "Politeness of Rev. A. Yates." Andrew Yates (1797–1844) was a Reformed Dutch clergyman who graduated from Yale in 1794 and taught at Union College, 1797–1801 and 1814–1825. See Sprague, *Annals*, 9:126–138. In 1825 Andrew Yates became Principal of the Yates Polytechny founded by his brother John B. Yates (1784–1836), a lawyer, and member of Congress (1815–1817) who was active in the construction of the Welland Canal (see *Biographical Directory of the American Con-*

P.S. Send me your account if you have any with Mr. Webster and I will make a settlement with him for you.   J. H.

---

gress). Their older brother, Joseph C. Yates (1768–1837) was Governor of New York from 1823 to 1825. To support the school John B. Yates apparently intended to use his large land holdings in Madison County.

The school is described by Franklin B. Hough, *Historical and Statistical Record of the University of the State of New York During the Century from 1784 to 1884* (Albany, 1885), pp. 731–732, as an example of "Manual Labor Schools." In this case farming was taught by practical demonstrations. But the presence of Alexander and other scientists as well as a professor of philology and ancient languages indicates that more than

practical vocationalism was involved. This is another instance (like Ezra Cornell's vision) of the idea of combining theory and culture with very down-to-earth practical work experiences. This was a fairly common and highly influential conception in nineteenth-century America and relatively rare in Europe.

After 1830, Stephen Alexander went to Albany, and Andrew Yates devoted his remaining years to aiding the organization of new churches. John B. Yates was unable to gain state support. In 1853 the Polytechnic Institute was incorporated by the Regents as an academy.

❧ 1826 ❧

T. ROMEYN BECK TO MARTIN VAN BUREN[1]

Correspondence of the Topographical Officer Stationed in Washington,
Records of the Office of the Chief of Engineers,
Record Group[2] 77, National Archives

Albany. March 10. 1826

Dear Sir

I am afraid you will think me troublesome but I rely in my present application on your kindness of disposition. I will be as brief as possible in stating what I venture to ask from you.

---

[1] Martin Van Buren (1782–1862), eighth President of the United States, was serving as Senator from New York at the time he received this letter. A lawyer, Van Buren was a major political figure in his generation best known today for his role in Andrew Jackson's administration and as Jackson's political heir. In 1848 Van Buren unsuccessfully ran again for the presidency on the Free Soil ticket. *DAB*.

In the context of Henry's career, two further observations are pertinent. Van Buren and his associates in the "Albany Regency" wielded considerable power in New York State

during Henry's adulthood in Albany and afterward. Henry was apparently known to some extent both to them and to their political opponents in the state. (Thurlow Weed [*DAB*], the Whig leader, knew Henry from the time they were apprentices in Albany.) He was able to work with either party if circumstances so required. Second, we have so far been unable to establish Henry's political adherence. There may appear in later volumes a document indicating Whiggery and another indicating support of the Democracy. We believe all the documents bearing on contacts with politicians show that both political par-

Mr Joseph Henry aged about 23 Years,[3] is a native of this city, of respectable parentage, but lost his father a number of years since. His worthy mother has by industry, supported him & his brother & sister during infancy & youth. Mr Henry learnt the trade of a silversmith[4] & made good proficiency in it, but having a great desire to advance in knowledge, entered himself in the Albany Academy,[5] studied Mathematics &c then for a support taught school in various parts of this county. With his earnings, he returned & again entered himself in the Academy. I employed him as my Chemical Assistant with perfect satisfaction, during the winter of 1823–1824. Last Spring, he was employed at my recommendation & that of others, as a principal surveyer of the projected *State Road*—in which duty I am authorized to say, he has acquitted himself to the satisfaction of the Commissioners. Mr Hammond will address the Secretary of War in a manner that will show his sense of his services.[6]

We have perceived by the papers, that it is proposed to increase the corps of U.S. Topographical Engineers,[7] & believing, that no individual can be

---

ties in the long run were equally responsive to intellectual needs and that Henry, *as a scientist,* had no need to assume a partisan pose. We also believe political concerns loom less in the Henry documents for the same reason that science looms less in the papers of political figures we have examined—that is, the documents simply reflect the intensity of the concerns of the men involved. The subject emphases do not necessarily prove anything about the politics of scientists nor the scientism of politicians.

[2] Hereafter RG.

[3] In fact, Henry was a few months past his twenty-eighth birthday.

[4] See *Coulson,* p. 12.

[5] There is very little knowledge about Henry's schooling and early occupation based upon contemporary sources. Much of what appears in print is based on later recollection. These are summed up in *Coulson,* pp. 15–20. We do know he entered the Academy in 1819 but have no knowledge of what conditions, if any, were imposed on an overage student. A sheet surviving in the Albany Academy Archives indicates Henry was absent some days in October 1822. From this letter of his teacher we now know that Henry was in the Academy for two separate periods during the years 1819–1822, the interval between being spent teaching in country schools. *Coulson,* pp. 16–17, is vague on dates but the most reasonable assumption is that Henry left the

Academy to tutor the Van Rensselaer children in 1822. This may conflict with the traditional account of a two-year stint there and Beck's statement (next sentence) that Henry assisted him in the winter of 1823–1824.

[6] See Hammond's letter of March 16, 1826, below.

[7] This document and the ones immediately following provide the surviving evidence of an unsuccessful attempt to find a position for Joseph Henry with the engineers of the U.S. Army. In retrospect, Henry's principal problem in the years between his leaving the Academy and the call to a professorship there in 1826 was simply how to support himself while continuing his professional development in the sciences. Suitable positions were relatively scarce in the United States of 1822–1826. One alternative was to seek employment in the emerging engineering profession which then was almost wholly what we now designate as civil engineering. The work on the Road Survey may very well have influenced Henry to try for an engineering career. By applying to the War Department, Henry's friends were proposing, in effect, to link his career to two important developments in American history: the Army Engineers as a scientific and technical elite prior to the Civil War; and the political dispute over internal improvements which ultimately comes down to the attitudes of Americans toward the uses of the natural environment. Both topics will

presented more worthy or under circumstances more interesting, I venture to ask your good offices in his favour. I have no doubt of his perfect competence, of his natural & acquired abilities, & his conduct & deportment are so modest & correct, that none who know him can avoid being prepossessed

---

recur, explicitly and implicitly, in later volumes of the Henry Papers.

In 1826 the Topographical Engineers were a "bureau" of the Engineer Department of the Army lacking the "corps" status of the Army Engineers of the Corps of Engineers. Oversimplifying the administrative complexities, the lack of "corps" status meant that the Topographical Engineers were not a part of the permanent complement of the Army with a position comparable to the other staff units. Attaining equal status with the Corps of Engineers was a principal organizational goal of the Topographical Engineers in 1826. It was a move in the direction of "corps" status (see the letter of Roberdeau to Barbour, March 17, 1826, below) which precipitated this application by Beck on Henry's behalf. In turn, this move for parity with the regular military engineers arose from pressures from the work on internal improvements, the principal function distinguishing the two bodies of engineers in the War Department.

Both bodies of engineers had Revolutionary War precedents. In that conflict, the predecessors of the Corps of Engineers were French officers, reflecting the eminence of that nation in this field since the days of Vauban. They were largely concerned with the construction of fortifications and other structures. "Geographers," of whom one was Henry's Albany associate, Simeon DeWitt, were also appointed to make surveys and to prepare maps and sketches. To minimize dependence on foreigners and for the sake of economy, the revived military engineers in 1802 were given control of the military academy at West Point which was retained until 1866. During this period the cream of the West Point graduates went to the engineers and, as one author stated, "the artillery and infantry had to take the leavings of the engineer corps." (James R. Jacobs, *The Beginning of the U.S. Army, 1783–1812*, [Princeton, 1947], p. 307.) Topographers, as such, reentered the U.S. Army during the War of 1812, and their role grew afterward as the building of coastal fortifications developed, explorations were sent into the West, and the demand developed for internal improvements.

There are instances of Army participation in construction projects very early in the history of the Republic, especially in connection with coastal fortification. The earliest work of this nature was usually under the direction of the Treasury Department. The Cumberland Road, for example, only came under the control of the War Department after 1828. After the issue of internal improvements flared in 1807, it was the Secretary of the Treasury, Albert Gallatin, who in 1808 issued a national plan for a series of roads and canals (*American State Papers,* Miscellaneous Series, *1*:724–741). In 1819, however, it was the Secretary of War, John C. Calhoun, then in his nationalistic phase, who responded to a request from Congress on transportation needs (*American State Papers,* Miscellaneous Series, 2:533–537). National defense justified the use of Army officers for mapping and construction projects; considerations of economy further justified their engaging in similar projects useful to the civilian sector.

Calhoun's report directly led to the passage of the Survey Act of April 20, 1824 (4 *Stat.* 22) authorizing the preparation of "surveys, plans, and estimates," for roads and canals of national importance and empowering the employment of civilians. (It is uncertain if Beck was applying for a commission for Henry or for a civilian post.) Although the program under the Survey Act was quickly embroiled in political disputes, its opponents, the Jacksonians, did not put an end to the program until 1838 and then under economic pressures arising from the panic of the previous year. In fact, more funds were spent on internal improvements in the Jackson and Van Buren administrations than in the previous period. (Henry G. Wheeler, *History of Congress, Biographical and Political*, 2 vols. [New York, 1848], 2:116.) What did change was the decreasing emphasis on a national plan and the increasing ad hoc nature of the surveys and construction projects conducted by the engineers.

In 1831 the Topographical Engineers were separated from the Corps of Engineers and made a separate bureau. When in 1838 the Survey Act of 1824 was repealed, the topog-

in his favour. In conclusion, I will only add that he is a nephew of M[r] M[c]Culloch[8] of the firm of Boyd & M[c]Culloch, Brewers.

> I remain with sentiments
> of great respect Yours
> T. Romeyn Beck

---

raphers attained corps status and all the internal improvements passed to their hands. The Corps of Engineers, with a few exceptions, was limited to the construction and maintenance of coastal fortifications. In 1852 internal improvements were revived with a new division of labor. The Corps of Engineers gained control of coastal harbor improvements on the Gulf and Atlantic, as well as works on rivers entering these waters. The sole exception was the Mississippi. The Topographical Engineers were "limited" to the Mississippi Basin (including its delta), the Great Lakes, the Saint Lawrence, the Rocky Mountains, and the Pacific Coast. In general, in the period 1824–1861 the Corps of Engineers were most active in heavy construction and on the coasts while the topographers were most active in the interior and in scientific work incidental to the settlement of the frontier. In 1863 the two bodies were merged.

The engineer officers of the War Department and their organizations played a significant role in Henry's career. During his teaching career West Point, with a curriculum influenced by the École Polytechnique, was not only the best engineering school in America, but may very well have been the best place in the nation to acquire a scientific education. Many of its graduates became friends and colleagues of Joseph Henry. As Secretary of the Smithsonian Institution, Henry would collaborate with the scientific surveys of the Topographical Bureau, and he would sit with engineer officers on such bodies as the Light House Board.

See Forest G. Hill, *Roads, Rails, and Waterways: The Army Engineers and Early Transportation* (Norman, Oklahoma, 1957); William H. Goetzmann, *Army Exploration in the American West, 1803–1863* (New Haven, 1959), and for an account stressing non-Federal actions, Carter Goodrich, *Government Promotion of American Canals and Railroads, 1800–1890* (New York, 1960). For the diminished national role of the Corps of Engineers after 1865, see Raymond H. Merritt, *Engineering in American Society, 1850–1875* (Lexington, 1970), p. 126–129.

[8] Hawthorn McCulloch (1772–1859) had been married to Henry's aunt, Jane Alexander McCulloch, who died in 1802. It is doubtful if Henry's relationship was close to McCulloch who was, apparently, well known to Van Buren. Munsell, *Coll. Alb., 1*:436.

BENJAMIN SILLIMAN, SR.,[1] TO T. ROMEYN BECK
Beck Papers, New York Public Library

Yale College March 14th, 1826

Dear Sir

Your favor of the 10th was this morning received enclosing the Geological Communication of M[r] Geddes[2] which I think valuable and will cheer-

---

[1] Benjamin Silliman (1779–1864), for fifty-one years Professor of Chemistry and Natural History at Yale, first prepared himself, after graduating from Yale College in 1796, for the bar. He was a tutor at Yale from 1799 to 1802, when he received the offer to be the first Professor of Chemistry at Yale. He was allowed to spend two years (1802–1804) in Philadelphia preparing himself at the medical school there, and he spent a year (1805–1806)

fully give it an insertion in the next number of the Journal of Science, which will not appear however sooner than the Month of May one being now in the press, which will appear in the course of a week. The Journal has been unexpectedly delayed by affairs connected with the printing office and not with my department. I forward by this mail a proof sheet of the "Botany of Illinois and Missouri" by Dr Lewis C. Beck[3] and fear that his patience has been almost exhausted by waiting for it. I will thank you to present my compliments to him & say that I hope he will forward the continuation seasonably.

As it is probable that I shall be obliged henceforth to take the whole concern upon myself of the "Journal of Science"—business & all, I hope that my friends and the friends of science will exert such influence as they may think the work deserves, for the purpose of extending its circulation that it may not be attended with hazard to the Editor.

I will thank you to say to Mr Geddes that I shall be pleased to receive from him any additional observations which he may have made concerning the interesting country, and practical pursuits of an Engineer in which he has been so much occupied.

> I remain dear sir
> Yours very respectfully
> B Silliman

---

in Europe buying apparatus and books for Yale. In 1806 he took up his duties as professor. Silliman did no significant research in chemistry, and his one major publication on the subject, *Elements of Chemistry*, 2 vols. (New Haven, 1830–1831) was, in the curt judgment of J. R. Partington, "unsuccessful" (*A History of Chemistry*, 4 vols. [London, 1961–1970], 4:76). Silliman's real contribution to science in America was on the administrative, popularizing, and political side. He played a major role in the creation of Yale's Medical School (1813) and in the founding of the Sheffield School of Science. He was the first president of the Association of American Geologists. His popular lectures on chemistry and geology (post 1836 in cities from Boston to New Orleans, including the first series of lectures at the Lowell Institute in 1839–1840) were public sensations. By far his most important service to the emerging scientific community in this country, however, was through his *American Journal of Science,* which first appeared in 1818. Silliman was a tireless and conscientious editor, and during the first three decades or so of the *Journal's* existence he made it into virtually the central voice of

American science. It was simultaneously "Silliman's Journal" and the *American Journal of Science*. Silliman in his role of editor gave valuable encouragement to Joseph Henry, as will appear in the correspondence between the two men later on in this volume. The *DAB* article on Silliman is judicious; for additional details see John F. Fulton and Elizabeth H. Thomson, *Benjamin Silliman: Pathfinder in American Science* (New York, 1947).

[2] James Geddes, "Observations on the Geological Features of the South Side of the Ontario Valley," *Silliman's Journal*, 1826, *11*: 213–218; this was the December number of the *Journal*. Geddes's paper was read before the Albany Institute, February 15, 1826, and was also printed in *Transactions*, Albany Institute, 1830, *1*:55–59.

[3] "Contributions Towards the Botany of the States of Illinois and Missouri," *Silliman's Journal*, 1826, *10*:257–264; 1826, *11*:167–182 (it is this installment, appearing in the October number, which Silliman refers to in the letter); 1828, *14*:112–121 (no more appeared, though the last page indicates that it was to be continued).

JABEZ D. HAMMOND[1] TO JAMES BARBOUR[2]
*Letters Received, 1826–1866 (file H 16) of the Office
of the Chief of Engineers, RG 77, National Archives*

Albany March 16, 1826

Sir,

In case it shall be deemed necessary to add to the corps of Civil Ingineers permit me to recommend as a candidate for that employment Mr. Joseph Henry of this City. He is a young man of excellent character and correct habits and highly distinguished for his advances in Science and particularly for his mathematical acquirements. Genl. Van Renssellear[3] to whom this young gentlemen is known will I presume call on you on behalf of Mr. Henry and make you acquainted with his merits.

> I have the honor to be with
> Great respect your
> Obed[t] Serv[t]
> Jabez D. Hammond[4]

[1] For Hammond, see the description of Henry's books of levels, July 19–December [15] 1825, footnote 3, above.

[2] James Barbour (1775–1842) served as Secretary of War from 1825 to 1828. He was active politically, serving as Governor of Virginia (1812–1815) and U.S. Senator (1815–1825). A supporter of J. Q. Adams, this post in the Adams administration was a way station between his original position as a Jeffersonian and his final allegiance to the Whigs. *DAB*.

[3] Stephen Van Rensselaer (1764–1839) was then serving in the House of Representatives.

[4] The War Department notation on the obverse of the letter and the entry in the Register of Letters Received, both in the Offices of the Secretary of War and the Chief of Engineers, incorrectly give the name of the sender of the letter as "John D. Hammond."

MARTIN VAN BUREN TO JAMES BARBOUR
*Correspondence of the Topographical Officer Stationed in Washington,
Records of the Office of the Chief of Engineers, RG 77, National Archives*

[March 17, 1826]

D[r] Sir,

The writer of the enclosed[1] is a gentleman of high respectability.[2]

> Yours,
> MVB

[1] Beck's letter to Van Buren, March 10, 1826, above.

[2] As Van Buren was a political opponent of the Adams administration, this one line letter of transmittal may have been either a tepid endorsement or a reflection of Van Buren's appraisal of the weight of his backing. He was, of course, a political opponent of the internal improvement policy of the Adams administration.

March 17, 1826

[ISAAC ROBERDEAU][1] TO JAMES BARBOUR

Correspondence of the Topographical Officer Stationed in Washington,
Records of the Office of the Chief of Engineers, RG 77, National Archives[2]

[March 17?, 1826][3]

Sir,

A letter is just now handed to me addressed Mr V. Buren to you,[4] containing a recommendation of Mr Henry of Albany for an appointment in the Topographical Engineers; it is a subject of much delicacy for me in the present state of the Corps to offer an opinion upon, at the same time it may be expected that a reply to the general principle of appointing Citizens to the Corps, should Congress agree to the modification of this dept as you have recommended it.[5] Under this impression and with the greatest deference I beg to observe, that there are officers who have for many years been in union with the Corps, whose talent & claims deserve primary attention, and that there are others in all respects well qualified, who are in anxious expectation of a transfer into it[6] whenever circumstances may render an increase necessary. Added to this the class which will graduate at West Point may & probably will produce some who have directed their attention to these pursuits in Sciences adapted to the duties assigned to that Corps. This being the case, there can be no vacancy for the appointment of a citizen,[7] be the claim to Science what they may without departing from the general principle, and leaving out of the Corps those who are now in serv-

---

[1] Isaac Roberdeau (1763–1829), a Lieutenant-Colonel and Chief of the Topographical Bureau. *DAB.* We are indebted to Mr. Elmer Parker of the National Archives for identifying the author from a comparison of the handwritings of this letter with the handwritings on manuscripts of other topographical engineers who were in a position to have written it.

[2] This is an unsigned fragment of what appears to be a draft of a letter to the Secretary of War. The letter itself is not in the records of either the Secretary of War or the Topographical Bureau in the National Archives.

[3] This date is assigned on the assumption that Van Buren's letter of the same date enclosing Beck's letter of March 10, 1826, was received in the War Department, and directly carried to Roberdeau, who immediately dashed off this response.

[4] Neither the records of the Secretary of War nor those of the Topographical Bureau register the receipt of this letter of Van Buren's. No reply or note of a reply were found in these sources or in the Van Buren Papers in the Manuscript Division of the Library of Congress.

[5] A reference to Barbour's proposal to give Corps status to the Topographical Bureau. See *Report of the Secretary of War . . .* (Washington, 1826), pp. 6–7, in *Documents Accompanying the President's Message to Congress . . . December 6, 1825* (Senate Document 2, 19th Congress, 1st Session). Barbour called for an increase based upon the demand for internal improvements. Beck's letter presumably was based on word of this proposal.

[6] Here Roberdeau is referring to Corps of Engineers and other Army officers who engaged in surveys from time to time.

[7] Especially since Barbour's plans called for an increase in commissioned personnel, not civilian engineers.

ice and who have assiduously endeavored to qualify themselves for the duties of the Top[ographical]. . . .[8]

[8] Here the text ends with "Top" in the original.

AMOS EATON[1] TO STEPHEN VAN RENSSELAER
Gratz Collection, Historical Society of Pennsylvania

Rensselaer School, March 25ᵗʰ 1826

Honorable friend,

A considerable number of our students, with the consent of their parents, have proposed taking a geological tour through the canal line,[2] during the May vacation. You will recollect that you told me to invite Prof. Cleaveland[3] to go through with me, whenever I took the last view, which was to have been last fall. He wrote that he could not go then, but would accompany me in the spring. Accordingly we are preparing to go in company, about 20, and take a portable kitchen on board a freight boat. We have ascertained that $20. each will be sufficient for the whole tour.

My object so far is to propose that Dʳ Scriven[4] be requested to wait for

[1] Amos Eaton (1776–1842) was the founder of Rensselaer Polytechnic Institute (RPI) and a leading geologist in America in the early decades of the last century. After graduating from Williams College (1799) he practiced law until sentenced to life imprisonment for forgery in 1811. Pardoned in 1815 by DeWitt Clinton, Eaton studied at Yale for two years with the elder Silliman and embarked on a career of lecturing and scientific odd jobs. In 1824, he founded RPI. *DAB*. See Ethel M. McAllister, *Amos Eaton, Scientist and Educator, 1776–1842* (Philadelphia, 1941). For the school he founded, see Samuel Reznick, *Education for a Technological Society* . . . (Troy, 1968). RPI was not founded, as some accounts state, to be the second engineering school in the United States. Eaton's desire was to train teachers who would instruct the people in applied sciences. Although civil engineering was introduced into the curriculum, the engineering aspect only became dominant after Eaton's death.

[2] For the canal tour see Henry's journal of May 2, 1826, below, and related documents.

[3] Originally, Parker Cleaveland (1780–1858)

of Bowdoin College, best known as a mineralogist; Chester Dewey (1784–1867) of Williams College, a naturalist and chemist; and Benjamin Silliman, Sr., of Yale, the editor of the leading American scientific periodical (*Silliman's Journal*) were expected to go but eventually withdrew. *DAB*. See George W. Clinton, "Journal of a Tour from Albany to Lake Erie in 1826," *Buffalo Historical Society Publications*, 1910, *14*:277–305, especially 277–278. The original manuscript is in the Buffalo Society of Natural Sciences.

[4] Possibly Thomas Edward Scréven (1796–1866). Scréven received his A.B. degree in 1815 from South Carolina College, then earned his M.D. from the College of Physicians and Surgeons in New York in 1818. We have no further clues regarding his activities in geology or his association with Eaton. Cecil Hampden Cutts Howard, comp., *Genealogy of the Cutts Family in America* (Albany, 1892), pp. 105, 213; *Catalogue of the South Carolina College* (Columbia, South Carolina, 1854), p. 27; *Columbia Alumni*, p. 196.

[5] William Buckland (1784–1856), a leading British geologist of the day. *DSB*. Buckland, a

his suit of specimens, until the month of June. As we are now to close the alluvial part of the survey, upon the plan of Buckland and Conybeare,[5] we can then send Dr S. a suit of the alluvial, or tertiary, formation; which will be much more interesting compleat. It is my intention to collect a number of the most perfect suits for you to distribute, and enough for sale to defray the expense of the expedition. These I intend to leave at bookstores in N. York, Boston, Albany &c. Not without your consent, however; but you will perceive, that this will accomodate many persons and save a little.[6]

I suppose Dr Blatchford[7] has written for your appointment of three examiners.[8] I will take the liberty to name several persons, who, I think, would be suitable. Professor Dewey of Williams College;[9] Judge David

---

clergyman, was Reader in mineralogy (1813) and geology (1819) at Oxford. From 1845 to his death Buckland was Dean of Westminster. He is best remembered for his advocacy of the geological reality of the Biblical deluge but his influence arising from his varied researches and his teaching went far beyond that position. His Bridgewater treatise, *Geology and Mineralogy Considered with Reference to Natural Theology* (London, 1836) and the earlier *Reliquiae Diluvianae* . . . (London, 1823) were important affirmations of natural theology. His close friend, William Daniel Conybeare (1787–1857) was also a clergyman active in geology although not as eminent an original investigator as Buckland. *DNB*.

At first glance, the reference of Eaton's to a "plan" of the two men seems to refer to a publication serving as a model for a geological survey. Of the two collaborative works of Buckland and Conybeare (as given in the Buckland bibliography, for which see *DSB*) neither that which Conybeare based on their joint observations (*Transactions of the Geological Society of London*, o.s., 1816, *3*:196–216) nor their joint paper, "Observations on the South-western Coal District of England," *Transactions of the Geological Society of London*, 2d s., 1824, *1*:210–316, is a likely model for Eaton's survey of the lands along the Erie Canal. Neither is cited in the published report (A. Eaton, *A Geological and Agricultural Survey of the District Adjoining the Erie Canal in the State of New-York* [Albany, 1824]). In his canal tour journal (see footnote 3, above), p. 289, George Clinton noted that Eaton referred to the "system so well established as that of Conybeare and Buckland" and in Henry's journal of May 8, 1826, below, a similar reference was made; certainly, Eaton is referring to a geological classification. We

have found no such Buckland and Conybeare or Conybeare and Buckland classification, strictly speaking. Buckland published a table of the strata in William Phillips, *A Selection of Facts . . . of the Geology of England and Wales* (London, 1818). The copy in the U.S. Geological Survey Library bears annotations in Joseph Henry's hand. The date of these annotations is undeterminable. (Henry did own a copy of Phillips' *Outline of Mineralogy and Geology* in the New York edition of 1816.) In addition to Robert Bakewell's classification (see *DSB*), Eaton cites the classification of Conybeare and Phillips in *Outlines of the Geology of England and Wales . . .* (London, 1822), vii. One can speculate that Eaton has merged the Conybeare and Phillips with the other writings of Buckland under the pressure, as it were, of the disputes over the distinctions between prediluvial, diluvial, and postdiluvial deposits. At least both Clinton and Henry discuss the alluvial and Buckland in this context.

[6] Attempts to finance research (or education) by selling specimens of rocks, plants, and animals were fairly common in nineteenth-century America.

[7] Samuel Blatchford (1767–1828) was a Presbyterian minister whose congregation was in Lansingburgh, New York, near Troy. Born in England, he came to America in 1799 and moved to Lansingburgh in 1804. He was the first president of Rensselaer Polytechnic Institute, serving from 1824 to 1828. See Sprague, *Annals*, *4*:158–168.

[8] That is, outsiders who would test prospective graduates of the Institute. Joseph Henry served as examiner later in 1826. See below, Eaton to Van Rensselaer, October 17, 1826.

[9] See note 3, above.

Birch of Troy;[10] Ebenezer Walbridge, Esquire of Lansingburgh;[11] Dʳ John Chester of Albany;[12] Prof. Joel B. Nott of Schenectady.[13] You may recollect others, whom you prefer. I mentioned these, that you might have their names before you for consideration. I hope you will appoint the whole three from among persons who are in no way concerned in the School. The sooner Dʳ Blatchford has their names the better, in order to give time for notifying them. If you should like M. Genet,[14] we should like him very well, or Mʳ Featherstonhawe.[15]

Our act of incorporation is not yet printed in the state paper. The preamble sets forth all that has been done in brief. The plan is perfectly successful in its operation. We have 25 students; nine of whom will probably take the Rensselaer Degree. Professor Ely[16] of Dr. Yates' Polytechny School of Chiteningo, has gone through one laboratory course. He is infatuated with our method. Says it is astonishing that this lecturing method was never thought of before. Every student gives five lectures each week. We have so far improved our plan, that 200 might be taught here at once.[17]

We are convinced, that we ought to have three terms. A recitation term in mid-winter, and experimental terms spring and fall. Our year ought to

[10] Not identified.

[11] Perhaps the Ebenezer W. Walbridge mentioned as an incorporator of an insurance company (1814) in A. J. Weise, *History of Lansingburgh, N.Y., 1670–1877* (Troy, 1877). The Rensselaer County Historical Society has identified him as an attorney holding various posts in the town of Lansingburgh, 1806–1830.

[12] John Chester (1785–1829) succeeded Blatchford as President for six months. He was a Presbyterian clergyman and also a Trustee of the Albany Academy (see above, Minutes of the Academy Trustees, January 31, 1817, footnote 1).

[13] Joel B. Nott (1797–1878) was the eldest son of Eliphalet Nott, the President of Union College (*DAB*). Joel Nott graduated from Union in 1817 and from 1820–1831 was successively Tutor, Lecturer, and Professor of Chemistry at his alma mater. After his resignation he farmed near Schenectady and briefly served in the State Legislature. We have found very little evidence of his chemical activities.

[14] See footnote 32, February 26, 1812.

[15] G. W. Featherstonhaugh (1780–1866) was an English geologist then residing in upstate New York. See W. H. G. Armytage, "G. W. Featherstonhaugh, F.R.S., 1780–1866, Anglo-American Scientist," *Notes and Records of the Royal Society*, 1955, *11*:228–235 and the com-

ments in George P. Merrill, *Contributions to the History of Geology* (Washington, 1906), p. 301 et passim. Featherstonhaugh's 1834 survey of the Ozark Mountains for the Topographical Bureau is regarded as the first formal recognition of geology by the Federal Government (Merrill, p. 323).

[16] Jonathan Ely was Professor of Practical Agriculture and the Natural Sciences at the Polytechny, for which see the note on Yates in the letter of Henry to Alexander, December 19, 1825.

[17] Amos Eaton was greatly concerned with methods of imparting knowledge. Here, he may sound as though he is merging the Lancastrian educational scheme of using the students with the lecture method now associated with the importations of German university ideals and techniques into America. The former may have some validity; the latter is doubtful. Eaton stressed learning by doing and by observing in the field. Because of the small size of the school, this was something like a present-day seminar. See Samuel Rezneck, "Amos Eaton, 'The Old School-master,' in Precept and Deed," *New York History*, 1958, *39*:165–178. Henry's own teaching methods were quite conventional and showed no evidence of having been influenced by Eaton's views.

begin the 3ᵈ Wednesday in July and our commencement should be the last Wednesday in June. This would make our experimental courses much cheaper on account of fuel. It would bring our agricultural operations to the best part of the season.

Will you be so obliging as to write me your pleasure in regard to Dʳ Scriven's geological specimens? We can easily make out a suit of the rock specimens in two hours; but the suit would be so much richer and so much more satisfactory with the specimens of Alluvial, or (as the English call it) the Tertiary formation, that I would imagine he would rather wait a little while for it.

The whole School are delighted to hear any thing from you. Would it be convenient to let us know, about what time we may expect you home?

The School has now taken on a character, and begins to appear like a durable establishment. The superior excellence of the plan is gradually becoming known. We are much puzzled about the governor's speech.[18] Why did he give exactly your plan (which he knew you had already put in practice) as if an original thought of his own? There is nothing different in his speech from your plan, but a few impracticable puerile appendages.

The Massachusetts commissioners have made a miserable report on the subject of a School intended to resemble yours.[19] It sounds well enough, till the mind tries it in practice. It cannot go, unless it is wholly changed in its most essential characters.

I have not lost a day from the School this term. I am among the students from sunrise till 9 in the evening. I think much more highly of the School, than I ever have.

I suppose you recollect, that our commencement is the last Wednesday in April.

Yours respectfully,
Amos Eaton.

[18] This probably refers to DeWitt Clinton's message to the Legislature of 1826, a copy of which is in the Henry Library. Clinton made a brief reference to the need for technical and vocational training, repeating a theme of the previous year's message. Clinton had endorsed the incorporation of Rensselaer Polytechnic Institute. No other possibility appears in Edward A. Fitzpatrick's *The Educational Views and Influence of DeWitt Clinton* (New York, 1911), No. 44 of the Columbia Teachers College Contributions to Education.

[19] Massachusetts, *Report of the Commissioners, Appointed by a Resolve of 22 February 1825* (Boston, 1826). As in the previous comment on Clinton, Eaton is somewhat obscure. The Massachusetts report recommended establishing a Seminary of Practical Arts and Sciences. The real difference between the Eaton plan and the New York and Massachusetts proposals was two-fold: Eaton stressed learning by experience, and he wanted to instruct teachers, not the actual practitioners of applied science. Eaton was in an awkward position when commenting on these contemporary proposals for vocational and technical education as some of the support for Rensselaer Polytechnic Institute derived from believers in direct education of practitioners, rather than followers of his pedagogic views.

April 14, 1826

EXCERPT,[1] MINUTES, ACADEMY TRUSTEES

Trustees' Minutes, 1:263–264, Albany Academy Archives

April. 14, 1826.

The Trustees met, pursuant to notice

Present

Philip S. Parker,	Henry R. Weed,
Chas R. Webster,	John W. Yates,
John Ludlow,	T. Romeyn Beck,
Eben. Baldwin,	The Recorder,

James McKown[2] Esqr having been appointed Recorder of this city, took his seat as a member of the Board . . . .

On Application of the Faculty

Resolved that Ryan's Astronomy[3] be added to Keith & Wallace on the Globes as a text book on the branch concerning which it treats.

A Copy of Cardell's English Grammar[4] & of Hart's Questions in Geography,[5] was presented in the name of Mr Cardell & on motion, they were ordered to be placed in the Academy Library . . . .

A Communication having been laid before the Board highly implicating the moral character & conduct of Professor O'Shannessy.[6]

Resolved that a Committee of five members be appointed to investigate the facts relating to the charges against Professor O'Shannessy—that they communicate to him the documentary evidence now before the board & after hearing such exculpatory evidence as he may introduce report the result of their inquiry to the board. *Resolved* that Messrs Yates, Baldwin, the Recorder, Mr Hawley & Mr Webster be that Committee.

---

[1] Portions of these minutes have been omitted where indicated.

[2] James McKown (1788 or 1789–1847), a local lawyer prominent in Albany politics who held the office of Recorder from 1826 to 1838, and from 1844 until his death. Munsell, *Ann. Alb.*, 5:103, and 10:380.

[3] James Ryan, *The New American Grammar of the Elements of Astronomy, on an Improved Plan* (New York, 1825).

[4] William S. Cardell (1780–1828) of New York published a number of educational works (*Allibone, 1:336*), including *Elements of English Grammar, Deduced from Science and Practice, Adapted to the Capacity of Learners* . . . (New York, 1826).

[5] Joseph C. Hart, *Geographical Exercises; Containing 10,000 Questions for Practical Examination on the Most Important Features of the Maps of the World and the United States* . . . (New York, 1824).

[6] This was the opening shot in an affair which was to lead to the vacancy at the Academy eventually filled by Joseph Henry.

April 24, 1826

On Motion

Resolved that Mr Ludlow, Mr Beck & Mr Bullions[7] be a Committee to revise the Statutes & report such alterations as they may deem necessary.

Adjourned.

[7] Reverend Peter Bullions (1791–1864), Presbyterian clergyman and classical scholar was born in Scotland and educated at the University of Edinburgh (M.A. 1813). Bullions was licensed to preach by the Presbytery of Edinburgh after four years of theological studies. He came to Argyle, New York, in 1818 where he was the ordained pastor. Bullions moved to Albany to become Professor of Latin and Greek at the Albany Academy from 1824 until 1848. While in Albany he was a member of the Albany Institute's Third Department. From 1832 until 1852 he preached at Troy; he was awarded an honorary D.D. by Princeton in 1837; and he was elected a Trustee of Rensselaer Polytechnic Institute in 1862, serving the last two years of his life. Bullions published a complete set of classical textbooks which were used extensively. See *Nason*, pp. 15, 92; *Herringshaw*, p. 170; *Academy Seventy-fifth Anniversary*, p. 69; *Howell and Tenney*, p. 684; *Princeton Catalogue*, p. 416; *Transactions*, Albany Institute, 1830, *1*, part 2: Appendix, p. 73; and Munsell, *Coll. Alb.*, 2:187.

MINUTES, ACADEMY TRUSTEES

Trustees' Minutes, 1:264–266, Albany Academy Archives

Albany. April 24. 1826.

The Board met, at the call of the Committee appointed on the charges against Prof. O'Shannessy.[1]

Present.

Jno W. Yates,	H. R. Weed,	Philip S. Parker,
Jno Ludlow,	Isaac Ferris,	T. R. Beck,
C. R. Webster,	Gid. Hawley,	E[benezer] Baldwin[2]

Mr Yates from the Committee to whom was referred the communication made to the board relating to Prof. O Shannessy Reported

That they gave him immediate information of the charge preferred against him & furnished him with copies of the letters which passed between Philip S. Parker Esqr & A. T. Freeman[3] of New York. That he ap-

[1] Michael O'Shannessy.

[2] The meeting was rather better attended than usual.

[3] Augustus T. Freeman is listed in New York City Directories for this period as a merchant. The letters exchanged between Parker and Freeman are in the Academy Archives. Parker wrote March 14, 1826, asking whether there was any truth "in a story now circulating" about O'Shannessy, who was supposed to have introduced Freeman to "a female of low *Character* and placed her under [Freeman's] care travelling in the Stage, from this City to New York." Parker asked for confirmation, for "if true Mr O'Shannessy's conduct deserves examination and I hope no feelings of fake delicacy will prevent you from informing us on the subject." Freeman replied March 27 that "last December O'Shannessy," learning that Freeman was returning to New York, "requested me to pay her every attention due to a *virtuous* and amiable Lady representing

129

peared before the Committee agreeably to their request, on the 15th inst. & denied the truth of M[r] Freeman's statement. That he entered into a detail of the circumstances, which, as he alledges, attended the transaction in question, and at the suggestion of the Committee, promised to reduce his account to writing, to be laid before the Board—that they have since received a letter from him, in which he declines entering into particulars, but repeats his allegation, that M[r] Freeman's statement is false.[4]

That they have also rec[d] a letter from him, addressed to the Trustees, tendering his resignation of the Professorship of Mathematics & Natural Philosophy in the Academy, in the words following, viz.

Gentlemen

After considering the proceedings of your body on the 15th inst, in connexion with former ones, I have been convinced that my interests will be best secured by retiring from the Institution, over which you preside. I therefore tender you my resignation as Professor of Mathematics and Natural Philosophy in the Albany Academy to take place at the expiration of the present Academic Year.

Signed

April 17. 1826.   M. O Shannessy

Under these circumstances, the Committee deemed it unnecessary to proceed farther in the investigation & agreed to recommend to the Board the adoption of the following resolutions.

Resolved that the Resignation by M. O Shannessy of the Professorship of Mathematics & Natural Philosophy in the Academy be & the same is hereby accepted, to take effect on the 31st of July next, being the close of the present Academic Year.

Resolved that the Board will proceed to fill the vacancy which will take place, in consequence of the above mentioned resignation, on Friday next & that the Clerk give due notice to all the members of the Board.

---

her to be the same and even more." Freeman, "not discovering anything to the contrary," placed her on their arrival "in a respectable Boarding house where she was recognized by a Gentleman of the City and reported to the Lady of the house as a notorious prostitute and one that had practiced similar impositions previously on others." Freeman was sure that O'Shannessy was "acquainted with her character" and if so "his conduct towards me is unbecoming a Gentleman and should an op-

portunity offer I shall have no hesitation of repeating the same to him."

[4] This letter, addressed to John W. Yates and dated April 17, 1826, is in the Academy Archives. O'Shannessy refused, "in consequence of particulars that have since developed themselves, which have the appearance of hostility towards me," to carry the thing further. "I am not at liberty to explain the matter fully, but shall at some future time." He never did, as far as is known.

Whereupon, the Board having considered said Report, *Resolved* unanimously to accept it & to adopt the resolutions proposed.

.   Adjourned to Friday
the 28th inst

JABEZ D. HAMMOND TO JOHN W. YATES[1]
Henry Papers, Smithsonian Archives

Albany April 28, 1826

Dear Sir,

Since I saw you yesterday I have searched for the letter I mentioned to you which I received from General Van Renssellaer[2] and which contained his opinion of M[r] Joseph Henry but cannot find it. I must have mislaid it. I had written[3] to M[r] Van Renssellaer requesting him to endeavor to procure a place for M[r] Henry in the U.S. Corps of Civil Engineers. In his reply M[r] Van Renssellaer according to my recollection stated in substance that he had called on the Secretary of War for the purpose of recommending M[r] Henry but that the Secretary had informed him that it was the intention of the Executive Department if a Law should pass to increase the Corps of Civil Engineers to take those who should be hereafter appointed from the graduates at West Point. Gen. V. Renssellaer added that he knew M[r] Henry very well, that he thought him a young man of great merit and that it would give him much pleasure to see him (M[r] H.) well provided for.

Altho' I do not claim to be a competent judge of M[r] Henry's scientific acquirements I hope you will excuse me for embracing the present occasion to state that he executed the business assigned him last summer by the Commissioners of the State Road with great accuracy, skill and ability and in a manner highly satisfactory to the Commissioners and I believe to the

---

[1] It is likely that this letter was written in support of Henry's candidacy for the position of Professor of Mathematics and Natural Philosophy at the Albany Academy. O'Shannessy submitted his resignation on the 17th of April; the Trustees, at the meeting of April 24, agreed to meet on the 28th to name O'Shannessy's successor. Yates had been chairman of the committee to investigate O'Shannessy. The conversation which Hammond mentioned as having taken place on the day before the Trustees met may have concerned Henry's qualifications for the professorship,

and this letter was probably given to Yates to confirm the conversation. Note, in the light of the O'Shannessy affair, the emphasis on moral qualities.

[2] Stephen Van Rensselaer (1764–1839), then in Congress.

[3] Neither Hammond's letter to Van Rensselaer nor the latter's reply has been found. For the attempt to find Henry a place with the Topographical Engineers, see above, T. R. Beck to Martin Van Buren, March 10, 1826, and related documents.

public. In relation to his moral qualities I must be permited to add that I never knew a person more free from faults or more amiable in his disposition.

> I am with great respect
> Your Obed[t] Serv[t]
> Jabez D. Hammond

MINUTES, ACADEMY TRUSTEES

Trustees' Minutes, 1:266–267, Albany Academy Archives

April 28, 1826

The Trustees met, pursuant to adjournment

Present

Jn[o] W. Yates,	Jn[o] Ludlow,	T. R. Beck,
Philip S. Parker,	P. Gansevoort,	Isaac Ferris,
The Recorder,[1]	Gideon Hawley,	E. Baldwin,
The Mayor,[2]	Cha[s] R. Webster,	W[m] James,
H. R. Weed,	Jn[o] Chester,	

On Motion

Resolved that the Trustees hereby request the Corporation of this city, to accept from them the vane & scroll lately taken down from the Old Gaol,[3] to be placed by the Corporation on such public building as they may designate.

The Board then proceeded to nominate & elect a professor of Mathematics & Natural Philosophy & on canvassing the ballots, it appeared that M[r] Joseph Henry of Albany was elected.

Whereupon Resolved unanimously[4] that M[r] Joseph Henry be & he is

---

[1] James M[c]Kown.

[2] James Stevenson.

[3] For the history of the Old Gaol in its relation to the Academy, see above, Minutes of the Academy Trustees, March 8, 1815, especially footnote 8.

[4] It is not known whether the *vote* was unanimous, or even whether there were other candidates. The fact that the entire Board was present suggests that the election may have been closely fought. The alternative is to suppose that they all appeared merely to acclaim Henry, a supposition which requires one to believe that a significant cross section of the Albany elite came to a usually indifferently attended Board meeting to swell the numbers of those voting for a (relatively) unknown young man of distinctly humble origins. There were others available who could have filled the position, Richard Varick De-Witt, for example. A third possibility is that the circumstances of O'Shannessy's departure made the selection of a successor a matter of great concern to the Trustees.

hereby appointed Professor of Mathematics & Natural Philosophy in the Albany Academy, at a salary of one thousand dollars per annum payable quarterly. Mr Henry to enter on the duties of his office on the first day of September next.

On application of M^r O'Shannessy, *Resolved* that the Clerk be authorized to furnish M^r O'Shannessy with a testimonial on the part of the Board of his scientific attainments in Mathematics & Natural Philosophy.[5]

Adjourned.

[5] This resolution was rescinded at the meeting of June 30, 1826.

FITCH'S[1] CANAL TOUR JOURNAL

Fitch Family Papers, Asa Fitch's Diary C:8–12,
Sterling Library, Yale University

May [2] 1826

The stove, cooking utensials, crockery &c was very tardy in being brought on board this morning, so that we did not get through the sloop lock until 11 o'clock. We were detained until about 1 in Troy, back of Fassett & Sheldon's[2] in taking the chemical apparatus of Hezekiah Hulbert Eaton[3] & Timothy Dwight Eaton,[4] & mr Arms[5] on board. *These boys & this* young man are to stay & lecture at different villages on our rout. Ate dinner below

[1] Asa Fitch (1809–1878) graduated from Rensselaer Polytechnic Institute in 1827, and thereafter studied medicine, taking an M.D. in 1829. He practiced medicine for a number of years in upstate New York, but his real passion was the study of insects, on which he published a number of papers. He was appointed (the first) New York State Entomologist in 1854 and held that position until 1870. *DAB; Nason,* pp. 178–181. See next document, footnote 1.

[2] John V. Fassett and Joseph D. Selden, "Dealers in Drugs and Medicines" (Troy City Directory, 1829), offered for sale portable kits of apparatus and chemical substances. These would take a student through two courses of lectures, and cost fifty dollars. Arthur J. Weise, *History of the City of Troy* (Troy, 1876), p. 148.

[3] Hezekiah Hulbert Eaton (1809–1832), son of Amos Eaton, attended Rensselaer Polytechnic (RPI) at its opening, and thereafter gave public lectures on chemistry in upstate New York and in Boston. After teaching at RPI (1829), he moved to Lexington, Kentucky, and in 1831 joined the faculty of the medical department of Transylvania University, where he lectured on chemistry and electricity. *Nason,* p. 134.

[4] Timothy Dwight Eaton (1807–1828) attended RPI and served there for a time as assistant in natural history. Ibid., p. 176.

[5] Stilman E. Arms (1803–1877) attended RPI, lectured in western New York, then studied medicine at Yale. In 1833 he set up practice in Elizabeth, New Jersey, where he remained the rest of his life. Ibid., p. 175.

the lower one of the nine locks. Here the most of the party, got specimens of the transition[6] argillite, which continues to the Cahoes falls.[7] All the distance from Troy to the Cahoes I came on foot, the boat was so slow whilst passing through the locks. I arrived at the falls, accompanied by Mr Oscar Hanks[8] full two hours before the boat came up. This gave me sufficient time to view them. The falls are not so high; but much wider than I expected to find them. Whilst standing on the bank (which I should judge was 120 or 130 feet from the foot of the falls) I could plainly feel the spray falling on my face & hands. The height of the falls is 70 feet. The river being low at this time, the water is broken into two distinct falls, near the middle by a projecting rock. The falls, with the surrounding scenery present a very grand & picturesque appearance.[9] On the opposite side of the river the rock rises full 50 feet higher I should think than the top of the falls. These are overgrown with green moss, & surmounted by pine spruce maple beech &c. I could at times partially perceive the rain bow, formed by the rays of the sun striking the rising spray. This spray resembles the smoke rushing from the mouth of a cannon, or more nearly perhaps, the steam rushing from the pipe of a steam boat. When I came on the bank against the falls, the sudden coolness of the air surprised me. When I had viewed this curiosity as long as I wished, I walked leisurely along; in company with Dr James Eights until the boat overtook us. The boat lay for the night in a small basin the south side of the mohawk, at the Lower aqueduct, in the town (I beleive) of Niskayuna. This day has been uncomfortably warm, for woolen cloths. After we had been to tea the rules drawn up by Pres[t] Blatchford[10] & Prof Eaton for the expedition were read to us. Dr Eights was appointed purveyor for the tour. Prof Eaton is commander, & an assistant is appointed daily by him to take notice of any ill conduct on board, to stop the boat at any place to be examined, to oversee the making of beds &c. Our rule is to arise at sun rise breakfast at 8 o'clock dine at 2 & drink tea after the boat stops for the night.[11] The following is a list of the members of the expedition.

---

[6] For Amos Eaton's theory of geological strata, see his various works listed in Ethel McAllister, *Amos Eaton* (Philadelphia, 1941), pp. 547–555, especially *Proposed Geological Nomenclature* (Troy, 1823).

[7] Cohoes Falls, just west of Troy on the Mohawk River.

[8] Oscar Hanks, of Troy, entered RPI in 1824 but did not complete the course. *Nason*, p. 549.

[9] ". . . diversion of the water of the Mohawk River for canal and power purposes has reduced the flow to little more than a trickle." Writers' Program of the Work Projects Administration in the State of New York, *New York: A Guide to the Empire State* (New York, 1940), p. 627.

[10] Samuel Blatchford.

[11] A more complete account of the rules was given by George W. Clinton in his diary, which appears in the *Publications of the Buffalo Historical Society*, 1910, *14*:273–305, pp. 283–284.

Stilmon E Arms A B R S[12]

Albert Danker[13]   "

H. H. Eaton   "

T. Dwight Eaton   "

Richard H. Hale[14] Memb. R.S.

Oscar Hanks, mem R.S.

Addison Hulbert[15] A B R S

S. C. Jackson[16] Member R.S.

P. C. W. T. McManus[17] A.B.R.S.

Wᵐ S. Pelton[18]

Prof A. Eaton

Sickles[19] pilot

B. F Root[20] A B R S

J. M. Trimble[21] Member R.S.

R. H Williams[22]   "

Charles Weston[23] mem. R.S.

Asa Fitch jun   "

Dr. Jas Eights

George W. Clinton

Daniel B. Cady[24]

Eleazer Hady[25]

Hildreth[26]

Henry[27]

Wm. Kane[28] capt

Sam[29] ——— cook

In all 24. Upon making up the beds in the cabin, I saw that it was almost impossible for all of the party to sleep there. At first, I had an idea of going

---

[12] The A.B. degree from the Rensselaer School.

[13] Albert Danker (1802–1868) graduated from RPI with the first class, and remained in Troy as a surveyor and civil engineer. *Nason,* p. 176.

[14] Richard H. Hale (d. 1849) attended RPI, then Union College, where he graduated in 1827. He attended the New York College of Physicians and Surgeons, and later practiced in Troy. It is not known where he took his M.D. *Nason,* p. 549; *Columbia Alumni,* p. 249.

[15] Addison Hulbert graduated from RPI in 1826 and became a mechanical engineer. *Nason,* p. 176.

[16] Samuel Clinton Jackson graduated from RPI in 1827. He was an "agriculturalist," according to ibid., p. 182, and moved to Galesburg, Illinois. He was still alive when Nason wrote (1887).

[17] Philip C. W. T. McManus, another RPI graduate (1826), studied law, then became a farmer. He died in 1882. Ibid., p. 176.

[18] William Snow Pelton (1807–1839), RPI class of 1826, studied medicine at the Rutgers Medical School, and practiced thereafter in Orange County, New York. Ibid., p. 177.

[19] This was perhaps the Abraham Sickles who was for many years one of the Albany town constables. Munsell, *Ann. Alb.,* 8:108, 113, 142; 9:155, 175, 192, 256.

[20] Bennet F. Root (1804–1879) graduated from RPI in 1826, then studied medicine at the Berkshire Medical College, receiving his diploma in 1832. In 1834 he moved to Michigan, where he practiced medicine until his death. *Nason,* p. 177.

[21] James M. Trimble enrolled in RPI in 1824 but did not graduate. He was from Hillsboro, Ohio. Ibid., p. 549.

[22] Richard H. Williams was a member of the class of 1826 but did not graduate. He was from Middlesex, New York. Ibid., p. 549.

[23] Charles L. Weston graduated from RPI in 1827, then studied law. He practiced for a time in Burlington, New Jersey, and later moved to Davenport, Iowa. He was still alive when Nason was writing. Ibid., p. 183.

[24] Daniel B. Cady was from Schoharie. He entered RPI in 1824, but did not graduate. Ibid., p. 549.

[25] Not identified.

[26] Fitch wrote only "Hildreth" originally, then added, probably later, in pencil, "Thomas?" We have not been able to trace Mr. Hildreth.

[27] Fitch wrote only "Henry" originally; as with Hildreth, he apparently added "Prof. Joseph" later. Henry had been professor for less than a week when Fitch wrote the entry; it is hardly likely that he would have been known as "Professor Joseph Henry" so early.

[28] Perhaps the William Kane who died at Albany in February 1849, at age 75. Munsell, *Ann. Alb.,* 1:344.

[29] Not identified.

to a tavern near by, & beging a small spot on the bar room floor to lay. But afterwards I joined, with two or three more, in erecting a kind of tent on the after deck, in which 4 of us were accomodated, in a manner, not the most uncomfortable. I had a cushion under me, & my cloak over me, & believe I did not awake during the night.

"NOTES OF A TOUR FROM THE HUDSON TO LAKE ERIE IN MAY AND JUNE OF 1826"[1]

Henry Papers, Smithsonian Archives

May 2[d] 1826

Left Troy at 20 minutes past 12. Took our clearance to Little falls. As a packet boat we were detained several hours in passing the nine locks[2] and arived about darke at the aqueduct. Between the junction & the river there are two double locks which in a short time will hardley be sufficient to pass the number of boates navigating the canal.

The rock we met with is[3]

---

[1] Later entries from this journal will be given as "Henry's Canal Tour Journal."

Amos Eaton was a great believer in field trips to teach geology. This journal of Henry's was created on one such field trip conducted in May and June of 1826. Three other journals survive for this trip: Amos Eaton's Journal (Journal E of the Geological and Agricultural Survey of the Erie Canal, in the New York State Library); George Clinton's Journal (see footnote 3 of Eaton to Van Rensselaer, March 25, 1826, above); and the diary of Asa Fitch, Sterling Library, Yale University. They will be cited hereafter as Eaton's, Clinton's and Fitch's Journal, respectively. Samuel Rezneck is the author of two articles on this tour of the Erie Canal: "A Traveling School of Science on the Erie Canal in 1826," *New York History*, 1959, *40*:255–269, based on Fitch's Journal; and "Joseph Henry Learns Geology on the Erie Canal," *New York History*, 1969, *50*:29–42, based on Henry's Journal. The tour was meant to combine both scientific field work and education in accordance with Eaton's pedagogic views.

The trip was made on the *Marquis De Lafayette*. At the end of the first day Eaton laid down the rules governing the excursion which were quite strict and explicit. In Eaton's pedagogy, learning by experience did not involve permissiveness. These rules are given in Clinton's Journal, pp. 283–284 (all Clinton references will be to the published text). The rules required that each day in rotation one of the students was to be appointed the assistant who was in charge of the party under the direction of the faculty, especially in matters of decorum. The rules also required that each member of the party keep a journal. Rezneck correctly notes that Henry's Journal, of the surviving student journals, was the most geological in content.

[2] These separated the Mohawk River from the Hudson River.

[3] The text simply ends. Eaton's Journal for May 2 states that he attempted to point out the order of superposition of various rocks along the route.

HENRY'S CANAL TOUR JOURNAL
Henry Papers, Smithsonian Archives

May 3[d] [1826]

Crossed the aqueduct at 5 o'clock and was called on deck by Mr. Eaton to be shown the Greywacke which rests on the Transision Argalite & extends beyond Rotterdam. On this rock we saw for the first mile *marley clay overlayed by bagshot sand. Mr E. thinks that the marley-clay is underlaid by plastic clay in some places. The plastic clay may be distinguished from marley by the latter's effervessing with acid.

The sandy plains between Albany & schenectaday according to Mr. E is *bagshot* sand underlaid by marley clay. This range extends from Sandy Hill almost uninterrupted to Coeymans. Bag-Shot sand was found to make a substantial bank to the canal contrary to the expectation of several of the canal commissioners.

The Graywacke is finely caracterized along the bank of the canal at this place (5 m[iles] W[est] of aqueduct) both the compact and slaty. This rock generally assumes a brown or redish tinge on exposure to the atmosphere this owing to the prote oxid of iron which it contains taking an additional dose of oxygen and becoming the peroxide. Half past 8 o C. At the 2[d] lock East of the Alexander's Bridge.

A little to the East of this place the graywacke presents a very irregular stratifigcation bending & raring in every direction similar to the rock described in Silliman's journal by Dr Steel[1] and is indeed the same range extending to saratoga lake where Dr S. made his drawing. Nearer the lock is a fine location of *diluvial* formation resting on marley strata in some

---

* This is the marley clay of Pierce[2] & the London clay of Conybeare.[3]

---

[1] John H. Steel, "Notice of Snake Hill and Saratoga Lake and its Environs," *Silliman's Journal*, 1825, 9:1–4. Steel (1780–1838), a physician, practiced medicine in Saratoga from ca. 1800 until his death. He was active in local and state medical societies. He had a keen interest in the natural history of his region, and published a number of works on mineral springs in and around Saratoga. William L. Stone, *Reminiscences of Saratoga and Ballston* (New York, 1875), pp. 278–306, 447.

[2] James Pierce, "Notice of the Alluvial District of New Jersey, with Remarks on the Application of the Rich Marl of that Region to Agriculture," *Silliman's Journal*, 1823, 6:237–

242. Pierce, who contributed a number of articles on geology and natural history to *Silliman's Journal* between 1818 and 1827, was a scientific wanderer; very little is known about him. He lived in New York City before 1820, and for a time in Catskill, New York, in 1821, where he took part in the activities of the Catskill Lyceum of Natural History (see his brief notice in *Silliman's Journal*, 1821, 3:237–238). His articles tell of his travels, which took him all over the Atlantic seaboard, from Maine to Florida.

[3] W. D. Conybeare and William Phillips, *Outlines of the Geology of England and Wales . . .* (London, 1822) part 1, pp. 22–36.

places & in others on the graywacke rock. This Diluvial consists of large rounded boulders of primative rocks.[†]

[†] According to the Geologists of the Day[4] the superincumbent class is divided into the The *ante diluvial Diluvial* & Postdiluvial. The Antediluvial which is lowest is supposed to have been formed before the Deluge, *Diluvial* formed by the deluge or some other cause which does not now exist. Postdiluvial is that division of the superincumbent class which is forming at pressent or has been formed by the same causes which exist at the present time.

The first of these divisions is subdividid into Plastic clay Marley or London clay & Bagshot sand.[5] Plastic clay is that used by the potter & is found in New Jersey.

[4] e.g., Conybeare and Phillips, op. cit., pp. xxviii–xxix, lvi–lxi. Though this broad tripartite classification might have been widely accepted, the subclassifications and the proper mode of identifying them were matters of sharp controversy. On this subject see Leonard G. Wilson, "The Emergence of Geology as a Science in the United States," *Journal of World History*, 1967, *10*:416–437.

[5] Conybeare and Phillips, op. cit., Plate after p. 2.

HENRY'S CANAL TOUR JOURNAL
Henry Papers, Smithsonian Archives

May 4th 1826

5 O'clock at Putnam's tavern on the canal in Rotterdam[1] at this place the graywacke of the Green mountain ridge meets (the calciferous sand rock of McClure & Eaton & the transition sandstone of Werner)[2] the calciferous sandstone of the McCombs mountain.

[1] This is the present location of the town of Rotterdam Junction, New York.

[2] William Maclure (1763–1840), geologist and patron of science, and Abraham Gottlob Werner (1750–1817), Professor of Mineralogy at the Mining Academy of Freiberg, author of the Neptunian Theory of the Earth, prolific writer on mineralogy and geology, and foremost in elevating geology to the rank of a real science. See *DAB* and Frank Dawson Adams, *The Birth and Development of the Geological Sciences* (New York, 1954), pp. 170–249. None of Maclure's or Werner's many publications appear to have been in Joseph Henry's library, but he need not have read them as much of Eaton's geological thinking was a result of, and a reaction to, their contributions. In the 1820s Eaton argued that geologists in America must be conscious of geological phenomena which are peculiarly American, not to be found in Europe. Thus, Eaton made frequent reference to the findings and classifications of geologists of European training, in part to stress differences in European and American strata. (Maclure was born and raised in Scotland, came to America in 1796, and served as President of both the American Geological Society and the Academy of Natural Sciences in Philadelphia.) Eaton clearly felt the need for the establishment of American geology, and stated so in his writings. See Amos Eaton, *A Geological and Agricultural Survey of the District Adjoining the Erie Canal* (Albany, 1824), pp. 155–157; Amos Eaton, *Geological Text-Book* (Albany, 1830), pp. iii–vii; and McAllister, *Amos Eaton*, pp. 283–285, 323–336. C. J. Schneer, "Ebenezer Emmons and the Foundations of American Geology," *Isis*, 1969, *60*: 439–450, dates the founding of an "American"

This rock becomes very interesting at Flint Hill where it contains quarts, hornstone calc-spar, rough agate, & hornstone containing specks of Carbonate of copper also hornstone running into semi opal.

This rock is overlaid by the Metaliferous limerock or the transition limestone of Werner which forms the bank of the canal about one mile East of schoharrie crick.

At about one mile west of Coenewago[3] on the south side of the canal a rock appears which resembles graywack slate so nearly that it is difficult to determine the difference. Mr E calls this calciferous slate. It rests on the metaliferous lime stone (transition lime stone of Werner) <*higher*> sometimes lower in the strata it passes into common graywack this rock in some places consistes of nearly one half carbonate of lime.

At Roots' Little nose[4] we met the first gneis rock which is the primative formation which suppoarts the transition to the east and is one of the primative ridges running from the McComb mountain to the south. On this <*ridge*> rock reposes the calciferous sandstone above this the Metaliferous lime stone still higher the calciferous slate which at higher elevation passes into common graywacke.

The large nose near Spraker is composed of sandstone towards the canal and on the west & south but the base rock or gneis appears on the south side of the hill.

---

geology from the next decade, especially the work of the New York State Survey. Schneer stresses Eaton's work on the canal but dates the "foundation" from the decision to switch from a mineralogical nomenclature to a "terminology based on type locality" plus the recognition of the importance of paleontological correlation. While Eaton never became paleontologically oriented and remained an adherent of the older nomenclature, his position cited above does presage the later developments. Although too complex and far afield from this volume for detailed treatment, the reaction of British geologists to Continental terminology was analogous to the reactions of Americans to the Europeans. Similarities were sought but, as differences were uncovered, a kind of nationalistic reaction occurred.

[3] Caughnawaga.
[4] A buttress of overhanging rock.

HENRY'S CANAL TOUR JOURNAL
Henry Papers, Smithsonian Archives

Friday May 5th [1826]

At spraker's Near Flat Brook. We [examined] this morning the hills on each side of the river; on the north side we found quarts containing anthersite coal & oxide of iron in veins also fortification agate and hornstone containing specks of carbonate of copper.

On the south side of the river we took specimens of the calciferous sand rock containing nodules & geodes of quarts common calcareous spar, & brown spar. This rock contains more carbonate of lime than the calciferous sand stone near Rotterdam and it is sometimes burned for lime.

Mr E this morning gave us a lecture on the general principals of Geology in which he observed that the Europeans were obliged to come to america to study the regular arraingements of rocks on a large scale.[1]

There are five or six primative ranges running through Europe which so disterbes the strata and forms [so] many different formations that the simplicity of the geological arrangement is rendered very obscure but in the northern part of the United States the straification is regular and extends many miles.

The rocks we have met with from the Hudson to 8 miles wes of schenectaday are based on the green mountain range. From this place West the rocks are based on spurs or ridges (called sometimes hogs back) from McComb's mountain.

The ranges on the East of the Hudson are very perfect in the primative & transition classes but dificient in the secondary. The ranges from McCombes mountain on the contrary are deficient in the primative & transition but exhibit the secondary in a very striking manner.

Friday 12 O'clock at Fort Plain,* Otsiquago[2] creek; about one quarter of a mile from the canal up the creek is a very interesting location of the transition rocks already mentioned; the rock next to the water is the calciferous sandstone which is surmounted by the metaliferous limestone containing stylastrites;[3] the sparry & shell variety occur. The shell variety alternates with the calsiferous slate whi[ch] form the upper stratum at this place.

* In 1782 a forte was built near this place.

[1] Not many did come, however. We might mention Johann David Schöpf (1752–1800) whose work is described briefly by George P. Merrill, "Contributions to the History of American Geology," *Annual Report of the Board of Regents of the Smithsonian Institution . . . Report of the U.S. National Museum* (Washington, 1906), pp. 208–209; John Finch of Birmingham, who made a geological tour in 1823 and reported his observations to the Academy of Natural Sciences in Philadelphia (see Leonard G. Wilson, "The Emergence of Geology as a Science in the United States," *Journal of World History*, 1967, *10*: 416–437, pp. 424–425); and, later on, Sir Charles Lyell (1797–1875), whose books on the subject are well known. (*Travels in North America, with Geological Observations,* 2 vols. [London, 1845], and *A Second Visit to the United States of America,* 2 vols. [London, 1849].) For the most part, geologists in Europe were content to read the reports of American geologists which were appearing in increasing numbers and to follow the progress of geology here by correspondence with their American colleagues. See Wilson, op. cit., pp. 416, 437.

[2] Otsquaga Creek.

[3] That is, fossil stylasters.

HENRY'S CANAL TOUR JOURNAL
Henry Papers, Smithsonian Archives

Saturday May 6th [1826]

Little falls.[1] The rock at this place has been called Granite but it is will characterised gneis of the sandy variety; about one mile to the west the calciferous sand stone is found resting on the gneis. A little to the west of this we find the Metaliferous lime stone which acording to Proffessor Eatons Map[2] dips under & is seen no mor on the south side of the canal to the west. Saturday 6 o'clock[3]—Furgason's Inn we left the boat at this place[4] to view the falls on starch factory creek. After walking about three miles through the woods we met the starch factory creek on which we found the slaty graywacke which resembles the second greywacke or calciferous slate but as it is over laid a little farther up the creek by millstone grit, saliferous rock, Grayband, & Feriferous slate. It must be the first gray wacke of Eaton.

---

[1] Little Falls in Herkimer County, New York. Water power from the gorge brought factories to Little Falls especially during the boom days of the Erie Canal.

[2] Insert in Eaton's *Geology of the Erie Canal* . . . (1824).

[3] Rezneck in his article on the Henry Journal says A.M. But Clinton's Journal for May 6 has the party leaving Little Falls at eight in the morning; Eaton's Journal clearly has the party almost at Utica (see next footnote), and

Fitch's Journal has the party arriving at three in the afternoon and almost immediately starting on the excursion which Henry describes here, returning between eight and nine in the evening. "P.M." is clearly correct, and Fitch's timing is probably right, given the distances both he and Henry mention.

[4] Three miles east of Utica according to Eaton's Journal, where Ferguson's Creek crossed the Canal.

HENRY'S CANAL TOUR JOURNAL
Henry Papers, Smithsonian Archives

Village of Utica   Sunday May 7th [1826]

The transition graywack is seen on the banks of the canal about two miles E of the village on the north side of the river.[1] I think there must be quarries of Metaliferous limestone as many of the Houses are built of this stone and the flag stones are generally of the same.

From the little falls to Rome the Canal in following the river takes a direction north of west and passes along the ridge of land formed by the out croppings of the different strata.

---

[1] The Mohawk River, which the canal followed westward to Rome, New York.

HENRY'S CANAL TOUR JOURNAL
Henry Papers, Smithsonian Archives

Monday [May] 8ᵗʰ 1826

Whitesbourrough. About one mile above this place we collected specimens of millstone grit from large boulder on the side of the canal near the Herkimer battle ground[1] which is on the side of the great swamp that extends from Whitesbourow to near Palmira. Mr E. thinks this swamp an excellent illustration of Coneybare's Diluvial formation[2] and proposes to call it the diluvial troughf. It is interrupted by gravelly ridges which run in a north easterly direction & form patches of arible land. The canal passes along the south side of this troughf.

[1] That is, the scene of the battle of Oriskany, in August 1777. See the *DAB* article on Nicholas Herkimer (1728–1777).

[2] See above, Henry's Canal Tour Journal, May 3 [1826].

LECTURE NOTES, HENRY'S CANAL TOUR JOURNAL
Henry Papers, Smithsonian Archives

[May 8, 1826][1]

Lecture on Alluvial formation

A science is a classification of general facts. Hitchcock's[2] geology is not scientific description.

The first man in America was Schoolcraft[3] after this Buckland & Coney-

[1] While these lecture notes are undated and entered in the back of Henry's journal, this date may be assigned on the basis that both Fitch and Clinton noted that Eaton gave this lecture then.

[2] "A Sketch of the Geology, Mineralogy, and Scenery of the Regions Contiguous to the River Connecticut . . . " (*Silliman's Journal*, 1823, 6:1–86, 201–236; 1824, 7:1–30) was the first of the publications of Edward Hitchcock (1793–1864), a noted American geologist, educator, and Congregational clergyman. In his geology he was largely self-taught, though he had both heard Eaton's public lectures and worked in Benjamin Silliman's laboratory at Yale. In 1825 he resigned from the ministry to become Professor of Natural History and Chemistry at the newly established Amherst College, serving later there as President (1845–

1854) and continuing to teach geology and theology until his death. Notable for his extensive geological and theological publications, he was primarily devoted to the reconciliation of science and orthodoxy. See footnote 7 of the Canal Tour Journal entry for May 10 [1826], *DAB, Poggendorff*, and Stanley M. Guralnick, "Science and the American College," (Ph.D. dissertation, University of Pennsylvania, 1969), pp. 274–276.

[3] Henry Rowe Schoolcraft (1793–1864), ethnologist, was to become most famous for his studies of the American Indians. Schoolcraft began his career with an interest in geology and mineralogy, in both of which he appears to have been largely self-taught; his only professional training seems to have come from his private tutor at Middlebury College in 1813, Frederick Hall (1780–1843), then Professor of

bear their system[4] cronological anti-diluvial diluvial & post-diluvial. Alluvial is the generic term including the whole and is derived from a word signifying to wash (in latin alluvium). Buckland is now living. Conybear[5] died last august in a fit. Flemming[6] attac[k]ed Buckland & Conybear.

All that part of the earth not rock and possessing a stratafyed structure are called anti diluvial. This formation could not be washed down.

Diluvial formation is an irregular mixture of andidiluvial matter mixed with animal & vegetable remains & deposited by a cause which does not now exist.

The third division is called postediluvial and is now forming by the disintegrating of rocks and chainging of rivers.[7]

Mathematics and Natural Philosophy. Schoolcraft's publications in geology were primarily concerned with the Midwest and Great Lakes regions, and the ones most likely to be under consideration in this lecture by Eaton were his *Journal of Travels from Detroit Through the Grand Chain of American Lakes to the Source of the Mississippi* (Albany, 1821) and his *Travels in the Central Portions of the Mississippi Valley* (New York, 1825). See Chase S. and Stellanova Osborn, *Schoolcraft, Longfellow, and Hiawatha* (Lancaster, Pennsylvania, 1942), pp. 306–317, 562; *Poggendorff, DAB, Herringshaw*, and *Catalogue of the Officers and Students of Middlebury College ... 1800 to 1900* (Middlebury, 1901).

[4] In lecturing Eaton seems to be referring to a general agreement between Conybeare and Buckland, as no such "system" was ever established through joint publication. See above, footnote 5 of Amos Eaton's letter to Stephen Van Rensselaer of March 25, 1826.

[5] The lecturer is confused here because the Conybeare who died in 1824 was John Josias Conybeare, also a geologist and theologian (b. 1779), and brother of William Daniel Conybeare. See *DNB*.

[6] John Fleming (1785–1857), *DNB*. See Henry's Canal Tour Journal, May 10 [1826], especially footnote 7.

[7] In two subsequent pages, Henry's jottings, not reproduced here, indicate that Eaton at some other time in the journey lectured on Frederick Pursh (1774–1820), the German-American botanist and explorer, and Linnaeus (1707–1778), the Swedish botanist.

HENRY'S CANAL TOUR JOURNAL
Henry Papers, Smithsonian Archives

Tuesday May 9th [1826] at Lenox
Started at 5 o'clock and arrived at Chitengo[1] about one Oclock PM. From Lenox to this place the banks of the canal are couloured by the argelacious

---

[1] Chittenango. This was reached by a small lateral canal off the Erie Canal described in this day's entry in Fitch's Journal.

oxide of iron[2] of a read or chocolate colour. About one mile West of canis-tota[3] the company visited a salt spring.[*]

Near the spring the banks of the canal are spotted with nodules of green ferruginous slate.

Chittenengo one o'clock [P.M.] visited the polytecnic school of Dr. Yates[4] & was very politely received by the faculty.[5] This place is interesting from the formation of calcarious tufa[6] and petrifictions of wood & leaves of the same substance; a large log on the side of the later canal from the main canal to Chittiningo is seen in a petrified state which Mr E supposed to have been a hemlock from the roughness of the bark.

These petrifactions are now forming as well as the tufa probably from the calciferous slate which formes the hill on the side of which the tufa is found; we collected specimens of wood the surface of which was only be-gining to petrify.

Plaster & Hydrolic Limestone is also found near this place.

[*] Mr. Clinton having walked a head of the boat passed this spring without noticing it.

[2] That is, a claylike material.
[3] Canastota.
[4] See the note on the school, Henry to Alexander, December 19, 1825.

[5] Including his first cousin, close friend, and future brother-in-law, Stephen Alexander.
[6] A porous rock deposited by streams.

HENRY'S CANAL TOUR JOURNAL
Henry Papers, Smithsonian Archives

Manlius centre[1] May 10th [1826] 5. o'clock. A number of beds of plaster is found at this place, the plaster is over laid at the bed above the tavern on the side hid by soft Hydrolic lime stone or perhepse the lias formation of the Europeans. Mr E says that in this state the higher beds of Gypsum are of a more slatey & earthy formation than the lower.

At the above mentioned place near the top of the hill is found a lime-stone which has the appearance of rotten wood eaten by worms and has been called by Mr. E & proffessor Nott[2] Vermicular lime stone. This stone

[1] Manlius, Onondaga County, New York. The party stopped overnight here after leaving Chittenango.

[2] Joel B. Nott of Union College assisted Eaton in the survey of the Erie Canal.

is found in beds from this place along the canal to salina[3] and perhapse extends to some distance on each side. It is sold for building stone under the name of Eaton stone.

The rock which appears along the canal from Manlius to Lockport except in some places where the out croping of the rock curves to the south is calciferous slate. This rock contans the plaster the vermicular lime stone & the chel[4] limeston in beds. According to Mr E the only chel limestone found in this country that does not contain horn stone is only found in beds.

The most profitable plaster beds are found in this region from Manlius to Onadago[5] hollow & is estimate to be about 40 square miles.

10 o' clock Syracuse. The solar evaporation company have very extensive vats for making salt[6] but as our stay was very short at this place we defered the exhamination of the workes until our return.

About 2 miles west of nine mile creek the canal passes through a bed shelly of marls & near the surface of the ground there is a stratum of black mold. Mr. E gave us a lecture on this substance and observed that this according to Buckland always separated the Diluvial from the Post diluvial. For an exposition of this subject see the contraversy between Flemming & Buckland in the Bostan Journal.[7]

---

[3] The former name of the northern section of the present city of Syracuse, New York.

[4] That is, shell.

[5] Onondaga.

[6] The salt springs in the Syracuse area attracted settlers in the late eighteenth century. The opening of the canal stimulated the development of the salt industry which was already appreciable, even in 1826.

[7] Eaton's journal for this date specifically discusses this, the point being that the Biblical deluge would have removed such a material of vegetable origin. Henry's reference is to the *Boston Journal of Philosophy and the Arts*, 1824, 2:315–332, 543–557, reprinting the article of John Fleming from the *Edinburgh Philosophical Journal*, 1824, *11*:287–305 and Buckland's reply, pp. 304–319.

Buckland, following Cuvier and others, believed in a universal deluge. Unlike Cuvier, he identified this deluge with the one described in the Bible. His diluvial theory then required a distinction between alluvial deposits prior to the universal flood, the diluvial deposits, and alluvial deposits after the flood.

Fleming criticized Buckland, using the evidence of extinction and geographic distribution of both surviving and extinct species. His general position was important conceptually since he was arguing against the use of science to construct natural theologies and in favor of uniform causes, rather than catastrophes like the universal deluge.

Interestingly, Buckland's reply cites the favorable review by Edward Hitchcock of Amherst of his *Reliquiae Diluvianae* in *Silliman's Journal*, 1824, *8*:150–168, 317–338; and Hitchcock appears in Eaton's *Geology of the Erie Canal*, pp. 159–163. Eaton's concern for interpretation of the alluvial deposits, like Hitchcock's, apparently originated in a belief in a universal deluge and a taste for natural theology.

For the diluvial controversy, see Leroy E. Page, "Diluvialism and Its Critics in Great Britain in the Early Nineteenth Century," in *Towards a History of Geology*, C. J. Schneer, ed. (Cambridge, Massachusetts, 1969), pp. 255–271, and C. C. Gillispie, *Genesis and Geology* (Cambridge, Massachusetts, 1951), pp. 122–125.

HENRY'S CANAL TOUR JOURNAL

Henry Papers, Smithsonian Archives

Rochester monday 15 May [1826]

We this day visited the lower falls of the Genesee river which affords the most interesting exhibition of the rocky strata of the West that can be immagined.

The lowes rock is secondary saltrock or the variegated sand stone of Werner. The next above which appears like a fillet around the ledge is *Grey band* (or Gray Feke) and is about four feet thick. Above this is a greenish slate called by M^r E Feriferous slate and is the lowes of the feriferous rocks between this rock & the next. Above is found the extensive iron formation. By comparing the two rocks described from rememberance with the rocks which I observed at Martin's Mills on the little Beaver Kill one of the head branches of a branch of the East branch of the Delaware river.[1] They appear to be the same & have the same relative situation but this country between the Hudson & Delawar has been called entirely transition. Much remains to be done in examining the rocks of our country and this place should be exhamined. At the falls above the Feriferous slate is the feriferous sand rock of Eaton and above this is found the calciferous slate or the (second graywacke of E). The upper falls at the Village is composed of the last mentioned rock the iron formation does not appear until half a mile down the river.

The saliferous rock is used for building stone in the village but it does not appear to stand well the exposure to the weather & sometimes scales off as may be seen by the facing of the aqueduct over the river which is formed of this rock.

Mr. E's views of the strata at this place is undoubtedly correct but the names which he has given to the new strata may meet with some opposition.

Below the lower falls a bridge of a single arch was thrown across the river of 352 feet span. The crown of the arch was between two & three hundred feet above the water. This bridge was built by a company of gentlemen in order to divert a portion of the travel from the East to the ridge road past the village of Carthage.

---

[1] Henry recollected here some of his observations on the State Road Survey, on Tuesday, August 23, 1825, near Lemuel Martin's Mills in the vicinity of Liberty, New York. Henry noted at this point: "sandston or fine Brecia resting on red sandstone is seen at the [Beaverkill] falls small veins of coal are found in a slaty rock which rests on the sandstone also yellow ocher in small quantities in a soft clay stone." Book of Levels No. 3, "From Neversink," no pagination, August 23, 1825, Henry Papers, Smithsonian Archives.

HENRY'S CANAL TOUR JOURNAL
Henry Papers, Smithsonian Archives

Wednesday [May] 17th [1826]

Holley Wednesday 17th from Rochester to this place the banks are coulered with the disintegrated saliferous rock & the feriferous sand stone: about 8 miles miles west of Rochester the feriferous slate is seen in the canal. At about 10 miles the bottom of the canal is formed of the saliferous sand rock which continues to the village of Holley. At this village the highest embank on the whole canal for a few rods is thrown over sand creek; gard gates are placed at each extremity of this high embankment to stop the water from running from the canal if the embankment should breake.

About three years ago at the saltlick a fiew rods from the embankment up the creek, teeth of the Mammouth were found which was mentioned in the papers at the time.[1] The one salt spring on the canal west of the genessee river is at this place, but more than fifty are already known between the canal & Lake Ontario. Most of these are north of the ridge road and are situated in a lower part of the rock which may perhape account for their saltness as they are geologically lower. According to Mr E['s] theory they must percolat through more salt rock than when nearer the surface.[2]

Pot & pearl ashes are manufactured at Holley. The work men informed me that the salt made with lime would make pearl ash & that they paid 25 cts mor on a hundred for ashes so made than without lime. This subject is not well understood. Where does the carbonic acid com from in the pearlash? What chemical change does the salt undergo in pearling & what in mel[t]ing to form pot ashes?[3]

At murry's basin 33 mils from Rochester we found mytolites[4] in a loose stone of sulferous rock.

[1] e.g., *The Albany Argus*, September 20, 1822.

[2] See Amos Eaton, *A Geological and Agricultural Survey of the District Adjoining the Erie Canal . . .* part I (Albany, 1824), pp. 102–114.

[3] Pearlash is obtained from potash, which is merely the ash from burned wood or plants, by a succession of processes of washing and calcining. Pearlash is in general richer in potassium carbonate than crude potash, for two reasons: first, because numerous impurities have been removed; and second, because during calcination the hydroxide is carbonated. The addition of lime does not cause "pearling"; in fact, it detracts from that process insofar as pearling is considered formation of potassium carbonate. The lime absorbs carbon dioxide, leaving the final product slightly caustic, that is, with a certain amount of potassium hydroxide. According to one authority, it was a peculiarly American practice to add lime, not for its aid to pearling as Henry implies, but because semicaustic pearlash was in demand with soapmakers. See Harlow Bradley, "Potash from Wood and Plant Ashes," *Metallurgical and Chemical Engineering*, 1915, *13*:841–846.

[4] Probably fossil mytilids.

Mr E observed that Conybere divided the saliferous rock into variegated sand stone & red marle.

HENRY'S CANAL TOUR JOURNAL
Henry Papers, Smithsonian Archives

Thursday May 18 [1826]

At Mr Shearer's store 6 1/2 miles East of Lock Port is a burning spring of coal gas which burns with a dense white flame. It is in a basin at the side of the canal and was discovered in excavating the canal. The gas issues directly from the alluvial soil and in greate abundance.

This Place is in the town of Royalton and has no local name we proposed to call it Gas-Port and left a direction for having this name written on the bridge. By making a reservoir with an inverted barrel an apparatus may be constructed which would be very interesting to travellers on the canal.

Mr E was much pleased to find it carburetted hydrogen.

This is the fourth spring at a small distance found along the canal all above and coming almost directly from the saliferous rock.

Note[1] on our return 'Gas port' was painted on the two sides of the bridge across the canal at this place.

At Lock-port we enter the region of Geodiferous Limestone. The geodes are seen all along the sides of the deep cutting west of the lock.

The mineral [c]ontained in them are dogtooth spar, cal. spar, sul. stron., sulphurettee of zinc & copper, and snowy & transparen and anhydrus gypsum, there are several varieties of the anhydrate the dogtooth spar sometimes is found running into arragonite; selling of minerals has become a business of some profit at this place & large quantitiees of them have been sent to New York. They are also exposed at Niagara falls by a grocer who if he does not understand the cemical composition of minerals at least knows full well how to sell they at a very high price—a piece of dog tooth spar about 4 inches long & twon broad he offered after giving a lecture on its rairness & Beauty to sell for three dollars.

[1] It seems apparent from the text as well as a change in handwriting that Henry wrote the rest of this entry into his journal at some later date. Clinton records in his journal that the party passed through Gas Port on the 26th of May, so it is reasonable to assume that Henry wrote this section then or shortly thereafter.

HENRY'S CANAL TOUR JOURNAL

Henry Papers, Smithsonian Archives

May [19th[1] 1826] We left the canal at the mouth of the tonewanta creek in a hired waggon and traveled 11 miles to the falls.[2] When I visited the falls in Oct 1825 they did not answer my expectations. Perhaps I did not view them with propper poetical feelings, but in this visit I have been mor fortunate.[3]

We firs crossed over Porters bridge to bath island a small island between the mainland & goat island. A house of refreshment & a biliard room are placed on this island at which the visitor pays 2/– for crossing the bridge.

This bridge is a curiousity & was built by Gen Porter & his brother.[4] It is placed in the current of the rapids & seams to be threatened every moment with distruction by the angry waters. By a little observation it will be seen however that each pier is placed either against a projecting rock or in the eddy of a rock above. These rocks are however all covered with the water and the bridge seams to stand the full force of the current. The Indian Chief Red jacket once crossed this bridge & after attentively exhaimining each pier exclaimed to Gen. Porter "Dam Yankey cheat every thing" pointing at the same time at the river.[5]

These piers were placed in their proper situations by first setting the ones near shore & then making a scaffold by projecting two long & stiff pieces of timber over it into the river a few feet above the water and loading the ends on the land with heavy stones. The skeleton of the next pier was then [c]aried to the extremity of these timbers and sunk in the stream against or behind a rock with stones.

The bridge was thus completed to this pier and the long timbers as before was projected from it & another pier sunk and so on. A shorter bridge connects bath island with goat island.

---

[1] Henry wrote "20th" but from the other surviving journals this is clearly an error, perhaps arising because the entry was actually written on the following day.

[2] Clinton and some others walked to Niagara Falls.

[3] i.e., during the road survey. This may be the first example of Henry's talent for sarcasm and irony. Clinton's Journal for this day confesses that although powerfully affected while at the Falls, he could recollect little of it later. Henry seems to say that he now had the rapturous romantic reaction expected of him.

[4] Peter Buell Porter (1773–1844), a lawyer and New York politician, had earned his military rank commanding militia in the War of 1812. He held various political offices thereafter and was Secretary of War in the administration of John Quincy Adams. *DAB.* His brother was Augustus Porter.

[5] This anecdote about the Seneca Chief Red Jacket (1758–1830), *DAB,* also appears in Clinton's Journal.

HENRY'S CANAL TOUR JOURNAL
Henry Papers, Smithsonian Archives

May 24th [1826]

Black Rock. We returned to this place last evening and crossed over to Fort Erie this afternoon which is about one mile above Black rock on the opposite side of the river.[1] The fort is now in ruins being partialy demolished by the Americans when they evacuated it near the close of the war: part of the walls are however standing and the line of the brest works belonging to the fort as well as the sites of the batteries & intrenchments of the British thrown up during the siege are stil to be seen. This fort was taken by the Americans on the night of the 3 of july 18—.[2] The British forces under General Drummond[3] attacked the fort on the 15th of August 18— and was repulsed with great slauter. Colo. Drummond[4] with a great number of men was blown up on one of the batteries at the same moment Capt. M[c]. Donough[5] was killed & Major Burdsel[6] was shot through the mouth. In our visits to this place we were so fortunate as to be accompanied by Maj. Frasier[7] a gentleman who in the sortie from this place distinguished himself so as to be promoted from a Lieutenant to a Maj. & aiddecamp to Gen. Porter.[8] In walking from the Ferry house opposite Black rock we were first shown the first battery of the British on the road about one mile from the fort and near the bank of the river. About one fourth of a mile nearer the fort farther from the river is the intrenchment of the seccond battery and almost directly in the rear of the fort about 350 yds distance is the third battery. These batteries are all connected by a line of brest-works together with a block house on the extreme right. We were led by the Maj to the third battery and shown the very gun on which he was standing & in the act of spiking it with the ram rod of his pistol when he received a wound in

[1] i.e., across the Niagara River on the Canadian side.

[2] Henry did not know the year, apparently, for he left it blank. The siege of Fort Erie took place in 1814. The events, which occurred essentially as Henry has recounted them here, may be followed in closer detail in Louis L. Babcock, *The Siege of Fort Erie* (Buffalo, 1899).

[3] Sir Gordon Drummond (1772–1854). *DNB*.

[4] William Drummond, commissioned in 1807, was a Lieutenant Colonel in the 104th Foot Regiment. Great Britain, War Office, *A List of All the Officers of the Army . . .* (London, 1812).

[5] Patrick McDonough, from Pennsylvania, was commissioned in 1812 and in 1814 was transferred to the artillery. Francis B. Heitman, *Historical Register and Dictionary of the U.S. Army, 1789–1903*, 2 vols. (Washington, 1903), *I*:433.

[6] Benjamin Birdsall, from New York, was a Captain in 1814, and was promoted to Brevet Major for distinguished service on the defense of Fort Erie. He was killed by a soldier in 1818. Ibid., p. 127.

[7] Donald Fraser entered the service in 1812. He received the rank of Brevet Major for gallant conduct during the siege. He resigned in 1816, and was later a paymaster and, after 1841, a customs officer at Niagara. Ibid., p. 276.

[8] Peter Buell Porter, for whom see above, May [19, 1826], footnote 4.

the leg with a musket ball. Two other eighteen pounders lying near were spiked with rat-tailed files which enabled the Maj to distinguish the one on which he received his wound. Thise guns were unmounted & the trunnions broken off by the Americans after taking the battery. The sortie was so un-expected that the soldiers had not time to discharge the cannon and they remain loaded at this day as we proved by running a pole into one of them & feeling the ball or wad. The sortie was made on the day[9] of september about three o'clock in the afternoon of a rainy day.

The Americans had been besieged for more than 50 days & the siege was carried on with skil & persaverance by the enemy. General Porter crossed the river with about 800 volunteers & indians & a sortie was agreed upon by himself and General Brown.[10] The enemy had almost surrounded them except on the south & south-West which was supposed to be an impassible swamp but it was found that it might be crossed without much danger by cutting down the small trees and thus forming a road by throwing them across the path: The enterprise of cutting this road was in trusted to Maj. Frasier then Lieutenant & another Young Lieut. with the promis of per-motion if they succeeded & threatned with being cashiered if they failed. It was necessary that this plan should be kept a profound secret. A few men therefore from each company was ordered into the wood in the rear of the fort under some pretence and then put under gard to prevent desertion until their service should be wanted. When all things were readdy, the party where led silently up to within a few rods of the enemys brest work and then commenced chopping towards the fort. The General in order to draw the attention of the enemy order the artillery to commense a brisk fire on the batteries near the river. Next day the troop were led to the charge along this road, the enemy were routed and the americans kept pos-session of the fort until near the close of the war. A few rods to the north we were shewn the spot where the oficers & men were buried that were killed at the assault on the fort. The place may be known, by a shallow trench about 4 rods long & 5 or six feet wide formed by the sinking of the ground on the decaying of the bodies. They were thrown in to the ditch in-discriminately, officers, non commissioned officers & soldiers. The bodies were placed head to foot crossway three & four deep with Col. Drummond on the right of the whole. The sinking of the ground showes that the mor-tal remains of these gallant soldiers are fast mingling with their mother earth & the demolishing hand of time is nearly as rapidly leveling the mon-uments of their labour and the reliques of their valour.

[9] Henry left blank the day of the month.
[10] Jacob Jennings Brown (1775–1828) was in the American military from 1809 until his death. He was General in Chief of the Army, 1821–1828. *DAB*.

HENRY'S CANAL TOUR JOURNAL
Henry Papers, Smithsonian Archives

Saturday May 27th 1826

Mr E related several annecdotes of Wasington Ervin[1] among others that the origin of his 'Death of a Friend'[2] was the death of Miss Matilda Holfman daughter of Mr Holfman Esq of New York. Ervin was engaged to be maried to this young lady when about eighteen years old and she eleven. Miss Holfman died at the age of eighteen of a consumption & Mr Ervin as ever since remained a batchelor & is now about 43[3] years old. Mr E. was his fellow student in Mr Holfmans office.[4]

[1] Washington Irving (1783–1859), the writer. *DAB*.

[2] Eaton was probably referring to passages in "Rural Funerals," *The Sketch Book* (New York, 1819–1820), in which Irving discourses at length on the deaths of friends. The *DAB* supports Eaton's account in suggesting that his comments therein on the death of a lover were inspired by the death of Matilda Hoffman.

[3] The figure is not clear in Henry's manuscript; it could be 43, 46, or 48. Irving was 43 in 1826.

[4] The events related in this paragraph, according to the *DAB* account of Irving, have been "oversentimentalized," though there is no doubt that they obsessed Irving as much as his biographers. Josiah Ogden Hoffman (1766–1837) was a prominent New York lawyer and judge of the New York superior court, 1828–1837. *DAB*. His daughter Matilda died of tuberculosis in 1809. For Eaton's law studies and his friendship with Irving, see Ethel McAllister, *Amos Eaton* (Philadelphia, 1941), pp. 20–24.

HENRY'S CANAL TOUR JOURNAL
Henry Papers, Smithsonian Archives

Rochester Monday May [29[th]][1] 1826. Le[f]t this place at 4 O clock P.M. with an addition to our party of Professor Rafinesque of the University of Transylvania, Ky.[2] The Professor is a short man stoutly formed and very plainly dressed. He appears to be about 40 years old and speaks the english very purely but with a strong French accent. His head is somewhat baled and he combes his hair directly across, has darke eyes & on the whole a pleasing countenance.

[1] Given as "30th" in original but from other journals this is the date of writing, not of the events described.

[2] Constantine Samuel Rafinesque (1783–1840), *DAB*, a naturalist then teaching at Transylvania University in Lexington, Kentucky. Rafinesque was born in Turkey of Franco-German parents. The brief account Henry gives of his arrival is substantially correct.

I learned nothing of his history but that he came to this country very young, returned to France and when coming again to America was shipwrecked and lost all his drawing, manuscripts, books &cc.

His fort appears to be zoology & botany and in these sciences he is very industrious but his usefulness is said to be much impaired by his proness to make new genera & species.[3]

He scetches very rapidly and took views of the upper & lower falls at Rochester.

 shell with a streight hinge he calls productus & belong to the great family of the terabratula; limestone interely made up of little shells he calls Lumacella formation from a word in the Spanish meaning small shells; shells with a narrow hing and ribed are terabratula.

According to Prof Raf. all venamus snakes may be known at the first sight by the broadness of the jaws which in the rattle snake the copperhead &c. are wider than the neck being inlarged in breadth by the poisoness fangs. I think this observation very important and should be bourn in remembrance.

[3] The conventional view of Rafinesque. To this add the conventional view that he never quite attained the discipline required for admission into the scientific community. Cf. Nathan Reingold, ed., *Science in Nineteenth-Century America* (New York, 1964), pp. 41–44.

HENRY'S CANAL TOUR JOURNAL
Henry Papers, Smithsonian Archives

[May] 31st [1826]

Palmyra. I left the canal at this place and took the stage for Albany via Syracuse, Manlius & Cherry Valley.[1]

In ascending the hill from Manlius towards Nelson the cornintiferous lime rock[2] is seen on the roadside about one mile from the village. Higher up the hill I collected a specimen of a slaty rock which appears to be Pyritiferous rock.[3] The calciferous rock appears much lower but I [may] be

[1] The rest of the party continued by the canal, reaching Troy on the tenth of June. See Clinton's diary, loc. cit., p. 305.
[2] See Amos Eaton, *A Geological and Agricultural Survey of the District Adjoining the* *Erie Canal* . . . , part I (Albany, 1824), pp. 136–138 for this term, which meant merely the presence of much hornstone.
[3] Ibid., pp. 139–145.

mistaken in the position of the limestone & this rock may be calciferous slate. Well caracterized cornintiferous lime stone is seen in several places between Cazenovia & cherry valley on the high ground.

Mr E Defines a faculty of the mind to be that power which produces any results different from any other result. Love Anger &c.[4]

[4] Henry has inscribed two large question marks just below this passage which seems an afterthought, not part of the journal strictly speaking.

TO [? GEORGE W. CLINTON][1]
Retained Copy, Henry Papers, Smithsonian Archives

Albany. June 7th 1826

Dear Sir

On my way home I stoped at Cherry Valley[2] long enough to make the following Geological section which I think is nearly correct. It crosses the falls of Bosman's creek and is parallel to the canal. These falls are estimated to be about 800 feet above the canejoharie level and are the same you refered me to. I collected specimens of each rock which I will send to Mr Eaton when I return from West Point.[3]

[1] Henry's notation at the bottom of this document reads "Copy to G W Clinton" and we have no further evidence that the letter was intended primarily for Clinton. It is possible that this single sheet was a letter to someone else, and that Henry noted on his retained copy that a copy was sent to Clinton. Nonetheless, it is fair to assume that Clinton was the recipient of a letter resembling this copy retained by Henry.

[2] Henry left the Erie Canal tour on May 31 at Palmyra, New York, to return to Albany by stagecoach, while Clinton continued on the tour. See above, Henry's Canal Tour Journal, [May] 31, [1826].

[3] For Henry's account of his trip to West Point, see the next document.

The seccond stratum is the same rock seen at the village and from which the cherry valley marble is taken. It resembles the metaliferous limestone but it evidently rests on one of the first or second graywackes & therefore cannot be that rock.

Please give the enclosed note to Prof. Eaton. If any other charges remain, I will pay them when I return.

HENRY'S JOURNAL OF A TRIP TO WEST POINT AND NEW YORK[1]

Henry Papers, Smithsonian Archives

Monday June 12 [1826]

I this morning in company with a Mr. Hide[2] from Bath in Maine visited the iron workes called the West Point foundry.[3] These works are owned by a company of gentlemen in New York one of which is Prof. Renwick's brother.[4] These workes are the most extensive of the kind in this state. Almost all the large iron articles from New York are cast at this place such as the principal parts of the steam engines & a large number of cannon for the United States are annually cast. The cannon are cast sollid in a pit with the large end down so that the pour is on the end. This part is cut off and the canon placed in a revolving collar on centres and made to turn round by water power with a slow motion. A large drill is pressed against the end equably by a weight. The boring is thus completed in a horizontal position in about one week. The canon are all proved by a United States Officer with a double charge of powder and two balls. The piece is discharged by a slow match against a bank. If they stand the proof the officer stamps them with the inspectors marke. A steam sylendar of 50 inches was laid on the

[1] This document consists of several sheets folded over once to make a sort of booklet. It contains entries from June 12, 15, 22, and 27, 1826.

[2] Probably one of the Hyde brothers, Jonathan (1772–1850) or Zina (1787–1856), both of whom were in the iron and steel trade. P. M. Reid, *History of Bath and Environs* (Portland, 1894), pp. 322–326.

[3] Founded in 1818 at the request of the government to manufacture cannons and munitions, the Foundry, as Henry states below, expanded its scope to include products for the civilian economy. Its high point was during the Civil War when its work force was 800–

1000. It continued to produce cannons for Spain and Latin American countries afterward but the coming of steel ordnance led to its closing in 1906. J. P. Lesley, *The Iron Manufacturer's Guide to the Furnaces, Forges, and Rolling Mills of the United States* . . . (New York, 1859), pp. 150, 213; William J. Blake, *The History of Putnam County, New York* (New York, 1849), pp. 244–245; J. S. H. Zimm et al., ed., *Southeastern New York*, 3 vols. (New York, 1946), 2:801, 908, 937, 947–948, 978.

[4] Either William Renwick (1799–1847) or Robert Jeffrey Renwick (1793–1875). Helen H. McIver, *Genealogy of the Renwick Family* (New York, 1924), pp. 3–4.

frames to be bored. This opperation would probably take two weeks. These sylendars are cast without a pattern by sweeping an outter & an inner molde in the manner of casting bells.[5] The machinery is propelled by a small stream of water falling on a water wheel of 38 feet in diameter. This wheel is certainly a great curiosity not only from its size but also from the beauty of its motion. A blast furnace is now erecting for smelting the silicious ore which abounds in the highlands around West Point, a mill for grinding blackining or coal dust for sprinkling the casting sand and another for beating the casting sand are nearly completed. The site of this work is badly chosen. The water power is insufficient at all seasons to propell all the work and there is a great want of room around the work as they are situated in [a] ravine. The houses of the work men are all situated on the hill above the foundry except one or two on the bank of a marsh which extends from the foundry to the island in front of West Point.

About 180 men are employed in these workes several of which receive 2 dollars & 50 cts. per day.[6] They are mostly Irish. The canon balls are cast in cast iron moldes after wards ground on grindstones and passed through a cylendar as a gage. They are then proved by raising them about 15 feet with a piling engine & dropping them on a piece of iron. If they do not break they are considered good. The chartered capital of the company

---

[5] Strictly speaking, sweeping an outer mold did not normally occur in bell casting in this period. By a pattern, Henry refers to a dummy of the object to be cast around which a mold was constructed. This was done in the casting of cannons Henry discusses above. Many cylinders were not cast by the use of patterns but a wooden profile or "batter board" was swept around on an axis to generate the inner shape as with bells. Then an outer shell or jacket was built up around the inner core, now filled with sand. A space was next made between the outer jacket and the inner sand core, perhaps by the lost wax process. This space was somewhat thicker than the desired size of the finished bell or cylinder, which required boring. This boring is what Henry refers to. A. Rees, *The Cyclopaedia* . . . (London, 1819), 6: "Boring of Cannon"; *10*: "Cylinder Boring"; *15*: "Foundery, casting of bells"; *Encyclopedia Metropolitana* (London, 1845), 8:650–655.

[6] A recent article by Nathan Rosenberg, "Anglo-American Wage Differences in the 1820's," *Journal of Economic History*, 1967, 27:221–229, based on Zachariah Allen's *The Science of Mechanics* (Providence, 1829), gives the daily pay of the best machine maker, forger, etc., at $1.50–$1.75. Victor S. Clark, *History of Manufactures in the United States*, 3 vols. (Washington, 1916–1929), *1*:389–397, gives somewhat higher rates for a founder in Pennsylvania, ca. 1823, who could make $1,000 per annum. Peter Temin, *Iron and Steel in Nineteenth Century America* . . . (Cambridge, Massachusetts, 1964), pp. 86–88, notes that most wages at an "iron plantation" in 1830 were about $20 per month but skilled workers received piece rates and earned rather more.

The West Point workers were very skilled and received top wages. This assumption is reinforced by what we know of the enlightened labor practices of the owners by the standards of the day. Blake, op. cit., 244–245, for example, noted that, "The men receive their wages every two weeks, and work but ten hours per day. If the necessity of the work requires them to work longer, they are paid accordingly. . . . The means and appliances sometimes attempted to be used by other manufacturing establishments to control the political sentiments of their workmen, are not countenanced here. . . ."

is one hundred thousand dollars but more than twice that sum is probably at present invested.

The chemical laboratory [at the Military Academy] is a room about 20 feet square. About one half is appropriated to the laboratory propper. The other half to the schollars seats which is fronted by a railing of pine rods. The whole room though small has a neate airy appearance. On the wall directly facing the audience is painted the different thermometrical scales. On each side of room shelves & glass cases are placed to contain apparatus & the minerological cabinet which is rather small although will chosen.

Assist. Prof. Prescot[7] has adopted a peculiar arrangement as regards his bottles. They are placed on a flight of perforated shelves resembling a flight of stairs. This arrangement is very convenient and occupies very little space. One article very necasary in teaching chemestrys is found in this room viz a black board on which the student is taught the atomic theory and all algebraical formula in chemestry. Indeed it appears to be one of the principles of teaching in this institution that every thing as far as practical should be demonstrated on the black board. The student is even required to draw all articles of chemical aparatus & explain them in this way.[8]

Attended the exhamination of Lieutenat Prescotts section in chemestry. This young gentleman bids fair to become one of the first chemests in the country. His mechanical & mathematical knowledge together withe his dexterity of manipulation give him a descided advantage over many of more reputation but less merit. The section was minutely examined on the atomic theory, the principles [of] galvinism & the facts relating to electromagnatism.

To expain the phenomina of electromagnitism suppose the two poles of

[7] Jonathan Prescott (d. 1837, aged 37) had been a West Point Cadet, 1818–1821, became Assistant Professor of Engineering, 1821–1822, then Assistant Professor of Chemistry, Mineralogy, and Geology, 1822–1826 at the school. From late 1826 he was on topographical and engineering duty. He resigned his commission in 1833. G. W. Cullum, *Biographical Register of the Officers and Graduates of the United States Military Academy*, rev. ed., 2 vols. (New York, 1879), *1*:264.

[8] "The division of classes into smaller sections, with more liberal use of the blackboard, began at the same time [1817], these beneficial changes being inspired by Major [Sylvanus] Thayer.

"The blackboard had been used long before this and was a favorite method of Mr. George Bacon, who was the civilian teacher of the Academy. Mr. Bacon gave to Cadet [Joseph Gardner] Swift in the autumn of 1801, a specimen of his mode of teaching at the blackboard...."

We take blackboards for granted. Henry noted their use because they were not common in 1826. It is a measure of the Military Academy's progressiveness in that day that blackboards were used there in 1801 and became common after 1817. The quotation is from *The Centennial of the United States Military Academy at West Point, New York, 1802–1902*, 2 vols. (Washington, 1904), *1*:244. The most recent serious history of the Academy is S. E. Ambrose, *Duty, Honor, Country: A History of West Point* (Baltimore, 1966).

a battery placed in the magnetic meridian and these poles united by a wire bent so as to form the three sides of a rectangular parallelogram with the angles above the poles of the battery. Now suppose a current of the electric fluid to pass from the negative pole in a spiral direction round the wire with the turns of the spiral running from left to right (the observer being supposed to face the north). Suppose this fluid to have an attraction for the north pole of the magnet and we can then explain all the phenomina of the variation of the needle. If the needle be placed above the conducting wire the current will carry the north pole to the East, if below to the West. If on the East side of the wire the north pole will be <*elevated*> depressed on the <*east*> west the same pole will be elevated.

For an account of several phenomena see 3[d] vol. of Hares Henry.[9]

Prof. Dana[10] informed me that all the electromagnetic phenomina may be shown by a battery composed of 20 plates of 10 inches square & that he used a needl mad bar-shaped about 4 inches long and 1/4 of an inch wide suspended on the edge so that the class might see every movement.

The rack for bottles, mentioned before, it should be observed, is labeled, Earths, Acids, Combustibles, Carbonates, Sulphates, Nitrates, etc. etc. Matrasses for wholding flasxs may be made as they are at the Point from the flag which formes the covering of oil bottles, or the husk of indian corn may be used for the same purpose.

---

[9] William Henry, *The Elements of Experimental Chemistry . . . The Second American from the Eighth London Edition, . . . Together with . . . A Theory of Galvanism by Robert Hare . . .* , 3 vols. (Philadelphia, 1823). A copy of the second edition is in Joseph Henry's Library (vols. 2 and 3 only). William Henry (1774–1836, *DNB*), chemist, is perhaps best known now for "Henry's Law" and for his close friendship and collaboration with John Dalton. Robert Hare (1781–1858, *DAB*), American chemist, influenced Joseph Henry. See below, Silliman to Hare, October 11, 1832.

The theory advanced in this paragraph is not found, however, in "Hare's Henry," but seems to be that expounded by Prescott. It is in fact a modification of Oersted's. Hans Christian Oersted (1777–1851), the Danish natural philosopher and physicist, whose discovery in 1820 of the effect of an electric current on a magnet began a new era in the science of electricity, will of course appear and reappear in these volun..es. It is sufficient here to point out that Oersted had said in the original communication of his discovery that "all the effects on the north pole [of the magnetic needle] . . . are easily understood by supposing that negative electricity moves in a spiral line bent towards the right, and propels the north pole, but does not act on the south pole." "Experiments on the Effect of a Current of Electricity on the Magnetic Needle," *Annals of Philosophy,* 1820, *16:*273–276. A similar left-handed spiral of positive electricity worked on the south pole. As far as Joseph Henry's brief description allows one to judge, Prescott (if it was Prescott) had adapted Oersted's ideas to a one-fluid theory of electricity ("*the* electric fluid").

[10] James Freeman Dana (1793–1827), chemist, was a graduate of Harvard (1813), Professor of Chemistry and Mineralogy at Dartmouth (1820–1826) and Professor of Chemistry at the New York College of Physicians and Surgeons (1826–1827). *DAB.* Dana was a member of the West Point Board of Visitors, for which see below, footnote 18.

Dr. Torrey[11] intends making one of Wallostons scales of chemical equivalents[12] & to use Mr. Thompson's new attomic numbers.[13] In forming the platina spunge Lt. Prescot makes use of the platina foil a narrow slip of which he dips into the moist precipitate[14] and heats it with the flame of a lamp & a blow pipe, then dips the foil into the precipitate again and so on until a ball is formed as large as a large sised pea. This is a very quick and sure method & attended with little trouble.

Mr. Canada[15] Mr. Kane[16] his Lady & myself visited the ruins of fort Putnam or fort Put as it is called for brevity. This fort was built during the revolutionary war. It commands the river up & down several miles & may will be called the Gibralter of America being placed on the pinacle of a crag of granite and defendid on the west by a perpendicular ledge of rocks more than one hundred feet high on the river side. Also the assent is steep. The fort by measurement is found to be about [?] feet[17] above tide & 450 above the plain of the point. It is now in a very delapidated condition not so much from time as the almos sacreligious parsimony of the person who

---

[11] John Torrey (1796–1873) was then serving as Professor of Chemistry, Mineralogy, and Geology at West Point. He is best known as a botanist but through most of his life earned a living as a chemist. Torrey, who first appears in a document at this point, became a close friend of Henry's and a colleague at Princeton. He will reappear, and prominently, in subsequent volumes. Although we have not located any evidence on the point, Torrey had connections with both Eaton and T. R. Beck and may have met Henry before this date. *DAB* and A. D. Rodgers III, *John Torrey, a Story of North American Botany* (Princeton, 1942).

[12] William Hyde Wollaston (1766–1828), chemist, physicist, and physiologist, was educated at Cambridge. He took an M.D. degree and practiced medicine from 1789 until 1800, when he abandoned medicine for science. *DNB*. His paper, "A Synoptic Scale of Chemical Equivalents," *Phil. Trans.*, 1814, *104*:1–22 described a scale which Lewis C. Beck and Joseph Henry later improved on. See below, L. C. Beck to Joseph Henry, April 15, 1827. Torrey seems not to have taken part in their effort.

[13] Thomas Thomson had recently published *An Attempt to Establish the First Principles of Chemistry by Experiment*, 2 vols. (London, 1825), by which he hoped to establish a correct system of atomic weights.

[14] This is apparently a description of the re-

actions when platinum is dissolved in aqua regia. After boiling in some HNO_3, the platinum is precipitated by sal ammoniac forming an ammonium-chloride of platinum. When heated, chlorine and ammonia are released, leaving behind a spongy mass of platinum. For a contemporary description, see L. C. Beck, *A Manual of Chemistry* (Albany, 1831), p. 380.

[15] Thomas Kennedy (1776–1832), a member of the Board of Visitors, a member of the Maryland legislature best known for his efforts (which succeeded in 1826) to remove the discriminatory aspect of the Maryland constitution which denied full rights to non-Christians. E. Milton Altfield, *The Jew's Struggle for Religious and Civil Liberty in Maryland* (Baltimore, 1924), pp. 6–43.

[16] John Kintzing Kane (1795–1858), *DAB*. Another member of the Board of Visitors, Kane was a Yale graduate (1814) who practiced law in Philadelphia. A Jackson supporter, Kane was Attorney General of Pennsylvania (1845) and a U.S. District Court Judge (1846–1858). He joined the American Philosophical Society in 1826; from 1828 until his death Kane was an officer of the Society, being its President, 1857–1858. He was the father of Elisha Kent Kane (1820–1857), the Arctic explorer. *DAB*.

[17] A space left for the number was never filled in.

owned the land before it was purchased by the U.S. The walls were torn down and carried to the plain for building stone but the transportation must have cost mor than stones might have been blastd for on the plain. This fort was commanded by a small battery on the hill directly in the rear; the remains of the works are stil to be seen. The front & south sides of the fort were lined on the inside by a row of bomb proof sells two of which have chimneys standing & were probably for the officers.

June 15 The Board of Visitors[18] this day gave a dinner to the accademic staff. Gen Houston[19] presided at one end of the table & Com. Chauncy[20] at the other. After the cloth was removed several toasts were given & the company repaired to the bank of the river to see the cadetts fire at a target on the opposite side of the river. Several bomb shells where thrown and burst in the air at a great hight. The sight was truly grand. On bursting a cloud of dense smoke was instantly formed & a report lowder than the cannon. The bomb could be plainly seen during the whole flight.

New York June 22, 1826

This evening visited Peals museum in Broadway.[21] This museum is owned by a son of Peal[22] of Philadelphia. It consists of three rooms the first appropriated to natural hystory the 2^d to Paintings. The third a lecture room in which Mr. Peal exhibited a number of experiments with oxygen &

[18] At this point we first learn of the Board from Henry. This was the occasion of their annual visitation to inspect West Point. Although we have no evidence on this matter, Henry's presence probably was no coincidental. Torrey or Prescott on the faculty might have invited him. Of the members of the Board, Henry may have known one whose name does not appear in this entry, James Dean (1778–1849) who had taught natural philosophy at the University of Vermont from 1820 to 1824. We have no evidence of any direct contact with James F. Dana before this date. Another member of the Board of Visitors, George Ticknor (1791–1871), the literary historian from Harvard, plays a very minor role subsequently in Henry's life in the squabble over the Smithsonian's library policy. See the Report of the Board of Visitors to West Point, 1826, in RG 94, National Archives, with its account of the stay at the Academy, June 5–24, 1826.

[19] Samuel Houston (1793–1863), *DAB,* better known for his role in winning Texas independence. At this date he was in the House of Representatives, serving on the Committee on Military Affairs, and was chosen President of the Board of Visitors. His title was by virtue of his 1821 election as Major General in the Tennessee militia.

[20] Commodore Isaac Chauncey (1772–1840), *DAB,* was then in command of the New York Navy Yard. He had charge of the naval forces on Lakes Ontario and Erie, 1812–1815. From 1821 to 1824 and from 1832 to 1840 Chauncey was on the Board of Navy Commissioners, a body which existed from 1815 to 1842 and had charge of naval supplies and the construction, equipment, and employment of naval vessels and armaments.

[21] This was the New York branch of the museum established in Philadelphia by Charles Willson Peale, the leading one in the nation at that date and highly influential in the subsequent history of museums in the nation. It originated in 1784–1786 when Peale added natural history curiosities to his portrait gallery. In 1810 his sons took over the management. The New York branch opened in 1825 but closed in the panic of 1837 when P. T. Barnum picked up pieces of the Peale museum empire. For the details of this story, see C. C. Sellers, *Charles Willson Peale,* 2 vols. (Philadelphia, 1947).

[22] Rubens Peale (1784–1865).

hydrogen gases. The experiments wher very neatly performed on a small scale in opperating with the compound blow pipe. He used substances about the size of a pea such as copper silver cast iron & lime. The copper burned with a blue flame, the silver also burned blue from the alloy contained in the sixpeny piece used in the experiment. The cast iron gave most vivid sintellations & the lime produced a light too intense for the eye to look upon (this is a beautiful experiment). His method of exploding hydrogen was also peculiarly neat. The mouth of the pistol was held down and a taper touched to the touch-hole. The gas then burned with a lambent flame from the hole but by turning the mouth of the pistol gently up the atmospheric air rushed in and mixing with the hydrogen produced an explotion very loud. The table on which the experiments were performed was lightened by gas & before each burner was placed a piece of horn to keep the light from the eyes of the audience and throw it on the table.

New York June 27th 1826

Mr. R Patten[23] informed me that he usually touched magnetic bars by placing a horseshoe magnet on a circle of bars & moving it round over every bar in the same manner that I have been in the habit of doing the same. He tolde me that he was about to make a compound horseshoe that would lift 150 lbs. He also stated that magnetic bars should always be made from steel that had been much hammered. He usually forges them from a large bar of steel. Some magnets do not magnetize as freely as others. In making a powerfull magnet the shape should be a horse-shoe and each bar should be as thin as a saw blade, magnatised separately and united all the north poles together with screws or rivetts of lead. Mr. P. sayes that he touches them repeatedly and then lays them by for a day or two & then touches them again until they have received the maximum of strength.

The points of the shoes are only hardened. He showed me one about 6 inches long & 2 inches thick that when first touched would lift 60 lbs. This magnet was incased in brass & composed of about 6 bars united by screws.

[23] Richard Patten (1792–1865), a maker and dealer in mathematical, surveying, and navigation instruments. About 1840 or 1841 Patten moved to Washington, apparently to provide instruments for Ferdinand Rudolph Hassler's Coast Survey. From 1849 to 1860 he was in Baltimore; he returned to Washington around 1862. From Silvio Bedini's forthcoming "Early American Mathematical Practitioners (A Biographical Dictionary)."

September 8, 1826

EXCERPT,[1] MINUTES, ACADEMY TRUSTEES
Trustees' Minutes, 1:274, Albany Academy Archives

Sept[r] 8. 1826

Professor Henry, being to deliver an Address[2] previous to entering on the duties of his office, it was resolved that the Trustees will meet at the hall of the Academy on Monday next at half past 9 am, that M[r] Hawley be requested to address Professor Henry on the part of the Board & that the Rev[d] M[r] Ferris be requested to officiate.

On Motion

Resolved that Professor Henry be allowed the use of the South West Room in the third story of the Academy, during the pleasure of the Board.

[1] Routine business has been omitted.
[2] For which see below, Henry's Inaugural Address to the Albany Academy, September 11, 1826.

MINUTES, ACADEMY TRUSTEES
Trustees' Minutes, 1:275, Albany Academy Archives

Sept[r] 11. 1826

The Trustees met, pursuant to adjournment

Present

| John W. Yates | P. Gansevoort | Isaac Ferris | Henry R Weed |
| G. Hawley | C R. Webster | John Ludlow | T R Beck |

In compliance with previous arrangements,[1] the Trustees met this day, in the hall of the Academy, when M[r] Hawley on the part of the Trustees delivered an address to the Professor Elect, after which Professor Henry read a Dissertation[2] of the importance of Mathematical Learning.[3] The Exercises were concluded with prayer by the Rev[d] M[r] Ferris.

[1] See the minutes for September 8, 1826.
[2] See next document.
[3] The addresses were published in the *Albany Argus and City Gazette*, September 18, 1826. Henry's was abridged, but Hawley's brief remarks appear to have been given in full. Hawley welcomed Henry to the faculty, and spoke of the significance of his position:

The department of Mathematics and Natural Philosophy . . . is one of the most important in this institution. It forms an integral part of the plan of education, now happily established here, which cannot be dispensed with without deranging the whole system. . . . Without intending to derogate from the importance and value of the classical department, the Trustees are free to acknowledge that they cherish with peculiar favor and regard that department of study which is best fitted to prepare the greatest

On Motion,

Resolved that a copy of the above addresses be requested for publication.
Adjourned.

---

number of pupils for the useful pursuits of active life: They consider this institution a local one, established for the special benefit of the city whose name it bears . . . ; they have, therefore, always regarded the English department with special favor, inasmuch as it is calculated to supply the wants of much the greatest number of our citizens; the clas-sical department being designed only for those who look to the learned professions for future occupation.

Hawley went on to impress upon Henry the seriousness of his obligations, adding however that since Henry had been a pupil in the Academy, and "received the greater part of [his] education under its instructors," he knew

what his duties would be. Henry's having attended the Academy, Hawley concluded,

is adverted to by the Trustees with peculiar satisfaction. It is considered by them a proof that the system pursued here, is capable of preparing youth for the highest duties to which they may be called in manhood.

In this short statement, Hawley gave as clear a statement of the educational policy followed by the Trustees as we have met with. It should be noted, however, that despite his attempt to make Henry a son of the Academy, Henry always represented himself as "principally self educated." See below, Henry to John Maclean, June 28, 1832.

INAUGURAL ADDRESS TO ALBANY ACADEMY, SEPTEMBER 11, 1826[1]
Draft, Henry Papers, Smithsonian Archives[2]

Henry's inauguration as Professor of Mathematics and Natural Philosophy at the Albany Academy was the first formal event in his career as educator and physicist. In accepting his position at the Academy, he expressed his understand-

---

[1] Henry's inauguration was an important occasion for the Academy. Gideon Hawley, Academy Trustee and Secretary of the Board of Regents, introduced Henry to the gathering. Hawley's remarks and parts of Henry's address were published in the *Albany Argus and City Gazette* on September 18 (for Hawley's introduction, see above, Academy Trustees' Minutes, September 11, 1826, footnote 3).

It is noteworthy that Henry was the only Academy professor ever to be so honored. According to Henry P. Warren, Principal of the Academy in 1913: "He was inducted into office with much form in our chapel, the only instance in the history of the Academy. Had the trustees an inkling of the fame that awaited the modest young professor?" *The Celebration of the Centennial Anniversary of*

the Founding of the Albany Academy (Albany, 1914), p. 25.

[2] This document appears to be a late or possibly final draft of Henry's remarks. Though the manuscript contains substantial revisions, the excerpts published in the *Argus* follow the corresponding passages in this draft almost verbatim (the *Argus* published approximately the last third of the draft). Except for the revisions, the manuscript is neatly penned, as if intended as a reading copy or as a publication copy for the *Argus*. The neat handwriting, not at all typical of Henry (the spelling too is above par), indicates he had made a special effort to write legibly and accurately.

The manuscript was extensively revised in both ink and pencil. Most of the revisions, which include several rewritten passages, are in Henry's usual scrawl. Some of the penciled

ing of scientific and mathematical traditions. Rather stiffly but confidently expressed, Henry's speech follows the typical lines of an inaugural address: he reviews the history of his discipline, considers its present state, and looks to the future. He begins with a historical overview of mathematics, taking advantage of this first opportunity to demonstrate his erudition. He then turns from the formal history to examples of current research, chiefly in the application of calculus to natural philosophy. While Henry almost never used higher mathematics in his published researches, his speech reveals that, despite his experimental bent, he recognized the importance of the mathematical approach to nature. After describing some of the more arcane aspects of mathematical physics, he then discusses the application of mathematics to technology and to the amelioration of man's estate. Impressed by recent progress in internal improvements, especially the construction of the Erie Canal, he optimistically foresees the merger in America of mathematics, science, and technology. In reviewing the history and progress of mathematics and natural philosophy, Henry is imparting received ideas and opinions. But it should be kept in mind that his account also reflects his own visions of the nature and future of the mathematical sciences and technology.

The branch of <*education*> learning it becomes my duty to teach has at all times in every civilized country been considered of great importance. It presents monuments of the human intellect, that chalenge the highest admiration & affords unlimited scope for talents & research.

To explain all the relations, boundaries & divisions of this science connected as it is with the whole circle of our knowledge, would be a design by far too extensive for a <*communication, circumstance*> occasion of the present kind & greatly beyond my abilities to execute. My intention is therefore merely to trace a rapid outline of its progres, to point out some of its many applications to the affairs of ordinary life, and to consider its

---

changes, however, may not have been made by Henry—perhaps by the editor of the *Argus*, perhaps by some unidentified friend.

We do not know how many drafts Henry made of his speech. Among his papers, there is only one other document relating to the address, a one-page fragment in Henry's hand bearing the label "accepting Prof: Albany Ac." The fragment contains what Henry may have used as an introduction to his remarks:

I receive the professorship which a liberal and enlightened board of trustees have done the honour to confide to my charge with feelings of gratitude & pleasure not unmingled however with anxiety. In thus publically accepting it I in effect give a pledge that I will discharge all its duties to the utmost of my power and always endeavor with the continuance & support of the present learned & experienced faculty to preserve the reputation & promote the honour of the Institution to which I am about becoming attached.

But I must beg for myself the indulgence which the candid & discriminating inhabitants of this city are allways willing [to] bestow in a first attempt in a new & untried pursuit.

The remainder of the document, written in pencil, duplicates passages in the main draft.

importance as a branch of education in its expanding influence on the mind.[3] A brief illustration of these topics it is hoped will not be thought unappropriate to this occasion.

Mathematics (in the strict sense of the term) is that science which has for its object the relations of quantities, or it is a comparison of those things that can be multiplied, divided or measured, such as extention duration & magnitude.

It has been divided into two kinds *pure* & *mixed*. *Pure* mathematics studies[4] the relations of quantities abstractly or considers them independantly of any substance actually existing. But *mixed* or physico-mathematics investigates these relations in connection with some known law of nature or with reference to the transactions of <*business in*> the affairs of society. Thus in surveying, its principles are applied to the measurement of land, in optics to the properties of light, in astronomy to the motion of the heavenly bodies. and in Political economy to the doctrine of annuites, the amount of interest &c.[5]

---

[3] On Henry's ideas of mathematics as a mental discipline, see below, footnote 46.

[4] Above "studies," "regards" is written in pencil.

[5] In this discussion of pure and mixed mathematics, Henry is invoking traditional ideas about the nature and classification of scientific knowledge. Pure mathematics applied mathematical deduction to abstract axioms and definitions without any reference to nature. Mixed mathematics, also termed compound or physico-mathematics, applied these same deductive procedures, not to abstract axioms, but to fundamental natural principles, discovered by observation, experiment, and induction. It normally included fields such as optics, acoustics, mechanics, astronomy, and hydrodynamics. In other words, what we now call mathematical or theoretical physics was then classified as a branch of mathematics. While the mixed sciences were distinguished from the more qualitative, experimental sciences such as chemistry, meteorology, and geology, the boundaries of mixed mathematics were neither precise nor fixed. When an experimental science became sufficiently mathematical, it too became a part of mixed mathematics. Note that Henry even included applied mathematical disciplines such as surveying and political economy among the mixed sciences. Usually, however, these applied fields were classified as "practical mathematics" or "applied science." In any case,

Henry believed that, to varying degrees, mathematics was intermixed with both the physical sciences and technology. For contemporary interpretations of pure and mixed mathematics, see the scientific encyclopedias and dictionaries cited below.

According to J. E. Montucla, the term mixed mathematics can be traced at least as far back as the seventeenth century. See Montucla's *Histoire des mathématiques*, 2d ed. rev., 4 vols. (Paris, 1799–1802), *1*:5, which gives Francis Bacon's usage of the term as an example. These notions of pure and mixed mathematics were still taken for granted in the eighteenth and early nineteenth centuries. They figured prominently in the scientific and mathematical dictionaries of Henry's day, which Henry, as a newcomer to science, undoubtedly read with care. For instance, in his "General Introduction" to the *Encyclopaedia Metropolitana* (vol. 1, 1818), Samuel Taylor Coleridge stressed the crucial importance of the distinction between pure and mixed mathematics in the general classification of scientific knowledge. Similar ideas of mathematics and physical science were outlined in other popular compendia such as Charles Hutton's *Philosophical and Mathematical Dictionary* (London, 1795–1796) and in Peter Barlow's *Dictionary of Pure and Mixed Mathematics* (London, 1814). An annotated copy of Barlow survives in Henry's library; and, as later parts of the address re-

Pure Mathematics has long been celebrated for the clearness & distinctness of its principles & for the rigour & beauty of its demonstrations. Unlike any other science it can [never suffer][6] a retrogresstion, for every truth when once developed by its rigid methods ever after becomes an immutable part of the science beyond the <utmost> power of sophistry to alter. Although its progress towards its present state of perfection has at times been extremely slow yet at no period has it actually declined & <it has *often moved with greate celerity*>.

Like that of many other branches of learning the origin of this science is lost in impenetrable obscurity.[7] Indeed we can scarcely conceive a state of society so rude as not to have made some advances at least in a knowledge of number & magnitude.

Nature has furnished <a great> & universal standard of computation in the fingers of the hand and all (most) nations have accordingly counted by fives and tens. The digits of both hands being enumerated the operation is repeated & this most probably gives rise to our present scale of decimal arithmetic.[8]

Geometry is said to owe its invention to the annual overflowings of the Nile.[9] The inundations of this river sweeping away those marks & bounda-

---

veal, Henry was particularly indebted to Barlow for his ideas about the development of mathematical thought.

As Professor of Mathematics and Natural Philosophy at the Albany Academy, Henry taught both pure and mixed mathematics. He taught mathematics from arithmetic through the differential calculus and the whole range of the physical sciences, including optics, astronomy, electricity, and magnetism. He also lectured on the applications of mathematics to the useful arts—to surveying, navigation, civil engineering, and architecture. *The Statutes of the Albany Academy* (Albany, 1829), pp. 9–15. For further details, see our notes to the *Statutes*, October 9, 1829, below.

[6] Henry actually wrote "can <*has never*> suffered."

[7] From the following remarks, we know that Henry was well versed in the popular history of science and mathematics. His library, as it survives today, also evidences Henry's historical interests; it includes a number of treatises on the nature and development of scientific thought, such as John Playfair's *Dissertation Second: Progress of Mathematical and Physical Science* (Edinburgh, 1819), Barlow's mathematical dictionary, and Tiberius Cavallo's *The Elements of Natural or Experimental*

Philosophy (Henry's Library contains the second American edition, Philadelphia, 1819). These books and others like them in Henry's Library were published before 1826. Although we cannot determine if Henry actually acquired them before that date, he obviously gleaned considerable historical information for his address from such general treatises. For his special debt to Barlow, see below, footnote 9.

[8] The above paragraph is faintly marked out. Henry may have intended to substitute another version, written on the verso of the preceding page, which reads:

Nature has furnished a universal standard of computation in the fingers of the hand. The digits of both hands being enumerated the operation is repeated and thus most probably arises our scale of decimal arithmetic which has been used by almost all nations although it is by no means the most simple or such would have been suggested were it not for some accidental association of the kind before mentioned.

[9] Henry clearly drew most of the following history of geometry from Peter Barlow's entry on "Geometry" in his *Dictionary of Pure and Mixed Mathematics,* which survives in Henry's

166

ries that designated the possession of property rendered it necessary to have some means of acertaining the lands of individuals after the subsiding of the waters. This may have led to the discovery of many important geometrical truths but is insufficient to account for the rise of the science itself which must be looked for only in the gradually progressive states of society.

The Greeks who received their knowledge from the Magi of Egypt had made considerable progress in the mathematics as a science more than 500 years before the birth of our saviour & encouraged by the free government & liberal institutions of this people Pythagoras the friend & pupil of Thales[10] began to enlighten the world with his discoveries. In arithmetic he invented the multiplication table; in astronomy he suggested the true solar system & in geometry discovered the 32^d & 47th prop. of Euclid. The last of these we are told gave him so much pleasure in the demonstration that in the fullness of his joy he sacrificed a whole hecatomb[11] to the muses.

Shortly[12] after the time of Pythagoras mathematics [science] was much extended by the celebrated problem of the *duplication of the cube*[13] the solution of which became through all Greece a subject of religious duty. It is said that the Atheniains being afflicted with the ravages of a pestilence consulted the oricles of Delos on the means of appeasing their gods. Its answer was "double the altar of Apollo." This being a perfect cube the question was at first thought easy but the mistake was soon discovered & all the learning & enginuity of the Greeks were unable to produce a complete solution. Their attempts however like those of the alchemists of more modern times were not entirely useless for several curious & interesting mathematical properties were the results of their repeated investigations.

It is however to Plato & the school founded by him[14] that geometry lies under the greatest obligation for its early advancements. So highly did this

---

Library. In some passages, Henry follows Barlow verbatim. Of course these descriptions of mathematics were part of the popular wisdom and could have been found in almost any scientific history, dictionary, or encyclopedia, such as the *Encyclopaedia Britannica* or Abraham Rees's *Cyclopaedia* (*The New Cyclopaedia or Universal Dictionary of Arts and Sciences*). The authors and compilers of all these works borrowed extensively from one another, often repeating each other's accounts verbatim.

[10] Pythagoras (ca. 580–500 B.C.), founder of the Pythagorean philosophical school at Croton. Thales of Miletus (ca. 639–548 B.C.), the Ionian philosopher. *Poggendorff*.

[11] Euclid's 32d proposition asserted that the three angles of a triangle are equal to two right angles. The 47th proposition was the Pythagorean theorem. A hecatomb was an ancient Greek sacrifice of usually one hundred cattle or oxen. (After the word hecatomb, "to the muses" is written faintly in pencil.)

[12] This paragraph was crossed out with a large X.

[13] The problem of constructing with compass and straightedge the side of a cube whose volume is twice the volume of a given cube. Henry may have derived his historical account of this problem from Barlow (s.v. "Geometry"). But almost all scientific dictionaries described the mythical origins of the attempts to double the cube.

[14] The Platonic Academy.

illustrious philosopher esteem mathematical learning that he ordered this incription to be engraved above the gates of his academy *"Let no one presume entre here who has not a taste for Geometry."* He introduced into the science a knowledge of those curves that arise from the different sections of a cone & many valuable inventions resulted from the labours of his school.

But in nothing is the genius & elegant inventions of the ancients better exemplified than in the elementary mathematical truths collected & arrainged by Euclid.[15] He was a member of the celebrated *<mathematical>* philosophical school at Alexandria in Egypt where a succession of learned & ingenious men kept alive the last embers of Greccian science after they had become cold & extinct in all those countries that then constituted the Roman Empire. He formed into one system all the scattered discoveries & inventions of his predecessors; begining with self evident principles & extending to the properties of the five mathematical solids he digested the whole into such admirable order & reasoned with such clearness & precision that even in the present advanced state of knowledge & at the distance of more than two thousand years the Elements of Euclid continue to form the most approved introduction to the studies of geometry & logic.

Nearly cotemporary with Euclid was Archimedes[16] of Syracuse whose name is familiar to every *tiro* in science & one that stands first on the list of inventive philosophers. His universal genius led him to the contemplation of every species of knowledge & nearly every branch of mathematics is indebted to him for various & important improvements. arithmetic, geometry, mechanics, optics & hydrostatics were alike the objects of his investigation & experienced alike the effects of his superior talents.

This was at the most brilliant period of ancient learning for after these *<great . . .>* fame presents few *<names>* others worthy of record; a taste for mathematics & literatur gradually declined until in the darkness of the middle ages mankind seam to have lost all desire for mental improvement as well as all sense of humanity. For several centuries the world scarcely produced one ornament or could boast one illustrious character to illumine the universal glume, so far from it that those days were spent in a dilligent search for the most valuable productions of antiquity not to treasure & preserve but to burn & destroy. In this fiend like spirit the Alexandrian library containing the works of the most eminent authours & all instruments of astronomical observation were entirely devoted to the flames by the savage fury of the Arabs. "The Calif Omar exclaimed, if they

[15] Euclid (ca. 330–260 B.C.), the Alexandrian mathematician and textbook writer. *Poggendorff*. The Alexandrian school of science flourished from the third century B.C. to about A.D. 200.

[16] Archimedes (ca. 287–212 B.C.), the most prominent mathematician and physicist of antiquity. *DSB*.

agree with the Koran they are useless, if not they should be destroyed."[17]
Thus it is always the pleasure & the pride of ignorance to level & demolish
what learning loves chiefly to cherish & promote.

But the dark ages appear to have been only an interval of repose ordered
by Divine providence for the restless mind of man & like the dreary night
of winter they preceded <*discoveries of the most momentous consequences
which*> the broadlight which the ensuing day of science has since desplayed.

The Arabians themselves were the first to catch again the sacred spirit of
learning that seamed to lingre in [the] consecrated East & they collected &
rekindled at Bagdat <*their capitol*> the expiring embers of that science
which they had almost extinguished in the ruins of *Alexandria*. From the
ninth to the 14th century the Eastern hemisphere furnishes no other guardians & promoters of learning than this people.

We[18] have thus far seen Mathematics [and] science flurishing only in the
East where like many a plant of the same clime it had grown more luxuri-
ous than beneficial[19] but we must now turn to view its <*progress in
strength and usefulness*> propigation as it spread through Europe continually to the West; for like the dianthus it appears to have always turned
its face to the declining[20] beams of the sun <*and not staid by seas its
branches have crossed the Atlantic & now furnish a spredding & a grateful
shade to our own fair country*>.

With the first dawn of learning a mathematical science of a name & a
character unknown to the geometers of Greece was received into Europe
from Arabia. As early as the 13th century Lenard a merchant of Pisa[21] visiting the East in the course of commertial adventures, returned to Italy enriched by the trafic & instructed in the sciences of these countries, brought
with him a knowledge of Algebra. The history of this branch of <*Science*> [?learning] in Europe from that period to the present time presents
the most brilliant collections of discoveries which have ever been at once
the fruit & the reward of genius. Other mathematical inventions apply each
to its own individual subject & cannot be brought to bear on any other; but

[17] Henry perhaps took the Caliph's words from Barlow's article on "Geometry" where they appear in a less dramatic form.
[18] On the back of the previous page Henry has written another version of this sentence: "We have thus far seen Mathematics <*flurishing only in*> the east but we must now turn to [? observe] its progress in the west where like the light of [? dawn] it constantly [. . .] on."
[19] "Useful" is faintly written above "bene-

ficial."
[20] Above this phrase, Henry or possibly someone else has written lightly in pencil: "following the course of the sun." And, next to the paragraph in the left margin, "Not good" is also written in pencil.
[21] Leonardo da Pisa (Fibonacci; ca. 1170–after 1240), Italian author of *Liber Abaci*, possibly the first work to introduce algebra and Arabic numerals to the West. *DSB*.

this extended by the Newtonian method of fluxions & the calculus of <*the french*> Leibnetze[22] becomes a universal instrument to operate on a variety of problems which could be touched by no rule of ancient geometry; and by the generality of its means brings under one point of view theorems & facts which had been previously considered isolated & independent. It was first applied to geometry for the purpose of assisting & suplying its defects but it has since ended with discarding that science almost entirely & usurping its place.

This calculus in the hands of modern philosophers has rather been considered as an instrument for the descovery of philosophical truths than as an independent & distinct object of study:[23] building upon principles established by the inductive methods taught by Bacon[24] it has been successfully applied to investigate the laws which govern the minutest particle of matter as well as to develope the grand principles which regulate the motion & preserve the harmony of the universe. A[25] popular therefore view of some of the labours performed by modern mathematicians & of a few of the discoveries made by means of the calculus which has almost exposed to light the whole mechanical arcana of nature, will better illustrate the progress & present state of the science than any farther attempt at a formal history.[26]

[22] As a student at the Albany Academy Henry learned the calculus in the fluxional notation. But he soon picked up the Continental techniques from French mathematical treatises such as S. F. Lacroix's *Traité élémentaire de calcul différential et de calcul intégral*. The third edition (Paris, 1820) of Lacroix exists in the Henry Library. Henry's heavily annotated copy of Lacroix, according to the book's inscription, was given to him by an Albany schoolmate, Thomas Hun, possibly before 1826. (Hun later became President of the Academy; see W. L. L. Peltz, *The Top Flight at Number One LaFayette Street* [Albany, 1939], pp. 75–76.) By 1829, according to the Academy *Statutes*, Henry was teaching the calculus from the English translation of a French text by Jean Louis Boucharlat. There was an English edition of Boucharlat published in 1820, *An Elementary Treatise on the Differential and Integral Calculus*, trans. R. Blakelock (Cambridge). No American edition is listed in either the Library of Congress *National Union Catalog* or in L. C. Karpinski's *Bibliography of Mathematical Works Printed in America through 1850* (Ann Arbor, 1940). But

since the text was used by the Albany Academy, we suspect an American edition was published.

Henry's first reaction was to associate the calculus with the French (along with Newton). But he quickly remembered his history and gave due credit to G. W. Leibnitz (1646–1716), the German mathematician and philosopher who developed the calculus independently of Newton and whose notation is now universal.

[23] Because of its early associations with scientific problems, the calculus was regarded more as an analytical tool of physics than as a purely mathematical discipline.

[24] Francis Bacon (1561–1626), English natural philosopher and jurist. *DSB*.

[25] At this point the *Argus* begins to excerpt Henry's address. The beginning of the paragraph is marked by a penciled asterisk. With a few exceptions which will be noted, these asterisks appear at the beginning and end of the passages which are excerpted in the *Argus*. The marks may have been made by the *Argus* editor or by Henry himself in preparing the copy for publication.

[26] Note that in discussing areas of current mathematical research, Henry is concerned

To measur the earth which appears to our senses by far the largest body in the universe and to determine its magnitude & figure is an enterprise that would seam greatly beyond the limited capacity of man. Confined as he naturally is to a particular country how is he to find the distance of places he can never visit or how traverse the whole circle of the <*earth*> globe when mountains, rivers & seas offer perpetual obsticles to his course? Difficulties however only serve to stimulate exertion & [an] enlightened man not confounded by the inadequacies of his <*natural*> physical powers finds in his intelligence a resource that admirably supplies all their defects. Mathematics furnishes him with a rule which applied to celestial observation enables him to determine the whole circumference of the terraqueous globe without quitting his own country or in some cases even the sight of his native habitation.

Not only this problem so interesting to geography and astronomy has been respectedly solved in almost every country but what may appear still more astonishing the weight & density of this great earth has itself also been accurately acertained.[27]

By[28] these calculations the earth is not only prooved to be an entire solid but the interior must be occupied by matter much more dense than any substance which composes its surface. This therefore completely excludes the possibility of the earth's interior being an inhabitable hollow or a reservoir of perpetual fire as some have most ludicrously supposed.[29]

---

solely with the physical applications of mathematics, that is with mixed, not pure, mathematics. Of course, physical research was more impressive and easier to convey to a general audience. Henry's stress on physics also reflected his belief that pure mathematics was more a mental discipline than a field for new research and discovery. See below, footnote 47.

[27] In 1798 the British scientist Henry Cavendish calculated the density of the earth by means of a torsion balance. *DSB*.

For the general scientific (chiefly astronomical) concern with the earth's density and configuration, see Sir George Airy's article on the figure of the earth in the fifth volume of the *Encyclopaedia Metropolitana*, 1845, pp. 165–242.

[28] This paragraph has been crossed out. A line has been drawn around it and the word "note" is written next to it in the left margin. The numeral "1" appears at the beginning of the paragraph, and a "2" at the beginning of

the next. Other numbers also occur at later points in the text but they do not seem to indicate any particular ordering of the text, nor do they always correspond to the *Argus* excerpting. Again, we cannot tell if Henry himself did the editing.

[29] Henry is repudiating the eccentric theory of Captain John Cleves Symmes (1780–1829) that the earth consisted of a series of concentric hollow spheres and was open at the poles. Symmes' ideas enjoyed a brief period of popularity but were soon dismissed by most serious scientists. See A. Hunter Dupree, *Science in the Federal Government, A History of Policies and Activities to 1940* (New York and Evanston, 1964), pp. 41, 56. Henry's reference to a "reservoir of perpetual fire" touches indirectly upon a major geological issue of the 1820s—the theory of the earth's residual central heat. While such theories had been around since the mid-eighteenth century, they

The heavenly bodies on account of their distance would appear if possible stil more excluded from the scope of human science: but "the firmament studed with sparkling lights"[30] has long been an object of wonder & study to mankind. In times too remote for the reccords of history, the stars <*must have been*> were observed to form clusters that always retained the same relation, position & names were given them descriptive of some fancied resemblance to things of a fabulous or <*divine*> terrestrial origin.

These constellations are now faithful pictures of all stages of civilization for "men in every age have written in the skye as on an album memorials of themselves & of the times in which they lived." The adventures of the gods & the inventions of men, the exploits of heroes & the fanccy of poets are here imperishably preserved and exhibited in glowing characters each night to the eyes of all nations.

The *Harpe of Orpheus,* the *figure of Orion* & the *Head of Medusca*[31] are as visible & unchanged to the inhabitance of this city as they were to the sheapherds of Chaldea, the priests of Egypt or the philosophers of Greece. Archturis a star celebrated in the book of Job shined last night as brightly in our western horizon as it did in the East in the times of Amos or of Homer.

Although the stars are usually compaired in number with the sand of the shoar and the leaves of the forest yet the modern astronomer with almost incredible labour has acertained the number & noted the position & magnitude of all those seen by the naked eye besides many visible only by the aid of the tellescope. This would seam to the casual observer rather as a work of curious speculation than as a subject of rational labour; but it is no less nessary in knowing the interesting changes that take place amoung the heavenly bodies than it is useful in advancing the art of navigation. For it is only a knowledge of the heavens that emboldens the <*sailor*> mariner to "push his bark from the shoar & fearlessly to spread his canvass to the wind."

The firmament presents to us another class of bodies called planets or wandering stars which do not preserve the same fixed position but moove

---

were especially vigorous in the 1820s, partly due to the uncovering of new experimental evidence. See Martin J. S. Rudwick, "Uniformity and Progression: Reflections on the Structure of Geological Theory in the Age of Lyell," in *Perspectives in the History of Science and Technology* (Norman, Oklahoma, 1971), pp. 214ff. Note that Henry's objection is not to the central heat itself but to the idea of a hollow fiery core.

[30] For this quotation and those which immediately follow, we have not identified the sources. We have searched Henry's personal library as well as other likely sources. In most cases, the ideas quoted were commonplace and Henry could have found them almost anywhere.

[31] i.e., the constellations Lyra and Orion; the Head of Medusa is in the constellation Perseus.

from one constellation to another performing a whole circle in the heavens in periodical times. They also have engaged the attention of philosophers & have been the objects of minute & careful observation; the invention of optical instruments & the improvements in calculation have brought them near to us & subjected them to the strict methods of mathematical reasoning. One general law has been observed to affect & govern every phenominon that takes place in their moovements & by means of which their distances, periods & magnitudes have been calculated & their respective weights & densities accurately estimated. Our globe so vast & so firmly rooted as it appears to the ignorant is prooved to be no more than one of the least of these bodies & in a rapid & constant state of motion both *rotary* & progressive.

The calculus applied to these recerches begins with investigating the laws of mechanical motion & equilibrium that govern matter on the surface of the earth and extens the same principles to all the planets that compose the solar system; pursues them through all the excentricities of their motions in eliptical & parabolical orbits & at last becomes able to refer every apparent irregularity & every complicated movement they present to the simple cause of universal gravitation,[32] thus forming a sublime system "that affords an example yet solitary in the history of human knowledge of a theory entirely complete; one that has not only accounted for all the phenomena that were known but has pointed out many others that observation has since recognised."

In the course of these investigations periodic changes have been discovered which require thousands of years for their completion. "What an idea" as it has been justly observed "does this give of that infinite power to whom such a space of time is but as a single day; & what an insight into the destiny of the human soul which although limited in its sublunary existance to a duration almost infinitely small has been endowed with faculties powerful enough to expound such laws."

The gigantic career leading to these discoveries was opened by Newton; pursuid with zeal by some of the most illustrious names that ever embellished the annals of science such as Euler, D'Alembert, La Grange & finally completed by La Place.[33]

---

[32] The first volume of a three-volume set of William Davis' edition of Newton's *Principia* (London, 1819) survives in Henry's Library. Davis' edition is based on Andrew Motte's translation. There is no indication of when Henry acquired the book.

[33] Leonhard Euler (1707–1783), Swiss math-ematician and physicist. *Poggendorff*; Jean le Rond d'Alembert (1717–1783), French *philosophe*, physicist, and mathematician, *DSB*; Pierre Simon, Marquis de Laplace (1749–1827), French mathematical physicist; Joseph Louis La Grange (1736–1813), French mathematician and physicist. *Poggendorff*.

This last philosopher not contented with the glory he had acquired as an original inventor, has since revised & illustrated the works of his predecessors, reduced them to one general method, and collected them into one grand work the *Mechanque Celeste*[34] which it is said does honour not only to the authour but the whole human race "& markes undoubtedly the highest point to which man has yet ascended in the scale of intellectual attainment."

A complete knowledge of this part of the higher mathematics requires such long & severe study with the application of such superior talents <*of the first order*> that few even of those reputed the most learned are intimately acquainted with its profound investigations. But since one great object of science is to ameliorate <*the natural*> our present condition by adding to those advantages we naturally possess it is fortunate that all problems valuable for their practical <*nature*> application can be deduced from principles of a much more elementary kind.

With such a knowledge only of pure mathematics as a student of this institution <*will*> can acquire in a few years of early & asiduous application he will be able successfully to pursue all subjects of a practical nature to which the rules of the science are applied.

And these in the affairs of life are neither few nor unimportant; for navigation, surveying, guaging & mensuration constitute only different branches of mathematical learning while geography, perspective & the whole circle of exact sciences depen entirely upon it for the establishment & exposition of their principles.[35]

It is also intimately connected with music & painting & sculpture & the labours of Dalton, Hauy, Bartholette[36] & others on the ultimate combinations of matter have almost ranked chemestry & mineralogy with the physico-mathematical sciences.

But in nothing do mathematical & philosophical principles appear more decidedly useful than in their application to the mechanic arts. To these they present in a condensed form the united experience of many ages. By a combination of theoretical knowledge with practical skill machines have

[34] *Traité de mécanique céleste*, 5 vols. (1798–1825). Henry's Library contains Thomas Young's *Elementary Illustrations of the Celestial Mechanics of Laplace* (London, 1821).

[35] Perhaps hoping that his students would not be intimidated by the mathematical sciences, Henry has artfully grouped the exact sciences with the "subjects of a practical nature" which can be deduced from relatively elementary mathematical principles.

[36] The English chemist John Dalton (1766–1844). *DSB*. Henry's spelling of Haüy is unclear, and the *Argus* printed the name as Hany. But Henry was obviously referring to the French crystallographer, Abbé René Just Haüy (1743–1822), *Poggendorff*. The first volume of Olinthus Gregory's two-volume translation (London, 1807) of Haüy's *Traité élémentaire de physique* (1804) survives in the Henry Library. Henry was also referring to the French chemist Claude Louis Berthollet (1748–1822). *DSB*.

been constructed no less useful in their <*productions*> results than astonishing in their operations. As one that may be allowed to stand *instar om-
nium* may be mentioned the steam engine that legitimate & gigantic of-
spring of mathematical & chemical science, at once more powerful than the
united force of the strongest & largest animals & more manigable than the
<*meakes*> gentlest & smalest. "And above all its" multiplied labours "the
propelling of vessells against the currents the winds & the waves of the
ocean"[37] is to us a most interesting object whether considered in its un-
paralleled usefulness or as an American invention completed & first tested
in our own state.[38]

The works[39] of internal improvement at this time so zealously prosecuting in all parts of the union emphatically teach us how mathematical &
mechanical knowledge may be applied not only to the necessities of ordinary life but to increase the power & promote the wealth of a nation.[40] The
successful completion of our canals & the contemplated construction of
roads & railways have turned upon us the eyes of every other state as afford-
ing a great example of public enterprise & industry & as furnishing engineers, mechanics, & contractors to execute similar workes in other parts of
the union.[41] The[42] tedious methods & the expensive plans of European

[37] The source of the quotation is unknown.
The *Argus* printed this passage with the quotation marks placed slightly differently.

[38] Henry is thinking of Robert Fulton's
Clermont, which negotiated the Hudson between New York and Albany in 1807. While
Fulton (1765–1815), *DAB,* demonstrated the
commercial feasibility of the steamboat, he
was anticipated in experimental steam navigation by other American inventors such as
John Fitch (1743–1798). *DAB.*

[39] The *Argus* printed the next two sentences
as they stand. But Henry wrote a slightly different version of the sentences on the backs of
two pages of the manuscript.

[40] For Henry and internal improvements, see
above, T. R. Beck to Martin Van Buren,
March 10, 1826, footnote 7.

[41] In the mid-1820s, the American transportation system was in a period of transition
and on the verge of a remarkable expansion.
The commercial success of the Erie Canal,
completed in 1825, launched a craze for canal
building throughout the nation. With the development of the steam locomotive, the railway, which was previously used by horse-
drawn vehicles, was also about to enter an
era of rapid development. The steam railroad,
which Henry is undoubtedly referring to,

would soon compete with the canal for public
support.

The opening of England's Stockton and
Darlington Railroad, the world's first general
transportation railroad, sparked the interest
of American officials and entrepreneurs. In
1825, the Pennsylvania Society for the Promotion of Internal Improvements sent the well-
known architect-engineer William Strickland
(*DAB*) to England to assess her expanding
railroad system. After observing the Stockton
and Darlington, Strickland reported that the
future of transportation belonged to the railroad, which he believed would soon supplant
the canal. Though skeptically received in
Pennsylvania, Strickland's report was prophetic. After 1825, Americans began to experiment extensively on steam railroads and
a railroad system came into being. In 1828, the
Baltimore and Ohio Railroad was chartered.
By 1830, it had laid 13 miles of track. George
R. Taylor, *The Transportation Revolution,
1815–1860* (New York and Toronto, 1951), pp.
34, 75–77. See also John F. Stover, *American
Railroads* (Chicago, 1961).

[42] There are three penciled x's around the
next two sentences, perhaps because the *Argus*
revised Henry's wording.

engineers have been found but ill to agree with the state of finance or the active character of the American people. Since with us great results must be produced with small means.

To teach therefore the practicle & scientific principles of engineering as adapted to this country becomes an important duty of the mathematical professor of this academy.[43] In[44] illustrating this branch & indeed every

---

[43] Perhaps chauvinism prompted Henry to dismiss European engineers as tedious and, by implication, unscientific. Actually, many French civil engineers (and scientists as well) were trained in the highly theoretical and mathematical curriculum of the École Polytechnique, the elite army engineering school established after the Revolution. Furthermore, many canals, bridges, roads, and mines in France were designed and constructed by graduates of the École des Ponts et Chaussées and the École des Mines, also known for their scientific and mathematical orientation. French engineering schools, especially the École Polytechnique, had a worldwide reputation and influence; following the French model, Germany established its first advanced engineering school in 1825, the Polytechnische Hochschule in Karlsruhe. Frederick B. Artz, *The Development of Technical Education in France, 1500–1850* (London and Cambridge, Massachusetts, 1966), pp. 228 (footnote 39), 234–245.

In describing the use of mathematics in American civil engineering, Henry was probably thinking of the mathematical approach to engineering instruction at the West Point Military Academy, which he had visited in June 1826 (see Henry's Journal entry for June 12, 1826). Ironically, West Point, too, was heavily influenced by the French example. Sylvanus Thayer, who became Superintendent of the Academy in 1817, restructured the engineering curriculum around French methods and French mathematical and scientific treatises. Claude Crozet, a graduate of the École Polytechnique, who taught engineering at West Point from 1816 to 1833, further emphasized the study of mathematics in the engineering curriculum. Henry was obviously deeply interested in the educational philosophy of the Academy. On his 1826 visit he met many of the professors there and by 1827 was himself seeking a professorship of chemistry at the Academy (see below, Henry to Bennett H. Henderson, July 25, 1827). By 1831 Henry was corresponding with his friend Charles Davies (1798–1861), a graduate of West Point

who taught mathematics there between 1815 and 1837 (see below, Henry to Davies, February 15, 1831). Henry had probably met Davies on his 1826 visit. Continuing the French tradition, Davies compiled popular mathematical texts of French origin, like his *Elements of Descriptive Geometry* (1826). (For Davies, Thayer, Crozet, and the mathematical tradition at West Point, see Sidney Forman, *West Point, A History of the United States Military Academy* [New York, 1950], pp. 41–53; and Florian Cajori, *The Teaching and History of Mathematics in the United States* [Washington, 1890], pp. 114–119.) Later, in 1850, Davies published a treatise on *The Logic and Utility of Mathematics* (New York, 1850), which concisely describes the system of mathematical instruction at West Point: "It is of the essence of that system that a principle be taught before it is applied to practice; . . . and that when such principles and such laws are fully comprehended, their applications be then taught as consequences or practical results. . . . In that system Mathematics is the basis–Science precedes Art–Theory goes before Practice–the general formula embraces all the particulars." (Pp. 3–4.) Henry's Library contains both the 1850 and 1869 editions of Davies' work.

By the 1830s, West Point graduates were serving on both military and civilian engineering projects. Although Henry probably viewed American engineering in terms of West Point, most civil engineers in the 1820s were practical men trained on the job. This was true of the Erie Canal, where most of the engineers were originally surveyors who learned canal building by experience. The Erie Canal, in fact, became an informal school which trained engineers for other internal improvement projects. Ronald E. Shaw, *Erie Water West, A History of the Erie Canal, 1792–1854* (Lexington, Kentucky, 1961), pp. 88–95; and Daniel H. Calhoun, *The American Civil Engineer, Origins and Conflict* (Cambridge, Massachusetts, 1960), pp. 24–53. It is hard to say how much mathematics the canal engineers applied to their work. The Chief Engineer of the Erie

other part of mechanical & natural science well selected experiments are of the utmost value. But this <*institution*> seminary so liberally endowed in all other respects is wanting in a philosophical aparatus. A lecture room has been fitted up and furnished with articles that illustrate many principles of chemical philosophy & the results continue to prove its greate &

Canal, Benjamin Wright, had a talent for mathematics. *DAB*. The other engineers undoubtedly picked up at least an elementary knowledge of geometry through surveying.

Before West Point and the Erie Canal began to augment the domestic supply of engineers, American civil engineering depended heavily upon European talent. The directors of early canal and river improvement projects eagerly sought the skills of European engineers. In fact, the Commissioners who planned the Erie Canal originally had considered recruiting a European, but nationalistic feeling and financial considerations ruled out the possibility. Daniel Calhoun, *The American Civil Engineer*, pp. 9–23, 26. On the national level, Simon Bernard (1779–1839), French military engineer and graduate of the École Polytechnique, served in the Corps of Engineers on the three-man Board for Fortifications. He also was appointed head of a three-man Board of Engineers for Internal Improvements (established by the Survey Act of April 20, 1824), which directed the Federal program of internal improvements between 1824 and 1831. See *DAB* and Major General William H. Carter, "Bernard," *Journal of the Military Service Institution of the United States*, 1912, 51:147–155. Henry must have been aware of the pervasive influence of the French engineering tradition in America. Undoubtedly his criticisms of European engineering stemmed partly from his nationalistic sentiments.

Perhaps by the "tedious methods and expensive plans of European engineers," Henry meant their concern for permanence and aesthetics—concerns ill-suited to the pragmatic needs of a young, expanding nation which lacked the capital for elaborate projects. About the construction of railroad bridges, for example, Carl Condit notes that European engineers were shocked by American pragmatic attitudes:

In the United States the criteria of adequate construction were always pragmatic, seldom either scientific or aesthetic: the minimum of material consistent with safety; the most rapid and efficient means of construction; design for expansion and relocation rather than permanence. It was a simple program, and if it seldom produced finished structural art, it could at least satisfy the demands of immediate mechanical utility.

American Building Art in the Nineteenth Century (New York, 1960), p. 103. Note that the American bridge engineer did not meet his practical needs by applying more science and mathematics. He simply built cheap, temporary structures.

American civil engineers were not, and would not soon be, as scientific as Henry envisioned. But Henry was outlining a program he thought essential for the future of American technology.

On American technology in this period, see Brooke Hindle, *Technology in Early America: Needs and Opportunities for Study* (Chapel Hill, 1966). For an examination of the role of science in nineteenth-century American technology, see Edwin Layton, "Mirror Image Twins: The Communities of Science and Technology in Nineteenth Century America," and Carroll Pursell, "Science and Industry in 19th Century America," both to be printed in the Proceedings of the Symposium on Science in Nineteenth Century America at Northwestern University in March–April 1970.

[44] There is some question about where Henry wanted to place this passage on philosophical apparatus. It and the beginning of the next paragraph are on an unnumbered page. The *Argus* article, though it does not include this particular passage, seems to justify the present order. The content of the paragraph also suggests this reconstruction.

It appears that Henry inserted the passage as an afterthought. Reviewing this part of his draft, he probably sensed a dramatic point where he could introduce his appeal for philosophical apparatus, as laboratory equipment was then called. As Professor at the Academy, Henry continually and successfully campaigned for additional laboratory apparatus. For the results of his efforts, see below, Henry's Descriptive Catalogue of Philosophical Apparatus Purchased for the Albany Academy, December 18, 1830.

increasing usefulness. It is however stil incomplete & for want of a few more articles many of the most interesting experiments of this science cannot be shewn. But I must be allowed to indulge the hope that the friends & guardians of this Academy with their usual zeal & enlightened policy will devise some means to supply these defficiencies.

Pure[45] mathematics requires no experimental illustration and from the effects it produces on the reasoning faculties is rendered more emenently useful as a branch of a liberal education. The powers of the mind are as much invigorated by frequent exertion as the limbs are strengthened by repeted action. Application & industry properly applied produce the most profitable kind of genius & the inventive faculty itself if not formed may be strengthened & improved by <practice> use & perseverance. Pure mathematics above all other studies serve to call forth this spirit of intellectual exertion. By an early attention to this science the student acquires a habit of reasoning & an elevation of thought which fixes his mind & prepares it for every other pursuit. And although in the active and more important duties of afterlife he may have forgotten every proposition in geometry & every principle in algebra still he will be much indebted to these early studies for that general discipline & enlargement of the understanding so necessary to his professional rise & usefulness.[46] There is no science says Dr Reid[47] better fitted to exercise & strengthen the reasoning powers than mathematics first because no other gives such scope to long & acurate reasoning & secondly because in this science there is no room for prejudices of any kind which may give a false bias to the judgement.

When a youth of moderate talents begins the study of Euclid every thing is new to him. His judgement is feeble & rests partly on the evidence of the thing & partly on the authority of the teacher. But every time he goes over the definitions the axiums and the elementary propositions, more light breaks in upon him; the language becomes familiar and conveys clear &

---

[45] An earlier draft of the beginning of this paragraph has been crossed out.

[46] Though there is no indication in the manuscript, the *Argus* omits most of the remainder of Henry's speech.

[47] Undoubtedly the philosopher Thomas Reid (1710–1796), the founder of Scottish Common Sense philosophy. *DNB.* We have not found the specific passage in Reid which Henry is apparently paraphrasing. But Reid expresses similar notions in his *Essays on the Intellectual Powers of Man* (Edinburgh, 1785), where he recommends the long chains of reasoning in mathematics for exercising and expanding the mind and praises mathe-

matics for its clear conceptions and freedom from sophistry. In the 1814–1815 Charlestown, Massachusetts, edition of Reid's collected works, which Henry may have consulted for this citation, the passages appear in vol. 2, p. 1 and vol. 3, pp. 254, 257.

In Henry's day, as it had been for centuries, pure mathematics was regarded and taught as a mental discipline. Such was the traditional function of mathematics in a classical education. See Florian Cajori, *Mathematics in Liberal Education, A Critical Examination of the Judgements of Prominent Men of the Ages* (Boston, 1928), passim.

steady conceptions. The judgement is confirmed; he begins to see what demonstration is and it is imposible to see without being charmed. He perceives [it] to be a kind of evidence that needs nothing else to strengthen it. He finds himself emancipated from bondage & exults so much in his new state of independence that he spurns all authority & would have demonstration for every thing. Experience however soon teaches him that this kind of evidence cannot be obtained in all cases & that in his most important transactions with the world he must rest contented with mere probability or at most with analogical reasoning.

The results produced on the mind by the sublime & enduring sceans presented in the study of astronomy have been so often and so abelly dwelt upon that it would be quite impossible for me to present them to you in a new or more striking form.

This therefore must suffer as a brief view of the extent, usefulness & effects of mathematical knowledge. It is not intended however by what has been said that other objects of inquiry are rendered unnessary by a knowledge of this science. Narrow minds indeed think nothing of importance but their own favourite pursuit & what suits not with their taste is folly & abserdity. But more liberal views exclude no branch of science or literature for they all contribute by various means to sweaten, to adorn & to embelish life.

But I fear I have too long trespassed on the patience of an enlightened audiance by a discussion of topics to them of so familiar & obvious a nature.[48]

[48] Certain of these themes, especially the application of scientific principles to the useful arts, appear in a more elaborate and mature form in Henry's Introductory Lecture on Chemistry, January–March 1832, below.

On the reverse side of this final page, there is another draft of the opening sentence of the address.

AMOS EATON TO STEPHEN VAN RENSSELAER[1]

Gratz Collection, Historical Society of Pennsylvania

Rensselaer School Oct. 17th 1826.

Honl friend,

You will recollect, that a fortnight from tomorrow our examination commences and continues two days. We have two candidates for the degree

[1] (1764–1839). This letter was quoted in part by Ethel McAllister, *Amos Eaton* (Philadelphia, 1941), p. 399.

of (r.s.) A.B.[2] and all the class are candidates for quarterly examination. I hope you will appoint examiners in season for us to give the necessary notice.

I wish not to interfere; but it would be my opinion that the fall examiners might be young men; and that men of higher and established reputations whould be troubled with it in June only, on the days preceding commencement. I hope you will not consider it an improper interference if I give my opinion in regard to a professor suitable for the duty.

> Mᵣ Henry, prof. Math. in Albany Academy.[3]
> Mᵣ Matthews,[4] teacher of the French School in Albany.
> Mᵣ Fisk,[5] teacher in Troy.
> Danˡ Gardner,[6] Esq. of Troy, a Schenectedy graduate.
> Matthew Henry Webster Esq. of Albany.

All these gentlemen are liberally educated, and have given more or less attention to the modern Sciences. Perhaps you will recollect a sufficient number, who are as well qualified. I mention them in aid of your recollection.

Please to address the
appointment to Prof. Blatchford

Yours respectfully
Amos Eaton
Sen. Prof.

---

[2] i.e., Bachelor of Arts, Rensselaer School. Eaton believed that the education that Rensselaer students received was distinctive enough to warrant a special designation.

[3] Newly appointed but known to Eaton at least from the Canal Tour.

[4] Frederick Matthews.

[5] Allen Fiske (b. 1789), an Amherst College graduate, first studied law, then opened a private school in Troy. He was principal of the Auburn, New York, Academy from 1832 to 1836. He was living in 1867. A. A. Fiske, *The Fiske Family* (Chicago, 1867), pp. 77–86.

[6] Daniel Gardner graduated from Union College in 1817. He practiced law in Troy until his death in 1863. *Union Catalog*, p. 15.

STEPHEN VAN RENSSELAER
TO SAMUEL BLATCHFORD
Amos Eaton Papers, New York State Library

Albany Oct 25—1826

Dear Sir

Permit me to recommend to you as Examiners for the ensuing Examination at the School over which you preside—Mᵣ Henry Professor of Math Albany Acʸ., Mᵣ Fisk of Troy, D. Gardner of Troy, Mathew H. Webster &

Mr Mathews Teacher Alb^y—& I also beg leave to suggest the propriety of inviting the Gov.[1] I will convey him to Troy. If he accepts his presence would give some eclat to the exhibition.

> With respect & &c
> Yours sincerely
> S V Rensselaer
> [In] Haste

[1] DeWitt Clinton.

❦ 1827 ❧

FROM ALEXANDER S. ALEXANDER
Mary Henry Copy, Henry Papers, Smithsonian Archives

Rochester, Feb. 11th, 1827

Cousin Henry

Surprise is one source of pleasure; an effect this letter may produce since the long silence between you and me has never been interrupted by any paper communication.[1] All the merit these lines can claim will be perhaps to produce an echo. I write to tell you I have seen an extract from your inaugural address and the only reason I was not more delighted was, that I could not see the whole of the production which is worthy of the Professor, a feast to the man of intellect as well as to the man of taste. From what I could gather from the "Argus" I must congratulate you on its success at the time of delivery, before a learned and polite auditory. May your Professorship be as splendid as its commencement was brilliant. . . .[2] Let me exhort you not to give yourself so exclusively to the dry bones of diagrams but consider that you are partly made for your friends and social intercourse.

> Yours most affectionately
> Alexander S. Alexander

[1] Henry, who had met Alexander in 1825, had promised to write to him, but apparently had not done so. See Henry to Stephen Alexander, December 19, 1825.

[2] Ellipsis points in Mary Henry's copy.

DIARY OF ASA FITCH

Fitch Family Papers, Asa Fitch's Diary E:43–48,
Sterling Library, Yale University

Albany   Sat 7 April 1827

Before breakfast we went to the lower extremity of the city, & came back on one of the rear streets. We then rambled about State, & the adjoining streets & visited I beleive, every bookstore in the city, in search of some person who was agent for the Casket a Philadelphia periodical.[1] I have been in the fidgets for a fortneit, to subscribe for this, but since I found no agent, I beleive my zeal for receiving it will subside, & perhaps expire. After breakfast we went to Morgans book-store,[2] where will be a book auction this evening. We received catalogues of the books, & concluded to stay to the sale. We had before intended to go out soon after noon. We next went to the Albany Academy. I gave my letter from Prof. Eaton to Dr Beck. He conducted us to the Library of the Academy of Sciences,[3] & handed down to us the transactions of the Philadelphia Society,[4] the Wernerian Society of Edinburgh, the New York Lyceum,[5] &c. He also provided me with pen & paper. Soon afterwards Prof Henry, who accompanied us to the west last spring, came in. He showed us through the different rooms of the building. The Cabinet of the Albany Lyceum. In this is several insects (2 or 300) but they are not labelled. They have a considerable number of shells the most of which are labelled, after the French naturalists. An extensive cabinet of Minerals is finely arranged. Here too are the specimens of the soils, collected & analyzed by Prof Eaton & Dr Beck while taking the Agricultural survey of Albany county.[6] They were just arranging a collection of coins, mostly copper, on cards. The Room for holding public examinations & exhibitions is large, & well seated. The Laboratory would contain a large audience. Our Chemical apparatus could not compare with what is here used. The school Library contains a considerable number of books, but not as many as that of the Academy of Science. After viewing

---

[1] *Casket: Flowers of Literature, Wit and Sentiment*, a popular monthly founded in 1826 by the publishers of the *Saturday Evening Post*. See F. L. Mott, *A History of American Magazines, 1741–1850* (New York and London, 1930), pp. 343, 544–545.

[2] Not identified.

[3] Fitch undoubtedly means the Albany Institute, an understandable confusion since the library and museum of the Institute were housed in the Albany Academy.

[4] Probably the Academy of Natural Sciences of Philadelphia.

[5] *Memoirs of the Wernerian Natural History Society of Edinburgh* had been published since 1808, while the *Annals* of the Lyceum of Natural History of New York dated from 1823.

[6] The results of the survey were published in Amos Eaton and T. Romeyn Beck, *A Geological Survey of the County of Albany, Taken under the Direction of the Agricultural Society of the County* (Albany, 1820). See above, Samuel Latham Mitchill to T. R. Beck, December 6, 1820.

the different rooms we returned to the one first mentioned. Here I looked over the different Zoological articles, & copied Says[7] new species of Coccinella. About 11 o'clock we left the Academy & went into the state Library,[8] which is public during the sessions of the Legislature. Here I cursorily examined a part of Wilsons American Ornithology,[9] with Bonapartes Continuation.[10] It is much the most elegantly executed work, I ever saw. A description of every known bird in America, with an engraving of it is here presented. The engravings are carefully & accurately executed, & most beautifully coloured.[11] Says American Entomology is not far behind it. There is only two volumes yet completed. In these, scarce the hundredth part of our insects are described. The work particularly the engravings is masterly. Mr Say does not hesitate to bring forward new species. In this, to a certain degree I think he is correct. Numbers of our insects are yet undescribed. After dinner we went into the assembly room. Mr. Root was near the end of a speech.[12] Had it been at a common academical exhibition he would have been hissed. We also heard short speeches from several of

[7] Thomas Say (1787–1834), zoologist, entomologist, conchologist. Say's grand-uncle, the naturalist William Bartram, aroused his interest in natural history, which he studied intensively after 1812. Say served as zoologist on numerous expeditions and held a nominal curatorship at the American Philosophical Society and a nominal professorship at the University of Pennsylvania (1822–1828). He published the first two volumes of his *American Entomology* in 1824 and 1825 and the third in 1828. Say's work was respected abroad and, as Fitch points out, the new species he proposed were widely accepted. *DAB.*

[8] Established in 1818 to serve the Legislature, the New York State Library soon began to supplement its core legal collection with holdings from other fields. As Fitch reveals, the sciences were well represented in the expansion and, by the mid-forties, the Library owned an excellent collection in mathematics, natural history, and the physical sciences. Henry showed a continuing interest in the Library's resources and owned copies of its 1846 published catalog and an 1861 supplement. Among the rich scientific holdings, the 1846 catalog lists works in mathematics, physics, chemistry, geology, botany, zoology, and medicine (studies in logic and metaphysics were also included in the scientific category). *Howell and Tenney*, pp. 688–690; *Catalogue of the New-York State Library* (Albany, 1846), pp. 219ff.

[9] Alexander Wilson (1766–1813) was a weaver, poet, and ornithologist. Born in Scotland, he came to the United States in 1794 and taught in New Jersey and Pennsylvania. Like Say, Wilson became interested in ornithology through William Bartram. The first volume of *American Ornithology* appeared in 1808 and volumes 2–7 by 1813. *DAB.*

[10] Lucien Jules Laurent Bonaparte (1803–1857), nephew of Napoleon, was a zoologist and ornithologist deeply interested in the principles of classification. During a brief stay in the United States (1822–1825), he devoted himself to the continuation of Alexander Wilson's work. In 1826, he published his *Observations on the Nomenclature of Wilson's Ornithology* (Philadelphia) and, between 1825 and 1833, *American Ornithology; or, the Natural History of Birds Inhabiting the United States,* 4 vols. (Philadelphia). *DSB.* The first volume of the latter work was prepared for press by Thomas Say.

[11] The engravings were made from Wilson's own drawings and paintings by Alexander Cawson. *DAB.*

[12] General Erastus Root (1773–1846), prominent New York political figure (at this time Speaker of the State Assembly) and Major General in the state militia. In 1795, Root published *An Introduction to Arithmetic for the Use of Common Schools. DAB;* James Pierce Root, *Root Genealogical Records, 1600–1870* (New York, 1870), pp. 155–156; and Edgar A. Werner, *Civil List of New York* (Albany, 1889), p. 433. He was also a corresponding

the other members, among them Sam¹ Stevens.[13] In about an hour they adjourned, & we returned to the Library room. . . .[14] After tea we went to the Book auction. The sales, were as high again as I had anticipated. Several fine works were sold. My bill amounted to $2.90. About half past ten we started on our return. As no stage leaves the city for Troy at this late hour, we commenced our journey on foot. We had got within about a mile of the half way house, when an Extra Stage overtook us. In this we returned the remainder of the way. The clock struck 12 as we got out at Babcocks.

---

member of the Albany Institute, to which he submitted reports on various scientific subjects. *Transactions,* Albany Institute, *1,* part 2: appendix, p. 68, and see below, Minutes for November 25, 1828.

[13] Representative from Tompkins County. Werner, *Civil List of New York,* p. 434.

[14] Here, we have deleted Fitch's remarks on some of the library's legal and literary holdings.

FROM LEWIS C. BECK

Henry Papers, Smithsonian Archives

Middlebury Vt. April 15th 1827.

My Dear friend

My time has been so constantly occupied since my arrival here[1] as to leave me no time for writing to you as I intended to have done some days since. There is such a barreness of Apparatus here that I am kept constantly on the run in preparing for my experiments. As to the scale,[2] you need not send any to this place at present. The Students who attend the courses do it, generally without any particular desire of becoming Chemists, but because they are rather obliged to do so. Few, therefore, will be likely to take hold in right earnest particularly as they have many other Studies to attend to.

As to what ought to be put on the back I am still somewhat in doubt but give you a rough sketch, which you may alter, amend, cut down &c in any way you think best.

"The Scale of Chemical Equivalents of which this is considered an

---

[1] Beck, who resided in Albany, was in Middlebury to give a course of lectures on chemistry in Middlebury College. He was at this time simultaneously Professor of Botany and Chemistry at the Vermont Academy of Medicine in Castleton and on the faculty of the Rensselaer School.

[2] Beck's and Henry's scale of chemical equivalents is further discussed in this letter; for

additional documentation, see the instructions for using the scale, September 1827, below, and the undated excerpt from Beck's Autobiography printed immediately after. Only one example of the scale is known to survive. It is at Transylvania College, and is described in Leland A. Brown, *Early Philosophical Apparatus at Transylvania College* (Lexington, Kentucky, 1959), p. 25.

improvement was an invention of Dr Wollaston.[3] It consists of a series of numbers commencing with 1 & increasing by one, written under each other, in such a manner that equal distances denote equal ratios. The distances between 100 & 200 is the same as between 1 & 2 because 100:200 :: 1:2. So also the distances between 100 & 300. Opposite to these numbers on the scale are now written the bodies of which these numbers are the equivalents & the distances between these, are the measures of the ratios of their combining quantities.

In the present scale Hydrogen is assumed as the radix in which respect it differs from that of Dr Wollaston.[4] When the slide is up all the substances are opposite to their atomic numbers, upon this supposition. By moving the slide we can instantly ascertain the proportions of the constituents of a compound whose weight is known. Suppose we have 100 parts of Carbonate of Lime & we wish to know how much acid & base it contains. Move the Slide so that 100 on it shall be directly opposite to Carb. Lime. The number opposite Lime will be 56 & opposite Carbonic acid 44. = to 100. Now if we wish to decompose this with any of the acids we can instantly ascertain the amount of each necessary to effect this object as of Liquid Sulphuric acid 98 parts & the result will be crystallized Sulphate of Lime 172 parts."[5]

You can add another illustration of its utility in analysis. One mistake I have noticed. Sulphate of Potash should be 88, I believe instead of 89.[6] But I have not the means of deciding correctly as my Brande is not at my elbow. Look at this if you please, & correct the mistake, if it is one. By all means sign our names to the above *"guide board"* or any other which you may adopt.

> In haste Your sincere
> friend
> Lewis C Beck.

---

[3] William Hyde Wollaston, "A Synoptic Scale of Chemical Equivalents," *Phil. Trans.*, 1814, *104*:1–22. The ways in which their own scale was considered an improvement over Wollaston's are specified in the directions for using it, September 1827, below, and in Beck's Autobiography, which follows.

[4] Wollaston based his scale on oxygen = 10.

[5] The combining weights in this paragraph were drawn mainly from William Thomas Brande, *A Manual of Chemistry* . . . (London, 1819). Henry's copy—the "First American, from the Second London Edition," annotated by William James MacNeven (1763–1841; *DAB*), three volumes in one, New York, 1821

—survives in his library.

Brande's equivalent weights were based on oxygen = 8 and water = 9 (1 hydrogen + 1 oxygen). Thus for example sulfuric acid was interpreted as being composed of 1 sulfur (= 16) plus 3 oxygen (= 3 x 8 = 24) plus 1 water (= 9), or 49, where we would write, balancing the *molecular* components, 2S(= 64) + 3O$_2$(= 96) + 2H$_2$O(= 36), or 196(= 2H$_2$SO$_4$). See Brande, op. cit., pp. 113 (sulfuric acid), 130 (carbonic acid), 192 (lime), 197 (carbonate of lime), 195 (sulfate of lime). That is, we balance molecules where they would balance atoms.

[6] Beck is right; see Brande, op. cit., p. 181.

FROM STEPHEN VAN RENSSELAER RYAN[1]

Henry Papers, Smithsonian Archives

Camp Experiment[2] } May 24th 1827
Fortress Monroe }

Dear Friend

I now fulfil my promise to you which I made before I left Albany last which was to write you an account of myself and situation.

I stopped at West Point where I saw all of your friends & who were all well; according to your request I told Lt Ross[3] that you intended to stop at the Point sometime during the Spring. He said that he should be extremely glad to see you and as he is a tolerably sincere fellow you may believe that what he says comes from the heart. I staid at the Point but two days and then continued my line of march for my post being as you may recollect under some what *pointed orders.* I arrived at this place the 13th of April after stopping at the different places on the road. I reported for duty in a half of an hour after I had arrived. This place is situated at the mouth of the Hampton Roads, where they enter the Chesipeak Bay. Two hundred miles from Baltimore about the same from Washington and

---

[1] Stephen Van Rensselaer Ryan (d. 1840), apparently of no relation to the Van Rensselaer family, probably became a friend of Joseph Henry's while they attended the Albany Academy together, Ryan completing his course in 1820. Entering West Point in 1821, he graduated sixth in his class in 1825 (Alexander Dallas Bache, who was to become one of Henry's closest personal and professional friends, was first in that same class). Ryan's activities after being commissioned in the artillery remain a mystery; however, we do know that he resigned that commission in 1833. By 1835 he became a Brigadier General in the Arkansas Militia. He served, perhaps simultaneously, as Transportation Agent for the U.S. Quartermaster Department in Napoleon, Arkansas, where he also engaged in business as a merchant. In this letter to Henry, it can be inferred that Ryan was undergoing special training in the newly developed weapons of the Artillery. See *Academy Seventy-fifth Anniversary,* pp. 80–81; Charles K. Gardner, comp., *A Dictionary of . . . the Army of the United States,* 2d ed. (New York, 1860), p. 392; Francis B. Heitman, *Historical Register and Dictionary of the United States Army,* 2 vols. (Washington, 1903), 1:855; George W. Cullum, *Biographical Register . . . of the*

United States Military Academy, 2 vols. (New York, 1868), *1:272.*

[2] So named as this place at Fort Monroe was primarily devoted to the testing of new ordnance.

[3] Edward C. Ross (1801–1851). Entering West Point from Pennsylvania in 1817, Ross graduated seventh in his class in 1821. He remained at the Military Academy as an Assistant Professor in Mathematics, also acting as Instructor for the Artillery School in 1824 (where he would certainly have met Ryan). From 1825 until 1833 he was the Principal Assistant Professor of Mathematics at the Academy. Resigning in 1839, Ross joined the faculty of Kenyon College as Professor of Mathematics and Natural Philosophy serving until 1848. He then became the popular first Professor of Mathematics at the Free Academy of New York City (later the City College of New York) until his death. See Cullum, op. cit., *1:213;* Gardner, op. cit., pp. 388–389; George Francis Smythe, *Kenyon College, Its First Century* (New Haven, 1924), p. 168; *Catalogue of the Theological Seminary . . . Kenyon College . . .* (Gambier, Ohio, 1847), unpaged; S. Willis Rudy, *The College of the City of New York: A History* (New York, 1949), p. 56.

eighteen from Norfolk, Virginia, to all of which places steamboats go. I had almost forgotten to state the distance to Richmond which is Ninety six miles and to *Yorktown* thirty miles by land, a steam boat goes from Norfolk to Richmond and a steam boat between the Point and Norfolk every day passage *fifty cents* so that you see we are not shut out of the world.

The Point on which the fortifications are building is of a white sand which is very loose so that the slightest breeze is always filled with it and is very annoying to the eyes and not very good for the clothes when we come off drill after there has been some considerable wind. We look as though we had been dusted over with flour, we drink rain water after it has passed through the sand which is thrown up into the works. Opposite the fortress are the works of the celebrated "Rip Raps." The works at this post are to be large and are well laid out but I cannot say *when they will be finished.* The Point is almost surrounded by water but of difficult approach on any side the water being shallow. I suppose that you know that the object of the school is to give instruction to the officers of Artillery. We have eleven companies of troops here and fifty five officers. We have been in Camp since the 23ᵈ of April, have had green peas ever since I arrived at the Post. Cherries and strawberries have been plenty for two weeks. This will give you some idea of the climate. Within a few days past we have the misfortune to have two six pounder's burst at one of which there [were] twelve officers practicing firing at the target. None were hurt as good Providence would have it though a piece weighing about two hundred pounds fell between two officers who were standing about three feet apart. The same piece came within five feet of me, a piece of the same gun weighing about forty pounds flew into our camp a distance of sixty rods at least. By the other gun which was burst one man was killed another is expected to die of his wounds and eight others were slightly wounded. Both times there [were] several officers present and as muc[h] exposed as the men but not one was in the least [harmed] which appears almost, *I will not [say] miraculous,* but I don't know what to say. I like the place very well and the commanding officer well also. We have company enough and that is tolerably good: my respects to enquiring friends write and direct to Fortress Monroe, Virginia.

Very truly your old friend
S. V. R. Ryan

July 25, 1827

TO BENNETT H. HENDERSON[1]

Retained Copy, Henry Papers, Smithsonian Archives

Albany July 25th 1827

Dear Sir

From the greate anxiety I feel on the subject of the appointment of the professorship of Chemestry in your institution,[2] I hope you will pardon me for requesting you in addition to the many polite attentions you shewed me while at the Point, to write me on the receipt of this whether Col. Thayer[3] has yet returned to the Point & whether you have heard any thing more concerning the appointment.

If Col. Thayer has not returned to the Point will you be so good as to immediatly forward to Washington the letter I left with you for the Sect. of war as it is of consequence that it should be in Washington as soon as possible since it has been refered to in other letters directed to the Heads of Department.[4]

Resp Your humble servt

Joseph Henry

[1] Lt. Bennett H. Henderson (1805–1832) served as Acting Assistant Professor of Ethics at West Point, 1826–1829. For two years afterward he was Judge Advocate of the Western Department, resigning from the Army shortly before his death in 1832. Charles K. Gardner, comp., *Dictionary of . . . the Army of the United States*, 2d ed. (New York, 1860), p. 225.

[2] West Point. We have no other information on this attempt of Henry's to go to what was obviously a better location for a man interested in science.

[3] Sylvanus Thayer (1785–1872) was Superintendent of the U.S. Military Academy from 1817 to 1833 and is generally credited with the elevation of West Point to a first-rank instituition. *DAB*. After leaving West Point, Thayer served as an engineer officer in New England. In 1867 he founded the Thayer School of Engineering at Dartmouth College.

[4] Henry's letter and the other letters supporting his candidacy have not been found in the records of the Academy, the Army Engineers, or the Secretary of War.

MINUTES, ACADEMY TRUSTEES

Trustees' Minutes, 1:306–308, Albany Academy Archives

August 9, 1827

Twice a year (in August and March) the Albany Academy conducted its annual and semiannual examinations and public distribution of prizes.[1] This minute is

[1] Records of these occur in the Trustees' Minutes in two forms: as a regular entry in its proper chronological position and as memoranda inserted in the Minutes (with other

for the first of the former attended by Henry as a member of the faculty; he participated in four additional annual examinations before his departure for Princeton. The 1832 examinations and the public distribution were canceled because of the cholera epidemic raging in Albany.[2]

Twice each year a committee of the Trustees would examine each and every class in the school on the assigned subject matter, quite often a specific text. We have no evidence of an actual examination and cannot say with certainty if the Trustees used written or oral tests or both. Nor is it possible to evaluate the quality and intensity of the Trustees' interrogations in the absence of any concrete evidence. Since the founding of the Academy, the Trustees, as a corporate body, had been conscientious; indeed, some had clearly devoted much effort to the affairs of the Academy. A reasonable assumption, therefore, is that these annual and semiannual examinations were serious appraisals of the performance of the students, not to mention the faculty. (In the 1827 Minutes, the examining committee reported with approval that the faculty "have not limited themselves to mere *memoriter* [from memory] instruction, but at every step, have endeavored to elicit the mind of the pupil, and make him thoroughly understand the subject of study.")[3]

On the basis of the examinations, a public distribution of premiums was made, usually on the next day. (In 1827 Henry's classes were examined on August 8.) Clearly, this was a civic ceremonial of some consequence in the early days of the Academy. The program for the ceremony of August 7, 1828, started with a procession formed at ten o'clock in the following order:[4]

MUSIC
Students of the Academy
Former Students
The Faculty
The Trustees
Former Members of the Board of Trustees
The Hon. the Corporation
The Regents of the University
Judges of the State and the United States Courts
Officers of the State Government
Parents and Guardians
Citizens and Strangers.

---

items) for the record. The former usually consist of text plus a clipping from a newspaper which gives the names of prize winners. The memoranda often have the printed program and notations as to which books were given to which students.

[2] For the epidemic, part of the great cholera epidemic of 1832, see Munsell, *Ann. Alb.*, 9: 249–256. See also Charles E. Rosenberg, *The*

Cholera Years . . . (Chicago, 1962).

[3] This occurs in the newspaper clipping from the *Argus* and is interesting as indicating what the Trustees regarded and announced as a desirable goal.

[4] From the printed program in the memorandum of 1828, Minutes, Academy Trustees, unpaged.

In 1829 the "La Fayette Guard," a uniformed company from New York City, marched also.[5] After an introductory prayer and music, members of the student body gave recitations from orations and writings literary, political, and moral,[6] these being interspersed by music at suitable intervals. (The Trustees would also award prizes for oratory on the basis of these declamations.) The premiums awarded were books. The surviving records in the Albany Academy Archives do not give enough information for exact bibliographic identification. From what little is given, premiums were usually books of travel, juvenile anthologies, and works of natural history. In 1827 thirteen copies of a book on "Nat. Philosophy," not otherwise identified, were awarded, apparently for the last time during Henry's tenure.[7]

The proceedings of these events provide a convenient summary of Henry's teaching load. In 1827 he taught one class each in trigonometry, the use of globes, algebra, and bookkeeping. In addition Henry had two classes of Euclid and seven of arithmetic. In 1829 in addition to the class in trigonometry and surveying, Henry had two classes each in Euclid, algebra, and physical geography, as well as seven in arithmetic. In 1831 there were single classes in "conic lectures," surveying, architecture, and a course described as encompassing differential and integral calculus, astronomy, descriptive geometry, and mechanics. These classes were in addition to two each in Euclid and algebra and six classes in arithmetic. Clearly, Henry was trying to expand the scope of his teaching. In 1831 the Trustees gave no premium for the conic lectures because the class had not usually recited together and recommended against establishing a premium for the calculus course because of insufficient enrollment.[8] This modest degree of success, coupled with the heavy teaching load, undoubtedly weighed heavily on a man who was increasingly anxious to spend more time on research.

---

[5] Minutes, Academy Trustees, August 6, 1829, *1*:340–343.

[6] About the only one of these possibly reflecting Henry's closest interests was the piece in 1828 on the character of William Herschel by Jean Baptiste Joseph Fourier, probably from the latter's éloge. See 1828 Memorandum, Minutes, Academy Trustees, unpaged. The éloge was given on June 7, 1824, and published separately that year.

[7] Memorandum for 1827, Minutes, Academy Trustees, unpaged.

[8] The course information is in the memoranda for 1827, cited above, 1829 (August 6, 1829, *1*:340–343) and 1831 (August 3, 1831, 2: 25–29). Henry's best students were complimented by the Trustees for their work in both courses, even though no premium was given. Henry and his students in 1829 were complimented for the maps they had constructed.

LEWIS C. BECK AND JOSEPH HENRY
DESCRIPTION OF A SCALE OF CHEMICAL EQUIVALENTS[1]
Henry Papers, Smithsonian Archives

[September 1827][2]

DESCRIPTION AND USE
Of the Scale.

The Scale of Chemical Equivalents, the invention of which is due to Dr. Wollaston,[3] is an instrument stamped with the accuracy and ingenuity of its author; and which has contributed, in an eminent degree, to facilitate the general study and practice of Chemistry.[4] The present scale differs from the original one, in the assumption of Hydrogen, as the radix or unity. Two principal advantages arise from assuming this substance as the unit.

1. We avoid fractional quantities,[5] and the whole scale, when the slider is properly placed, becomes a table of atomic weights.[6]

---

[1] The description was printed on a long piece of paper which was pasted on the back of the scale. The paper measures 18½″ × 4½″.

We have seen (above, Henry's Journal of a Trip to West Point and New York, June 12, [1826], especially footnotes 11 and 12) that John Torrey intended to construct such a scale. An additional impetus may have come from the scale devised by David Boswell Reid (1805–1863; *DNB, DAB*), chemist at Edinburgh who later came to the United States. Reid's scale was marketed with a pamphlet, *Directions for Using the Improved Sliding Scale of Chemical Equivalents; with a Short Explanation of the Doctrine of Definite Proportions* (Edinburgh, 1826), a copy of which is in the Henry Library, though we do not know when he acquired it. There are similarities which suggest that Henry probably had Reid's pamphlet by him when he wrote his description (see below, footnote 6). His other authorities were William Thomas Brande, *A Manual of Chemistry* . . . (London, 1819) and Thomas Thomson, *An Attempt to Establish the First Principles of Chemistry by Experiment*, 2 vols. (London, 1825). Of course, Henry used L. C. Beck's suggestions, too; see Beck's draft of the description in his letter to Henry, April 15, 1827, above.

[2] This is the publication date printed at the end of the scale. Beck's letter of April 15, 1827, above, makes it clear that he and Henry

were working on the scale through the first half of 1827.

[3] William Hyde Wollaston, "A Synoptic Scale of Chemical Equivalents," *Phil. Trans.*, 1814, *104*:1–22.

[4] Wollaston hoped that his scale "will at least serve for a specimen of the extreme facility of mechanical approximation, which may very frequently be advantageously substituted for computations, that are often more laborious than the accuracy of our data warrants; and if it tend to introduce into more general use, that valuable instrument the common sliding rule, it will be the means of saving no inconsiderable portion of time to those who are engaged in scientific pursuits." Ibid., p. 18.

[5] The assumption that atomic weights were all whole numbers when hydrogen was taken as unity was part of "Prout's Hypothesis." On this, see W. H. Brock, "The Life and Work of William Prout [1785–1850]," *Medical History*, 1965, *9*:101–126. It is interesting that Beck and Henry make no mention of Prout; they follow Brande in this. Reid discussed Prout briefly (p. 7) and Thomson wrote his *Attempt* with the avowed purpose of establishing Prout's hypothesis. See J. R. Partington, *A History of Chemistry*, 4 vols. (London, 1961–1970), *4*:222–232.

[6] Reid, op. cit., p. [i]: "In order to render [the scale] as extensively useful as possible, a great many additions have been made, while,

2. These atomic numbers exhibit for the most part, in reference to hydrogen, the specific gravity of gases and other chemical substances supposed to be in an aeriform state, and also the combining ratios of their weights under the same volume.[7]

MATHEMATICAL CONSTRUCTION

It will be observed that the slider of the scale is graduated into divisions and subdivisions continually decreasing in length, from 8 at the top to 330 near the bottom. These divisions correspond in relative lengths to the differences of the logarythms of the numbers placed opposite them. They were protracted by assuming a convenient length as unity, and transferring from a scale of equal parts the distances corresponding to the differences of the logs. of the several numbers on the slider. Thus the distance between 8 and 9, or between 10 and 20, is a linear representation of the excess of the log. of the latter over that of the former of these numbers.

Now since the division of numbers is performed by taking the difference of their logs, and since the several divisions on the scale represent the difference of the logs, of the numbers placed opposite them, it follows, that the distance between any two numbers will be equal to the distance between any other two that give the same quotient by division. But numbers which give the same quotient have the same ratio to each other, therefore equality of ratio on the scale is expressed by equality of distance.

Thus if one leg of a pair of compasses be placed at 8 and the other opened to 16, and the instrument be transferred as a measure to any other part of the scale, its extremities will be found to rest only on numbers that have the same ratio as those from which it was tranferred; as 10 and 20, 30 and 60 &c.

But the same thing may be performed by placing marks on the fixed part of the scale to represent particular openings of the compass, and by merely moving the slider past these, the several numbers which have the same ratios will be indicated. Thus, marks at oxygen and sulphur on the fixed part

---

at the same time, it has been very much simplified, by taking hydrogen as a standard of comparison, instead of oxygen, by which fractional numbers are avoided, formerly a source of very great inconvenience."

[7] Notice that Henry said "for the most part." Strict connection between the specific weights of gases and their atomic weights required the intervention of Avogadro's hypothesis, that equal volumes of gases under similar conditions contain the same number of gas molecules. None of the authors that Henry drew on made use of this hypothesis (though Prout had: see Brock, op. cit., p. 106). Brande, for example (p. 161), gave two tables, one for gases whose specific gravities in terms of hydrogen = 1 are identical with their atomic weights in terms of the atomic weight of hydrogen = 1, and one for exceptions. The vicissitudes of Avogadro's hypothesis and the vexed problem of the atomic weights in the first half of the nineteenth century are subjects too complicated to go into here. See Partington, op. cit., 4:199–232.

correspond, when the slider is in a proper position, to 8 and 16. Now if the slider be moved so that 10, is at the upper mark, the lower will be opposite 20, &c. as in the above case.

CHEMICAL EXPLANATION

The application of the logametric scale to Chemistry is founded on the most important fact in this science; which is, *that all bodies whether simple or compound, that enter into Chemical combination, always unite in weights or in multiples of weights that have the same constant ratio to each other.* And as these relative weights have the same effect in forming neutral compounds and in producing other chemical changes they are called chemical equivalents, and may be expressed in numbers referable to a common standard taken as unity. On this scale the least combining quantity of hydrogen is taken as the unit; and as eight times as much oxygen by weight enters into combination with hydrogen to form the chemical compound water, oxygen will be expressed by 8, and water by 9. If, therefore, the slider be so placed that 8 near the top of it coincides with the upper oxygen, the whole scale becomes a synoptical table of these chemical equivalents, having hydrogen as its radix. Thus 16 is the equivalent for Sulphur, 17 for Ammonia, 24 for Sodium, 70 for Barium, 110 for Silver,[8] &c. &c. These substances were placed opposite the respective numbers on the slider as they have been determined by Thompson, Brande and other approved authors.

In order to diminish the length of the scale and render it more portable, it commences with oxygen 8, instead of hydrogen 1, and 10 atoms of hydrogen are placed opposite 10 on the slider. For the same reason 2 carbon, the atomic weight of the atom of which is 6, is placed opposite 12.

Again, as water and oxygen enter into combination in several definate proportions, 2 oxygen is placed opposite 16, 2 water opposite 18; 3 ox. opposite 24; 3 water opposite 27, &c, &c.

* These have also been called atomic weights, because philosophers have supposed that in all cases of chemical combination and union takes place between the ultimate atoms of bodies. This is the basis of the Atomic Theory.[9]

[8] These weights were cited by Reid (see table, pp. 21–26) and Thomson (see tables at the end of vol. 2); Brande (see tables, pp. 154–160, 413–454) cites a different figure for silver. In general, here and in the examples below, Henry used atomic weights which were identical in Brande, Thomson, and Reid (who probably took his from Thomson anyway). Where there was conflict, Henry followed Thomson, presumably because Thomson's determinations were more recent and because

they were all whole numbers.

[9] Since there is no corresponding asterisk in the text, we do not know exactly which passage this footnote refers to. We assume it would be the second sentence, ending with "unity."

Throughout this period there was uncertainty about the logical status of the atomic theory: was it a theory of matter or a set of rules governing chemical combination? Beck and Henry reflect this dilemma by using in

EXAMPLES AND ILLUSTRATIONS

1. Without moving the slider, the scale shows us that 50 is the equivalent number for carbonate of lime; this substance consisting of carbonic acid and lime, we find the equivalent of the former to be 22, and of the latter 28–50. Any denomination may be given to these numbers, as ounces, grains, parts, &c. But if we wish to ascertain the constituents of any other number of ounces, grains, or parts, as 100 for example, we have only to place 100 on the slider at carbonate of lime; and carbonic acid is then opposite 44, and lime 56; which are the proportions of these ingredients in 100.

2. Suppose we wish to ascertain the constituents of 100 parts of nitrate of ammonia. Move the slider so that 100 is at nitrate of ammonia, which we find has 1. *W.* before it, indicating one proportional of water. Then 1. water on the scale, is opposite 11.3, on the slider; ammonia opposite to 21.2, and dry nitric acid to 67.5. The constituents of 100 parts of nitrate of ammonia are, therefore, 11.3, water; 21.2, ammonia, and 67.5 dry nitric acid, =100.

3. When oxygen at the top is at 8 on the slider, sulphate of potash is at 88, which is therefore its equivalent number. In order to decompose this, we may take nitrate of barytes, the barytes having a greater affinity for sulphuric acid, than the potash. The quantity requisite for the decomposition is 132, being the number at nitrate of barytes; and the amount of sulphate of barytes resulting from this decomposition will be 118. We can also ascertain the quantity of nitrate of barytes necessary to decompose 50, 100, 150 or any other number of parts or grains of sulphate of potash, by placing either of the above numbers on the slider opposite to sulphate of potash and then finding the number of nitrate of barytes.

To find the composition of the metallic salts, we ascertain the amount of acid and *oxide* of the metal. Thus nitrate of silver is equivalent to 172, and consists of dry nitric acid, 54, and oxide of silver, 118, =172. So also we find 100 parts of sulphate of barytes to consist of dry sulphuric acid, 34, and baryta or oxide of barium, 66. And in all cases where *W** is not prefixed to the salt it is then supposed to consist of a base united to a dry acid.

LEWIS C. BECK,

JOSEPH HENRY.

* See abbreviations on the face of the scale.

---

their main text the term "equivalent," and relegating the "atomic theory" to a footnote. "Equivalent" was a term thought to be neutral on the question of the reality of atoms, a term expressive of chemical facts which held true whether "philosophers" were right or not about what "takes place between the ultimate atoms of bodies." The subject has been well treated by David M. Knight, *Atoms and Elements* (London, 1967).

EXCERPT FROM LEWIS C. BECK'S AUTOBIOGRAPHY[1]

Beck's Autobiography, 4:9–11, Lewis C. Beck Papers,
Rutgers University Library

During this year (1827) Mr. Joseph Henry, then a Professor in the Albany Academy, (now Secretary of the Smithsonian Institution) & myself, published *"A Scale of Chemical Equivalents,"* which we constructed under the direction of Dr. Wollaston, the celebrated English Chemist. Our Scale was nearly twice the length of Wollaston's & contained the names of more than double the number of substances.[2] It was also more neatly made.

Mr. Henry arranged the divisions on the slider & furnished the account of the Mathematical Construction. I arranged all the substances according to their atomic weight, & made the entire copy for the engraver, a work which of course required great accuracy.

The Scale was engraved on Copper at considerable expense. One great difficulty in the way of the accuracy of the Scale, was in attaching the printed part to the wood work, in such a manner that the exact ratios should be preserved in every position of the slider. The scale was at length engraved on bank paper & put on by Mr. Wilson,[3] a globe maker, who was accustomed to this kind of work. Still many of them were, upon trial, found to be inaccurate & these were laid aside.

There were published at first some 6 or 8 dozen of these Scales, & being considerably in demand, we prepared a Second edition. In this several new substances were introduced. But Wilson had, I think died in the mean time & we were obliged to employ another person to complete the work. He did not succeed very well—he, indeed, had no idea of the accuracy required, & the result was, that many of them were useless. Out of about 150, perhaps not more than 100 were fit for use.

From the expense & trouble which attended the construction of these scales, they were necessarily sold at a considerable price. I scarcely know whether the sales were sufficient to meet the expenses, but this did not at that time enter into our calculation.

---

[1] Dated May 1851.

[2] Wollaston nowhere says in his paper how long his scale was; from his Plate I, however, depicting the scale, it appears that eighty separate substances were included.

[3] *Howell and Tenney*, p. 600: "The first globe manufacturer in the United States was James Wilson, who was born in Londonderry, N.H., in the latter part of the eighteenth century, and died in Bradford, Vt., in extreme old age. . . . About 1820 his sons, John and Samuel Wilson, established a globe manufactory in Albany. . . . So much did they improve the art of globe-making as to elicit the admission of English manufacturers, that their globes were geographically and mechanically superior to their own. John Wilson died in 1833, and his brother Samuel near that date."

TO ÉLIE MAGLOIRE DURAND[1]
Retained Copy, Henry Papers, Smithsonian Archives

Albany Sept. 11, 1827

Dear Sir

I send by the bearer Mr. Robinson[2] one Dozen Chemical scales. We cannot afford [to sell] them for less than one dollar & twenty five Cts a piece by the wholesale. You can therefore fix your price accordingly.

Respectfully yours
Joseph Henry

[1] Élie Magloire Durand (1794–1873), probably known to Henry as Elias Durand, a French pharmacist and botanist. After having had considerable training in chemistry and having acted as a commissioned pharmacist in the French Army, Durand came to America in 1816, led a nomadic life for several years, and finally settled in Philadelphia with his own drugstore. His store quickly became famous not only for its fashionable imported furnishings but also for Durand's commitment to pharmacy as a profession and a public responsibility. At the center of the Philadelphia medical circle, Durand introduced many foreign medicines and developed several of his own. He cultivated a keen interest in American flora and was a member of both the Academy of Natural Sciences and the American Philosophical Society. Surely Henry and L. C. Beck could have wished for no more influential marketplace for their chemical scales. See *DAB* and Venia T. and Maurice E. Phillips, comps., *Guide to the Manuscript Collections in the Academy of Natural Sciences* (Philadelphia, 1963), p. 259.

[2] Not identified.

TO [LEWIS C. BECK][1]
Lewis C. Beck Papers, Rutgers University Library[2]

Albany Frid. Sept 21, 1827

Dear Sir

Although as usual I am busily engaged in applying *birch* to one end and *arithmetic* to the other yet I have plenty of time to collect a few notes on the subject of *brome* (alias the essence of st-k)[3] or to execute with pleasure any order within my means that you may be pleased to intrust me with.

The facts I send were collected from the annals of Philos & Brand's Jour.[4] They do not contain an account of the nature of the compounds of

[1] Beck was then teaching at the Vermont Academy of Medicine, Castleton.

[2] A Mary Henry copy is in the Smithsonian Archives, indicating that a retained copy once existed. The text does not materially differ from the original received by L. C. Beck, allowing for the limitations of Miss Henry's transcribers.

[3] Was "stink" a taboo word in polite Albany circles at this date?

[4] William Thomas Brande (1788–1866) had served as one of the joint editors of the Royal Institution's *Quarterly Journal of Science and Art*. The Mary Henry copy says "Repertory

brome as you desired. On this point the books give little more than a description of the different processes of forming them, which I thought would not be very interesting at present and I have therefore merely given the names of the several substans with which the brome unites.[5]

As to the scale I have sent one doz. to Philadelphia[6] and half a doz. to Dr. Hadley,[7] also left one at Webster's and another at Dr. Meggs';[8] the woodwork of 1½ doz more is completed and before they are varnished I will correct iodine with a pen. Finally the copy right which you concur in thinking necessary shall be secured.

The aurora has also been seen here several times displaying its fantastic flirtations amoung the clouds and stars of the north since the grand exhibition of the 28.ᵗʰ ult. The knowing ones of this city have been likewise engaged in theorizing on the cause of that phenomenon & three opinions principally seam to prevail; the first is that it was only a lunar rainbow; the second that it was merely a reflection from a cloud, of the aurora; and the third which appears to me as plausible as the other two is that it was a sign in the heavens that Mrs. Whipple should have been hung with Jessy Strang.[9] (By the by I have seen a very striking likeness of Strang done by Collins).[10]

---

of Arts" which is doubtful. Brande was a chemist and a colleague of Faraday at the Royal Institution. Two of his early works survive in the Henry Library and could conceivably have been purchased in Albany: *Dissertation Third: Exhibiting a General View of the Progress of Chemical Philosophy . . .* (Boston, 1818) and *Manual of Chemistry* (New York, 1821).

[5] Apparently Henry enclosed a list of literature references which no longer exists in the Beck papers. From Beck's *A Manual of Chemistry* (Albany, 1831), pp. 117–119, one can get a convenient summary of the state of chemical knowledge of bromine as of the date of publication. Bromine had been recently discovered, and Beck was obviously anxious to keep up with developments.

[6] For Beck and Henry's collaboration on the scale of chemical equivalents, see above, L. C. Beck to Henry, April 15, 1827, and related documents; the dozen scales were going to Elias Durand (see preceding document).

[7] James Hadley (1785–1869), a physician, for many years a professor at the Fairfield and Geneva Medical Colleges. Franklin B. Hough, *American Biographical Notes* (Albany, 1875), p. 183.

[8] Probably Richard M. Meigs.

[9] Jesse Strang and Elsie D. Whipple were accused of the murder of John Whipple, Elsie D. Whipple's husband. On July 27, 1827, Strang was found guilty by a jury with only needed, in Munsell's words, "a few minutes absence" to reach this verdict. Strang was hanged on August 24, 1827. Munsell, who probably witnessed the event, described it later as follows:

Jesse Strang was executed in the Hudson Street ravine, a few rods above Eagle street. The hills on either side were densely crowded with spectators, as many as 40,000 having collected, some of them from a great distance. He was attended upon the gallows by the Rev. Wm. B. Lacey, and the cord which sustained the drop was cut by the sheriff, Conrad A. Ten Eyck. It was the last public execution in Albany. The principal avenues to the city were thronged during the fore part of the day with people from the country. The number of vehicles entering from the north was 1100 by count and 175 were left by the road side above the Patroon's bridge. The citizens had never seen anything to equal it.

Apparently many of the citizens regretted not having seen a double hanging. Munsell, *Ann. Alb.*, 9:158–159.

[10] William Collins, a portrait painter active

On looking over the different journals I find eight accounts of auroral arches similar in almost every respect to the one seen here. They all extended across the heavens in an east & west direction, or at right angles to the magnetic meridian, and nearly all moved in the same manner to the south. Prof. Hansteen's observations on the aurora as well as on the magnetism of the earth, published in the Edin. Jour. are very interesting: he asserts from repeated observation, that the aurora is formed of luminous beams moving parallell to the direction of the dipping needle; and that the centre of the arches formed by these beams, is always the same as the magnetic pole of the earth; these observations are certainly corroborated by the appearance of the arches above mentioned.[11]

I wish to direct your attention to an experiment mentioned in the historical sketch of electro-magnetism given in the Annals,[12] which I think has considerable analogy to the auroral arch. It is this. A wire is bent so as to form nearly a complete circle of about 16 inches in diameter. The two ends are made to approach & are placed in two cups of mercury one above the 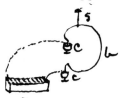 other so that the whole apparatus may be perpendicular to the horizon and the wire at liberty to turn on its points. When a current of the galvanic fluid is passed through the bent wire, after some oscillations it places itself in a plane perpendicular to the magnetic meridian and thus in mineature, as it appears to me, represents the auroral arch. There is certainly a striking analogy particularly when viewed in conjunction with M. Ampere's Theory of the magnetism of the earth, which he supposes to be merely caused by currents of electricity circulating in planes at right angles to the magnetic north & south.[13] But be this as it may I am sure that there "are more things in

* NOTE: In the above marginal sketch (a) the trough (b) the wire (c,c) the cups & (s) a silk thread to suspend the wire.

in Albany, 1827–1832. George C. Groce and David H. Wallace, *The New York Historical Society's Dictionary of Artists in America, 1564–1860* (New Haven, 1957), p. 141.

[11] Christopher Hansteen (1784–1873); director of the observatory at Oslo, very active as an observer, experimenter, and theorist in matters involving terrestrial magnetism and other geophysical phenomena, in this case the aurora. The reference here is to "On the Aurora Borealis and Polar Fogs," *Edinburgh Philosophical Journal*, 1825, *12*:83–93, 235–238 and "On the Number and Situation of the Magnetic Poles of the Earth," ibid., 1825, *12*: 328–334. Henry would soon do work on auroras himself (see below, footnote 10 of Albany

Institute Minutes, September 21, 1830).

[12] [Michael Faraday], "Historical Sketch of Electro-Magnetism," *Annals of Philosophy*, 1821, 2:195–200, 274–290; 1821, 3:102–121. The experiment is by Ampère and is described by Faraday on pp. 279–280 and later discussed on pp. 115–116.

[13] Ampère's theory of the earth's magnetism was described by Faraday (see preceding note, p. 116). It assumed that magnetism is caused by currents of electricity and that, in the case of this planet, the arrangement of materials in the earth acts as a battery producing electrical currents whose characteristics result in the various properties of terrestrial magnetism.

heaven & earth" connected with electro-magnetism "than are yet dream't of in philosophy."

Give my respects to Mrs. B. and be assured that

I remain your sincere Friend
Joseph Henry

TO JOHN TORREY

Retained Copy, Henry Papers, Smithsonian Archives

Albany Thurs. Oct. 4ᵗʰ 1827

Dear Sir

Your letter of the 28ᵗʰ[1] only came to hand this day and I hasten to inform you that your troughs[2] which, I have retained so long are still in my possession. I beg you will pardon my remissness in not sending them, or writing before this time; as we were disappointed in performing the experiments on the body of Strang,[3] & I had an impression that you would not want <*the troughs*> them before the first of Nov. A gentleman of my acquaintance leaves here for New York on tuesday next, with whome I will send them & you will probably receive them on Wednesday. This time I hope will not be too late for any arraingements you may have made concerning them as I should regret extremely that your kindness to me should be met on my part with any thing that would cause you an inconvenience.

I am much obliged to you for your notice of the errors on the scale. Sul. copper according to Thompson should have been 125 instead of 152 as it is on the scale.[4] Silica was taken from Brand's tables (32)[5] but I agree with you in thinking that silicon would have been better. These errors shall be

---

[1] Not found.

[2] i.e., galvanic troughs.

[3] Apparently Henry had conducted disappointing galvanic experiments on the recently executed Strang or was prevented from doing so. Galvani's discovery of "animal electricity" had prompted a rash of experiments on electrically induced muscle contractions. And, as the chemist Andrew Ure revealed in an 1819 article ("Account of Experiments on the Body of a Criminal after Execution," *Quarterly Journal of Science*, 1819, 6:283–284), the corpses of recently executed criminals were common subjects. The experimental goals were twofold: to develop techniques of electrical therapy (Ure even foresaw possibilities of reviving the dead) and to discover the precise nature and role of electricity in the body,

undoubtedly Henry's main purpose. In a later volume, we will encounter Henry conducting similar experiments on an executed criminal in New Jersey.

[4] Henry is referring to sulphate of copper in Thomas Thomson's *An Attempt to Establish the First Principles of Chemistry by Experiment*, 2 vols. (London, 1825), 2:376, 516. Using oxygen as the atomic weight unit, Thomson lists copper sulphate at 15.625. Since Henry uses a hydrogen radix (one-eighth the weight of oxygen) copper sulphate comes out to 125.

[5] Cf. William Thomas Brande, (see Henry to [L. C. Beck], September 21, 1827, footnote 4). Thirty-two is the equivalent weight which Brande ascribes to silica in *A Manual of Chemistry* (New York, 1821), p. 453.

corrected before any more impressions are taken from the plate and in the mean time should you discover any more will you be so good as to give us further notice.

Respect. Yours
Jos Henry

FROM LEWIS C. BECK[1]
Henry Papers, Smithsonian Archives[2]

Castleton Oct 7. 1827

My Dear friend.

I received your letter & the accompanying documents in time to deal out a dose of Bromine to the class, for which I am much obliged to you; & in return promise, that should I ever be so fortunate as to obtain any I will send you the first parcel as a valuable addition to the stock of Chemical perfumery.

As to Northern lights & arches & zones, they have altogether disappeared since the Equinox, which I look upon as a convincing proof that they must have had an intimate connexion with the affair of Strang & Mrs Whipple. Your electro-magnetic theory therefore must be given up.[3]

light,—the formation of Chloriodic acid by the direct combination of Chlorine & iodine, & the subsequent decomposition by means of this acid of Ammonia, forming muriatic acid & iodide of nitrogen, the latter of which I obtained & exploded, &c. *Note.* I do not believe that phosphorus will burn in the vapour of iodine. I think I gave it a fair trial, & no combustion took place until the phosphorus was in actual contact with the solid iodine. While upon phosphorus I performed an experiment which I noticed in Henry, the rationale of which I am somewhat puzzled about. A piece of phosphorus introduced into a vessel of pure Oxygen gas is not luminous under ordinary pressure & temperature.[4] When, however, the density of the gas is diminished either by means of the air pump or by[5] . . . .

---

[1] Replying to Henry's letter of September 21, above.

[2] A fragment of the top of the sheet containing the first and a later page of the letter.

[3] The end of the first side of the fragment. The text following is on the reverse and apparently is from a discussion of Beck's chemical work.

[4] The reference is to William Henry's *The Elements of Experimental Chemistry*, 2 vols. (Philadelphia, 1822), 2:1–3. (This volume is in the Henry Library.) In Henry's account he briefly mentions three supposed combustion products (2:3). We have no way of knowing exactly what Beck was puzzled about.

[5] The word "phosphorus" on the next line is visible on the fragment.

MINUTES, ALBANY INSTITUTE
Institute Minutes, Albany Institute Archives[1]

Wednesday Octr 10th 1827

Institute met pursuant to adjournment.

The Minutes of the last meeting were read & approved.

Donations since last meeting were read consisting of Various valuable Gold & Silver coins deposited.

Mr George Clinton read an Essay on the properties of light.[2]

Mr Mayell exhibited a perspective view of the Engine used in the Steam Boat Victory, also a model of the boiler used on that vessel accompanied with an explanation of both.[3]

Mr Henry read a paper on some modifications of Electro magnetic Apparatus, accompanied with Experiments.[4]

Adjourned

[1] After April 5, 1826, that is page 31, the pages of Volume I of the Minutes of the Albany Institute are no longer numbered. Our citations will give only the date of the meeting.

[2] This paper apparently was never published.

[3] William Mayell's lecture was never published.

[4] Henry's paper was published in the *Transactions*, Albany Institute, 1830, *1*:22–24.

"REMARKES ON SOME OBJECTIONS TO MATHEMATICAL REASONING WHICH APPEARED IN THE ANTIDOTE FOR OCT. 20th 1827"[1]
Miscellaneous Henry Papers, Smithsonian Archives

The following are some remarkes on the examples aduced by Mr Mason in support of the asser[tion] that there are objections to mathematical evi-

[1] Henry's remarks are undated, but we assume they were penned on or near the date of the article in question. This issue of the *Antidote*, an Albany newspaper, and subsequent issues in October and November 1827 are not known to survive in any American library. Although we cannot tell if the *Antidote* also published Henry's remarks, the first sentence of the manuscript was twice revised as if Henry intended to submit his reply to the newspaper. Henry's thoughts on infinity and the infinite divisibility of matter are clearly not original. He is simply presenting and elucidating ideas gleaned from his general reading on science and philosophy—ideas which, in the tradition of public enlightenment, he possibly hoped to convey to the readership of the *Antidote*.

On the nature of the text following the asterisks, see footnote 5.

dence more puzzeling and unanswerable than can be alledged against moral reasoning.[2]

The first example given is "It is *mathematically* demonstrated that matter is infinitely divisible; that is, has a infinite number of parts. A line then of half an inch has then a infinite number of parts. Who does not see the absurdity of an infinite half inch, etc. etc."[3]

The term infinity upon which the quibble in this sophism is made to turn, like many other terms used in science, has a different signification from what it has in a moral or a metaphysical sense. Infinity in the most extended, and perhapse the propper sense of the term is that which is so great that nothing can be added to it, or supposed to be added. In this sense it is used in speak[ing] of the infinite wisdom & goodness of the Almighty. But this meaning of infinity is not applicable to mathematics for the object of this science is the comparison of the relations of quantity & such quantity only as can be conceived & defined by the human mind. No idea can be formed of a quantity so great that nothing can be added. Such a quantity therefore, although we may believe in its existance, can never be the subject of mathematical reasonings.

But the term infinity has another signification & is defined by the mathematician to be that which is great beyond any asignable limits. In this sense the series of numbers 1, 2, 3, 4, 5, 6 etc. etc. may be said to be infinite.[4]

* * * * *

Those[5] who have attempted to prove that matter is infinately divisible have not attended to the idea for which infinity stands and by that neglect have laid themselves open to objections that they knew little how to answer. But if we attend to the idea of infinity in its sense as explained by Lock[6] & others we shal not meet with the same difficulty.

---

[2] While the full context of his article is unknown, the unidentified Mr. Mason is obviously defending recondite moral and theological concepts from scientific criticism on the ground that many basic mathematical ideas appear equally if not more, inscrutable.

[3] Henry also wrote this excerpt from Mason on the cover-sheet of the document.

[4] Note especially Henry's insistence on separating the precise, quantitative discourse of mathematics and science from other realms of discourse. From Henry's wording, it appears that he drew the mathematical definition of infinity from a reference work he frequently consulted in Albany—Peter Barlow's *Dictionary of Pure and Mixed Mathematics* (London, 1814).

[5] The remainder of the text is from a separate undated document, labeled "scraps on infinity," found among the Miscellaneous Henry Papers, Smithsonian Archives. Mary Henry dated the document 1827. Although the specific evidence for her dating is unknown, the content of the manuscript suggests it was originally part of Henry's reply to Mason. It appears that Henry is simply turning from the mathematical concept of infinity to the physical question, raised by Mason, of matter's infinite divisibility.

[6] The English philosopher John Locke (1632–1704). See his *An Essay Concerning Human Understanding* and *A Treatise on the Conduct of the Understanding*, chapter 17: "Of Infinity." In the 1853 Pittsburgh and

Whoever thinks on a cube of an inch in diameter has a clear and positive idea of it in his mind and can also frame one of ½ an inch, or ¼ or ⅛ and so on, till he has the idea in his thoughts of something exceedingly small but this small as it may be reaches not the extreme limits of minuteness, for after he has continued this halving in his mind & has diminished his idea as much as he pleases, he has no more reason to stop, nor is one jot nearer the end of such division than when he began. Nor[7] is there any thing insignificant [or] subtle in saying that we must be careful to distinguish between the infinite divisibility of matter & matter infinitly divided.

The first is nothing but an endless progression of the mind in dividing the parts of matter as long as it pleases; but to talk of matter as infinitely divided, is either taking it for granted that in our division of it we must come to an end at last, and this is begging the quest[ion], or else it is supposing the mind has already passed over and has actually a view of all the parts of matter, which an endless division can never totally represent to it, which carries a plain contradiction.

Philadelphia edition which we have consulted, the chapter occurs on pp. 137–144.

[7] In these final remarks, Henry is paraphrasing and embroidering upon a passage in Locke's *Essay*, chapter 17, sec. 7, p. 139. He is applying Locke's analysis of the infinity of space to the divisibility of matter. In sec. 12, pp. 140–141, Locke deals specifically with the concept of matter's infinite divisibility. Henry owned the second volume of the 1825 New York edition of the *Essay*. The first volume, which contains the passage in question, does not survive in his library.

1828

MINUTES, ALBANY INSTITUTE
Institute Minutes, Albany Institute Archives

Feb[y] 13. 1828

A Special meeting of the Institute having been called, the death of DeWitt Clinton,[1] one of the Honorary Members was announced, whereupon the following resolutions were proposed & unanimously adopted

---

[1] We have already alluded to DeWitt Clinton's role in New York's state and local politics, his promotion of the Erie Canal, and his view of the interdependence of science and economic development (see above, T. R. Beck to J. W. Francis, February 26, 1812, especially footnote 33). To the Albany Institute, of course, the death of DeWitt Clinton meant the loss of one of the influential founders. We have already noted that Henry kept a collection of Clinton's pamphlets in his library, a few of which bear Henry's annotations (see

Resolved that in common with our fellow citizens of the state, & nation, we lament the death of De Witt Clinton, late Governor of this State.

Resolved that as humble members of a vast community throughout the civilized world, whose efforts are directed to the advancement & diffusion of Science, we deeply deplore the loss of which our common cause has sustained in the death of one of its most distinguished patrons & successful cultivators.

Resolved that as a first tribute of respect to the memory of the illustrious dead, we will attend the funeral & wear the usual badges of mourning for thirty days.

Resolved that we will cause a marble tablet, with an appropriate inscription, to be placed in the hall of the Society, in honour of our distinguished member, & that Messr's L. C Beck, C R. Webster, & Mayell[2] be a Committee to carry this resolution into effect.

Adjourned.

---

ibid.). Clinton's interest and activities in science, although strictly in the tradition of amateur studies in natural history, were prime influences in the young lives of the nation's earliest professional scientists such as Henry, Beck, and others.

[2] William Mayell.

MINUTES OF THE TRUSTEES OF THE ALBANY LANCASTRIAN SCHOOL SOCIETY FEBRUARY 16, 1828–SEPTEMBER 17, 1832
Manuscript Division, New York State Library

Joseph Henry served as a Trustee of Albany's Lancastrian School Society for nearly five years, having been first elected on February 16, 1828. While never a member of any committees of the Trustees during his appointment, he did serve as Secretary to the Trustees from February 1830 until February 1832, being succeeded in that capacity by Matthew Henry Webster. The minutes of the Trustees during Henry's Secretaryship, comprising eight pages, thus appear in Henry's hand.

The minutes consist mostly of the proceedings of annual meetings for the election of Trustees and the recording of the annual report from the principal teacher, W. A. Tweed Dale.[1] The reports depict the increasingly desperate position of the school's attendance and finances, a condition brought about allegedly

---

[1] See above, Minutes of the Albany Institute, February 2, 1825, especially footnote 5.

by the creation of the Albany common schools through the state system.[2] Owing to the routine nature of most of the business recorded in the minutes, and especially the lack of evidence of Henry's personal concern or activity, printing of the minutes in this volume is not warranted.

Henry's election to the Lancaster School Trustees, although an honor, must have come as a surprise to none of his contemporaries. A majority of the Trustees were active members of the Albany Institute along with Henry, and the cooperation established between the Lancaster School and the Academy undoubtedly contributed to Henry's involvement. His election to the Trustees, and his subsequent service as Secretary, does signify, however, Henry's increasing acceptability and involvement in community affairs as his accomplishments in science and education came to be known.

[2] See the Minutes of the Academy Trustees for April 8, 1822, printed above, and footnote 3, for a brief history of the Lancaster School and its relationship with the Academy.

EXCERPT, AMOS EATON TO BENJAMIN SILLIMAN, SR.
Gratz Collection, Historical Society of Pennsylvania

Troy, Feb. 26. 1828.

Dear Friend,

The travelling by land and water has been greatly interrupted by wind and ice for some time. I have generally received your letters by the morning Albany mail, at 7 o'clock on the third day from the New Haven post mark. Your last was one whole week on the way. Even the rapid N. York and Albany line detained my last letter from there five days.

I hope you received the box of plates and synopses (850 each, as the printer said who packed them) by stage. I went to Albany to send it by water, as our Troy folks were all discouraged by the floating ice. I learned at Albany, that the little steam boat, which had left Albany the day before, was stopped nearly opposite Hudson. The other boat would not go until the fate of that could be ascertained. No sloop would then go either. I went to consult Mr Baccus.[1] He, and all others who often transmit packages, advised the stage conveyance; as the river might be difficult a long time at this season. So I entered the box at half a passenger, and saw it entered regularly on the way-bill. A printed card of direction, and strong lettered name, Prof. Silliman, Yale College, marked on the box with black oil paint. I am

[1] E. F. Backus (1770–1859), a bookseller and publisher in Albany who later moved to Philadelphia. Munsell, *Ann. Alb.*, 8:82.

thus particular; but the box might have miscarried; for I was told, that the Albany, Hartford, and New Haven lines were all independent and all met at Norfolk, and that the roads were very bad.

In regard to my name, I supposed it was sufficient at the head of the Synopsis, which is to precede the statement of facts addressed in support of it.[2]

If you have no choice, I should like a running head something like this, to cross the opposite paper.

Geological	Nomenclature.

or

Geological Nomenclature	For North America.

If you have no choice on the subject, we (I mean Beck, Henry, Clinton and Eights)[3] are inclined to the opinion, that it would be best to pass over your June number, and not appear again until your September number.[4] That is, not get the manuscript into your hands until the last of July or first of August. We have two short reasons for this. 1st We intend to go through the Erie Canal in our vacation, which begins on the last Wednesday in June.[5] 2d We hope to see some attacks upon the proposed nomenclature in the June number; which we would like to meet indirectly in our continuations in the Sept. number....[6]

[2] Amos Eaton, "Geological Nomenclature Exhibited in a Synopsis of North American Rocks and Detritus," *Silliman's Journal*, 1828, *14*:insert between 144 and 145 and "Geological Nomenclature, Classes of Rocks, etc.," ibid., pp. 145–159, 359–368.

[3] L. C. Beck, Joseph Henry, G. W. Clinton, and James Eights. Henry's contributions to the article cited above are acknowledged at the start. On p. 154 he is specifically cited for

helping to trace the Lake Erie rocks to the Catskill Mountains.

[4] The article appeared in the July 1828 issue.

[5] This did not occur. According to Samuel Rezneck, "A Traveling School of Science on the Erie Canal in 1826," *New York History*, *40*:256, the next tour occurred in 1830.

[6] The remainder of the letter concerns two of Eaton's sons.

EXCERPT,[1] MINUTES, ACADEMY TRUSTEES

Trustees' Minutes, 1:314–315, Albany Academy Archives

March 14, 1828

A Communication from the Faculty was presented, proposing certain works as Textbooks & requesting certain modifications in the Statutes, which after being considered, were determined on as follows,

[1] Routine business and motions on classics texts are omitted.

Resolved that Euler's Algebra[2] & Davies' Descriptive Geometry[3] be adopted as class books in the Academy.

Resolved that Professor Henry be allowed to instruct a Class in Day's Trigonometry.[4]

---

[2] [John Farrar, comp.], *An Introduction to the Elements of Algebra . . . Selected from the Algebra of Euler,* 2d ed. (Cambridge, Massachusetts, 1821). This book was mentioned in Henry's Report to the Trustees of June or July 1829 (below, see especially footnote 7), and the *Statutes* of 1829.

[3] Charles Davies, *Elements of Descriptive Geometry* . . . (Philadelphia, 1826). Curiously, this text by Davies was not mentioned specifically in Henry's Report to the Trustees of June or July 1829. It was, however, listed as a textbook in the 1829 *Statutes.* The omission may be at a gap in the Mary Henry text (foot-

note 12 of the Henry 1829 report).

[4] Jeremiah Day, *A Treatise of Plane Trigonometry* (New Haven, 1815). Apparently a popular treatise, the book had twelve printings by 1858; the edition most likely referred to here is that of 1824. Note the wording of this resolution, implying that Day's book, unlike the above-mentioned "class books" in algebra and descriptive geometry, was to serve as a special supplement to Henry's teaching. It was not mentioned in Henry's report to the Trustees in 1829 and was not listed in the 1829 *Statutes.*

EXCERPT,[1] MINUTES, ALBANY INSTITUTE

Institute Minutes, Albany Institute Archives

April 3. 1828.

Mr Henry read a paper on Light & vision with Experiments on the Thaumatrope,[2] a newly invented philosophical Instrument.

On motion

Resolved that it will be proper to commence the publication of the Transactions of the Institute.

---

[1] A few lines on donations and on the reading of the minutes have been omitted.

[2] The thaumatrope, an ancestor of the motion-picture projector, demonstrated the illusion of the "persistence of vision." In its earliest form, it consisted of a small disk which was held by two threads and which bore a different image on each side. When the disk was spun (thaumatrope means "wonder-turner") the eye saw only a combined image. Its invention is generally attributed to John Ayrton Paris in 1827. An English physician and scientist with a flare for popular writing (in 1831 he wrote a eulogistic biography of

Humphrey Davy), Paris popularized the new device in his "novel," *Philosophy in Sport Made Science in Earnest; Being an Attempt to Illustrate the First Principles of Natural Philosophy by the Aid of Popular Toys and Sports* (1827). While a commercially successful toy, the thaumatrope and its optical principles caught the interest of scientists such as David Brewster, Charles Babbage, John Herschel, William Hyde Wollaston, and Michael Faraday. Experimenting on the device in 1828, Henry was abreast of the British discoveries in the persistence of vision.

Resolved that a Committee of publication be appointed by ballot.
Messrs S. De Witt
T. R. Beck &
Ja⁸ G. Tracy
were duly appointed said Committee.

Adjourned.

EXCERPT,[1] MINUTES, ACADEMY TRUSTEES
Trustees' Minutes, 1:316, Albany Academy Archives

[April 11, 1828]
A Class in the Academy being desirous of studying Civil Engineering & the Professor of Mathematics having recommended Sganzin's Work[2] for that Subject therefore,
Resolved that he be allowed to instruct the class in the same.

[1] Routine business has been omitted.
[2] M. I. Sganzin, *An Elementary Course of Civil Engineering* (Boston, 1827), translated from the third French edition. This book has survived in Joseph Henry's Library and bears his annotations.

EXCERPT,[1] MINUTES, ALBANY INSTITUTE
Institute Minutes, Albany Institute Archives

July 10, 1828
Ordered that copies of the Transactions as published be forwarded in the name of the Institute to the following Societies & Individuals & that the Treasurer pay the expense of the same:

1 D⁻ Brewster[2] Editor of the Edinburgh Journal of Science
2 Professor Jameson[3] " " Edinburgh New Philosophical Journal
3 Editors of the Philosophical Magazine & Annals of Philosophy,[4] London

[1] Routine business is omitted.
[2] Sir David Brewster (1781–1868) was editor of the *Edinburgh Journal of Science* from 1824 to 1832. See *DNB* and Henry Carrington Bolton, *A Catalogue of Scientific and Technical Periodicals, 1665–1895*, 2d ed., Smithsonian Miscellaneous Collections, vol. 40 (Washington, 1898), p. 187.
[3] Robert Jameson (1774–1854), mineralogist, edited the *Edinburgh New Philosophical Journal* from 1826 until his death. See *DNB* and Bolton, op. cit., pp. 187–188.
[4] From 1827 to 1832 the *Philosophical Magazine and Annals of Philosophy* was edited by Richard Taylor (1781–1858) and Richard Phillips (1778–1851). They united their journal with Brewster's *Edinburgh Journal of Science* in 1832. See *DNB* and Bolton, op. cit., p. 445.

4 Professor Brande.[5] Editor of Quarterly Journal of Science, London
5 New York Lyceum of Natural History[6]
6 American Philosophical Society, Philadelphia
7 Academy of Natural Sciences   "
8 Literary & Philosophical Society[7] New York
9 New York Historical Society[8]   "
10 American Academy of Arts & Sciences,[9] Boston
11 Professor Sillimans Journal[10]
12 Connecticut Academy[11]
13 Dr Jones Editor of the Franklin Journal[12]
14 Natural History Society,[13] Montreal
15 Ferrusac's Journal[14]

[5] William Thomas Brande. *The Quarterly Journal of Science, Literature and the Arts,* sometimes known as *Brande's Quarterly Journal of Science,* was published by the Royal Institution from 1820 through 1827. (Bolton, op. cit., p. 803.) The Albany Institute had not by this time received word of the end of this publication.

[6] For a description of the publications of the New York Lyceum, the American Philosophical Society, and the Academy of Natural Sciences, see footnote 23 of Minutes, Albany Institute, October 13, 1824, above.

[7] The Literary and Philosophical Society of New York was founded in 1814 and began publishing its *Transactions* in that year. Bates claims that the "society's membership gradually passed over to the Lyceum of Natural History of New York. . . ." Ralph S. Bates, *Scientific Societies in the United States,* 3d ed. (Cambridge, Massachusetts, 1965), p. 41.

[8] The New-York Historical Society, founded in 1804, published its *Collections* from 1809–1830. Bates, op. cit., p. 41, mentions that the society about 1816 "embarked temporarily on the collection of natural history specimens."

[9] The American Academy of Arts and Sciences, founded in 1780, began publishing its *Memoirs* in 1785 and continued them well into the twentieth century.

[10] Of course, the *American Journal of Science,* edited by Benjamin Silliman.

[11] Established in 1799, the Connecticut Academy of Arts and Sciences began publishing its *Memoirs* in 1810, although upon the coming of *Silliman's Journal* in 1818 most of the Academy's papers were published there. See Bates, op. cit., pp. 14–15.

[12] Thomas P. Jones (1774–1848), editor of the *Journal of the Franklin Institute* from

1826 until his death, was also a U.S. Patent Office supervisor and examiner. See *DAB* and Bolton, op. cit., p. 27.

[13] The Natural History Society in Montreal was founded in 1827, but we have found no evidence that the society published any journal before 1856. See Bolton, op. cit., p. 147, and *The Canadian Naturalist and Geologist,* 2d ser., 1883, *10*:239.

[14] Established in 1823, the *Bulletin général et universel des annonces et nouvelles scientifiques* was published by Baron de Férussac, or André Étienne Just Paschel Joseph François Férussac (1786–1836). *Poggendorff.* According to Bolton (op. cit., pp. 135–136, 140–141), from 1824 to 1831 the *Bulletin* was divided into eight sections, each one being a publication in its own right; they were:

Section I	Bulletin des sciences mathématiques, physiques et chimiques
Section II	Bulletin des sciences naturelles et de geologie
Section III	Bulletin des sciences médicales
Section IV	Bulletin des sciences agricoles économiques, [etc.]
Section V	Bulletin des sciences technologiques
Section VI	Bulletin des sciences géographiques, statistiques, d'économie publique et des voyages
Section VII	Bulletin des sciences historiques, antiquités et philologie
Section VIII	Bulletin des sciences militaires.

16 Revue Encyclopedique[15]

At a date later than this document, perhaps during the 1837 trip to Europe, Joseph Henry acquired a number of books originally in the library of this bibliographic service, some bearing notations indicating use in preparing entries.

[15] Begun originally in 1792 as the *Magasin encyclopédique* in Paris, the journal had been renamed several times before it was known as the *Revue encyclopédique;* during the years 1819 to 1831 the journal was edited by Marc Antoine Jullien (1775–1848). Bolton, op. cit., pp. 343–344.

EXCERPT,[1] MINUTES, ALBANY INSTITUTE

Institute Minutes, Albany Institute Archives

Oct[r] 3[d] 1828

H. G. Spafford having requested the Institute to Examine an Invention[2] which he has recently made on motion of Dr. TR Beck,

Resolved That Stephen Van Rensselaer, Simeon De Witt, Oliver Kane,[3] Charles R. Webster, Richard V. De Witt, & Joseph Henry be a Committee on the part of the Institute to Examine & Report on such Invention.

Simeon DeWitt Exhibited a hydrostatic balance being a modification of the usual apparatus for ascertaining the Specific gravity of water.[4]

And also a Silver coin of the Colony of Massachusetts—1653.

Dr. T. R. Beck gave notice that he intended to deliver a course of Lectures on Mineralogy, in Connection with Prof. Henry and invited the members of the Institute to attend.[5]

Adjourned.

[1] Notes concerning routine business and donations are omitted.

[2] Horatio Gates Spafford (1778–1832), author of the widely used *Gazetteer of the State of New-York, Carefully Written from Original and Authentic Materials* (Albany, 1813), was a corresponding member of the Institute. Hough, *American Biographical Notes*, p. 370 and *Transactions*, Albany Institute, 1830, *1,* part 2: appendix, p. 69. The invention has not been identified; it appears in neither the published literature nor in U.S. patent records. Nor do we have the report on it.

[3] Oliver Kane (1767–1842) was a member of the Institute and trustee of the Albany Academy from 1830–1834. Munsell, *Ann. Alb., 10*:326. *Transactions*, Albany Institute, 1830, *1,* part 2: appendix, p. 74. *Academy Seventy-fifth Anniversary*, p. 66. Henry Hun, "A Survey of the Activity of the Albany Academy" (unpublished manuscript, 1922–1935, Manuscript Division, New York State Library and Archives of the Albany Academy).

[4] The hydrostatic balance was used to weigh a body in water in order to determine its specific gravity. For a description, see *Encyclopaedia Britannica*, 8th ed., s.v. "Balance." The reference to finding water's specific gravity is probably a secretary's error since water had generally been accepted as the unit of specific gravity. DeWitt's modification of the apparatus is unknown.

[5] In Minutes of the Albany Institute for August 22, 1828, Beck was granted the use of the Institute's mineralogical collection for lectures on mineralogy. We have found nothing more on this additional Beck-Henry lecture course.

TO HARRIET ALEXANDER[1]

Family Correspondence, Henry Papers, Smithsonian Archives

Albany Nov. 15th 1828

My Dear Cous.

On the receipt of your letter,[2] I hastened, with pleasure, to execute the commission which you were so kind as to intrust to me; but I have not been fortunate enough to find any cloth of the required width. I have however sent a piece, of about a yard in breadth, which I hope will answer; if it do not please return it and I will try again.

Mr. Ryley had left Town before your letter reached me, and I have therefore, forwarded the cloth by the stage.

As to the price—according to your request, I have charged the same with due [. . .] will at some future period, [. . .] the account in *propria persona* with interest added in conformity with the law, in such cases, mad[e] and provided.

If, at the time when I present the account, it should not be convenient for you to make immediate payment, I will accept as security of the debt, a bond and mortgage on your real or *personal* property.

On the subject of promises, when am I to have the pleasure of performing the one, which depends on your coming to Albany? Do not delay too long as I am very anxious, as soon as possible to completely retrieve my character and to reinstate myself in your good opinion as a person of the strictest veracity.

Excuse me for taxing your patience with this scrawl, which with all your "cleaverness" I fear you will not be able entirely to decypher. Indeed both Stephen and myself would do well to take a lesson from you in the "art chirographical" for permit me to tell you that I was no less agreeably surprised at the receipt of a letter from you, than pleased with the beauty, & the correctness of its execution.

Yours etc
Jos. Henry

[1] Harriet Alexander (1808–1882). Harriet and Stephen were the children of Maria and Alexander Alexander, the latter being a brother of Ann Alexander Henry, Joseph Henry's mother. Thus, Harriet Alexander and Joseph Henry were first cousins. They were married on May 3, 1830. Subsequent letters will depict their courtship and early years together. Their letters to one another are important sources on both family activities and Henry's career. Genealogical information is in Robert Gaylord Lester's unpublished genealogy of the Alexander family in the files of the Henry Papers project and in William H. Eldridge, *Henry Genealogy: The Descendants of Samuel Henry . . . and Lurana (Cady) Henry . . .* (Boston, 1915), pp. 128–129.

[2] Not found.

P.S. Give my love to your Mother. I am very glad to hear that her health is so much improved. I hope she will soon be well enough to visit Albany. Remember me to your Aunt.[3]

All well here I believe—Adieu

J. H.

[3] Miss Nancy Connor, the sister of Harriet's mother, Maria Alexander. Records in City History Center, Schenectady City Hall.

EXCERPT,[1] MINUTES, ALBANY INSTITUTE

Institute Minutes, Albany Institute Archives

Hall of the Institute
Nov[r] 25th 1828

Gen[l] Root made some observations on the subject of Thermometers to show the inaccuracies of the present mode of usage & construction of those instruments.[2]

D[r] L C Beck exhibited the new table of Chemical Equivalents, prepared by himself & M[r] Henry.[3]

M[r] Henry exhibited a philosophical balance on a Simple Construction mentioned in Brewster Journal of Science[4]—the balance was made by D[r] Ten Eyck of this city.

Gen Root made some observations on the Solar spots of 1816 showing that from personal observation & those appearances there was reason to believe that there was a double revolution of the Sun, on its axis & at right angles to it.

Adjourned.

[1] Routine business and the list of donations have been omitted.

[2] Erastus Root, whose remarks apparently were never published.

[3] Probably a revision of the scale of chemical equivalents described in Beck's letter of April 15, 1827, to Henry, above. A later discussion of the same subject is in Lewis C. Beck, *A Manual of Chemistry* (Albany, 1831), pp. 33–34.

[4] See William Ritchie, "On an Extremely Cheap and Delicate Hydrostatic Balance," *Edinburgh Journal of Science*, 1826, 5:118–120.

❦{ 1829 }❦

EXCERPT,[1] MINUTES, ALBANY INSTITUTE
Institute Minutes, Albany Institute Archives

March 18, 1829.

The Institute met pursuant to Adjournment.

First Vice President in the Chair.

Minutes of the last meeting were read and approved.

Mr. Ames[2] made a communication on the principles of a machine for *Dressing Hemp and Flax,* invented by Mess.[rs] Watson, Blossom, and Burnet, of Salem, Washington County and exhibited a model of the same which was explained by Mr. Burnet.[3]

Professor Henry made a communication on *Daniel's Hygrometer,* introduced one of said instruments, and illustrated its principles and importance.[4]

---

[1] The list of donors and other routine matters from the end of these minutes have been omitted.

[2] Julius R. Ames (1801–1850), a miniaturist and the son of the better-known miniaturist Ezra Ames. He was a member of the Third Department of the Institute. A graduate of Union College (1820) and an attorney, Julius R. Ames was later the author of *The Bible of Nature and Substance of Virtue* (Albany, 1842) and various abolitionist pamphlets. George C. Groce and David H. Wallace, *The New York Historical Society's Dictionary of Artists in America, 1564–1860* (New Haven, 1957), pp. 7–8; Albany City Directories, 1832–1850; *Union Catalog,* p. 19.

[3] J. Y. Watson, J. Blossom, and A. Burnett were granted a patent on April 21, 1829, for a Hemp and Flax Breaking Machine.

[4] John Frederic Daniell (1790–1845), who will appear in subsequent volumes, especially in connection with the battery bearing his name, was very active in various meteorological researches, like Henry and other contemporary physical scientists. From 1831 until his death, Daniell was Professor of Chemistry at King's College, London. *DNB.*

Daniell's device is a dew point hygrometer in which a surface is artificially cooled to form dew. It consisted of two glass bulbs joined by a wide tube. One bulb contained a thermometer. This bulb was gilt and polished and was half filled with ether. The rest of the apparatus is devoid of air, and the other bulb is covered by a thin cloth. When this cloth-covered bulb is cooled by pouring a few drops of ether on it, the inside ether begins to condense on the cloth-covered side and to evaporate on the other side. As the temperature of the gilt bulb drops, dew appears. The mean of the temperatures of dew appearance and dew disappearance (when the cooling is stopped) is the dew point. For a discussion of the attempts to measure atmospheric humidity, see W. E. K. Middleton, *Invention of the Meteorological Instruments* (Baltimore, 1969), pp. 81–132. In later describing Daniell's hygrometer in his Descriptive Catalogue of Philosophical Apparatus Purchased for the Albany Academy (see below, December 18, 1830, Article No. 19), Henry used a somewhat less precise method of determining the dew point.

Not having Henry's text, we cannot state what he thought the importance of the instrument was. Daniell (see Middleton, op. cit., p. 117), felt the device would lead to weather forecasting. While Daniell's book, *Meteorological Essays and Observations* (London, 1823), pp. 139–205, contains an essay on the new hygrometer, it is likely that Henry came across the device in his reading of the *Quarterly Journal of Science, Literature and the Arts* ("Brande's Journal") where the invention was first announced ("On a New Hygrometer . . . ," *8*:298–336). In later issues Daniell

Dr. T. R. Beck read a paper on the English Language, in relation to *Americanisms.*[5]

The Recording Secretary of the Second Department reported, the resignation of Mr. Joseph Henry as one of the Curators: and that the Department had elected Dr. *Philip Ten Eyck,*[6] to supply the vacancy.

A letter from Lt. Ingalls, U.S. Army, corresponding member of the Institute, was read by Dr. L. C. Beck; and on motion was referred to the Curators. . . .[7]

---

gave further reports of his work with the instrument (9:128–133, 268–278; *10*:123–144; *13*: 76–91; *17*:46–71). From one of Henry's surviving notebooks of the period (No. 6123 of the Henry Papers computer control system), we know he was reading through "Brande's Journal" roughly around this date and noting references to electricity and magnetism (see pp. 53, 68, 74–78, 101–102 of this notebook). While dew point hygrometers continued in use, they did not solve the forecasting problem. The wet and dry bulb psychrometer in which evaporation from a moist surface reduces the temperature was also coming into use at this period. An interesting aspect of Middleton's work is to note how many leading physical scientists of the last century interested themselves in hygrometers and other meteorological instruments.

[5] Subsequently printed as "Notes on Mr. Pickering's 'Vocabulary of Words and Phrases, Which Have Been Supposed to be Peculiar to the United States,' with Preliminary Observations," *Transactions,* Albany Institute, 1830, *1*:25–31. This is one of the few contributions of the Third Department to the *Transactions.* The work of John Pickering (1775–1846) was published in Boston in 1816. Beck's purpose was twofold. On the one hand he was anxious to correct British charges against American propensities to produce neologisms; at the same time, Beck did not want American English to become a dialect markedly different from the mother language.

[6] Philip Ten Eyck (1802–1892), who succeeded Henry, would later collaborate with him in his experiments and then again succeed Henry when the latter resigned the chair of Math-

ematics and Natural Philosophy at the Academy in 1832. Ten Eyck held the professorship until 1848. Little is known of him. Born in Albany, he entered the Albany Academy in 1815 and acquired an M.D. degree at the College of Physicians and Surgeons in 1825. The collaboration with Henry is apparently his sole scientific contribution. Cuyler Reynolds, *Hudson-Mohawk Genealogical and Family Memoirs,* 4 vols. (New York, 1911), *1*:414; *Academy Seventy-fifth Anniversary,* pp. 20, 70, 77; *Columbia Alumni,* p. 202; Henry Hun, "A Survey of the Activity of the Albany Academy" (unpublished manuscript, 1922–1935, Manuscript Division, New York State Library and Archives of the Albany Academy).

[7] Thomas R. Ingalls (1798–1864), a corresponding member of the Institute, was a West Pointer (1818) and taught mathematics there in 1821. From 1822 to 1829 he was in the Artillery. In 1826 Ingalls received the M.D. from the Vermont Academy of Medicine. Ingalls resigned his commission in 1829 and from that date until 1833 he was Professor of Chemistry and Natural History at the University of Louisiana. From 1833 until 1836 he practiced medicine in New Orleans and served as Professor of Chemistry at the Medical College in New Orleans. In the years 1839–1841 Ingalls was President of Jefferson College of Louisiana. From that date until his death we presume Ingalls was in private practice. G. W. Cullum, *Biographical Register of the Officers and Graduates of the U.S. Military Academy,* 7 vols. (Boston, 1891), *1*:279.

The communication is "On the Luminous Appearance of the Oceans," *Transactions,* Albany Institute, 1830, *1*:8–9.

HARRIET ALEXANDER TO STEPHEN ALEXANDER

Mary Henry Copy, Family Correspondence,
Henry Papers, Smithsonian Archives

[March? 1829][1]

My dear Brother,

I've received your kind letter the night before last when we were just wishing to hear from you. We were rejoiced to hear of your safe arrival although we can hardly realize that you have been with us; it seems like a pleasant dream.

Joseph Henry and I went to Galway the morning after you left and found all our friends well and surprised and happy to see us. I was surprised to find how much I enjoyed it so soon after being separated from you but I can assure you I wished for you very frequently. We returned on Monday evening.

Our Social Club meets here this afternoon. Many good resolutions have been made by us on the commencement of the year which will no doubt improve us if put into effect. Our meetings for drawing and reading will so be renewed and continued. We will often think of and be obliged to you as caterer.

Cousin Joe very kindly forwards me an Albany paper weekly called the Albany Times and Literary Writer.[2] I will forward it to you if you say so. I have just finished transcribing your lectures. Mama thinks you will eclipse your eyes in calculating eclipses. One piece of intelligence pleases me much that your thermometer is broken. It will prevent you from mounting that hill in all weathers. Yesterday and today have been gloomy days to me. I have felt lonely and need I say I have wished for you, but have reasoned myself into the belief that it is best for you to be where you are. Looking back upon those years of undervalued bliss which we have passed together, ignorant of the world and of its disappointments when my happiness and love centered wholly upon you, I am sometimes surprised at the willingness with which I part from you, and the pleasure I enjoy when absent from you. But so it is. We know all is for the best and submit cheerfully.

---

[1] The *Albany Times and Literary Writer* mentioned in the text started publication on December 27, 1828, and ceased publication with the issue of April 18, 1829 (No. 17 of this weekly). "March" appears faintly on the document, perhaps representing what was on the original. *Howell and Tenney*, p. 376.

[2] Only four issues are known to survive, Nos. 13, 15, 16, and 17 of March 21, April 4, April 11, April 18, 1829, all in the New York State Library. The publisher, James McGlashen (1803–1833), may have been a friend of Henry's. (Munsell, *Ann. Alb.*, 9:271.) Most of the contents are reprints from British journals. To this were added local poetry, news notes, book reviews, and a miscellany of fillers. Albany lost little with its demise.

Often when our *large family* has collected around the work stand in these long winter evenings we amuse ourselves with conjecturing what Stephen is doing; we see you in your *sanctum sanctorium* reading or in a thinking posture. Sometimes I take a walk with you up the hill to observe the weather or down to the Post Office to receive a letter. Sometimes I take you to see my friends but not often for that is dangerous. You do not know how often they enquire for you. Really it makes me feel quite proud. Do not let it excite your vanity.

I have learned the *primo* of a fine duet; you can learn the secundo when you come.[3]

---

[3] The text ends at this point.

EXCERPT,[1] MINUTES, ALBANY INSTITUTE
Institute Minutes, Albany Institute Archives

Wednesday, April 1. 1829.

On Motion of Dr. T. R. Beck,

Resolved, That a committee be appointed to solicit some member or members of this body, to deliver occasional Lectures, with the use of the Philosophical Apparatus attached to the Institute. Whereupon, Mr. Kane, Dr. L. C. Beck and Professor Henry were appointed said committee.

Mr. Kane from the foregoing Committee, reported—That Dr. L. C. Beck and Professor Henry had assented to the requirements of the Institute; and would deliver a lecture at the next meeting, on *Electricity* and *Galvanism*.[2]

Dr. Lewis C. Beck gave notice of his intention, at a future meeting, of offering some remarks to the Institute on the *Forest Trees* of this State.

---

[1] That portion of these minutes concerning routine business and the payment of dues has been omitted.

[2] Henry presented a lecture-demonstration on electricity at the next meeting (see April 15 Minutes below), but there is no evidence of Beck's collaboration. Since Beck would be giving his own lecture on botany to the Institute, perhaps he helped prepare the electrical lecture, but left the actual presentation to Henry. In any case, Beck had some interest in electricity and magnetism. In 1827 he submitted a paper to the Institute on magnetism, which remained unpublished (Institute Minutes, February 14, 1827). His *A Manual of Chemistry* also included a section on galvanism and electromagnetism (Albany, 1831), pp. 79–107.

EXCERPT,[1] MINUTES, ALBANY INSTITUTE
Institute Minutes, Albany Institute Archives

Wednesday 15 April 1829.

Dr. L. C. Beck read a communication on the Forest Trees of the State of New York so far as the same are embraced in the genus Quercus or Oak the number of which are 15–13 trees & 2 shrubs.[2]

Mr. Joseph Henry made some remarks on the science of Electro & thermo-magnetism which he illustrated with Experiments performed by means of some modifications of the usual Instruments.[3]

Dr. T. R. Beck from the Committee[4] appointed to superintend the publication of Vol. I of the Transactions of the Institute made the following Report.

That at a period simultaneous with their appointment on the 3ᵈ of April 1828,[5] a subscription was commenced for defraying the expense of publishing the first number of said Transactions, so that the Institute should not be rendered responsible for the same. The Conditions were that for every dollar subscribed, 4 Copies of said Nᵒ should be received. In conformity with this arrangement Nᵒ 1 has been published, consisting of 24 pages containing papers by Messrs. S. Dewitt, Lieut. Ingalls, L. C. Beck, and J. Henry. The amount paid on said subscription and also for sales to individuals of Nᵒ 1 has been as follows. . . .[6]

The Expense of publishing said Nᵒ 1 according to an a/c rendered by Messrs Websters and Skinners amounts to $26.50

Receipt of Sale by messrs W&S   22.50

Leaving a Balance of   4.00

The Committee are happy to State that the Nᵒ has been received in a favourable manner both at home and abroad. The Edinburgh Journal of Science,[7] The Franklin Journal,[8] and Sillimans Journal[9] have each ex-

---

[1] The formal opening paragraph which follows immediately in the original is here omitted, along with other matters at the end of these minutes.

[2] Apparently never published. L. C. Beck closed his paper "On the Geographical Botany of the United States," read March 26, 1828, with a brief reference to the large number of species of oak in the country. *Transactions, Albany Institute*, 1830, *1*:21.

[3] Apparently never published. We have no reliable evidence on just what Henry did.

[4] Simeon DeWitt, T. R. Beck, and James G. Tracy.

[5] See the Institute Minutes of that date, above.

[6] We omit the list of twenty-nine subscribers, including Joseph Henry who paid $1.25 for five copies of the first number.

[7] Thomas R. Ingalls' "On the Luminous Appearance of the Ocean" appeared in 1828, *9*: 330–331, in abstract. Simeon DeWitt on terrestrial magnetism was excerpted and commented on by David Brewster, 1829, *10*:22–24.

[8] The *Journal of the Franklin Institute*, 1828, *2*:164–166, had a notice of the publication of the first number and an extract of the Ingalls paper.

[9] DeWitt's article on the variation of the magnetic needle is partially reprinted in

tracted articles from it. A copy of the number has been deposited with the Librarian for the Library of the Institute and the remainder of the Edition is in the hands of the Committee of Publication.

A general impression appeared to prevail among the members of the Society that the above result was satisfactory as to the feasability of publishing a volume of Transactions. Accordingly a subscription paper was prepared in the following words.

> "The first number of the Transactions of the Albany Institute having been published by private contribution the Committee of Publication deem the present a proper time to ascertain wether the members wish the Transactions to be continued. A subscription for one hundred Copies at three dollars each is necessary for this purpose. The volume will certainly not be completed before December 1829 and possibly not until some time after that period.[10] It is understood that the monies already subscribed and paid for the first N° shall be deducted from the present subscription and such members as may wish it, may pay for each N° as it is published and an account of their payments will be kept by the printer. The volume to consist of 300 pages."

The Institute by a vote passed July 10, 1828 resolved to subscribe for sixteen copies and directed their distribution to sundry Scientific Societies most of whom have formerly sent their Transactions, and also to various Scientific journals, foreign and domestic.[11]

In addition to this up to the date of the present report 85 Copies are subscribed for by various individuals.

The Committee now deemed it right to ascertain the amount for which said volume could be printed. It was stipulated to consist of not more than six numbers (including N° one already published). That said additional numbers (in the whole volume not to exceed 300 pages) should be printed in a style equal to N° 1. That no extra charge should be made for tables of figures, or for printing in smaller type and that each of said N°ˢ should have a cover similar in quality and appearance to that of N° 1 with such

---

Silliman's Journal, 1829, *16*:60–63, with a piece of Nathaniel Bowditch's, pp. 64–69, casting doubt on DeWitt's observation of the retrograde movement of the needle. After Bowditch's death, the Albany Institute in 1841 requested Henry to investigate the discrepancy in the findings of the two men. Referring to Elias Loomis' "On the Variation and Dip of the Magnetic Needle in Different Parts of the United States," *Silliman's Journal,* 1838, *34*: 290, Henry confirmed the validity of DeWitt's observations. Albany Institute Minutes of January 28, 1841, and January 12, 1842. See Henry's Deposition of May 19, 1832, below, footnote 12.

[10] The volume appeared in 1830.

[11] See the Institute Minutes for July 10, 1828, above.

printing on it as the Committee might direct. It was further agreed that the Committee should be altogether responsible for any engravings they might choose to add and lastly the time for publishing said numbers was to be at the pleasure of the Institute, agreeing however that proper exertion should be made to complete the same by the 1st of May 1830. In conformity with these preliminaries, the following estimate has been received from Websters and Skinners (the original hereunto annexed)

Estimate.

"For printing Transactions of Institute, 276 pages residue of volume 1st 300 copies in 5 Nos with printed covers, additional to each number.

Websters & Skinners to collect the Subscriptions from Subscribers in the City on the publishing of each number and to apply the avails in discharge of the debt as above. But in event of insufficiency of collections, the Institute to make good all deficiencies, on the publication of the last number."

It appears from the above that the expense will be as follows

For Nº 1 already published	$ 26.50
For the remaining five Nºs	360.00
	$386.50
Recd by Messrs Websters & Skinners on Nº 1	$ 22.50
Subscription of 85 subscribers _____ _____ __	255.00
Subscription by institute for 16 Copies _____	48.00
	$325.50
Leaving about 20 copies to be subscribed for	$61.00

These are the facts which the Committee desire to present to the Institute and on which they request their decision as to the expediency of pursuing the publication of the 1st volume of the Transactions.

In favour of this, the Committee would present the arguments, of increase of reputation and utility gained by a Society in appearing before the public, of advantage to the Library by exchanging for the publications of other Societies, of the possibility of some pecuniary advantage since the 40 additional copies (including those subscribed for by the Institute) subscribed for and taken on will pay all disbursements and leave at least 150 copies in the possession of the Institute to be sold or exchanged for other property. This last however will be slowly realized.

On the other hand the objections to pursuing the publication are that the Institute must become responsible for the balance that is not collected, that at all events, it must now become responsible for at least 36 copies or $108, with the contingencies of paying the same by future subscriptions, and lastly the consideration that the exercise of selection in the publishing of papers, has often lead to deadly feuds in Societies and occasionally to their subversion.[12]

The Committee of Publication however are decidedly of opinion that the attempt should be made. On their part they can only promise impartiality and decision to the best of their powers, if entrusted with the publication of the projected volume. They have agreed to attend to all the details of distribution and thus relieve the Institute of all expenditure on that head. They further feel confident that with a trifling exertion on the part of members the numbers required to fill up the subscription list can be readily obtained.

It must however be distinctly understood that the choice is a perfectly free one. The Committee have occurred no additional debt, beyond that for N° 1 and which will clear itself except printing the Charters and a Catalogue of the Library; each of which are now passing through the press. And they must not neglect to add that Messrs Websters & Skinners have with Liberality printed 50 additional Copies of the above as a donation to the Society, in addition to the 300 copies struck off in contemplation of pursuing the publication of the volume.

The Committee offer the following resolution. *Resolved,* that the Committee of Publication be directed to pursue the publication of volume one of the Transactions. And that the Institute will guarantee the expenses of Printing the same, according to the terms proposed by Messrs Websters & Skinners.

(Signed) S. De Witt Chairman

Whereupon

After considering said Report, it was *Resolved* that the same be agreed to & that the resolution proposed by them be adopted.

The Committee of Publication further

Report

That an accurate Catalogue of the Library was deemed a subject worthy of early attention in the proposed Transactions and indeed of necessity whether the same be published or not. They have therfore prepared with the assistance of the Librarian and Curators a complete Catalogue[13]

---

[12] These passages can be viewed as an extension of the discussion on publishing in the Institute Minutes of October 13, 1824, above.

[13] This catalog was reprinted in the first volume of the *Transactions* in pp. 7–24 of part 2, Appendix. From the index of donors in the catalog we learn that Henry gave the Institute the Abbé Nollet's *Leçons de physique expérimentale,* 6 vols. (Paris, 1759).

up to the present date—a printed Copy of which accompanies this report. . . .[14]

The Library according to the printed Catalogue consists at the present date

of	671 vol
of 108 Pamphlets bound in	11 vols
amounting to _____	682 vols

and also 7 unbound pamphlets.

At the formation of the Institute the Library contained 329 volumes shewing an increase of 353 volumes since that period to the present. . . .[15]

One suggestion more, the Committee beg leave to make. Four Periodicals are now taken by order of the Institute., viz

> The London Philosophical magazine[16]
> The London Repertory of Inventions[17]
> The Philadelphia Franklin Journal[18] &
> Silliman Journal

All these are Scientific. Should not a literary Journal be taken?[19]

> (Signed) T. R. Beck on behalf
> of the Committee

Albany April 15. 1829.

I hereby receive the Library of the Albany Institute, according to the printed Catalogue accompanying this report—With the exceptions stated above.

> Librarian. . . .[20]

---

[14] At this point we omit the list of books charged out and missing.

[15] Here we omit the list of duplicates the Institute proposes to dispose of.

[16] *The Philosophical Magazine* . . . edited by Richard Taylor and Richard Phillips resulted from the 1827 merger of *The Philosophical Magazine and Journal* with the *Annals of Philosophy,* a leading British scientific periodical.

[17] *The Repertory of Patent Inventions* . . .

started in 1825 as the continuation of a journal originating in 1794. As its title indicates, this periodical was quite utilitarian.

[18] The *Journal of the Franklin Institute.*

[19] We cannot state if Beck's query resulted in an additional subscription to a literary journal.

[20] Joseph Henry. At this point we omit the remaining text on routine business of the Institute.

FROM ISAAC MOTT[1]

Miscellaneous Manuscripts, New York Historical Society

Albany May 10th 1829

Mr Joseph Henry

I have the pleasure of informing you, that you were elected a member of the Polyhymnian Society[2] at our last meeting, and that our next meeting will be held on thursday evening next at 7 O clock in my School room.

Respectfully Yours

Isaac Mott Sec

[1] Isaac Mott (1801–1842), from a family of Hicksite Quakers, was a teacher in Albany, along with his brother Joseph P. Mott and two sisters, from 1824 until sometime in 1829. The Albany City Directory for 1828–1829 lists his occupation as "teacher, Albany High School." According to a family genealogy, the Motts actually opened up two schools, one for boys and another for girls, in the upper part of a private home in Albany. Thomas C. Cornell, *Adam and Ann Mott: Their Ancestors and Their Descendants* (Poughkeepsie, 1890), pp. 134, 219. Before the establishment of a widely based system of public education, Albany relied partially upon schools which were typically unincorporated and operated by a few teachers, sometimes even individual teachers, in privately owned quarters (see *Howell and Tenney*, p. 694). In the late 1820s Albany was apparently proud of "several" small "private schools of high character" besides the Albany Academy, the Albany Female Academy, the Albany Female Seminary, and the Lancaster School (see "City Schools," *Albany Argus*, August 25, 1828, p. 2). Mott and his brother were resident members of the Second Department of the Albany Institute, but neither seems to have been particularly active in Institute activities (see the Minutes of the Albany Institute, 1826–1831, and *Transactions*, Albany Institute, 1830, *1*, part 2: Appendix, p. 73). As of 1830 Isaac Mott no longer appears in the Albany City Directories. Other than to cite the obvious connections which Henry and Mott had at the Albany Institute and perhaps as fellow educators in the Albany community in the 1820s, we can shed no further light upon their relationship.

[2] The Polyhymnian Society appears to be a genuine obscurity. As Polyhymnia was the Greek Muse of the sacred lyric, we suppose that the Society had some concern with literature and/or music. Our search through newspapers, city directories, local histories, and various other sources has revealed nothing about the nature of this society.

TO STEPHEN ALEXANDER

Family Correspondence, Henry Papers, Smithsonian Archives

Schenectady May 13th 1829

Dear Cous

We arrived at Schenectady this morning at ½ past 6 o'clock after a pleasant although rather a cold passage. Your Aunt & the two "Darkies" were all well and very happy to hear from you. Nothing singular has transpired since we left home except that the packet-boat in which we went to Utica in attempting night before last to pass the Schoharie creek was carried over the dam by the current into the river. Fortunately no lives were lost but a greater part of the baggage is either missing or damaged.

I was much pleased with an articles on canals translated from the French in an olde vol. of Silliman's Journal[1] which I met with on the canal boat. The authour proves several facts which to me were entirely new as well as quite paradoxical. Among these the following may serve as puzzles for a class in Engineering.

To pass from a higher to a lower level much less water is required where the fall is distributed among several locks of small fall than when the whole depression is taken at once by one lock of great fall. Again in passing boats from a sumit level along a canal where there is a scarcity of water it is possible so to proportion the draft of the boat or the quantity of water which it displaces to the fall of the locks & the depth of the canal that the expenditure of the water shall be minus or so that a quantity of water will actually <*pass*> be raised from the lower to the higher level. The same effect may be produced in all cases where the descending boats pass heavily loaded & the asscending ones return empty or with a light freight.

I met with a person on the boat from Fredonia in Chataqua Co. who informed me that the village is still in part lighted with native gas. There is an abundance of the gas but the gasometer they now have will not supply more than about one hundred lights. A company of men at this village contracted with the Government to supply with this gas the lighthouse lately erected on a point of Lake Erie about 5 miles from Fredonia. After [putting in][2] about one mile of iron tube to con[duct the] gas they found that they could not made it descende any farther. They have since abandoned the project & now light the house with oil. I think it would be no very difficult matter to calculate the pressure required on a gasometer of given capacity to force the gas down any distance through a pipe of known diameter the relative specific gravity of the gas & the atmosphere being known. Is it not probable that this [failure] was owing to using too large a gasometer which would act against the <*weights*> <*pressure on*> the gas in the pipe like the power of the hydrosta[t]ic paradox.

If the top of the light-house be nearly as high as the source of the gas, or the gasometer, would not the gas continue to flow with a small pressure in a manner similar to water rising to its level in a bent tube?

[1] M. P. S. Girard, "Memoir on Navigable Canals, Considered in Relation to the Rise and Fall, and the Distribution of Their Locks," *Silliman's Journal*, 1822, *4*:102–124. Translated by J. Doolittle from the *Annales de chimie*, July, 1820.

[2] A corner of the page has been torn away; we have added here and in another instance soon to follow language appropriate to the context.

I have not yet found my cloak. It was not the "Buffalo" but the Niagra that we got on board of on monday evening. The Buffalo passed us about one o'clock the next [?morning][3] & has perhapse left my cloak at the [embarkation] place. Excuse this scrawl from

Your aff[ectionate cous J. H.]

If you receive my cloack please to keep it until you come to Albany and if it be not too much trouble I wish you would write to me concerning it and other matters.

---

[3] As in footnote 2, the words bracketed here are our speculations as to what was lost when the corner was torn. In the case of the closing we have used initials and language like those in other letters to Alexander in this period.

TO THE ACADEMY TRUSTEES[1]

Mary Henry Copy, Henry Papers, Smithsonian Archives

[ca. June or July 1829][2]
To the Trustees of the Albany Academy

Gentlemen:

In compliance with a request from Dr. T. R. Beck, the principal of the Institute, that I would transmit to your board an exposition of the system of teaching persued in the Academy, I respectfully submit the following.

Before entering on a detail <*of the studies persued and*> of the manner

---

[1] The text of this document is published here on the basis of Mary Henry's copy, no original of the message having survived. The document from which Mary Henry copied appears to have been a draft which Henry retained, as she apparently faithfully reproduced deleted passages.

[2] This date is assigned because it was during these two months that the Trustees' Committee was busily preparing a description of the present state of education at the Academy and some proposals for improvements. The Committee was formed at the Trustees' meeting of April 10, 1829, "to inquire into the propriety of relieving the Principal from his attendance upon the younger scholars in the English Department." Originally consisting of Rev. John Ludlow, Philip S. Parker, Alfred Conkling, and Gideon Hawley, the Committee acquired the aid of James Stevenson when, on June 12, 1829, the Board "Resolved, that the power of the Committee . . . be increased so to as revise & report on the general course of study now pursued & that they report such improvements & alterations as they may deem necessary & proper." The results of their scrutiny, which had been aided by such reports as this one from Henry, were reported to the Trustees on August 10, 1829. The Board promptly endorsed the Committee's proposals for reorganization, ordered that the public be informed, and published new *Statutes* on October 9, 1829; for a discussion of the *Statutes*, see the entries for the *Statutes* of September 14, 1819, above, and October 9, 1829, below. This report of Henry was submitted to the Committee but was never copied into the minutes of the Board. Minutes, Academy Trustees, *1*:333–337, 343–349.

of teaching <*them*> I would solicit the indulgence of the board in permitting me <*to make a few general remarks on some principles of Education which appear to have a particular bearing on the subject and*> to state the views of education on which this system is founded. . . .[3]

It is a law of our nature abundantly proved by observation that in early life, when the reasoning faculties are but partially developed, the principle of imitation is the most powerful and the most active and that also at this period the mind is susceptible of acquiring habits of action of industry and of mental expertness which <*shall*> have an important influence on the character and destiny of the future man. The child by an almost instructive power of imitation learns to express its wants in correct and, where proper models are present, even in elegant language and that too without being able in the least degree to understand the simplest principle of philology. With equal facility many mechanical habits of rapid and correct mental action are formed at this time which can scarcely be acquired at any subsequent period.

As life advances and the judgement and reasoning faculties are developed the principle of imitation and the power of forming mental habits become more and more feeble. The Mother-tongue is the most early and the most correctly learned <*of any other after*> and he who has not in early life acquired the habit of reading spelling and a rapid performance of the first four rules of arithmetic will never acquire them but at <*the expense*> an immense sacrifice of time and labor. On the other hand, experience warrants the assertion that no system of Education, however perseveringly applied can render a boy of ordinary talent capable of thoroughly understanding the demonstrations of Euclid before the age of nine years and even were the thing possible it would probably be at the expense of some important faculty of the mind left uncultivated.

From these views, for the truth of which I appeal to every person practically conversant with the business of Education, it is evident that the different faculties and powers of the mind are not simultaneously but successively developed and consequently that some periods of life are better suited to particular acquirements than others. It is not however intended by this remark that only a single faculty of the mind should be cultivated at one time but that the most important, according to the order observed in nature, should each in its proper season be the prominent although not the exclusive object of attention and that no faculty should be cultivated at the expense of another. According to these views <*of education as soon as*

---

[3] The marks which Mary Henry made at this point indicate that she probably omitted at least a phrase and possibly one or more sentences.

the> a boy <*enters the academy at the age of eight years he*> should commence his mathematical studies by forming the habit of mathematical expertness in resolving and combining large sums of figures and as this habit so essential to a proper combination of practical skill and[4]

On these principles the plan of teaching in the mathematical department of the Academy is founded. The boy on his entrance is put into a class and commences with the addition of a small number of figures which is gradually increased until he can add with rapidity and correctness a long column. At the same time he is made to commit to memory the addition and multiplication tables. . . .[5]

After <*having gone through*> the arithmetic has been gone through two or three times and the student become familiar with the practice of principles as far as they can be explained without reference to higher principles of mathematics, Bonicastle's algebra[6] is commenced and studied in connection with arithmetic. Simple illustrations are given at first by operating alternately with figures and letters but here as in arithmetic the student is trained into a habit of resolving with ease the most difficult examples in the book. After Bonicastle has been read twice through as far as Quadratics, if the boy is of proper age, Euclid[7] is begun and particular pains are taken to initiate him as soon as possible into the spirit of the work; to let him see what demonstration is and he cannot see it without being charmed. He is required to draw the diagrams without reference to the book and to designate the different parts not by letters but by figures promiscuously placed. Whenever the proposition will permit, the diagram is varied in shape and position from that given in the book and in all cases where one part of a theorum of Euclid is inferred from a similar part previously demonstrated, the student is required to demonstrate the part so inferred. The student is thus taught to depend upon his knowledge of principles rather than upon memory in his demonstrations. About four propositions are given each day as a lesson and the text of those passed over are repeatedly reviewed. In this manner the first book is read through four or five times. This book is given special attention <*so particularly dwelt*

---

[4] Mary Henry's copy ends in such a manner, obviously incorrectly.

[5] As in the preceding case, it appears that Mary Henry's copy has an omission at this point of indeterminate length.

[6] John Bonnycastle, *An Introduction to Algebra* (New York, 1818). According to the inscription in his copy of the key, Henry came to possess the *Key to Bonnycastle's Algebra* by William Davis, 2d ed. (London, 1810) in

1827. The Albany Academy library had the 1811 printing of "Bonnycastle's Algebra." See "Inventory of Library, Philosophic Apparatus, Etc.," Minutes, Academy Trustees, 2:491, and footnote 5 for the document of September 1, 1821.

[7] John Playfair, *Elements of Geometry, Containing the First Six Books of Euclid* (New York, 1819).

upon> not only from its practical importance but also because it affords the most perfect chain of logical reasoning that can be presented to the student. Every time he goes over the axioms, the definitions, and the propositions, new connections and new facts become apparent. The second book is read but twice and then reviewed with algebraical demonstrations. The third and sixth books are repeatedly reviewed as they are important in a practical point of view and are often referred to in a subsequent part of the course. The fourth book is not considered as essential and is not therefore so much dwelt upon. In the fifth book algebraic demonstrations are substituted in place of those of Euclid as they are easier and much more explicit.

While the student is reading the first book of Euclid he continues arithmetic and Algebra. Practical examples of the latter are taken from Bonicastle and the theoretical principles recited from Euler.[8] The rules of arithmetic are now investigated by algebra and correct notions of ratio, proportion, infinite series and the abstract principles of numbers are given in short lectures in connection with the recitation from Euler. After the three first books of Euclid have been studied plane trigonometry is commenced and the student is made familiar with its application to the measurement of heights and distances. He is also taught the mensuration of superfices particularly as applied to survey and is exercised in the practical use of the quadrant, the compass and other mathematical instruments by the actual employment of them in the field.[9] During this time he recites daily in Euclid and algebra but has discontinued arithmetic.

When the six books of Euclid have been read and some principles taught from La Croix's Algebra,[10] the analytical plane and spherical trigonometry

[8] [John Farrar, comp.], *An Introduction to the Elements of Algebra . . . Selected from the Algebra of Euler*, 2d ed. (Cambridge, 1821). The compiler of not only this volume but also several others cited below, John Farrar (1779–1853) was a mathematician, physicist, and astronomer. Receiving his B.A. degree from Harvard in 1803 and his M.A. in 1806, he backed away from his intended career in the ministry to become the Hollis Professor of Mathematics and Natural Philosophy at Harvard in 1807. Holding that position for nearly thirty years, he distinguished himself as a great teacher, a fellow and officer of the American Academy of Arts and Sciences, and a publisher of textbooks which had wide usage in American colleges. His texts were mostly his own compilations and translations of astronomical and elementary mathematical literature of Europe. While not a man known for his original thinking, Farrar's energy and devotion to publishing these textbooks, known collectively as the "Cambridge Course of Mathematics and Mechanics," brought a sense of contemporary science into the American college course. Ill health prevented Farrar from continued productivity in the final twenty years of his life. See *DAB*, and Stanley M. Guralnick, "Science and the American College, 1828–1860" (Ph.D. dissertation, University of Pennsylvania, 1969), pp. 262–263.

[9] According to the *Statutes* of the Academy, the book to be used was John Bonnycastle, *An Introduction to Mensuration and Practical Geometry* (Philadelphia, 1818). See above, footnote 5 of September 1, 1821.

[10] John Farrar, trans., *Elements of Algebra by S. F. LaCroix* (Cambridge, Massachusetts, 1818). A copy of this edition was in the Albany Academy library, and one still remains in

of the same author[11] is begun and also his application of algebra to plane geometry and to conic sections or the equation of curves. . . .[12] The next work in order is the Cambridge Topography[13] and in this the part on nautical astronomy has especial attention as an exercise of the principles of spherical trigonometry. During the last three years, three classes have been instructed in Cavallo's Philosophy[14] and one in Biot's Astronomy[15] with the use of Delambres and Burckhardt's astronomical tables.[16] In one case the Enfield's philosophy[17] has been used and also the Cambridge treatises on differential and integral calculus.[18]

In[19] order to give some knowledge of the principles of natural philosophy, astronomy, the use of the globes and physical geography to those who do not study theoretical knowledge can be best acquired between the age of eight and nine *<with more facility than at any subsequent period it should by no means be neglected but>* it should be considered the most prominent object of attention during the first year of the Educational course. At the same time however the child should be repeatedly exercised in simple practical problems which may serve as an entering wedge gradually to expand the mind. From nine to twelve more theoretical instruction should by degrees be mingled with the practical examples but the habit of rapid operation should still be exercised and confirmed.

Henry's Library. Minutes, Academy Trustees, "Inventory of Library, Philosophic Apparatus, Etc.," 2:492.

[11] The edition most likely referred to is in Henry's Library and bears annotations which signify that Henry learned from this book as well as taught from it. It is [John Farrar, trans.,] *An Elementary Treatise on Plane and Spherical Trigonometry . . . from LaCroix and Bezout* (Cambridge, Massachusetts, 1820).

[12] Again, it seems that Mary Henry omitted something.

[13] [John Farrar,] *An Elementary Treatise on the Application of Trigonometry to Orthographic and Stereographic Projection . . .* (Cambridge, Massachusetts, 1822). On the flyleaf this book is titled "Topography."

[14] Tiberius Cavallo, *The Elements of Natural or Experimental Philosophy*, 2 vols. (Philadelphia, 1819). See above, footnote 5 of September 1, 1821.

[15] John Farrar, comp., *An Elementary Treatise on Astronomy* (Cambridge, Massachusetts, 1827), "Selected from Biot's Traité Élémentaire d'Astronomie Physique," 2d ed. (Paris, 1811).

[16] While several astronomical tables of Jean Baptiste Joseph Delambre (1749–1822) and

Johann Karl Burckhardt (1773–1825) appeared in the thirty years preceding the writing of this report, it does not appear that they ever published jointly. Furthermore, no American or English editions have been identified. Thus, it remains a mystery as to what editions were in use here. See *Poggendorff*.

[17] William Enfield, *Institutes of Natural Philosophy* (Boston, 1802). The foregoing, the first American printing of the second British edition, is the volume surviving in the Henry Library. However, from Henry's annotation in this volume it appears that the edition used at the Academy may well have been the third American edition, printed in 1820. Henry noted that a review of this edition appeared in *Silliman's Journal*, 1821, 3:125–157.

[18] John Farrar, translator, *First Principles of Differential and Integral Calculus or the Doctrine of Fluxions . . . Taken Chiefly from the Mathematics of Bézout* (Cambridge, Massachusetts, 1824).

[19] This paragraph has been reproduced exactly as it reads in Mary Henry's copy, but the reader will note that its meaning is extremely confused. We can only conjecture that the copyist skipped a line or more.

At the age of twelve or thirteen a boy of ordinary capacity who has been properly taught may commence algebra and pursue it in connection with arithmetic, the one branch assisting to illustrate and explain the other but here also he should be made perfectly familiar by repeated exercise with every elementary algebraic process. At the age of fourteen, and scarcely before, the student may begin Euclid and from this period to the end of his course his pursuits would be almost exclusively an exercise of the reasoning faculties. He should be required to demonstrate every principle that forms a part of his studies and taught to become a profound reasoner as well as an expert mathematician. During the whole course nothing should be passed over superficially nor should the student be pushed on too rapidly. He should learn thoroughly every step in its proper order for it is a maxim perhaps more useful in mathematics than in war that no advances <are to> should be made while anything remains unconquered behind.

FROM JAMES O. MORSE[1]
Correspondence, Albany Institute Archives

Cherry Valley Aug. 10. 1829

Dear Sir

I enclose you a brief paper which unless you think it wholly devoid of merit, is at the service of your Institute.[2] It is as you will see a very hasty production, but it may possibly furnish to you and your worthy associates some hints which may serve as stimulents to further investigation of a part of our State of which but little is generally known.

Respectfully
Your friend
James O. Morse

[1] James O. Morse (1788–1837), a wealthy lawyer described as having political and literary tastes and, apparently, one of Henry's friends in Cherry Valley, New York. He was a graduate of Union College, 1809. John Sawyer, *History of Cherry Valley* (Cherry Valley, 1898), pp. 62–63, 93, and *Union Catalog*, p. 6. See an incidental mention of Morse in footnote 3 of the Description of Henry's Books of Levels, July 19–December [15] 1825.

[2] Probably Morse's "Observations on the Great Graywacke Region of the State of New-York," *Transactions*, Albany Institute, 1830, *1*:84–85, read to the Institute on October 28, 1829.

TO MARIA ALEXANDER[1]

Family Correspondence, Henry Papers, Smithsonian Archives

Albany August 15th 1829

My Dear Aunt

The stage leaves Albany for Middleburgh[2] on Sunday Wednesday and Friday and returns on the next day. The fare is twelve shillings each way which is some what less than the cost of a private conveyance, but I think that the travelling would not be quite so pleasant. If you conclude to go do not fail to command my attendance as an escort to yourself and your fair Secretary.[3] I will be ready at any time during the next week as I shall not leave Albany until the week following.

I have made some inquiries concerning the bills of the Green County[4] Bank and learn that the time of their redemption expires on the first day of september next. The Brokers will give 25 cts. on a dollar, so that you can have 30 shillings for your 15 dollars. If they are sent to the Receivers at Cattskill you will stand a small chance of getting more and you may per-hapse draw less. They must however be disposed of before the first of sep-tember as they will be worth nothing if returned after that time.

Mr Ames[5] has finished the alteration of the miniature and has much im-proved its appearance: he has changed the colour of the coat to black with-out altering its fashion and also retouched the back ground. It was not thought advisable to do any thing to the hair but the shading given to the other parts of the picture has placed the head more in relief, and made the original likeness considerably more distinct. Mother knew it immediatly and has taken the charge of it until Harriet and yourself come down. We[6] had a delightful ride to Albany on tuesday both in respect to our stage company and a pleasant temperature of the weather. The Lady whom you saw in the stage was Mrs. Walton on a trip to Albany to take her daughter Mrs Beck to Schencetady. The remainder of the day after our arrival was also rather pleasantly passed. We first dined at 'Our house' w[h]ere the

---

[1] Mrs. Maria Alexander (1769–1852), wife of Alexander Alexander (1764–1809; Ann Alexander Henry's brother), was the mother of Stephen and Harriet Alexander. This letter was addressed to Maria Alexander in Schenectady. See typed notes on Henry ancestry in Family Correspondence, Henry Papers, Smithsonian Archives.

[2] Middleburg, New York, about thirty miles west of Albany.

[3] Harriet Alexander.

[4] Greene County adjoins the southern border of Albany County.

[5] Julius R. Ames, miniaturist. See above, Excerpt of Albany Institute Minutes, March 18, 1829, footnote 2. We think this may be a reference to the surviving miniature of Henry.

[6] From the context of the letter, we can assume the traveling party consisted of Henry, Stephen Alexander, and Christian B. Thümmel (see next footnote).

handkerchiefs were properly marked according to your directions. Afterwards visited Mr. Ames with the miniature, and the Barber with Mr Thümmel's[7] head; we next took tea with Mrs Shankland[8] and in the evening went to see Maelzels grand exhibition of the conflagration of Moscow.[9] At half past nine I bid good-by to the two Gentlemen at the Eagle Tavern where they had taken lodging in order to start with the stage at one o'clock the next morning. The remainder of their tour through the *"Land of steady habits"*[10] you will probably learn from the letters from Stephen.

Please give my love to Harriet & Miss Conner[11] (I wish she would permit me to call her *Aunt* Conner as Miss, is rather too cold and formal). I hope Harriet has intirely recovered from her indisposition and that you and she will soon visit Albany.

> I am with much Respect
> And Affection
> Your Nephew
> Jos. Henry

P.S. Please direct your *little cleark*[12] to inform me what I am to do with the bills.   J H

P.P.S. All well.

---

[7] Christian B. Thümmel (1802–1881), clergyman. Thümmel was undoubtedly born and raised in Germany. At some time between 1825 and the date of this letter, Stephen Alexander probably became a close friend of his at the Yates Polytechny in Chittenango, New York. In 1830, Thümmel became an assistant professor and librarian at the Hartwick Seminary (about 5 miles south of Cooperstown, New York), serving until 1832. In 1831 Union College awarded Thümmel an honorary A.M. degree. Thümmel and Stephen Alexander were apparently close associates and may have engaged in phrenological studies together; but since we can imagine no need for taking a phrenological bust to the barber, we assume that the purpose of the visit was related to Thümmel's personal grooming. We have no further clues as to his subsequent activities.

Henry Hardy Heins, *Throughout All the Years, The Bi-Centennial Story of Hartwick in America, 1746–1946* (Oneonta, New York, 1946), pp. 44, 45, 162. *Union Catalog*, p. 41.

[8] Probably Mrs. P. V. Shankland; see footnote 3 of Henry to Harriet Henry, June 4, 1830.

[9] Maelzel's Exhibition opened the night before (August 11, 1829) in Knickerbocker Hall. Featuring a "Bass Fiddler," "Speaking Figure," and "Automaton Rope Dancer," the exhibition concluded "with the Evacuation and Conflagration of Moscow. . . , [a] scene never before exhibited in this country." *Albany Daily Advertiser*, August 11, 1829, p. 2.

[10] Connecticut.

[11] The addressee's sister Nancy Connor who had been living there in Schenectady.

[12] Henry is referring to Harriet.

TO WILLIAM CAMPBELL
Mary Henry Copy, Henry Papers, Smithsonian Archives

Albany Sep. 25th 1829

I have an idea of preparing an article for the next number of the Transactions of the Institute on the topography of the State of New York.[1] I propose to give sectional tables of all the heights and distances that I can procure. May I request that you will send me an abstract of the principal points of your survey along Susquehanna from Otsego Lake to Binghamton. I intend giving secular views in a tabular form.

I have taken the temperature of several wells and find that they scarcely differ in temperature when similarly actuated and near the same place. I consider this an excellent method of readily finding the mean temperature of a place. As the result, my observations give precisely the temperature of Albany.

[1] See *Transactions*, Albany Institute, 1830, *1*:87–112.

THE STATUTES OF THE ALBANY ACADEMY[1]
Albany Academy Archives

October 9, 1829

On this date the Trustees approved a revision of the 1819 *Statutes.*[2] Although the basic pattern established in the early years persisted, the Academy in this formal document attained maturity. While the early vision of the school was not literally realized, many of the hoped-for elements now existed in a flourishing condition. The Academy had achieved its classic state or even a golden age to which its annalists could rightly point with pride.[3] Devoted Trustees undoubtedly deserved some credit. If any one person was responsible for this success, it was the Trustee who also served as Principal, T. Romeyn Beck. We assume that Henry, as one of the senior faculty, had some role in the developments leading to the 1829 *Statutes;* that Henry's was the hand penning the lines relating to the instruction in mathematics and in natural philosophy is the only assumption we care to make.

The new text was both more explicit and elaborate than its predecessor, especially on the organization of the Academy, curriculum, and student discipline.[4]

[1] Printed, 31 pp.
[2] See above, September 14, 1819.
[3] Many passages of this nature occur in the previously cited volumes commemorating the seventy-fifth and centennial anniversaries of the Academy.
[4] Although the regulations on pp. 26–30 of the 1829 *Statutes* are quite detailed and strict

Where the previous *Statutes* had two Departments of Classics and of Mathematics with an English (i.e., elementary) School attached to the latter, there were now four numbered departments. The First Department was Beck's. "English and Natural Sciences" was its area of concern, or what was previously characterized as the nonelementary, nonmathematical, nonclassical curriculum. The development of the courses of the First Department from nearly nothing in 1819, when Henry enrolled, to its 1829 impressive state was the most obvious and most significant change in the Academy. It was Beck's triumph. The Second Department, Classical Studies, was in the hands of Peter Bullions. Henry's was the Third Department concerned with Mathematical Sciences. Both of these departments now offered a more elaborate array of courses, essentially in the pattern going back to the early years of the Academy. A Fourth Department was the elementary school section of the Academy. If any one aspect of the Academy was responsible for the issuance of a revised *Statutes,* it was the creation of this department. Public pressures for a system of tax-supported common schools loomed far larger in the revision than what seems most interesting to modern eyes, the overlap with the colleges.

No clues to this are apparent from the 1829 *Statutes* which concentrates on the offerings beyond the elementary level. Students had a choice of three "courses" or arrangements of the subjects "in order to render the studies pursued more directly subservient to the different objects which Students may have in view in future life." Again, the courses were numbered. The First was called the General Course; the Second was the English and Mathematical Course; and the Third was the Mercantile Course. Each Course was to start after the completion of the work in the Fourth Department.[5] As the General Course included all of the studies of the first three departments "except such as are peculiarly Mercantile," we here reproduce a chart from pp. 24–25 of the *Statutes.* (See pages 234–235.)

From its prominence in the *Statutes,* we can infer that the eight-year General Course was the pride and joy of Trustees and faculty. An Albany boy received a splendid education comprehending the subjects of all three advanced departments. To be more precise than the language quoted previously, only penmanship, taught in all three departments, and the newly introduced work in French

---

on disciplinary matters, regulation No. 25 did allow the faculty to introduce what we would now call an honor system. Corporal punishment was administered, as was common then. In his monograph, *Melville's Early Life and "Redburn"* (New York, 1951), pp. 51–56, William H. Gilman discusses the experiences of Herman Melville who entered the elementary school part of the Academy on October 15, 1830, stressing the harshness of the discipline and the sternness of the atmosphere. At the 1863 fiftieth anniversary celebration, Herman Melville showed up to take an honored place in the procession, his supposed wounds of body and spirit at the Academy healed by time. With admirable prescience his fellow alumni welcomed Melville as a world famous author. Official business kept Henry in Washington. *Celebration of the Semi-Centennial Anniversary of the Albany Academy* (Albany, 1863), pp. 11, 66–67.

[5] The description of the departments and the courses is taken from chapter 3 of the *Statutes,* pp. 6–18.

COURSE AND ORDER OF STUDIES.

General Course.

1st. DEP.—English and Natural Science.	2d DEPARTMENT—Classical Studies.	3d DEPARTMENT—Mathematical Science.
	1st Year. Latin Grammar, Corderius, Historia Sacra, Turner's Exercises (begun,) Latin Reader, Irving's Universal History.	
	2d Year. Latin Reader continued and Turner's Exercises, Cornelius Nepos. Irving's Grecian and Roman Histories, and Roman Antiquities.	
	3d Year. Caesar, Ovid, Latin Prosody. Turner's Exercises, Translations. Irving's Grecian Antiquities, Mythology and Biography. Greek Grammar.	
4th Year. Geography. English Studies, including Grammatical Reading, Declamation and Composition.	**4th Year.** Sallust, Virgil, Latin Prosody. Exercises, Translations, Synonymes. Ancient Geography, Adam's Roman Antiquities. Greek Grammar, Jacob's Greek Reader, Anthon's Greek Exercises.	**4th Year.** Arithmetic. Physical Geography.

5th Year.
History in general. Constitution of the United States. Constitution and parts of the Statutes of the State of New-York. English Studies continued as above.

6th Year.
Rhetoric and Belles Lettres. Technology, or the application of Natural Science to the Useful Arts. Chemistry and Mineralogy. English Studies as above.

7th Year.
Natural History. Elements of Criticism and Logic. Chemistry and Mineralogy. Reading of English Classics and English Studies.

8th Year.
Natural Theology. Evidences of Christianity. Moral Philosophy and Political Economy. English Studies as above. Chemistry.

5th Year.
Livy, Cicero's Orations, Horace, Prosody. Single and double Translations, Comparative Grammar, Synonymes. Graeca Majora, 1st v. Anthon's Gr. Exercises. Ancient Geography, Roman and Grecian Antiquities.

6th Year.
Cicero de Officiis and De Republica. Horace—Satires and Epistles. Terence. Graeca Majora, 1st & 2d vols. Greek Exercises. Translations, &c. as above.

7th Year.
Cicero de Oratore & de Natura Deorum. Tacitus, Horace Art of Poetry, Terence. Graeca Majora, 1 & 2d v. Homer's Iliad. Translations, &c. as above.

8th Year.
Tacitus. Quinctilian. Juvenal. Persius. Graeca Majora, 2d vol. Longinus. Translations, &c. Comparison of Styles.

5th Year.
Arithmetic continued. Algebra begun. Use of the Globes. Construction of Maps. Practical Geometry. Mathematical Geography.

6th Year.
Algebra contin'd. Euclid. Plane Trigonometry, with application to Heights and Distances. Perspective. Architecture. Technology, or the application of Mathematical and Mechanical Science to the Useful Arts.

7th Year.
Technology contin'd. Geometry of Solids. Mensuration, Surveying and Navigation. Analytic plane & spherical Trigonometry. Application of Algebra to Geometry, including Conic Sections and the Equation of Curves in general.

8th Year.
Descriptive Geometry. Application of Trigonometry to Nautical Astronomy and Topography. Differential Calculus. Mechanics. Physics, including Optics, Electricity, Magnetism, and Electro-Magnetism. Astronomy and Civil Engineering.

were omitted, besides the bookkeeping and mercantile arithmetic offered in Henry's Third Department. Although not stated, the General Course was the college preparatory course. Every classical student was automatically enrolled in the General Course; only a classically prepared student could qualify for admission to the established liberal arts colleges of the day.[6] Put another way, every classical student who went through the last five years of the General Course, or any appreciable portion of these years, was well grounded in mathematics, the sciences, and the early nineteenth-century analogues of our courses in the humanities and the social sciences. Men so educated were not likely to perceive any necessary incompatibility between the classics and the sciences.

Students in the English and Mathematical Course completed their work in five years. As this course consisted of everything in the General Course except the classics, we suspect that the first three classical years of the General Course were sometimes taken jointly with work in the Fourth Department by boys obviously bright enough for college or so destined by family status. It seems unlikely that Beck, Bullions, and Henry would immediately thrust English and Mathematical boys out of the Fourth Department into the fourth-year curriculum while making their General Course peers wait three years. Except for the Classical Studies of the Second Department, students in the English and Mathematical Course had identical training as the General Course scholars. Presumably, the absence of Latin and Greek simply indicated the lack of any intention of going to college. Although "objects . . . in view in future life," to which the particular courses were "subservient," appears highly vocational to modern eyes, the particular array of subjects in the English and Mathematical Course does not suggest specific occupations, unlike the situation in recent decades.

Even the four-year Mercantile Course does not seem particularly vocational by modern standards.[7] The Classics were omitted. Otherwise the Mercantile Course was quite similar to the English and Mathematical Course. The Third Department simply dropped the work for the eighth year of the General Course; bookkeeping and mercantile arithmetic were introduced in the offerings of the fifth through seventh years; and in a few instances some of the tougher mathematical courses were skipped. In the Mercantile Course's second year (the equivalent of the General Course's fifth year) mathematical geography was omitted. In the third year Mercantile Course students had the same nonclassical work as their peers in the other two courses. In the fourth and last year Henry omitted the trigonometry and analytical geometry of the General Course but substituted the physics of the eighth year and a "popular course" in mechanics and astron-

---

[6] George Frederick Miller's *The Academy System of the State of New York* (New York, 1969), pp. 57ff, discusses the college entrance requirements, calling attention to two important points for the argument developed below. The curriculum of the academies, especially the better ones like the Albany Academy, tended to go beyond the college preparatory level. Not all of the students enrolled in the advanced courses went on to college, raising an important point. If not a stepping stone to college, what was the purpose of these courses?

[7] The Mercantile Course is outlined on pp. 14–15 of the *Statutes*.

omy. The latter may be identical with the astronomy and civil engineering of the General Course's eighth year. The only concession Beck made in his contribution to mercantile education was to drop his seventh-year subjects and instead give the eighth-year course. Natural theology, the evidences of Christianity, moral philosophy, and political economy were apparently deemed more essential to a future business career than natural history, criticism, and logic.

When the enrollment figures are broken down by course, the results are not fully enlightening. The statistics below start the year before Henry joined the faculty and are carried forward in time a few years after his departure to demonstrate any trends. The numbers for 1825–1828 are not wholly comparable even to one another, let alone the later figures. The data for the quarters starting with the September 1828 quarter and ending with the June 1834 quarter have gaps. By far the most serious for our purposes is the absence of information on the number of students in the Mercantile Course. They were probably few and are counted in with the English and Mathematical scholars. Despite lacunae, the figures given are useful, particularly because they reflect not only the nature of the Albany Academy, but aspects of public policy in education.

From its start the Board of Regents encouraged the academies to prepare the young for college. Funds were given by New York State for these schools as far back as the eighteenth century. In 1817 the Regents formalized their interest in encouraging college preparation (i.e., the classics), by specifying that the number of classical scholars was to determine the distribution of the state aid ("the literature fund"). Academies thereafter kept records and reported the number of classical scholars. In 1827 the State Legislature, in an unusual move, specifically changed the method of apportionment; hereafter students in higher English studies were to be counted as well as the classical scholars. Public policy in the state now supported not only Peter Bullions' efforts but also the labors of T. R. Beck and Joseph Henry.

Ordinarily, the State Legislature left apportionment of funds to the discretion of the Regents.[8] At that period the University of the State of New York had no responsibility for elementary education. The broadening of the basis of appor-

---

[8] Frank C. Abbott, *Government Policy and Higher Education, A Study of the Regents of the University of the State of New York, 1784–1949* (Ithaca, 1958), pp. 17ff, 36. Miller, op. cit., pp. 24–29. Franklin B. Hough, *Historical and Statistical Record of the University of the State of New York...* (Albany, 1885), pp. 80–93, 444–456, 526–573.

All of the State aid to the Academy in this period went for the salary of the faculty. The sum was never larger than a few hundred dollars. Legislation in 1830 modified the apportionment by pupils in the higher branches of study by giving each senatorial district an equal amount of aid, no matter what the number of pupils involved. Even so, in 1831 the Academy received $313.70.

Apparently, the Albany Academy in this period did not profit from another form of the Regents' largesse. As early as 1790 the Regents made funds available for the purchase of scientific instruments and books. The practice ceased in 1830 only to be revived in 1834. In the next half century the Regents distributed $157,609.20 to the academies who were required to raise an equal sum. In these years the Albany Academy did receive such support. Although the sums granted to particular schools seem modest to twentieth-century eyes, the cumulative impact of this aid was probably quite considerable. Hough, op. cit., pp. 512–526.

Course Enrollment, Albany Academy, 1825–1834[9]

	1825	1826	1827	1828
Whole no. of students at date of report	137	141	137	153
Whole no. of students during year	193	191	—	—
Average no. of students for each term	136	132	—	—
Whole no. of classical students at date of report	64	48	—	—
Average no. of classical students for each term	65	53	—	—
No. of students claimed by the trustees to have pursued classical studies, or the higher branches of English education, or both, for 6 months of the year*	—	—	79	81
No. of students allowed by the regents to have pursued said studies for 6 months of said year*	—	—	75	80

Blank spaces reflect the differences in categorizing and reporting data from year to year.

* The report in 1828 gave these figures for 4 months.

[9] As part of its visitation rights, the Board of Regents could and did require reports from the academies. When the apportionment of funds was determined by the number of students, these reports became more detailed. An example of such a report is printed below in the Trustees' Minutes of January 27, 1832. The reports from the academies became the basis for various statistical tabulations and charts in the annual reports of the Regents to the State Legislature. Although useful in many respects, this information is all we have for the years 1825–1828. The figures given are from the following: *New York Senate Journal,* 49th Session, January 1826, pp. 611–618; *New York Senate Journal,* 50th Session, January 1827, Appendix B; *New York Senate Journal,* 51st Session, January 1828, Appendix B; *New York Senate Journal,* 52nd Session, January 1829, pp. 431–445, Appendix I. Starting with the school year of 1828–1829, T. R. Beck presented a detailed financial report to the Trustees giving the income from tuition. As the tuition for each student was not the same but varied with the work taken, we have used these figures to formulate this table. We assume that "English" means those in the English and Mathematical Course. Unfortunately, the data does not differentiate between Mercantile Course students and the English and Mathematical students. For example, in the September 1828 quarter Beck reported the following:

Of the Students attending during the

	Total	Class.	Eng. & Math	4th
Sept. '28	153°	56*	96	—
Dec. '28	172°	61	111	—
March '29	151°	59	92	—
June '29	137°	55	82	—
Sept. '29	195#	60*	81	52
Dec. '29	217#	54	99	61
March '30	237	63	112	62
June '30	247	58	116	73
Sept. '30	251	64	121	66
Dec. '30	257	65	125	68
March '31	250	70	109	71
June '31	240	57	86	97
Sept. '31	240	49*	102	88
Dec. '31	241	51	94	96
March '32	229	48	86	95†
June '32	238	48	69	121
Sept. '32	210	46	64	100
Dec. '32	230	51	69	110
March '33	230	55	68	107
June '33	213	40	62	111
Sept. '33	250	37	85	128
Dec. '33	271	39	90	142
March '34	267	50	93	124
June '34	242	45	75	122

° This total is the sum of Classical & English students only, irrespective of enrollment in the 4th Department for which the figures are unknown.

* In addition, one student was engaged in both Classical and English studies.

Total of 195 includes one French student; total of 217 includes three French students.

† Illegible in Minutes. This figure arrived at by subtraction of Classical and English students from the total.

September Quarter 1828	Cash Rec^d	Add $3.50 rec^d of Erwin 3.50
52 were classical at $7.50—43 Paid.		$811.25
7 Free 2 Unpaid	$322.50	
90 were English at 5.50 82 Paid		
2 Free 6 Unpaid	451.00	The greater tuition for classics was common
4 were Classical (half-Quarter)		in the period according to Theodore R. Sizer,
at $3.75. 3 paid 1 unpaid	11.25	ed., *The Age of the Academies* (New York,
6 were English (half-Quarter)		1964), p. 23. The sources of our table for 1828–
at 2.75 All paid	16.50	1834 are the Trustees' Minutes of February
1 Half the Quarter English &		12, 1830 (*1*:362), February 17, 1831 (2:2–3), May
Half the Quarter Latin	6.50	26, 1832 (2:28–29), July 12, 1833 (2:84–85), May
153		15, 1834 (2:109–110), May 28, 1835 (2:143–144).

tionment was specifically linked to the desire to provide more teachers for an expanded common school system to increase educational opportunities in the state. Classical scholars destined for college and the learned professions were not likely to man the common schools and the academies. The academies were not particularly successful as a source of trained teachers and eventually lost this function to the normal schools.

One consequence of the 1827 legislation was a general rise in the enrollment of the Albany Academy (from 137 in 1825 to over 200 by the academic year when the *Statutes* were adopted). Two trends are visible in the 1825–1834 period. The number of classical students (and, therefore, the number in the tough, prestigious General Course) shows a slow but steady decline. There is an initial rise through the September 1831 quarter followed by a leveling off, leading to a slow decline. The Fourth, or elementary, Department, on the other hand, climbs fairly steadily in both absolute and relative terms. In the September 1829 quarter the fifty-two elementary students were slightly more than one-fourth of the total; by the June 1834 quarter the 122 boys in the Fourth Department were a shade over half the total school population. When Henry left the Academy in October 1832, the advanced portion of the school was in a period of decline, as far as numbers were concerned. How much of a decline this was from the standpoint of the academic program, we cannot state because the data does not allow us to estimate the number of Mercantile Course students counted with the English and Mathematical students. In the year 1834, the Regents reported on statewide trends since the 1827 increase in the literature fund. The total number of academy students had doubled, roughly in accord with the situation at the Albany Academy. But while the Academy had a relative decline, the number of students throughout the state in classical and higher English studies had increased fivefold.[10]

By the winter of 1828–1829, the movement for a common school system supported by public funds was strongly underway in the city of Albany.[11] In addition to the Albany Academy, the Female Academy, and the Lancaster School, there were a number of private, one-man, schools in Albany. Yet one-half of the city's children received no schooling. The agitation in Albany was part of a more general statewide movement which in 1830 resulted in legislation authorizing, among other things, a school district for each ward in Albany. As a Trustee of the Lancaster School, Henry obviously was involved in this public question, but we have located no surviving documents of his bearing explicitly on this matter.

---

[10] *Annual Report of the Regents of the University of the State of New-York, 1834* (Albany, 1835), p. 8.

[11] This account is indebted to William Esmond Rowley's 1967 Harvard dissertation, "Albany: A Tale of Two Cities, 1820–1880," pp. 103–112. See also Lawrence A. Cremin, *The American Common School, An Historic* Conception (New York, 1951) and Bernard Bailyn, *Education in the Forming of American Society* (Chapel Hill, 1960). For a revisionist view of the common school movement, see Albert Fishlow, "The American Common School Revival: Fact or Fancy?" in Henry Rosovsky, ed., *Industrialization in Two Systems* (New York, 1966), pp. 40–67.

The Lancaster School was widely denounced, as was the whole concept of providing education to the disadvantaged as an act of charity. The Trustees and Faculty of the Academy somehow had to accommodate to the pressures for common schools while maintaining the essentials of an educational scheme they obviously favored.

On August 8, 1829 the Trustees issued a report explaining the changes later embodied in the 1829 *Statutes*.[12] Apparently answering doubts about the creation of the Fourth Department and the public role of the Academy, they stressed the extension of the course of studies in both the elementary and advanced departments. The separation of the elementary students into a new department was justified as relieving Beck and Henry of heavy duties previously borne. Henry, the report stated, "has, in fact, to attend daily to 160 recitations; if so, how can he acquit himself in such a manner as even to satisfy his own laudable ambitions." After this seeming concern for Henry's research the report noted that the new arrangement would make the English education (which included mathematics) on a par with the work in American colleges, inducing more youths to attend the Academy. As an additional move to meet the demands for greater educational opportunities, the report picked up the theme of the 1827 legislation, offering to give one year's free education to six young would-be teachers in common schools. The report concluded:

It is a primary object with the trustees of the Academy, to establish and pursue a system of education so full and comprehensive as to enable every pupil, who seeks it, to obtain a good education here, without the risque or necessity of resorting to other places. To that end, various departments of instruction have from the commencement of the institution been established in it, and under the modifications now introduced, while the classical department remains the same as heretofore, the other departments are increased in number, and the spheres of instruction in each is materially enlarged. The trustees, without intending to derogate from the importance and value of the classical department, nevertheless, freely acknowledge, that they cherish, with at least an equal degree of favor and regard, the other departments in their Academy; which are fitted to prepare the greatest number of pupils for the usual pursuits of active life. They consider their institution a local one, established for the special benefit of the city, by whose extraordinary munificence it has been most liberally endowed; it is open and free for the admission of pupils from every class of the community; and while it possesses the means, it offers to use them, to impart instruction corresponding with the wants and objects of every individual in

---

[12] The copy of the text of the report in the manuscript minutes is a clipping from the *Albany Argus* of August 21, 1829, p. 2, columns 3 and 4 from which we have taken the quotation given below. The Committee of the Trustees submitting the report was appointed on April 10, 1829, to come up with a new plan for the Academy specifically to relieve Beck of the pressures of teaching the younger boys.

the city. The mechanic arts and mercantile pursuits, with every other occupation in civil life, are regarded with equal favor. As the institution has been endowed out of the public treasury of the city, it ought not to exist otherwise than as a public school, accessible, alike, to every class of our citizens. It was originally established as such; as such it has ever since been, and still is conducted and maintained; and as such it is hoped the public will regard and sustain it.

In his master's dissertation on early Albany schools,[13] John T. McClintock points out that very few students apparently went through the entire course of study in the Academy. The high turnover of students, coupled with the low tuition in the elementary portion ($3 and $4 per quarter in 1829), meant that the Academy provided some education, at least, to a wide range of the Albany public, not merely the sons of the well-to-do. The Academy also granted scholarships to bright, poor boys from the Lancaster School and, later, the public common schools. When this practice ended in 1868 after Albany founded its public (or free) high school, the Albany Academy became a purely private institution whose outermost reach was college preparation.[14] It was all in a common American pattern. Many educational institutions originally founded with some degree of public support and ostensibly for a broad purpose of the society survived to become largely the preserve of the well-to-do; newer, less prestigious schools served a wider segment of the public.[15] Was it only coincidental that the Fourth Department enrollment started rising appreciably after the victory of the common school movement?

If the evolution from quasi-public service to private privilege is a familiar one in American history, what about the educational pattern in the Academy during its classic phase? Two elements of the pattern are noteworthy: the curriculum and the commitment to educate a wide age spectrum—from the elementary school to what we now might designate as the junior college level. The secondary literature in the history of education is not too helpful in explaining these characteristics. The most recent relevant work, *The Age of the Academies*,[16] has an interpretive introduction by the editor, Theodore R. Sizer, placing the academies in relation to the public high schools which succeeded them. Despite a number of proper disclaimers,[17] a reader of Sizer is likely to come away with two

---

[13] "Albany and Its Early Nineteenth Century Schools," Harvard Graduate School of Education, 1967, passim.

[14] *The Celebration of the Centennial Anniversary of the Founding of the Albany Academy, May 24, 1913* (Albany, 1914), pp. 25–28.

[15] Admittedly, a sweeping assertion like this is not easily documented, especially in a footnote. What we have in mind is the public support given to Ivy League universities in their early years, such as the funds the Board of Regents made available to Columbia Col-

lege, and the recent findings that many older state universities had student bodies largely derived from families in quite comfortable circumstances.

[16] Theodore R. Sizer, ed., *The Age of the Academies* (New York, 1964).

[17] Perhaps the most important for our purpose is the statement on page 19, "The academy was the American's compromise between practical education and the education traditionally held valuable."

distinct impressions. The first is genealogical—the academies arose in large measure from the model supplied by the writings of John Milton and Benjamin Franklin who thereby somehow become the ancestors of the American high schools. The second related impression is that utilitarian pressures produced a vocational curriculum. Even Sizer's own evidence does not unequivocally support his splendid genealogy. For our purposes it is sufficient to note that the pattern of British education in the previous century provided ample precedent for the educational program of the Albany Academy.[18] Involving Milton and Franklin simply gives a respectable foundation for the imputation of utilitarian vocationalism. Here, too, the pattern in the mother country before independence raises doubts about assumptions of American conditions uniquely predisposing educational authorities to deviate from a nonvocational to a vocational curriculum. As previously noted, the Albany Academy curriculum had very little of a specifically vocational nature. The Sizer interpretation probably arises from reading present concerns into past language about the relationship of abstract learning or theory to practical affairs.

There are, for example, a number of instances in the manuscript minutes of the Board of Regents in which theory and practice are mentioned. In 1790 the Board urged that "Science & Literature deserves the patronage of a free and enlightened people" as essential to "public happiness" and "the common prosperity."[19] At a later date the Regents regretfully noted that America lacked universities for the instruction in "professional and other knowledge immediately connected with the business of life."[20]

Accompanying the rising demand for better common schools by 1826 was a movement for educating the practitioners of agriculture, mechanics, and the other useful arts. The response of the Regents was a proposal that the professors at the colleges "and perhaps the Academies at Albany and the principal villages" give brief courses of lectures to mechanics and others, as a logical supplement to the common school system. Using the apparatus provided by the Regents, the lectures would effect a "more intimate union of the efforts of Scientific and practical men." Quite similar to Henry's views in his January–March 1832 introductory chemistry lecture, below, the Regents cite fairly simple chemical examples, not the rather more sophisticated situation Henry sees. What is noteworthy is that the Board, like Henry, took for granted a rather direct connection between scientific knowledge and utility. The way to get practical results, therefore, was to teach what passed then as scientific theory.[21]

When this topic recurred in the Regents' deliberations in 1830,[22] the prosper-

---

[18] Here and in what follows we are greatly indebted to Nicholas Hans, *New Trends in Education in the Eighteenth Century* (London, 1951).

[19] Minutes of the Board of Regents, February 19, 1790, *1*:17–19, in the Office of the Commissioner of Education of the State of New York, Albany, New York. All citations are

to the original manuscript minutes. In this case and in several of the following footnotes, the texts are printed in the annual reports of the Board with minor revisions.

[20] Ibid., April 10, 1822, *2*:291.

[21] Ibid., January 12, 1826, *3*:100–105.

[22] Ibid., April 6, 1830, *3*:306–309.

ity of Europe was ascribed as "principally owing to the knowledge which science has diffused among the inhabitants of that continent."[23] But "in our higher schools [i.e., the colleges], science is taught rather as an accomplishment than as a useful branch of knowledge; and as those who study it are generally destined for the learned professions, it holds but a subordinate grade in their acquirements, and seldom sheds its light upon those branches of productive labour which it is calculated most to benefit." Since the colleges were not doing the job, the Regents proposed using part of the literature fund to support special schools of applied science (i.e., agriculture and the mechanic arts). As to the academies, rather than suggesting a change in curriculum towards the vocational, the Regents wanted to spend more money on scientific books and philosophical apparatus.[24]

Around the time when Henry was publicly stating his faith in science and its applicability to the wants of life in the early months of 1832 the Regents in preparing their annual report took particular pains to discuss the development of science and mathematics in the curriculum of the academies:[25]

A reference to the abstract [of the status of the academies] will show that it is not only extremely diversified, but that it embraces, in many of the academies, almost every branch of education which enters into the course of our colleges of the highest grade; that the difference between them is not so much in the nature of the studies, as in the extent to which the course is respectively carried. It may, perhaps, occur to those who examine with minuteness that part of the abstract which exhibits the course of study, that mathematics and the physical sciences enter into it in a degree disproportioned to literature and the moral sciences. The fact is not disputed; and it is conceived that it is to be traced to the condition of society in the United States, and the nature of our occupations. Education, like every thing else, when unrestrained by positive regulation, naturally takes the direction of individual interest. The physical resources of New York—of the whole country, indeed—are in a course of active development: no part of the globe presents so wide a field, or offers higher rewards for the application of physical science. Literary pursuits, on the other hand, are almost always the companions of leisure and wealth; and it is to be expected that many years will elapse before they will enter as largely into our course of education as those sciences which are applicable to the ordinary business of life.

This peculiarity in the course of academic education in this State is not adverted to with a view to intimate that it is desirable to change its direction by legislative measures. On the contrary, it deserves to be considered,

---

[23] Henry comments on the scientific basis of European (particularly British) technology in his Introductory Chemistry Lecture of January–March 1832, below; see especially footnote 19 where this topic is considered in greater detail.

[24] On the philosophical apparatus, see footnote 8, above.

[25] Minutes of the Board of Regents, February 28, 1832, 3:362–369.

whether it be not safer to leave education in its higher branches, to take its general direction from the necessities and demands of the country—whether the only purposes for which the arm of government can be advantageously interposed, be not to bring the benefits of elementary education within the reach of the greatest possible number of persons, and to place its higher branches, with regard to patronage, on a basis of exact equality. The Regents would not be understood as undervaluing the utility of classical studies, much less the importance of those departments of knowledge which come within the definition of moral science. They intend only to advert to the ascendancy of other branches of education, as the natural result of our social condition: and without claiming too much for our national literature, which is, however, rapidly improving, they conceive that we have a conclusive reply to the reproach of a want of genius, sometimes cast upon us, by appealing to more than one living example of literary distinction in natives of this State, who command, in an eminent degree, the attention and patronage of Europe. With us, as every where else, a demand for the productions of literature, like those of science and art, is all that is necessary to secure them; and it is worthy of reflection, whether any effort to create a demand for them by legislative arrangements would not be an unwise diversion of intellectual labor from more useful channels; if individuals find it for their interest to become mathematicians or civil engineers, and this would not be the case unless the country needed their services as such, whether it would not be unjust to the community to attempt, by legislative encouragement, to make them classical scholars or linguists. The provisions of the act of April 1827, which place classical studies and the higher branches of English education, including moral and physical science, on the same level, with regard to a participation in the benefits of the literature fund, afford all that can reasonably be demanded of the government, by opening the various channels of instruction to a fair competition.

An ascription of narrow vocationalism, of an unthinking catering to utility, does not adequately describe the situation. Perhaps "occupational egalitarianism" is a more useful concept. Almost from its inception the Board of Regents had given preference to students going to college and to the colleges themselves. Concretely, this meant education in the classics and preparation for careers in medicine, the law, and the ministry. Not all graduates of the early colleges in New York (and elsewhere in the nation) went into these three learned professions. For a number, it is true, college education provided a cultural adornment. Nevertheless, a principal justification for the existence of colleges in the United States up to this time was to provide a supply of properly trained professionals. By 1826–1827, the State of New York started to amend its educational policy so that public support would be equally accessible to all vocations. As seen previously, this took two principal forms: first was the expansion of aid to academies to include students in the higher nonclassical subjects; second was the movement to promote lectures and then special collegiate-level schools for agriculture and the mechanic arts. What this meant ultimately was that occupations were or should become equal in terms of public support and in requisite advanced training. Occupational egalitarianism was very American, perhaps uniquely so; the nature of the academies was traditional in a British sense.

Modestly appearing in Albany and elsewhere in the nation, occupational egalitarianism was an important trend. Placing all occupations requiring training on the same level as the older learned professions implied a kind of classlessness, but not necessarily an equivalence of power and prestige. Each occupation, by virtue of its requisite formal learning, became a profession, and each was equally professional in the eyes of its practitioners and of the society at large. Occupations lacking professional status in America strove to attain this level by virtue of a suitable educational program and all the trappings associated with such status. To the Regents the proper educational program for most vocations involved a thorough grounding in basic scientific principles. In the next century Abraham Flexner would sourly comment on what he considered the pseudo-scientific pretentiousness of "non-academic" subjects in the American universities.[26] Given his viewpoint—from the German university—Flexner never perceived the phenomenon as a means of leveling upward.

Obviously, not every occupation could achieve an equivalent of professional status. Obviously, not all professions became equal in terms of social status, financial rewards, and influence. The Regents' minutes of February 28, 1832, quoted previously, made a distinction between the "scientific" and the "literary" occupations. Clearly, "science" was given the palm because of its utility. Ultimately, this preference would have beneficial consequences for scientists, but, at the same time, yield serious vexations. Behind the preference was a rather simplified view of science and a naive faith in its easy utility. Joseph Henry and his kind gave allegiance to science because of an intellectual preference, not primarily out of respect for a useful accumulation of data. Henry wanted other human activities to become imbued with both the spirit and substance of his kind of science. But as this occurred in the American context, Henry's science became simply one of many equal modes of "science," not its highest form. For Henry and other scientists, this was to be a source of conflict.

While perhaps signaling a future trend in American society, the Albany Academy's curriculum in 1829 embodied older educational forms and social assumptions. The particular range of courses offered was quite like the offerings of many British schools of the previous century, particularly what Nicholas Hans

---

[26] Abraham Flexner, *Universities: American, English, German* (New York, 1930), pp. 39–218. Flexner's particular criticisms are often quite just. What he fails to appreciate is that the universities and colleges in the United States often have functions beyond research and the training of the learned. The proliferation of colleges and universities in the United States indicates to us that they took over the role briefly exercised by the academies—providing a broad general education and a diversity of special skills for which there is a felt need in American society.

has designated the "private schools." In these British schools there was clearly an intention to prepare youths for adult life, often combining "a liberal education with technical training."[27] Quite a number had a range of subjects much like the Albany Academy. Even the particular array of courses taught by Joseph Henry had many British precedents. The mathematician Charles Hutton (1737–1823), whose books Henry owned in Albany, gave courses nearly identical with the Third Department's.[28] A twentieth-century reader can even suspect a relationship to the tri-partite Scottish curriculum.[29] All that was happening in Albany when the Academy was founded was that a number of the leading citizens wanted the children of the city to receive a good general education according to the familiar example of schools in the mother country.

The references encountered previously about the utility of mathematics are not properly interpretable as merely reflections of practical pressures. After all, the classic curriculum, including mathematics, was not simply designed to produce cultured gentlemen but also to yield lawyers, ministers, and physicians. Not only equity between occupations was involved in expanding the nonclassical curriculum. Few would go on to a college for the learned professions, and very few other collegiate institutions existed for other professions (Rensselaer Polytechnic Institute being one of these few). Consequently, we can assume that many people in 1829 and earlier regarded the academies as the only place possible for most men in the community to receive an education above the rudiments.[30] Except for the relatively few going on to college and the learned professions, the academies were to provide all the educational requirements of the community beyond the elementary skills in reading and writing. To meet the needs of the community in one institution clearly required more than the classics —the prerequisites of the three established professions—but a fairly broad range of subjects. Surveying and mercantile arithmetic hardly encompassed the needs ,of American communities in the early years of the Albany Academy. Future leaders of these comunities also had to know moral philosophy, mathematics, and literature, subjects somehow "subservient to . . . future life."

The presence of the elementary school and the role of the Albany Academy in the community is clarified by the preceding assumptions. If one school was to take care of most of the needs for "higher" education, why not place the very young in the hands of those who would, in any event, instruct them in later years? It was an economical way of guaranteeing the quality of early education.

---

[27] Hans, op. cit., especially his chapters 3–5. The quotation is from page 65. The British situation in the previous century displays a greater degree of specialization; that is, there were an appreciable number of schools with a specific vocational and technical orientation. Given the British precedent, the pressure for schools for the practical arts and for vocational courses does not seem a uniquely American phenomenon but an evolution from an early, generalized educational program to a more complex, specialized curriculum.

[28] Ibid., pp. 109–110.

[29] George E. Davie, *The Democratic Intellect, Scotland and Her Universities in the Nineteenth Century* (Edinburgh, 1961), p. 14.

[30] Comments bearing on this point are in *The Celebration of the Centennial Anniversary of the Founding of the Albany Academy, May 24, 1913* (Albany, 1914), pp. 17ff, 21, 28ff.

247

The enlightened self-interest of the community, if not Christian charity, also called for opening the doors to bright but poor boys—like Joseph Henry. Careers were open to talent. From the statistics given here, derived from the annual reports of the Trustees, most of the scholarship students in the early years were placed in the General Course and given the best education the Academy could provide.[31]

Free Scholars, September 1829–June 1834

	Total	C	EM	4th		Total	C	EM	4th
Sept. '29	9	8	1	—	Sept. '32	7	3	2	2
Dec. '29	9	9	—	—	Dec. '32	8	3	3	2
March '30	[12]*	9	3	—	March '33	8	3	3	2
June '30	13	10	2	1	June '33	6	3	1	2
Sept. '30	12	9	2	1	Sept. '33	7	3	2	2
Dec. '30	12	9	2	1	Dec. '33	8	4	2	2
March '31	11	9	1	1	March '34	8	5	1	2
June '31	[7+]*	6	[?]*	1	June '34	7	5	—	2
Sept. '31	10	4	4	2	C—Classical Students				
Dec. '31	10	4	4	2	EM—English & Mathematical				
March '32	10	4	4	2	Students				
June '32	8	4	2	2	4th—Fourth Department (i.e.,				
					elementary) students				

* Figures illegible.

Comparisons are hazardous at far retrospect. These Free Scholars in Albany may well have received the best education then available in the State of New York. The Albany Academy had the most extensive curriculum, and the largest faculty and student body in the state. Its plant and endowment surpassed all others.[32] The senior faculty—Beck, Bullions, and Henry—were a very able group. The years of Henry's association with the Academy were a golden age for a particular educational concept. Expansion of the colleges, the burgeoning of the common schools, and the later appearance of the public high schools made the concept obsolete except in one respect. Judging by the experience of the State of New York, the nonvocational curriculum of the public high schools was strongly influenced by the precedent of the academies.[33]

[31] Ibid., p. 24, comments on the good academic performance of the free scholars.

[32] *Annual Report of the Regents of the University of the State of New-York, 1831* (Albany, 1832), insert chart abstracting the returns of the academies. Interestingly, only one school in the state had more higher branch scholars, the Albany Female Academy.

[33] See Miller, op. cit., pp. 46ff, 53–57, 86–99.

Ann Alexander Henry (1760–1835), circa 1829, Joseph Henry's mother.
This miniature, now in the Smithsonian Institution,
is attributed to Ezra Ames (1768–1836).

Lithographie par Deroy

Dessiné d'après nature par J. M.

Ville d'Albany Capitale de l'état de New York.

Albany Capital of the state of New-York.

Urbs Albany Caput provinciæ New York.

Stadt Albany Hauptstadt in New-York.

Imp. Lith. et B.... dirigée par Noël ainé & Cie.

View of Albany, 1828, from Jacques Gérard Milbert, *Itinéraire pittoresque du fleuve Hudson* . . . (Paris, 1828–182
Courtesy of the Library of Congress.

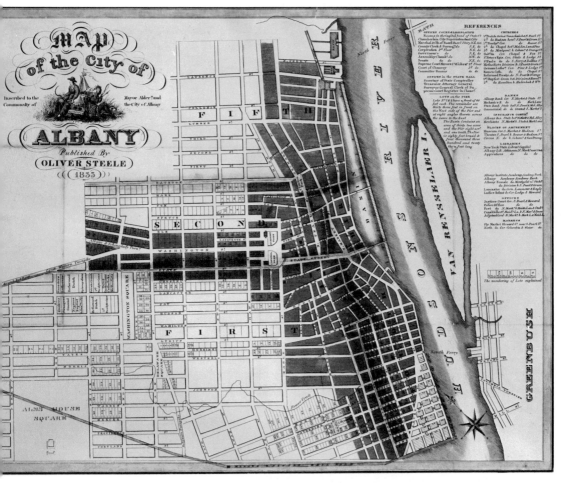

"Map of the City of Albany, Inscribed to the Mayor, Alder^n., and Commonalty of the City of Albany,"
published by Oliver Steele, 1833. Courtesy of the Library of Congress.

Lewis Caleb Beck (1798–1853), n.d.,
by J. H. Shegogue (1806–1872).
Courtesy of the Rutgers University
Art Gallery.

Theodric Romeyn Beck (1791–1855), 1829,
by Henry Inman (1801–1846).
Courtesy of the Pennsylvania Academy
of the Fine Arts.

Stephen Van Rensselaer (1764–1839), 1829.
Attributed to John Livingston Harding.
Courtesy of the New-York Historical Society.

Simeon DeWitt (1756–1834), circa 1830,
by Henry Inman (1801–1846).
Courtesy of the Albany Institute
of History and Art.

Prof. Silleman   Albany Dec 10th 18[30]

    Dear Sir

        I have been engaged for some time
past in a series of experiments on Electro Magnetism
and particularly in reference to the developement
of great magnetic power with a small galvanic
element. The results I wish to publish if
possible in the next No. of the Journal of
science. I am anxious that they should
appear as soon as possible since by delay=
=ing the publication of the principles of these ex=
=iments for nearly two years I have lately had the
mortification of being anticipated, in part by
a paper from Prof. Moll in the last No of Br
Brewster's Journal.

        Please inform me if I shall be too
late for the next No. of the Journal if I send a
paper within two weeks of the date of this letter — it
will probably make five or six pages — If it be

Letter from Joseph Henry to Benjamin Silliman, Sr., December 10, 1830. Courtesy of Yale University.

not too late I should like to have a small
wood cut of a powerful magnet which I am
constructing on electro-magnetic principles.

Both Mrs. Henry and myself retain a lively
recollection of the many polite attentions we received
in New Haven last spring We join in a respectful
remembrance to your self and family
                    I am with much respect
                    Your humble servt
                         Joseph Henry
Professor Silliman

The large electromagnet constructed by Henry in early 1831 for Benjamin Silliman, Sr., of Yale College. This electromagnet is now in the Smithsonian Institution.

EXCERPT,[1] MINUTES, ALBANY INSTITUTE
Institute Minutes, Albany Institute Archives

Albany. Oct[r] 28. 1829

A Special meeting of the Institute.

A Communication from Ja[s] O. Morse of Cherry Valley a Corresponding Member on the Great Graywacke Region of the State of New York was read.[2]

M[r] Joseph Henry read a Communication on the Topography of the State of New York.[3]

---

[1] Routine business has been omitted.

[2] See James O. Morse to Joseph Henry, August 10, 1829, above.

[3] This paper was published by the Albany Institute in its *Transactions*, 1830, *1*:87–112. In slightly revised form it was published as introductory material in David H. Burr's *Atlas of the State of New York* (Albany, 1829), pp. 21–29. See Burr to Henry, November 25, 1829, below.

TO HARRIET ALEXANDER
Family Correspondence, Henry Papers, Smithsonian Archives

Albany Nov. 12th [1829]

A Mon Cher Cous.

Agreeably to one of my pr—s[1] I send you the "Token for 1829"[2]—please accept it as a pledge that the rest shall all in due time be performed.

My eye is almost intirely well—nothing contributed more to the cure than an application of *brandy*.[3]

Yours &c

Jos. Henry

PS My compliments to your Mother & Aunt. J H

---

[1] Promises?

[2] *The Token and Atlantic Souvenir, a Christmas and New Year's Present* was published annually in Boston from 1829 to 1838.

[3] Externally? Despite this medicinal need for liquor, Joseph Henry hardly appears to have been a wayward young man. Although no evidence has surfaced in manuscripts, within a year of this letter Henry was active in the temperance movement. Late in October 1830, Henry was elected Vice President of the Albany Young Men's Temperance Society. *Albany Argus*, October 27, 1830, p. 2.

FROM DAVID H. BURR[1]

Henry Papers, Smithsonian Archives

New York Nov 25 1829

Dear Sir

Yours of the 22[2] has just been received. I acknowledge my remissness in not answering your former letters & hope that you will forget & forgive.

The delays in the appearance of my Atlas[3] have been greater than I anticipated but whether the delay is Chargeable to any one in particular I am uncertain but certainly not to you and I feel extremely grateful for the assistance you have so kindly afforded me.

I received Several copies of the Atlas on Monday. I directed one to be left with M[r] Van Rensslaer[4] (Surveyor Generals office) who promised me

---

[1] David H. Burr (1803–1875), cartographer. Born probably in Bridgeport, Connecticut, Burr's education remains a mystery. It is unknown when he and his family moved to New York State, but we do know that Burr studied law at Kingsboro and was admitted to the New York bar. Becoming a member of the militia in 1824, he was appointed aide-de-camp to Governor DeWitt Clinton. Apparently with the aid of Clinton, he was designated Deputy Surveyor of the State Road Survey in 1825. In 1827 the legislature of the state directed Surveyor-General Simeon De-Witt to verify and authorize the publication, at state expense, of Burr's *Atlas*, which was then a work in progress, based on the findings of the survey of 1825, the Simeon DeWitt map of 1802, and reports from local surveyors solicited through circulars. The *Atlas* was the second of its sort for a state, and among the last ever to be engraved; both it and the large map of the state were to be published tardily in 1829. The Introduction to the *Atlas* contains a sizable section (pp. 21–29) on an overview of New York topography, which is only a slight revision of the paper Henry delivered before the Albany Institute on October 28, 1829, "Topographical Sketch of the State of New-York, Designed Chiefly to Show the General Elevations and Depressions of Its Surface," *Transactions*, Albany Institute, 1830, *1*:87–112. As a handsomely engraved product, *An Atlas of the State of New York* (Albany, 1829) won fame for its compiler in cartographic circles. From 1832 until 1846 Burr served in Washington as Topographer in the Post Office Department (especially helping to locate post offices in

poorly mapped territories and states) and as Geographer to the House of Representatives. Simultaneously, he worked to compile and publish *A New Universal Atlas; Comprising Separate Maps of All The Principal Empires, Kingdoms and States Throughout the World; and Forming a Distinct Atlas of the United States* (New York, [1835?]), and he published frequent revisions. After a brief trip to Europe in hopes of having his revised *Universal Atlas* published there, he returned home to become first the U.S. Deputy Surveyor to Florida, then to hold a similar position in Louisiana, and then to act as Geographer for the U.S. Senate. In 1855 Burr was appointed the first Surveyor-General of the Utah Territory; there he became deeply involved with the tensions and conflicts between the Mormons and Federal authorities, serving the latter for three years. Weakened by exposures, trials, and fatigue, he returned to Washington an invalid and died December 25, 1875. See Walter W. Ristow, "Simeon DeWitt, Pioneer American Cartographer," in *Kartengeschichte und Kartenbearbeitung*, ed. Karl-Heinz Meine (Bad Godesburg, 1968), pp. 110–113; see also information on Burr in the Bibliography of Cartography File, Map Division, Library of Congress.

[2] Not found, like the other letters mentioned immediately afterward.

[3] *An Atlas of the State of New York* (Albany, 1829).

[4] Mr. Bernard S. Van Rensselaer (d. 1879), who is listed in the Albany City Directory for 1831–1832 as the Surveyor-General's Clerk. A resident of Albany at this time, he entered the Albany Academy in 1815 and graduated

to show it to the Editor of the Argus.[5] I presume he will attend to it. Mr Croswell has promised as soon as the work appeared to notice it. If an article appears in the Argus will you send me a Copy of it.

You are perfectly at liberty to take such impressions of the mountain elevations as you wish. Tell Mr Clark[6] to use care & not injure the plate in doing so. If you find any errors I shall be much obliged to you if you correct them.

The profile of the Champlain Canal will be shown on the plate forming the NW Corner of the Large Map. I had the Erie Canal twice inserted because the first is so distorted in length.

I have the pleasure to add that Mrs Burr presented me last Friday with a fine Daughter & both are doing well.

When you come we shall be happy to see you here and have you stay with us.

I am as ever Yours

D. H. Burr

P.S. Please bring or send me one of your Topographical Scetches.

---

from Union College in 1821. By the time of his death he had become Deputy Surveyor-General. See *Union Catalog*, p. 22 and *Academy Seventy-fifth Anniversary*, p. 78.

[5] Edwin Croswell (1797–1871), journalist and politician, was at this time beginning to come into political power through his editorship of the *Albany Argus* and friendly relationship with the Albany Regency. He continued to edit the *Argus,* with the help of his cousin, Sherman Croswell (1803–1859), until 1854. Although the *Argus* was long the voice of the Democratic Party in New York State, there is no reason to believe that Henry's or Burr's efforts to have the *Atlas* announced were politically directed. See *DAB* and *Howell and Tenney,* pp. 359–360.

[6] Undoubtedly Asahel Clark (d. November 19, 1835), engraver and partner in the firm of Rawdon, Clark & Co., who did the engraving for Burr's *Atlas of New York*. Asahel Clark was a nonresident and corresponding member of the First Department of the Albany Institute. See *Transactions*, Albany Institute, 1830, *1*, part 2: Appendix, p. 66. Albany City Directory for 1825 and Munsell, *Ann. Alb.*, *10*:250. See also George C. Groce and David H. Wallace, comps., *The New York Historical Society's Dictionary of Artists in America 1564–1860* (New Haven, 1957), pp. 129, 726.

TO STEPHEN ALEXANDER[1]

Family Correspondence, Henry Papers, Smithsonian Archives

Albany Dec. 5th 1829

My Dear Stephen

After a very long delay I at length commence to fulfil the promis which I made of writing as soon as leasure would permit. You must not think

---

[1] For Stephen's reply, see his letter of [March 13–15?, 1830], below.

however that I have been so much engaged that I could not have spared a few moments to devote to you before this time. On the contrary my conscience accuses me of having much less profitably employed many hours and also of having wasted many more in not paying due attention to that proper distribution of time which in a great measure constitutes the grand secret of doing much with apparent ease and leasure.

After having made this confession I must be allowed to add in some justification of my tardiness that my labours have been more arduous during the last three months than at almost any other period of my life. We have more than 200 pupils in the Academy and have introducd several new studies which have occupied considerable extra time.[2] The work on which I was engaged when you were in Albany proved to be a labour of much more magnitude than I expected at the commencement that it would be. It has only been published within the last three weeks and is scarcely yet before the public owing to the unforeseen difficulties in printing and binding a work of such magnitude.[3] Several copies have been exhibited in New York and are highly spoken of by the different papers of that city. I have published my Topographical sketch of the State in the transactions of the Albany Institute with additions and corrections.[4] The compilation of the several tables and the other facts in this paper cost me considerable labour but I hope the article will be in some degree useful both as it regards the subject of internal improvement and the study of the climate of the State, particularly in connexion with the meterological observations made by the several academies. The configuration of the surface of a country you know has a great influence on its mean temperature as well as on the direction of its prevailing winds.

At the last meeting of the Institute Dr. T. R. Beck proposed you as a corresponding member of the Society; you will of course be elected as such at the next regular meeting. It is hoped by the publishing committee that you will favour the transactions in the next or a subsequent number with a paper either on your new method of finding the longitude or on some other subject which you may deem of interest to the public.[5] You must not always bury yourself among the hill of Chittenango or suffer your torch of knowledge to shine only within the walls of the Polytechny. I hope that

---

[2] Minutes, Academy Trustees, August 9, 1827 (see above), discusses the range of courses taught by Henry.

[3] Henry's "Topographical Sketch" was first published as the Introduction to David H. Burr's *An Atlas of the State of New York, Containing a Map of the State and of Several Counties* (New York, 1829).

[4] Henry's "Topographical Sketch of the State of New-York," published in *Transactions*, Albany Institute, 1830, *1*:87–112.

[5] See Harriet's letter of March 25, 1830, footnote 3, below.

you receved the Phrenological bust[6] in good order, the names of the different organs refered to on the skull I will add (if I can get them and have
room) as an appendix to this letter.

After having thus finished all communications of an ordinary kind I
must now call your attention to a subject of a much more serious nature.
I allude to my engagement with Harriet. I am confident that it would have
been much more proper for me to have spoken to you on this subject when
your were in Albany. I have often regretted that I did not do so as I was
only detered by those feelings of an unmanly kind which perhapse [a] delicate subject generally produces but which should not have prevented me
from speaking freely with you; I thought at that time that I could communicate my sentiments more freely by letter but now that I have commenced
I scarcely know what to say. I feel that it is an affair that very nearly concerns the temporal happiness of several individuals besides ourselves. Your
mother and your aunt are both devotedly attached to their children and
would be rendered miserable by any misfortune that should befal either you
or your sister. Harriet has had offers which certainly in pecuniary and perhapse in other points of view would be much more advantageous than the
present. These considerations have made me more anxious about the result
of the connexion than under less peculiar circumstances I might perhapse
have been. With regard to myself I am fully confident that I shall be both
happier and better by the union. My only source of anxiety is that Harriet
may not be as happy as she deserves or that she may not be as fully so as I
wishe she may be. Connubial happiness in some degree depends upon
worldly success and this is not always within the reach of personal exer-
tions for while much depends on individual labours much also proceeds
from the dispensations of that providence over which human power has no
controll.

I hope from the first that I have been fully impressed with the responsibilities and importance of this connexion. I have certainly endeavored to
act in such a manner that Harriet might be as little as possible under the
influence of any feelings which might bias her judgement in making her
decision. And even now although I am confident that my future happiness
depends principally on this event were she to repent in the slightest degree
of having made the engagement or were any serious objection raised on
your part or on that of the family I would instantly relinquish all claim
and suffer her again to decide a new.

Give me your sentiments on this subject frankly and if I have not been

[6] For a study of phrenology during Henry's
lifetime, see John D. Davies, *Phrenology, Fad*
and Science: A Nineteenth-Century American
Crusade (New Haven, 1955).

as explicit on some points as you may deem necessary inform me of it and I will indevour to state my views and feelings more clearly and fully.

> With sentiments of the highest Respect
> I am Affectionatly
> Yours
> Joseph Henry

PS Dr T. R Beck has gone to Fairfield to delver his annual course of lectures which circumstance renders my labours in the Academy just at the present time more than ordinarily active.[7]

NOTE I have kept this letter on hand several days after writing it in order that I migh add the refferences to the Phrenological bust. I am however at last obliged to close it without obtaining a copy. I loaned the refference which I receved with the bust to Isaac Jackson[8] and he has gone to Pittsfield. I will send it in my next letter. J. H.

General Beck[9] has been almost constantly confined to his room for the last two months and I think it probable that he will not survive this winter.[10]

[7] T. R. Beck lectured on medicine at the Western College of Physicians and Surgeons in Fairfield, Herkimer County, between 1815 and 1840.

[8] Isaac Wilber Jackson (1805–1877), educator, author, was born in New York. He attended Albany Academy with Henry, graduated from Union College in 1826, and tutored Union students from 1826 to 1831 when he became Professor of Mathematics and Natural Philosophy. Several texbooks in mathematics grew out of his lectures at Union, one of which went through eight editions. *Her-ringshaw*, p. 522; *Union Catalog*, pp. xii, 30; *Academy Seventy-fifth Anniversary*, p. 81; Stanley M. Guralnick, "Science and the American College, 1828–1860" (Ph.D. dissertation, University of Pennsylvania, 1969), pp. 278–279.

[9] T. R. Beck's brother, Nicholas F. Beck died on June 30, 1830, age 34. He was the Adjutant General of New York State. Munsell, *Ann. Alb.*, 9:312.

[10] Henry penned this statement, apparently an afterthought, in the margin on the first page of his letter.

TO HARRIET ALEXANDER[1]

Family Correspondence, Henry Papers, Smithsonian Archives

Albany Dec. 25ᵗʰ 1829

My Dear Harriet

For the last three weeks I have been constantly looking forward to this day with the liveliest anticipations of hope and in truth no Christmas since

[1] Part of this letter is printed in *Coulson*, p. 45, who frequently changed Henry's spelling and punctuation to conform to modern usage.

the days of my boyhood has ever appeared so pleasant in prospect as this. But now that it has come instead of hastening to enjoy it with you as I fondly anticipated I am unexpectedly obliged to embarke in a few moments for New York. My stay in that city however will be no longer than is necessary to transact some business for the academy and if nothing happens I shall probably be in your presence on next wednesday evening when I hope soon to loose in the pleasures of your company the reccollection of every circumstance but the one on which I base my every hope of future happiness.

Do me the favour to accept the accompaning annual. And be assured that with Sentiments of the highest esteem and feelings of the warmest kind I am My Dear Harriet

Your's devotedly
Jos. Henry

P.S. Agreeably to your Mother's request I have made enquiry concerning Quinces but can find none; they are a very scarce article and have sold as high as four dollars per hundred this last season.

There are several kinds of fruit advertised in Albany in a preserved state. Will not some of these answer instead of Quinces? If so please to write me so that I may receive your letter when I return to Albany and I will take what you order to Schenectady when I go up.

In great haste
Yours
J Henry

P.P.S. No person opens letters addressed to me you may therefore write at any time between this and next tuesday.

⊰{ 1830 }⊱

TO STEPHEN ALEXANDER

Family Correspondence, Henry Papers, Smithsonian Archives

Schenectady Jan 8th 1830

My Dear Stephen

Although I have not received a letter from you since I last wrote,[1] yet I will so far depart from the established rools of ettequette in such cases

---

[1] See Henry's letter to Alexander of December 5, 1829, above, and a later response of Alexander's on [March 13–15?, 1830], below.

made and provided as again to intrude upon your philosophical reveries with something in the shape of a letter.

I have been in Schenectady for several days past and have made a long as well as a very pleasant visit to the little hospitable old city that has the honour of being your birth place. I return to Albany this afternoon where I hope to find a letter in waiting for me from Chittenango. If I do not I shall almost conclude that you have *"cut my acquaintance."*

Dr Joslin[2] has been engaged during the long College vacation in giving a course of Anatomical lectures to the students & citizens. He has not been able as yet to procure a subject for dessection although he went to New York for that purpose.[3] He is therefore obliged to demonstrate the several parts from the comparative anatomy of animals. I attended his lecture on the brain in which the several parts of that organ were shown from the head of an ox. I was surprised to see a considerable resemblance between the brain of this animal and that of man.

The difference appeared to be more in the size than in the form. We have very remarkable weather for this season of the year. The Hudson is still open or has only been closed within two days past since which time I have not heard from Albany. I spent the first part of the vacation in New York. I went down on Christmas; the river was entirely free from ice and the city had the appearance and almost the *"feel"* of Summer.

You have seen before this time the Governors Message[4] and are no doubt

[2] Benjamin Franklin Joslin (1796–1861), physician, author, and educator, graduated from Union College in 1821. He stayed in Schenectady tutoring Union students in mathematics from 1822–1824, then spent two years in New York City at the College of Physicians and Surgeons, which awarded him a medical degree in 1826. From 1827 to 1837 he was professor of Mathematics and Natural Philosophy at Union College and held the same chair at New York University from 1838 to 1844.

While at Union, Joslin edited the American edition of Dionysius Lardner's *A Treatise on Hydrostatics and Pneumatics* (Philadelphia, 1832), published his own *Meteorological Observations and Essays* (Albany, 1836), and wrote an article on "Irradiation," *Transactions,* American Philosophical Society, n.s., 1831, *4*:340–349. Despite his apparent preoccupation with mathematics and science, Joslin continued to practice medicine and in 1842, while at New York University, was converted to homeopathy. *Union Catalog,* pp. xii, 21; Stanley M. Guralnick, "Science and the

American College, 1828–1860" (Ph.D. dissertation, University of Pennsylvania, 1969), pp. 280–281, and especially Benjamin Franklin Bowers' *Address on the Life and Character of the Late Benjamin F. Joslin, Delivered before the Homeopathic Medical Societies of New-York and Brooklyn* (New York, 1862).

[3] At this date the only legal way of obtaining a human corpse for teaching anatomy was to get the body of an executed criminal. Grave robbing did occur, but Joslin's unsuccessful attempt probably involved a clandestine arrangement with the manager of a pauper institution (e.g., a charity hospital). See John Blake, "The Development of American Anatomical Acts," *Journal of Medical Education,* 1955, *30*:431–439.

[4] Enos Thompson Throop (1784–1874), lawyer, New York jurist and politician, was at the time of this letter both Lieutenant Governor and Acting Governor, owing to Martin Van Buren's resignation of the office to become President Jackson's Secretary of State. *DAB.* Just prior to assuming the governorship to which he had been elected (1830–1832), Throop

highly pleased with the direct (not collateral) puff which his excellency has given your Institution. It will probably be of considerable service to the Polytechny in making it more extensively known and justly appreciated. Give my respects to Mr Thumel[5] and tell him that I hope his *"imperfect knowledge of the English language"* has not prevented the entire recovery of his arm.

I am with affection and esteem Yours Jos. Henry

On[6] the first pages of this letter is a list of the [phrenologi]cal organs on the bust which I sent to you.[7] The classification is from Comb's Phrenology.[8] It [was co]pied by Harriet from one furnished to her by Dr Joslin.

---

delivered the annual Governor's Message to the Legislature on January 5, 1830. The paragraph which Henry alluded to was undoubtedly the following:

Among the matters of interest relating to this subject [domestic agriculture and manufactures], and which promise to satisfy the desires of those patriotic individuals, who have labored to introduce more science into practical agriculture, I notice, with pleasure, the dawnings of a scientific agricultural education. A school for that purpose is established in Oneida county, which has placed itself in the class of literary institutions under the care of the regents of the university. Students are there instructed in scientific and practical agriculture; are compelled to go through all its manual operations, and pay for their instruction by labor. A principle, similar in some respects, is introduced into the polytechnic at Chitteningo, founded by and under the superintendence of Doctor Yates. In his school, which is designed to carry a pupil through all the sciences, he has provided for the instruction of such youth in the principles of husbandry, and other branches of education, as will volunteer to labor for their tuition and support. It is also deserving of notice that he has admitted the students to a share in the government of his school. He has established a miniature legislature for passing laws, and courts for trying offenders, where all the forms of election, legislation, and judicial proceedings are observed. The students are represented in one branch of their legislature; the faculty form another, and the principal has a veto. A judge is appointed from among the officers, to preside in the court, for the trial of offences against their laws, with an appeal from the decisions of the court to the faculty and principal.

Legislative Documents of the Senate and Assembly of the State of New York, 53rd Session, 1830 (Albany, 1830), pp. 13–14.

[5] So spelled. Christian B. Thümmel, for whom see Henry to Maria Alexander, August 15, 1829, footnote 7.

[6] These three sentences were added to the first page of the letter along the left margin, apparently after Henry had finished writing on the other side. The sheet has been torn at those points in the text where brackets appear, presumably a result of the seal being broken.

[7] The list, apparently an enclosure, has not been located. It was discussed in Henry's letter to Alexander of December 5, 1829, above.

[8] George Combe (1788–1858), *Elements of Phrenology* (Philadelphia, 1826), first American edition from the second Edinburgh edition, improved and enlarged. The first Edinburgh edition was published in 1824. For Combe, see *DNB*.

DIARY OF ASA FITCH[1]

Diary 8, page 76, Fitch Family Papers, Sterling Library, Yale University

[February 8, 1830]

Monday 8th Spent part of the forenoon in the Assembly Chamber & the State Library. Was rejoiced to find in the latter Says Monograph of American *Cerainbyces*[2] in the A. Phil. Soc. Trans. & some other papers on Entomology. Went to the Alb. Academy, & renewed the term for which I take Samouelle's Entomologist.[3] Profs. Henry & Bullions[4] attended Dr. M's. Lecture[5] this P.M. Made myself know to the latter, who is well acquainted with father.

[1] The entry for February 8, 1830, is printed here in its entirety.

[2] More properly, Thomas Say, "Descriptions of Insects of the Families of Carabici and Hydrocanthari, *Latreille*, Inhabiting North America," *Transactions*, American Philosophical Society, 1825, 2:1–109.

[3] George Samouelle, *The Entomologist's Useful Compendium; or, an Introduction to the Knowledge of British Insects* (London, 1819), a widely popular work of entomology in its day.

[4] Classics Professor at the Albany Academy; see above, Minutes, Academy Trustees, April 14, 1826, footnote 7.

[5] Dr. Alden March (1795–1869), surgeon, anatomist, and teacher of surgery. A native of Massachusetts, March was awarded his M.D. degree from Brown University in 1820, whereupon he commenced practicing surgery in Albany. Simultaneously he was a professor at the Vermont Academy of Medicine, 1825–1831. He was a principal leader in establishing medical education in Albany, participating in the Albany Medical Seminary, 1827–1833, lec-

turing on anatomy since 1821, presiding over the Albany Medical Society, 1832–1833, and heading the movement, from 1830 until its success in 1839, for establishing the Albany Medical College and Albany City Hospital. The lecture which Fitch, Henry, and Bullions attended was "introductory to his course of anatomy, in which he discussed at length the importance of establishing a hospital and medical school in Albany." Munsell, *Ann. Alb.*, 9:200. The lecture was published in 1830, entitled *A Lecture on the Expedience of Establishing a Medical College and Hospital in the City of Albany*. See *DAB*; Howell and Tenney, pp. 210, 213–214, 220; *Brown University Historical Catalogue, 1764–1914* (Providence, 1914), p. 587; Munsell, *Coll. Alb.*, 2: 220–229 and 4:61–63; Emerson Crosby Kelly, "Development of Medical Education in Upstate New York: The Albany Area," *New York State Journal of Medicine*, 1955, 55:2264–2268; idem, "The Doctors March to Armsby of Albany," *Bulletin of the History of Medicine*, 1956, 30:32–37.

TO HARRIET ALEXANDER

Family Correspondence, Henry Papers, Smithsonian Archives

Albany Feb. 9th 1830

My Dear Harriet

Although our parting was rather colder, than is compatible with that warmth of feeling, with which I always wish to regard you, and which I now find to be most essential to my own happiness; still I am confident, from a knowledge of your character, that you will not receive unkindly this communication, or be disposed to consider it an unnecessary intrusion. I know that you will believe it is, only prompted, by a sincere wish, to dispell any unpleasant reflection, which my abrupt departure, and some previous improper expressions, may have left upon your mind.

Perhaps other feelings than those which now actuate me, may for a moment, have suggested a sullen silence; but *My Dear Harriet* I vallue too highly, those feelings with which I am happy in believing we mutually regard each other, to suffer them for an instant to be disturbed, by an unmanly or improper reserve.

In reviewing our past intercourse, I find much to sensure and to regret, in my conduct; it has often been careless and inconsiderate: At first I treated you with much aparent coldness and reserve; and several times since I have acted with a rudeness, highly improper, towards the woman whom I love and respect. But this has not arrisen, from any want of a proper estimation of your worth, or from the slightest intention to manifest indifference, or disrespect; on the contrary. I have from the first regarded you with increasing esteem and affection; and have never intentionally or willingly given you either pain or offence.

It is however far from being enough, that I have not directly intended wrong; for I should have guarded each word, and each action, so as not to have given, if possible the slightest cause of disquiet; and that too more particularly at the commencement of our intercourse. *"A little thing can blast an infant blossom, and the breath of the south can shake the rings of the vine, when they first begin to curl like the locks of a lisping boy; but when by time and consolodation, they stiffen into the hardness of a stem, they can then endure the storms of the north, and the rough blast, and the loud noise of a tempest, and never be broken."*

Precisely such in my opinion is the Character of female attachment: At first every harsh word has the power to shake and alarm it; and the more tender its nature, the more sensitive it is, to the slightest breath of suspition, or unkindness. But it does not always continue thus, for when constancy has been tested by experience longer that the *whims* of fancy can last or an unstable attachment, formed without esteem, can exist, the affection becomes confirmed, by confidence, as well as habit; and a quick reply, a trifling error, or even one unkind expression has no power to disturbe it.

The attachments of men are perhapse of a less affectionate but of a more unyielding nature. They are not so permenantly affected by those little annoyances which sometimes ruffle the temper, but leaves undisturbe the heart. I have no fear that any offence, which your nature is capable of giving, can interrupt for more than a moment those feeling with which I now almost habitually regard you: but still I must acknowledge that you do possess the power, in a very considerable degree, of giving me pain; and when I am smarting under the lash of your displeasure, I may show for an instant a spirit of rebellion but one kind word, or one smile of reconciliation will I am sure never fail to call me back to my allegiance.

Perhapse you will think me too confident and [? may be], somewhat, mischieviously inclined to put me to the trial—I am certain that I would stand the ordeal; but pray you in pity, do not unnecessarily, give me the pain of the experiment.

I have one small request to make before closing this letter and that is, that you will answer it, if it be with but two lines.[1] I am sure you would not refuse this little favour if you knew how much pleasure it will give me particularly in the present state of our affairs.

I am *My Dear Harriet* as ever with sentiments
  of love and esteem

Your's devotedly
Joseph Henry

N.B. My Love to your Mother and Aunt.
I trusted to the merchant for the size of the patern of your aunt's dress. I now fear that it is too small. Tell her not to have it made until I come to Schenectady and I will bring a few yards more.

Adieu J. H.

----

[1] For Harriet's reply, see her letter of February 16, 1830, below.

EXCERPT,[1] MINUTES, ALBANY INSTITUTE
Institute Minutes, Albany Institute Archives

Albany. Feb[y] 11. 1830

Professor Henry gave a Lecture on Electricity, accompanied with experiments. . . .[2]

----

[1] The routine notices about donations, accounts, discussions of a system of penmanship, and a law on incorporation of lyceums are omitted.

[2] We have no knowledge of what this lecture consisted. The most reasonable guess is that Henry was demonstrating his work on increasing the lifting power obtainable from small galvanic elements.

FROM HARRIET ALEXANDER[1]
Family Correspondence, Henry Papers, Smithsonian Archives

Schenectady Feb. 16th 1830

My Dear Joseph,

I received yours on Saturday last[2] and would have answered it immediately, had not a sore finger disabled me.

It was quite an agreeable although rather an unexpected favour and met with a cordial reception, as a proof of your continued esteem and a relief from many unpleasant [*written above:* apprehensions] feelings relative to the impression my, at best, foolish and inconsistant conduct, may have made on you at your last visit; particularly, as your grave phiz and cold air at parting bespoke no little dissatisfaction and which I will acknowledge, for a moment, heightened my displeasure. But a very little reflection, soon convinced me that *I* was the offender. I can scarcely tell, what at first displeased me, some mere trifle which ought to have passed unheeded; impute it not to any act of yours but rather to that inability of temper which so often involves me in difficulty. I regret the inquietude, which I fear, it has occasioned you, but fear I should be half inclined to repeat the offence if I could be assured of it its being followed by so pleasing a communication.

Mary Ann La Grange is with us at present, to whom I have made some important disclosures, but strange to tell she evinced no surprise.

Love from Mother and Aunt. Excuse the shortness (is that a proper word) of this scrawl & believe yours truly

Harriet.

---

[1] *Coulson,* pp. 44–45, prints an incomplete version of this letter which he mistakenly dates February 11, 1828.

[2] Henry's letter of February 9, 1830, above.

TO HARRIET ALEXANDER
Mary Henry Copy, Family Correspondence,
Henry Papers, Smithsonian Archives

[March] 5, 1830[1]

I owe you a thousand thanks for the pleasure and delight afforded me by your frank and generous reply to my letter. If after every storm comes such

---

[1] While the Mary Henry copy bears the date "Feb. 5th 1830," this letter followed that of Harriet to Henry, February 16, 1830, above, and probably bore the date we give to it.

a calm I care not dear girl how often you ruffle the more irritable parts of my temper. I intended to have expressed my gratitude in a much more pleasant manner to myself in a visit to Schenectady last Saturday, but on that day and during this week I was occupied too much with lectures and our semi-annual examination. I have at present the pleasure of reflecting that my visit is yet to come and that shortly too, as I am determined that no ordinary circumstance shall interfere next Saturday evening.

With regard to the word "Shortness" which occurs at the close of your letter permit me to make a few remarks. Although this term is often improperly applied, yet I think there are cases where it may be used with grammatical as well as moral propriety. As an example I cite the following quotation from an author[2] whose opinions are entitled to your most particular attention. "When we have once resolved to perform an action, highly proper in itself and which is intimately connected with all our phases of terrestrial happiness, it is certainly wise considering the general mutability of human affairs, to make the shortness of the delay, in some degree, correspond with the importance of the transaction." In this didactic sentence I find no gramatical error and I sincerely hope that you will be fully impressed with the truth and importance of its moral correctness. It is true indeed that the same sentiment has been expressed with more brevity by the Bard of Avon without the use of the word "Shortness" thus. "Since it is to be done: it were well done; that it were done quickly." As I quote from memory the latter sentence may not be precisely in the words of the author.[3] We can however settle that point on Saturday evening as well as discuss the whole subject which you may perceive is a great favorite with me. In the mean time, the hours will move with slowest pace, my dearest Harriet until I can in person assure you that I am with love and gratitude

Devotedly yours—Jos Henry

P.P.S. Do not be from home on Saturday.

---

[2] Unidentified.

[3] Henry grasped the essence of, but garbled Shakespeare's familiar lines. In *Macbeth,* act I, scene 7, line 1, Macbeth says:

"If it were done, when 'tis done, then
 'twere well
It were done quickly."

TO HARRIET ALEXANDER

Mary Henry Copy, Family Correspondence,
Henry Papers, Smithsonian Archives

March 11th 1830 Albany

My dear Harriet,

I hope that your mother continues better and that before this time with your affectionate care she has so far recovered as to exchange the solitude of her chamber for the cheerfulness and comfort of your snug little sitting room. I would be extremely sorry not to find her in good health and spirits on my next visit, ready as she always has been to give me a cordial welcome.

That Mother and Aunt both tell me you are an excellent sick nurse and in this particular I most readily subscribe to their opinion for that you are an excellent nurse is in strict accordance with my preconceived ideas of your character and permit me to say I consider this one of the most estimable as well as amiable faculties which can be possessed by a woman. It is one which promptly finds its own reward in the feelings of gratitude it inspires, for there is no kindness so sensibly felt especially by our own sex as that rendered in the hour of sickness. I say particularly by our own sex, since from some peculiarity in our nature we are less capable of deeply sympathizing in the distresses and misfortunes of our fellow creatures than you are. We have consequently more cause for surprise and gratitude when we find ourselves the objects of that benevolence we have the power only in a partial degree to extend to others.

This is the third time I have attempted to write to you since last week and since I have been interrupted, you must not think my employments or pursuits have for an instant displaced the thoughts of you or of the tender relation in which we now stand to each other. On the contrary I may say in truth that you occupy at present more of my thoughts than is compatible with a very rapid advance in my studies. The thoughts of you have proved powerful rivals to Chemistry and Mathematics,[1] which formerly occupied a much larger share of my contemplations. I now find it almost impossible to confine my attention to an abstract subject for any length of time as it is liable to be diverted by the slightest association which savours of our union.

If I do not deceive myself you promised to write to me at least concerning your Aunt's health.

---

[1] But not physics?

FROM STEPHEN ALEXANDER[1]
*Mary Henry Copy, Family Correspondence,
Henry Papers, Smithsonian Archives*[2]

[March 13–15?, 1830][3]

I rejoice to hear of the happy completion of the work on which you have spent so much time and labour with less intermission in fact than (as I feared) a due attention to your health would justify. Your topographical sketch I consider both an interesting and important acquisition to the geography of the state and especially useful in perfecting the science of meteorology.[4]

With respect to any conversation with me on the subject of your engagement with my beloved sister I can excuse your reserve, since the prevalence of a similar feeling prevented me from relieving your embarrasment by first introducing the subject. Your union shall not meet with the least objection on my part. Although I would not myself marry my own cousin, I still cannot say that such a thing ought not to be done. If therefore your affections are placed upon each other, your happiness shall not be marred by wanting my consent. Connubial happiness you have justly intimated depends not only on human exertion as connected with worldly success but also upon the smiles of a Divine Providence; Permit me however most affectionately to remark that the principal source of true happiness you have omitted to notice. The great creator has so formed the human soul that it can never be completely happy but in communion with Himself and his own infinite perfections. Deem me not officious if to him who shortly expects to enter into a very near connection with one of the objects most dear to me on earth and in view of the intense interest the subject should awaken, I earnestly beg leave to recommend as of surpassing excellence and the only true source of happiness that religion whose legitimate effect is peace on earth and whose design is "good will towards men" which in prosperity constitutes life's charm, in adversity its solace. . . .[5]

---

[1] This is Stephen's reply to Henry's letter of December 5, 1829, above, regarding his engagement and plans to marry Harriet. It also appears to be the letter from Stephen mentioned by Joseph in his letter of March 18, 1830, below, which means that Stephen probably wrote it between the 13th and 15th of March 1830.

[2] This text is obviously not complete but whether a few lines or a few pages are lacking is now unknown.

[3] In a hand other than the transcriber's this fragment is dated "Probably March or April 1830."

[4] Joseph Henry, "Topographical Sketch of the State of New-York, Designed Chiefly to Show the General Elevations and Depressions of Its Surface," *Transactions*, Albany Institute, 1830, *1*:87–112; read before the Albany Institute on October 28, 1829.

[5] Mary Henry's ellipses.

The bust you were so kindly pleased to send came safely covered with Electro-magnetic wire. I leave a small corner to Mr. Thümmel,[6] who has something to say to you.[7] "In case our Polytechnic breaks up Stephen and myself have resolved to marry each other and go to the Western wilds won't you join us."

[6] Christian B. Thümmel, for whom see above, Henry to Maria Alexander, August 15, 1829, especially footnote 7.

[7] At this point we have the following Mary Henry interpolation: "Mr. Thümmel is a professor in the school a warm friend of the two young men [i.e., Henry and Alexander]. His good wishes are pleasant to Henry. . . ."

FROM HARRIET ALEXANDER

Mary Henry Copy, Family Correspondence,
Henry Papers, Smithsonian Archives

March 16, 1830

Dear Joseph,

I have some faint recollection of a promise to write to you reporting Aunt's health, which you may think I have forgotten but as my letter was to be confined to that subject I was disposed to delay that I might have the more to communicate. Aunt was quite ill the night you left but by the timely application of the usual remedies was relieved. On Tuesday we moved her, the bed, easy chair, and all the sick appendages to the room below where she is at present very comfortably occupying her usual seat at the window knitting.

From the patient we are led by a very natural process to think of the *nurse*. I think I may be permitted to give you the *sage* advice, never flatter a nurse for fear you may receive heartless attention. I cannot refrain from adding another passing remark, [even] if it is not immediately connected with the subject: Do not place implicit reliance on the representation of partial relatives for fear you should be deceived. I should like to add much more on other subjects that would perhaps be equally interesting did not my promise compel me to be *mum*. Believe me yours truly

Harriet

P.S. We are much obliged for the package you sent. Shall expect your excellency on Saturday next.

TO HARRIET ALEXANDER

Mary Henry Copy, Family Correspondence,
Henry Papers, Smithsonian Archives

Albany March 18ᵗʰ 1830

My dear Harriet,

I was most agreeably surprised this evening on my return from the Academy to find two letters on the table directed to me.[1] The receipt of a letter at any time and from almost any person is to me a circumstance of considerable interest. In the present case I need not say how much that interest was heightened when I recognized the writing of Stephen and yourself. I have had only time to read attentively that part of Stephen's long and interesting communication which relates to the subject nearest my heart. What he says you shall know when I visit Schenectady.

I am happy to hear that the invalid is so far recovered from her severe indisposition as to be able to resume her usual seat and to beguile the tedium of recovery by occupation. I will be careful to make no remarks on the character of the *nurse* as you may be disposed to think, however sincere they may be, that I do not pay due attention to your first *sage* admonition. With regard to the second grave advice, I will only say that if ever I should happen to be deceived by the representation of partial friends in any thing relative to you I hope, nay I am certain, that you will be so compassionate as always to continue the deception since "where ignorance is bliss it is folly to be wise."[2]

You will excuse the *"shortness"* of this letter. I must hasten with it to the [post] office or it will not reach you before the writer. I am my dearest Harriet, as I hope through life to be

Only yours,

J

P.S. I find at the bottom of Stephen's letter from Mr. Thümmel[3] [where] he says that if the *"Politicking"* keeps up Stephen and himself have resolved to *marry each other* and go to the Western Wilds. He does not state which of the two is to assume the gown.

---

[1] Probably Stephen's letter of [March 13–15? 1830], and Harriet's letter of March 16, 1830, above.

[2] From Thomas Gray's *Ode on a Distant Prospect of Eton College,* published in 1742.

[3] See the conclusion of Stephen's letter of [March 13–15?, 1830], above.

266

HARRIET ALEXANDER TO STEPHEN ALEXANDER

Mary Henry Copy, Family Correspondence,
Henry Papers, Smithsonian Archives

Schenectady March 25, 1830

Joseph seems pleased with the communication he received from you.[1] He has promised to let me see it at some future time. From his importunity seconded by the arguments of my mother I have at length consented that the matter which has so long occupied our thoughts shall be consummated as early as the first of May, on one condition—that my brother can be here at that time. Please let us know. Many plans for the future have been proposed. The last, which appears the best for all parties, we wish to subject to your consideration. It is that our Mother sell this house and move to Albany.[2]

Doubtless it will be a trial to leave this place to which we are all much attached. This home, every corner of which is endeared to us, and our circle of faithful friends with whom we have held such long and familiar intercourse. But this is as nothing compared to the trial of parting with my mother, of breaking up our dear little family. If she will go, the family will be still united, with the addition of another affectionate member who will perhaps relieve her of some care and then there will be the same home for my dear brother to pass his vacations.

Please let us know what you think of the plan. I leave it entirely to Mother, shall neither persuade or advise. It will be a great change for us all. I feel it to be a very solemn step for me attended with great responsibilities and duties. May we all seek the guidance of a higher power. Mother particularly desires your opinion [or] your objections if you have any to the proposed plan.

Love from Mother and Aunt and that Heavens best blessings may rest upon you is the wish of

Yours as ever
Harriet

P.S. Dr. Beck was much pleased with the communication you proposed sending to the Institute.[3]

---

[1] Stephen's letter of [March 13–15?, 1830], above.

[2] The copy indicates a gap here.

[3] Probably "Elements of the Solar Eclipse of February 12th, 1831: Together with a Particular Calculation for the Latitude and Longitude of Albany," read before the Institute on September 21, 1830, and published in *Transactions*, Albany Institute, 1830, *1*:243–50. We have no way of knowing whether Harriet is referring to T. R. or L. C. Beck. Both men were physicians and both were active in the Albany Institute.

TO HARRIET ALEXANDER

Family Correspondence, Henry Papers, Smithsonian Archives

Albany Saturday Morning
April 3ᵈ 1830

My Dear Harriet

My last lecture, in our present course is anounced for tuesday next; and as I shall be occupied the whole of this day, in arranging my lecture, and preparing my illustrations, I cannot possibly leave the city, and shall not therefore have the pleasure of seeing you until next saturday.

You can scarcely imagine My Dear Harriet how much I am delighted with the plan suggested at my last visit.[1] I think your Mother is not much opposed to it, and by some solicitation may be induced to acquiesce. The only obstacle is the attachment which she and your Aunt have formed for Schenectady, a place endeared to them by all the pains, & pleasures of Memory. I have spoken freely on the subject with Mother and Nancy. They think under all circumstances that it will be by far the best arrangement and provided it merits entirely with your Mother's approbation they wish it may go into operation.

The only gloomy forebodings I have ever had in reference to our union have arisen from the reflection that circumstances would oblige me to separate you from those whom you hold the most dear and to introduce you to the cares of a family with which (however you might love) you could scarcely ever assimilate either in habits or feelings. The present plan as I now view it hapily obviates all difficulties. You will not be separated from those who in their declining years require your affectionate attention and I shall be surrounded by those I most love and esteem. I do not ask an answer to this, but I need not say that a line from you will be very acceptable. Have you any commands or any commission for me to execute? I shall have leasure after tuesday to devote all my extra time to you.[2]

My time at present will not permit me to say more on this subject and I can only assure you My Dearest Harriet that

I am with the most ardent attachment
as ever devotedly Yours
Jos. Henry

---

[1] We cannot be sure when Henry visited Harriet last. The plan suggested was probably that Harriet's mother and aunt move to the Henry home in Albany following Harriet's marriage to Joseph. See Harriet's letter of March 25, 1830, to Stephen, above.

[2] The preceding three sentences were appended in the right margin, near the words which they here follow.

P.S. I send the last new novel to you & the other book to your Mother. Although I do not approve of much reading of the novel kind yet I think under present circumstances to prevent too serious thought on a certain subject you may safely indulge a little.

(In great haste)   J. H.

EXCERPT,[1] MINUTES, ALBANY INSTITUTE
Institute Minutes, Albany Institute Archives

April 8, 1830.

The Institute met pursuant to adjournment.

President of the First Department[2] in the Chair. The Minutes of the last Meeting were read and approved.

The following Communication was announced by the President, viz

Albany, 5th April 1830

To Simeon DeWitt Esq.

First Vice President of the Albany Institute

Sir,

I have understood that it would be desirable to complete the Mineralogical Collection of the Albany Institute. If the Sum of $200, in four annual payments, will aid in effecting this, and also in procuring works on the Science, I offer it to the Institute.

With much respect
Your obedt. Servant
William Caldwell[3]

---

[1] Routine business has been omitted from the end of these minutes.

[2] That is, Simeon DeWitt, elected President of the First Department for the year at the January 13, 1830, meeting. Minutes, Albany Institute, January 13, 1830.

[3] William Caldwell (1776–1848) was the son of a Revolutionary War General, James C. Caldwell. James Caldwell settled in Albany where, after the Revolution, he established himself in lumbering, in tobacco manufacturing, in mercantile operations, and in a grocery store. At about the turn of the century, the elder Caldwell handed these successful industries to his son William, the former departing Albany to develop the town of Caldwell, New York, now known as Lake George. William maintained the Albany-based businesses, among which was the largest tobacco manufactory in the area, while at the same time he established and operated iron and grist mills in his father's developing town. William Caldwell was a member of the Second Department of the Albany Institute, but we have no further information on the nature of his interest in science or education. Caldwell also made a substantial contribution for science education at the Albany Academy, for which story see below, Excerpt of the Minutes of the Academy Trustees, February [19], 1831. See Munsell, *Ann. Alb.*, 4:322; Munsell, *Coll. Alb.*, 4:405, 427, 435; Reynolds, *Alb. Chron.*, p. 579; *Howell and Tenney*, pp. 603, 620–621, 625; William H. Brown, ed., *History of Warren County, N.Y.* (Board of Supervisors of Warren County, 1963), pp. 69–71, 209–211;

Whereupon,

It was unanimously *Resolved,* That the thanks of the Institute be presented to Mr. Caldwell for his very liberal donation of $200 for the completion of the Mineralogical collection, and for procuring works on that Science.

The Corresponding Secretary announced the receipt of a letter from Cyrus Bryant[4] Esq. Corresponding Member, communicating one from the Baron Ferrussac,[5] of Paris, acknowledging the receipt of the 3d Number of the Transactions of the Albany Institute.

A Communication from Mr. Molinard,[6] on the elastic force of Steam, being a translation of Dulong's Report[7] to the Academy of Sciences of Paris, was received and read.

Dr. L. C. Beck made some observations on the Combustion of Spongy Platina, with experiments.[8]

Professor Henry exhibited a new modification of the Whirling Table,[9] which he illustrated by experiments.

W. Max Reid, *Lake George and Lake Champlain* (New York, 1910), p. 307; and Codman Hislop, *Albany: Dutch, English, and American* (Albany, 1936), pp. 210, 233.

[4] Cyrus Bryant (b. 1798) of Cummington, Massachusetts, was a corresponding member of the Institute's Second Department. Born in Cummington, he studied at the Hadley Academy and then entered the Rensselaer Polytechnic Institute, graduating from the latter in 1829. He "lectured on natural sciences at Northampton, Mass.; also at Princeton, Ill., as well as several other places in Massachusetts and Illinois; was circuit clerk of Bureau County, Illinois, and master in chancery, same county and state." He died in Princeton, Illinois. See *Nason*, p. 186; and *Transactions*, Albany Institute, 1830, *1*, part 2: Appendix, p. 70.

[5] For information relating to the transmission of the Institute's *Transactions* to Baron de Férussac, see the Excerpt of the Institute Minutes, July 10, 1828, especially footnote 14.

[6] Julian Molinard (1796–1863) was Professor of Modern Languages at Albany Academy in 1830 and from 1839 to 1859. He was elected a member of the Albany Institute in 1840. See Munsell, *Coll. Alb.*, 2:141; *Academy Seventy-fifth Anniversary*, pp. 69–70; and Minutes, Albany Institute, April 2, 1840.

[7] Pierre Louis Dulong (1785–1838), "Recherches sur la chaleur specifique des fluides élastiques," delivered in 1828 and published in *Annales de chimie*, 1829, *41*:113–158.

[8] While it does not appear that L. C. Beck ever published a paper on this particular subject, he did discuss the phenomenon in his *Manual of Chemistry* (Albany, 1831), pp. 125, 380. See also above, Henry's diary entry of June 12, 1826, especially footnote 14.

[9] We cannot be sure exactly what modification Henry demonstrated; it may correspond to that mentioned below in item No. 6 of the Descriptive Catalogue of Philosophical Apparatus Purchased for the Albany Academy, [December 18, 1830].

FROM HARRIET ALEXANDER

Family Correspondence, Henry Papers, Smithsonian Archives

Schenectady April 13th 1830.

Dear Joseph

Be not alarmed. Alls well. I only have another *favour* to *request* which is that you will send to Mrs Ludlow's[1] for a *Bandbox* of which has been left there for my ladyship and if you have not too great an aversion to travelling with that troublesome appendix of a lady I shall be much obliged to you if you will bring it with you next Saturday when we expect pleasure of a visit from you.

No remarkable changes have taken place since your departure. We are all well. Love from all to you and In great haste

Believe me yours as ever
Harriet

[1] This may be Mrs. John R. Ludlow, whose husband was the minister of the First Reformed Dutch Church in Albany from 1823 to 1834 and a Trustee of the Academy during those same years. See Excerpt, Minutes, Academy Trustees, September 9, 1825, footnote 3, above.

TO HARRIET ALEXANDER

Mary Henry Copy, Family Correspondence,
Henry Papers, Smithsonian Archives

April 19th 1830 Albany.

My dear Harriet:

I was engaged in arranging the Academy Library until after three o'clock on Saturday; also owing to the negligence of our penny post, your letter of the 13th did not reach me until evening. You must not therefore impute my non appearance in Schenectady on the expected day to any aversion I may have to travelling with that most tantalizing of all companions a lady's band box. On the contrary had I received your note earlier in the day it would have prompted me to procure a passage in an express stage, the lateness of the hour prevented my making the effort.

Perhaps I was the more anxious to promptly execute this commission from the consideration that it is possible "knowing as you do the natural antipathy of our sex to the above mentioned article" that the request was partly made in order to test my gallantry. Be that as it may I sincerely regret that circumstances prevented my visit. I have taken the liberty of looking at the bonnet and must be allowed to say I much admire the taste displayed in its choice. It is certainly beautiful and I cannot refrain from adding, that I am sure it will exhibit in all its native sweetness the face which in my eye is interesting beyond all others. The bonnet will be delivered the afternoon or Friday evening or Saturday morning next in person. I shall demand the fee for my commission. It is possible that I shall be so scrupulous in my dealings as even to refuse bills on the Mohawk bank as a lawful tender.

Monday Evening—9 o'clock. I have just returned from a most delightful ride on horse back which extended nearly to Troy and now sit down to my letter in a very pleasant state of body and mind. In reviewing my letter it seems almost too trifling to be addressed to you when we are so shortly to form the most important as well the most tender of all connections. The truth is I am not much inclined at this time to be in a serious mood. My feelings on the subject of our union have become modified by time and circumstances. I do not now view the approaching event with as much anxiety for the result as formerly, and although the thoughts of it are almost constantly with me, they are only associated with the pleasurable reflections which arise from a perfect confidence in the genuineness of our attachment. With such a state of mind and the fact of my enjoying better health then at any other period during the last six months, it is not surprising that I feel inclined to look at the sunny side of the *present* and to cherish high hopes of enjoying in the future as much domestic happiness as is consistent with our present state of existence.

Devotedly & [Wholly] Yours

TO STEPHEN ALEXANDER

Mary Henry Copy, Family Correspondence,
Henry Papers, Smithsonian Archives

Albany April 23. 1830.

My dear Stephen:

Do not imagine that I have delayed an instant in answering your interesting letter[1] because I thought such a delay in any degree excusible by your previous silence. On the contrary so far from not admitting the suffi-

---

[1] See Stephen Alexander to Henry, [March 13–15?, 1830], above.

ciency of your apology, I am about to urge a similar one for not having before expressed my acknowledgement of the contents of your letter. . . .[2]

Harriet has informed you how very necessary your presence will be on a certain occasion and indeed to me the affair would appear almost improper and deprived of much of its interest were you not present. Permit me my dear cousin to assure you I duly appreciate your generous consent to my union with your beloved sister—to a union the result of which I know is intimately connected with your own happiness and which in one particular at least is at variance with your opinions of a proper connection.

Dr. Beck is much pleased with your proposition to furnish an account of the eclipse, thinks the American Almanac[3] will not suffer detraction in the least through the interest of your paper. Many thanks for your solar tables. I owe you much on the score of tables which I have never acknowledged. Do not disappoint us by not coming before the first Monday in May.[4] Surely Dr. Yates[5] will not be so unreasonable as to object to your absence on such an occasion.

Before closing, let me say that every sentence of your letter was received with the same feelings with which I am sure it was penned. I know my dear Stephen that you have always been warmly interested in my prosperity and would do much to promote my happiness; indeed I sometimes almost fear that you have consented to my union with Harriet more from love than prudence; be this as it may—whatever may be my faults of character I trust I am not deficient in a reciprocation of a like feeling towards you. I am with affection and esteem, Yours

Joseph Henry

---

[2] Mary Henry's ellipses indicate that she excluded some of Henry's acknowledgments.

[3] In writing to Stephen, Harriet Alexander also informed him that Beck was enthusiastic about this astronomical project. See her letter of March 25, 1830, above, especially footnote 3. *The American Almanac and Repository of Useful Knowledge for the Year 1831* (Boston, 1830) was to be published about November.

A copy of this Almanac survives in the Henry Library, and a section, pp. 5–26, is devoted to the prediction of the eclipse of February 12, 1831, at certain points in the United States.

[4] That is, the 3rd of May.

[5] The Reverend Andrew Yates, for whom see Henry to Stephen Alexander, December 19, 1825, above, especially footnote 8.

HENRY'S NOTES ON A TRIP TO YALE[1]

Henry Papers, Smithsonian Archives

May 6th 1830

One of the most interesting articles of apparatus in the Phylosophical room of the college is a working moddle of the hydrolic ram made principally of brass with a reservoir and air vessel of glass.

a the air vessel

b the glass reservoir

e c d the tube

x a pupit valve[2]

r a basin to cach

the waste water

Prof Olmsted[3] mentioned an experiment to illustrate centrifugal force of a very interesting kind. A small quantity of quick silver is placed in a

receiver and made to revolve rapidly by the untwisting of a string. When the motion has acquired a certain velocity, the mercury rises from the bottom and forms a ring of metal around the circumference of the receiver. I propose to give motion to the cylinder by attaching it to my modification of the whirling table.

The Prof also showed me the torsion ballance of Coulom,[4] one con-

---

[1] Joseph Henry and Harriet Alexander had been married on the morning of May 3, 1830. They traveled to Yale via New York City. On their return, they would have a short sojourn in New York. For Henry's date of marriage, see the Albany *Argus*, May 4, 1830, p. 2, "Married."

Henry's original title reads: "Notes on objects in Yale College May 6th 1830." Many of the apparatus described in this document were subsequently purchased by Henry for the Albany Academy and appear in his Catalogue of Philosophical Apparatus, December 18, 1830, below. *Annals of Yale College, from Its Foundation to the Year 1831, to which Is Added an Appendix, Bringing It Down to 1838*, 2d ed. (New Haven, 1838), pp. 233–262, discusses the apparatus at Yale, the chemical laboratory, origin and content of the mineralogical

and geological cabinet, the department of natural philosophy, and the societies and libraries attached to the institution at the time of Henry's visit.

[2] i.e., puppet or lift valve.

[3] Denison Olmsted (1791–1859), Professor of Mathematics and Natural Philosophy at Yale from 1825 to 1836, after which he taught principally astronomy until his death in 1859. Olmsted authored textbooks on natural philosophy and astronomy for the lower school grades, and published two college texts from his lecture outline for Yale students and his notes: *An Introduction to Natural Philosophy* (New Haven, 1831), and *An Introduction to Astronomy* (New Haven, 1839). DAB.

[4] i.e., Charles Augustin de Coulomb (1736–1806).

structed in Paris. It is similar to the plate given of it in the Cambridge Phylosophy;[5] the larger cylinder is about 9 or ten inches in diameter, the smaller about one inch. The graduation is of Paper, the index is a stick of shellack with a pith ball on one end & a nob of shellack on the other. It is suspended by a very fine silver wire.

This instrument is so dellicate that merely breathing on a ball will cause the index to move around the arch. Prof. O. uses it to show the electricity produced by evaporization.

In order to make the rise of the boards of the Hydrostatic bellows apparent to a class Prof. O. ataches to the upper board a compound lever so as to operate the index in the machine for determining the expansion of mettals by heat.

The bottom of the ballance of Columb is cemented into a wooden dish covered with sealing wax. The apparatus consists of a cylinder of glass open at both ends; the upper is covered with a plate of glass, the lower in the dish. The diameter of the cylinder is about 12 or 13 inches instead of 9 or 10 as mentioned before.

In company with Dr Tulley[6] I visited the Gymnasium of the Messrs Dwite.[7] It is on the sound at the place where the steam boat for N.Y. lands. The house was erected for a tavern and was purchased by Mr Dwite for 8 thousand dollars, the original cost was 30 thousand. The Gymnasium at present contains about 90 students who pay from 250 to 300 dollars annually. At the present there is a vacation and consequently we did not see the school in operation. We were however shown the different rooms and the domestic arrangment of the establishment. The students are all assembled for study in a large building called the school house and are never permitted to get their lessons in their own rooms but during the day they are constantly under the eye of the instructor. The upper story of the school

---

[5] A reference to the electricity and magnetism text of John Farrar in 1826, a translation of sections of Jean Baptiste Biot's *Précis élémentaire de physique* of 1824. Henry is referring to figure 5 which is discussed on page 14 and in a note by Farrar, pages 365–367. Henry's copy is extensively annotated, but not at these passages.

[6] William Tully (1785–1859), Professor of Materia Medica and Therapeutics at Yale. See Harriet Henry to Stephen Alexander, May 7, 1830, footnote 12, below.

[7] The New Haven Gymnasium, conducted between 1828 and 1831 by Messrs. Sereno and Henry Dwight, sons of Timothy Dwight (1752–1817). This academy opened its doors in May 1828 to boys from the ages of six to fourteen and sought to prepare them either for college or commercial life. Located in the Steamboat (or Pavilion) Hotel on the waterfront, the institution was patterned after the German gymnasiums. In addition to the regular faculty, Professors Silliman and Olmsted of Yale served as lecturers in mineralogy and astronomy, respectively. Rollin G. Osterweis, *Three Centuries of New Haven, 1638–1938* (New Haven, 1953), p. 228.

house [is] divided into lecture rooms & classes are called from the large room below in order to recite. One plan was mentioned by Mr Dwite which he considered as very conducive to good government. It is that each boy is seated with his back to the instructor and the consequence is that before he begins to play he must turn his face towards the teacher.

The next morning after our arrival we visited the Colleges in company with Dr Tulley & Mr. Baldwin.[8] We were first shown into the library, which contains about 9000 volumes. The names of the Donors are placed above the books around the room. Among a number of names thus arranged I noticed that of Bishop Berkley[9] the celebrated metaphysician. Our time was so limited that we could not devote as much time to the examination as we wished.

From the library we passed to the philosophical hall where we were shown the aparatus. The most interesting article of this collection is Atwoods machine[10] for the illustration of falling bodies. Prof. O informed me that the results of the experiments with this machine perfectly agree with the calculations from theory or do not differ by a quantity which can be recognised by our senses. I do not think the aparatus is quite as extensive in Yale College as that in Union but the articles are perhapse better chosen and are of a superior kind.

From the philosophical room we repaired to the Cabinet; this is the most extensive collection of minerals in this country and includes the most rare as well as the most valuable specimens of the mineral kingdom. One thing in the arrangement strucke me as peculiarly useful to the student. The different varieties of the same mineral occupied one case or a department of a case by itself in a conspicuous part of which is placed the primative form of the mineral as well as the most common seccondary forms in moddels of wood. The floor of the cabinet is entirely covered with square tables of about 4 feet in diameter on which are placed cases with minerals. A sufficient space is left between each to permit a passage. On the bottom

---

[8] Possibly Simeon Baldwin (1761–1851), or his son Roger Sherman Baldwin (1793–1863), both of whom lived in New Haven at this time. The elder Baldwin was a graduate of Yale, preceptor of an academy in Albany in 1782, member of the U.S. Congress, 1803–1805, and Mayor of New Haven in 1826. At sixty-eight, however, he was far removed from Henry's generation and that of William Tully who although Henry's senior by twelve years was twenty-four years younger than Simeon Baldwin. On the other hand, Roger Sherman Baldwin at thirty-seven was but four years older than Henry. He had graduated from Yale in 1811, was prominent in local politics, and had practiced law in New Haven since 1814. *DAB.*

[9] George Berkeley (1685–1753). *DNB.*

[10] An apparatus designed by George Atwood (1745–1807) to demonstrate the laws of uniformly accelerated motion due to gravity. Atwood's machine was constructed with pulleys, so that a weight suspended from one of the pulleys descends more slowly than a body falling freely in air but still accelerates uniformly. *DSB.*

of the case a little pillar is placed, on the top of which there is a lable of card.

The chemical lecture room [apparatus] was next viewed, the most striking of which was the great defflagrator[11] of Dr Hare of Philadelphia. The apparatus was placed in a backroom and the galvanic influence conveyed by lead tubes into the lecture room, the whole circuit made by the fluid through the coils and the lead tube. Of this we were informed by Prof Silliman. Our time was so limited that we did not stay minutely to inspect the apparatus but was to have called the next day when Prof. Silliman would escort us. Something however prevented & I have now to regret that I did not see more of the Laboratory.

On one of the recitation halls they are now erecting a tower to serve as an observatory in which are to be placed the great tellescope & transit instrument now making for Yale College[12] by Dolland[13] of England (a grandson of the inventor[14] of the achromatic glass). The tower is an octagon with a window in each side and two opening in the direction of the meridian for taking higher altitudes than can be seen from the window. The whole erection is intended to be an imitation of the temple of the winds.[15, 16]

---

[11] A deflagrator is a battery, described below in Henry's Catalogue of Philosophical Apparatus, December 18, 1830, footnote 4.

[12] In 1828 through the donation of a nearby resident, Yale purchased a Dollond refractor of five-inch aperture, the finest telescope in America for almost a decade to come. David F. Musto, "A Survey of the American Observatory Movement, 1800–1850," *Vistas in Astronomy*, 1968, 9:87–92.

[13] George Dollond (1774–1852), optician, invented an improved altazimuth, 1821, "a double altitude instrument," 1823, and an at-mospheric recorder. *DNB*.

[14] John Dollond (1706–1761), for whom see Henry's Catalogue of Philosophical Apparatus, December 18, 1830, footnote 3, below.

[15] Henry was referring to the Tower of the Winds at Athens (ca. 100 B.C.) now believed to have served as a water clock.

[16] Appended to this document are several Henry sketches and a note to send Mr. Davis' logbook to Mr. Baldwin by way of the boat to New Haven. We do not know the meaning of this note of Henry's.

HARRIET HENRY TO STEPHEN ALEXANDER

Mary Henry Copy, Family Correspondence,
Henry Papers, Smithsonian Archives

New Haven May 7. 1830

My dear Brother

In fancy I have placed you immediately before me. . . .[1] It is with the greatest difficulty that I can convince myself that I am awake. The events

---

[1] Mary Henry's ellipses indicate she omitted something here.

of the past week seem like a dream. But four days since we parted and now between us miles intervene and so varied have been the scenes, it seems impossible.

We reached New York in safety. . . .[2] Landed at five in the morning and after having escorted Jane[3] to the residence of the Blue eyed lady[4] who was still sweetly slumbering, proceeded without delay to the New Haven boat. The morning was foggy and the number of passengers small. Tired from the excitement of the previous day and separated from every friend save the one to whom I had just been united in the dearest bonds, the importance of the step which I had taken seemed to rush upon me with redoubled force. The reflection that the happiness and in a measure the spiritual and temporal happiness of one dear to me was intrusted to me was a solemn one. Visions of the past too glided before me. Every childish joy in which you had participated and all the trifling eras of my life passed in pleasing review. You will think perhaps it was a gloomy day, but I can assure you it was not. A sense of unworthiness for such exceptional pleasure gave me almost pain. Who is blessed as I am? A Mother kind, anxious, devoted to my happiness. A husband I had better not eulogize at present and a brother all kindness. . . .[5]

But perhaps something about our journey will be more interesting than my thoughts. It is unnecessary to attempt a description of the different places through which we passed, as they have all been viewed by you. We entered this city a short time before the Governor,[6] who was met by the military and escorted by a large number of the citizens into the city. This is the fourth election.[7] We had the unexpected pleasure of seeing the gentleman. The legislature of the State is now in session. Monsieur Joseph has gone to the house. He has met with several of his friends, who have laid him under many obligations by their kind attentions. On Monday[8] morn-

---

[2] As above, these are Mary Henry's signs of omission.

[3] We conjecture from the context that Harriet is referring here to Jane Olive Alexander (b. 1807), unmarried at this time, the youngest of ten children of John Alexander (1760–1841), Harriet's and Stephen's (also Joseph Henry's) uncle. Unpublished Alexander Family Genealogy by Robert Gaylord Lester in the Henry Papers files.

[4] Unidentified.

[5] Again, Mary Henry's ellipses.

[6] Gideon Tomlinson (1780–1854), was Connecticut's Governor from 1827 to 1831. From 1818 to 1827 Tomlinson was a Representative in the U.S. Congress, and in 1831 he resigned his governorship to serve in the U.S. Senate until 1837. See *Herringshaw* and *Biographical Directory of the American Congress*.

[7] This does not make sense; we assume it is a transcribing garble of Mary Henry's cohorts.

[8] "Monday" must be either Harriet's slip of the pen or Mary Henry's transcribing error. As Joseph and Harriet were married in Schenectady on Monday, May 3, and arrived in New Haven on Tuesday, May 4, at the earliest, then it seems more likely to have been Wednesday or Thursday, May 5 or 6, when this visit took place. Indeed, Henry recorded the visit on May 6, for which see the preceding document.

ing we visited the library, laboratory, philosophical hall of the College and we were introduced to Professors Olmsted[9] and Silliman[10] with both of whom Joseph was very much pleased and with whom he has passed part of his time every day. Prof. Silliman expressed much at his introduction to Joseph with whom he said he was acquainted by reputation. He called upon us with his daughter yesterday morning and politely offered to attend us to any part of the city and went with us this afternoon to see some specimens of statuary, executed by a self taught American artist,[11] a man of great genius who works without a model. His two principal figures are Jephthah and his daughter; the latter which is unfinished is beautiful. Her position, drapery and particularly the expression of her countenance, a mingling of surprise, disappointment and joy are admirable. I do not know when I have seen anything that pleased me more. Last evening we called at Prof. Silliman's. I am delighted with him. I do not recollect whether you saw him when you were here. We intended to leave for Bridgeport this morning but were unable to obtain a passage. We will leave this evening to reach New York on Saturday, and home by Wednesday evening. I am delighted with this city. I should like to remain if all near and dear to me could be here. Do dear Brother write soon. Present my acknowledgements to Mr. Thümmel for his kind wishes.

P.S. We leave tomorrow morning, have just engaged to attend a small party this evening at [William Tully's],[12] a friend of my good man's—there is a

[9] Denison Olmsted (1791–1859), for whom see above, Henry's Notes on a Trip to Yale, May 6, 1830, especially footnote 3.

[10] Of course, Benjamin Silliman (1779–1864), for whom see footnote 1, Silliman to Beck, March 14, 1826, above.

[11] The sculptor whose work they saw was undoubtedly Hezekiah Augur (1791–1858), who turned his skill at a hobby, wood-carving, into an artistic career, when he struck financial difficulties. His *Jephthah and His Daughter* was an outstanding piece in early neo-classical sculpture. See *DAB* and George C. Groce and David H. Wallace, comps., *The New York Historical Society's Dictionary of Artists in America, 1564–1860* (New Haven, 1957), p. 16.

[12] Although Mary Henry has left this blank, we conjecture that the hospitable friend was William Tully (1785–1859), physician and educator (see below, Henry to Benjamin Silliman, December [2]8, 1830). Tully was born in Saybrook Point, Connecticut, and he attended Yale, graduating in 1806. He then studied medicine under several prominent New England physicians, and began his practice in Connecticut in 1811. In 1824 he was appointed President and Professor of Theory and Practice and Medical Jurisprudence in the Vermont Academy of Medicine in Castleton, retiring from the presidency in 1830 but continuing to teach there for eight more years. In January 1826, he moved to Albany, where he began practicing as a colleague of Dr. Alden March (for whom see above, the diary of Asa Fitch, [February 8, 1830], especially footnote 5). Tully had probably been a resident member of the Albany Institute, for when he removed to Yale in 1829 to become Professor of Materia Medica and Therapeutics he became a corresponding member of the Institute's Second Department. He remained at Yale until 1842, later moving to Springfield, Massachusetts, where he died. Tully was a prolific writer and was considered to be one of the most learned and scientific physicians in New England during his time. See *DAB* and *Transactions*, Albany Institute, 1830, *1*, part 2: Appendix, p. 73.

real old wife's expression. Said personage sends his love to you is at present engaged in writing.[13] I wish you could become acquainted with Prof. Olmsted. He is a very scientific and exceedingly pleasant man. I will look out for that pair of black eyes you spoke of. I will examine every pair I see. What a sly rogue you are Stephen. One would suppose from your grave phiz that you never looked at a lady with any interest. I shall watch you closely after this.

[13] If Henry was engaged in writing a letter to Stephen Alexander, then we have failed to turn up such a manuscript. Perhaps Harriet is rather referring to Henry's recording the day's observations at Yale, for which see above, May 6, 1830.

TO HARRIET HENRY

Mary Henry Copy, Family Correspondence,
Henry Papers, Smithsonian Archives

May [18], 1830[1]

My dear Wife

I arrived in New York last evening at seven o'clock after a tedious day's sail. The weather was too cold to remain on deck and I was obliged to confine myself to the cabin. . . .[2] I have had several invitations to dine but have excused myself and taken a meal at a public house. . . .[3]

Went with Prof. Green[4] to College of Physicians & Surgeons passed an hour very pleasantly in the laboratory of the College. Met Prof. Davies[5] of West Point—promised to stop at the Point on my way home. Saw Prof. Ross[6] of West Point on the Steamer yesterday—he insisted on my bringing my

[1] While Mary Henry has dated this letter May 11, 1830, we have assigned the date May 18, from the context of both this letter and Harriet Henry's letter to Stephen Alexander, immediately following this entry.

[2] Mary Henry's ellipses, indicating she omitted something here.

[3] Again, Miss Henry's marks of omission.

[4] Undoubtedly Jacob Green, for whom see below, Joseph Henry to Jacob Green, February 3, 1831.

[5] Charles Davies (1798–1876), educator and author, entered West Point in 1815 and was trained in artillery and engineering. Upon his graduation, Davies was appointed Assistant Professor of Mathematics at West Point and later was appointed Assistant Professor of Natural and Experimental Philosophy. In 1823 he became the Professor of Mathematics, remaining until 1837. He later held appointments at Trinity College and Columbia College. His publications were many. He published a series of widely used mathematical textbooks, from *A Primary Table Book* to *Elementary Geometry and Trigonometry,* and he prepared editions of Adrien Marie Legendre's *Geometry* and Pierre Louis Marie Bourdon's *Algebra.* See *Herringshaw,* and Charles K. Gardner, *Dictionary of the Army of the United States* (New York, 1860), p. 141.

[6] Edward C. Ross, for whom see above, Stephen Van Rensselaer Ryan to Henry, May 24, 1827, footnote 3.

trunk to his house when I came to the Point. I met Prof. Renwick[7] according to appointment. He was very kind, offered me the use of any book in his library to take to Albany. Spoke very highly of my experiments on magnetism &c &c, finally introduced me to the Atheneum[8] in the Library of which I have passed the last two hours.

[7] James Renwick, Sr., for whom see above, John McVickar to T. R. Beck, April 18, 1822, footnote 3.

[8] The New York Athenaeum, founded in 1824, was intended to act as a "sister" institution to Liverpool's Royal Institution, by which arrangement members of one institution could enjoy the privileges of membership in the other. The Athenaeum aspired to the "Cultivation of Science, Literature, and the Arts," and it boasted a library and reading rooms to which a stranger might be admitted for up to six months if a member sponsored him. James Renwick acted as Corresponding Secretary of the Athenaeum upon its founding. See Henry Wheaton, *An Address, Pronounced at the Opening of the New-York Athenaeum, December 14, 1824,* 2d ed. (New York, 1825), p. 1, and *Constitution and By-Laws of the New-York Athenaeum* (New York, 1825), pp. 3, 14, 15.

HARRIET HENRY TO STEPHEN ALEXANDER

Mary Henry Copy, Family Correspondence,
Henry Papers, Smithsonian Institution

Schenectady May 18, 1830

My dear Brother

We returned on Wednesday last. I have intended to write before this but calls and other things have prevented. We reached New York Saturday evening. On Monday morning we went to Coleman's book store for the remainder of the plates and passed an hour very pleasantly in looking at some very beautiful engravings,[1] and we visited a private collection of pictures brought from London, some of which are executed by celebrated Italian and Spanish artists.[2,3]

The last thing on Tuesday was to visit the Academy of Design.[4] After

[1] We do not know what "remainder of the plates" refers to. The reference is to the bookseller William A. Colman at 237 Broadway whose establishment was known for its art materials.

[2] Apparently a reference to the Abrahams collection which is briefly discussed in Thomas S. Cummings, *Historic Annals of the National Academy of Design* (Philadelphia, 1865), p. 118.

[3] Here Mary Henry inserts "[Then follows an account of various dinner engagements calls &c.]."

[4] The National Academy of Design was founded in 1825 as the New York Drawing Association, receiving its present name on incorporation in 1828. For many years (1826–1845, 1861–1862) its President was Samuel F. B. Morse, who plays a significant role in Henry's later life. Because of Mary Henry's editing (see preceding note), we cannot say if the two men met in 1830 but that appears doubtful. Mary Henry, mindful of Morse's role in Henry's career, would have noted any such early

leaving there, we hastened to the boat. Reached Albany Wednesday morning and without stopping came directly here to find my mother and Aunt well. Thursday Friday and Saturday we received, and there seemed no end to the calls. Joseph left Monday to return Friday when said calls will be returned and so will end all this wedding ceremony. Were it not for this, I believe I would forget I am married, not withstanding Joseph's charge to the contrary. The events of the last fortnight seem more like a confused dream than reality. I am glad to hear the cake arrived safely. I suppose it has already shared the fate of its predecessors, quick consumption, the disease which seems to prevail among cakes since they rapidly disappear.

As ever, Harriet.

---

contact. The National Academy of Design is significant as the first organization in America whose membership was limited to professional artists. No comparably limited organization of scientists existed in America in 1825 nor for many years afterwards. See Eliot C. Clark, *History of the National Academy of Design, 1825–1953* (New York, 1954).

TO HARRIET HENRY

Mary Henry Copy, Family Correspondence,
Henry Papers, Smithsonian Archives

Albany May [19–20] 1830[1]

My dear wife,

Since I left Schenectady[2] with gloomy weather and absence from the object most dear to me on earth time has passed with slow and heavy pace. Although I am aware each passing minute is an item expended from my alloted portion of mortal life, yet I cannot refrain from wishing the period between this period and next Friday annihilated so that at the present moment I might have the pleasure of your presence.

There is little danger my dear Harriet in my present state of feeling that I could forget in absence I am a "married man." A sense of lonliness, a feeling of anxiety which not even the active duties of my profession can repress, constantly remind me of the interest I have in the welfare of another and emphatically tell me my destiny is connected to a second self.

---

[1] It is clear from the context that the letter was written during the week of May 17, and from the context we assume it was written a day or two after Henry's letter to Harriet above, to which we have assigned the date May 18, 1830.

[2] The Henrys did not yet have a home of their own. Harriet remained with her family in Schenectady while her husband taught in Albany and commuted to her on most weekends.

I do not think we can essentially be disappointed in each other. We have not allowed our minds to form unreasonable expectations of the married state. Our fancies have not been sickened with visions of happiness human nature can never hope to enjoy, nor have we imagined perfections in each other which belong only to the beings of fiction and romance. On the contrary I believe we have coolly reflected on the trials and difficulties of the state, as well as warmly anticipated its enjoyments.

While my eyes, which find to please so much more in you than in any other woman, are not blinded entirely to the fact that you may possess some of the weakness of your sex, I love you the more because you are not perfect. And although the defects of my character have been too glaringly displayed to escape even your notice yet I hope, nay I am sure you look upon my faults with an eye of extenuation. Let us perpetuate our present feelings by a rigid adherence to our resolution of implicit confidence and by considering our marriage as a bond of perfect friendship, in which the faults and weakness of each are to be met on the part of the other by a spirit of gentle reproof and compassion. To my beloved wife, with the most tender regard.

P.S. If I am not in Schenectady before ten o'clock I beg my darling will not sit up for me. I may not leave Albany until the ten o'clock stage.

TO HARRIET HENRY
Family Correspondence, Henry Papers, Smithsonian Archives

Albany frid. June 4th 1830

My Dear Wife

I start this afternoon for New York, in the steam-boat New Philadelphia, and will of course expect to see Mother & you on my return or at the fartherest on tuesday next. Do not let mother change her mind relative to comming down. I have informed Mrs Beck & (indirectly) Mrs Ludlow[1] that she will be in town next week. Her *non*-appearance will therefore cause some disappointment. Mrs Ludlow was so kind as to send a person to inform me that a house is to be let in Pearl street but I do not think the location would be agreable or convenient. Your Mother however can see it when she comes down. General Beck is now so feeble that he is almost con-

[1] Perhaps the wives of T. R. Beck and Reverend John Ludlow.

stantly confined to his bed. Dr. Beck requests me to inform his brother[2] in N.Y. that it is not probable that he will live more than eight or ten days. Mother has entirely recovered from her attack and is now enjoying her usual health. I have not heard from Shankland's[3] family this week.

Excuse the shortness of this letter as I have penned it in a room with nearly a hundred noisy boys[4] who are constantly interrupting me with questions and complaints.

If I should have a spare moment while in N.Y. I will probably, I should say I will certanly, write to you but if you do not hear from me, be not allarmed as my time will be much occupied.

Be careful of your health—Give my love to Mother & Aunt also to the Misses Ryley. And be yourself assured that

> I am My Dear Harriet
> Your Affectionate
> Husband
> Jos. Henry

PS You will receive this letter tomorrow. Will it be asking too much if I request that you will write to me on the same day that I may have the pleasure of hearing from you immediatly on my return. J H

---

[2] Probably John Brodhead Beck (1794–1851). A graduate of Columbia College (1808), John Brodhead Beck received his M.D. in 1817 from the College of Physicians and Surgeons. His dissertation on infanticide was used by T. R. Beck in the treatise on medical jurisprudence. In 1826 John Brodhead Beck became Professor of Materia Medica and Botany at the College of Physicians and Surgeons. *DAB*.

[3] The Shanklands who appear to be personal friends of Harriet and Joseph are Peter V. Shankland (1803–1852) and his wife Susannah (1802–1838). Peter Shankland occupied various positions in local government such as Chamberlain of Albany and Clerk of the County. Susannah Shankland, usually referred to as Susan, seems to have suffered from a protracted illness, as the state of her health will be discussed in family correspondence below and in subsequent volumes of the Henry Papers. Munsell, *Coll. Alb.*, *4*:115; Munsell, *Ann. Alb.*, *4*:293; *9*:219, 233, 267; *10*:247, 261, 273, 277.

[4] In the letter Henry originally wrote "scholars" but crossed this out and redefined his charges.

TO HARRIET HENRY

Family Correspondence, Henry Papers, Smithsonian Archives

> Albany Wed.
> June 23ᵈ 1830

My Dear Wife

Contrasted with the pleasure I enjoyed in your company last week, the present one, with gloomy weather, and sickness in the family, appears to

have passed, thus far, very heavily. Mother is now much better, but yesterday, and monday, the weather affected her unfavourably. Jack[1] is worse and I fear will scarly be able to stand the attack. Dr Wing however thinks he will recover. General Beck is extremely weak and is not expected to live from day to day. Dr. Beck and myself are to watch with him to night. I have not seen Mrs Shankland since my return from Schenectady, but I intend visiting her this evening. The next no. of the Transactions of the Institute has been put to press without Stephen's paper on the eclipse which will be published in the following No. This arraingment will give him time to prepare it in the best manner, and also allow him to superintend the printing, and the engraving himself, when he comes to Albany.[2]

I hope you have not refused to take the charge of the African School during this week. It gives me pleasure to see that your acquaintances as well as myself properly estimate your qualifications and that you have the will as well as the power of being useful;—nevertheless I hope you have not been so intensely engaged as entirely to forget that you have a husband and one too, who would not willingly stand seccond in your thoughts, even to a work of benevolence. If Mother continues better & Jack should not become dangerously ill, I will if a passage can be procured, be in Schenectady on friday evening if not on saturday forenoon.

I believed you promised an answer to this. You will probably receive it tomorrow morning, before gowing to school, and as you will have but a few moments to write in, I do not expect a long letter; I shall however be much disappointed if I do not receive a few lines.

Give my love to Mother and Aunt; tell them I have done nothing farther concerning the house, and I am confident that [there] will be no difficulty in procuring one, at any time when they are ready to move. I have written this letter in my room, but have not taken up my abode permanently in this place, nor do I intend to do so until mother is completely recovered. I now use it as a study during the daylight.

> I am My Beloved Wife as ever
> With Esteem
> Your affectionate
> Husband
> Joseph Henry

---

[1] Unidentified.

[2] This appeared as "Elements of the Solar Eclipse of February 12th, 1831 Together with a Particular Calculation for the Latitude and Longitude of Albany," *Transactions*, Albany Institute, 1830, *1*:243–250.

TO HARRIET HENRY
Mary Henry Copy, Family Correspondence,
Henry Papers, Smithsonian Archives

July 1ˢᵗ 1830 Albany

My dear Wife

My usual letter was prevented last evening. I was called to General Beck's[1] where I had promised to watch last night. The General as you have probably heard died last evening. . . .[2] This is the first deathbed scene I have ever witnessed and I do assure you I never before had so vivid a realization of my own mortality.

[1] General Nicholas F. Beck, for whom see above, Henry to Stephen Alexander, December 5, 1829, footnote 10.
[2] Mary Henry's ellipses indicate she omitted something here. It would have been unusal for Henry to write a letter so short as this, and we may assume that Mary copied only a brief excerpt from the original.

FROM HARRIET HENRY
Family Correspondence, Henry Papers, Smithsonian Archives

Schenectady Aug 3ᵈ 1830.

My Dear Husband.

Your Sister[1] when I was in Albany very kindly offered to superintend the cleaning of the House of which offer Mother will gladly acept & feel very grateful to her if she will procure a woman, or women as she sees fit, as soon as convenient to clean the house—let her do it as she thinks best, she not [to] be very particular & may leave the washing of the paint in the second story untill we come. Charge all expenses to [?Mother.]

If Nancy should be so engaged that it would be inconvenient for her to attend to it please let us know & Mother will be down, but if she can you need not expect any of us this week. Mr Frash will be down the last of the week with a load of furniture.

And another favour which we have to beg is that you will please to call at the Insurance Office & pay the end[orsement]—you will see by examining the note that it perhaps expires on Thursday.

If you or James[2] have time Stephen would be much obliged to either of

[1] Nancy Henry.   [2] James Henry.

you that will come upon Dibly & Brown[3] & see if the Books he expected from N.Y. have arrived & please let him know *when you write* which I think you promised to do this week.

Don't you think I have been quite sociable. If we were to remain in Schenectady much longer & business should continue I fear I would become quite a scribbler.

Aunt has been quite unwell yesterday. Mother is much better. Steph in very good spirits this morning. I think he will not return to Chitanango.

You I suppose are very much engaged this week—please write if it is only a few lines. We shall expect you on Friday afternoon. Do not disappoint us if you can and we have been planning a family visit to Mrs Van Slyck[4] on Saturday next. Love from all to all. Excuse this as I fear the mail will be closed. And believe me dear husband with affection & esteem, Yours as ever

Harriet

[3] The Albany City Directory for 1831–1832 lists a firm of merchants, Dibble and Brown, at 43 Quay; the 1832–1833 Directory gives the name as Dibblee and Brown. They are not listed in sources we have examined as book-sellers but may have had this as a sideline. Another possibility is that Dibblee and Brown acted as shipping agents for merchandise, including books.

[4] Not identified.

TO HARRIET HENRY

Mary Henry Copy, Family Correspondence,
Henry Papers, Smithsonian Archives

Albany [August 5?, 1830][1]

I received your letter last evening but engagements until very late prevented my answering the same night . . .

My sister has taken charge of the cleaning of the house and has this morning employed two women who will finish it this week . . . I am happy to hear there is a prospect of Stephen's being with us. I have been planning several pursuits in which we can jointly engage and have in anticipation appropriated one of the rooms of our new house for our study and library.

In regard to your becoming "quite a scribbler," let me tell you I am of opinion that to converse well, is as important to a woman as to write well, and although I am always made happy by the receipt of a letter from you,

[1] The manuscript lacks the salutation and bears the date "July 1830." It is, however, a reply to Harriet Henry's letter of August 3, 1830, above.

I would much rather learn your thoughts directly by the sound of your voice than at a distance by means of your pen. When you come to Albany you shall have my permission to talk as much as you please.

I hope this letter will be read with the same warm feelings with which it is written. I will confess that our separate and unsettled state and the business of the last three days have almost made me forget I am a married man. The receipt of your letter and the pleasure of answering it has forcibly reminded me that I am united to one, with whom, always to love and be beloved, is the highest anticipated pleasure of my life.

Your devoted J

TO HARRIET HENRY

Family Correspondence, Henry Papers, Smithsonian Archives

New York Monday
Afternoon Aug 30th 1830

My Dear Harriet

I know that you have begun to despair of hearing from me by letter as I promised; but you will be satisfyed with my punctuality when I tell you that I send this by the first boat that has left N.Y. since yesterday morning at 7 o'clock an hour when as you may well suppose I was fast locked in the arms of Morpheus.

We arrived here safely at half past 9 o'clock on saturday evening without meeting with any unusual occurrence except being detained on the bar five miles below Albany & in sight of the city more than two hours.

Mrs. Ring & [?her] sister[1] insisted on my making their house my home during my stay in N.Y. and I was the more easily persuaded to accept their kind offer as I felt rather unwill during the whole of saturday and was fearful of a more severe attack.

The Ladies have prescribed for me & I am almost entirely well to day— I did not leave the house yesterday.

The rain to day has prevented Prof. Renwick and myself from making the observations on magnetism which were the principal object of my visit

---

[1] This actually reads "Mrs Ring and his sister" but has been edited as above because of the later reference to the "the Ladies." In any event, we have not identified the Rings.

to N.Y. We are to meet tomorrow morning for that purpose at 6 o'clock in the college yard if the weather will permit.[2]

Mr Van Rensslaer & his son[3] came abord the steam boat at West Point. Tell Stephen that I spoke to him about the loan of his chronometer for astronomical observations. He said that he had none at present but that he had ordered one which would cost four or five hundred dollars & which was expected every day and that we could have the use of it as often and as long as we pleased.[4]

I will leave for Albany on tuesday evening. Excuse the "shortness" to this letter as Mr Turnbull[5] is waiting for me to accompany him to see a scotchman[6] who has an extensive collection of Philosophical apparatus.

I am My Dear Wife as
Ever Your
Devoted

Give my love to all the   Husb
members of both families. J. H.   Jos

---

[2] See below, Minutes of the Albany Institute, September 21, 1830, especially footnote 11, for Henry's and Renwick's interest in terrestrial magnetism.

[3] Stephen Van Rensselaer, Jr.?

[4] In Henry's notebook (No. 6123) there is an entry of November 17, 1831, bearing Van Rensselaer's name concerning a silver pocket chronometer of Parkinson and Frodsham which may be the one referred to here.

[5] John Turnbull; see below, Turnbull to Henry, August 16, 1831.

[6] Not identified.

EXCERPT,[1] MINUTES, ALBANY INSTITUTE

Institute Minutes, Albany Institute Archives

Special Meeting   Sept 21 1830
The Institute met pursuant to notice
        The 1st Vice President in the Chair
A Communication from Prof. Joslin of Union College on the apparent radiation of cold was read.[2]

---

[1] Names of new members and several persons "probably elected some years since, but there is no minute of it," have been omitted from the end of these minutes. Among the names given are two close friends and associates of Henry's, Asa Gray and Benjamin Silliman, Sr. The remainder of these minutes, also omitted, concerns routine business.

[2] Benjamin F. Joslin, "On the Apparent Radiation of Cold," *Transactions*, Albany Institute, 1830, *1*:236–242. For information on Joslin, see footnote 2, Henry to Stephen Alexander, January 8, 1830; on the paper see below, Joslin to Henry, October 16, 1830.

A Communication from D[r] Mease[3] of Philadelphia on the Penitentiary System was read.[4]

The Rev. D. Brown[5] read a Communication on the importance of general instruction in the Useful Sciences which on motion was referred to a Committee consisting of Messr's Mayell,[6] Henry, & C. R. Webster.[7]

A Communication from Stephen Alexander Esq Corresponding Member was read, being the Elements of the Solar Eclipse of Feb[y] 12, 1831— with a particular calculation for the Latitude & Longitude of Albany. . . .[8, 9]

M[r] Henry exhibited Professor Hansteen's[10] (of Norway) Apparatus[11] for

---

[3] James Mease (1771–1846), physician, scientist, author, was born in Philadelphia. A graduate of the University of Pennsylvania (1787), he received his medical degree from the same institution in 1792. Mease wrote, edited, or compiled several medical works, although he is principally remembered for his contributions to literature unidentified with his profession. Of his printed works, *The Picture of Philadelphia, Giving an Account of Its Origin, Increases and Improvements in Arts, Sciences, Manufactures, Commerce and Revenue* (Philadelphia, 1811) is best known. But his *A Geological Account of the United States, Comprehending a Short Description of Their Animal, Vegetable, and Mineral Productions, Antiquities and Curiosities* (Philadelphia, 1807), a physical and commercial geography, was a valuable compilation and a pioneer work in its field. *DAB*.

[4] Published as *Observations on the Penitentiary System, and Penal Code of Pennsylvania, with Suggestions for Their Improvement* (Philadelphia, 1828).

[5] Reverend David Brown, who we know was a resident member of the Institute but whose name is not listed in the Albany City Directories or in any of the Albany local histories. As far as we can tell, his remarks on this occasion were never published.

[6] William Mayell, a hat manufacturer who lived in Albany and was active in the Institute.

[7] Charles R. Webster, publisher of the *Albany Gazette*.

[8] Published in *Transactions*, Albany Institute, 1830, *1*:243–250. For Stephen's observation of the eclipse and his findings, see Isaac W. Jackson to Joseph Henry, February 16, 1831, footnote 8, below.

[9] Two paragraphs concerning routine donations to the Institute are omitted here.

[10] Christopher Hansteen, Director of the Observatory at Oslo, and an active observer, experimenter, and theorist in matters pertaining to terrestrial magnetism. *Poggendorff*.

[11] Henry describes this apparatus as being two magnetic needles, each "suspended, according to the method of Hansteen, in a small mahogany box, by a single fibre of raw silk. The box was furnished with a glass cover, and had a graduated arc of ivory on the bottom to mark the amplitude of the vibrations. It had also two small circular windows, diametrically opposite to each other, through which the oscillations of the needle could be seen." Hansteen had given two such needles to Captain Edward Sabine, who substituted a needle of his own for one of the Hansteen needles before passing them to James Renwick, Sr., Professor of Natural Philosophy and Experimental Chemistry at Columbia, who gave the needles to Henry.

On Renwick's request, and with the assistance of Stephen Alexander, Henry in September 1830 began a series of observations with the Hansteen apparatus to determine the magnetic intensity of Albany. In the course of these, he unexpectedly "witnessed a disturbance of the magnetism of the earth, in connection with an appearance of an aurora." Two years later, he published his findings. See Sabine's "Observations on the Magnetism of the Earth, especially of the Arctic Regions; in a Letter from Capt. Edward Sabine, to Professor Renwick," *Silliman's Journal*, 1830, *17*:145–156; and Joseph Henry, "On a Disturbance of the Earth's Magnetism, in Connexion with the Appearance of an Aurora Borealis, as Observed at Albany, April 19th, 1831," ibid., 1832, *22*:143–155.

Captain, later Sir Edward, Sabine (1788–1883) was a leading investigator of terrestrial magnetism who later became head of the Royal Society and the British Association for the Advancement of Science. *DNB*. Henry will meet Sabine later, and the close relationship that grows between them will appear in

ascertaining the magnetic intensity at various places & described the manner used in observing the same.

---

subsequent volumes. For James Renwick, Sr., see John McVickar to T. Romeyn Beck, April 18, 1822, footnote 3, above.

"OBSERVATIONS TO DETERMINE THE DIP OF THE MAGNETIC NEEDLE MADE WITH AN APARATUS LOANED TO ME BY PROF RENWICK OF COLUMBIA COLLEGE," SEPTEMBER 25, 1830[1]

Notebook [6123], pages 12–14, Henry Papers, Smithsonian Archives

The needle was first unmagnetized by touching it in a contrary direction with a powerful magnet, and observing where it ceased to possess the power of attracting iron filings. It was afterwards presented to a delicately suspended sewing needle, which had been magnetized, but it shewed no signs of polarity.[2]

[1] The date is given at the end of this description of experimental procedures, preceding the data noted in footnote 7 below. Magnetic dip (or inclination) is the angle made with the horizon by a magnetic needle free to rotate in a vertical plane. Henry probably took the dip measurements in conjunction with the magnetic intensity observations he began in the latter part of September 1830. The observations were being made for Renwick, as indicated in Henry's article, "On a Disturbance of the Earth's Magnetism, in Connexion with the Appearance of an Aurora Borealis, As Observed at Albany, April 19th, 1831," *Silliman's Journal*, 1832, 22: 145, 148–149. The article includes a simple, well-known trigonometric formula correlating the angle of dip with the horizontal and vertical components of the earth's magnetic force. Henry also discusses the formula in his notebook (pp. 123–124), where he remarks: "Apply this method [of calculation] with the dipping needle in the Academy. These formulas have been investigated by myself, but similar [ones] may be seen in the Ency[clopaedia] Metrop[olitana]." He is citing Barlow's article on magnetism (see below, footnote 3). Henry may have been looking for variations in magnetic dip at Albany, for,

according to his article, he had witnessed auroral and magnetic disturbances during his observations in the fall of 1830.

At another point in his notebook, Henry lists some of the numerous references he consulted on terrestrial magnetic phenomena. The citations are occasionally followed by Henry's own brief comments. Although most of the references concern terrestrial magnetic intensity, a few, by Sabine, Hansteen, and others, deal with magnetic inclination, its long-term variations and its relation to magnetic intensity. Henry also cites Peter Barlow's *An Essay on Magnetic Attraction and On the Laws of Terrestrial and Electro Magnetism*, 2d ed. (London, 1824), which survives in the Henry Library. Barlow's work includes trigonometric computations on magnetic inclination. He computes, for example, annual dip variations and then compares theoretical with experimental results.

[2] In another notebook entry (p. 41), Henry remarks on William Scoresby's method of inducing and destroying magnetism by hammering (see Scoresby's "Experiments and Observations on the Development of Magnetical Properties in Steel by Percussion," *Phil. Trans.*, 1822, pp. 241–252; 1824, pp. 197–221). Henry wrote, "Would not this be a good plan

The needle thus freed from magnetism, was accurately ballanced by the adjusting screws, so that it would remain in almost any position. In this adjustment it was found that the pieces of glass or agate on which the axis of the needle turns, was not parallel to the line joining the two zeros of the graduated limb, & that when the instrument was placed horizontal, the needle rolled on its axis toward the north. To obviate this defect, the spirit level on the top was altered so as to be parallel to the edge of the agate. The needle was then magnetized and carefully placed on the agate edges.[3]

The instrument was previously placed in the direction of the magnetic meridian with its graduated face to the east. After making a few ocilations, it settled at a degree which was read by means of a magnifying glass, and the divisions estimated by the eye to within 5′ of the truth; the limb of the instrument being divided to half degrees.[4] The degrees were read both at the top and bottom in order to correct by the mean of the two, the error of eccentricity.[5] In the first series of observations, three sets of observations were taken with the needle in the above position; it was drawn a little out of the line of the dip each time by a magnet, & then suffered to come to rest. The whole instrument was next turned about until its graduated limb faced the west, & <*three*> four observations were then made as before. After this the needle was removed from its place, & the poles reversed by touching them with two strong magnets; <*three*> four observations were then repeated with the face of the needle to the east & west as before.[6] The

---

for freeing the dipping needle of its magnetism previous to adjusting it? It is probable that if the blow be too violent, transverse magnetism will be induced in the direction of the shorter axis of the bar. Repeat this exp."

[3] The Renwick apparatus is similar to that described by Henry Cavendish in "An Account of the Meteorological Instruments Used at the Royal Society's House," *Phil. Trans.*, 1776, *66*:395–401. The dipping needle rotated in a vertical plane on a horizontal cylindrical axis, the ends of which rolled on agate planes. The needle was suspended at the center of a vertical graduated circle which indicated the needle's angle with the horizon. The circular frame—or "limb"—rested on a flat stand, equipped with levels and adjusting screws so that the apparatus could be adjusted to the horizon. To eliminate gravitational forces, the needle had to be accurately balanced; the Cavendish apparatus employed a mechanical balancing device invented by John Michell (*Phil. Trans.*, 1772, p. 47). Excellent illustrations and descriptions of these instruments can be found in P. M. Roget, *Treatises on*

Electricity, Galvanism, Magnetism, and Electro-Magnetism (London, 1832), pp. 74–82, and in Peter Barlow's article on magnetism in the *Encyclopaedia Metropolitana*, 1845, *3*: 767–770. References in Henry's notebook indicate he consulted the earlier edition of the *Metropolitana* on terrestrial magnetism.

[4] i.e., the instrument was equipped with a vernier scale.

[5] The eccentricity of the needle's axis to the center of the graduated limb.

[6] Changing the orientation of the apparatus was a standard way of compensating for errors in the balancing of the needle and in the construction of the apparatus. See Roget, *Treatises*, pp. 76–77. In another notebook entry (p. 42), Henry mentions the dipping needle of Daniel Bernoulli, an instrument designed to minimize errors due to an imbalanced needle. Henry read about the Bernoulli needle in an article in the *Repertory of Arts and Manufactures*, 1823, *43*:111, based upon John Robison's description in *A System of Mechanical Philosophy*, 4 vols. (Edinburgh, 1822), *4*:290–292. Robison owned an instrument of

first series of observations were made in the French room of the Academy, the degrees noted to $\frac{1}{4}$°. The second series were observed in the Academy park near the tree in the middle of the inclosure. In all these observations I was assisted by Dr P. Ten Eyck.[7]

---

this kind, about which Henry remarks in his notebook (p. 42): "I have no great faith in this needle, but perhapse I do not view it properly. Will it not be worth the tryal, if I get the loan of the West Point needle to compare it with that instrument." Daniel Bernoulli's instrument is also described in Roget, *Treatises*, pp. 78–79, which drew upon the Robison account; we have no information on the West Point needle.

[7] Following this excerpt are two series of measurements taken in the manner described above. The readings were taken on September 25, 1830, at 10 A.M. and 4 P.M.

EXCERPT,[1] MINUTES, ACADEMY TRUSTEES

Trustees' Minutes, 1:385–387, Albany Academy Archives

Albany. Octr 8. 1830

The Trustees met, pursuant to adjournment

Present

| Mr James, | Mr Webster, | Mr Beck, |
| Mr Conkling, | Mr Hawley, | Mr Parker, |

The Examination of sundry works of Mr Hassler, designed as Text Books, having been requested

Resolved that the Principal & Professor of Mathematics[2] be requested report their opinion of the same to the Board. . . .[3]

---

[1] Portions of these minutes dealing with routine business have been omitted.

[2] T. R. Beck and Joseph Henry.

[3] Henry's report on the mathematical works of Ferdinand Rudolph Hassler (1770–1843) is printed below, where biographical information on Hassler may also be found; see "To the Academy Trustees," November 12, 1830. The Board had called for a report on Hassler's works earlier (Minutes, Academy Trustees, July 13, 1827); the task was entrusted to a committee, which apparently never reported.

FROM BENJAMIN F. JOSLIN

Henry Papers, Smithsonian Archives

Union College, Oct 16ᵗʰ 1830

Dear Sir

Will you have the goodness to send me that volume of the Traite de Physique[1] as soon as you can spare it, and have a convenient opportunity to send it.

In case you should think fit to publish [the] paper[2] which I communicated to the institute I beg leave to suggest slight alteration if it is not too late. I should prefer having the text terminate with the argument in favour of Prevost's theory,[3] and put the subsequent part in the form of a note omitting however altogether the sentence in the said note which is quoted

---

[1] It is not clear just which work Joslin is asking for. The best known work of the day with a similar title was J.-B. Biot's *Traité de physique, expérimentale et mathématique,* 4 vols. (Paris, 1816), the basis of some of Farrar's translations. Volume 3 of the 1816 edition is also in Henry's Library but the presence of H. Vethake's name indicates Henry probably acquired the volume after coming to Princeton. E. Peclet's *Traité élémentaire de physique,* 2d ed., 2 vols. (Paris, 1830) is in the Henry Library. It is possible that Henry had volume 2 in Albany; there are two inscriptions in the work, one in the manner of his early writing. This volume covered light, in addition to electricity and magnetism.

[2] See Minutes, Albany Institute, September 21, 1830, above, footnote 2. The contents are briefly discussed below. What is most interesting about this work is not its subject matter but its approach. Joslin, who was mathematically inclined, casts his arguments in the form of a mathematical proof. Two thought experiments are given. No experimental data whatsoever appears. Given the correctness of his assumptions, the conclusions follow. This is markedly different from Henry's style.

[3] Pierre Prévost (1751–1839), Professor of Philosophy (1793) and Physics (1810) at the Academy at Geneva. *Poggendorff.* Prévost's theory was an explanation of the apparent radiation of cold in terms of the caloric theory which avoided acceptance of the hypothesis that cold was a separate substance, instead of being the absence of heat. Sir John Leslie in his article on cold in the seventh edition of the *Britannica* (reprinted, pp. 342–345, in *Treatises on Various Subjects of Natural and Chemical Philosophy* [Edinburgh, 1838], a copy of which is in the Henry Library) traces the experiments on radiation of cold back to Della Porta, to the Accademia del Cimento in Florence in the next century, and to M. A. Pictet of Geneva in 1781. *Poggendorff.* Prévost postulated that, as the quantity of caloric radiated is proportional to the difference in temperature of the bodies, a warmer body radiates more than a cold body, receiving less caloric in return. Therefore, the temperature of the warm body will drop and the radiation of cold is only apparent. See P. Prévost, "Suite des considérations sur le mode d'action du calorique," *Bibliothèque britannique,* 1804, 26:205–219.

Joslin was defending this theory against the criticism of John Murray in *Elements of Chemistry,* 2d ed., 2 vols. (Edinburgh, 1810), *I:*145–147, and of the anonymous reviewer of Sir John Leslie's *An Experimental Inquiry into the Nature and Propagation of Heat* (London, 1804) in the *Edinburgh Review,* 1805–1806, 7:63–91. Joslin, who was obviously out of date, probably got onto this from the article on "Cold" in the *Edinburgh Encyclopedia* (1830 ed.), 6:731–743, especially pp. 737–739. At least, the language in the printed article shows signs of borrowing from this source. For a recent article bearing in part on Murray, see Patsy A. Gerstner, "The Reaction to James Hutton's Use of Heat as a Geological Agent," *The British Journal for the History of Science,* 1971, 5:353–362.

from the Edinburgh Review.[4] I should wish the note then to commence thus:[5]

The foregoing investigation suggests a general formula for expressing the ratio of the reflecting to the absorbent & projecting powers, or at least the law according to which these powers vary. Is not this the only sense &c

Please give my respects to Prof Alexander

> I am sir very respectfully your
> Friend
> B F Joslin

[4] See previous footnote.

[5] Joslin's desires were disregarded. The printed text simply continues beyond the defense of Prévost with Joslin's derivation of a general law.

GEORGE CHILTON[1] TO T. ROMEYN BECK

T. Romeyn Beck Papers, New York Public Library

N. York Oct 30. 1830

Dear Sir,

I received yours this day. The Reflectors[2] were sent, [via][3] Steamboat North America, on Thursday which you probably have received by this time. They would have been sent sooner had I not waited for the glass, ordered by Mr Henry (for the Tortion balance).[4]

Mr Henry saw a deflagrator in my garret which may have appeared to a disadvantage. It consists of 5 troughs each containing 44 double copper cells with each a sheet of zinc in the center. The size of the plates 7 by 3 Inches is the size of Hare's. The zinc is new and will last a dozen years at least, without removal, and then may be removed at a trifling expense. The

[1] George Chilton (1767–1836), chemist and inventor of scientific instruments, was born in England and came to New York at age thirty. Although Chilton published seven papers on chemistry and mineralogy and became established as a popular lecturer on science, he was most devoted to the maintenance of an instruments store in New York. He not only manufactured his own instruments but also imported materials and philosophical apparatus. He was aided in his operations by his son, Dr. James R. Chilton, who maintained the business after the death of his father in 1836 and who will appear subsequently in later activities of Henry. *Silliman's Journal*, 1837, *31*: 421–424.

[2] Undoubtedly the parabolic mirrors used in the demonstrations of experiments on radiant heat; their cost was $25.00. See Henry's Descriptive Catalogue of Philosophical Apparatus below, [December 18, 1830], footnote 18.

[3] A word or symbol at this point is illegible, but we assume it has approximately this meaning.

[4] A plate of glass which Henry had ground for Coulomb's balance, costing $2.25. See ibid., footnote 33.

whole is fitted in frame work which is easily taken to pieces. It has 5 well made troughs for acid and 5 additional ones for water to plunge the plates when not in use.

I have been thus particular in my description with the hope that it may suit you to have it.[5] If it should not, I shall be obliged to advertise it as I have no room to show it. The price 75 dollars.

Yrs sincerely
G. Chilton

[5] We have found no record indicating that any such purchase was made. See ibid., as well as the Miscellaneous Albany Academy Accounts in the Henry Papers, Smithsonian Archives.

TO HARRIET HENRY

Mary Henry Copy, Family Correspondence,
Henry Papers, Smithsonian Archives

Nov. 6th 1830 Albany

My dear wife,

I owe you nothing on the score of forgetfulness although a variety of engagements have prevented an immediate answer to your kind and affectionate letter. You have certainly been a very good girl in writing so promptly. I hope soon to pay you in part with a profusion of that coin which passes current only between ourselves. For the first two or three days after your departure I was very lonely and almost inclined to be displeased with myself and everything around me. Your letter had a soothing effect and the assurance that you are happy in the enjoyment of your friends has in a measure reconciled me to your absence.

Stephen has almost this instant finished writing the introduction to the eclipse. The whole will be sent to the printer tomorrow. Your mother is much pleased at the prospect of seeing the *end* of the eclipse, neither the beginning nor the middle is half as interesting to her although equally important in an astronomical point of view.

Tell your friends they need not feel obliged to me for the visit of my wife. I constantly wish her home and am so very selfish as to determine not to let her remain longer than two weeks. Existence would almost be insup[erable][1]

[1] The copy ends at this point.

TO THE ACADEMY TRUSTEES
Miscellaneous Records, Albany Academy Archives

Albany Nov 12th 1830

Gentlemen

In complyance with a resolution of your board directing a report on Hasler's Mathematical works[1] I respectfully submit the following.

Mr Hasler[2] is well known as a person of great attainments particularly in mixed or the higher departments of practical mathematics. His plan of the survy of the coast of the United States and his report of that part of the work which he was permitted to execute have received the unqualified approbation of the first astronomers and topographical engineers of the world.

For a few years past Mr Hasler has held an office under the excise department of New York[3] and as this employment does not exclusively occupy him he has employed his extra time in preparing for the press different parts of an elementary course of mathematics. Of this course the following parts have appeared viz *Elements of Arithmetic;*[4] *Elements of Geometry;*[5] *Elements of Plane* & *Spherical Trigonometry;*[6] *A Popular Exposition of the System of the Universe and a Portable Volume of Tables.*[7] These works are all far superior to the majority of book on thes subjects and although entitled *elements,* in many cases give profound views of the different branches of which they treat.

To begin in order with the arithmetic. It contains the most logical & phlosophical exposition of the subject which I have ever seen and it is from the principles given in this book that I have been in the habit for some time past of explaining to my puples the rationality of the rules of arith-

---

[1] See Excerpt, Minutes, Academy Trustees, October 8, 1830, above.

[2] Ferdinand Rudolph Hassler (1770–1843), geodesist, mathematician, and first Superintendent of the United States Coast Survey. He was born in Aarau, Switzerland, emigrated to America in 1805, and within two years began an association with government efforts to survey the coasts of the United States that continued intermittently until his death. Henry's friend, Alexander Dallas Bache, was Hassler's successor. *DAB;* and Florian Cajori, *The Chequered Career of Ferdinand Rudolph Hassler* (Boston, 1922).

[3] Specifically, Hassler was performing the duties of gager in the New York Custom House. *DAB.*

[4] *Elements of Arithmetic, Theoretical and Practical; Adapted to the Use of Schools, and to Private Study* (New York, 1826), which went through nine editions by 1843 and in 1834 was published in Switzerland.

[5] *Elements of the Geometry of Planes and Solids* (Richmond, Virginia, 1828).

[6] *Elements of Analytic Trigonometry, Plane and Spherical* (New York, 1826).

[7] *A Popular Exposition of the System of the Universe, with Plates and Tables,* 2 vols. (New York, 1828). Volume 2 is entitled *Plates and Tables to the Popular Exposition of the System of the Universe,* which explains Henry's reference to a "Portable Volume of Mathematical Tables."

metic.[8] Some idea may be formed of the estimation of this work among men of science from the fact that it is the arithmetic on which the students are examined previous to their admission in to the Military School of West Point.[9] The subject is treated in some what of a synthetical manner; the most important principles and rules on modes of operation are given in the form of propositions and *printed* in *italics;* the explanation or demonstration of these are given immediatly after.

In refference to its introduction into the Academy as a book of general use or one to be substituted in the place of those now used I would remark that it appears to me to be a work better calculated to give clear & logical ideas to the teacher than to assist much in advancing the knowledge of the young puple. It is certainly an admirable work for those who have made some advance in the study or who have already in a considerable degree acquired the habit of abstract reasoning but I should think it almost useless in the hands of a boy under *ten* or *eleven* years old as being above his capacity. I do not however wish to be understood from this remark that a boy of ten or eleven cannot be made to comprehend most of the truths contaned in this work. On the contrary I may say from experience that by *oral* communication & by questioning on the subject of the lesson a teacher may give a puple of that age a thurrow knowledge of the principles of this science but I believe it is only by oral instruction & that often repeted that he can be made perfectly to understand them.

Another objection to the adoption of Mr Hasler's arithmetic as a book of general use, is that it is almost exclusively a book of principles containing but few practical examples; while these from the manner of teaching in the Academy require to be very numerous.

Almost every abstract principle of arithmetic as taught in the Academy is given from the mouth of the teacher to each class accompanied with illustrations on the black board, after the principles of a rule have been thus explained and the student questioned on the subject of the lesson one or two pages of practical examples from the arithmetic are always given for the next days lesson. It is therefore absolutely necessary that the book used should contain a great variety and number of such examples under each rule. For this reason Daboll's arithmetic[10] is now used and it is only used

[8] For Henry's thoughts on the teaching of mathematics at Albany, see his letter of [June or July 1829] to the Academy Trustees, above.

[9] From 1807 to 1809 Hassler had taught mathematics at West Point. When, in 1809, the Secretary of War decided that the law did not authorize the employment of civilians at the Military Academy, he became Professor of Natural Philosophy and Mathematics at Union College. *DAB.*

[10] Nathan Daboll, *Daboll's Schoolmaster's Assistant, Improved and Enlarged: Being a Plain Practical System of Arithmetic, Adapted to the United States,* stereotype ed. (Albany, 1821), which went through many editions and was published for several years after Daboll's

as a book of examples: The principles of the science & the explanation of the rules are given after the manner of Hasler and Colburn.[11] Besides the examples in Daboll the teacher is in the habit of giving each class in course several hundred extra examples from his own head or selected from Bonnycastle,[12] Hutton,[13] & others. With the addition of mental arithmetic the same plan is persued by Mr Carpenter[14] in the 4th department & the Boys under his charge are making very rapid improvement in the first rules of arithmetic.

The forgoing objections I have stated personally to Mr Hasler and he at the time thought of compiling a book to accompany his arithmetic consisting wholly of examples with a few short practical rules. A cheap work of this kind would render Haslers arithmetic much more valuable and be a great acquisition to the teacher.

From the above remarks it will be perceved that I do not think it advisable to introduce Hasler's Arithmetic as a book to be generally used in the academy or in other words that each boy persuing this study be required to purchase a copy.

There is however a class of students in the Institution to whom it may be very valuable. I allude to the young men who enter the academy for a short time in order to review their arithmetic and also those who are fitting themselves for the business of teaching. I would reccommend that they in almost every case be required to procure a copy of this work. It may also perhaps be given to the highest class in arithmetic or to those who are about to commence the study of algebra. On this point however I do not wish to speak descidedly without having made an experiment & I must confess that I feel an unwillingness to reccommend the multiplication of book unless absolutly necessary.

The next book is the Elements of Geometry which is designed as a substitute for Euclid. With this work I am but imperfectly acquainted & shall not attempt a particular description. There are several authours on this

---

death. Henry may have used the edition cited here, but we have no way of knowing for sure.

[11] Warren Colburn, *Arithmetic: Being a Sequel to First Lessons in Arithmetic*, 3d ed. (Boston, 1826), was being used at Albany Academy at this time. For Colburn, see *DAB*.

[12] John Bonnycastle, *An Introduction to Algebra* (New York, 1818).

[13] Charles Hutton, *A Course of Mathematics, for the Use of Academies, as Well as Private Tuition*, 4th American ed. rev., cor., and enl., 2 vols. (New York, 1825–1826), is in Henry's Library.

[14] George Washington Carpenter (1811–1910) was Surveyor of the city of Albany. In 1823 he entered Albany Academy and was a tutor in the same institution from 1830 to 1835. According to *Coulson*, p. 43, Carpenter was a former pupil and assistant of Henry's at the Albany Academy. See Henry Hun, "A Survey of the Activity of the Albany Academy" (unpublished manuscript, 1922–1935, Manuscript Division, New York State Library and Archives of the Albany Academy); *Academy Seventy-fifth Anniversary*, p. 69.

department of mathmatics which have been introduced into Colleges & academys in this country instead of Euclid. The one in most common use is LaGendres Geometry.[15] The reasons stated for the prefference given to this book is that Euclid does not contain a sufficiant number of elementary truths for [the] present state of the science & that his demonstrations are often prolix and sometimes unnescessarily precise. In answer to these objections it may be stated that one of the principal objects in the study of the mathematics is the improvement of the reasoning faculties. Now there is no work at least as far as my knowledge extends which can be compared with Euclid for the precision of its definitions or the strict & severe logic of its demonstrations. It is moreover a work which is in a manner identifyed with all the mathematical and metaphysical writers of the last century who refer to its propositions by quoting their No. and Book. The first part of Euclid should therefore I think be taught in every college & academy; additions should undoubtedly be made to sute the present state of the science and other demonstrations may be advantageously substituted in place of those of the 2nd & 5th Books.

The next two books are the Astronomy & the Analytic trigonometry. The introduction of these at present would be attended with some inconvenience as the Cambridge course of Mathematics[16] have been introduced and are now in use. The prefference was given to this series of books because they contain the only complete course of mathematics of any extent to be procured in this country or indeed which exists in the English language. The several parts of this work are connected with each other by an almost constant refference from one volume to the other; to teach therefore one part from a different authour would be attended with considerable difficulty both to the Instructor and the pupil. This objection will not exist if Mr Hasler completes his whole course which if it be found better to answer the purpose may be addopted entere.

The last work which remains to be noticed is the vol. of Mathematical tables. These I have had occasion to use almost constantly for three or four weeks past and can therefor state explicitely that they are a very valuable acquisition to the mathematical student as well as to the practical engineer. Since my engagement in the Academy I have often experienced the want of a work of this kind as in the mathematical works now used no table of any degree of acuracy is to be found. The student has only had recourse to

[15] A. M. Legendre, *Elements of Geometry and Trigonometry, with Notes,* trans. by David Brewster (New York, 1828), which is in the Henry Library.

[16] Meaning the entire range of textbooks compiled and translated by John Farrar. See Henry's letter of [June or July 1829] to the Academy Trustees, footnote 8, above.

the imperfect tables prefixed to Gibson's Surveying[17] & Bowditches Navigation.[18] These only extend to 4 and 5 places of decimals and are consequently inapplicable to any very exact calculation.

The introduction of this work will I am confident have a tendancey to induce a habit of more exact numerical calculation and enable the student to become more intimatly acquainted with the use of logarithmetic tables. The price of this vol. is $2.50 and it is more minute in some cases and almost as extensive in every way as Hutton's Mathematical tables[19] which cannot be procured in this country, and if ordered from England will cost at the least $10.

In conclusion therefore I would reccommend that Hasler's Arithmetic be used for the older students in the academy & that each student when commencing the study of Trigonometry or the higher parts of algebra be required to procure a copy of Hasler's Mathematical tables.

> I am Gentlemen with much
> Respect Your
> humble serv[t]
> Joseph Henry

---

[17] Probably Robert Gibson, *A Treatise of Practical Surveying, Which Is Demonstrated from Its First Principles*, 2d New York ed. (New York, 1803).

[18] Nathaniel Bowditch, *The New American Practical Navigator* (Newburyport, Massachusetts, 1802), which quickly superseded its predecessors, became a standard reference work for seamen throughout the world, and, in revised form, is still widely used. The latest edition available to Henry would have been the fourth, published in New York in 1817.

[19] Charles Hutton, *Mathematical Tables; Containing the Common, Hyperbolic and Logistic Logarithms . . .*, 7th ed. (London, 1830). The edition cited here was the latest available to Henry.

TO BENJAMIN SILLIMAN, SR.[1]

Silliman Family Papers, Sterling Library, Yale University

Albany Dec.10th 1830

Prof. Silliman
    Dear Sir

I have been engaged for some time past in a series of experiments on electro-magnetism and particularly in reference to the development of great magnetic power with a small galvanic element. The results I wish to publish if possible in the next No. of the Journal of Science. I am anxious

---

[1] Henry's retained copy of this letter, dated one day earlier, is in the Smithsonian Archives. It has been printed in Nathan Reingold, ed., *Science in Nineteenth-Century America: A Documentary History* (New York, 1964), p. 65.

that they should appear as soon as possible since by delaying the publication of the principles of these experiments for nearly two years I have lately had the mortification of being anticipated in part by a paper from Prof. Moll in the last No of Brewster's Journal.[2]

Please inform me if I shall be too late for the next no. of the Journal if I send my paper within two weeks of the date of this letter—it will probably make five or six pages. If it be not too late I should like to have a small wood cut of a powerful magnet which I am constructing on electro-magnetic principles.

Both Mrs. Henry and myself retain a lively reccollection of the many polite attentions we receved in New Haven last Spring. We join in a respectful remembrance to your self and family.

I am with much respect
Your humble serv
Joseph Henry

[2] Gerrit Moll, "Electro-Magnetic Experiments (Formation of Powerful Magnets by Galvanism)" *Edinburgh Journal of Science,* 1830, *3:*209–218. Moll (1785–1838) was a Dutch physicist at the University of Utrecht. *Poggendorff.* Reingold, *Science in Nineteenth-* *Century America,* pp. 62–65, discusses the impact of Moll's article on Henry and the problem of conflicting claims for priority in scientific discovery between American and European scientists.

FROM BENJAMIN SILLIMAN, SR.
Henry Papers, Smithsonian Archives

N Hav. Dec[r] 17 1830

Dear Sir

Yours of the 10th [1] reached me a few hours since. I write by return of mail to say that as Prof Molls memoir is already printed in this N[o] of the Journal[2] it is the more important that yours should appear also. Although we are already arrived at the *Miscellanies* I will reserve a form for you at the very end where you can come in by way of appendix.[3] As a week is already

[1] See above.
[2] Gerrit Moll, "Electro-Magnetic Experiments," *Silliman's Journal,* 1831, *19:*329–337. Both Henry and Silliman had noted this piece on its original publication in Britain. Moll, like Henry, was aware of the work of William Sturgeon. His paper is markedly different in style from Henry's. Henry is detailed and factual; Moll is more "literary" in his range of allusions. And Henry's results were more spectacular in terms of lifting power.

[3] Joseph Henry, "On the Application of the Principle of the Galvanic Multiplier to Electro-Magnetic Apparatus, and Also to the Development of Great Magnetic Power in Soft Iron, with a Small Galvanic Element," *Silliman's Journal,* 1831, *19:*400–408.

gone since you wrote I trust that your paper may be forwarded with very little delay & may I beg the favor that you will steal a few hours to complete it with the least possible delay & let it come by mail & *you need not pay the postage*. Pray write on receipt of this what we may expect unless the piece is about ready.

I am gratified that your visit was agreeable to you & present my respects to Mrs Henry & my kind regard to yourself. I am writing at college or my family would join.

Yours with sincere
esteem
B Silliman

Pray give your title correctly on the first page of the piece.

HENRY'S DESCRIPTIVE CATALOGUE OF PHILOSOPHICAL APPARATUS PURCHASED FOR THE ALBANY ACADEMY[1] [DECEMBER 18, 1830][2]

Albany Academy Accounts for Philosophical Apparatus
Henry Papers, Smithsonian Archives

In his Inaugural Address Henry briefly interrupted his survey of the mathematical sciences with an appeal for additional philosophical apparatus, which he deemed indispensable in teaching the mixed and experimental sciences (see above, September 11, 1826). On March 12, 1830, it was recorded in the Minutes of the Academy Trustees (2:371–373) that $362 had been donated or subscribed for the purchase of new scientific apparatus. The seventeen donors and subscribers were prominent figures in the Albany business, scientific, and educational community, including a number of Academy Trustees. Stephen Van Rensselaer, President of the Albany Institute, and John T. Norton, Academy

---

[1] This document, except for the last few lines, is not in Henry's hand.

[2] Though this document is not dated, a detailed account of expenditures which accompanies it bears the date December 18, 1830. In the first part of these accounts, T. R. Beck listed the donations and total expenditures for the apparatus. The itemized account of expenditures which followed was examined by a Trustees' Committee of Accounts and found to be "correct and duly supported by vouchers." Below, the accounts are used in determining the prices of the various articles of apparatus. Hereafter, these official accounts are cited as Account of Expenditures. This document and the vouchers, which we also cite below, are in the Henry Papers, Smithsonian Archives, File Box 28, in the Folder "Albany Academy Accounts for Philosophical Apparatus, 1827–1831."

Trustee, were the largest contributors at $50 apiece. It was resolved that James Stevenson and T. R. Beck "be a Committee to ascertain the price of various articles of Philosophical Apparatus and that they report which it would be most expedient to purchase." Henry, who was responsible for buying and cataloging the apparatus, undoubtedly encouraged the donations and advised Stevenson and Beck on the most suitable purchases.

By December 1830, the Trustees had allocated a total of $392 for the apparatus, of which Henry had spent $347.66. The additional funds came from two new subscribers, Alfred Conkling, member of the Albany Institute, and William James, Academy Trustee. The following document is Henry's report on the newly purchased apparatus. Accompanying this descriptive catalog was a detailed account of donations and expenditures. Both documents, along with the vouchers for the individual purchases were submitted to a Trustees' examining committee in December and read into the Trustees' Minutes for January 28, 1831 (2:396–397). These financial records, which we have not printed, contain information on the prices and manufacturers of the various items of apparatus, information included in our annotations to Henry's Catalogue.

Under Henry's direction, the Albany Academy acquired an excellent collection of philosophical apparatus, which we suspect compared favorably with collections at leading American colleges. Henry had visited Yale in May 1830 with an eye toward finding good apparatus for the Academy, noting that Yale's collection was better than Union's and that its mineralogical cabinet was the best in this country (see above, Henry's Notes on a Trip to Yale, May 6, 1830). Obviously impressed by what he had seen at Yale, Henry soon acquired many of the same items for his classes in Albany. Henry's collection could not have rivaled in size or quality that of West Point, which imported much of its apparatus from Europe and, at this date, had the best collection in the United States. Yet, from observation of the West Point apparatus which survives at the National Museum of History and Technology (Washington, D.C.), we can say that the articles in Henry's Catalogue were typical of the apparatus in the West Point collection. Furthermore, Henry noted that a few pieces in his Catalogue were the largest in this country. Since many of the courses he taught at Albany were college level, Henry undoubtedly wanted a cabinet of similar quality.

As will be seen, most of the items in Henry's Catalogue were familiar pieces of school apparatus used to demonstrate well-known principles in the sciences and practical arts. Almost all figured prominently in standard works on mechanics, such as Jacob Bigelow's *Elements of Technology* (Boston, 1829), and Olinthus Gregory's *A Treatise of Mechanics, Theoretical, Practical, and Descriptive*, 3d ed., 2 vols. (London, 1815)—works which survive in the Henry Library. Indeed Henry probably consulted these standard treatises in selecting his teaching apparatus. While most items were for demonstration, Henry might well have used a few pieces (e.g., the electrical machine, deflagrator, and torsion balance) for his original researches in electricity and magnetism. He may have used other articles, such as the hygrometer, in his meteorological observations for the Regents.

At the Albany Academy, Henry inaugurated a regular and continuing program for buying philosophical apparatus. The Academy Trustees resolved on March 12, 1831, that the Principal and Instructors of the Academy "present annually to the Board at its monthly meeting in June, a catalogue of the Library, Philosophical & Chemical Apparatus, & other personal property belonging to the Academy & under their general care & supervision." (Minutes, Academy Trustees, 2:12.) Accordingly, a second brief report, noting the purchase of electrical apparatus, was presented to the Trustees on June 10, 1831 (Minutes, Academy Trustees, 2:17–19). The Academy's catalog of philosophical apparatus in 1839, which included far more than Henry's original inventory, showed that the Academy's collection of apparatus continued to grow under Henry's successor, Phillip Ten Eyck (Minutes, Academy Trustees, 2:503–511).

No. 1. An Achromatic Dolland Telescope with 3 eye pieces, one for terrestrial views, which magnifies about 40 times; and 2 for celestial objects, one of which magnifies about 70 & the other 110. The diameter of the object glass is $2\frac{7}{10}$ inches and the focal distance 3 feet, 8 inches. The tube of the instrument is of brass with a plain brass stand; the whole packed in a mahogany case. Price $140.[3]

No. 2. A large cylindrical electrical machine, mounted on a table with a drawer; the diameter of the cylinder is 16 inches; accompanying it are

---

[3] John Dollond (1706–1761), the British optician, was the inventor of triple achromatic object-lenses for telescopes. His family was still producing optical instruments in 1830. *DNB.* Henry may have purchased an imported telescope from Dollond of London, but the name "Dollond" was often used in a generic sense for achromatic telescopes.

According to a receipt given to T. R. Beck on July 6, 1830, the telescope was obtained from Benjamin Pike and Benjamin Pike, Jr., in New York City. Proprietors of Benjamin Pike & Son, the Pikes were opticians, philosophical instrument makers, and importers of apparatus. According to an 1863 eulogy, Pike, Sr. (1777–1863), was born in London and came to New York City in 1798, where he established his well-known business in 1805. The eulogy adds that "for half a century his store was the headquarters of scientific men, and he was the companion of Fulton, Eckford, and others whose genius has done credit to our country. He manufactured models and instruments for them, and he was really the great pioneer manufacturer of philosophical instruments in America." "Death of Benjamin Pike, Sen.," *Scientific American,* 1863, n.s., 8: 346. We suspect that Pike was a colleague of

inventors and mechanics, rather than scientific men in the modern sense. Eckford is Henry Eckford (1775–1832), the New York City shipbuilder, who built the *Robert Fulton,* which made the first successful steam voyage from New York to New Orleans and Havana in 1822. *DAB.* Less is known of Benjamin Pike, Jr., who later assumed control of the business. In 1848, Pike, Jr., published a catalog of the apparatus he made, imported, and sold: *Pike's Illustrated Descriptive Catalogue of Optical, Mathematical, and Philosophical Instruments,* 2 vols. (New York, 1848). A second edition, which we have frequently cited below, appeared in 1856. The catalog is an excellent source for descriptions and illustrations of a wide range of contemporary scientific apparatus (about 1200 items are listed). In the preface to this work (1856 ed., 1:iii, iv), Pike states "he is not a man of letters, but a mechanic,—a practical workman . . ." who has "devoted himself from early youth to the manufacture of these instruments on a somewhat extensive scale. . . ." Pike, Jr., adds that his collection of instruments is "not surpassed, if equalled, by any in the country, for extent, style, quality, or *cheapness.* . . ."

two detached conductors of varnished tin and one fixed conductor of wood covered with tinfoil. To this is attached a large brass Electrometer. The cylinder of this machine is unusually large and is perhaps the greatest in diameter of any in this country.[4]

No. 3. A large working model of Mongolfiers Hydraulic Ram. The tube for the passage of the water is one inch in diameter, made of lead and painted black; the valves are of brass; accompanying it is a block tin tube

---

[4] Cylindrical machines generated static electricity and the electrometer measured the quantity of static charge. For a general description of these devices, see the *Encyclopaedia Britannica*, 8th ed., s.v. "Electricity." The 16-inch cylinder of Henry's machine was indeed large. Joseph Priestly's electrical machine, one of the largest known cylindrical generators, had a 12-inch cylinder. (Priestly's machine is now in the collection of the National Museum of History and Technology in Washington, D.C.) However, it should be noted that cylindrical machines were eighteenth-century vintage and were largely superseded in the nineteenth century by plate electrical machines, also described in the *Encyclopaedia Britannica*.

Henry's Account of Expenditures and a receipt of June 5, 1830 show that the glass cylinder and its mounting were bought from Benjamin Pike for $25. Other vouchers show that an additional $17.49 was paid to the following craftsmen for parts and labor:

Robison [? Robinson] (for carpenter's work)
—unidentified
G. W. Carpenter (for glass rods)
—probably the surveyor
George Washington Carpenter,
for whom see above,
Henry to the Academy Trustees,
November 12, 1830, footnote 14.
Thomas Brown (for work done on the machine)—listed in the 1830–1831 Albany City Directory as a "scourer."
John Watson (for finishing the machine)
—an Albany carpenter. Albany City Directory, 1830–1831.

In the following year, Henry obtained another important piece of electrical equipment. At the Trustees' meeting of January 28, 1831, it was proposed to use the remaining funds and any further donations for purchasing a "powerful galvanic apparatus & also Electromagnetic Apparatus, if possible." (Minutes, Academy Trustees, 2:397.) By June 1831, further donations permitted the construction of a Galvanic Deflagrator with 300 plates, a large galvanic battery invented in 1821 by the chemist Robert Hare (1781–1858; see below, Silliman to Hare, October 11, 1832). The deflagrator is described above, Chilton to Beck, October 30, 1830, and in Silliman's *Elements of Chemistry*, 2 vols. (New Haven, 1831), 2:651–653. According to Silliman, it consisted of a series of zinc plates within flat copper cases, which were suspended by beams and levers so that they could be immersed and removed from the acid simultaneously. The levers and simultaneous immersion allowed the power to be turned on and off instantaneously without loss of energy. The powerful battery generated intense heat, enough to ignite or deflagrate various substances. Silliman also describes other forms of the Hare deflagrator, which underwent several modifications. According to the "Second Report on the Purchase of Philosophical Apparatus" (June 3, 1831, Albany Academy Archives) which was included in the Trustees' Minutes of June 10, 1831, Phillip Ten Eyck oversaw the construction of the large battery and the following merchants and craftsmen were involved in the construction:

To W. Humphrey & Co. for
  Zinc & Copper $55.81
To Peter Smith for 10 days work,
  soldering, etc. $20.49
To Jnº McHench for Wood-work, etc. $24.00
To William Gladding for painting,
  troughs, etc. $ 2.00
To L. Pruyn & Co. for vises, etc. $ 2.23
To W. A. Wharton for a three-gallon
  electrical jar and tin foil $ 4.14

Ten Eyck received $25. All but one of the above appear in the Albany City Directory, 1830–1831, 1831–1832: William Humphrey of Humphrey & Co., hardware merchants; Peter Smith, coppersmith; McHench is unidentified; William Gladding, painter; Lansing Pruyn of L. Pruyn & Co., hardware merchants; W. A. Wharton, druggist.

12 feet long for forcing the water through. This model will raise a small, continued stream to the height of 40 feet.[5]

No. 4. A Hydrostatic Bellows, the top and bottom 18 inches in diameter made of black walnut—the sides of strong leather. A perpendicular tube 5 feet long for pouring in the water is attached by a coupling screw, to another tube which is connected with the bottom.[6]

No. 5. An article of apparatus intended to show the method of converting continued circular motion into a variety of reciprocating motions. This may be called a model of *Cams* and was designed to illustrate a part of the chapter in *Bigelow's*[7] Technology, on the Elements of Machines.

No. 6. A modification of the Whirling Table intended to show a class of interesting experiments on the whirling of bodies suspended by a string which cannot be exhibited by the ordinary whirling table. It consists of a vertical wheel about 18 inches in diameter, which communicates motion

[5] Joseph Michel Montgolfier (1740–1810), the French inventor of the warm-air balloon, introduced his *bélier hydraulique* in the *Journal des mines*, 1802–1803, *13*:42–51, and 1803–1804, *15*:23–37. *Nouvelle biographie universelle*.

The hydraulic ram was used to demonstrate that the momentum of water could raise a small amount of water to a considerable height. When water flowing through a pipe reached sufficient velocity, a valve was forced shut, suddenly diverting the water into a chamber containing air and a small amount of water. The shock of the diverted water compressed the air in the chamber, which in turn forced a small amount of water up into a connecting vertical tube. This machine, which Henry had seen at Yale (see above, Henry's Notes on a Trip to Yale, May 6, 1830) is described and pictured in Bigelow, *Elements of Technology*, p. 323. In his *Treatise of Mechanics, Theoretical, Practical, and Descriptive,* 3d ed., 2 vols. (London, 1815), *2*:238–241, Olinthus Gregory treats the theory of the ram and notes that Montgolfier suggested the device could be used to drain mines.

In the accompanying Account of Expenditures, this article is listed at $10. According to a voucher of November 4, 1830, work and parts for the machine were provided by Peter Smith, an Albany coppersmith. Albany City Directory, 1830–1831.

[6] Since the pressure of water depends only on its depth, a small weight of water in the vertical tube generated sufficient pressure in the bellows to support large weights placed on top of the bellows. A common piece of apparatus for showing hydrostatic principles, the bellows are treated in James Ferguson's *Lectures on Select Subjects,* Robert Patterson's revised edition, originally edited by David Brewster, 2 vols. (Philadelphia, 1806), *1*:121. The bellows are pictured in Ferguson's volume of plates, X, fig. 6. Henry had seen an example of the apparatus at Yale.

In Ten Eyck's 1839 catalogue of philosophical apparatus (Minutes, Academy Trustees, *2*:503–511), this item is listed at $5. According to a voucher of November 4, 1830, the coppersmith Peter Smith furnished parts for the machine. Among Henry's financial records for the purchase of philosophical apparatus (Smithsonian Archives, File Box 13), there is a second account of donations and expenditures, apparently not submitted to the Committee of Accounts. This account contains further details on Henry's purchases. (Hereafter this document will be cited as the unofficial record of expenditures.) In these other accounts, it is noted that William Story provided the leather bellows for the apparatus. In the Albany City Directory, 1830–1831, Story is listed as a bellows-maker on Vine Street.

[7] Bigelow, *Elements of Technology,* chapter 11: "Elements of Machinery," pp. 237ff. The cams are listed in the 1839 catalogue of apparatus at $4.

to a horizontal arm by means of a cord: this arm in time sets in motion a vertical spindle to which is attached the string supporting the whirling body.[8]

No. 7. A Working Model of Barker's reaction mill, made of tinned iron painted black, with a wooden frame. In this form of the mill, the water is admitted at the top.[9]

No. 8. Another form of Barker's Mill in which the water rises from below to the arms by means of a reservoir at one side. This modification has the advantage of not supporting the heavy column of water which occupies the shaft of the other form of the mill.[10]

No. 9. Paradoxical balance invented by Desagulliers, to show the absurdity of a self moving machine on mechanical principles. Two weights, one on each arm of the balance, may be placed at any distance from the centre of motion, without disturbing the equilibrium. This article also illustrates the principle of a kind of balance used by druggists.[11]

No. 10. Apparatus for illustrating the doctrine of the percussion of elastic and non-elastic bodies, made of cherry and furnished with 5 ivory balls, one inch and a half in diameter. For experiments on non-elastic bodies, balls of putty or clay are substituted for the ivory ones.[12]

---

[8] Another common piece of school apparatus, the whirling table illustrated principles of central forces. See Ferguson's *Lectures*, *1*:30 and plate IV, fig. 1. There are no records showing the manufacturer or price of the machine, only a voucher of July 24, 1830, indicating that an unidentified Robert Robertson fixed the whirling table for $0.75.

[9] Water poured into the top of a vertical pipe is emitted at the bottom through two openings on the opposite sides of a horizontal tube which is made to rotate by the impulse of the ejected water. The device is something like a modern lawn sprinkler. Invented by a Dr. Barker, the machine employed the "reaction" of water to turn millstones. See, for instance, Gregory's description in *Treatise*, 2:113 and plate IV, fig. 3. Sir John Leslie considers the theory of the reaction mill in his *Elements of Natural Philosophy*, 2 vols. (Edinburgh, 1823), *1*:349ff. The 1839 catalogue of philosophical apparatus lists the price at $3. Peter Smith was paid for parts, according to a voucher of November 4, 1830.

[10] According to Gregory, the modification was invented by James Rumsey, an American, and Segner, a German. *Treatise*, 2:114. Like the original machine, the modified mill appears in most standard treatises on mechanics.

[11] In his *A Course of Experimental Philosophy*, 2 vols. (London, 1734–1744), *1*:146–147, the English scientist John Theophilus Desaguliers (1683–1744; *DNB*) uses this balance to illustrate general principles in statics, especially the concept of virtual velocities. He later refers to this apparatus (pictured on plate 14, fig. 7) in a theoretical argument against perpetual motion (p. 175). For a history of the concepts of virtual velocity, virtual displacement, etc., see Erwin N. Hiebert, *Historical Roots of the Principle of Conservation of Energy* (Madison, 1962), chapter 1.

Henry must have been eager to acquire a device disproving perpetual motion, in view of his hostility toward the unschooled mechanics who were forever seeking his advice on perpetual motion machines. See below, Henry to J. R. Henry, July 9, 1831.

The price is $3 in the 1839 catalogue.

[12] According to a bill of August 31, 1830, the ivory balls were bought for $2.50 from George and James Chilton in New York City, for whom see above, George Chilton to T. R. Beck, October 30, 1830. The total price of the apparatus in the 1839 catalogue is $7.

No. 11. Hero's Fountain made of tinned iron painted black. For a description of this article see Biglow's Technology. Page [322].[13]

No. 12. Holbrook's school apparatus consisting of Diagrams, Geometrical solids &c. For particular description see accompanying pamphlet.[14]

No. 13. A portable wooden case containing 72 wide mouth bottles with specimens of the articles used in the [arts]. These are intended to illustrate a chapter in Technology.[15]

No. 14. An Electrical Battery consisting of 9 ½ gallon jars in a wooden case.[16]

No. 15. A large Cryophorus consisting of two glass globes about 8 inches in diameter, connected by a hollow tube about 3 feet long. The tube rests on a wooden support. This article is one of the largest of the kind, ever exhibited in this country.[17]

No. 16. A pair of parabolic Mirrors of brass, two feet in diameter for experiments on the radiation of heat. Each mirror is supported on a mahogany foot stand, with an adjusting screw for raising or lowering it.[18]

---

[13] Bigelow treats Hero's Fountain, discussed in most essays on hydrostatics, on p. 322 of his *Elements of Technology* (Henry left out the page number). The fountain employed water and air pressure "to raise water, or to project it in the form of a jet." A noteworthy feature of the device was that the spout was above the reservoir of water. Bigelow and Gregory (*Treatise*, 2:220) state that the same principle was used to raise oil in lamps and to irrigate land. The machine is attributed to Hero of Alexandria (284–221 B.C.), the Hellenistic mathematician and scientist. *Poggendorff.* The coppersmith Peter Smith furnished parts for the apparatus. Voucher of November 4, 1830.

[14] Manufactured by the Holbrook School Apparatus Co. of New York City. See F. C. Brownell, *How to Use Globes in the School and Family*, 2d ed. (New York and Chicago, 1860). Henry bought this demonstration apparatus directly from the Albany booksellers Little and Cummings, who gave him a receipt for $10 on July 17, 1830. For Little and Cummings, see below, Silliman to Henry, January 6, 1831, footnote 3.

[15] i.e., Bigelow's *Elements of Technology*, chapter 1: "Of the Materials Used in the Arts." The collection, itemized in Henry's unofficial record of expenditures, consisted chiefly of various dyes and pigments. According to the Account of Expenditures, the total collection was bought from Chilton's for $19.46.

[16] Listed in Henry's Account of Expenditures at $11.

[17] William Hyde Wollaston, "On a Method of Freezing at a Distance," *Philosophical Transactions of the Royal Society of London*, 1813, pp. 71–74. Wollaston's cryophorus (i.e., frost bearer), which became the model for Daniell's hygrometer (Article No. 19), illustrated two well-known physical principles: (1) the boiling point of a fluid is lowered when the vapor pressure over the fluid is reduced, and (2) evaporation from a fluid cools the remaining fluid. The two globes and connecting tube were evacuated. One globe contained a small amount of water. The empty globe was then cooled in ice water, which condensed the water vapor within. The reduction in vapor pressure caused evaporation and cooling of the water in the other globe. The new vapor was then condensed and the process continued until the water froze. Much smaller than Henry's, Wollaston's original cryophorus had a two- or three-foot tube but only one-inch globes.

According to a voucher of July 31, 1830, Chilton made the cryophorus for $5.

[18] The manuscript is torn here; we have read the complete description from the 1839 catalogue, which repeats most of Henry's original inventory.

The mirrors, bought from the Chiltons for $25 (bill of August 12, 1830), demonstrated, for instance, that heat could be focused; it was also shown that the focused heat could ignite various substances.

No. 17. A Water hammer, an article of apparatus for showing the percussion of Water, when excluded from air. This is also one of the largest kind.[19]

No. 18. A small Weighing Machine, on the principal of the Dinamometer. The body to be weighed draws out a graduated scale from which the weight is read. The tube of the instrument contains a spiral spring which is compressed in proportion to the weight applied to the hook below.[20]

No. 19. Daniels Hygrometer. This instrument, the most perfect Hygrometer ever invented, is on the principal of Dr. Wollaston's Chrysophrus, and like that instrument consists of two glass balls connected by a hollow tube; one of the balls contains a small quantity of Ether, into which dips the end of a small Thermometer inclosed within the tube. The instrument is used by dropping Ether on the outside of the empty ball which causes, by its evaporation, a reduction of temperature within. Cold is then produced in the other ball in the same manner as in the Chrysophrus; when the temperature of the ball containing the Ether becomes a certain degree lower than that of the surrounding atmosphere, moisture or dew is deposited on its outside; the temperature noted by the enclosed thermometer at the moment of the deposition is called the dew point; it is this temperature that is requested to be registered in using the instrument and from which we estimate the comparitive moisture of the atmosphere. In order to preserve from accident this delicate instrument it has been fastened to a mahogany foot & surrounded by a small wooden frame.[21]

No. 20. Davy's Safety Lamp of the usual form, which is too well known to require a particular description.[22]

---

[19] Bought from Chilton for $3, according to the voucher of August 12, 1830. In Pike's 1856 *Catalogue*, *1*:222, the apparatus is described as an evacuated 12-inch glass tube containing three or four inches of water. When the tube is shaken vertically, "the water, rising a few inches and sinking suddenly to the bottom of the tube, produces a sound like that arising from the stroke of a small hammer on a hard body, whence the name of this instrument, the action of which depends entirely on the exclusion of the air, so that the water moves in a dense mass."

[20] The dynamometer was a precise spring balance used in the laboratory. Henry's weighing machine cost only $0.37½. Account of Expenditures.

[21] i.e., John Frederic Daniell (1790–1845), whose hygrometer is discussed above, Minutes, Albany Institute, March 18, 1829, foot-

note 4. Henry may have used the hygrometer both for demonstration and for his own work in meteorology.

[22] The English chemist Humphry Davy (1778–1829) wrote a series of articles on the invention of the safety lamp in the *Philosophical Transactions of the Royal Society of London*, 1816, pp. 1–22, 23–24, 115–119. In 1815 Davy was asked to design a lamp which could illuminate coal mines without igniting the explosive firedamp, the gas released in mines by the decomposition of coal and other organic substances. Davy established that firedamp consisted chiefly of methane and discovered that it would ignite only at a high temperature. After less than three months of research, Davy found that a fine wire sieve surrounding a gas lamp cooled the flame sufficiently to prevent any explosions. *DSB*. In his Introductory Lecture on Chemistry (Jan-

No. 21. A small Mirror which distorts an object, in one direction. This is a cheap article, which serves to illustrates a principle in Optics.[23]

No. 22. A Glass Jar about one foot high and three inches in diameter, intended to be used for experiments in Hydrostatics.[24]

No. 23. Filtering Stand for supporting glass funnels made of Cherry.

No. 24. Stand supporting a large glass funnel, which contains an air thermometer. This apparatus is used to show the slow conduction of heat, downwards in water.

No. 25. Two Cherry frames, one about 3 & the other 4 feet high, intended to support a set of brass pullies and some other mechanical powers.[25]

No. 26. Architectural drawings, pasted on thick cards. One of these is a large and accurate perspective view of the three Grecian orders; it is of much use in explaining to a class the peculiar distinctions of this part of architecture. Another is an outline drawing of the comparitive elevations of the most celebrated edifices in the world.[26]

(Omitted through Carelessness)[27]

27. Leslie's Differential Thermometer[28]

---

uary–March 1832, below) Henry cites Davy's safety lamp as an example of the utility of basic science.

A voucher of August 12, 1830, shows that the lamp was bought from Chilton for $2.50.

[23] Distorting mirrors of all sizes and varieties were popular demonstration items in college laboratories. The price listed in the 1839 catalogue is $2.50.

[24] Bought from Chilton for $0.50 (August 31, 1830). In Henry's Account of Expenditures, the item is described as a glass jar for "floating images." The apparatus is described as follows in Benjamin Pike's *Catalogue*, *1*:230–231: The tall glass jar is nearly filled with water and covered with an elastic diaphragm. The images are colorful glass figures—a man, a balloon, a car, etc.—with a small hole at the bottom through which they are partly filled with water so that they just float in the jar. When the diaphragm is pressed, water is forced into the hollow figures, compressing the air within. The figures then slowly sink. When the diaphragm is released, the air in the figures re-expands; the figures again float to the surface.

The apparatus, a variation on the more commonly known Cartesian diver, demonstrated principles of buoyancy and Pascal's law that water pressure is exerted equally in all directions.

[25] A similar piece of apparatus is pictured in Pike's *Catalogue*, *1*:281.

[26] i.e., the Doric, Corinthian, and Ionian Orders. The drawings and card-backing were obtained from Little and Cummings and from Websters and Skinners (see above, Minutes, Albany Academy, June 11, 1816, footnote 1). The architectural drawings apparently were made originally by the aforementioned Holbrook School Apparatus Company. From the existing accounts it is difficult to tell the price of the apparatus, but it cost between $4 and $11. Unofficial record of expenditures; Henry's Account of Expenditures; see also Ten Eyck's 1839 catalogue.

[27] The following items, added after the original document was completed, are written in Henry's own hand.

[28] A delicate instrument used to detect minute differences in temperature. A simple modification of the air thermometer or the hygrometer, it consisted of two hollow glass bulbs connected by a U-shaped tube, containing a small amount of sulfuric acid tinged with carmine. The instrument measured the temperature difference between the two bulbs: when one bulb was warmer, the expansion of the air inside it forced the sulfuric acid solution higher in the other side of the tube. John Leslie used his differential thermometer in an extended series of experiments on the

28. Nicholsons Specific Gravity Apparatus[29]
29. Wollaston's Steam Apparatus[30]
30. Specimens of Palladium & Cadmium[31]
31. Box of Scales & Weights[32]
32. Plate of Glass for Coulombe's Balance[33]

---

theory of heat. *An Experimental Inquiry into the Nature and Propagation of Heat* (London and Edinburgh, 1804). Four dollars in the 1839 catalogue.

[29] A modified hydrometer used to find the specific gravity of both solids and liquids. See Olinthus Gregory, *Treatise, 1*:378–379, and plate XVI, fig. 8. William Nicholson (1753–1815), the English scientist, inventor, and editor of the *Journal of Natural Philosophy* (1797–1815), wrote and translated many books on chemistry and natural philosophy. *DNB*. In the Account of Expenditures, the article is listed at $1.50.

[30] As described in Pike's *Catalogue, 2*:97, the apparatus "is a small but neat contrivance of Dr. Wollaston, to illustrate the principle of the condensing steam engine." It consists of a flask with a steam-tight piston in its neck. Ether or water is in the bulb of the flask. As the fluid is boiled and condensed, the piston moves up and down. Purchased from Chilton for $2. Voucher of August 12, 1830.

[31] Palladium was discovered in 1803 by the English analytical chemist William Hyde Wollaston (1766–1828), who separated the metal from platinum. Cadmium was discovered in 1817 by Friedrich Stromeyer (1776–1835), Professor of Chemistry and Pharmacy at Göttingen. Both metals were discovered by very elegant techniques of chemical separation. Mary Elvira Weeks, *Discovery of the Elements*, 6th rev. ed. (Easton, Pennsylvania, 1956), pp. 429–432, 529–535. In his *Elements of Chemistry*, Silliman remarked that cadmium "is an interesting metal" but that he was "not aware that cadmium has been obtained in this country. . . ." (New Haven, 1831), 2:223.

[32] Purchased from Chilton's for $1.50. Voucher of August 12, 1830.

[33] i.e., the torsion balance of the French physicist and engineer Charles Augustin Coulomb (1736–1806). Coulomb used a delicate torsion suspension for precise quantitative measurements in electricity and magnetism. *DSB*. See also C. Stewart Gillmor, *Charles Augustin Coulomb: Physics and Engineering in Eighteenth Century France* (Princeton, 1972).

The Coulomb balance was an important piece of research apparatus, though it could of course be used simply to illustrate principles of static electricity. Bought from Chilton's for $2.25, according to the voucher of August 12, 1830.

EXCERPT,[1] MINUTES, ALBANY INSTITUTE

Institute Minutes, Albany Institute Archives

Albany. December 20. 1830

Professor Henry made a Communication on Electro Magnetism, accompanied with experiments. In one of these, he exhibited an iron bar, which with its armature weighed about 20 pounds & on immersing the galvanic

---

[1] The election of corresponding members, the donation of specimens, sundry communications, and a report on a planned guide to Albany are here omitted. Henry's paper was not printed by the Institute in its *Transactions*.

coils connected with it, into acid, it was found to possess a magnetic power capable of raising upwards of 700 pounds. . . .²

---

² This is clearly an account of the experiment Henry later reported in *Silliman's* *Journal*, 1831, *19*:405 (exp. 15) in much greater detail than this bare announcement.

FROM ISAAC W. JACKSON
Henry Papers, Smithsonian Archives

[December 20–31?, 1830]¹

Dear Sir,

I presume you are pursuing your Elec Mag. investigations with your usual success. How do you explain the *vast* difference between the weights sustained by one pole & by both poles, acting together?² The magnetic power does not appear to be developed till the poles are united, or only a slight degree of it. This I presume is not true to the same extent in common horse shoe magnets. I inquired of Mr Joslyn³ if he knew the ratio between the weights sustained by one & both poles together in ord. magnets, & he is confident that tho not ½, it is very far from being near your result.⁴ The next time I see you which I presume will be about New Years, you'll

---

¹ The original of this letter bears no date, except Henry's notation indicating that he received the letter in December 1830. We conjecture, however, that Jackson witnessed Henry's demonstration of the powerful electromagnet at the December 20, 1830, meeting of the Albany Institute, of which Jackson was a member (for notice of that meeting, see excerpt above). From the context of the letter, it must have been written before the "New Year" and it therefore preceded Henry's published account of these experiments in the January 1831 number of *Silliman's Journal*.

² The problem to which Jackson is referring was probably demonstrated at the Institute and was mentioned by Henry in his article in *Silliman's Journal* (*19*:406):

In these experiments a fact was observed, which appears somewhat surprizing, when a large battery was attached and the armature touching both poles of the magnet, it was capable of supporting more than 700 lbs.

but when only one pole is in contact it did not support more than 5 or 6 lbs., and in this case we never succeeded in making it lift the armature (weighing 7 lbs.). This fact may perhaps be common to all large magnets, but we have never seen the circumstance noticed of so great a difference between a single pole and both.

³ Of course, Benjamin Franklin Joslin, Professor of Mathematics and Natural Philosophy at Union. See Henry's letter to Stephen Alexander, January 8, 1830, especially footnote 2, for more about Joslin.

⁴ Jackson's reaction to Henry's problem is interesting, as it shows that he anticipated a simple mathematical proportion between the lifting powers of single and double poles. Revealing at that time the lack of theoretical understanding, the problem since then has required a far more sophisticated treatment. It is interesting also that Jackson, like Joslin perhaps, and like many scientists at the time,

have the whole matter disentangled. Till then I'll say no more about a subject of which I know so little. If you can spare time, you will much oblige me by looking at page 15th art 25 of Farrars topography. It appears to me there is an error in his mode of projecting the perpendiculars to the ecliptic.[5] Pray look at it & write me by Averil.[6]

The formula not demonstrated I mentioned to you is on page 118 nt *177*

$$\sin\tfrac{1}{2}C' = \sqrt{\frac{\sin\tfrac{1}{2}(C + c - c') \cdot \sin\tfrac{1}{2}(C + c' - c)}{\cos c \cos c'}}$$

$$\text{putting } c - c' = \delta \qquad C - (c - c')$$

$$= \sqrt{\frac{\sin\tfrac{1}{2}(C + \delta) \cdot \sin\tfrac{1}{2}(C - \delta)}{\cos c \cos c'}}$$

$$\& \sin(\tfrac{1}{2}C + \tfrac{1}{2}\delta) \cdot \sin(\tfrac{1}{2}C - \tfrac{1}{2}\delta) = (\sin\tfrac{1}{2}C \cos\tfrac{1}{2}\delta + \cos\tfrac{1}{2}C \sin\tfrac{1}{2}\delta)$$
$$\times (\sin\tfrac{1}{2}C \cos\tfrac{1}{2}\delta - \cos\tfrac{1}{2}C \sin\tfrac{1}{2}\delta)$$
$$= \sin\tfrac{1}{2}C^2 \cos\tfrac{1}{2}\delta^2 - \cos\tfrac{1}{2}C^2 \sin\tfrac{1}{2}\delta^2$$
$$= \sin\tfrac{1}{2}C^2 - \sin\tfrac{1}{2}\delta^2 \text{ Hassler Page 40}^{\text{th}}$$
$$\text{L N}^{\underline{o}} 1$$

$$\cos c \cos c' = \overline{\cos\tfrac{1}{2}(c + c')}^2 - \overline{\sin\tfrac{1}{2}(c - c')}^2$$

$$= \overline{\cos\tfrac{1}{2}(c + c')}^2 - \overline{\sin\tfrac{1}{2}\delta}^2 \text{ Hassler page 43 M 15}$$

---

assumed that the properties of the electro-magnet would be quite different from those of common magnets.

[5] Jackson is referring to John Farrar's *An Elementary Treatise on the Application of Trigonometry to Orthographic and Stereographic Projection . . .* ; first published in Cambridge, Massachusetts, in 1822, with subsequent editions in 1825, 1833, and 1840. We know that Henry must have been familiar with this work, as he mentioned using it for teaching in his report to the Albany Academy Trustees [ca. June or July 1829], printed above (see especially footnote 12). While we have no evidence of how Henry replied to Jackson's query, we do know that Farrar's fourth edition (1840) continued publication of the same misstatement which troubled Jackson about a decade earlier.

The problem which Jackson raised here is somewhat more simple than his solution implies. Where Farrar's note 177 says that ". . . the cosines of small angles vary very slowly

. . . ," the statement should have read ". . . the sines of small angles vary very slowly. . . ." Thus, Jackson is correct in saying that the reason assigned for the trigonometric step is not correct. While Jackson cited F. R. Hassler's *Elements of Analytic Trigonometry* (New York, 1826) in his demonstration, the trigonometry used here is standard, and he could have cited other contemporary works.

[6] Chester Averill (1804–1836), through the politeness of whom Jackson sent this letter to Henry, according to a note on the cover sheet. Born in Litchfield, Connecticut, Averill entered Union College in 1824. Upon graduating with a B.A. degree in 1828, he remained at Union as a tutor and instructor, becoming an adjunct professor of chemistry and ancient languages by July 1831. He also lectured in botany and mineralogy, being appointed full professor in 1832. See Thomas C. Reed, *A Discourse on the Character of the Late Chester Averill* (Schenectady, 1837), pp. 7–53.

$$\text{\& hence } \sin\tfrac{1}{2}C' = \sqrt{\frac{\overline{\sin\tfrac{1}{2}C}^2 - \overline{\sin\tfrac{1}{2}\delta}^2}{\cos\tfrac{1}{2}(c+c')^2 - \sin\tfrac{1}{2}\delta^2}} = \frac{\sin\tfrac{1}{2}C}{\cos\tfrac{1}{2}(c+c')} \quad\text{\textit{nearly}}$$

* omitting $\sin\tfrac{1}{2}\delta^2$

Read the 177th article—the reason assigned there is not the correct one.

Have the goodness to drop me a line by Averil respecting the projection of the Secondaries to the ecliptic, and another matter that you may think interesting. Respects to Mrs. Henry & Mrs Alexander & you both.

I W Jackson

I should have written to Mr Alexander before this, respecting *the Observatory*,[7] but have been waiting for Doctor Nott[8] [to] return from N.Y. with whom I asked to have some conversation on the subject. I shall be down Deo volente about New Years.

You <*may*> will not have time to write me by Averil. Write then as soon may be.

---

[7] It is possible that Stephen Alexander, recently returned to the Albany area after the closing of the Yates Polytechny in Chittenango, New York, was anxious to establish an observatory nearby, and that he had passed word of his interest, maybe through Henry, on to Jackson at Union. As the President of Union, Eliphalet Nott (see next footnote) had established a reputation for his program of scientific education, as well as for his fund raising and the resulting physical expansion of the College. Alexander may have optimistically viewed Union as a reasonable possibility for the erection of an observatory. We have found no evidence of a movement at Union for an observatory at this early date; however, throughout this period in the early nineteenth century many efforts were made at other locations to establish astronomical observatories, and nearly all failed. An account of the American Philosophical Society's abortive attempts can be found in Whitfield J. Bell, Jr., "Astronomical Observatories of the American Philosophical Society, 1769–1843," *Proceedings of the American Philosophical Society*, 1964, *108*:7–14; for a broader view of the observatory enthusiasm, see David F. Musto, "A Survey of the American Observatory Movement, 1800–1850," *Vistas in Astronomy*, 1968, *9*:87–92.

[8] Eliphalet Nott (1773–1866), a Presbyterian clergyman, educator, inventor, and college president. While pastor of the First Presbyterian Church in Albany from 1798 to 1804, he won repute as one of America's greatest orators. Nott also participated in the movement which culminated in the founding of the Albany Academy in 1813. From 1804 until 1866 Nott served as President of Union College in Schenectady, distinguishing himself as a fund raiser and builder of the physical campus, as well as the initiator of a scientific course of study as alternative to the classical curriculum. See *DAB*.

TO BENJAMIN SILLIMAN, SR.

*Daniel C. Gilman Collection, Library, Johns Hopkins University
and Benjamin Silliman Papers, Historical Society of Pennsylvania*[1]

Albany Tuesday Evening
Dec. [2]8th 1830[2]

Prof. Silliman
Dear Sir

I have just finished my paper & will send it by the next mail which closes at 8 o'clock tomorrow morning. I hope the delay has caused you no inconvenience. As it has been written in great haste please make any verbal alteration necessary or cause My friend Dr Tully[3] to do so. If there be anything improper in the concluding paragraph in relation to Prof. Molls paper let it be omitted.

If the paper be too late for insertion in the next No of the Journal I wish to publish it in the Transactions of the Albany Institute. The paper is somewhat longer than I supposed it would be before collecting the facts together. I have however left out every thing not directly applicable to the subject and have been as brief as possible. I should like much to have the sketch of the magnet inserted but if it be too late or there be little room I have no objections to having it omitted.

I am Sir Respectfully
Yours &c
Joseph Henry

P.S. Please correct in a note the mistakes made in a former No of the Journal[4] that I belonged to the Rensselaer school. I have always been associated with Dr T R Beck in the Albany Academy.

P.P.S.[5] If it would be any object to you I should like to superintend the

---

[1] While the first sheet of this letter is filed in the Gilman papers at Johns Hopkins, the second sheet, which begins with the "P.P.S.," was found in three pieces filed in a "Miscellaneous Papers" folder in Box 1 of the Silliman Papers at the Historical Society of Pennsylvania. For further discussion of the probable history of the second sheet, see below, footnotes 5 and 8.

[2] The original reads "Dec. 8th 1830," but it is clear from the context that this was a response, penned on Tuesday, December 28, to Silliman's letter to Henry of December 17, 1830, for which see above. It should be noted, too, that the cover sheet was postmarked "Dec 29."

[3] William Tully, M.D., for whom see above, Harriet Henry to Stephen Alexander, May 7, 1830, footnote 12.

[4] Henry is referring to *Silliman's Journal*, 1829, *16*:371, where in the "Intelligence and Miscellanies" it is stated, "10. Dr. Wollaston's scale of chemical equivalents.—We have already mentioned [*14*:202, 203 (1828)] that an improved edition of this very useful instrument has been published by Professors Beck and Henry of the Rensselaer school. . . ."

[5] Here begins the second sheet of the letter. From the abnormally poor spelling and the rough construction of his thoughts, we can almost feel Henry's drowsiness and his haste to write this P.P.S., make the sketch, seal the

construction[6] for your lecture room of a Galvanic magnet on my pla[n] which will support 1000 or 1200 lbs. The whole expense will be about 30 or 35 dollars. Please write me on this subject.[7]

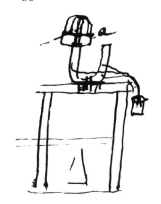

I should perhape have mentioned in my paper that[8] by inverting the <*large*> magnet it sets in motion a very large revolving cylender of March & Ampere.[9]

The cylender (a) is 6 inches in diam[eter] and supported on a piece of soft iron. The horse shoe is inverted by merely turning the top piece of the wooden frame. This interesting experiment is thus exhibited on a very large scale. It is scarcely worth while to insert this in the paper sinc several thin[g]s more interesting have been omitte[d].

Please excuse this scrawl as I am writing without a candle just after day-break.   J.H.

---

letter, and hurry to the post office by 8:00 A.M. The entire P.P.S. was undoubtedly written on that short winter morning.

[6] Henry first wrote, "I should like to construct for your lecture room," but corrected the statement before mailing the letter to say he would instead superintend the work.

[7] Indeed, Silliman did. See below, Silliman's reply to Henry, January 6, 1831. The magnet which Henry eventually constructed for Silliman is on exhibit at the National Museum of History and Technology, Washington, D.C.

[8] The peculiar history of this letter is probably explained by the fact that this sheet was cut into three pieces, this sentence constituting one of the fragments. Furthermore, the portion of this sentence which precedes this footnote was crossed out, and that portion beginning with "by" was printed verbatim at the bottom of Henry's article in *Silliman's Journal, 19*:408. Thus, it appears that Silliman separated this sheet from the first and probably filed the first, then cut out the statement from the "P.P.S." which he wished to print. The fragments of the second sheet were not reunited with the first sheet, which came to the Gilman papers at Johns Hopkins University, but were placed with that portion of the elder Silliman's papers now in the Historical Society of Penn-sylvania.

[9] The reference is to the revolving apparatus of James Marsh (1790–1846), an assistant of Peter Barlow's at Woolwich. Marsh published an account of an improved design of Ampère's rotating cylinder in the *Philosophical Magazine and Journal*, 1822, *59*:433–453. His improvement consisted in permitting both the inner and outer cylinders to rotate. Ampère's design (see *Annales de chimie et de physique*, 1821, *18*:331–333, and fig. 20) permitted rotation of only one element. While producing a more impressive demonstration, Marsh's design did not add anything to the scientific principles involved. Ampère had devised his apparatus in response to Faraday's demonstration of electromagnetic rotation (see L. P. Williams, *Michael Faraday* [New York, 1965], pp. 151–168). Of course, Henry here made no attempt to improve upon the qualities of the rotating apparatus, nor did he pretend that any new light would be shed upon the principles involved. Henry's purpose was to make the demonstration still more impressive through the use of his powerful electromagnet. Silliman was sufficiently enthusiastic about the possibilities of classroom demonstration to mention the subject in his response to Henry of January 6, 1831, printed below.

⊰{ 1831 }⊱

FROM BENJAMIN SILLIMAN, SR.
Henry Papers, Smithsonian Archives

New Haven Jan 6 1831

My dear Sir

Your paper is done (figure etc) & I hope you will find it correctly printed.

It is a highly important & interesting paper & will undoubtedly be printed in the foreign Journals & I shall be much gratified in quoting the results in my chemical book.[1] As I must finish the electro-magnetic notices next week if there is any thing you would wish to add it may be in time; especially I should like to know it if you should carry the lifting power higher even than you have done. I shall be much obliged by receiving such an apparatus as you are kind enough to offer to have constructed for me. In order to exhibit it to my classes before the breaking up of the Medical School the instrument must be here the last week in Feb[y] as the lectures end on the 26th of that month & I should have opportunity to become a little familiar with it by experience begun a few days earlier. I should like to have it fitted so as to shift for the revolving apparatus on the top & if any other apparatus admits of convenient adaptation to it for the purpose of exhibiting electrical & magnetic currents & revolutions[2] I should like it & will cheerfully pay any additional expense. As my time of preparation with it must of course be short, I will thank you to send me a memorandum of directions for the experiments to enact that I may lose no time in groping.

Would it not form an interesting addition as regards the impression to be made on a class if an armature were provided admitting of a hook from  a rope passing round a pulley wheel & then let 2–3–4.–5 *etc* persons pull—adding to the number till it should become affectual: a *shifting* beam might be adjusted—provided its permanent fixtures would [not] interfere with the scale for the weights. The frame would be easily fixed to the *floor by hooks.*

I shall have 50 copies of your memoir done up for you to distribute among your friends & I will direct that they go in M[r] Littles[3] bundle.

---

[1] Benjamin Silliman, Sr., *Elements of Chemistry*, 2 vols. (New Haven, 1831). The references to Henry's work are in 2:680–683.

[2] See the comment to which Silliman is responding in the "P.P.S." of Henry to Silliman, December 28, 1830, and footnote 8, printed above.

[3] Weare C. Little (?–1885), a bookseller, was

I found room only to crowd in two lines with respect to the revolving experiment[4] & shall be pleased to receive a notice of that or any facts for the April N^{o}.

I remain dear sir yours very truly & respectfully

B Silliman.

---

then a partner in the firm of Little and Cummings. Munsell, *Ann. Alb.*, 9:233, 234, 243. The firm came into existence in 1828. In addition to acting as Silliman's agent in Albany, Little was a successor of E. F. Backus in the publication and sale of law books. *Howell and*

Tenney, p. 702.
[4] A reference to the lines which Silliman excerpted from Henry's letter to him of December [2]8, 1830, and printed at the end of Henry's article, at the bottom of page 408. See that letter printed above, especially footnote 8.

TO BENJAMIN SILLIMAN, SR.

Daniel C. Gilman Collection, Library, Johns Hopkins University

Albany Jan 15th 1831

Dear Sir

Yours of the 6th inst[1] was received three days since. I am happy to learn that you think my paper an interesting one and shall consider myself honored by any quotation you may please to make from it in your book on Chemistry. I have no other results to communicate at present as I have not made any experiments on this subject since I sent the paper but from those before made I think it is certain that no greater result than that stated (750 lb) can be obtained by a piece of iron of the size used in these experiments or in other words the iron appears to be magnetized to perfect saturation.

I commenced to day with the construction of your large magnet by drawing the plan of the iron part & it is now in the hands of the forger. I found some difficulty in procuring in Albany a piece of iron of the size and some little delay will also be caused by having to send to New York for copper wire of the proper diameter since the navigation of the Hudson is interrupted by ice.

The whole apparatus can be finished by the first week of next month. I am some what at a loss to know how I shall forward it to New Haven at this season of the year but perhaps you can direct some method of conveyance or I may possibly find some person with whom I can send it. I will try the method you suggest with regard to exhibiting the power of the magnet by

[1] See above.

several men drawing at a rope. I would however propose a slight alteration in the method of applying the power which would consist in having a pul-ley fixed to the floor directly under the magnet and a second pulley to the ceiling of the room—a rope passing through these from armature would hang like a bell rope. Several men might hang their weight on this and the number be increased until the armature separated. By this arrangement each person could pull no more than his weight and as it would sustain 4 or 5 ordinary sized men the exhibition would be interesting. I usually show the power of the magnet by suspending from it by means of the scale beneath ten 60 lb weights which it readily sustains. On withdrawing the cup containing the diluted acid from the small battery the whole weight falls with a great noise.

The journal has not yet reached Albany. I have no fears with regard to the accuracy of the printing of the paper. Please accept my sincere thanks for the agreeable and unexpected favour of the 50 copies to distribute among my friends.

> I am Sir with much respect
> Your humbl serv.
> Joseph Henry

FROM NATHANIEL SCUDDER PRIME[1]
Henry Papers, Smithsonian Archives

Mount Pleasant[2] Jan. 22nd 1831

Dear Sir,

Having a private opportunity to Albany, I write to request the favour which I intimated when I had the pleasure of seeing you last.

I wish a set of magnets similar to those I saw you use.[3] If you can have

---

[1] Prime (1785–1856) was a Presbyterian clergyman and a Princeton graduate (1806). He is described as an advocate of temperance and moral reform. *Appleton's Cyclopedia of American Biography.*

[2] Westchester County, New York.

[3] We have no information on Prime's visit with Henry, or whether Prime saw Henry's demonstration before the Albany Institute.

a set prepared for me, my brother in law[4] who will hand you this, will pay you for them.

I am aware that this is putting you to great trouble, but I can procure none that please me so much as yours. If, however, it should ever be in my power, I shall always be ready to reciprocate the favour.

Yours respectfully
Nathl. S. Prime

P.S. If you can favour me with any new suggestions or experiments on Electro-magnetism,[5] it will add to other favours.

---

[4] Not identified.

[5] Prime does not figure further as a scientist in electromagnetism or any other branch of knowledge. Nor do we know if Henry provided magnets. Throughout his career Henry would receive analogous letters from non-scientists and young people. He could never tell if the interest expressed in science would develop into something serious. We suspect he tended to reply encouragingly to such letters as a way of stimulating research.

FROM BENJAMIN SILLIMAN, SR.
Henry Papers, Smithsonian Archives

New Haven January 25th 1831

Dear Sir

I thank you for your prompt attention to my magnet[1] & am pleased with your modification of the pulley & as it happens it will exactly suit the fixtures in my laboratory; it will admit also of the common square board or scale of the grocers upon which either weights or men can be placed.

As regards the sending, the river will doubtless remain closed & there is I suppose no other way than to have the frame & all packed (in pieces of course) in a strong box & let them come over land by Hartford or Litchfield; the latter will be the most driest & to prevent imposition I shall be obliged to you to have the fare settled (by weight if they prefer it) & marked in the box & I will pay it here and your own bill anywhere & in any way you may perfer with many thanks for your kindness.

As the river closed just as the Journal was going away I fear it has met with delay but have written to New York to have it expedited. When you write me again respecting the magnet be so good as to mention whether the

---

[1] Purchased by Silliman from Henry for Yale College. See Henry's letter of January 15, 1831, to Silliman, above, and footnote 6 in Isaac W. Jackson's letter of February 16, 1831, to Henry, below.

Journal & your extra copies have arrived.[2] I am not sure whether Dr Teneycks name should have been placed in the title;[3] if so pray apologize if it is an omission certainly not intended & perhaps an apology may be due to you for placing it with yours in the chemistry.[4] Had there been time I would gladly have sent you the abstract (brief of course) made of the most remarkable facts for the chemistry—but time did not admit of it. If agreeable to receive payment for your communication be so good as to note it in the bill for the magnet and excuse me if I am wrong in naming it; it is perhaps safer to err on that side than on the other.[5]

> I remain dear Sir
> with much respect
> your obt & oblg^d Servt
> B. Silliman

[2] Copies of Henry's article on the development of great magnetic power with a small galvanic element, published by Silliman in January 1831 (*19*:400–408).

[3] Dr. Philip Ten Eyck, who frequently collaborated with Henry, and whose name does not appear in the by-line of the above-mentioned article.

[4] See Silliman's *Elements of Chemistry*, 2 vols. (New Haven, 1831), *1*:680.

[5] Henry did not request payment for the article. See his comment at the close of the letter to Silliman of March 28, 1831, below.

TO JACOB GREEN[1]
Henry Papers,[2] Smithsonian Archives

Albany Feb. 3rd 1831

Dear Sir

I send by my brotherinlaw Mr Alexander some of the apparatus which I promised you last summer. I would have sent it soonner but could not for want of an oportunity. They consist of two magnets and an article to show

[1] Jacob Green (1790–1841), *DAB*. A chemist, Green graduated from Rutgers in 1812. He came to Albany soon afterward. The Albany City Directories list him as a bookseller (1815) and an attorney (1816). While there, Green actively participated in the Society for the Promotion of Useful Arts, one of the predecessors of the Albany Institute. In 1814 he was one of the Counsellors of the Society; in the same year Green was elected to the standing Chemical Committee of the Society. As he was no longer listed as a Counsellor in 1817, we assume he left Albany around that date.

From 1818 to 1822 Jacob Green was Professor of Experimental Philosophy, Chemistry, and Natural Philosophy at the College of New Jersey (Princeton) where his father, Ashbel Green, was then President.

In 1825 he joined the faculty of Jefferson Medical College in Philadelphia as Professor of Chemistry. Yale gave Green an honorary M.D. in 1827.

Green was a friend of T. R. Beck's from the Albany days and undoubtedly had other friends in common with Joseph Henry. Green continued his contacts with his Albany friends

the deflection of the needle. The horse shoe is one I constructed some time since and which in some degree illustrates my method of making strong electro-magnets with small galvanic plates; it is not however on the most improved plan as you will see by comparing it with my paper on electro magnetism appended to the last No of Sillimans Journal. You may perhaps consider it somewhat powerful as I have succeeded in making it sustain a weight of 40 lbs with the galvanic coil at present attached to it. This was

however under the most favourable circumstances. You will find no difficulty in making it lift 25 or thirty lbs. It will be necessary for you to procure a piece of soft iron ¾ of an inch or more in thickness for an armature or lifter ((a) see fig.). A loop of wire should be passed over it to which the weight is to be fastened. N B The armature must be filed perfectly flat so that the contact may be perfect.

Mr Alexander goes to the southern part of Delaware to observe the great eclipse of the 12th inst. He leaves Albany on rather a short notice & has not provided himself with a portable telescope. He expects to procure one in New York. If he does not may I request as a particular favour that you will indeavour to borrow one of small power for him in your city. I will be responsible for any damage it may sustain. I hope however that he will obtain one in N Y and not be obliged to trouble you.

and published in the *Transactions* of the Albany Institute. In addition to his chemical research, Green published papers in botany. He also published two early American works on subjects related to Henry's principal intellectual interests, both surviving in Henry's Library. With Ebenezer Hazzard, Green wrote in 1809 *An Epitome of Electricity and Galvanism.* The copy in the library was presented by Green in 1826 or later as the inscription is to "Prof J. Henry." More likely as an influence on Joseph Henry is Jacob Green's *Electro-Magnetism, Being an Arrangement of the Principal Facts hitherto Discovered in that Science* (Philadelphia, 1827). Two copies are in the library, Henry's and Torrey's, neither bearing annotations. Green's book is a clear, readable account and fairly up to date. By 1827, Henry's reading probably encompassed all the facts, and more, in the volume. Nevertheless, as a handy summarization, it was undoubtedly read and consulted.

Green played a significant role in Henry's transfer to Princeton (see John Maclean to Henry, July 10, 1832, below). As letters in subsequent volumes will show, Jacob Green was regarded by Henry as a friend whose opinions mattered.

Transactions, Society for the Promotion of Useful Arts, vols. 3 and 4, *passim; Princeton Catalogue,* p. 29; and E. F. Smith, *Jacob Green, 1790–1841, Chemist* (Philadelphia, 1923).

[2] This is the original letter addressed to Green and carried by Stephen Alexander but never delivered personally. On the obverse of the second page is Alexander's note:

Mr. A. regrets that he was unable to find Prof. Green at the place indicated by the directory; he has, in consequence, left the apparatus at Carey & Hart's bookstore. Mr. Henry mentioned that the stand of the horseshoe magnet was not sufficiently elevated for the introduction of the max. weight which the magnet would sustain.

From file markings, Green apparently did receive this letter with the apparatus. The presence of the document in Henry's papers may have resulted from Mary Henry's collecting activities.

You have seen my paper in Silliman. I am now constructing a magnet on the same plan which will lift 1000 lbs or more, if there be no fallacy in my former experiments. If you will pay the cost of materials & the Black-smith work I will construct a magnet for you which will lift (with a coil of zinc & copper of the size attached to the magnet I now send) 2 or 3 hundred lbs. There are several other articles which I can not construct at present but which you may have made in Philadelphia. Among these are the following

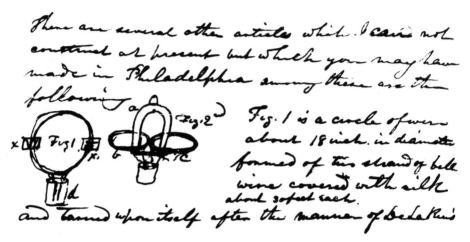

Fig. 1 is a circle of wire about 18 inch. in diameter formed of two strand of bell wire covered with silk about 30 feet each and turned upon itself after the manner of De La Rive's ring.[3] This apparatus is suspended by a fiber of silk with the plates of zinc & copper in a cup of acid. It after a few oscillations settles in [pos]ition at right angles to the magnetic meridian. (a) Fig 2nd is a piece of soft iron bent into the form of a horseshoe; (b) and (c) are two coils of wire about 5 or six inches in diameter with the ends soldered to the zinc & copper of a small coil.

When the coil is placed in acid & the ends of the horse shoe, dipped into the rings (or coils) of wire it instantly becomes a strong magnet although the galvanic currents are several inches distant.

---

[3] A. A. De La Rive (1801–1873), a Swiss physicist, was a friend of Faraday and, later, of Joseph Henry. He was Professor of Physics at the Geneva Academy. The reference is to "Notice sur quelques expériences électromagnétiques," *Bibliothèque universelle* (*Science et arts*), 1821, *16*:201–203. A silk covered copper wire is coiled to form a small ring and the ends of the wire are joined to small plates of copper and zinc protruding through both ends of a cork. When placed in dilute acid, the ring becomes magnetic or, as Faraday put it, "presents all the phenomena of a mobile conducting wire." (*Quarterly Journal of Science*, 1822, *12*:185.) Note that while De La Rive coiled a single wire, Henry, perhaps hoping to achieve larger electromagnetic effects, used *two* wires connected in parallel. Parallel wiring was also a distinguishing feature of his large electromagnets.

Mr A. will give you any information you may wish on this subject.
N.B. Do not forget the *quid pro quo* but send me the book you promised.[4]

With much Respect Yours
Joseph Henry

[4] Which book was promised is unknown to us.

TO CHARLES DAVIES
Retained Copy, Henry Papers, Smithsonian Archives

Albany Febry. 15th 1831

Dear Sir

I can scarcly hope that you will pardon me for not answering you letter[1] before this time. It was received 10 days after its date but my time since has been unusually occupied; bisides the ordinary duties of the Academy, which require about 7 hours daily, Dr Beck & myself are giving a course of Lectures on Chemistry and Physics. I have also been engaged in a series of experiments on electro-magnetism. These persuits have so completely occupied my time, during the last two months, that the present is almost the first leisure moment I could command.

In answer to your queries respecting arithmetic, I would say that the one I would prefer should be partly synthetical.[2] The rules and the most important principles should be printed in italics, after the manner of the texts of Euclid. The demonstrations of these rules and principles should be given afterwards in common type. My reason for this arrangement is that arithmetic is taught in the Academy to boys from 6 to 12 years of age.[3] It is first principally taught as an art, the pupil is required to commit to memory all the rules and is drilled upon the practice of them until he is quite expert. As he becomes more advanced in years the *rationality* of the rules are more dwelt upon. Our first object in teaching arithmetic is to make the pupil an expert accountant and afterwards gradually to induct him into a knowledge of its Philosophical principles. According to a new arrangement in the Academy, the boys are drilled in the first four simple and com-

---

[1] Not found.

[2] Henry expressed a like preference in the discussion of F. R. Hassler's works; see his report to the Academy Trustees, November 12, 1830, printed above. Davies, no doubt, took Henry's recommendation seriously, for his first book on arithmetic was organized as Henry

outlined: *Mental and Practical Arithmetic* (Hartford, 1838).

[3] For Henry's description of the teaching of mathematics at the Albany Academy, see his report to the Academy Trustees, [ca. June or July 1829], printed above.

pound rules <*of arithmetic*> before they enter my department and until this time they require no arithmetic except for learning the tables. The only arithmetic which is in common use in the academy at present is Dayboll's[4] and this is only used as a book of examples as indeed it is good for nothing else. I <*am in the habit of writing*> write at each recitation the rule on the blackboard and at the same time explain its principles. The class has then given it a page of examples from Dayboll, which each member is required to work out before the next recitation.

I prefer Hasler's Arithmetic or one on his plan to any I have seen. It has been adopted as one of the books to be used in the Academy but I only put it into the hands of some larger boys or young men who enter the academy for a short time to qualify themselves for teaching a country school. I can do nothing with it when given to boys 10 or 11 years old. It would be an excellent book for us were there an appendix or companion prepared to it consisting of only the parts that are printed in italics and the remaining part filled with practical examples. We could then use the book of examples for the younger boys, making them commit the rules and when they were a little more advanced give them the book of principles. I do not expect that you will entirely agree with me in opinion as to our plan of teaching arithmetic. You will probably think it too mechanical but you must recollect that we have to deal with children and not young men in this study and also that arithmetic is both an art and a science. The principles of a rule may be partly explained or demonstrated by a boy who cannot work a problem by it of any considerable length with eather correctness or expidition. If you do not think I have treated you too ungentlemanly by delaying my answer so long pleas write me again on this subject. N.B: I made an observation on the eclipse.[5] The day was cloudy but a break enabled me to obtain a good observation of the begining and the time was noted by an excellent clock with a mercurial pendulum. I am now making a series of observations to establish the true time and the rate of the clock.

Accompaning this letter I send you a copy of my paper on Electro-Magnetism. Prof. Silliman was so good as to send me fifty copies for distribution among my friends. I am at present engaged in some experiments on the same subject but shall not be able to do much with them until after we have finished our course of Lectures.

If you think any suggestions from me would be of any use I will cheer-

---

[4] Nathan Daboll, *Daboll's Schoolmaster's Assistant, Improved and Enlarged: Being a Plain Practical System of Arithmetic, Adapted to the United States* (Albany, 1821). See Henry's report to the Trustees of November 12, 1830, especially footnote 10.

[5] Henry communicated his observations on the solar eclipse of February 12, 1831, to the editors of the *Albany Argus*. They appeared in the issue of February 15, 1831, p. 3, col. 2.

fully give them. I cannot however give *you* any thing on the principles of the science but I may have derived some knowledge from the practice of teaching which may not be intirely useless in a practical point of view. I intend visiting the Point early in the Spring in order to inspect your new articles of apparatus and if possible to make a few observations on magnetism.

I am Sir with much Respect & Esteem Yours &c
Joseph Henry

FROM ISAAC W. JACKSON[1]
Mary Henry Copy, Henry Papers, Smithsonian Archives

Schenectady Feb. 16, [1831][2]

Your paper was a glowing prize for Mr. Silliman.[3] It is worth all the attempts at original experimental investigation that have ever been recorded in his journal. It will undoubtedly attract that attention abroad which it so richly merits.[4]

I presume you are very busy now. Have you completed the apparatus of Silliman[5] and what are its effects?[6] On what have you been lecturing and to how large audiences?[7] With what success I need not ask. I should like to hear particulars.

I wish you resided some fifteen miles nearer to us—par example—in one of the wings of the new college. The railroad will approximate us tho. The old colleges have been clothed in a new dress and look smiling as a young bridegroom coming forth his chamber.

I will want you sometime to have made for me a set of electro-magnetic

[1] This letter is obviously incomplete. Above the date is a badly garbled note that says: "We may add if only to introduce a very close and dear friend of Henry, an enthusiastic scrap from a letter from Prof. Jackson of Union College, Schenectady." For I. W. Jackson, see Henry's letter of December 5, 1829, to Stephen Alexander, footnote 9.

[2] In view of Jackson's reference to Henry's paper, below, which he describes as a "glowing prize for Mr. Silliman," the date must be 1831 as Henry's article on the development of great magnetic power with a small galvanic element was published by Silliman in January of that year. See the next footnote.

[3] Joseph Henry, "On the Application of the Principle of the Galvanic Multiplier to Electro-Magnetic Apparatus, and Also to the Development of Great Magnetic Power in Soft Iron, with a Small Galvanic Element," *Silliman's Journal*, 1831, *19*:400–408.

[4] The copy indicates a gap here.

[5] The magnet Benjamin Silliman purchased from Henry for Yale College.

[6] See Joseph Henry and [Philip] Ten Eyck, "An Account of a Large Electro-Magnet, Made for the Laboratory of Yale College," *Silliman's Journal*, 1831, *20*:201–203.

[7] This probably refers to the lecture series on chemistry given by T. R. Beck and Henry during the winter of 1830–1831.

apparatus. It is a subject that never took much with me but I must have a little electricity and magnetism in my head. This however at your leisure and after your present investigations shall have extended the bounderies of the science.

I hope Alexander has had a fine day for the eclipse. Have you heard from him?[8]

---

[8] On September 21, 1830, Stephen Alexander had read a paper before the Albany Institute entitled "Elements of the Solar Eclipse of February 12th, 1831: Together with a particular Calculation for the Latitude and Longitude of Albany," *Transactions*, 1830, *1*:243–250, in which he used known solar and lunar tables to predict the "particular Eclipse for Albany" and eventually compute the latitude and longitude of the city. Sometime before Jackson wrote this letter, Alexander went to Berlin, Maryland, to observe the eclipse. In August 1833 he presented his findings to the Institute in a paper called "Astronomical Observations Made at Berlin, Worcester County, Md. (February, 1831), with Some of Their Results," *Transactions*, 1852, *2*:84–96.

EXCERPT,[1] MINUTES, ACADEMY TRUSTEES
Trustees' Minutes, 2:4–6, Albany Academy Archives

Albany. Feb[y] [19] 1831

The Committee to whom was referred the subject of a Communication from William Caldwell[2] Esq[r] of this city, announcing to the Board, through one of its members, that he had deposited with its Treasurer, the sum of one hundred dollars as a donation to the Academy, upon the condition that the interest thereof "be annually bestowed as a premium on the best scholar in Mathematics & Natural Philosophy in the Academy, such scholar to be of at least four years standing & such premium to consist of a book or books, or of a gold or silver medal."

Report

That this handsome donation ought in their opinion to be accepted and gratefully acknowledged by this board. The Committee cannot doubt but that it will add new impulse to honorable ambition and promote a spirit of generous rivalry among the students in the pursuit of the noble and useful studies which it is especially designed to encourage.

The Committee recommended that the money be invested in the stock of one of the Banks of this city.

---

[1] The bulk of these minutes consists of a report of the accounts of the Academy, 1829–1830, and a report on several elementary texts.

[2] William Caldwell (1776–1848), who previously made a $200 contribution to the Albany Institute. See above, Excerpt of the Minutes of the Albany Institute, April 8, 1830, especially footnote 3.

The donor, having under the limitations above mentioned, submitted it to the Board to determine, of what the premium shall consist, the Committee have deemed it their duty to direct their attention to this point and are unanimously of opinion that it should be a medal of gold.

The Committee are further of opinion that the premium ought to be denominated the *Caldwell Premium* in honour of the liberal donor, And in order to carry into effect the foregoing suggestions, should the Board concur with them in opinion, the Committee submit the following resolutions.

Resolved that the donation of one hundred dollars presented to the Academy by William Caldwell Esqʳ of this city be accepted by this Board upon the conditions prescribed by him.

Resolved that the Trustees entertain a high sense of the liberal and enlightened spirit so honorably and judiciously displayed by the donor upon this occasion and that he is eminently entitled to the thanks of the Board.

Resolved that the money be invested by the Treasurer of the Board in the stock of one of the banks of this city, as soon as an opportunity for such investment upon reasonable terms shall be presented.

Resolved that in additions to the premiums already provided for by the existing Statutes of the Academy, there shall be a premium to be denominated the *Caldwell Premium,* consisting of a gold medal of not less than five, nor more than seven dollars in value, bearing the inscription "*Caldwell Premium*" and such other appropriate devices and inscriptions as shall thereafter be prescribed by the Board, which shall be awarded annually on the day of public speaking, to the best scholar in Mathematics & Natural Philosophy in the Academy, of at least four years' standing.

Resolved that the Senior Trustee be requested to communicate a copy of the foregoing resolutions to Mʳ Caldwell.

> A. Conkling
> John Ludlow } Committee
> Philip S. Parker

Whereupon

Resolved unanimously that the above report be accepted and the resolutions contained in it adopted.

March 12, 1831

FROM BENJAMIN SILLIMAN, SR.[1]
Henry Papers, Smithsonian Archives

New Haven Mar. 12 1831

Dear Sir

I write to know whether you have any thing for the ensuing N° of the Journal on galvano-magnetism; if you have made any advances you should not withold them (in justice to yourself) as there will be other laborers in the same field. I have some short notices on the subject from D^r J W Webster[2] & from Dr Hare[3] which will appear in April. If you have any thing I should like to receive it as soon as may be.

As the river is now open I trust that our machine can come around by water & I observe that one of our New Haven sloops advertises to visit Albany soon; perhaps it may come by her but I would not wish you to hurry the affair as our medical school is now broken up but I shall have much pleasure in showing your results to the college classes. [I] remain dear Sir

yours very truly

B Silliman

I hope the pamphlets came safely to you & that the short abstract of your memoir in the 2^d Vol of the Chemistry is correct.

---

[1] For Henry's response, see below, March 28, 1831. This exchange is also printed in Nathan Reingold, ed., *Science in Nineteenth-Century America* (New York, 1964), pp. 65–68.

[2] John White Webster (1793–1850), physician and chemist, achieved notoriety through a bizarre homicide. Webster earned his B.A. from Harvard in 1811 and his M.D. there in 1815. From 1824 until 1849 he taught chemistry at Harvard, which career was terminated when he was accused of a macabre murder of a creditor. He was convicted upon largely circumstantial evidence and hanged for the crime. While such an ending might have appeared to be a blatant setback for science at mid-century, Webster had not distinguished himself as a first-rate chemist or teacher and, despite a reasonably prolific early career, he had published only one paper and no books since 1841. Publish or perish, however, was not involved in the execution. See *DAB* and the Royal Society *Catalogue*.

Webster's reactions to Henry's article appear in *Silliman's Journal*, 1831, 20:143–144. Webster repeated Henry's experiments and marveled at their applicability to the "mechanic arts." He also suggested that there would be a greater economy in using sealing wax instead of silk in constructing the electromagnet, and he later reported to Silliman, in time for inclusion in this number, that he was able to suspend 112 pounds some twenty-one hours after the plates were removed from the solution and dried. Of course, Webster did not communicate his findings to Henry personally but chose rather to report his findings to *Silliman's Journal*, which was acting as a center for such exchanges.

[3] Dr. Robert Hare (1781–1858), American chemist who was at this time, and for most of his career, at the University of Pennsylvania. For more about Hare and his relationship with Henry, see below, Silliman to Hare, October 11, 1832, especially footnote 1.

Not yet a personal acquaintance of Henry but a close friend of Silliman, Hare apparently wrote to the latter on three occasions between February 24 and March 17, 1831, relating his attempts to build upon Henry's experiments. Hare had constructed "an apparatus, upon a small scale, in imitation of that of Prof. Henry," and he reported to Silliman the ways in which he varied the construction and the effects of these changes. See *Silliman's Journal*, 20:144–146, for Hare's findings. The significance of *Silliman's Journal* as the center for scientific exchange and communication in America is again shown.

TO BENJAMIN SILLIMAN, SR.[1]
Retained Copy, Henry Papers, Smithsonian Archives

Albany March 28th 1831

Dear Sir

I take the opportunity of my friend Dr Powers[2] going to New Haven to send the long promised magnet. I found it impossible with my other engagements to have it finished before the close of your medical term and therefore concluded to wait until the river opened. Dr Powers has seen our[3] method of operating with it and has been so obliging as not only to take charge of its conveyance but has also promised to attend the fitting of it up at New Haven.

The frame we have used in our experiments is too small, we have therefore concluded not to send it. Dr P. however can have one constructed to suit your Lecture room for but little more expense than the transportation of one from here would ammount to be the steam boat.

We have also sent but one battery[4] as the other used in our experiments (see paper)[5] belonged to the academy. We have no time before Dr P's departure to have another constructed.

---

[1] This is Henry's reply to Silliman's letter of March 12, 1831, above. Both letters are printed in Nathan Reingold, ed., *Science in Nineteenth-Century America* (New York, 1964), pp. 65–68.

[2] Titus William Powers (?–1863). Having attended the Albany Academy from 1817 until 1819, Powers entered the College of Physicians and Surgeons in New York City in 1825. He earned his M.D. degree in 1831 from Yale, where he was a student of William Tully, another of Henry's friends. A resident member of the Second Department of the Albany Institute in 1830, Powers was made a fellow of the College of Physicians and Surgeons in 1833. A resident of New York City from 1831 until 1847, according to the city directories, he was a practicing M.D. except in the years 1839–1844, when he was listed as a commission merchant. He died, unmarried, in Savannah, Georgia, in 1863. See Henry Hun, "A Survey of the Activity of the Albany Academy" (unpublished manuscript, 1922–1935, Manuscript Division, New York State Library and Albany Academy Archives); *Columbia Alumni*, p. 79; *Catalogue of the Officers and Graduates of Yale University in New Haven, Connecticut, 1701–1904* (New Haven, 1905), p. 206; *Catalogue of the Officers and Students in Yale College, 1830–31* (New Haven, 1830), p. 9; New York City Directories, 1831–1847; *Transactions*, Albany Institute, 1830, *1*, part 2: Appendix, p. 74. Powers remains obscure. In New York he maintained his friendship with Henry, and his letters to Henry will appear in subsequent volumes of the Henry Papers. He does not appear to have played an active role in any of the New York scientific institutions, nor, apparently, did he publish anything on science or other subjects in the more prominent journals.

[3] Henry includes, of course, Philip Ten Eyck in the use of "our" and, later, "we."

[4] Henry and Ten Eyck were sending a cylindrical battery which they found to be the best source of power for the electromagnet. While several other types were used in the experiments, it is reasonable to assume that Henry and Ten Eyck would send the type of battery best suited for their demonstrations. Of course, they would have preferred to send two cylindrical batteries so that the demonstration of the reversing of polarity could have been performed with the apparatus as sent, but circumstances did not permit. See the article cited in the next footnote.

[5] Henry is here referring to the paper which originally accompanied this letter and which

The power of the magnet may be shown to a class in the manner you proposed with a rope and a pulley.[6] We have however exhibited it by piling on the scale beneath the magnet about ¾ (say 1500 lbs) of the maximum weight which it will support. After showing that the magnet fairly sustains this, by slowly withdrawing the acid from the battery we suffer the whole to fall about 5 or 6 inchches. This never fails to produce a great sensation among the audience as before the fall they can scarcely believe that the magnet supports the weight. We send one large revolver;[7] the experiment would be more striking if two were used as they would turn in different directions.

The sec^d vol. of Your Chemistry was received only about 6 or 7 days ago. I am much gratified with the analysis of my paper and am pleased that you have mentioned Dr Ten Eycks name as you have done.[8] In justice to myself however I must add that it is the opinion of those of my friends who are acquainted with the whole affair that my name alone should stand on the title of the paper. The communication was drawn up by myself and all the experiments detailed in it except those credited to Dr. Ten Eyck were devised solely by me. To Dr Ten Eyck belongs the merit of arranging the mechanical part of the apparatus.

The large magnet described in the last paper[9] was constructed entirely by my own hands except forging the iron. The plan of the frame was made by Dr Ten Eyck and also the drawing made by him. The experiments with it were performed by both. In regard to the magnet we send to you, the plan was drawn by myself and the forging done under my direction. The winding with wire was done by Dr Ten Eyck. We mutually experimented with it. I have been thus explicit that you may understand what share each has had in the affair and also to answer a passage in one of your letters.[10] *<In the accompanying account of the magnet>* I wish you would publish the account of the present magnet as an extract of a letter to you (if you

---

is printed in *Silliman's Journal*, 20:201–203, "An Account of a Large Electro-Magnet, Made for the Laboratory of Yale College."

[6] See above, Silliman to Henry, January 6, 1831, where Silliman suggested this manner of demonstration.

[7] Referring to the revolving apparatus of Marsh and Ampère. See above, Henry to Silliman, December 28, 1830, the "P.P.S." section and footnote 9.

[8] Henry is citing Silliman's *Elements of Chemistry*, 2 vols. (New Haven, 1831); in the second volume Henry's experiments are dis-

cussed on pp. 680–683.

[9] Of course, Henry's paper in *Silliman's Journal*, *19*:400–408, which he transmitted to Silliman along with his letter of December 28, 1830, printed above.

[10] The question of proper credit for the work in which Henry and Ten Eyck collaborated was raised first in Silliman's letter to Henry of January 25, 1831, printed above. Silliman subsequently attempted to clarify the problem in an editor's note on the first page of the paper, where he paraphrased Henry's message. *Silliman's Journal*, 20:201.

consider this mode not improper).[11] I was much gratified with your kindness in sending me fifty copies of the paper and consider myself much more than *paid for my communication*[12] by this and other instances you have shown me of good feeling.

Did my pecuniary circumstances permit I would gladly send you the magnet free of expense but this I cannot well afford. My experiments have already cost me considerable. The several items of expense without counting my own labour (which of course is sufficiently paid by the honour of constructing it) will ammount to 35 Dollars. This may if you please be transmited to me by Dr Powers and if you wish I will send a bill of particulars. The paper is perhapse too late for the journal you will perhapse give it a place in the apendix and may find leisure to make a few experiments with it yourself before the publication of the next number.

I am Sir with much respect

Yours Jos Henry

I[13] commenced last fall a series of observations on the intensity of magnetism at Albany and used the needles furnished to Prof. Renwick by Cap. Sabine. I have since had a number of similar needles constructed and shall resume the obs. next month. The results I should be pleased to communicate to the Journal with the consent of Prof. Renwick.

[11] Apparently Silliman had no objection, for the account was published as if it were an extract.

[12] Henry is undoubtedly referring to Silliman's comment in his letter of January 25, 1831 (printed above), "If agreeable to receive payment for your communication be so good as to note it in the bill for the magnet. . . ."

[13] Silliman revised Henry's words in this postscript and printed the edited version as a "P.S." to the letter, the supposed extract of which was the paper describing the Yale magnet. See *Silliman's Journal, 20:203.*

FROM BENJAMIN SILLIMAN, SR.
Henry Papers, Smithsonian Archives

New Haven April 5, 1831

Dear Sir

I have to regret that I was out of town while Dr Powers was here but on my return I found that everything had been judiciously arranged by him & Mr Shepard[1] & I have had the pleasure of witnessing some of the effects, al-

[1] Charles U. Shepard (1804–1888), *DAB.* Shepard was a mineralogist who was serving as Lecturer in Botany at Yale at this time. He attended Brown and Amherst. In 1833 he became Lecturer in Natural History at Yale and from 1834 to 1869 (with the exception of

though not at the maximum, which no doubt we can attain as soon as we have the requisite leisure. I am greatly gratified & obliged & feel that you are entitled to much more than reinbursement of expenses. As however you decline compensation permit me to add the trifling acknowledgement of $5 in addition to the 35$ & to request that you will if you choose, regard it as a trifling aid towards your future experiments. If contributions from the friends of Science to enable you to go on in a field, in which I think you should, if possible, anticipate competition & rivalry, are desirable, I will, with pleasure, contribute & will if possible invite others to do the same.[2] At your leisure I will thank you to inform me of the safe arrival of the money. The items of the bill are of no consequence except for information to others; it might be well, if convenient, therefore, to mention the cost of the iron, the forging, & the wire & its envelope, but I would [not] have you take any trouble about it & a more general statement is sufficient without being very precise. Be so good as give my particular thanks to Dʳ Powers & to say to him that I am very much obliged by his kind & useful attentions & will cheerfully contribute towards the expense of his journey if he will inform me what I ought to pay.

I was so fortunate as to get your notice inserted as an appendix,[3] although the Journal was printed & I have directed the printer to send you 50 copies by mail & I should be willing that your particular friends should have them before the Journal arrives. I hope I have not done wrong in inserting in a note your claims & those of Dʳ Ten Eyck; it is but justice to you both.[4]

I shall be happy to hear from you always & particularly in relation to magnetism & your proposed observations, about the publication of which you will observe I have not committed you. I am gratified that the abstract in the chemistry pleased you; I only regret that your late results could not have been inserted. I remain dear Sir your very satisfied and obt servant

B. Silliman

---

the Civil War years) Shepard concurrently taught chemistry at the South Carolina Medical College. In 1847 (after a few years of lecturing there) he moved to Amherst. He was a notable mineralogical collector.

[2] Henry's reply does not survive. There is no evidence indicating that Henry agreed and that Silliman raised a fund to support Henry's electromagnetic researches.

[3] Joseph Henry and Dr. [P.] Ten Eyck, "An Account of a Large Electro-Magnet, Made for the Laboratory of Yale College," 1831, 20: 201–203. A separate account must have ac-companied the letter of March 28, 1831, above, to which Silliman added the note at the end of the letter when he printed the piece.

[4] As a note on page 201 of the above, Silliman inserted an account of the contributions of Henry and Ten Eyck to this magnet, taken, with little editing, from Henry's letter to him of March 28, 1831. Both Henry and Ten Eyck were apparently dissatisfied by Silliman's editorial actions. From the letter of Silliman to Henry, July 21, 1831, below, Ten Eyck was not mollified by the footnote. Nor was Henry.

$20 Enclosed 1 bill No 1161 B. U S. Phil. Decr 4—1828 Hartford Branch
$20 ——————————— 1288 ——————— Mar 31—1829 ———————
$40—in two bills as above

EXCERPT,[1] MINUTES, ALBANY INSTITUTE
Institute Minutes, Albany Institute Archives

April 11. 1831

L. C. Beck read a notice of the discovery & properties of Bromine, & exhibited several experiments with that substance.[2]

Mr Henry gave an account of a large magnet recently constructed for the laboratory of Yale College, with a detail of sundry experiments performed with the same.

Adjourned.

[1] Notes to the effect that minutes of the last meeting were read and approved, a list of donors since the previous meeting, and the names of two new members are here omitted.

[2] A new chemical for members of the Albany Institute, perhaps, but not for Beck and Henry. See Henry's letter of September 21, 1827, above.

DIRECTIONS FOR AN EXPERIMENT
WITH THE VIBRATING NEEDLE, APRIL 19th 1831[1]
Rhees Collection, Henry E. Huntington Library and Art Gallery

Directions

1. Note carefully the arc by placing the eye in such a position that the suspension fiber & the arc to be noted come in the same time. Observe

[1] The document was folded into a booklet. These directions, for measuring the earth's magnetic intensity with the Hansteen needle, appear on the left-hand pages. A series of intensity measurements taken in the Albany Academy Park are recorded on the facing pages. We are omitting these readings. The date we have given is actually written on the right, above the experimental data. It is possible, therefore, that Henry wrote the accompanying directions at another time.

We have compared this document with a number of contemporary articles and treatises on terrestrial magnetism, and, to our knowledge, the directions were composed by Henry. We know, however, that Henry read widely on this subject and, conceivably, he may have copied the directions from a source unknown to us. Among the works Henry read on terrestrial magnetism was his copy of John Farrar's *Elements of Electricity, Magnetism and Terrestrial Magnetism* (Cambridge, Massachusetts, 1826), consisting of selections from J.-B. Biot's *Précis élémentaire de physique*. The section

when the point of the needle swings no farther than this line. This will give the vib[rations] corresponding to the arc.[2]

2. If the case be of glass breathe on it before vibrating the needle to dispell any electricity the glass may have acquired by carrying.

3. Before commencing to count after carrying the instrument any distance suffer the apparatus to stand 15 or 20 minutes until it acquires the temperature of the air as it will have been heated by the body in carrying. This precaution is necessary as a few degrees in temperature varies the rate of the needle.

4. To set the needle in motion take a piece of soft iron about or nearly a foot long. Hold it in the position of the dip and then bring the lower end near the south pole of the needle. A bar of soft iron is better than a magnet

---

on terrestrial magnetism, including a discussion of the vibrating needle, is heavily annotated (pp. 210ff). In addition, one of Henry's early notebooks (Henry Papers Control No. 6123) contains his reading notes on magnetic intensity experiments and a list of references he consulted on the vibrating needle. Among the many references were articles by the leading theoreticians and experimentalists on terrestrial magnetism, such as Hansteen, Sabine, Arago, and Humboldt. While Henry read extensively on the theory of the earth's magnetic intensity (especially on the disturbing effect of the aurora borealis), he was also deeply concerned with experimental procedures. At the beginning of notebook 6123 (pp. 5–7), Henry copied "Directions for observing the Magnetic intensity with the horizontal needle," directions which differ from those given in this document. According to Henry, the passage, which is undated, was taken from "a paper from Capt. Sabine (probably) to Prof. Renwick." The paper, which we have been unable to identify, may not have been published (in any case, it is not the letter from Sabine to Renwick published in *Silliman's Journal*, 1830, 17:145–156). At another point in the notebook (pp. 105–110), Henry copies verbatim one of Hansteen's descriptions of an experiment with the vibrating needle, even copying down Hansteen's extensive tables of data. See "Account of the Recent Magnetical Discoveries of Professor Hansteen to M. Rumker, Director of the Nautical Academy of Hamburgh," *The Edinburgh Philosophical Journal*, 1821, 4:295–300.

Henry published the results of these and other observations in *Silliman's Journal*, 1832,

22:143–155, "On a Disturbance of the Earth's Magnetism, in Connexion with the Appearance of the Aurora Borealis, As Observed at Albany, April 19th, 1831." This document presents data taken at 12:52 P.M., before the auroral and magnetic disturbances began; not yet aware of the aurora, Henry was simply checking for daily variations in the magnetic intensity. (Henry's notebook also contains intensity readings for September and October 1830, which Henry alludes to in his article.) Henry's continuing interest in the aurora and its influence on terrestrial magnetism will be evident in a number of subsequent documents.

[2] For a general description of the apparatus, designed by Hansteen, see above, September 21, 1830, footnote 10. Henry's experimental procedures are outlined in his article, cited in footnote 1 above. Above his experimental data, Henry notes he is using Needle XI, one of the needles lent by Renwick. Following usual procedures, Henry set the needle vibrating, as in direction No. 4 below, and commenced his observations when the needle's oscillations diminished to thirty degrees of arc. He then measured the time required for 300 vibrations of the needle, taking readings after every tenth vibration. The intensity of the magnetic force was then determined in the same way that gravitational forces are calculated from the oscillations of a pendulum (i.e., the intensities are proportional to the square of the number of oscillations). See the theoretical discussion in P. M. Roget, *Treatises on Electricity, Galvanism, Magnetism, and Electro-Magnetism* (London, 1832), pp. 82ff.

and cannot alter the intensity of the needle. The bar should be about 10 or 12 inches long.

5. The thermometer if the case be not made of iron should be placed as near the apparatus as possible or at least in such a position that its temperature may be affected by the heat of the observer's body in the same degree as the needle[3] is.

---

[3] Henry recorded the temperature at the beginning and end of the experiment. In the article cited in footnote 1, Henry gives the formula, obtained by Hansteen, for adjusting the experimental results to standard temperature.

We have omitted an unrelated fragmentary note attached to this document.

FROM JAMES RENWICK, SR.
Henry Papers, Smithsonian Archives

Columbia College New York
23ᵈ April 1831

Dear Sir

My friend Dʳ W H Ellett,[1] whom I am happy to have an opportunity of introducing to your acquaintance will hand you this letter. He is about making a tour to the Westward and has undertaken to make some experiments on Magnetic Intensity.[2] I have therefore to request that you will deliver him the apparatus and the instructions for its use that accompany it. Should you have had any new needles made it will perhaps be well to let at least one of them accompany Dʳ Ellett.

I am Dear Sir
Yrˢ sincerely
Jaˢ Renwick

---

[1] William Henry Ellet (1806–1859) was a graduate of Columbia College (1824) who was a lecturer in chemistry there (1830–1832) at the time of this writing. From 1832 to 1835 he was Professor of Elementary Chemistry in his *alma mater*. Ellet held the chair of chemistry, mineralogy, and geology at South Carolina College, returning to New York in 1848. He won a prize for an essay on compounds of cyanogen as a student and while in the South developed a method of manufacturing guncotton. From 1854 to his death, Ellet acted as Consulting Chemist to the Manhattan Gas Co. *National Cyclopedia of American Biography, 11:*37.

[2] Apparently not published.

EXCERPT,[1] MINUTES, ALBANY INSTITUTE
Institute Minutes, Albany Institute Archives

Albany. April 25. 1831.

Mr Alexander read an account of the Annular eclipse of Feby 12th as observed at Berlin, Worcester County (Maryland) accompanied with drawings illustrative of the same.[2]

Mr Henry exhibited some experiments with a large electro-magnetic magnet & having the instantaneous reversion of the poles, by merely changing the direction of the galvanic current.

He also exhibited an Apparatus for determining the Magnetic Intensity of the Earth by means of the vibrations of a small needle, suspended by a silk fibre in a box with a glass cover. This apparatus was invented by Professor Hansteen of Norway & was sent by Capt. Sabine[3] to this country to be used in the contemplated Southern Expedition.[4] Accompanying the box are two needles, the one constructed by Professor Hansteen & the other by Capt. Sabine. From the mean of a great number of observations it is found that the rate of the Hansteen needle (or the time which it requires to make 300 Vibrations) is at Albany 978'.[5] At London the rate of the same needle is 956'. The rate of the Sabine needle at Albany is 830'; its rate at London is not known.

Mr H. mentioned that in the course of the observations with these needles, on two occasions the time of vibrations was strangely altered without an apparent cause. The first was observed at the time of the solar eclipse on the 12th of February. The Hansteen needle was then found to make 300 Vibrations in 130 Seconds of time less than its usual rate (of 978'). It is possible that this was caused by some accidental disturbing cause. None however is known to exist.

This circumstance is now stated in order that the fact may be recorded & that attention may be directed to it at the time of the next solar eclipse in 1832.[6]

The second was on the 19th of April, when an observation was made with

---

[1] We have omitted the first portion of these minutes dealing with routine matters and with a report by a committee gathering materials for a history of Albany.

[2] Stephen Alexander published his observations on the solar eclipse in "Astronomical Observations Made at Berlin, Worcester County, Md. (February, 1831), with Some of Their Results," *Transactions,* Albany Institute, 1833–1852, 2:84–96.

[3] The Sabine-Hansteen apparatus is described above, Minutes, Albany Institute, September 21, 1830, footnote 10.

[4] The 1829 exploration of the Antarctic under Captain Nathaniel B. Palmer. See above, Minutes, Albany Institute, May 5, 1824, footnote 16.

[5] i.e., seconds.

[6] In July 1832.

the same needle at 5 O Clock pm. The time of 300 Vibrations was found to be 10 seconds less than the usual rate. At about 9 pm. of the same evening, an auroral arch was seen in the south. A short time afterward the whole northern hemisphere was covered with beams of light, which crossed at the Zenith. As it was thought that this might have influenced the needle, a set of observations was made in the same place at 10 O Clock, while the aurora was most active. The time was then one second greater than the mean rate.[7]

Adjourned.

[7] Henry published his observations of the disturbances in "On a Disturbance of the Earth's Magnetism, in Connexion with the Appearance of an Aurora Borealis, as Observed at Albany, April 19th, 1831," *Silliman's Journal*, 1832, 22:143–155.

EXCERPT,[1] MINUTES, ACADEMY TRUSTEES
Trustees' Minutes, Albany Academy Archives

April 27. 1831

An Application was made in behalf of William Dunlap Esq[r2] for leave to exhibit his painting of the Attack on the Louvre in the Large Room of the Academy, which on motion was granted.

[1] We have omitted from the minutes a number of topics of a routine nature.

[2] William Dunlap (1766–1839), noted playwright, theatrical manager, painter, and historian. Having lost sight in his right eye as a child, Dunlap determined to pursue a career in art. While studying in London, Dunlap developed an interest in the theatre. He made several attempts at a career in the theatre upon his return to New York, but he was forced to resort to painting to maintain solvency. While he had been a member of the reactionary American Academy of the Fine Arts, he joined with a group of progressives in founding the rival National Academy of Design in 1826. *The Attack on the Louvre* was painted by Dunlap in the winter of 1830–1831, depicting vividly the revolutionary movement of the previous summer. Apparently the picture was shown at the National Academy of Design, and at that time (1831) Dunlap was made Vice President and Acting President of the Academy, which office he held until his death. Despite its popularity in New York, however, the painting was an absolute failure on the road. See *DAB* and Oral Summoner Coad, *William Dunlap, A Study of His Life and Works* (New York, 1962), especially p. 111.

Dunlap may have met Henry in connection with the exhibition of his painting at the Albany Academy, but we have no specific evidence of their contact at this time. There is evidence that a meeting did occur late in 1832. The noted educator James C. Welling (1825–1894; *DAB*), paying tribute to his personal friend Joseph Henry after the latter's death in 1878, relates a story of an encounter between Dunlap and Henry shortly before the call to Princeton, in which Dunlap cheered a dispirited Henry by saying: "Albany will one day be proud of her son." *A Memorial of Joseph Henry* (Washington, 1880), p. 184. Dunlap's diary entry for October 8, 1832, confirms a meeting with Henry, and although the diary does not contain Welling's phrase, it does note another prophetic evaluation of Henry: "His name will be enroll'd with those of Franklin, Silliman, Rittenhouse & other Americans who have transmitted light from the West to the East, and from the region to which light has

The Principal requested permission of the Board to resign the Lectureship on Chemistry to which he had been appointed in October 1818,[3] which on motion, was accepted.

On Motion

Resolved unanimously that D[r] Lewis C. Beck be & he is hereby appointed Lecturer on Chemistry under the regulations adopted for the same in December 1819.

---

been travelling for ages to that whence it emanated." William Dunlap, *Diary of William Dunlap*, ed. Dorothy C. Barck, *Collections of the New-York Historical Society*, 1931, *64*:620. Coulson uncritically relates both versions of the encounter, ignoring the apocry-

phal odor that attaches to both. *Coulson*, pp. 93–94.

[3] For notice of the establishment of the chemistry lectureship and of T. R. Beck's appointment to it, see the Trustees' Minutes of October 27, 1818, printed above.

FROM PENFIELD AND TAFT[1]

Henry Papers, Smithsonian Archives

Crownpoint 30th May 1831

M[r] Henry

Sir as we have no convenience for bending Large Irons we send the one Made for your Magnet in a Straight Draft, presuming they have better con-

---

[1] Allen Penfield (1785–1872) and Timothy Taft (1796–1877) were New Englanders who came to the Crown Point area around 1826. When iron ore was discovered, they established a forge in 1828. Taft sold his interest in 1834. We suspect that this letter and the one of June 27, 1831, below, were written by Penfield. With the opening of the Champlain Canal, the Penfield and Taft ore beds and other properties in the Lake Champlain region were developed and remained in production throughout much of the last century.

A serious problem facing iron mine owners was the separation of the iron from its ore. A Samuel Browning of Franconia, New Hampshire, had obtained two patents for "Magnetic Cylinders" (October 13, 1810, and November 25, 1814), devices for separating iron from crushed ore by means of magnets. Although the patents had expired (fourteen years being the term of patents then), a special act of Congress on March 3, 1831, revived Browning's 1814 patent for an additional fourteen years. Presumably, the interest

of the northern New York iron masters in magnetic ore separation was behind this action, but we have not located any records of Browning; the records of the House and Senate in the National Archives contain no further information beyond what is in print; and the destruction of the Patent Office records in the 1836 fire removed from our view assignment records which might have given enlightening financial and technical information.

A clue to the owner of the Browning patent is a small clipping from an undated, unnamed newspaper pasted on a page in a Henry notebook (No. 7169, p. 172). James Creighton Odiorne of Boston here announced his ownership of the patent, warns against infringers, and offers to supply magnetic separating machines. Odiorne (1802–1879) was a Yale graduate, 1826, with master's degrees from that institution and King's College, Nova Scotia, as well as an A.B. (ad eun.) from Harvard. In 1828 he became a partner with his father, George Odiorne, in an iron and

veniences at Mr Townsands Shop[2] & will do it better to your satisfaction. The Large Draft Weighs 112 ^lb the other 40 ^lb. We shall be at Albany in a few Days & will call on you & shall wish an Experiment tryed on a peace of Iron which we shall have. If the Large Draft is not sufficient deep to take of one end it can be Made perfectly Sound by taking a Heat & up setting it.

yours in haste
Penfield & Taft

---

nail business. An active Anti-Mason, Odiorne was a founder in 1832 of the New England Anti-Slavery Society, being elected Vice President. Having a "fondness for statistical and historical investigations," Odiorne was a member of both the American Statistical Association and the Boston Society of Natural History. James Creighton Odiorne, *Genealogy of the Odiorne Family: With Notices of Other Families Connected Therewith* (Boston, 1875), pp. 75–77, 115–117.

Henry's involvement was, for him, technologically simple. A large number of magnets were variously mounted on the cylinders. Prior to his involvement, the magnets were recharged by being stroked against a more powerful magnet. Penfield and Taft wanted to find a simpler, more effective way of magnetizing the components of the separator. Henry undoubtedly used his powerful electromagnet for this purpose and, as will be seen below, constructed an electromagnet for use at Penfield and Taft's plant at what is now Ironville, New York. This may very well have been the first industrial application of electricity.

See Richard S. Allen, "Separation and Inspiration . . . ," an unpublished 1967 research report of the Penfield Foundation, Ironville, Crown Point, New York, a copy of which is in the files of the Henry Papers, and Elmer E. Barker, "The Story of Crown Point Iron," *New York History*, 1942, 23:410–436.

[2] A reference to the firm of Isaiah (1777–1838) and John Townsend (1783–1854). The firm began its operations in 1804 and it was prominent in cast iron manufactures, an Albany specialty during the last century. Both brothers were very prominent in the business community. John was Mayor of Albany twice, 1829–1831 and 1832–1833. *Howell and Tenney*, pp. 663ff and Munsell, *Ann. Alb.*, 9:190, 194, 267–268, 271, 283.

GERRIT MOLL TO MICHAEL FARADAY[1]

Faraday Papers,[2] Institution of Electrical Engineers, London

Utrecht 7 June 1831.

My dear Sir!

All I can say in answer to your kind letter of 30th last,[3] is that you have my full authority to print my paper, where and in such a form as you may

[1] Michael Faraday (1791–1867), *the* experimental physical scientist of the last century and Henry's great contemporary. Because of the many connections between the researches of Henry and Faraday, the latter will appear (and significantly) in subsequent volumes. L. Pearce Williams's recent *Michael Faraday, a Biography* (New York, 1965) is the best introduction to Faraday's work and to the relevant literature.

[2] The original of this document is an unsigned, three-page text on a sheet folded into four pages. The address is on the fourth page, as well as a seal (a letter M) to which is attached part of the last page of the text. From the folds, it is highly unlikely that Moll had an additional sheet with text.

From the absence of a signature, the gaps

think proper. I am however with you, of opinion, that if it is to have any good effect, this must arise principally from the circumstance of its being written by a foreigner.[4] I have however not the slightest objection, if it is at all thought expedient, to let the editor of the Quarterly publish it as he pleases; only I do not wish to see any alterations made in my statements. I was indeed exceedingly astonished to see the Quarterly adopt Babbage's

---

in the text where Moll left spaces for numerical data, and the two added notes of June 9 and 10, we speculate that Moll held up mailing the letter to complete his additional experiments but mailed it out in haste so that Faraday could act on the reply to Charles Babbage (for which see below, footnotes 4 and 5). In so doing we think he forgot the missing data, as well as the signature.

[3] Not found.

[4] This work by Moll was published as *On the Alleged Decline of Science in England by a Foreigner* (London, 1831) with an introduction by Faraday. It was a reply to Babbage's *Reflections on the Decline of Science in England* (London, 1830). Babbage (1791–1871), *DNB*, was an English mathematician best remembered for his attempt to construct a calculating machine on principles now widely recognized as basic to computer technology. Babbage will appear subsequently in the Henry Papers.

The motives of Babbage and the consequences of his book are too involved for elucidation in a footnote. in the Henry Papers. His principal targets were the stagnating Royal Society and the comparative neglect of research by the British government. For further details, see Nathan Reingold, "Babbage and Moll on the State of Science in Great Britain, a Note on a Document," *British Journal for the History of Science*, 1968, *4*: 58–64; and L. Pearce Williams, "The Royal Society and the Founding of the British Association for the Advancement of Science," *Notes and Records of the Royal Society*, 1961, *16*:221–233. Faraday did not agree that science was declining in Britain nor did a number of other prominent British scientists. He consequently welcomed the defense by a foreigner. A prominent aspect of the pamphlet war on this issue was that Babbage and his supporters cited the French example to make their points. Moll, on the contrary, was virulently anti-French, perhaps largely because of the experiences of the Netherlands under French occupation during the Napoleonic era.

Both Babbage's work and the Moll rejoinder are in the Henry Library. The former was in Henry's possession while he was in Albany; we cannot state when Henry acquired the Moll pamphlet. At some later date, probably after he moved to Washington, Henry had the two works bound together. Except for writing in Moll's name on the title page, Henry made no annotations or marks on the Moll work. On the contrary, the Babbage work has a few scorings in the margin, one comment, and some text was carefully copied by Henry into a notebook (No. 6123). There is a high degree of probability that these notices of the Babbage text took place in the Albany period.

On pages 133–140 of his notebook, Joseph Henry copied or paraphrased slightly Babbage's treatment of "Frauds of Observers" (pp. 174–183 of the original). At this point (p. 140 of notebook) Henry notes that he had neglected to put in a portion properly preceding the section on frauds. This is "Of Minute Precision in Observation" from pages 167–169 of the Babbage text. This appears on pages 140–142 of the notebook. The most significant deviation from the original in this section is that a quote from Delambre is translated from the French given by Babbage. Henry is, as usual, meticulous in noting a deviation from the source and does so by writing, "[trans by J.H]." From this note we confirm a rising suspicion that Henry had somehow learned French. Henry next copied and paraphrased pages 170–174 of Babbage "On the Art of Observing" into pages 143–146 of his notebook. These sections of Babbage are just what a young, conscientious scientist might find fascinating. Both how to do "observing" and how not to treat the data are discussed. Throughout his career Henry would have a great concern with the reliability and misuse of data. Babbage's influence in this regard was certainly not unique, but, coming at so early a stage in Henry's life, we cannot avoid inferring much importance from this reading.

From the details of scientific work, Henry's scorings in the margin next indicate an interest in the proper role of the professional

notions, and even going byond them. I would have been much less surprised if it had been the Edinburgh, but something strange must have
crossed the minds of the editors of the Quarterly, to allow such things to
find their way, in a Journal which has a right to call itself so eminently
english.[5]

I have been toiling very much these days, in endeavouring to repeat the
American electro-magnetic experiments,[6] but without success. I could not
convince myself that by increasing the number of coils the power of the
temporary magnet was increased in the least degree. First, the horse shoe
of weak iron of 16 inches long, and one inch in diameter, was coiled round
with 79 feet, of brass bell wire of $\frac{1}{16}$ inch diameter, in 5 different and suc-

---

scientist. Here too, Babbage touched on persistent themes in Henry's career. On page 10
of the *Decline* . . . Henry notes Babbage's view
that the opinion of the profession as a whole
is more valuable than the estimations of individuals because of personal rivalries and jeal-
ousies within the profession. Babbage then
states (and Henry scores the margin) that "The
pursuit of science does not, in England, constitute a distinct profession." Because of this,
there is no authoritative professional opinion,
and amateurs are given scientific posts (again
Henry scores the margin). This complaint will
reappear in subsequent volumes but about
American conditions.

In defining the proper role of the professional cultivators of science, Babbage makes
two points noted by Henry. He differentiates
the true scientist (pp. 126, 131) from the mere
routine observers and calculators and also
from the inventor who seeks a monopoly for
private gain. In the first case, Babbage asserts
the primacy of discovering new principles and
laws over merely accurately recording "the
facts which nature has presented." In his
later career Henry would not assume an egalitarian stance in science. As we shall see in
later volumes, Henry believed, to paraphrase
him, in weighing rather than counting scientific opinions. This belief, present implicitly
in Babbage, would have important consequences in the egalitarian society of republican America, greater than in a limited
monarchy where hierarchical stratifications
were endemic.

In the second case, Babbage does not deny
the right of a discoverer to seek profit by a
legal monopoly from a patent or from keeping a discovery secret. Quite clearly, Babbage
sets greater value on those who make known
discoveries as part of "the permanent endow-

ment of the human race." But there is an
ambiguity or tension in the text, and we
cannot help but wonder if Babbage's words
were in Henry's mind when he was writing
the letter to Rogers of November 4, 1831,
below. This is a theme which will recur in the
Henry Papers.

Finally, on page 207 of Babbage, Henry
notes the pointlessness of the long anecdote
about Davy and Wollaston on whether or not
it was worthwhile to test if two volumes of
hydrogen and one of oxygen will convert to
water if condensed by pressure to the specific
gravity of water. Biot had already performed
the experiment showing they did indeed form
water. Henry cites the account given in the
Philosophical Magazine, 1805, *21*:362–364. As
the undated anecdote refers to the work of
Jacob Perkins (*DAB*) which was published in
the *Phil. Trans.* in 1826, pages 541–547 (or,
less likely, the earlier publication in the same
in 1820, pp. 324–330), Henry clearly has a
point. Again, this is an example of something
recurring in his professional life. He read
widely, had a retentive mind, and had few
compunctions about pointing out lack of originality.

[5] This is a reference to the generally lauda-
tory review of Babbage in *Quarterly Review*,
1830, *43*:305–342. Faraday was not successful
in getting a rejoinder published which may
explain why his preface to Moll, dated August
1831, contains a statement that the text had
been in his possession at least four months.
The "Edinburgh" is *The Edinburgh Journal
of Science* edited by David Brewster (*DNB*),
who was a vociferous champion of the de-
clinarians.

[6] i.e., Henry's, as reported in *Silliman's Journal*, 1831, *19*:400–408.

cessive coils, making in all 251 turns, and weighing about 5 lb in all. The galvanic apparatus consisted of a copper trough in which a zink plate of [?][7] feet square was inserted. I supported about 56 lb.[8]

The same horse shoe, which I had used in former experiments, was coated with silk, over this was coiled an iron spiral of [?] inch thick making [?] turns. Over this coil a second silk coating was put and over this second silk bag, a second coil, similar to the first. Using the same galvanic apparatus of my former experiments, the horse shoe was unable to carry an anvil of 202 lb, but it very freely took 180 lb. Therefore no increase of power whatever was obtained. Finding myself thus foiled in this attempt, I endeavoured to try what effect a very small galvanic apparatus would have, on a large horse shoe.

A horse shoe of 24 inch in length (when stretched out) and weighing about 29 lb. and 2 inches thick, was coated in silk and surrounded with *one* coil of iron wire of [?] inches thick. The galvanic apparatus was a small brass trough with a zinc plate of 9 inch square, the weight supported by the temporary magnet was about 8¾ lb. A larger horse shoe of 3 inches thick,

and 22 inches arch was now taken, coated, as usual, with silk, and a spiral of iron coiled round it ¾₁₆ of an inch thick, and making 165 turns. The weight of this horse shoe and coil was about 102 lb. It was first ascertained that the horse shoe did not possess magnetism sufficient to support a sewing needle, and a miniature galvanic trough was put in action, its zinc plate had no larger surface than ⅞ square inch.

and this sketch represents its real size. The horseshoe, by the means of such a feeble power, became capable of supporting 7 lb. The conducting fluid (¹⁄₆₀ nitric and ¹⁄₆₀ sulphuric acid diluted) did not exceed one drachm,[9] it was little more indeed than a thimble could contain.

This experiment appears rather curious, especially as it would seem that, when large galvanic apparatusses are used, the force which the same magnet acquires, does not increase very materially when a stronger galvanic power is used. In all these experiments I always use, *one* zink plate in a copper trough.

I shall be very happy to learn whether you have been more successful in

---

[7] Blank left unfilled by Moll. In this paragraph and the ones following, it is not clear if Moll is exactly reproducing Henry's apparatus. Three similar blanks occur later in the text.

[8] Here Moll is not clear about the connections to the battery, an essential point.

[9] An older spelling of dram, a small measure of liquid.

repeating the American experiments.[10] My anvil of 202 lb is still a limit to which I have been gradually approaching, but which I have not yet been able to reach.

9th June My temporary magnet supported today 240 lb. I could not go beyond. The zink plate had 7 square feet surface.

10th June 1831 It supported 254 lb, but I could not obtain more.[11]

---

[10] Volume I of *Faraday's Diary 1820–1862*, 8 vols. (London, 1932–1936) covering the years 1820–1832 has no explicit reference to Joseph Henry; we presume Faraday knew of the work in Albany and think it likely he would have tried the experiments.

[11] These results are still not comparable to Henry's.

FROM JOHN R. HENRY[1]
Henry Papers, Smithsonian Archives

Shippingport. Ky.[2] June 25th 1831

Dear Sir

Permit me through the acquaintance heretofore existing between yourself and my father (Francis Henry[3] of Cooperstown) to address you upon the subject of your new and powerfull magnet. There is a mechanick living in Louisville who has for a long time been engaged in efforts, to accomplish the same, and has failed. He now wishes if possible to purchase from you

---

[1] John R. Henry appears in the records of the Louisville and Portland Canal Company, chartered in 1825 to bypass the rapids on the Ohio River near Louisville, Kentucky. (Note that Henry wrote "L & P. Canal" below his signature.) According to the journal of his assistant Increase A. Lapham (1811–1875; *DAB*), J. R. Henry took the job of assistant engineer on the Canal in October 1827 and, in the following year, became chief engineer. He came to the Canal from Rochester, New York, but, as his letter reveals, may have originally come from Cooperstown. The two-mile long Canal, the first major improvement on the Ohio River system, was opened for business in 1830 and completed in 1831. Henry probably left the area soon after the completion of the project, since he is listed in the 1832 Louisville City Directory but not in those of 1836 or 1838. We have no information on Henry's subsequent activities or on any further connections with Joseph Henry.

The Journals of Increase Lapham, in the custody of the State Historical Society of Wisconsin, have been edited and are now being published. See Samuel W. Thomas and Eugene H. Conner, eds., "The Falls of the Ohio River and Its Environs: The Journals of Increase Allen Lapham for 1827–1830," *The Filson Club Quarterly*, 1971, *45*:5–34, 199–226 (two additional installments are forthcoming). For a financial and administrative history of the Canal, see Paul B. Trescott, "The Louisville and Portland Canal Company, 1825–1874," *Mississippi Valley Historical Review*, 1958, *44*:686–708.

[2] i.e., Shippingsport, a small village at the western end of the canal.

[3] According to the records of the New York State Historical Association of Cooperstown, New York, Col. Francis Henry lived in Cooperstown, where he was one of the founders of the county agricultural society. In his reply to J. R. Henry (see below, July 9, 1831), Joseph Henry acknowledges the acquaintance of his father, but we have not discovered the nature of their relationship.

the original, but should he fail in this, he wishes that the principals upon which it is constructed should be so far explained as to enable him to construct a similar one, and for which he will pay you whatever sum of money you think proper to demand. He is a very ingenious man and in pursuit of the perpetual motion.[4] Please address me upon the subject. I have collected a great number of petrefactions at this place and have many to spare, if you think they would be desirable in your Institute, I will send a box.

> I am Sir your Ob^t & Humble Servant
> Jno. R. Henry Esqr
> L & P. Canal

[4] We have not identified the Louisville mechanic, one of the many inventors to ask Henry for information on his electromagnet (see Henry to J. R. Henry, July 9, 1831).

FROM PENFIELD AND TAFT
Henry Papers, Smithsonian Archives

Crownpoint 27th June 1831[1]

Mr Joseph Henry

Sir we send by James King[2] Esqr Six double points & four single points, which we wish you to Magnetise & we will send for them soon, if they opperate well wish you to write us immediately. We wish you to Make a Machine that will answer to Magnetise the Points for Our Machine. We think a Small Machine will answer our Purpose. We shal Leave it to you to Make Such an one as will answer . . .[3] purpose. We shall wish to have it done in the course of 3 or 4 weeks. We shall be at Albany in about 4 weeks & shall then Like to get the Machine.[4]

> yours with Esteem
> Penfield & Taft

NB We calculate to fasten the double points on to the cillender with a screw.

[1] See the prior letter of May 30, 1831. No reply of Henry's survives to that letter or to this one in either the Henry Papers or the Allen Penfield Collection at Ironville, Crown Point, New York.

[2] According to Allen (see footnote 1 of May 30, 1831), James King (1789–1841) represented Penfield and Taft in the legal dispute arising from the revival of the Browning patent of 1814. King, a Princeton graduate (1807; A.M. 1810), was an eminent Albany attorney. From 1823 until his death King was a Regent of the University of the State of New York, serving as Chancellor from 1839. Franklin B. Hough, *Historical and Statistical Record of the University of the State of New York During the Century from 1784 to 1884* (Albany, 1885), pp. 783, 787; and *Princeton Catalogue*, p. 119.

[3] A hole in the document occurs at this point where once there was a word.

[4] Allen, op. cit., states that Henry did build an electromagnet for Penfield and Taft.

FROM EBENEZER EMMONS[1]

Henry Papers, Smithsonian Archives

Wms College July 3ᵈ· 1831

Prof Henry

Sir

Permit me to introduce Mr A. Clark, Principal of the High School in this place.[2] I do this for the purpose of obtaining your assistance in procuring articles for putting up apparatus for Electro Magnetic experiments. The principle article I want is wire of suitable size & of sufficient length to exhibit magnetism on a scale similar to that detailed in A.J. of Science. Please to give Mr C. those directions for conveniently putting up the apparatus which your experience approves, as far as you are willing should be made public.

I am Sir yours
with high esteem & respect
E. Emmons

[1] Ebenezer Emmons (1790–1863) was an important, if controversial, figure in the early history of American geology. Born in Middlefield, Massachusetts, he had degrees from both Williams College (1818) and Rensselaer Polytechnic Institute (1826). Emmons studied medicine at the Berkshire Medical School but supplemented his income from practice by serving as Lecturer in Chemistry at Williams starting in 1828 and as a junior professor at RPI in 1830. He continued his connection with Williams until 1852 at which date he was Professor of Obstetrics. He was appointed Professor of Chemistry at the Albany Medical College in 1838.

Emmons was strongly influenced by Amos Eaton's geological views. In 1836 he became geologist on the Survey of New York, leaving in 1842 to become custodian of the state collections at Albany and later State Agriculturalist. Emmons is given credit by some for the development of the New York system of classification and its nomenclature. His Taconic system was very controversial, and a geological map prepared under his guidance was subjected to violent attack leading its compiler, George T. Foster, unsuccessfully to sue Louis Agassiz and James Hall for libel in 1850. Joseph Henry was a witness for Agassiz and Hall. Emmons became State Geologist of North Carolina in 1851. *DSB* and *DAB*. For Emmons' date of appointment to the New York Survey, see the Diary of William L. Marcy, entry of June 2, 1836, Marcy Papers, Library of Congress.

[2] Alonzo Clark (1807–1887), physician, was born in Chester, Massachusetts. He was graduated from Williams College in 1828, and from the College of Physicians and Surgeons in New York in 1835. Afterward he settled in New York City where he became an eminent practitioner. Clark held the chair of Pathology and Materia Medica in Vermont Medical College, of Physiology and Pathology in the College of Physicians and Surgeons from 1845 to 1855, and of Pathology and Practical Medicine in the same institution from 1855 to 1885, where he was also Dean and President of the faculty from 1875 to 1885. Howard A. Kelly, *A Cyclopedia of American Medical Biography, Comprising the Lives of Eminent Deceased Physicians and Surgeons from 1610 to 1910*, 2 vols. (Philadelphia, 1912), *1*:181–182.

TO JOHN R. HENRY

Retained Copy, Henry Papers, Smithsonian Archives[1]

Albany July 9th 1831

Dear Sir

I am happy in having an oportunity of furnishing a son of my friend Col. Henry of Cooperstown with the information required in your letter of the 25th ult.[2]

The magnet you have probably reference to was constructed by me (or under my direction) for Yale College and is now in the laboratory of that Institution as a permanent part of the apparatus. My method of forming these powerful magnets is by no means a secret as I have published detailed accounts of my experiments and discoveries in the 19th & 20th vols. of Sillimans Journal of Science;[3] & these have since been republished both in France and in England so that the invention is now fully before the scientific world.[4] These magnets are constructed on a new principle and are entirely different from the ordinary steel magnets, with which every person is familiar.

The one referred to was formed of a bar of soft iron 30 inches long and bent into the form of a horseshoe. Around the bar about 800 feet of copper bell wire are coiled in 26 different pieces. Through these wires a stream of electricity is made to pass from a small galvanic battery soldered to the ends of the wires. The magnetism is induced in the soft iron by the electricity.

The whole subject belongs to a new department of science lately discovered called electro-magnetism which has excited much interest in Europe but is very little known in this country.

---

[1] The copy is incomplete; on the back of the second page, Henry wrote: "Copy (in Substance) to Mr. Henry of Kentucky on Mag. —1831."

[2] See above, June 25, 1831.

[3] "On the Application of the Principle of the Galvanic Multiplier to Electro-Magnetic Apparatus, and Also to the Development of Great Magnetic Power in Soft Iron, with a Small Galvanic Element," January 1831, *19*: 400–408; and Joseph Henry and Dr. [P.] Ten Eyck, "An Account of a Large Electro-Magnet, Made for the Laboratory of Yale College," April 1831, 20:201–203.

[4] By the date of this letter, excerpts from the Henry-Ten Eyck article appeared in the *Journal of the Royal Institution*, May 1831, *1*: 609–610. In October 1831, a report on the same article appeared in the *Philosophical Magazine, 10*:314–315. However, prior to the date of this letter, we have found no mention of either article in the French scientific literature. We have checked through the French and French language periodicals listed in H. C. Bolton, *A Catalogue of Scientific and Technical Periodicals*, 2d ed. (Washington, 1897) and through the journals of French scientific societies catalogued by Samuel H. Scudder, *Catalogue of Scientific Serials . . . , 1633–1876* (Cambridge, Massachusetts, 1879). A few months after this letter, the Henry-Ten Eyck article was reported in a well-known Swiss journal, De La Rive's *Bibliothèque universelle des sciences, belles-lettres et arts*, October 1831, *48*:226–227. It was also noted in the German scientific journal, the *Annalen der Physik und Chemie*, 1832, 24:638–639.

The striking results of my experiments however have had a tendency to render the subject more popular among men of science in America and other and doubtless more important improvements will be made.

It will perhaps be impossible for me to give such a description of the method of forming the magnets to a person unacquainted with the principles of Electro-magnetism as will enable him to construct one and if I were to attempt it no good could result to a person attempting to form a perpetual motion on any mechanical or magnetic principle. By a refference to the publications I have mentioned however he may perhapse glean sufficient information particularly if he is in any way acquainted with galvanism to construct a magnet on my plan. Or if he is very anxious to have one constructed I will superintend the work. The expense will however be considerable as the one made for Yale College cost in materials and mechanical workmanship more than $50. But I advise him to save his money if he only wants the magnet for a perpetual motion as all his experiments in regard to that object will certainly fail.

It is a fact that does not tell much for the diffusion of Knowledge among the mechanics of this country that there are at the present time many ingenius but illiterate mechanics engaged in attempts to invent self moving machines.[5] Since the news of my magnet has gone abroad I have had several similar applications from persons at a distance but have in each case discouraged their projects.[6]

---

[5] Henry's impatience with American inventors and mechanics continued to grow; early in the following year, he launched a full-scale attack against them in a public scientific lecture at the Albany Academy. See his Introductory Lecture on Chemistry, January–March 1832, below.

For contemporary preoccupations with perpetual motion, see Thomas P. Jones, "Observations on the Attempt to Construct Machines of the Kind Usually Intended by the Term Perpetual Motion; with Notices of Some of the Particular Machines which Have, at Different Times, Been Proposed for the Attainment of this Object," *Journal of the Franklin Institute*, 1828, 2:318–327. This journal, edited by Jones, was then the foremost inventors' magazine in America.

[6] No such applications survive among Henry's papers.

FROM CHARLES BARTLETT[1]
Henry Papers, Smithsonian Archives

Utica July 9. 1831.

Professor Henry
   Sir

At a late meeting of the Curators of the New York State Lyceum[2] held pursuant to notice at the Washington Hall in this Village for the purpose of appointing persons to lecture before the Lyceum at its first annual meeting, which will be held on the 2nd Wednesday in August next 12 o clock at noon at the court room in this Village, you was unanimously appointed to lecture on the following Subject, Viz

"On the introduction of the Study of the Natural Sciences with our common Schools."

Knowing that the objects of this Lyceum are duly appreciated by you, and being persuaded that your compliance with the appointment will greatly contribute to the attainment of these objects you will permit me as the organ of the Curators respectfully to urge your acquiescence.[3]

I am with great respect
Your Obt Servant
Chas Bartlett

[1] Charles Bartlett, the Recording Secretary of the New York State Lyceum, Utica, New York, appears in the 1829 Utica City Directory as the principal of a High School; in 1832 the title of his school was the Utica Gymnasium.

[2] Organized the day previously, the New York State Lyceum was part of the movement founded by Josiah Holbrook which was largely educational in orientation. The lyceums were local clubs mainly devoted to the dissemination of knowledge, not the encouragement of research. It was an ancestor of the Chautauqua Movement of the late nineteenth century. The Utica group played an impor-tant role in the movement. In the August meeting, to which Henry was invited by this letter, a call was issued for a meeting in New York City to form a National or American Lyceum. The call was successful, unlike the call to Henry. See, New York State Lyceum, *Proceedings of the First Annual Meeting* (Utica, 1831), especially, p. 11 (a copy was kept by Henry in his library); Carl Bode, *The American Lyceum, Town Meeting of the Mind* (New York, 1956); Cecil B. Hayes, *The American Lyceum* (Washington, 1932), p. 6 (U.S. Office of Education, Bulletin No. 12, 1932).

[3] For Henry's reply, see below, July 20, 1831.

FROM WILLIAM M. CUSHMAN[1]
Correspondence, Albany Institute Archives

Albany July 15th 1831

Dear Sir,

Allow me to present to the Institute through you a curiosity I obtained while at the South engaged in my profession. Having never seen a similar aboriginal relic of so large a size, I was induced to present it to that body, thinking it might have some interest with the curious among its members.

Permit me, Sir, to add the following remarks, which as they are mere speculations, I hope will be received as such; and pardoned if erroneous.

Indian Battle Axe. (probably)

One day last March, while in the performance of field operations on the New-Castle and Frenchtown Rail Road upon the top of a hill about half a mile south of Frenchtown on Elk River, Maryland, my attention was accidentally directed to a large decayed stump; at the root of which I observed a stone of a somewhat singular shape and appearance. It was picked up and immediately recognised as an Indian axe,[2] perhaps battle axe: at the time some speculations of the following import were made and they may perhaps be warranted by the facts below enumerated.

Near where it laid were two depressions sunk some few feet below the surface communicating with each other by a neck or rather strait, (the figure 8 will give a good idea of the form of the ponds and their connexion) which we had hitherto regarded as ponds whose only inmates were the frog and the lizard; and therefore not very inviting to the curious. The margin of this place was hemmed round by rows of the Sour Gum tree, with no place of access except on one side, from the impenetrable breaks of green briar climbing and twining round them.

---

[1] William McClelland Cushman (1810–1874), a student at the Albany Academy, was a civil engineer. In 1828 he was engaged in surveying for the projected railroad between Boston and the Hudson. In 1830 and 1831 he was working on the New Castle and Frenchtown Railroad in Maryland and Delaware. He later was engaged in New England and in the Albany area. A. W. Cushman, *A Historical and Biographical Genealogy of the Cushmans . . .* (Boston, 1855), p. 360–361, identifies Cushman as a student of Henry's; indeed he attended the Academy from 1823 until 1829. See Henry Hun, "A Survey of the Activity of the Albany Academy" (unpublished manuscript, 1922–1935, Manuscript Division, New York State Library and Albany Academy Archives).

[2] An early example of a typical event in Henry's later role as Secretary of the Smithsonian Institution. Many offers of Indian artifacts were received by Henry in Washington. His concern for preserving evidence of the original inhabitants of the land impelled Henry to become a leading patron of ethnology.

Prior to the coming of the whites, this area was the hunting ground of the Susquehannock Indians. Stone artifacts were frequently found in this area. George Johnston, *History of Cecil County, Maryland* (Elkton, 1881), p. 5.

This discovery led me to take a different and far more interesting view of this singular spot than formerly, viz.

Might not (I conceived) this have been dug out by the aboriginal inhabitants of the State as an encampment—a place of rendezvous for indians placed to watch the operations of their troublesome "white faces" at Frenchtown: while here perhaps upon this stump this axe had been made the guillotine to dispatch unfortunate captives. At worst it has every indication of having been used for such a purpose, for the head is evidently stained with blood—the soft nature of the stone permitting it to stain so deep that the lapse of many years has not been able to remove it.[3]

I will now state some reasons for making these surmises.

1^{sty} This Hill is the highest ground for several miles in circuit, thus giving scope for observation upon the movements of the Whites or other enemies.

2dly It was sunk below the surface as a retreat to screen themselves from view while at intervals they were on the watch of their antagonists.

3dly On the margin of Elk River innumerable flocks of Duck resort to feed upon a weed growing in the bed of that stream. I have seen the surface darkened with their number, chiefly Canvas-back.[*] This fact united with that of the fine fishing ground, would perhaps justify the supposition, seeing that hunting and fishing were the red mans only subsistence. It was in this neighbourhood the celebrated "Indian Queen" held her court—and here too some of her exploits were performed.[4]

I send also a specimen of lignite obtained from the same neighborhood,

---

[*] The mode of shooting the Canvas-back is this.

A light canoe is obtained just deep enough to keep its upper edge a few inchs above the water: in the bow a small swivel[5] is placed heavily loaded: in front a flock of stuffed duck skins are made to float as a decoy. Thus equipped, the sportsman, lies down in his boat and either suffers it to drift out into the stream or propels it gently with paddles, until the decoy flock induces their unsuspecting mates to join their party, when the swivel is discharged—frequently killing forty or fifty at a shot. It is also a remarkable fact this water fowl never comes near the shore on the Sabbath—because, I was told, this was the time idlers took to make havoc among them, showing an instinctive dread which this part of the creation, more than any other, have good cause to exercise.

---

[3] Human blood on the stone would have weathered away long before 1831. The "guillotine" possibility is rated by a modern specialist on this area, C. A. Weslager, as "sheer speculation."

[4] In his paper, "Wynicaw—a Choptank Indian Chief," *Proceedings*, American Philosophical Society, 1944, 87:398–402, C. A. Weslager names four Indian "Queens" on the Eastern Shore of Maryland and other Indian "royalty" show up in various colonial sources. None were, however, holding court in the Elk River neighborhood to our knowledge. We are indebted to C. A. Weslager of Brandywine College for his expert advice.

[5] Sometimes referred to as the Poacher's Gun. It is an oversized shotgun with a 1-inch to 1¼-inch bore mounted on a swivel which fired 30 to 50 pounds of shot.

buried about 15 feet below the surface. Large elliptical masses were dug up and for the most part embeded in a very pure alumin of which the accompanying is a specimen. A gentlemen who had been engaged in the manufacture of porcelain during the last war, when foreign manufactures were interdicted by the embargo, told me the clay very strikingly resembled that used for that purpose.

I am Sir
Very respectfully
Your obed Sevt.
Wm. M. Cushman

TO CHARLES BARTLETT
Retained Copy, Henry Papers, Smithsonian Institution

Albany July 20th 1831

Charles Bartlett Esq
> Dear Sir

I have the honor of receiving your letter[1] informing me of my appointment by the Curators of the New York State Lyceum to deliver a lecture on the subject of the introduction of the study of the Natural Science into our common schools.

Please sir inform the gentlemen curators for me that I feel deeply interested in every effort to diffuse useful knowledge among our citizens generally believing as I do that this diffusion is the principal, if not the only means of promoting individual happiness as well as national prosperity and that I know of no better method of accomplishing it than by raising the character of our common schools.

With these views it would give much pleasure to embrace the present opportunity of aiding as far as my abilities would permit the designs of the State Lyceum but I find myself under the necessity of declining the appointment as it will be entirely incompatible with my present circumstances.[2]

My duties in the Academy will detain me in Albany during the first week in August and I have a previous engagement which will [detain me] the whole of the second week.

Please tender to the Curators my thanks for the honor they have con-

---

[1] See above, July 9, 1831. [2] Most of the "appointees" also declined.

ferred on me and acept yourself my acknowledgments for the polite and friendly communication.

> I am sir with great respect
> Your Obt serv-
> Joseph Henry

FROM BENJAMIN SILLIMAN, SR.
Henry Papers, Smithsonian Archives

New Haven July 21, 1831

Dear Sir

I hope you have found your paper[1] correctly printed in the last number of the Journal. The machine is an elegant one & I doubt not will do you credit. I shall be happy to hear from you again on the subject or on any other & shall be happy to insert any thing from you in the October Nº of the Journal.

I understood from the remarks made by a young gentleman from Albany[2] a few weeks ago here—reported to me by Mʳ Shepard[3]—that Dʳ Ten Eyck was dissatisfied with the statement made in the April Nº of the Journal respecting his concern in the magnetic apparatus & moreover that I had mistaken your intentions in publishing the statement which you sent me.[4] If I erred in this respect I regret it as I misunderstood your wishes & was actuated solely by the desire to do you both exact justice. It was my intention to write Dʳ Ten Eyck a note by Mʳ Webster,[5] but I believe it will answer every purpose if you will be so kind as to shew him this letter & add that if any thing can be noted in the October Nº of the Journal which will tend to set the matter right, it will give me pleasure to insert it. I set a high

[1] Henry's "On a Reciprocating Motion Produced by Magnetic Attraction and Repulsion," *Silliman's Journal*, 1831, 20:340–343. By rigging an electromagnet on a pivot and reversing the polarities, Henry constructed a rudimentary electrical machine, the principles of which are embodied in our everyday direct current motor. While Henry conceived of his invention as little more than a "philosophical toy," he was certainly correct in stating that "it is not impossible that the same principle, or some modification of it on a more extended scale, may hereafter be applied to some useful purpose." (20:340.) See W.

James King, *The Development of Electrical Technology in the 19th Century: 1. The Electrochemical Cell and the Electromagnet*, United States National Museum Bulletin 228 (Washington, 1962), pp. 260ff.

[2] Matthew Henry Webster. See Henry's letter to Silliman of February 28, 1832, below.

[3] Charles U. Shepard, for whom see above, Silliman to Henry, April 5, 1831, especially footnote 1.

[4] See above, Henry to Silliman, March 28, 1831.

[5] Matthew Henry Webster.

value upon what you & Dr Ten Eyck have so handsomely done & of course I could have no other wish than that you should both stand fairly & fully before the public in relation to this interesting subject. Mr Webster will inform you that your magnet performs admirably well & excites great interest among the students & all who see it or hear of it.

I remain dear sir with great respect yours very truly

B Silliman

FROM JOHN TURNBULL[1]

Mary Henry Copy, Henry Papers, Smithsonian Archives

New York. Aug. 16. 1831

I had the pleasure of travelling upon the Rail Road which to me was a real satisfaction. For after all the actual inspection is worth all that can be said or written upon the subject. Although it differed in no material particular from what I expected still the reality is better than all the descriptions which can be made of it. Our motion was slow, it is true, only 8 miles an hour but enough to satisfy curiosity. I looked at the engine and found that fanners had been made instead of bellows as you recommended.[2] The prin-

---

[1] Though identified in this fragmentary document simply as J. Turnbull, the author of the letter must be Henry's friend John Turnbull, whom Henry mentions briefly in his letter to Harriet of August 30, 1830, above. In a February 23, 1835, letter to John Torrey (Torrey Papers, New York Botanical Garden Library), Henry describes Turnbull as a young Scotsman who lived for a time in Albany. The Albany City Directories of 1826 and 1827 list him as a teacher. Though he did not teach at the Albany Academy, he may have met Henry, given the small size of the Albany educational community. Later Turnbull ran a lottery in New York at 210½ Broadway. He appears in the New York City Directories from 1827–1828 to 1830–1831. We have no information on Turnbull's connections with the American or Scottish scientific community (except for his acquaintance with the Scotsman in New York with the collection of philosophical apparatus, mentioned in the above-cited Henry letter), but he frequently served as a go-between for Henry and the Edinburgh physicist James David Forbes (1809–1869). *DNB*. When Turnbull sailed

to visit Scotland in the summer of 1834, Henry asked him to take a Hansteen magnetic needle to Forbes (Henry to Forbes, June 30, 1834; Forbes Papers, St. Andrews University Library). In 1835, Forbes had Turnbull, then in Edinburgh, send a package (possibly containing the Hansteen needle) to Henry via one of Turnbull's friends in New York. Henry to Torrey, cited above.

[2] The early date of the letter and the reference to fanners almost certainly identifies the railroad as the Baltimore and Ohio (B.&O.), the first American railroad to be open to public use. Following the English example, virtually all American locomotives relied on the exhaust of steam to create the draft for the locomotive boiler. However, the early B.&O. locomotives, the so-called "Grasshoppers" which had vertical boilers and pistons, used fans powered by small turbines operated on exhaust steam. John H. White, Jr., *American Locomotives, An Engineering History, 1830–1880* (Baltimore, 1968), p. 112.

We do not know what prompted Henry's recommendations. In January 1831, the B.&O. Directors sponsored a competition for the

cipal defect is thought to be the smallness of the steam chamber which it is intended to be remedied by one of larger dimensions.[3]

most efficient locomotive (the competition was won by Phineas Davis, who introduced the fans and the vertical boiler). Perhaps one of the contestants—or the B.&O. Directors—sought Henry's advice. Edward Hungerford, *The Story of the Baltimore and Ohio Railroad*, 2 vols. (New York and London, 1928),

1:105–108.

[3] Before 1870, almost all locomotive boilers were too small for the cylinder size. Because American tracks were weak, small boilers were needed to lessen engine weight. John H. White, Jr., *American Locomotives*, p. 93.

FROM BENJAMIN F. JOSLIN
Henry Papers, Smithsonian Archives

Schenectady Aug. 29th 1831

Dear Sir,

At your request I send you a short account of the arora borealis as it appeared in the city of N. York Apr. 19th about 9 P.M.

It was peculiarly interesting on account of the actual meeting of the luminous columns in the magnetic meridian at the point in the direction of the dipping needle toward which they usually tend. The luminous matter occupied the whole northern half of the visible celestial hemisphere, and was very much condensed near the point of convergence. Some of the eastern corruscations were at times transiently curved as though their middle parts (as was probably the case,) were driven eastward by the impulse of the westerly breeze which was blowing at the time. A luminous band was at one time extended across the heavens at right angles to the meridian and 30° south of the zenith. This had at times an oscillatory motion in a north & south direction. It passed near the moon, around which was one of the larger halos. The sky had been previously clear. The converging rays appeared to meet at the star δ Leonis.[1]

In haste your Friend   B F Joslin

P.S. I find from my Journal that it was entirely cloudy on the 22[d] & 23[d] Sept. and no arora was of course seen. Nor was there any here (at least 9 PM) Oct. 15th. It was clear that evening. B. F. J.

[1] In Henry's paper, "On a Disturbance of the Earth's Magnetism, in Connexion with the Appearance of an Aurora Borealis, as Observed at Albany, April 19th, 1831," *Silliman's Journal*, 1832, 22:143–155, this passage appears on page 149 with slight editorial revisions by either Henry or Silliman.

FROM WILLIAM CAMPBELL

Henry Papers, Smithsonian Archives

Cherry Valley 5ᵗʰ Sept 1831

Dear Sir

Your Favour of the 30ᵗʰ ultimo[1] was duly recᵈ. I remember having observed the extraordinary Aurora Borealis you mention, and I find that I have noticed it in my meteorological Journal as having occured on the evenining of the 19ᵗʰ April. It was very brilliant as observed at this place, assuming a variety of forms, and at one time forming a stupendous arch crossing the heavens from East to West and at an other time radiating from a point South of the Zenith.[2] The memoranda I made at the time is not as minute as I wish now it had been; but my recollection of its appearance is very distinct.

I remain yours &c
William Campbell

[1] Not found.

[2] Henry used Campbell's observations on the aurora in his "On a Disturbance of the Earth's Magnetism . . . ," *Silliman's Journal,* 1832, 22:149.

FROM JOHN GIBSON[1]

Henry Papers, Smithsonian Archives

Black Rock [N.Y.] Sep 24ᵗʰ 1831

Dear Sir

I beg leave to trouble you to send me a little information. I have just engaged to build two 80 horse power Engines for a new boat on Lake Erie. This is the first boat of a new line which is just formed by a company of the

[1] Gibson had an ironworks in Black Rock, New York (now part of Buffalo). We have not succeeded in identifying him precisely or in learning more about his relationship with Joseph Henry. The Buffalo and Erie County Historical Society could not find any secondary references to Gibson. From this letter we know he built steam engines and was engaged in building boats on the Great Lakes. The Northwest Ohio-Great Lakes Research Center, Bowling Green, Ohio, has cross-indexed all names of owners, builders, and captains on vessel enrollments issued at Buffalo, 1816–1842; Gibson does not appear here either.

The Peter B. Porter Papers at the Buffalo and Erie County Historical Society contain four documents (C-179, D-116, D-163, and X-3) pertaining to Gibson. From these we know that in 1829 the firm was known as Gibson, Johnson and Ehle; that the name was changed in 1833 to Gibson, Grayson, and Co.; and that in 1836 the firm was in financial trouble. It was involved in the construction of harbor works in Black Rock.

357

most wealthy and powerful merchants at Buffalo, Detroit, and along the Lake.[2] I have an interest in the line and intend doing all the Engine work. I am now collecting all the practical information in regard to the best boats now in operation. There is some difference of opinion about where it is most advantageous to place the Paddle wheels. Some think in the middle of the boat, others nearer to the Bow, and others again nearer to the Stern.[3] My own opinion is that nearer to the Bow than the Stern is the best but in this I may be mistaken. My object at present is to trouble you to examine some of the best Boats on the Hudson in this respect and inform me as soon as you can, as I am now drawing a plan of the Boat and machinery.

Any other information you can conveniently furnish will be acceptable. Business is very brisk with me, and for the first time in my life I have the offer of more work for the ensuing winter than I can undertake. In addition to these Engines above mentioned I have the offer of 4 Fifty horse power Engines for two other Boats in Canada besides several kinds of land engines. I intend being in Albany in the course of next month for the purpose of engaging hands for the winter etc. Mrs G has not been very well since I last wrote you but is now getting better. This place has been generally very healthy.

Remember us kindly to all friends and believe me Yours truly

John Gibson

PS I have understood that the Paddles of the North American are far forward of the center of the Boat. J G

---

[2] Several combinations existed with extensive shipping interests; we cannot identify precisely which one Gibson refers to.

[3] At this date the location of the paddle wheels was still in dispute among boat builders. In his 1824 report on American steamboats, Jean Baptiste Marestier noted that some boats place the wheels amidship and others about one-third from the bow (*Memoir on Steamboats of the United States of America,* trans. S. Withington [Mystic, 1957], pp. 10–11). Louis C. Hunter, *Steamboats on the Western Rivers,* reprint ed. (New York, 1969), pp. 96ff, 169, notes that weight distribution was a principal factor in steamboat design. The location of the paddle wheels and the engine machinery were clearly key factors. As boats increased in length, the machinery was shifted from the earliest position amidship to about a third the length from the bow. The side wheels themselves were shifted in time to about one-third from the stern.

Hunter's account is based on inland waterways, but both the early builders in the Mississippi Valley and Gibson on Lake Erie at first looked to the East for technical precedents. Gibson did not contemplate a stern wheel. Although stern wheels were in use at this date, side wheels were generally preferred.

For Henry's reply, see the letter of October 18, 1831, below.

FROM CHRISTIAN B. THÜMMEL[1]
Henry Papers, Smithsonian Archives

Hartwick Seminary, Octbr 8ᵗʰ 1831.

My dear Sir,

Your letter[2] should have been answered sooner, had circumstances permitted it; I trust however my answer will not be too late. I returned here about a week ago, & inquired immediately for your letter, but it had not been received at the Cooperstown Postoffice, till at length two days ago I happened to find it in the obscure Postoffice in this place, into which once in a great while one of my letters strays and generally remains there safely deposited till good luck brings it by some means or other into my hands. So in future please to be particular in directing for me to the *Cooperstown Postoffice*. And now to the inquiries in your letter.

First in regard to the Aurora Borealis on the 19th of April last, I find in our Metereol. register the following: April 19th Therm: Morn: 50. Aftern: 64. Even: 46. Wind. A.M. *W*. P.M. *S*. & the next morning *N.W*. Rain, in the morning. Splendid Aurora Borealis.[3] A nucleus about in the Zenith moving to the South, with bright rays in every direction, about half past 8 P.M. So far the Journal. Both Rev. Mr Miller[4] & myself admired this Aurora Borealis, the most beautiful I ever witnessed; the nucleus was clear & compact remaining stationary for some time, till it began to move, then the rays darted forward in every direction like crystals, and soon overspread the whole sky, assuming again various shapes & figures. Secondly as to Stephen's inquiry about the temperature. I find in his letter,[5] which I succeeded in hunting up after a long search, the following. The sudden change of Temperature which accompanied the Eclipse was very sensible to the feelings.[6] The thermometer in a situation sheltered from the wind & in the shade sank from 38 degrees to 30 & shortly after the end had risen to 33½.

---

[1] See above, Henry to Maria Alexander, August 15, 1829.

[2] Not found.

[3] For Henry's interest in the relation between the aurora and the weather see below, Alexander to Henry, April 21, 1832, footnote 4. Henry used Thümmel's observations in his paper "On a Disturbance of the Earth's Magnetism . . . ," *Silliman's Journal*, 1832, 22: 149.

[4] Probably Rev. George B. Miller (1795–1869), Professor of Theology and Principal of the Hartwick Seminary. Henry Hardy Heins, *Throughout All the Years, the Bi-Centennial Story of Hartwick in America, 1746–1946* (Oneonta, New York, 1946), pp. 159, 162.

[5] We have not found Stephen Alexander's letter to Thümmel.

[6] The reference is to the solar eclipse of February 12, 1831. For Alexander's work on that solar eclipse, see above, Jackson to Henry, February 16, 1831, footnote 8. In his paper read to the Albany Institute in August 1833, Alexander included data on temperature variation during the eclipse. ("Astronomical Observations Made at Berlin, Worcester County, Md. [February, 1831], with Some of Their Results," *Transactions*, 1833–1852, 2:84–96.)

So far the answer to your inquiries. I should like to fill this sheet in some way or other but know hardly how: News do not grow here at all, & the old things you all know as you live in the Capital & near the Capital & City Hall. I reached of course Canajoharie in safety & found Mrs. Thümmel expecting me & in health. In Canajoharie I preached twice to some German Emigrants who had been 2 years in this country, learnt very little of the English language & had heard no German sermon in all that time.[7] They were highly gratified to hear the Gospel once more preached to them in their own language, & had come, at least some of them on a Sunday before to a Luth. Church at Stone Arabia 4 miles from Canaj. where I preached German in the Afternoon to the old Mohawk Germans. Here in Hartwick we go on as usual, our term has but just commenced & we have not yet our whole complement of Students, numbering only 35 at present. Will you please inform me what Compend of Universal History you use in the Academy, or which you think the best Compend. Tytler[8] is used here which I do not like. Letter from home, which I received on my arrival here informed me of the health & well being of my mother & brother & sister; news of course the most gratifying to me. My noble Grandduke of Oldenburgh Paul has just taken his third wife a daughter of the ExKing of Sweden. His royal Highness the Grandduke perhaps fears soon to become himself an Ex-Grandduke, & thinks it best to take the daughter of an ExKing. By the bye the ExKing is said will make my native place, [. . .] his residence; what an honour! Other political news I know not. Stephen has long since heard, *that the Dutch have taken Holland,* whether they ever will take Belgium [. . .] A question Leopold will probably try hard to [. . .][9]

Stephen will of course read this letter, & consequently [. . .] consider it as also written to him & send me soon an answer. Mrs Thümmel joins me in sending her compliments to all the members of your respected family & entertains with me the hope of soon having the pleasure to see at least some of them at our house. It will prove a pleasant excursion this winter by good sleighing in the *hollow days,* as one of our [. . .][10] Students used to write.

With much respect
Yours
C B Thümmel

[7] Thümmel himself was obviously a German immigrant.

[8] Alexander Fraser Tytler, *Elements of General History, Ancient and Modern,* 3 vols. (Edinburgh and London, 1801–1822). The first American edition appeared in 1823.

[9] Here and at the end of the previous sentence, a portion of the document has been torn away where the letter was sealed.

[10] The illegible word here could possibly be Chickeniny, perhaps the garbled name of an Indian tribe.

TO JOHN GIBSON

Retained Copy, Henry Papers, Smithsonian Archives

Albany Oct 18th 1831[1]

Dear Sir

An engagement at the time prevented my attending immediately to your queries[2] respecting the position of the paddle wheels of the steam Boats on the Hudson. I have since made some enquires myself and am indebted to Dr Ten Eyck who has been at the trouble to measure in a rough way the distance from the stem post and stern post of the shaft of each boat on the river. The following is his report on the subject.

*Constitution	26 }	From shaft	23 From shaft to
	24 }	to stem post	stern post
*Constellation	26 }		
	30 }		25
Albany	21		35
*De Witt Clinton	21 }		
	32 }		38
*North America	33½		31½
*John Jay	21		22
New Philadelphia	25		44
Ohio	32 }		
	44 }		30

* Those marked (*) have their boiler before the shaft. Also in the above where two numbers are given the larger No arises from the fact that these boats have been lengthened by the addition of false bows.

If I were to give an opinion from my own views of the subject or a priori from general principles I would say as near the centre as possible would be the best position. By the centre I mean the position of the largest transverse section of the boat. If it be placed much in advance of this the water from the wheel will be piled up as it were before the boat & thus impede her progress. If near the stern the wheel will produce a partial vacum of water or a negative pressure as it is called which will also much increase the resistance.[3]

---

[1] On the second page of this document, Henry dates this letter "Nov 7th 1831," apparently the date when the outgoing copy was written and sent.

[2] See Gibson's letter of September 24, 1831, above.

[3] Henry apparently did not consider the matter of weight distribution, only the re-

I believe however that there is some advantage in steering in having the wheels before the centre but how much before can only be told by experiment & observation.

---

sistance offered by the shape of the boat structure. Although the early trend was toward the bow or at the center, later boats placed the wheels a third of the length from the stern. Contrary to Henry's assertion in the next paragraph, this location improved steering. See footnote 3 of Gibson's letter of September 24, 1831.

TO JAMES D. NICHOLSON[1]
Retained Copy, Henry Papers, Smithsonian Archives

Albany Oct 18ᵗʰ 1831

Dear Sir

The notice of my election as an academician of the Northern Institute and Academy of Fine Arts[2] came to my residence at a time when I was out of Town. It was accidentally mislaid and has only come to light almost at the present moment.

Please inform the Institute that I regret not having sooner acknowledged my sense of the honour confered and that I accept with much pleasure the "degree of Academician & Associate of that body."

I am Sir Respectfully
Yours etc
Joseph Henry

[1] James D. Nicholson, listed in Albany City Directories (1830–1832) as a printer. Nicholson published the *Albany Literary Gazette,* which appeared briefly from September 1831 to April 1832 under the editorship of John P. Jermain. Reynolds, *Alb. Chron.,* p. 500.

[2] The Northern Institute and Academy of Fine Arts was founded in Albany in 1831. Munsell, *Ann. Alb.,* 5:261. We have not been able to determine how long the institute survived or its functions. Ezra Ames, a well-known portrait painter in Albany, is listed in Albany City Directories (1833–1834) as its President; James D. Nicholson appears as its Corresponding Secretary. Although Nicholson's incoming communication does not survive, we suspect that he was serving in this capacity when he informed Henry of his election as academician of the institute.

TO WEARE C. LITTLE

James T. Mitchell Collection, Historical Society of Pennsylvania

[November 1831][1]

Mr Little Please send by the bearer[2] a copy of the American Almanac.[3]

Jos Henry

[1] On the reverse of this little note, someone, perhaps Weare C. Little, has written "Novr 1831." Underneath, in a different hand is an identification of Henry—"Prof^r of Natural philosophy at Princeton: one of the ablest men of his day"—just what a dealer or autograph collector would write.

[2] Unknown to us.

[3] This copy survives in Henry's Library.

The American Almanac and Repository of Useful Knowledge for the Year 1831 was published in Boston by Gray and Bowen. The copyright notice, on the reverse of the title page, is dated November 11, 1830. Henry's interest was undoubtedly because of the extensive section on the eclipse of February 2, 1831 (pp. 4–26) and other astronomical data. The work is unannotated.

TO JAMES COCHRAN[1]

Retained Copy, Henry Papers, Smithsonian Archives

Albany Nov 3rd 1831

Dear Sir

Surveyor General De Witt has been so kind as to address a letter to you on the subject of a lot of land in the town of Hanniball.[2] The lot belongs to Mr Alexander and his sister my wife. It has been suffered to remain unattended to for many years from the circumstance of the owners being minors.

Mr Alexander & myself have lately purchased at considreable expense the part sold for taxes and wish now to dispose of the whole lot. A Professional Gentleman[3] who has satisfied himself of the validity of our title has

[1] James Cochran (1769–1848), lawyer, soldier, politician, was born in Albany. He graduated from Columbia College, New York City, in 1788; was commissioned major in the army by President John Adams; was Regent of the University of the State of New York, 1796 to 1820; elected to the House of Representatives, March 4, 1797, to March 3, 1799; and was a member of the State Senate from 1814 to 1818. Cochran moved to Oswego in 1826, was Postmaster of that city from 1841 to 1845 and editor of a local newspaper for several years. *Biographical Directory of the*

American Congress. For Cochran's reply, see his letter of November 9, 1831, below.

[2] A small town twelve miles south of Oswego, in Oswego County, New York.

[3] Daniel Cady (1773–1859), lawyer, judge, congressman, was born in Columbia County, New York. Cady studied law in Albany and established a law practice in Johnstown (then in Montgomery County), New York. He was a member of the State Assembly from 1808 to 1813, when he became District Attorney of the Fifth District. Elected as a Federalist to the Fourteenth Congress (March 1815–March

offered to purchase the whole at the rate of 6 dollars per acre in cash and will himself be at the expense of ejecting the persons who now possess the lot. Our Friend Mr De Witt advises that before we make the sale we request you to inform us if the property cannot be disposed of to better advantage or if there be any posibility of your being able in your Prof. capacity to find a purchaser in a short time who will pay 1000 or 1500 $ down and the remainder in instalments secured by mortgage or otherwise. Please answer this as soon as convenient as we are required in a short time to give a definite answer to the Prof before mentioned. I will make such an arrangement with the Surveyor General that on application to him your compensation for Prof services will be paid.

> I am Sir with much
> Respect Yours &c
> Joseph Henry

PS Address to me at the Albany Academy.　J. H.
We have been informed that most of the timber used in constructing one of the dams in the Oswego river was cut from this lot and that the persons who cut the same are responsible.

1817), he decided after one term to resume his practice in Johnstown. From 1847 to 1855 he was Justice of the State Supreme Court, and in 1856 served as President of the State Electoral College. *Biographical Directory of the American Congress.*

TO MR. ROGERS[1]
Retained Copy, Henry Papers, Smithsonian Archives

Albany Friday Evening
[November 4] 1831[2]

Dear Sir

I extremely regret that Messrs Townsend's workmen have disappointed me in finishing the steel horse shoe magnet as they promised; it was to be

[1] This letter begins in a straightforward manner—another Henry description of an electromagnetic device or procedure. About halfway through, the text takes an unexpected turn, making this a unique and biographically important document.

Identifying the addressee, "Mr. Rogers," becomes a significant task. Henry's retained copy gives little help as both the full name and location of "Mr. Rogers" are absent. So

far as we have been able to determine, this transaction about a magnetic ore separator does not involve Penfield and Taft with whom Henry worked earlier in 1831 (see the letters of May 30, 1831, and June 27, 1831, above).

From the text we know the following about "Mr. Rogers": he is in iron mining and has a forge or foundry associated with the mining operation. We can further assume from the letter that Rogers is located relatively con-

finished last Saturday without fail, yet not withstanding I have been at the Furnace two or three times every day since, I have not been able to get the magnet before this evening and not then until after standing over the workman from three until 6 o'clock. I am afraid that the delay has cost you much inconvenience and in order to save time I will send the horse shoe magnet alone tomorrow morning. I have charged it this evening & find that it operates well in charging small pieces of steel like your magnetic points. It will probably be found sufficiently powerful for your purpose and with care in using will serve in its present state to charge all your points. The reason why I do not send at the same time the Galvanic magnet is that I met with an unexpected difficulty in completing it. According to promis I was engaged in a copersmiths shop with it the whole of Saturday and Monday. After three o'clock after it was completely finished as I supposed on trying it I was much surprised to find that it would operate only with comparitively little power. I was at first much at a loss to account for this anomaly until after some reflection I concluded the defect might exist in

---

veniently to Albany so that mail and parcels can pass between him and Henry. This clearly indicates the Adirondack iron mining region where magnetic ore separators were coming into use. Henry's correspondent has one which may or may not be in actual use. An important piece of information about "Mr. Rogers" turns out to be of no use in identification—he "had" a patent (see footnote 5, below).

The only person we have located who fits these criteria is James Rogers, Sr. (1804–1880), but this identification is offered on a tentative basis. No other likely "Rogers" is known to us in the Adirondack mining region. James Rogers, Sr., was the founder and principal manager of what later became the J. and J. Rogers Iron Company which by 1869 was rated the largest firm of its kind in New York State. The other "J. Rogers" of the company name we can omit from consideration as he was named John Weed in 1831 and only changed his name to Rogers in 1844. Other Rogerses—relatives of James Rogers, Sr.— apparently had minor roles in the launching of the firm in 1831–1832.

In 1830 James Rogers, Sr., opened a store in Keeseville, New York, in the mining region. In 1831 he and his partners were making iron at Black Brook, New York. If this identification is correct, at Black Brook there was a magnetic ore separator in operation or being developed by Rogers in consultation with Joseph Henry. The firm prospered and

acquired additional mining properties and expanded its activities to include sawmills. In 1836 J. and J. Rogers had a magnetic ore separator at their Palmer Hill property which was unsuccessful and replaced by a gravity separator. By 1869 the firm had over 50,000 acres and the "aggregate revenue" of the partners was $200,000 annually. The firm was an integrated one and produced a wide variety of products from about 22 tons of iron a day produced by their furnaces.

By 1869 James Rogers, Sr., was obviously a man of means. If this identification is correct, in 1831 he was shrewd enough to enlist the best investigator of electromagnetism in America in the improvement of the separation process. And he may have even flirted with the idea of achieving a stronger position in the iron industry by acquiring control of the basic separator patents. *Leading Citizens of Clinton and Essex Counties, New York* (Boston, 1896), pp. 430–431; *History of Clinton and Franklin Counties, New York* . . . (Philadelphia, 1880), pp. 245, 247, 253; Winslow C. Watson, *The Military and Civil History of the County of Essex, New York* (Albany, 1869), pp. 441–447; and David H. Newland, *Geology of the Adirondack Magnetic Iron Ores* (Albany, 1908), Bulletin No. 423 of the New York State Department of Education.

[2] The corner of the sheet bearing the date is torn off. The date given here was written by Henry in his file notation on the last page of the manuscript.

the zinc employed in the construction: there being no sheet zinc in Albany but the small quantity you saw me experimenting with I used cast zinc but this from some subsequent experiments I find to produce a different result from the other. This fact is very interesting in a philosophical point of view and at leasure I intend to investigate the cause as it may lead to some curious results. Sheet zinc is abundent in N.Y. and I have sent for a supply. It will be received tomorrow and I shall then be able to forward your Galvanic magnet next week, but as I observed before I do not think you will have much use for it particularly if the steel horseshoe magnet be properly hardened and you be careful in useing it, never suffering it to remain when not employed without its poles connected by a piece of soft iron. From the delay in getting it finished there was no time left to have the face of the ends ground perfectly flat as they should be in order to operate most powerfully: You will observe that it holds most strongly when the edge of the plate of soft iron is turned towards the faces because in this position the contact is most perfect. In touching your *points* observe the following directions. Place the *point* or bar on a flat board; then place the horse shoe perpendicularly upon it with the two poles equidistant from the extremities of the bar—thus move the horse shoe backwards & forward two or three times from one extremity to the other using some pressure; turn the bar and rub the other side in the same manner without sep arating the magnet. I mean to say that the bar should be turned with the other side to the magnet without separating it from the attraction of the magnet. All violent separations of a magnet and a piece of iron or steel tends much to weaken the power; it will be best therefore as soon as a bar has been rubbed on both sides to apply another bar before the first is removed. This will in part nuteralize the power of the horseshoe and the separation can then be made without weakening either the magnetism of the bar or of the horseshoe.

On the same principle it will be improper to suffer any person to apply iron to the magnet & then forceably pull it off. The armature or soft piece of iron should be sliped off when the magnet is required to be used. I am the more particular in these instructions as I do not think the magnet was sufficiently well hardened to retain its magnetism well without careful usage. If you find any difficulty write me and I will give you further instructions with regard to charging it again. N.B. In giving your *points* the most powerful charge remember to have both poles of the horseshoe on the bar. You will probably be able with a little practice to charge seven in a minute.

Since you were in Albany I have thought considerably on your machine and have made some experiments in relation to it. I have also seen My

Friend Mr Tracy[3] who informed me that you were anxious that I should communicate my views on the subject to no person. You need be under no apprehension on this score for although I have heretofore been perfectly free in giving to the public any Knowledge I might possess of use and although I have considered it almost below the dignity of science to ask pay for my Knowledge yet I now conceive that I have been rather too free for my own interest and that the subject of magnetism is worth something more to me than mere fame.[4] As however I do not wish to devote much time to the subject of your machine without a fair prospect of remuneration, I have thought best before commencing to make particular inquiries in relation to the validity of your patent[5] or of any that I might obtain for the application of Galvanism to the same purpose. The following opinion which comes from the best authority in the state[6] on the subject you may rely on as correct and I communicate to you in a spirit of perfect candor. 1st no patent can be held for the application of an old power with which the public have been long acquainted although it may not before have ever been applied as stated in the specification of the patent. A case was lately decided in this District directly to the point in which the application of an old principle was pattented to a new purpose—the patent was not sus-

---

[3] Probably James G. Tracy. See footnote 14 of May 5, 1824, above.

[4] "Mere fame" for science is what Henry wanted all through his life. Here for the first and (so far as we now know) the only time Joseph Henry wavers and is tempted to abandon science for money. We have no idea why Henry considers this possibility? Were the Henrys pinched for money? Was he discouraged by the prospect of a lifetime at the Academy? Were his relations with members of the Institute becoming tense, perhaps because of the Ten Eyck dispute? Throughout the rest of his life Henry would be an apostle of disinterested research, a model of the true scientific spirit for his American contemporaries. Having overcome temptation himself, was he inclined, in later years, to display less tolerance towards those who succumbed?

[5] At this date the only patent in effect for the use of magnetism for the separation of iron from its ore was the Browning patent (see footnote 1 of Penfield and Taft's letter of May 30, 1831, above). The patent had expired but was renewed by special act of Congress on March 3, 1831. The next patent issued for iron ore separation was issued to Joseph Goulding, Reesville, New York, on July 18, 1832; it was probably for a gravity

separation process, not the use of magnetism.

As in the case of the identification of James Rogers, Sr., as the addressee, the surviving evidence does not help. The implication of the text is that Rogers had the rights to the Browning patent. The relationship of Rogers to James C. Odiorne is unknown to us. What we do know from Richard S. Allen's study of Penfield and Taft (p. 6) is that the iron men in the north country "made plans to band together and fight any infringement suit, but there is no record of Browning ever having pressed his claims." Penfield and Taft had been advised by counsel that the Browning patent was void. A further implication from this text is that one of the iron men in the Adirondack region was behind the revival of the patent and was seriously considering exercising his monopoly rights. We have no further evidence on why Rogers did not press his patent claims, if indeed they were his to press. The strong opposition of his peers coupled with doubts of the patent's validity may have been sufficient to outweigh the expectations of profit.

[6] Another mystery. Among Henry's friends and acquaintances in the Institute and Academy were a number of leading attorneys. We cannot point to any of these as being preeminent in reputation as a patent attorney.

tained.[7] This principle of law you will observe naturally affects the validity of your patent.[8]

[7] As explained in the next footnote, the interpretation of the patent law stated by Henry is at variance not only with current practice but with the established legal doctrine at the time this letter was composed. We are assuming Henry has not garbled what "the best authority in the state" told him. The case in question remains unidentified. Since 1819 the former Federal circuit courts, whose boundaries coincided with those of the district courts, had original jurisdiction in patent litigation. Unfortunately, there are no surviving records of the Circuit Court for the Northern District of New York, then sitting in Albany, prior to 1837. The legal reporting system of the day was not too thorough; few cases from the Northern District of New York at that period are noted in the volumes we have examined.

[8] Henry's first point is obscured to a modern reader by the use of terms such as "power" and "principle" in unfamiliar and archaic senses; in the case of principle, two quite distinct connotations are present here (or three, if one counts "principle of law") and in the judicial opinions on patent law. Another source of obscurity is that Henry's interpretation of the law is not true today and was contrary to the prevailing legal doctrine in 1831. In this extended footnote, we will first briefly dwell on the semantic problem, then rephrase Henry's meaning before discussing the points of patent law at issue. Some of the implications of Henry's misunderstanding will appear here and in the two succeeding footnotes.

An archaic definition of power is "a simple machine." The power or simple machine is an embodiment of an inherent property or effect of nature. Put another way, a simple machine is a source or means of supplying energy. Inventions could consist of a combination of powers (that is, simple machines) or of a power (or inherent property of matter) embodied in a novel manner and/or applied in a novel way. Principle does have the connotation of a general or fundamental truth as when we speak of the "principles of physics." In this sense there is an overlap with terms like "theory," "hypothesis," and even "fact." *Webster's Third New International Dictionary of the English Language, Unabridged* gives the following definitions, obviously derived from patent law: "natural law or laws applied to achieve or produce a result by an artificial device: the laws or facts of nature underlying and exemplified in the working of an artificial device." An additional definition of principle is "the mode of construction or working of an artificial device." In both terms, but especially in the use of the word principle, there is an ambiguity in that each is used in two senses: as an abstract property of nature and as a technological concept given concrete embodiment. It was a minor confusion in the development of patent law; to Henry and like-minded scientists the issues raised were quite serious.

Following his unknown authority, Henry construes the law to mean that if a scientific principle is well known, no new patent is valid even though for a completely novel application. If we give his meaning correctly, it appears that only one patentable application is legal for each newly found power or principle. Under this construction of the law, the Browning patent in the hands of Rogers, for example, was void because the power or principle of magnetism acting on iron was an old one, even if its application to iron ore separation was novel. What Henry does, in our opinion, is to blur the two meanings of principle, invariably tending to use the term in its scientific sense so that the patent system is viewed from the vantage point of scientific advances. While this usage is quite consistent with the statements in his 1826 Inaugural Address, Henry simply misconstrues the spirit and the development of patent law. From its very beginning in the reign of James I, Anglo-American patent law encouraged applications per se; the patent law did not exist to stimulate the growth of abstract truth or general principles. In fact, as we shall see below, Henry interpreted the law as placing the scientist, as scientist, at a decided disadvantage in acquiring patents.

Basically, one cannot patent scientific knowledge as such. Early American decisions cited the well-known British case of *Boulton and Watt* v. *Bull,* in which one of the points at issue was the distinction between the use of the word "principle" as an abstract property of nature and as an embodiment of a technological concept: "Undoubtedly there can be no patent for a mere principle; but for a principle so far embodied and connected with corporeal substances, as to be in a con-

2nd If any discovery in science be communicated to the public through any periodical or other publication so as to become public $<property>$ Knowledge no patent can be sustained for the application of that discovery

---

dition to act, and to produce effects in any art, trade, mystery, or manual occupation, I think there may be a patent." A recent discussion of Watt's views on patent law showing his concern with this issue is Eric Robinson, "James Watt and the Law of Patents," *Technology and Culture*, 1972, *13*:115–139. Robinson shows that the issues involved were still being debated in Britain at least as late as 1829. The point was reaffirmed in an 1810 Circuit Court decision in Georgia involving Eli Whitney: "A patent is not grantable for a principle merely, but only for an application of a principle, whether previously known or not, to some new and useful purpose."

The distinction between a scientific principle and what was legally patentable was clearly given on two subsequent occasions. An 1817 Circuit Court decision in Pennsylvania noted that: "A patent for 'an improvement in the art of making nails, by means of a machine which cuts and heads the nails at one operation,' is not a grant of an abstract principle; nor is it the grant of the different parts of any machine, but of an improvement applied to the practical use, effected by a combination of various mechanical powers to produce a new result." In April 1831 the Circuit Court for the Eastern District of Pennsylvania in another case involving Eli Whitney asserted:

> Nor is a discovery of some new principle, theory, or elementary truth, or an improvement on it, abstracted from its application a new invention. But when such discovery is applied to any practical purpose, in the construction, operation or effects of machinery or composition of matter, producing a new substance, or an old one in a new way, by new machinery, or a new combination of the parts of an old one, operating in a peculiar, better, cheaper, or quicker method, a new mechanical employment of principle already known, the organization of a machine embodied and reduced to practice on some thing visible, tangible, vendible, and capable of enjoyment, some new mode of practically employing human art or skill. It is a 'discovery,' 'invention,' or 'improvement,' within the acts of congress . . . .

And finally, in 1853 in one of the telegraph patent cases in which Henry had more than a passing interest, the decision flatly noted that "the discovery of a principle of natural philosophy or physical science is not patentable."

Clearly, Henry is mistaken in his views. There is ample evidence of the issuance of valid patents for both improvements in the application of known scientific principles and for new applications of old principles. In both cases the law then required, as it does now, that the inventions be novel and useful, as well as an appreciable advance over the prior state of the art. (For further comments on this last requirement, see footnote 10, below.) Although mistaken, Henry's views follow naturally from his interpretation of the nature of science and its relationship to technology as given in his Inaugural Address and further amplified in his introductory chemistry lecture several months after this document was composed (see below). Henry believed that discovery of scientific principles was all-important, not the concrete embodiment of these in practical applications. Not only was the discovery of principles of science important for its own sake, but, according to Joseph Henry, the way technology should and did advance was by deriving particular applications from general truths of nature uncovered by natural philosophers. It is our opinion that the difference in attitude of scientists like Henry and of the society at large toward patents, inventions, and inventors throughout the nineteenth and early decades of the present century was an important factor in the belief of scientists that America was indifferent to basic research. This belief will play a significant role in Henry's actions at both Princeton and the Smithsonian. For a discussion of this theme, see Nathan Reingold, "American Indifference to Basic Research, a Reappraisal," to appear in the Proceedings of the 1970 Conference on Science in Nineteenth-Century America at Northwestern University.

Discussion of the evolution of patent law is difficult because of the nature of the legal literature. Examples of the case reporting system and systematic treatises are quite often composed in an ahistoric fashion, almost as though the entire content of the field were simply an unfolding of matter implicitly present in the Statute of Monopolies of James

to the arts of life. This principle you will also observe will prevent me from holding a patent for the application of Galvanism to the separation of iron.[9] You will perceive readily that it will be for your interest that this

---

I. Very few minority decisions are given nor is there any systematic coverage of decisions reversed on appeal for this early period. Without a major research effort, we cannot say if a significant minority of jurists and attorneys shared Henry's general position at some time in the past. The tenor of the patent literature suggests—and correctly, we suspect—that the question of the role of scientific principles was not particularly significant except in a few isolated cases. In a number of other cases, the citation of the doctrine of nonpatentability of scientific principles is very casual, a truism not worth lingering over.

For the patent law see Thomas Green Fessenden, *An Essay on the Law of Patents for New Inventions*, 2d ed. (Boston, 1822) in general and pp. 69–130 for the discussion of *Boulton and Watt* v. *Bull;* the quotation above from the opinion of Chief Justice Eyre is taken from p. 101; Willard Phillips, *The Law of Patents for Inventions* (Boston, 1837); *Federal Digest*, vol. 49.

Particular cases cited above are: after the British opinion we next gave *Whitney* v. *Carter,* Circuit Court, Georgia, 1810, Federal Case 17, 583; following that was *Gray* v. *James,* Circuit Court, Pennsylvania, 1817, Federal Case 5718; the second case involving Eli Whitney is *Whitney et al.* v. *Emmett et al.,* cited in 1 Baldwin 303, from the Circuit Court of the Eastern District of Pennsylvania, 1831, but the text used was from the decision as given in Federal Case 17, 585; the telegraph case is *O'Reilly* v. *Morse,* 56 U.S. 62. See also the 1851 decision, In re Henry [not Joseph Henry], Federal Case 6371.

[9] Again Joseph Henry misconstrues the patent law in such a way as to place the scientist at a particular disadvantage. The ideology of science stresses publication; the scientist is under an obligation to add his results to the known body of knowledge. If a scientist does this, Henry says, he is barred from taking out a patent and presumably so is anyone else. If we combine this point with the purport of the first one, it would seem that valid patents can result under two circumstances: the original scientific discoverer can apply for a patent before publication; prior to the discovery of a scientific principle an inventor might stumble upon an application in complete ignorance of the truths of nature involved. As to the first,

Henry had already published. The law, however, was not concerned with the publication of philosophical principles but whether a particular technological concept was known to have been reduced to practice. An 1816 decision in Pennsylvania noted, "The discovery must not only be useful, but new; and it must not have been known and used before in any part of the world to sustain the patent" (*Evans* v. *Eaton,* Federal Case 4559). Justice Story in an 1817 Circuit Court case in Massachusetts (*Bedford* v. *Hunt,* Federal Case 1217, cited in 1 Mason 305) had declared that the mere speculation of a philosopher or mechanician will not deprive an inventor of a patent. But if the speculation is put into even limited use, this will void a patent. As long as Henry had not published an account of an electromagnetic application of his contrivance, it was still possible for him to receive a valid patent, all other legal criteria being met. As to the second circumstance, Henry did not believe this happened frequently, and he clearly did not consider this the best way to attain technological progress. See both the next footnote and the introductory chemical lecture.

If Henry misconstrued the patent law, others in his circle did not. In the Lewis C. Beck Papers at Rutgers is an undated, incomplete manuscript text of a lecture on the "Separation of Iron Ore by the Magnet." From internal evidence the lecture was delivered in Albany during the early years of interest in the possibility of using magnetism in iron ore mining, that is sometime after 1831. We have not succeeded in determining the precise date of this lecture. It may even have been part of the lecture series in which Henry participated with Beck in the early months of 1832. Beck had hunted through the literature and come up with two published references to devices for the use of magnetism to separate iron from its ore. The first is to a patent issued to a William Fullerton and described in the *Repertory of Arts and Manufactures*, 1794, *1*:297; the second is to a description of a device by a J. D. Ross in the *Transactions* of the Society of Arts, 1813, *28*:206. Beck declared the Browning patent void since the particular application was well known in principle and exemplified in practice. "The peculiar arrangement of the magnets & accompanying apparatus can certainly form no part of the claim of Mr.

opinion coming as it does from so good authority should be kept a secret and indeed this is the advise given by the person himself. He says the most proper way of acting in this case is to improve the machine as much as possible and to fassion it in different manners and to take out patents for the alterations and improvements and this is the only way of securing to <*yourself*> the alterings of the machine.[10] According to these views if they

---

Browning. But if so, there are many other ways in which magnets might be constructed and arranged so as to produce the desired effect." While this opinion must have pleased the iron mining men of the Adirondack region (Mr. Rogers excepted), Beck's words must have increased Henry's uneasiness about collaborating with Mr. Rogers.

[10] At this point Henry discloses a serious inconsistency in his interpretation of the patent law. He has limited the validity of patents to inventions which are the first applications of scientific principles and further has limited the issuance of valid patents to one application per scientific principle. He now goes on to cite his unknown authority to the effect that alterings (not further defined) of the original contrivance will yield valid patents. If you are interested in encouraging scientific work, this seems strange; if you are interested in encouraging improvements in existing arts, such a legal doctrine is quite reasonable. And the law does indeed grant patents for improvements in existing devices, creating a major problem for the courts. In practice, how does one determine that a proposed improvement is not only new, but that its newness is of such dimensions as to merit the grant of a legal monopoly? The development of this legal issue could not have satisfied a Joseph Henry. In 1817, in the Circuit Court of Massachusetts, Justice Story had declared that an improvement need not necessarily be superior in all respects but simply "useful" in contradistinction to mischievous or immoral (*Lowell* v. *Lewis*, Federal Case 8568).

Later decisions were somewhat more elaborate but hardly spelled out objective criteria. In 1840 an Ohio decision said: "A patent for an improvement in a machine which had been previously patented to another person cannot protect the right of the patentee, unless the improvement be substantially different in principle from the original invention" (*Smith* v. *Pearce*, Federal Case 13089). *Winans* v. *Denmead* in 1853 asserted that: "To change the form of an existing machine

and by means of such change to introduce and employ other mechanical principles or natural power or a new mode of operation and thus attain a new and useful result is the subject of a patent" (56 U.S. 333). Somewhat more elaborate is the language of *Huggins* v. *Hubby*, an 1861 case in Ohio: "To sustain a patent for an improvement, it must effect the same object a better, cheaper, more expeditious, or more beneficial manner than the instrument improved, or it must effect some further or other beneficial object in connection with the former" (Federal Case 6839).

What this meant to the scientifically inclined is that the law was skewed to the benefit of the inventor to the point of giving legal monopolies for very minor alterings of devices. L. C. Beck was clearly dubious also. In his autobiography the astronomer Simon Newcomb gives an example of the reaction of research scientists to the standards of invention of the Patent Office. He had helped with the cooling of the air in the White House while President Garfield lay there stricken with the assassin's bullet. Afterward an inventor had claimed infringement since his patent claimed "about every possible way in which ice could be arranged for cooling purposes," including placing the blocks on supports as Newcomb did. Newcomb commented: "In a word, the impression I got was that the only sure way of avoiding an infringement would have been to blindfold the men who put the ice in the box, and ask them to throw it in pellmell." Simon Newcomb, *The Reminiscences of an Astronomer* (Boston, 1903), pp. 357–363.

Even more important to a Henry than the legal standard of invention were the implications of the development of the patent law, reflecting as it did public attitudes. Too often, the references to the work of science were prefaced with terms such as "mere." Henry had no objection to the grant of property rights to encourage invention. As shall come out in later volumes, he did object to the exaltation of the inventor and the downgrading of the role of the scientist. The development of the patent law simply did not accord with

agree with yours I should like first to make some experiments with a view of improving your machine.

I am still confident that I can form a machine on Galvanic principles which will effect powerfully the separation of iron but on mature reflection I think I can greatly improve the operation of yours so as to make it as powerful as the other and with less expense.

For this purpose I should like to have a drawing or a model of the machine in its present state and with your improvements. I should not probably alter the moving principles of the machine but should principally confine my experiments and alterations to the form, to the position & the sizes of the magnets.

Perhapse it would be well for me to have a model of the Galvanic machine constructed and take a patent for the same to prevent others from seazing upon it as well as to strengthen at least in appearance your patent for I understand it is agreed upon that you will join me in this patent as well as in my experiments. Write me as soon as convenient and state your views & propositions deffinitly on the subject and we will make arrangements for commencing operations.[11] I should like to have constructed in Albany as a test under my direction not a model but a working cylinder of a machine. The magnets could be forged at your establishment and the work filled up here. I have made some calculations and drawings of a modification of your machine which I think will be a great improvement. It however must of course be tested by experiment.[12]

---

his belief in the importance of science and that applications should ideally derive from scientific principles. Two later decisions illustrate the gap between Henry and his fellow scientists on the one hand and the world of the inventor on the other. In an 1849 ruling in Pennsylvania the court declared:

He who first discovers that a law of nature can be applied to produce a particular result, and having devised machinery to make it operative, introduces it to his fellowmen, is a discoverer and inventor of the highest grade. He may assert and establish his property, not only in the formal device, for which mere mechanical ingenuity can at once, as soon as the principle is known, imagine a thousand substitutes, but in the general principle which his machinery was the first to embody, to exemplify, to illustrate, to make operative, and to announce to mankind. This is not to patent an abstraction, but rather the invention, as the inventor has given it to the world, in its

full dimensions and extent (*Parker* v. *Hulme,* Federal Case 10, 740).

An 1870 case in Massachusetts further declared: "An inventor or discoverer of a new and useful art may have a valid patent although ignorant of the philosophical or abstract principle involved in the practice of the art" (*Piper* v. *Brown,* Federal Case 11, 180).

[11] We have found no further examples of the Henry-Rogers correspondence.

[12] From Henry's letter to Silliman of March 28, 1832, below, we know he was still working on the application of electromagnetism to iron ore processing in the following spring. In L. C. Beck's unpublished lecture referred to in footnote 9 there is a reference to a machine of this nature which Beck himself conceived. We have no conclusive evidence of either Henry or Beck participating in the other's work in this area. We cannot explain why Henry now thinks he can obtain a patent after his enunciation of contrary principles.

November 8, 1831

FROM PARKER CLEAVELAND[1]

Henry Papers, Smithsonian Archives

Brunswick (Me) Nov. 8, 1831.

Dear Sir,

Will you have the goodness to inform me what was the expense of the Electro-magnetic apparatus, which you made for Yale College, described in Sillimans Journal vol. 20, p 201.[2]

Also please inform me, whether you would be willing to prepare a similar one for our College, and if so, *how soon* it could be in readiness.

Have the goodness to write me as soon as convenient; and should the College be able to purchase, I will reply immediately.

Yours with much esteem

P. Cleaveland

[1] Parker Cleaveland (1780–1858), scientist, author, educator, was born in Byfield, Massachusetts. He attended Dummer Academy, and in 1799 graduated from Harvard College. In 1803, while studying for the ministry, Cleaveland accepted a tutorship in mathematics and natural philosophy offered him by Harvard. He remained there until 1805 when he was appointed Professor of Mathematics and Natural Philosophy at Bowdoin College, in Brunswick, Maine. Cleaveland's *Elementary Treatise on Mineralogy and Geology* (Boston, 1816) was the first American work in this field and was well received in Europe. Upon the founding of the Medical School of Maine, administered by Bowdoin, he turned to teaching materia medica. He will appear subsequently in Henry's letters. See *DAB*.

[2] For Henry's response to this query see his letter to Cleaveland of November 16, 1831.

FROM JAMES COCHRAN

Henry Papers, Smithsonian Archives

Oswego November 9th 1831

D[r] Sir

Your letter of the 3[d] instant,[1] I received yesterday. There is no doubt that upon a subdivision of your lot into 50 or 100 acres, you can sell to settlers at $10 per acre—and might get perhaps, one fifth of the purchase money down, and the rest in four or five equal yearly installments with interest. In such case you would be obliged to prosecute by ejectment the present tenants, which would be attended with a little delay. Indeed you could not get judgment against them untill after June Circuit. At June

[1] Henry's letter of November 3, 1831, above.

Circuit next summer, you could have a trial and a verdict, and at the next Supreme Court your judgment.

Now, it is submitted to you whether you had not better accept of the proposition of your professional friend and take six dollars per acre cash, he to prosecute the tenants. It is a question which you and Mr. Alexander can determine for yourselves, better than any other can, because a decision by you would depend much upon your business or occupation. At all events, I advise immediate measures against the tenants, whose title is a late fabricated one, to take off the timber. Since I wrote to you, they have doubled their teams, and are committing dreadful depredations upon the timber. I see no reason why you may not put a stop to these depredations by application to the Court of Chancery.

The injury done the lot by the state agents in repairing the dam did not amount to much. The timber cut was principally hemlock, and for the purpose of getting brush from the branches of the Trunk. If I can afford you any asistance by way of advice or otherwise respecting your lot, I will do it with pleasure. My present opinion is, that you had better sell at $6. per acre cash, unless you can find it convenient to wait for your money at $10 to settlers.

> Very respectfly
> Your ob[t] S[t]
> James Cochran

TO DANIEL CADY[1]
Retained Copy, Henry Papers, Smithsonian Archives

Monday Evening Nov 14th 1831

Dear Sir

We have received through the Surveyor General an account of the lot in Hanneball. This information has been tardy but is somewhat satisfactory. His informer states that the land can be sold and he thinks readily for 10 to 12 dollars per acre, one fifth of the money down, and that there are two worthless persons in possession of it who are cutting off the timber that we will be at some expense and trouble in dispossessing them. We feel ourselves under much obligation to you for the manner in which you have acted in this affair and in particular for the disinterested information you

---

[1] On the final page of this document, Henry wrote the following: "Draft of a Letter to Cady relates to Lot in Hanniball, Nov 14th 1831."

have now given us in relation to the trespassors. We wish to dispose of the lot and are desirous under these circumstances that you should be the purchaser.

We have been considreably disappointed in our first calculations concerning the number of acres. Had there been 475 as we supposed it would have ammounted at 6 dollars per acre to $2850. If there be as is suppose[d] only 375 acres it will ammount to 2250. Cannot you afford in justice to yourself to give us $2500 for the lot, which is about the mean between our former expectations and your last offer. It is not necessary that the whole sum should be payed down. We should like to have about one half in cash & the remainder at any time which might suit your convenience.

We have procured a deed acknowledged in due form from Mr. [? Kiersted]² and now wish immediatly to settle the affair as the persons in possession must be stoped in their depridations.

Please write immediatly.

---

² Unidentified.

TO PARKER CLEAVELAND¹
Retained Copy, Henry Papers, Smithsonian Archives

Albany Nov. 16ᵗʰ 1831²

Dear Sir

The magnet constructed under my direction for Yale college cost Prof. Silliman 40 dollars.³ I wrote him before paying the different bills that it would cost 35 dollars. He generously sent 40 but even with this sum after paying all the bills I found myself minus about 5 dollars. A part of the above expense however was incurred by experiments to determine the proper length of the wires & the size of the battery proper for the quantity of iron.

I have lately had forged a large horseshoe weighing 101 lbs which I intend fitting up for some contemplated experiments on the identity of elec-

---

¹ Henry is replying to Cleaveland's request of November 8, 1831, above.
² On the back of the letter, Henry has dated the copy November 17.
³ See Henry's correspondence with Silliman in January and April 1831, above, and Henry and Ten Eyck, "An Account of a Large Electro-Magnet Made for the Laboratory of Yale College," *Silliman's Journal,* 1831, 20:201–203.

tricity and magnetism.[4] It will be much more powerful than any heretofore made being almost double the weight of the Yale College magnet (59½ lb). I shall probably have it completed in about three weeks. I would despose of it to the college if they choose to purchase at the cost of material and manual labour and this will probably ammount to from 50 to 60 dollars as the iron work alone comes to 30 dollars.

I have in possession the magnet described in my first paper published in the American Journal.[5] It will support 700 lbs & may perhaps be sufficiently large for your purpose. I will despose of it to the College for 30 dollars and would prefer doing this to sending my large one as I could then experment with it at my leisure. I will however act in accord with your wishes and if you would prefer it I will have constructed a magnet of the same size as that of Yale College & charge the actual cost of materials & workmens wages.[6]

I have lately improved the form of the little machine described in the July No of Sillimans Journal.[7] A article of this kind can be constructed in Albany for about 15 dollars, the permanent magnets being the most costly part of the apparatus. As they require to be powerful they are made of a number of pins fastened together with screws.

I am sir with much
Respect Yours &c

[4] By "experiments on the identity of electricity and magnetism," Henry probably meant the attempt to produce electricity from magnetism. In the surviving Henry documents, this is the first mention we have found of his electromagnetic induction experiments, though we suspect he had been considering the experiments earlier.

The large magnet may be the one referred to in his 1832 paper announcing his discovery of electromagnetic induction, "On the Production of Currents and Sparks of Electricity from Magnetism," *Silliman's Journal,* 1832, *22*:403. According to the article, he had begun to construct the large magnet in August 1831 but was unable to use it for his induction experiments: "I was, however, at that time, accidentally interrupted in the prosecution of these experiments, and have not been able to resume them, until within the last few weeks, and then on a much smaller scale than was at first intended." Since he ultimately used a smaller magnet in these experiments, the larger magnet may have never been completed.

[5] "On the Application of the Principle of the Galvanic Multiplier to Electro-magnetic Apparatus, and Also to the Development of Great Magnetic Power in Soft Iron, with a Small Galvanic Element," *Silliman's Journal,* 1831, *19*:400–408.

[6] For a detailed description of Cleaveland's magnet, which would be about the same size as Silliman's, see below, Henry to Cleaveland, May 8, 1832.

[7] "On a Reciprocating Motion Produced by Magnetic Attraction and Repulsion," *Silliman's Journal,* 1831, *20*:340–343.

TO DANIEL CADY

Retained Copy, General Manuscripts, Rare Book Collection,
University of Pennsylvania Library

Albany Tuesday Nov. 22nd 1831

Dear Sir

Your letter of the 18[th1] came to hand on saturday last. Mr Alexander &
myself have considered with some attention your offer of $6.66 per acre for
the land, to have the Lot surveyed and to pay the taxes on the present year
on condition that we will give you what you can recover from the prosecution of the persons who have trèsspassed on the lot. By this proposition you
offer in addition to your former offer of 6 dollars per acre about 270 dollars
(allowing the lot to contain 375 acres)[2] for our chance of recovering [$]1000
or more. What this chance is, in the uncertainty of the law and what the
cost of failure would be you know much better than we do. But if it be an
even chance can not you afford to give us $6.66 per acre for the land and
one half of what you may recover from the prosecution. According[ly], as
we now view the subject this appears to us quite as favourable a proposition to your interest as the one you made us at first of 6 dollars per acre.
Besids if it can be so arranged we would rather not give up all interest in
[the lot] for by so doing, since it would be made in our names, we would
have the full oblique of the suit with but little of the benefit.

I am hopin[g] that we will soon be able to make a setlement of the affair
that will be satisfactory to both parties.[3]

I am sir with much
Respect & esteem Yours
Joseph Henry

[1] Not found.
[2] Actually, at 66 cents an acre more for 375
acres the figure is closer to $250.
[3] The next mention of property in Hannibal appears in Daniel Cady's letter of April
20, 1832, to Henry, below. Although other
letters may have passed between them in the
intervening months, none are known to us.

FROM PARKER CLEAVELAND

Henry Papers, Smithsonian Archives

Brunswick Nov. 25, 1831.

My dear Sir,

We are much obliged by your favor of Nov. 16.

On deliberation, we should prefer to have a magnet constructed on the plan of that for Yale College, certainly not less, and should it weigh 10 or 12 lbs more, there would be no objection.

As electro magnetic appr. is sometimes apt to be a little *capricious,* we should consider it a favor to have you test its powers, before you send it.

Permit me also to remark, that it may be important to us to have it made, as soon as your convenience permits, on account of conveyance by water down your river to the city. Although I should not use it at my Lectures before the *first* of Feb. yet passages by water from N. York to Boston or Portland are slow and not very frequent in the winter. I shall write you again as to a place of deposite in the City.

With much esteem
Yours etc. P. Cleaveland

FROM PARKER CLEAVELAND
Henry Papers, Smithsonian Archives

Brunswick Me. Dec.ʳ 8, 1831.

My dear Sir,

I wrote you Nov. 25 stating what kind of magnet we should prefer. When completed, it may be sent to *John P. Thurston,* Merchant, *South Street, N. York.* I can not ascertain the No. of his store, but believe it to be *about 56.*

Please have the apparatus well secured in a *strong box,* and direct it *to me,* care of *N. & L. Dana & Co. Merchants, Portland, Me.*

If you send it to Mr. Thurston by an honest man, who will be sure to find Mr. T's store, and leave it with him, I should like to have you pay the freight down to the city, and put it into my bill.

When you send it, please write me by mail, and let me know the whole expense, and whether freight is included. Also inform me if a draft on the *American Bank in Boston* will answer in payment. Such a draft made payable to you on *your order* is *perfectly safe on both sides,* if Boston money will answer your purpose. If not, I will inclose U.S. bills.[1]

Also please inform me how you usually estimate the weight supported by the magnet or rather what sort of weights you use in the scale. And gen-

---

[1] That is, in notes of the Bank of the United States, the only nationally circulating currency.

erally, if there is any thing in the management of the apparatus in *first trials,* which would not be *perfectly* obvious, you will oblige me by directing my attention to those points.[2]

> With much esteem
> yr servt
> P. Cleaveland

[2] For Henry's reply, see his letter of May 8, 1832, below.

HENRY NOTEBOOK ENTRY

Notebook [6123], page 177, Henry Papers, Smithsonian Archives

Dec 20th [1831]

On reading Mr DeWitts paper (manuscript)[1] on the functions of the moon, I am struck with the remark that the moon exercises some influence on the light of the sun reflected from her.

It is possible that the rays of light in passing near the moon in the time of an eclipse, may undergo some change in refference to *polarization* or *depolarization.* Can not this be determined by the ordinary methods of experimenting on polarized light.[2]   J. H.

[1] Simeon DeWitt published a paper, "Observations on the Eclipse of 16 June, 1806 . . . ," in the *Transactions* of the American Philosophical Society, 1809, 6:300–302, in the form of a letter to Benjamin Rush dated April 25, 1807. On March 2, 1825, DeWitt read this piece with an extensive addition to the Albany Institute which later published it in its *Transactions,* 1833–1852, 2:70–83. Presumably, Henry had the manuscript of the address in 1831.

[2] This is apparently a reference to DeWitt, pp. 80–81, in the Institute *Transactions,* op. cit. Henry's old friend was struck by the spectacular appearance of the corona. Like others, DeWitt incorrectly postulated a lunar atmospheric explanation which had been discredited in the previous century. Aware of these objections, DeWitt argued against them by postulating a uniform density of the lunar atmosphere.

DeWitt's presentation had two distinctive contributions. He assumed, first of all, that the moon was continually giving off emanations which became visible during the eclipse. Assuming a beneficent Creator who arranged phenomena, DeWitt, secondly, postulated a kind of interchange between the sun, moon, and earth. In this train of thought he relied heavily for support on analogies from the living world. It seemed reasonable and probable to him that the sun's rays, during eclipses, carried something tangible or an "impulse" from the moon to the earth.

Henry, a man of a different mold, simply translated DeWitt's speculations into the question of an experiment on the possible polarizing effect of the moon on sunlight during an eclipse. We have no evidence of his ever conducting such a test nor was this normally part of the observations performed during solar eclipses at that period.

FROM EDWARD HITCHCOCK[1]
Henry Papers, Smithsonian Archives

Amherst College (Mass.) Dec. 28ᵗʰ 1831

Sir,

My object in addressing you at this time is to make an enquiry in respect to the construction of an Electro-Magnet similar to that described in the American Journal of Science Vol. 20 p 201. I wish to know whether any artist in Albany or elsewhere constructs magnets of this kind & at about what price. Or if not can I get one constructed here by a tolerably ingenious artist from your description so as to exhibit to good advantage the wonderful powers of the instrument. I wish very much to be able to show one to my Class next term & have therefore presumed to trouble you without a personal acquaintance, with these enquiries.[2] By answering them you will much oblige your humble servant.

Edward Hitchcock

[1] For biographical information, see above, Lecture Notes, Henry's Canal Tour Journal, May 8, 1826, especially footnote 2.

[2] For Henry's reply, see below, January 27, 1832.

⁂{ 1832 }⁂

HENRY'S INTRODUCTORY LECTURE ON CHEMISTRY [JANUARY–MARCH 1832][1]
Miscellaneous Notes, Henry Papers, Smithsonian Archives

It is usual in commencing a course of lectures on any subject to set fourth in an introductory its nature and particular advantages as an object of study. In the present instance however we shall not confine our remarkes

[1] Henry's manuscript, loosely bound in a gray booklet, is entitled simply "Introductory." The text itself is undated, but "1840" appears faintly on the gray cover. The date appears to be in another hand and erroneous in any case. Internal evidence clearly places the manuscript in Henry's Albany period. It is conceivable that he used the same text again at a later time for some occasion unknown to us. From the opening paragraph, we know that Henry's lecture inaugurated a course on chemistry—probably the public chemistry course delivered jointly by Henry, T. R. Beck, and L. C. Beck, which the latter mentions in his unpublished autobiography of 1851 (Lewis C. Beck Papers, Rutgers University Library, pp. 33–35). Beck notes that in 1831 he was "appointed Lecturer on Chemistry at the Albany Academy. This was in a measure a nominal appointment & its duties were discharged by deliv-

to chemestry a knowledge of which is so manifestly applicable to the every day business of life and the importance of which has been urged in this place by a person far more capable than I am to do it justice.[2] A portion of the time generally allotted to an exercise of this kind will be devoted to a brief exposition of the importance of the study of Mechanical Philosophy a branch of <*general*> Physical science intimatly connected with all the arts and with the developing of the human mind and progress of civilization.[3] The remaining part of the lecture will be occupied in exhibiting the articles of apparatus procured during the last season to illustrate mechanical & physical science.[4] We are induced to adopt this course because we

---

ering a few lectures in conjunction with my Brother & Prof. Henry, before a popular audience during the winter season." Beck's first lecture, surviving in the Rutgers University Library, is entitled "Introductory to the Chemical Course. Albany Academy" and is dated January 1832. Since, in the first paragraph, Henry seems to be referring to Beck's lecture, we assume that Beck spoke first and that the Henry manuscript, therefore, should be dated January 1832 or later, but sometime during the winter season. No other lectures by Henry or the Becks in this series have been found.

[2] Apparently a reference to L. C. Beck's "Introductory to the Chemical Course," now in the Rutgers University Library. Unlike Henry, Beck confined his lecture to the development of chemistry. Approximately half of his lecture was devoted to the technological applications of chemistry, a subject which Beck introduced with these remarks:

> But it is not only to the more enlarged & correct views concerning the scope & purpose of Chemistry that we are to ascribe its advancement & the important rank which it now holds among the sciences. Though these alone might have had the effect of securing the attention of many votaries of science, they never would have led to that general interest which it now appears to excite. We are to look for the reason of this in the fact that ever since Chemistry has shaken off the trammels of error & superstition, it has been constantly contributing to the wants of society—it has been constantly contributing to the improvement & extension of the arts.

Just a few years before the Henry-Beck lectures, similar beliefs in the immediate utility of chemical knowledge were confidently expressed in a New York Regents' report to the State Legislature on the "practical usefulness" of scientific education at the Rensselaer School. Taking chemistry as a case in point, the report recapitulated the importance of chemistry for agriculture, asserting that "the principles of chemical science are so intimately blended with this great and primary branch of labor, that there are but few operations of the farm which are not materially profited by its aid," including soil analysis, fertilizers, and so forth. The report also described the dependence of many manufacturing industries on chemistry. Iron and steel production, the manufacture of glass, porcelain, and earthenware, tanning, soapmaking, and brewing were all cited to show the utility of chemical principles. Board of Regents' Minutes in the custody of the Office of the Commissioner of Education of New York, Albany, New York, March 11, 1828, *3*: 201–204.

Although the links between chemical science and technical developments were then taken for granted, the precise nature of the interrelationship has recently come under scrutiny. On the complexity of this interaction in a specific case—the production of sal ammoniac in the eighteenth century—see Robert P. Multhauf, "Sal Ammoniac:: A Case History in Industrialization," *Technology and Culture*, 1965, *6*:569–586.

[3] The phrase given here is a revision of an earlier Henry wording which reads: ". . . connected with <*chemestry both in its application*> to the useful arts and in its development of the laws of nature."

[4] On the philosophical apparatus at the Albany Academy, see above, Henry's Descriptive Catalogue of Philosophical Apparatus Purchased for the Albany Academy, December 18, 1830.

consider that this department of science, & particularly the higher parts of it, has not received that attention in this city and indeed in this country which its importance demands. This science does not afford to the lecturer the advantage of fixing the attention of his audience by a series of brilliant experiments as in chemestry.[5] On the contrary its illustrations are of such a nature as to appear dull and uninteresting to those who are averse or are unhabituated to mental exertion.

But if it fail to please the idle or the inattentive in this respect it cannot but reccommend itself to <all> the reflecting by its importance in a practical point of view for certainly that species of knowledge which adds to our comforts and convenience which extends our power over matter, the elements and the brute creation and which applies directly to the wants of every individual cannot be uninteresting to an inquiring mind in whatever form it may be communicated.

The mechanic arts upon proper reflection must awaken the curiosity and the interest of all who are dependent upon them for the necessaries or the luxuries of life and these will comprise every member of the civilized part of mankind. The advancement also of these arts must be felt as an object of great importance both to nations and individuals. Now without the application of correct scientific knowledge to this purpose they must ever remain stationary or their advance be extremely slow.[6] This position will

---

[5] A comment, we suspect, on the contemporary popularity of the public chemistry lectures then being given across the United States by men of all occupations and educational levels. According to Wyndham Miles, from the mid-1700s to the late 1800s public courses were given on all subjects in the arts and sciences. Often featuring spectacular demonstrations, the chemistry lectures drew some of the largest audiences. The most prominent chemist to give such courses, Benjamin Silliman, lectured to the public from 1834 to 1857. "Public Lectures on Chemistry in the United States," *Ambix*, 1968, *15*:129–153.

Though Henry is dealing in this lecture with the more austere parts of chemistry and physical science, the Henry-Beck lecture series belonged to this tradition of public enlightenment.

[6] Undoubtedly Henry's confident pronouncements on the utility of science were designed in part to elicit public support for basic science. It is widely believed that pure science was poorly supported during the first half of the nineteenth century and that, as George Daniels has put it, scientists were

compelled to "sell" basic science to the public on the grounds of its utility (George H. Daniels, "The Pure-Science Ideal and Democratic Culture," *Science*, 1967, *156*:1699–1705). Yet, to view science and technology solely in these terms perverts the basic spirit of Henry's statements about the technological and social benefits of science. It also distorts the views of many of his scientific contemporaries. We must emphasize that Henry seems sincerely and intimately concerned with the practical results of scientific research. Although committed personally to basic science, Henry, like some of his colleagues, regarded applied science as a legitimate and important concern of the scientific community.

Henry's deep-rooted belief that the useful arts should and actually do depend wholly on discoveries in pure science followed directly from the scheme of human knowledge he delineated in his Inaugural Address to the Albany Academy (see above, September 11, 1826, especially footnote 5). There, Henry described a continuum between pure and applied disciplines, asserting that principles and discoveries in "pure" fields, epitomized by mathematics, infuse the so-called

appear evident when we reflect that every mechanic art is based upon some principle of one of general laws of nature and that the more intimately acquainted we are with these laws the more capable we must be to advance and improve <*the useful*> arts.

---

mixed disciplines and ultimately the practical arts. The extent to which a field embodies abstract principles is a measure of its maturity. Henry never precisely spelled out the patterns of interaction between abstract and applied researches; we surmise from this lecture, however, that he believed that all authentic and original discoveries in the mechanic arts were made by scientists or at least by men in firm command of scientific principles. Somehow, the theoretical discoveries are then "reduced to practice" (Henry is never quite explicit as to how this reduction occurs), whence they are exploited by engineers, practical men, and artisans. In asserting that every mechanic art is "based upon" fundamental natural principles and laws, Henry does not mean to say that every invention and practical art merely embodies these principles implicitly, a trivial assertion. Rather, he suggests that before a useful art can advance, its underlying principles must be formulated and extracted theoretically.

As we shall see, Henry's conception of technology stemmed not only from his theory of knowledge but from his interpretation of the historical development of technology, to which he devotes the bulk of this lecture. Some of his historical examples do indeed reveal important links between technology and science, but none follows Henry's scheme in any clear-cut way. In seeking historical precedent for his views, Henry surely encountered many cases in which invention manifested no obvious relationship with basic science. But it appears that Henry dismissed most such advances by denying their fundamental novelty or importance. See, for example, his remarks below on the steam engine, in which he dismisses over 300 patents as mere gadgets, accepting as original and significant only those modifications he regarded as truly scientific. By definition, he excludes from scientific technology all purely empirical, trial-and-error developments.

Although not yet systematically attacked, the problem of the interrelationship between theoretical science and technology promises to become a major historical issue. To what extent were scientists on both sides of the Atlantic concerned with the applied arts?

Were scientific theories actually applied to craft and industrial processes? These interrelations have been studied for a number of historical periods, especially the Industrial Revolution. Although isolated interactions are admitted, historians generally agree that theoretical science played only a minor role in technology before the mid-1800s. However, the recent study of A. E. Musson and Eric Robinson, *Science and Technology in the Industrial Revolution* (Manchester, 1969), attempts to show that artisans, mechanics, and manufacturers in the Industrial Revolution were more scientific than previously thought. An interpretation of the role of science in manufacturing in late eighteenth-century France is offered by C. C. Gillispie, "The Natural History of Industry," *Isis*, 1957, *48:* 398–407, who discerns no direct impact of scientific theory on the great technological advances in France during that period. The American case has been studied by Kendall Birr, "Science in American Industry," in *Science and Society in the United States*, eds. D. Van Tassel and Michael G. Hall (Homewood, Illinois, 1966), pp. 35–43. Birr, too, sees few connections between the major achievements in technology and science before mid-nineteenth century. Concerned with these same issues, Edwin Layton contends that technology was not directly dependent on science in nineteenth-century America; rather, the communities of technology and science, while exhibiting parallel structures, were essentially independent. Information passed between the two communities by indirect means, primarily by scientist-engineers who belonged to both communities. "Mirror Image Twins: The Communities of Science and Technology in Nineteenth-Century America," to be published in Proceedings of the Symposium on Science in Nineteenth-Century America held at Northwestern University, 1970. The general historical studies of the relations between theory and practice are usually oversimplified and imprecise; the complexities of this interaction have been brought out most clearly in detailed examinations of specialized technologies, such as Robert Multhauf's analysis of sal ammoniac production in eighteenth-century France, cited above, footnote 2. In

The loom and the plough, the wind mill, the water wheel, and the steam engine are all instances of the application of the principles of science to practical purposes and each has received from the abstract labours of the Philosopher their greatest improvements. The plough of Jefferson.[7] The

---

any case, the interaction between science and technology obviously was far more complicated than Henry indicates.

Henry's intense but naive beliefs were embraced by a number of his contemporaries. His good friend Alexander Dallas Bache later enunciated similar beliefs in his *1856 Anniversary Discourse Before the American Institute, of the City of New York:* "empiricism is the lowest form of knowledge. Science generalizes, and the scientific mechanic, instead of looking for separate solutions for every problem, solves many from one principle. It is easier to work down than up." Quoted in Howard S. Miller, *Dollars for Research: Science and Its Patrons in Nineteenth-Century America* (Seattle and London, 1970), p. 79. Abbott Lawrence, industrial entrepreneur, patron of science, and benefactor of Harvard's Lawrence Scientific School, actively promoted the application of theoretical science to American industry. Miller, *Dollars for Research*, pp. 77ff. For additional contemporary statements of this position, see the remarks of Edward Everett, future President of Harvard College, at the opening of the Mechanics' Institute in Boston in 1827: "An Essay of the Importance to Practical Men of Scientific Knowledge, and on the Encouragement to Its Pursuits," published in *The American Library of Useful Knowledge* (Boston, 1831), pp. 59–105.

Though uncommon in early nineteenth-century America, Henry's implicit faith in the immediate utility of theoretical science became the stuff of a pervasive mythology. This view culminated in 1945 with a highly influential report by Vannevar Bush, Director of the U.S. Office of Scientific Research and Development. Bush's *Science, the Endless Frontier: A Report to the President* (Washington, 1945), pp. 13–14, postulated a direct relationship between basic research and practical progress:

Basic research [Bush contends] leads to new knowledge. It provides scientific capital. It creates the fund from which the practical applications of knowledge must be drawn. New products and new processes do not appear full-grown. They are founded on new

principles and new conceptions, which in turn are painstakingly developed by research in the purest realms of science.

Today, it is truer than ever that basic research is the pacemaker of technological progress. In the nineteenth century, Yankee mechanical ingenuity, building largely upon the basic discoveries of European scientists, could greatly advance the technical arts. Now the situation is different.

A nation which depends upon others for its new basic scientific knowledge will be slow in its industrial progress and weak in its competitive position in world trade, regardless of its mechanical skill [as printed in original].

By the late nineteenth and twentieth centuries this view of technology was no longer entirely a myth, especially with the establishment of science-based industries in electricity and chemistry. And yet, Edwin Layton questions the accuracy of the Bush doctrine even in the twentieth century. "Mirror Image Twins," pp. 3–4.

[7] See Thomas Jefferson's "The Description of a Mould-board of the Least Resistance, and of the Easiest and Most Certain Construction," *Philosophical Transactions of the Royal Society of London,* 1799, *4*:313–322. According to G. E. Fussell, Jefferson designed his mould-board on mathematical principles. "The Agricultural Revolution, 1600–1850," in *Technology in Western Civilization,* ed. Melvin Kranzberg and Carroll W. Pursell, Jr., 2 vols. (New York, London, Toronto, 1967), *1*:135. As for Jefferson's notion of the relations between theory and practice, Hugo Meier writes that

Suspecting that an English man of science might question the devotion of a scholar to the improvement of so humble an instrument as the plow, Thomas Jefferson carefully explained to the president of the Board of Agriculture in London that "the combination of a *theory* which may satisfy the learned, with a *practice* intelligible to the most unlettered labourer, will be acceptable to the two most useful classes of society."

"Technology and Democracy," *Mississippi Valley Historical Review,* 1957, *43*:620–621.

loom has occupied the attention of a Cartwright.[8] The proper form of the vanes of the wind mill employed the calculus of a Burniuli.[9] The water wheel is now constructed on principles deduced from the scientific investigations of Smeaton[10] and the steam engine on those of Black & of Watt.[11] The proper construction of a road and of the carriage that moves upon it are interely dependant on the most strict scientific principles. Canals require a still higher order of scientific knowledge. So does the vessel navigated by steam and still more the rail way with its rapid mooving car.[12] And how astonishingly have these arts of loco-motion improved within a few years or since the more abstruse principles of science have been applyed to them. Compare the present time with the period not long since when men of the most robust constitutions prepared themselves for a journey of 150 miles from this city by making their wills & [settling] their worldy concerns. Now by the improvement of science & its applications to the arts there is no part of our own country or of the civilized world which is not easily and readily accessible to the most delicate constitution or the most fastidious habit. But it is not alone in the increased facilities of personal conveyance that we are to seak the value of the application of science to the advancement of arts. Commerce is also thus extended and the bonds of union among the several parts of the same nation as well as the individual members of the whole great family of mankind are strengthened and expanded.

In former days the arts of distant countries were never interchanged and their productions only with extreme difficulty; now there is no discovery in

[8] Edmund Cartwright (1743–1823), British, the reputed inventor of the power loom. *DNB*.

[9] Probably Daniel Bernoulli (1700–1782), the Swiss physician, mathematician, and natural philosopher.

Many eighteenth-century scientists were interested in the theory of windmills, chiefly as a problem in fluid dynamics. The reference is probably to Bernoulli's *Hydrodynamica* (1738), which treated some of the mathematical problems involved with the form and position of windmill sails. See the reference to Bernoulli in James Ferguson's *Lectures on Select Subjects*, Robert Patterson's revised edition, originally edited by David Brewster, 2 vols. (Philadelphia, 1806), 2:263, which Henry owned. Whether such theoretical speculations had any real impact on the technological development of windmills remains an unanswered question.

[10] The British scientist-engineer John Smeaton (1724–1792). According to Abraham Wolf, *A History of Science, Technology, and Philos-* ophy in the Eighteenth Century, 2d rev. ed. by D. McKie (London, 1952), pp. 588–592, Smeaton did apply scientific principles of a high order to the theory of waterwheels and his designs had a significant impact on the actual development of waterwheel technology. Constructing laboratory models of waterwheels in 1752 and 1753, he attempted to determine what weight and velocity of water was required in order to produce the maximum output of power. Also working on the theory of windmills, Smeaton published his results in *An Experimental Inquiry Concerning the Natural Powers of Water and Wind to Turn Mills and Other Machines, Depending on a Circular Motion* (1759).

[11] For Black and Watt and the development of the steam engine, see below, footnote 21.

[12] For other Henry statements about the importance of scientific principles in engineering and in the construction of railroads and canals, see his Inaugural Address of September 1826, especially footnotes 40 and 42.

any civilized country that may not in a few months be introduced into all others; nor any necessary or luxury of life peculiar to any clime that may not be obtained and enjoyed in almost any other. But I cannot better illustrate this part of my subject than by quoting a passage from a popular[13] author of the day speaking of the effects of commerce & science on individual comfort. He says a man of small fortune in London (or Albany if you please) may cast his looks around and say with exultation and with truth I am lodged in a house which affords me conveniences and comforts which even Kings could not command a few centuries ago. For me the silk worms of China, Italy and France exert their art and for me the looms of Nankin, Lyons and Florence labour. For me the sheep of Saxony and Spain are shorn and the clothiers of Gloster and Yorkshier ply their shuttles; for me the cotton of Carolina and Bourbon is rolled upon the spindles of Manchester; For me is raised the flax of Munster, the hemp of Russia and the sugar cane of the Indies. For me blossoms the spicy forests of Sumatra and the Moluccas, the Coffee gardens of Java and Cuba. To warm me steam engines are raising from the depths of the earth its mineral fuel and to give me light the whale is persued to his most secret haunts among the eternel ice of either pole.

Would time permit the importance of mechanical science in connection with other departments of knowledge might be dwelt upon. In passing however <*to another part of our subject*> we will only remark that from it the intellectual philosopher draws his most striking illustrations. Without the knowledge of mechanical arts on which depend the welth and the power of a nation no value would be placed upon Political Economy; or, <*if man were*> to a hoard of savages interely destitute of useful inventions or the principles on which they are founded, the most sublime system of ethics would be disregarded. Mechanical science also furnishes the most powerful extrinsic argument which can be adduced in support of the truth of revealed religion. No person capable of fully appreciating the force and clearness of inductive reasoning can rise from the perusal of Paley's Natural Philosophy baised upon the mechanism of nature without being roused to a more lively sense of the existance and attributes of the Deity.[14]

[13] The unnamed author, probably British, has not been identified.

[14] The widely influential English natural theologian and Utilitarian philosopher William Paley (1743–1805), Archdeacon of Carlisle. *DNB.* Surviving in Henry's Library is an annotated 1819 edition of Paley's *Natural Theology: Evidences of the Existence and Attributes of the Deity, Collected from the Appearances of Nature* (Hallowell, England), of which the first edition appeared in 1802. In the beginning of the book Henry wrote his signature and the date April 1823. According to the 1829 *Statutes* of the Albany Academy (see above, October 9, 1829), courses were taught in Natural Theology and in the Evidences of Christianity, for which the Paley text was probably used. Henry's Library contains volume one of Paley's *The Principles of Moral and Political Philosophy,* 2 vols. (Ex-

Important as the study of Mechanical Philosophy must appear to every well informed mind it is a fact that there is a general tendancy among men of mere practicle skill particularly in this country to undervalue it and to consider scientific principles as mere hypothises from which no practical benefit can be derived.[15] But these persons do not recollect or are ignorant

---

eter, 1829), listed as a textbook in the 1829 *Statutes* of the Academy. Paley's argument from design was currently in vogue in both Britain and the United States. George Daniels points out that American scientists of this period "were careful to stress that the moral and religious aspects of science were as valuable to society as was its practical utility." *American Science in the Age of Jackson* (New York and London, 1968), p. 48.

[15] Henry's spirited attack on the ingenious mechanic becomes one of the major themes of his lecture and a recurring theme in his later career. As we have observed, Henry was neither opposed nor indifferent to the useful arts, but simply insisted that they be properly pursued—that inventors, mechanics, and engineers base their work upon the discoveries of theoretical science. Henry was convinced apparently that American inventors and mechanics generally were hostile to the application of science to technology. (Henry lashed out at the "ingenius but illiterate mechanics" once before; see his letter to J. R. Henry, July 9, 1831, above.) Their hostility, he believed, was symptomatic of a widespread American prejudice against not only the pursuit of theoretical science but also its application. A denunciation of such public prejudices occurs later in this lecture. Henry contrasted the American case with the European, especially the British, in which he believed the useful arts were properly dependent on scientific knowledge. (Science and technology in British manufacturing are considered below, footnote 19.)

Were Henry's impressions an accurate reflection of American attitudes toward technology and invention? Precisely what prompted his reactions against the ingenious mechanic? As yet the historical evidence is too meager and the historiography too confused to answer such broad questions with any assurance; our analysis can only be tentative and suggestive. In "Technology and Democracy, 1800–1860," *Mississippi Valley Historical Review*, 1957, *43*:618–640, Hugo Meier maintains that Americans in the first half of the nineteenth century were in general skeptical about the utility of basic sci-

ence. Meier cites the example of Thomas Green Fessenden, editor of the *Register of Arts*, who dismissed scientific theorizing as useless, and the editors of the *Useful Cabinet,* who eschewed all "refined philosophical speculations" (p. 621). Linking this antipathy to theoretical science with American democratic and pragmatic ideals, Meier repeats de Tocqueville's observation that "those who cultivate the sciences amongst a democratic people are always afraid of losing their way in visionary speculation. They mistrust systems; they adhere closely to facts and the study of facts with their own senses." In the curt judgment of George Daniels, "The American public has always had difficulty recognizing the connection between abstract science and useful technology." *American Science in the Age of Jackson* (New York and London, 1968), p. 48.

Actually documenting these alleged prejudices against the application of science to the arts is a difficult and intricate task. First of all, any such prejudices were usually spoken, not written; American artisans and inventors have left historians little in the way of an ideological literature. What literature does survive has rarely received historical scrutiny. Analysis of these attitudes is further hindered by changes and ambiguities in the definition of science. Henry notwithstanding, we suspect that American inventors regarded themselves as men of science, a notion based on a naive identification of science with empiricism. If inventors were attacking anything, it was not science per se, but a theoretical approach such as that of Henry. Probably the public accepted the inventor's scientific self-image and his empirical view of science. (Again, the historical evidence known to us on public attitudes is wholly inadequate for any firm judgments.) Such attitudes may have arisen from pragmatic biases in America but also, we suggest, from an ignorance of Henry's concept of science and technology or of any alternative view. During this period, theoretical scientists such as Henry were relatively scarce in America, even within the small scientific community.

This muddling of science, empiricism, and

of the fact that almost every art particularly it be of extensive utility is founded on the accumulated discoveries of scientific men for centuries.

Thus when a ship carpenter after a few years of apprentiship finds himself enabled to project and construct a vessel capable of resisting the utmost force of the wind and the waves of the ocean; When the sailor who has acquired the art of directing this ship to any point of the compass and of forcing his way by a series of diagonal movements into the teeth of opposing winds; When by an easy and almost mechanical observation and by a simple calculation he can determine his position in the midst of the trackless waters—they are both unwilling to acknowledge their obligations to science. The very names and the history of the Philosophers to whom they are indebted for all that is valuable in their respective arts are interely unknown to them.

The ship carpenter would be much surprised were he told that the curves which serve to form the molds of ships <sides> which he describes with so much ease and facility has employed in their invention the sublime calculus of a *Euler*.[16] The sailor would be no less astonished on being in-

---

invention persists to the present and continues to confuse the historiography of science and technology. Typical of the popular heroic accounts of American inventors and scientists, the recent *Those Inventive Americans* (ed. Robert L. Breeden, The National Geographic Society, 1971) groups Henry indiscriminately with a host of empirics and mechanics. This placement nullifies the attempt by Carroll Pursell (the author of the Henry article in the volume) to delineate accurately Henry's attitude toward technology and inventors. There is a similar imprecision in the scholarly literature. For instance, Hugo Meier (in "Technology and Democracy," cited above) argues that Americans were predisposed toward applied, utilitarian, and pragmatic science but fails to differentiate the various meanings of such terms. Frequently he refers to the crude empiricism of unschooled mechanics which Henry deplored; other times, he deals with the more scientific technology of, for instance, Jacob Bigelow, who came closer to Henry's idea of applied science. Meier fails to mention Henry's own ideal of technology which was expressed in print later in his career.

Whatever the popular attitudes toward theoretical science, mechanics and inventors were coming into increasing esteem—a trend which doubtlessly fueled Henry's resentments. Even if more than pure empirics, mechanics were receiving acclaim which Henry considered dis-proportionate to their contribution. By ignoring the primary role of science in technology, Americans had limited technological progress while depriving the scientific inquirer of his due social and economic rewards.

[16] Leonhard Euler (1707–1783), the Swiss mathematician and physicist, was one of the many theorists who wrote treatises on the theory and practice of shipbuilding. According to George Naish, Euler had written extensively "on the form of ships and why they sail to windward" and "was regarded as the great authority on ship-design." "Ship-Building" in *A History of Technology*, ed. Charles Singer et al. (Oxford, 1958), 4:577. Naish adds, however, that these mathematical theories of shipbuilding seldom worked out in practice and were largely ignored by the shipbuilders themselves, who remained faithful to their empirical methods. Views similar to Henry's about the necessity of applying theory to shipbuilding can be found in Isaac Newton's correspondence. Newton even had something to say about the "Vulgar Mechanik" who "can practice what he has been taught or seen done, but if he is in an error he knows not how to find it out and correct it, and if you put him out of his road, he is at a stand. . . ." See Newton to Hawes, May 25, 1694, in *Correspondence of Isaac Newton*, eds. H. W. Turnbull and J. F. Scott, 4 vols. to date (Cambridge, 1959–1967), 3:359–360.

formed that the instruments and the methods of calculations he employs and that he easily learned in a few months had engaged for centuries the attention of a succession of men of abstract science most of whom perhaps had never set foot on shipboard.

When a discovery is once made and reduced to practice thousands may be taught to apply it and that too without any intellectual exertion. The apprentice boy acquires all that is previously known in his particular art with far less labour than it cost the men of science to add a single fact or a single invention to the common stock. From the facility which continued practice gives, the <*practical*> operative mechanic is often inclined to plume himself upon those attainments which consist rather in a habitual dexterity [of] fingers than any acquirement of the mind and to regard with contempt the principles scientific, what he snearingly denominates merely book knowledge.

The prejudice indulged by men of practical <*operation*> ditail against the theoretic inquirer is said to be more prevalent in this country than almost any other. Although we have some mechanics possessing extensive scientific knowledge yet they are extremely scarse amoung us. We have practical men in great numbers without theory and theoretic men without practice. Now it is evidently the union of these two in the same individual from whom we must expect the greatest & most successful efforts of art. But this prejudice is not confined to the mechanic. It is also often indulged by men from whom we might reasonably expect more <*reasonable*> liberal views by men in power or who have the direction of works of great public utility.[17] That this prejudice does obtain in any country is extremely unfortunate since it prevents mere practical men from seaking that learning which can alone enable them to unite the qualifications of both classes and it deters men of science from acquiring that practicle skill which will make their theoretical knowledge most valuable.[18] England although no longer the mistress of the ocean is still the queen of the mechanic arts and in no country is there a more intimate combination of scientific knowledge with practical detail and there is no part of the civilized world <*to which its manufactors do not add some of*> which has not borrowed from her inventors many of the comforts and luxuries of life.[19]

---

[17] Here, Henry may be thinking about political leaders in charge of internal improvements or about the patent law, which he believed favored the gadgeteer and put the scientific discoverer at a great disadvantage. See above, Henry's letter to Mr. Rogers, November 4, 1831, and especially footnote 8 to that document.

[18] A good counter example to the notion that Henry was solely an apostle of pure scientific research. See also footnote 6 above.

[19] Similar admiration for Britain's supposedly scientific technology was expressed a few years earlier in a report made to the New York State Board of Regents. Demonstrating the immediate utility of chemistry, the report

As an objection to these remarkes it may perhaps be said that the mere practical engineer often executes with complete success work of great and public utility but on examination it will generally be found that such works are servile imitations of constructions of a similar kind to what he has had ready access. Let him be required to act in some untried exigency where he has no precedent and see how soon his slender resources will fail him. Under such circumstances would not his practical acquisitions be much more valuable did he add to them such a knowledge of mechanical philosophy as would enable him to bring untried principles to his aid or to profit by the experience of others as detailed in books of science.

It is also indeed true that occasionally men of great native talents may without the aid of learning effect wonders: for instance it is said that a material improvement of the steam engine connected with the opening

---

noted that in Great Britain "there are but few extensive manufacturing establishments which are not directed in their operations by a practical chemist." Board of Regents' Minutes, March 11, 1828, 3:204.

Henry may have been accurate in his comparison of American and British technology as of 1832. However by mid-century there was new respect for American technology on both sides of the Atlantic, largely as a result of the American exhibit at the great Crystal Palace industrial exposition in London in 1851. The starkly utilitarian American exhibit met with initial disdain but soon aroused the curiosity of British manufacturers. The British were especially impressed by the McCormick reaper, American machine tools, Colt's repeating pistols, and the rifles manufactured by Robbins and Lawrence, which featured finely machined interchangeable parts. The British respect for American technology—at least in certain technological fields—was reinforced by their observations of American machinery at the New York Exhibition in 1853. Nathan Rosenberg, *The American System of Manufactures* (Edinburgh, 1969), pp. 6–23.

The reference to England's loss of mastery of the oceans is baffling unless Henry is reflecting American pride at the showing of U.S. Navy vessels in the War of 1812 or perhaps the feats of the clipper ships.

David Landes points out difficulties in the view of British technology here expressed by Henry. British industrialists of the nineteenth century, Landes indicates, resisted improvement and expansion of the stunted system of scientific, technical, and vocational education

in England. Many feared that technical instruction would undermine the value of trade secrets and some believed that school-trained technicians would arouse the resentments of unschooled foremen and craftsmen trained by on-the-job apprenticeship. Most industrialists felt that such instruction would be essentially useless:

. . . they were convinced the whole thing was a fraud, that effective technical education was impossible, scientific instruction unnecessary. Their own careers were the best proof of that: most manufacturers had either begun with a minimum of formal education and come up through the ranks or had followed the traditional curriculum in secondary and sometimes higher schools. Moreover, this lesson of personal experience was confirmed by the history of British industry. Here was a nation that had built its economic strength on practical tinkerers —on a barber like Arkwright, a clergyman like Cartwright, an instrument-maker like Watt, a professional "amateur inventor" like Bessemer, and thousands of nameless mechanics who suggested and effected the kind of small improvements to machines and furnaces and tools that add up eventually to an industrial revolution. She was proud of these men. . . .

The Unbound Prometheus; Technological Change and Industrial Development in Western Europe from 1750 to the Present (Cambridge, 1969), pp. 344–345.

Henry's criticisms of American technology would seem to apply with equal force to England.

and shutting of the valves was made by an idle boy who constructed it in order to enjoy his play.[20] But of such instances very few occur in the history of inventions and that they have taken place is from their example a circumstance rather productive of injury than of good. The truth is that men of such commanding genius as to dispense with the ordinary modes of acquiring knowledge are extremely rare. The Shakesperes of Science are as few as those of Literature: for one that has fallen by chance or unassisted talent upon a fortunate discovery thousands have improved the arts by the aid of calculations baised upon the strictest scientific principles. Permit me to illustrate this assertion by a few instances.

The great improvements made in the Steam Engine by Watt were not the productions of a fortunate conjecture or an accidental discovery. On the contrary they were baised on the scientific recerches of Dr. Black on the principles of latent heat. Although the theory of these improvements were soon established it required the laborious efforts of a whole life of continual study and scientific experiment to bring the engine to the state of perfection in which he left it.[21]

[20] The story of the idle but clever Humphrey Potter is a persistent legend in the history of the steam engine, apparently originating in J. T. Desaguliers' *A Course of Experimental Philosophy*, 2 vols. (London, 1734–1744), 2:533. Desaguliers recounts Potter's reputed improvement of the Newcomen engine (in 1713) to show the importance of chance discovery in the development of the steam engine:

> If the Reader is not acquainted with the History of the several improvements of the Fire-Engine since Mr. *Newcomen* and Mr. *Cawley* first made it go with a Piston, he will imagine that it must be owing to great Sagacity, and a thorough Knowledge of Philosophy, that such proper Remedies for the Inconveniences and difficult Cases mentioned were thought of: But here has been no such thing; almost every Improvement has been owing to Chance, as I shall shew in the Notes, where I shall give a History of those Improvements. (2:474)

Desaguliers' description was since repeated and embellished. The story appeared, for instance, in Adam Smith's *The Wealth of Nations* (pp. 9–10 of the 1937 Modern Library edition, New York, ed. Edwin Cannon). In *A Treatise of the Steam Engine* (London, 1827), John Farey reprints Desaguliers' account, adding that a man named Potter went on to build an engine in Hungary in 1720

(p. 128). Henry might have learned of Potter from two contemporary books on the steam engine which survive in his library: Robert Meikleham [Robert Stuart], *Descriptive History of the Steam Engine*, new ed. (London, 1829), p. 66, and Elijah Galloway, *History of the Steam Engine*, 2d ed. (London, 1828), p. 23. The former cites Desaguliers as his source.

H. W. Dickinson, noting that Potter is almost better known than Newcomen, concludes that the engaging legend cannot be confirmed. He suggests that Desaguliers, who obtained his information second hand from the surveyor Henry Beighton, perhaps garbled Beighton's account, confusing a buoy in the valve mechanism with the boy Potter. *A Short History of the Steam Engine* (New York and Cambridge, 1939), p. 41. But, in his introduction (unpaged) to a new edition of Dickinson's *Short History* (London, 1963), A. E. Musson states that the Potter story may be true after all. He cites new evidence uncovered by Edward Hughes in "The First Steam Engines in the Durham Coalfield," *Archaeologia Aeliana*, 1949, 27:44. It must be said, however, that Hughes' bit of evidence is unconvincing.

[21] The Scottish physician and chemist Joseph Black (1728–1799), who discovered the principle of latent heat, and the Scottish inventor and instrument-maker James Watt (1736–1819). Legend has it that Black's discovery of latent heat led to Watt's invention

So profound were the views on which these improvements were founded that although more than half a century has elapsed since the time of Watt yet no material alteration has been made in the engine notwithstanding more than 300 pattents have been granted for fancied improvements in this machine.

The cotton gin to which the commercial wealth of this country is more indebted than to any other mechanical invention was the production of a man [of] liberal education and extensive scientific knowledge. Mr. Whitney's attention <*as I am have been informed by a person who in this city who know well*> was directed to the subject by a friend and after a seclusion of several weeks he produced his finished plan.[22]

The attention of our countriman Fulton was directed to the subject of steam navigation by Chancellor Livingston and to this he applied with energy all the powers of his mind together with all the mechanical skill and scientific knowledge acquired by previous recerches.[23] The result I need

---

of the separate condenser, a claim made by Black himself and his student John Robison. However, the legend has proved to be false; Watt, never really a student of Black's, later denied that his knowledge of latent heat inspired his invention. Yet Watt, who demonstrated considerable scientific skills, maintained that Black taught him "to reason and experiment in natural philosophy." Henry E. Guerlac, *DSB*, s.v. "Black."

[22] While Eli Whitney (1765–1825) was residing on the plantation of Nathaniel Greene in Georgia, Greene's widow suggested that he build a machine to separate the seed from green seed cotton—a device which she correctly believed would revolutionize Southern agriculture. Phineas Miller, the manager of the Greene plantation, encouraged Whitney to continue work on the gin and to secure a patent, which he eventually obtained in 1794. *DAB*.

While Whitney's mechanical skills were long recognized, less is known of his scientific knowledge. He attended Yale from 1789 to 1792, perhaps to prepare for law. We know that all Yale students were then required to take at least some courses in science and mathematics. Relying on no particular evidence except possibly conversation and reminiscences, Denison Olmsted, who held chairs of mathematics and natural philosophy at Yale between 1825 and 1859, stated that, at Yale, Whitney "devoted more attention to the mathematics, and especially to mechanics, theoretical as well as practical, than to the

classics." An interesting comment on contemporary ideas about the education of inventors and mechanics, Olmsted gives two (probably apocryphal) quotations to the effect that Whitney's mechanical genius could only be ruined by a college education. *Memoir of Eli Whitney, Esq.* (New Haven, 1846), pp. 9-11.

[23] After working briefly in Philadelphia, Robert Fulton (1765–1815), artist, civil engineer, and inventor, went to London in 1786 to earn his livelihood as a painter. There he kept abreast of all new developments in engineering and science. In 1793, he gave up art for engineering, first turning to canal building and later to the invention of a submarine. His early interest in the steam propulsion of boats was revived by Robert R. Livingston (see above, Beck to Francis, February 26, 1812, footnote 19), whom he met in Paris. Livingston, then U.S. Minister to France, had been concerned with steam navigation and held a monopoly granted by the New York legislature for the steam navigation of state waters. In 1802, Livingston provided the funds for Fulton's work on the steamboat and, in 1807, Fulton's *Clermont* successfully navigated the Hudson between New York and Albany. *DAB*. Like Fulton, Livingston had scientific interests. According to H. W. Dickinson, he had already conducted experiments on steam power before meeting Fulton. *Robert Fulton, Engineer and Artist; His Life and Works* (New York, London, Toronto, 1913), pp. 134–135. Livingston was also interested in

scarcely say was the attainment of an object incalculably valuable not only to this country but to the whole civilized world.

Other instances are furnished by the inventions of Sir Humphrey Davey. The first of these is his safty lamp. [After] an explosion taking place in a coal mine in Northumberland by which many valuable lives were lost the public called loudly for some invention by [which] such accidents might be prevented in future. Davey after a number of experiments on the nature of the fire damp & a profound investigation of the principle of flame constructed the lamp which fully answers the intended purpose.[24]

The second is his improvement in the copper sheathing of vessels, this becoming quickly coroded by the salt water and requiring to be often renewed. Davey was required to suggest a remedy. On investigation he was soon successful in showing that this action of the salt water was a galvanic phenominon and not contented with pointing out the approximate cause he immediately proposed a remidy and this consisted in merely applying to the inside of the copper plate a small quantity of tin.

It is propper to mention that although this remedy completely prevented the corosion of the copper yet by presenting a clean surface free from verdigrease the sides of the ship become covered with barnacles and sea shells which greatly impead its motion through the water. The <*invention*> plan consequently has not been introduced into general use. This circumstance in principle militates nothing against the invention since it fully answer the purpose intended.[25]

Many other instances of the same kind might be furnished from the history of the inventions of the last half century but these it is thought will be sufficient to shew how dependent men even of the first rate talents are upon science as the bases of their inventions and if it be so essential to these how much more so must it be to minds of an ordinary character. Without a knowledge of science the artizan is little more than a labouring machine.

---

scientific agriculture, paleontology, and, in 1791, organized what was later known as the Society for the Promotion of Useful Arts, a predecessor of the Albany Institute. *DAB.*

From the existing secondary works on Fulton and Livingston, it is impossible to determine the scientific attainments or theoretical knowledge of either man. The passing references to their scientific erudition do not indicate the precise nature and extent of their knowledge.

[24] On Davy's invention of the safety lamp, see above, Henry's Descriptive Catalogue of Philosophical Apparatus Purchased for the Albany Academy, December 18, 1830, footnote 22.

[25] Among a number of articles on this subject, Davy published "On the Corrosion of Copper Sheathing by Sea-Water, and on Methods of Preventing This Effect; and on Their Application to Ships of War and Other Ships," *Philosophical Transactions of the Royal Society of London,* 1824, pp. 151–158.

Davy's frustration is not surprising; barnacles, algae, and fouling-organisms in general still constitute one of the major unsolved problems in today's naval technology.

Possessed of it he appears to catch a spark of the Promethian fire of genius and arts, manufactures and even civilization is advanced by his efforts.

Besides[26] the advancement of the useful arts science produces other important practical results. It not only teaches us what has already been done in the way of inventions in every part of the world and what we may reasonably expect to further accomplish but it also points out to us what projects are at variance with the laws of nature and what we can never hope to attain.[27] And in this respect it is of the utmost importance to societies and individuals by repressing the premature zeal of ignorant although perhaps ingenius inventors.

We may safely assert that out of every hundred fancied improvements in arts or mechanics in this country ninety at least if not ninety and nine are either interely useless or such as have been known and in use for many years in Europe. Those who are skeptical on this point we refer to the Journal of the Franklin Institute <*published in*> of Philadelphia. They need only read over the list of patents published in this work in order to be convinced that an enormous expenditure of time, of ingenuity and of fortune is yearly lavished on the most futile attempts to inovate and improve.[28]

A more general descemination of scientific knowledge by convincing such inconsiderate inthusiasts of their real ignorance or by showing them that their fary land has long been occupied would save them perhaps from impending ruin and would relieve the public from the distraction of having its attention perpetually <*distracted*> excited by unworthy objects. It is obvious then that if any study be of value to us as a nation it is that of science applied to the useful arts. By its prosecution we may be placed on the

---

[26] We have omitted an earlier version of the next two paragraphs which Henry crossed out.

[27] Henry found perpetual motion enthusiasts particularly vexing. See above, Henry to J. R. Henry, July 9, 1831.

[28] The Franklin Institute, founded in 1824, was one of the many mechanics' institutes flourishing in the 1820s and 1830s. At first devoted to popular education, the Franklin Institute soon distinguished itself from its sister organizations by embarking on highly scientific technological investigations, such as its well-known study of steam boiler explosions between 1830 and 1837. Bruce Sinclair, *Early Research at the Franklin Institute; the Investigation into the Causes of Steam Boiler Explosions, 1830–1837* (Philadelphia, 1966), p. 3 and passim. Also see Sinclair's " 'Science with Practice; Practice with Science:' A History of the Franklin Institute, 1824–1837" (Ph.D. dissertation, Case Institute of Technology, 1966).

Beginning in 1828, the *Journal of the Franklin Institute* began to publish listings of American, British, and French patents; its editor Thomas P. Jones was the Superintendent of the Patent Office. Henry's Library contains a run of this journal, beginning with volume 1 of the new series, 1828. Some of the volumes bear annotations.

Jones's list of patents not only served to communicate and publicize recent inventions to subscribers, but, since an 1836 fire destroyed most Patent Office records, it has also become one of the most important sources for pre-1836 American patents.

For Henry's views on the inadequacies and inequities of U.S. patent laws, see above, Henry to Mr. Rogers, November 4, 1831.

same level if not on a higher [level] with the most improved nations of Europe. By it alone our native talent for inventive [tasks] may be properly directed and successfully applied to the promotion of our national welth and power.

But it is not alone the practical parts of science or those immediatly applicable to the purposes of life that should be studied. Speculative science should also receive its share of attention. Those who possess the genuine spirit of investigation and who have tasted the satisfaction arising from an advancement in intellectual acquirements are contented to proceede in their researches without inquiring at each step of their progress what they gain by their [? newly discovered] lights and to what practical purposes they are applicable; they receive a sufficient gratification from the enlargement of their views of the universe and experience immediatly that pleasure which others wish to obtain more circuitously <*by its means*>. To minds of this stamp the extension of science becomes an object of the most absorbing interest. An object too in the persuit of which as much heroism has been often desplayed as that exhibited in the field of battle or on the stormy deep. Even the alchymists of old grouped their way amidst tremendous elements which not infrequently gave them most durable proofs of the energies of nature. A lost eye, a dismembered limb, or a scorched and crisped visage, bore frequent testimony of the conflicts they carried on with the powers of darkness. Men of science have indeed learned to control these ordinary dangers but often they encounter others of a no less formidable character. Some have ascended the air in balloons, others have climbed to heights to which the eagle never soars. Others have braved the terrors of a polar winter and some have descended into the glowing craters of a burning volcanoe.

But to those who are incapable of appreciating the incentives to daring enterprises like this and who cannot consceive why science should be prosecuted so enthusiastically for its own sake I would say the study of no department of [science] however remote it may at first sight appear from practical application but what has in some manner an indirect bearing on the wants or luxuries of society. The discovery which now appears as an isolated fact or the principle which at present is regarded as a mere <*hypothesis*> object of idle curiosity may here after in the progress of science become a new moving power in <*nature*> mechanics or a general law of nature leading to many important practical results.[29]

---

[29] That Henry's concern for the utility of science did not at all imply a de-emphasis of pure science is evident from this passage. All theoretical inquiry, Henry maintains, is ultimately relevant to the useful arts.

Thus the science of pure or speculative mathematics beginning with points, lines and surfaces <*of such a*> nature <*as*> to be mere abstract conceptions of the <*mind*> and which[30] have no tangible existance in nature is at length applied to almost every department of human inquiry and to almost all the ordinary transactions of life. Many branches of this science were investigated to a great extent before any practical use was made of them and they have since been applied to subjects apparently the most remote from their nature.

The first facts of the science of electricity were discovered by Thales of Myletus[31] 500 years before the Chris[tian] era and these in the 18th Century after assuming in the mind of Franklin the form [of] a connected theory[32] led him to the most astonishing results ever recorded in the history of discoveries or inventions: to the art of defending human habitations from the lightnings of the heavens. How little could the Myltian Philosopher anticipate from his labours such brilliant results or how far from his thoughts must have been the idea that dry sparkes which he was developing by friction on bits of amber were in reality the incipent bolts of Jove.[33]

How contemptable in the eyes of the heroes and statesmen of antiquity would have appeared the labours of that man who devoted his life to investigate the properties of the magnet; little could they anticipate that this humble mineral in after ages was destined to change the form and condition of human society in every quarter of the globe. The magnet was known nearly two thousand years before it was applied to any purpose of practical utility. During that time the ocean was a fearful and trackless abyss and voyages were confined to short excursions along the shore. But when magnetic polarity was applied to the aid of navigation man seamed to acquire a new sense. Guided by it <*Vasco de Gama*> Columbus lead the way to a new world and an <*fresh*> impulse was given to the human mind which had been slumbering for centuries.

These instances should teach us to dispise no persuit in science because

---

[30] The phrase originally read "surfaces of such a kind as can only be conceived of in the mind but which. . . ." Along the left margin, Henry inserted "W[ith] Appalon the properties of the conic sections were discovered more than 2000 years ago." He means the Greek mathematician Apollonius of Perga (second half of third century B.C.–early second century B.C.), author of the *Conics. DSB.*

[31] The Greek philosopher Thales (639–548 B.C.) is said to have recognized that amber, after being rubbed, was able to attract light bodies. *Poggendorff.*

[32] Benjamin Franklin (1706–1790) advanced the theory that electricity consisted of a single particulate subtile fluid. The deficiency or excess of electrical fluid in a body determined its electrostatic charge.

For an affirmation of Franklin's theoretical orientation in science, see I. B. Cohen, "How Practical was Benjamin Franklin's Science?" *Pennsylvania Magazine of History and Biography*, 1945, 69:284–293.

[33] This sentence was originally somewhat confused; two slightly different versions are here interwoven.

its utility cannot be immediately perceived because cui bono cannot be answered by pointing to a golden harvest. <*Many*> Most discoveries are unproductive until the progress of science in after years directs their application to purposes of practical utility.

<*Such discoveries*> They may be compared to the acorn; buried for a time in an arid and secluded soil accidentally stimulated by some genial ray of sunshine [and] rains of heaven. It strikes its roots into the earth, and shoots upwards its branches to the day, humble indeed in its first appearance and slow in its progress to maturity but destined at length to become a mighty oak stretching its arms amid the skys, the ornament, the strength and glory of a forest.[34]

---

[34] After this point, a page of manuscript is razored out of Henry's text. At the top of the final page appears the ending of a sentence apparently begun on the previous torn out page. The phrase reads: "northern part of Siberia in order to make a series of <*mag-*

netic> observations at the magnetic pole of the earth," perhaps a reference to Hansteen's Siberian trip. Following this is a slightly revised version of Henry's concluding paragraph.

EXCERPT,[1] MINUTES, ACADEMY TRUSTEES
Trustees' Minutes, 2:34–37, Albany Academy Archives

Albany. Jan[y] 27. 1832.

The Board met, pursuant to adjournment

Present

W[m] James	C R Webster
G. Hawley	Ja[s] Stevenson
A Conkling	Oliver Kane
J. Ludlow	R V DeWitt
I. Ferris	Arch. Campbell[2]
	T R Beck

The Minutes of the last meeting were read & approved.

---

[1] Various routine matters have been omitted from the end of these minutes.

[2] Archibald Campbell (1779–1856), born in Scotland, came to the United States at the age of twenty-one. He began his career in Albany in Solomon Southwick's printing establishment (see above, Academy Trustees' Minutes of January 31, 1817, especially footnote 5),

but he spent most of his life in the State of New York's Department of State. Campbell was prominent in many Albany affairs, among which he acted as a Trustee of the Lancaster School Society, founder and President of the St. Andrews Society, Trustee of the United Presbyterian Church, and Trustee of the Albany Academy from 1831 until 1847. In addi-

The Principal in compliance with the requisitions of the Statutes,[3] presented a draft of the Annual Report of the Board to the Regents of the University, which after being read was unanimously adopted & ordered to be signed by the Senior Trustee & Clerk & transmitted the Regents of the University.

The Report is in the following words
To the Regents of the University of the State of New York
The Trustees of the Albany Academy, established at Albany, in the County of Albany
Respectfully Report
That the state & condition of their Academy on the 30th of November 1831, was as follows,

Permanent Funds

Academy Lot & Building .... (estimated Value) $90,000
Other Real Estate .... D⁰   D⁰   8,600
Library, Philosophical & Chemical Apparatus   D⁰   D⁰   1,550
Other Personal Estate (including $100, permanently
  invested in the Canal Bank)[4] 7,400

$107,550

---

tion, he was active in forming an association in December 1828 to erect a vault in Albany to protect human cadavers from being stolen for dissection before burial; for a note on this problem, see above, Henry to Stephen Alexander, January 8, 1830, especially footnote 3. Munsell, *Ann. Alb.*, 8:338; 9:177, 203; *Coll. Alb.*, *1*:431; *Academy Seventy-fifth Anniversary*, p. 66.

[3] The New York State Legislature had enacted by this time several provisions which established the academy system through the Board of Regents of the University of the State of New York. Basic to the legislation was the creation of the Literature Fund in 1790; under the direct administration of the Regents, the Fund was to be allocated annually to academies throughout the state in proportion to their numbers of classical scholars. By means of the statute of 1827, the Legislature increased the Fund considerably and the number of pupils studying higher English branches were to be counted in apportioning aid. The regulations as they had developed in the hands of the Regents were

compiled and only slightly changed in the revised statutes of 1830, the statutes referred to here in the Trustees' report. By this time a full report of the activities and status of each academy was a prerequisite for aid from the Regents (see footnote 10 below). George Frederick Miller, *The Academy System of the State of New York* (Albany, 1922), pp. 26–29; Franklin Benjamin Hough, *Historical and Statistical Record of the University of the State of New York* (Albany, 1885), pp. 30–31, 80–83.

[4] The Canal Bank was incorporated in Albany in 1829. John T. Norton, its first President and also an Albany Academy Trustee, was absent from this meeting. Also among both the Academy Trustees and the fifteen directors of the bank was Richard V. DeWitt. *Howell and Tenney* (p. 531) reports that "the failure of this bank in July, 1848, was memorable as the first failure of a banking institution in Albany." See below, Academy Trustees' Minutes, October 16, 1832, especially footnote 6.

January 27, 1832

Revenue

Tuition Money rec^d for the Year ending Novr 30. 1831	$4389.19
Interest of Income of permanent funds rec^d during the Year	1194.00
	$5583.19

Debts

The Debts contracted by the Academy & remaining unpaid on the said Novr 30. 1831	$1423.00

Money, rec^d from the Regents

Amount of money rec^d from the Regents since the Annual Report	$306.50

This sum has been expended in the payment of the salaries of Teachers

Teachers.		*Salaries*
1. T Romeyn Beck. Principal.	A House &	$1250.
2. Rev. Prof. Bullions. Prof of Languages.	A House &	$1200
3. Joseph Henry. Prof. of Mathematics & Nat Phil.		$1000
4. Henri Picard.[5] Prof. of Modern Languages		550
5. George W. Carpenter[6] Tutor.		500
6. Samuel McArthur.[7] Tutor		300
7. Griffith W. Griffiths.[8] Assistant Tutor		200
8. Benjamin F. Foster.[9] Instructor in Penmanship		300
9. Lewis C. Beck. Lecturer on Chemistry Receives fees for Attendance.		
		$5300

[5] Henri Picard was Professor of Modern Languages at the Academy from 1831 until 1835. *Academy Seventy-fifth Anniversary*, p. 69.

[6] George Washington Carpenter, for whom see above, Henry's Report to the Academy Trustees, November 12, 1830, especially footnote 14.

[7] Reverend Samuel McArthur (d. 1881) was a graduate of Union College with the A.B. degree in 1834. He tutored at the Academy, 1831–1833 and 1834–1835. See *Union Catalog* and *Academy Seventy-fifth Anniversary*, p. 70.

[8] Griffith W. Griffiths (b. Albany, 1814), entered the Academy from the Lancaster School in 1827, graduating in 1831. He acted as tutor at the Academy from 1831 until 1834. See *Academy Seventy-fifth Anniversary*, p. 70, and Henry Hun, "A Survey of the Activity of the Albany Academy" (unpublished manuscript, 1922–1935, Manuscript Division, New York State Library and Albany Academy Archives).

[9] Benjamin Franklin Foster (1803–1859) was teacher of penmanship at the Academy from 1831 until 1833. He became well known for his system of penmanship and he authored more than a half dozen books on related topics. See *Academy Seventy-fifth Anniversary*, p. 69; Munsell, *Coll. Alb.*, 1:464; Edwin M. Snow, M.D., *Alphabetical Index of the Births, Marriages, and Deaths Recorded in Providence*, 42 vols. (Providence, 1879–1919), 3:202.

The whole number of students (including classical & all others) belonging to the Academy, on the said 30ᵗʰ of November—1831 .... was 240.

The whole number of students belonging to the Academy on the said 30ᵗʰ of November 1831, or who belonged to it during part of the year ending on that day & who are claimed by the Trustees to have pursued for four months of said year or upwards classical studies, or the higher branches of English education or both, according to the true intent & meaning of the ordinance of the Regents of the 18ᵗʰ of March 1828[10] .... was 129.

A true list of the names, ages & studies of the said students, so claimed by the said Trustees to have pursued classical studies, or the higher branches of English Education or both, is herewith annexed duly verified by oath, as required by the law of the state & the requisitions of the Regents

By Order of the Board
Wᵐ James. Senʳ Trustee

T Romeyn Beck   Clerk

The Principal also presented meteorological Observations for the Year 1831, kept at the Academy, which were also ordered to be transmitted to the Regents of the University.[11]

[10] It was in the Regents' Ordinance of March 18, 1828, that the academies of New York were required to submit to the Board a full report of all facets of their operations, including even the meteorological reports. The Academy Trustees' report printed here answers all the questions in the exact form which was specifically requested. See Miller, *The Academy System of the State of New York*, pp. 25–26.

[11] These were the observations recorded by Henry and T. R. Beck under the Regents' meteorological program for the academies. See above, Academy Trustees' Minutes of September 9, 1825, especially footnote 7.

TO EDWARD HITCHCOCK
Retained Copy, Henry Papers, Smithsonian Archives

Albany Jany 27ᵗʰ 1832

Dear Sir

Your letter[1] was received the first of the present month but as I was at that time engaged in superintending the construction of a large Galvanic magnet for Prof. Cleaveland[2] of Maine I concluded to defer my answer until its completion that I might write you more particularly in reference

[1] Hitchcock's letter of December 28, 1831, above.

[2] Parker Cleaveland's electromagnet is de-scribed below, Henry to Cleaveland, May 8, 1832.

to the price &c. I fear however that your patience has been too much taxed by the delay.

"A tolerably ingenious artist" with some care would find no very great difficulty in constructing a magnet similar to the one made under my direction for Yale College. It requires considerable attention in winding and in insulating the wires in order that the greatest effect may be produced with a small galvanic power. The Yale College magnet was formed of a square bar of Sweed's[3] iron three inches on a side and wound with 26 strands of copper wire of the ordinary size used for house bells. The wire was covered with cotton (silk is prefferable) thread similar to the covering of bonet wire. This covering was effected by stretching a strand of wire of thirty feet between a small steel swivel fastened in a vise and the spindle of a common spinning wheel. While one person turned the wheel rapidly another guided the silk along the wire and in this manner a strand of thirty feet could be covered with cotton or silk in about 8 or 10 minuts.

In constructing other magnets I have since used instead of cotton thread a coating of varnish composed of gum lack and mastic but in these cases the precaution was taken of weaving as it were a layer of silk cloth between the adjacent spires of the coil. The process was simply this, the horse shoe was first covered with strips or ribbons of old silk attached to the iron by a coating of varnish. One extremity of a varnished strand of wire being fastened to the horseshoe with strong thread it was passed once around the magnet with the end of a flap of loose silk under it. The flap of silk was then turned back and another turn or spire of the wire wound on, so as to be under the silk; the third spire passed above the silk & the 4th under it and so on. In this way each spire was separated from the other by a coat of varnish and also a thickness of silk. The wires were put on in succession each occupying in a magnet of the size of that of Yale College about two inches and after the entire length of the magnet was covered with one thickness of wire the whole was again wound with stripes of old silk and then received a coat of the varnish a second, [a] third, and towards the ends a fourth thickness of wire was thus put on. One caution is very necessary to be observed that the different ends are not confounded with each other and it becomes some what of a difficult matter to distinguish which should be soldered to the zinc & which to the copper if some method to distinguish them be not adopted from the beginning. This will be evident when it is recollected that there will be in a large magnet constructed on this plan from 50 to 60 projecting ends. The plan I have last persued was to seize a loop on the first end of the first wire which may be denominated the zinc

---

[3] i.e., Swedish.

end & the extremitty of this wire which was left projecting after the proper length was coiled on the wire was straightened and called the copper end. The straight end of a second wire was tied to this and then wound in a contrary direction to the first and its last end was marked with a loop or zinc [?terminal]. The first end of the third wire was tied to the last end of the 2nd and also marked with a loop. The third wire was likewise wound in a contrary direction to the 2nd and so on through the whole series of wires. Upon little reflection it will be evident that if all the looped ends be soldered to the zinc of a battery & the straight ones to the copper that the galvanic current will circulate in the same direction through the whole system.[4] The advantage of this method is that two zinc & two copper ends project together and may be secured as one end and at the same time insure the circulation of the fluid throughout the whole length of the wire without the chance of passing in a short direction from one to the other. And this is a very important consideration as I was once for a considerable time much puzzled to account for the failure of a magnet which was at length discovered to be owing to a zinc & a copper end coming in contact before they projected from the coils of the magnet. The galvanic current in this case passed directly from one to the other instead of making the intire circuit of the wires.

In forging the horseshoe the whole should be well rounded on the edges so that the wire may come in as close contact as possible with the surface of the iron. The faces of the horseshoe should be filed perfectly flat as also that of the lifter & then ground together. In respect to the cost the following is a statement of the actual expense of Prof Cleveland's magnet. For Iron, Forging & finishing the Horseshoe & lifters weighing 80 lbs $16, for wire about $6, for silk & varnish $2, winding 12, battery $5—making in all about 41 dollars.

---

[4] That is, each strand of wire was independently attached to the terminals of the battery to produce a parallel circuit.

TO PARKER CLEAVELAND
Retained Copy, Henry Papers, Smithsonian Archives

Albany Febry 14th 1832

Dear Sir

The magnet you requested me to construct for your College was finished the last of December but as the Hudson closed very unexpectedly and indeed before the receipt of your last letter I could not forward it to New York according to your direction.

I would have written before this had there not been several prospects of the river opening before the first of the present month. There is however little indication at this time of an early spring and the river may remain closed until the last of March. Please therefore inform me if you can defer much longer the exhibition of the magnet or if it be necessary even at an increased expense to forward it by the stage.

I have not fully tested the maximum of its lifting power but as far as the experiments have been made it fully answers my expectation. I think however that a larger Galvanic battery will be required than the one which I have attached to the apparatus in order fully to develop the greatest magnetic intensity. There is no sheet zinc in Albany & I shall not be able to procure any until the river opens.

I will write particularly in reference to the construction of the magnet and the manner of experimenting with it when I send the article.

I exhibited your magnet yesterday afternoon to a number of the members of our state Legislature together with several other gentlemen who were apparently much gratified with the experiments.

> With Much Respect
> Yours &c
> Joseph Henry

P.S. May I request that you will inform me if there is any record of an aurora borealis having been observed at Brunswick or any other part of your state on the evening of the 19th of April 1831.[1] There was a very brilliant one seen in almost every part of the state of New York which was observed to produce a remarkable effect on the intensity of terrestrial magnetism at Albany. I am anxious to learn how extensively it was seen particularly in an east and west direction. Any information will be considered interesting.   J.H.

I have not yet collected the different bills of iron, wire, copper &c but the whole will be about $40 exclusive of transportation.

---

[1] On January 26, 1832, Henry had presented a paper to the Albany Institute on the aurora borealis of April 19, 1831, and in April 1832 his remarks appeared in *Silliman's Journal*, 22:143–155, under the title "On a Disturbance of the Earth's Magnetism, in Connexion with the Appearance of an Aurora Borealis, as Observed at Albany, April 19th, 1831."

FROM PARKER CLEAVELAND
Henry Papers, Smithsonian Archives

Brunswick Feb. 22, 1832

My dear Sir,

Yours of the 13[1] is just rec^d. As I can get my magnet almost any week from the city,[2] I think you may safely defer sending it, until your river opens. My course continues til the middle of May. In this case, I should hope that you would be able to obtain some zinc and construct the battery of such zinc, as will best develope the magnetic power.

When you write, let me know the whole expense, including, *if you can conveniently,* the transportation to Mr Thurston, there in the city, and say whether I shall send you a draft on a Boston Bank or United States Bills. We cannot find N. York money here.[3]

The evening of the 19th of April, 1831, was cloudy, a thick stratus resting on the earth; and about 10 O'Clock thunder with roars and much lightning in this place.[4]

Yrs with much esteem
P. Cleaveland

[1] Henry's retained copy, which we print above, is dated February 14. We assume that the original outgoing letter to Cleaveland bore the earlier date. It has not survived.
[2] New York City.
[3] In this period, notes were still issued nationally by the Bank of the United States, but the bulk of the paper currency was issued by private, state-chartered banks, whose notes circulated locally.
[4] See Henry's letter of February 14, above.

TO BENJAMIN SILLIMAN, SR.
Retained Copy,[1] Henry Papers, Smithsonian Archives

Albany Feby 28th 1832

Dear Sir

I have lately read a paper before the Albany Institute on the subject of the influence of the Aurora borealis on the magnetism of the earth as observed at Albany on the evening of the 19th of April 1831.[2] I am requested by the Chancellor of the Regents[3] of the University of the State to publish

[1] According to Henry's filing note, the copy contains "the substance" of the original outgoing letter.
[2] Noted in Minutes, Albany Institute, January 26, 1832.
[3] Simeon DeWitt.

the paper in an appendix to the annual meterological Report of the Regents.[4]

My object in addressing you at this time is to ask if it would be consistant with your usual practice in such cases to publish the same article in the next no. of the Journal[5] & if so would there be sufficient time for me to send my paper after the receipt of your answer.

If published in the next no. it would appear about simultaneously in both publications. The Report will not be printed under six weeks from this time. I would prefer publishing the paper alone in the journal as it would have a sufficiently wide circulation without the appearance of wishing to make it more public than its importance would merit but I do not wish to decline publishing in the Report for I intend making the paper as it were the basis of a petition to the Regents for funds to purchase an apparatus for observations in terrestrial magnetism.[6]

Would that I could close this letter without alluding to the subject of your last letter.[7] I hope you have not imputed my long silence to any improper feelings. So far from these I have always been confident that you have ever been actuated towards me by the most kind motives. The truth is your last letter refered to a most disagreeable affair and I was not at the time of its receipt in a state of mind to answer it properly. I have been very delicatly and unplesantly situated in reference to my magnetic experiments & my feelings have been so deeply wounded that even at this time I find I cannot refer to the subject without most unplesant associations. It is unnecessary for me to trouble you with a detail of the circumstances which led to other persons being connected in any way with me in these experiments and it must suffice at present that I assure you that to the best of my apprehensions of right I have done ample justice to those named in my papers & while I deeply regret that the experiments should have been the cause of any unplesant feelings between myself & them I must insist on justice being done to myself.

With regard to the conversation between Mr Webster[8] of Albany & Mr Shephard[9] I am informed by a person who was present at the conversation

---

[4] "On a Disturbance of the Earth's Magnetism, in Connection with the Appearance of an Aurora Borealis, As Observed at Albany, April 19, 1831," *An Abstract of the Returns of Meteorological Observations Made to the Regents for the Year 1831. Annual Report of the Regents of the University of the State of New York* (Albany, 1832), pp. 107–119.

[5] The article appeared in April 1832, 22: 143–155.

[6] Not found among the surviving Minutes

of the Regents.

[7] See above, Silliman to Henry, July 21, 1831.

[8] Matthew Henry Webster (1804?–1846), known as Henry Webster; identified above, "Licence for Begging for the Lyceum," February 24, 1823, footnote 3.

[9] i.e., Charles U. Shepard (1804–1888). See above, Silliman to Henry, April 5, 1831, footnote 1.

that Mr. Webster represented the affair much to my discredit.* I do not believe that he would intentionally do me wrong but he was unacquainted with circumstances & if he told only what he knew he could not do me justice.

As to the note you published from my letter[10] although not intended for the public eye it was neverthless *strictly* correct. It was written in direct answer to an inquiry (made by your self in a letter which is now before me) "if Dr Ten Eycks name should not have been placed on the title of my first paper."[11] No apology could possibly be made to Dr Ten Eyck in a subsequent No of the journal as you suggested since the note was written by me. I would have been better pleased had it not been published as it has been made the ostensible cause of an unjust censure: it has however done no injustice and as it is the truth must stand on record as such. I am confident in publishing the note you only intended to do me justice. These experiments cost me much time and thought and instead of the results producing pleasure they have been a source of much anoyance and many wounded feelings. It is not of Dr Ten Eyck in particular that I complain for I believe that he regrets as much as I do that a disagreement has arisen between us. I do not however think he has acted with strict propriety in the affair and I believe I have much more cause to complain of him than he has of me. We are now on friendly terms & there appears to be a disposition on the part [of] some other person,[12] of whom I think I have cause of complaint, to observe a conciliatory course. The disagreement therefore which it is possible in some measure arose in the first place from a misunderstanding will probably be forgotten. It would perhaps have been the wiser course for me to have never again aluded to it but I thought it improper to close a letter to you again without noticing the subject of your last letter. I am now willing to forget & forgive but at the same time shall be somewhat tenacious of my rights in reference to magnetism.

I am sir with much Respect
Yours Sincerely
Joseph Henry

<*Perhaps*[13] *I have said more on the subject of the last page of my letter than is necessary for the occasion as I do not wish unnecessarily to again*> I know not how my character stands with Mr Shephard since the communication of Mr. Webster but rather than again have cause to allude to the

---

[10] "An Account of a Large Electro-Magnet Made for the Laboratory of Yale College," *Silliman's Journal*, 1831, 20:201. Henry's letter of March 28, 1831, is printed above.

[11] Silliman to Henry, January 25, 1831, above.

[12] Henry Webster?

[13] These remarks were written along the left margin of the first page of the letter.

subject I would prefer that he retain his present opinion until he has an oportunity by coming better acquainted with my character to form a more just opinion.

* The person who gave me this information was Mr. Horace Webster.[14] I have never since spoken to Mr. Henry Webster on this subject as I could not without mentioning my authority.

[14] Horace Bush Webster (1811 or 1812–1843), attorney, Yale graduate (M.A. 1831), appointed Albany City Attorney in 1843. Munsell, *Ann. Alb.*, *10*:340–341; Reynolds, *Alb. Chron.*, p. 553. *Catalogue of the Officers and Graduates of Yale University, in New Haven, Connecticut, 1701–1904* (New Haven, 1905), p. 89.

FROM BENJAMIN SILLIMAN, SR.

Henry Papers, Smithsonian Archives

New Haven Mar. 5, 1832

Dear Sir

I have been told that you have been constructing a larger galvanic magnet then those of which notices have been published.[1]

I write to inquire whether there is any thing that you would like to have published in the Am. Journ. for April as to any extension or new application of your discovery. I am informed that you have applied it to the separation of fragments of magnetic iron from mixtures of other things.[2]

Do you recollect what acids you employed & of what strength as regards dilution with water when you lifted the ton.

I lifted over 1000 at a public lecture last week & I have not yet been able to go beyond this. There seems to be a little curve [on] the face of the magnet—on one side—which prevents its touching the armature except in certain points. I think however that I can have the grinding down repeated here at our manufactory of arms.[3]

I have added two chains to protect the armature from falling. They are long enough to allow of the fall of the scale with the weights & are secured to the armature by drilling in, endwise above the centre of gravity & then screwing in an eye at each

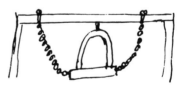

[1] See Henry's references to this larger magnet in "On the Production of Currents and Sparks of Electricity from Magnetism," *Silliman's Journal*, 1832, *22*:403.

[2] See above, Penfield and Taft to Henry, May 30, 1831.

[3] Silliman probably meant the firearms factory established by Eli Whitney (1765–1825)

end. I have also added a copper cylinder to contain the acid; this cylinder is hung by weights & pullies fixed to the frame & is in equipoise with the acid in;[4] both these additions I find convenient.

I have a short iron lever of Swedes iron about 9 feet long; two or three men bear down upon the remote end until the weight is in place & then the lever is removed & more weight added by hand. If you have any improvements I should like to know them. Has your Institute published any N⁰ recently? Have you seen any notice of your magnet in the foreign Journals? I have not & have been surprised & disappointed.[5] Have you pursued your magnetic observations as formerly suggested?[6]

Hoping to hear from you when convenient

I remain dear sir
Yours very truly
B Silliman

P.S.[7] After I had put this letter into the P.O. I found yours of Feb 28[8] in my box & now open mine to say that I will publish your paper provided it arrives in season & is not longer than the moderate space which I have remaining for the next No will allow: please send it forward as soon as may be by mail & I will pay the postage* & if by misfortune it should fail of insertion in the April N⁰ it shall go into that of July altho' it should appear first in Albany. Send it on however as soon as practicable & I trust I can get it in: please say also how many copies you wish struck off for yourself. I am much grieved that your very meritorious & brillant achievement in electro-magnetism should have been a source of pain to you & that I although with pure intentions which I observe you justly appreciate should have been auxiliary to it. In the honesty of my heart I intended to do justice to both yourself & D⁰ Ten Eyck & supposed that you mutually understood each

---

* I was writing under the impression that it was to be in MS. I recollect now that you will send a proof. The sooner the better.

---

in the New Haven suburb of Whitneyville. Obtaining in 1798 a government contract to produce 10,000 muskets, Whitney made one of the first attempts in America to introduce specialized machinery and interchangeability into the manufacture of firearms. *DAB.* When Whitney died in 1825, his nephew Eli Whitney Blake (1795–1886) continued the business with one of his brothers until 1836. Blake, a student of physics and mathematics, introduced a number of innovations into arms manufacturing. *DAB.*

[4] The pulleys allowed Silliman to raise and lower the acid to and from the galvanic plates. In Henry's original setup, the cup of acid was placed on an adjustable stand at-tached to the frame. Since the Silliman magnet had two batteries, so that the current and the magnetic poles could be reversed, there may have been two cups of acid.

[5] For notices of Henry's experiments in foreign journals, see Henry to John R. Henry, July 9, 1831, footnote 4.

[6] i.e., terrestrial magnetic observations, which Henry mentioned in "An Account of a Large Electro-Magnet, Made for the Laboratory of Yale College," *Silliman's Journal,* 1831, 20:203.

[7] The postscript was crossed out in pencil by Mary Henry or one of her transcribers.

[8] See above.

other. Of what was said to Mr Shepard your late letter gives me the first intimation which I have had as Mr Shepard never named it to me, & on calling on him today I find that no impressions were made on his mind unfavorable to you by Mr Webster's remarks which Mr Shepard says were only to that effect—that it was not your intention that I should publish *that* note & that Dr T. E. felt hurt by it: Mr Shepard entertains toward you only sentiments of great respect for your moral and social worth and for your great ingenuity and scientific acumen which produced your beautiful magnet. *Here* it excites unqualified admiration & an audience of 300 looked at its performance last week with astonishment. I have no more room & little time because we are in the midst of our public examination for medical degrees. I approve entirely of your determination not to permit your right as a scientific inventor to be weakened & while as an impartial editor I am of course ready to do justice to all parties I am always particularly happy in giving celebrity to your discovery. In much haste, very truly

Your friend & servant

B S.

TO BENJAMIN SILLIMAN, SR.

Retained Copy,[1] *Henry Papers, Smithsonian Archives*

Albany March 28th 1832

Dear Sir

I found it impossible to procure a proof of my paper[2] before last Saturday afternoon the printing of the meterological report having been defered by a press of other matter. I fear the paper will be found too long for insertion in the present No of the Journal. If however you cannot give it a place at this time I hope you will consider it worthy a publication in the next No following as I wish to give it rather more circulation than it will receive in the Regent Reports. I think it desirable that the attention of observers should be more particularly directed to the subject at the present time since it is probable that the Aurora is now passing through one of its

---

[1] From Silliman's letter of April 26, 1832, below, we know this is Henry's retained copy. We also know from the file note on the final page of the document that it is not a verbatim copy of Henry's outgoing letter.

[2] "On a Disturbance of the Earth's Magnetism, in Connection with the Appearance of an Aurora Borealis, As Observed At Albany, April 19, 1831," *An Abstract of the Returns of Meteorological Observations Made to the Regents for the Year 1831. Annual Report of the Regents of the University of the State of New York* (Albany, 1832), pp. 107–119, subsequently printed under the same title in *Silliman's Journal,* 22:143–155.

periods of maximum intensity and that the oportunity which is now offered to study its influence on the needle will soon be passed. Please to state that the paper is from the Report of the Regents of the University in 1832 to the Legislature of the State of New York. Also make the following corrections. In the 3ᵈ paragraph counting from the end of the paper and in the last sentence of it, instead of evening read evenings. In the first footnote in the first column strike out the words *of science*.

In answer to your inquiries relative to my farther experiments in magnetism I have little definite to communicate at the present time. I have not abandoned entirely the subject but have been prevented by circumstances from prosecuting a series of experiments which were commenced on a very extensive plan. I had partially finished a magnet much larger than any before made and had constructed a kind of a reel on which more than a mile of copper wire was wound. I was obliged to abandon the experiments on account of the room in which my apparatus was erected being wanted for the use of the Academy and it has not been convenient to resume them during the winter.[3] I have however constructed a magnet for Prof. Cleaveland of Maine of about the same power as yours and have introduced some improvements in the method of winding &c. I have also been considerably engaged in attempting to apply the principles of electro-magnetism to the separation of iron from its matrix in a manner similar to the magnetic machine now in use in the northern part of this state. My plan is very simple and I think efficient but whether it will ever superceed an improved machine with permanent magnets I am not certain. I do not feel at present disposed to hazard much in experiments on a large scale in reference to it and will probably do nothing further with out some more definite arrangement with the present proprietor[4] of the separating machine, who has visited me several times for the purpose of confering on improvements on his machine. I have furnished a number of Electro-magnets for touching the magnets in the machines now at work and have I think suggested some important improvements in the construction of the separating machine. I think the apparatus could be made a very valuable affair were it properly formed on scientific principles and the management of it given to a person who understood the subject of magnetism & mechanics. It is at present in a

---

[3] The nature of the experiments discontinued by Henry remains a mystery to this day. Minutes of the Albany Academy Trustees, September 17, 1831, mention taking a room from Henry to be used by George W. Carpenter's Fourth Department, but we cannot be sure it was the room housing Henry's apparatus. These may be the electromagnetic induction experiments mentioned in Henry's article, "On the Production of Currents and Sparks of Electricity from Magnetism," *Silliman's Journal*, 1832, 22:403.

[4] This may be James Rogers, Sr., for whom see Henry's letter of November 4, 1831, footnote 1, above.

very imperfect state although exciting considerable interest among Iron founders.

I have given considerable attention to the subject of terrestrial magnetism and have with the assistance of Mr. Alexander my relative made a number of observations on the intensity at the top and bottom of a high hill. The result of these I have not yet calculated and do not know if they will produce anything interesting.[5] The subject of terrestrial magnetism in this country affords a wide field for observation and experiment and should I be successful in procuring a suitable apparatus from the Regents, I intend doing something myself by making a tour along the boundary line between New York and Pensylvania to determine the change in the variation of the needle during the last 50 years. The variation for the time this line was surveyed is inscribed on stone monuments at intervals as I am informed from the Delaware river to Lake Erie.[6]

I cannot inform you of the precise strength of the acid used in producing the maximum result with your magnet. The acid and water was not measured but mixed in such quantities as to act powerfully on the zinc. Our object was to produce a saturation of magnetism and this was found to be affected in the greatest degree at the first moment of immersion of the battery. To measure the power at this instant the scale below the magnet was loaded with about 1000 lbs. A heavy weight was then placed upon the end of the lever which was made to act as a steelyard with a force of 1000 lbs additional to the weight placed on the scale. The long end of the lever was lifted by two persons until the armature came in contact with this end of the magnet, the acid was suddenly raised, the lever quickly lowered, and a small sliding weight rapidly moved along the lever. The point on which this weight rested before the fall of the weights was noted as indicating, when added to the weights before described, the full power of the magnet. The action of the acid did not continue more then half a minute during the experiment.

In order to produce the greatest effect the battery was not used for several hours before the experiment. I should suppose that you would find no

---

[5] So far as we know, the results of these observations were never published. Henry's interest in the effect of altitude on magnetic intensity may possibly be attributed to the efforts of Horace Benedict de Saussure (*Poggendorff*) and Jean-Baptiste Biot (*DSB*). On August 24, 1804, Biot had made a balloon ascent with Joseph Louis Gay-Lussac (*Poggendorff*) to determine whether magnetic intensity of the earth decreased at great altitudes, as had been suggested by de Saussure's

experiments in the Alps. After timing the oscillations of a magnetized needle at various altitudes, Biot and Gay-Lussac concluded that up to 4,000 meters there was no change. See Joseph Louis Gay-Lussac, "Relation d'un voyage aérostatique fait par MM. Gay-Lussac et Biot, le 6 Fructidor XII," *Journal de physique, de chimie, d'histoire naturelle et des arts*, 1804, 59:454-461.

[6] We have no indication that Henry ever pursued this idea further.

difficulty in making it support acording to your plan of using it 1500 lbs. There is one position in which the armature fits best. It was not well ground and when you have it worked more perfectly let the artizan be careful that he does not bruise the wires or force them too close together so as to destroy the insulation. I had much difficulty in detecting the cause of a failure of one of my magnets which after much labour was found to be the touching of a strand of wire with another in an opposite direction.

Respectfully your ob^t serv
Joseph Henry

EXCERPT,[1] MINUTES, ALBANY INSTITUTE
Institute Minutes, Albany Institute Archives

Albany. April 12, 1832

The Institute met, pursuant to adjournment.
Mr Butler[2] 3rd Vice President in the Chair
The Minutes were read & approved. . . .
Mr Henry made a Communication on Weights & Measures.
Mr Butler also made some explanatory remarks on the same subject. . . .[3, 4]

---

[1] Routine business has been omitted.

[2] Benjamin Franklin Butler (1795–1858), a New York lawyer and politician associated with Martin Van Buren. He was Attorney General of the United States, 1833–1837, and Acting Secretary of War, 1836–1837. *DAB. Transactions*, Albany Institute, 1830, *1*:153–232, has the expanded text of an 1830 discourse of Butler's before the Institute on the general objects of the Institute.

[3] We have no evidence on what Henry said or on Butler's comments.

[4] The remainder of these lengthy minutes is omitted. Two points merit mention in abstract. The Treasurers of the three Departments gave their reports indicating that the Second Department (natural history) spent about twice as much as the First (natural philosophy) with the Third having slightly less than the First. Some idea of the small size of the Institute is gained by the statistics that $132.71 was paid out by the Treasurer who retained a balance of $29.49.

In a second interesting transaction, these minutes list books purchased from a $150 gift of R. V. DeWitt, a total of seventy-five volumes. Some were bought at auction, others from the dispersal of an estate.

EXCERPT,[1] MINUTES, ACADEMY TRUSTEES
Trustees' Minutes, 2:42–43, Albany Academy Archives

Albany April 13. 1832

On Motion

The following works were directed to be text Books in the Mathematical Department,

Boucharlat's Theorie des Courbes
Lardners' Hydrostatics & Pneumatics[2]

---

[1] Routine business has been omitted.
[2] J. L. Boucharlat, *Théorie des courbes et des surfaces du second ordre*, 2d ed. (Paris, 1810); and Dionysius Lardner, *Treatise on Hydrostatics and Pneumatics* (London, 1831); both of which are in the Henry Library.

FROM PARKER CLEAVELAND
Henry Papers, Smithsonian Archives

Brunswick April 18, 1832

My dear Sir,

I rec[d] yours of Feb. 22,[1] saying that the magnet was ready, but the Hudson closed. You also intimated, that you should like to have a larger Galvanic App[aratus] attached. I wrote immediately,[2] that I thought you might venture to wait till the river was open, so that the magnet could go down by water and you obtain sheet zinc to enlarge the Gal. Appr. Navigation has now been going on some weeks between N. York and Portland, and I am daily looking for the magnet. Indeed I feel a little anxious to receive it, as my Lectures will close in about 4 weeks.

You will please write me when you send it, stating the whole charge and such directions as may be convenient for its use.[3] What sort of weights do you employ?

Yrs with much
esteem
P. Cleaveland

---

[1] See above, Henry's letter of February 14 (the date of Henry's retained copy) which evidently reached Cleaveland on February 22.
[2] See Cleaveland's letter of February 22, above.
[3] See Henry's reply of May 8, 1832, for his description of the apparatus.

April 20, 1832

FROM DANIEL CADY

Henry Papers, Smithsonian Archives

Oswego 20th April 1832

Dear Sir

I have been at this some days, but on account of the continued rains, [could not] sooner forward to you a survey of Lot 15.[1] I hope it will enable you to induce the Comptroller[2] to deduct a part of the Taxes. I shall be detained in this Country a few days longer & will then be in Albany to complete the business between us.[3]

I am Dear Sir
Yours respectfully
Daniel Cady

[1] On the reverse side of this document is the following notation by Henry: "From D Cady enclosing survey of Lot No 15 Hann., April 1832." Cady's survey, however, has not been found.

[2] Silas Wright (1795–1847) served as Comptroller of the State of New York from 1829 to 1833. Of New England background, Wright was graduated from Middlebury College in 1815, then read law and was admitted to the New York bar in 1819. Practicing law in Canton, New York, he became active in local politics and rose to the rank of brigadier general in the militia. As a state senator, 1824–1827, Wright was anti-Clintonian, anti-canal; as a U.S. Representative, 1827–1829, he ascended to leadership in Martin Van Buren's Albany Regency. Wright served subsequently as a U.S. Senator (1833–1844) and as Governor of New York (1845–1847). *DAB.* Scattered references in later Henry letters indicate that Wright and Henry were personal acquain-

tances, but we have no evidence of their having met at the time of this transaction.

[3] Henry's letter of May 7, 1832, to James Cochran, below, indicates that the Hannibal lot was sold. We can only assume, however, that the purchaser was Daniel Cady. In the Rare Book Collection of the University of Pennsylvania Library is a Henry letter that says: "We are in no immediate want of the ballance you mention as being inconvenient to pay at the present time. You can therefore make such arrangement in reference to it as will best suit your own convenience. The lot has fallen far short of what we anticipated and I am informed there is no remedy." In closing, Henry wrote: "I have paid the taxes but have made as yet no settlement with the comptrooler concerning the charge for too much land." The letter is dated May 1, 1832, and is similar in detail to those written earlier by Henry to Cady.

FROM STEPHEN ALEXANDER

Family Correspondence, Henry Papers, Smithsonian Archives

At nine o'clock P.M. April 21st, [1832], the sky being nearly covered with intensly dark clouds a brilliant tinge of Aurora appeared in the north while a loosely connected mass of auroral matter resembling a row of cirrocumulous clouds extended nearly across the heavens.[1] The form of this seemed to be in some measure dependent upon occasional breaks in the mass of clouds before mentioned. The intensity of its light was variable, the matter appearing occasionally to become more dense at its western extremity. Its altitude when first observed was about 60°. As the clouds dispersed, patches of auroral matter could be perceived through their interstices varied by occasional nuclei of greater density and when the atmosphere became, to a considerable extent, clear (at about 20[m] past 9) a beautiful softened tinge of light was visible in almost every part of the celestial hemisphere appearing however rather faint in the directions of the Zenith and southern horizon. There appeared some tendency to form a corona in the direction of the dipping needle, nothing well defined could however be detected.[2] General motion of the mass of luminous matter seemed to take place in a southern direction. Its points of greatest brightness were commonly near the western & south-western positions of the horizon (opposite page).[3] At ½ past nine the light was almost wholly confined to the northern portion of the sky, its greatest altitude being about 35 degrees. At ¼ past 10 the appearance had become very faint and of the form of an arch (the crown of which was about [5] degrees high) with a well defined dark space immediately below it. A diffused light of greater extent was visible for some time afterwards, which was followed by a repetition of phenomena nearly similar to those above described. The wind which was northerly, was very strong about the time that the aurora was most active but suddenly moderated almost as soon the light became confined to one quarter of the heavens.[4]

S. Alexander

[1] As Alexander's postscript indicates, Henry too was diligently studying this brilliant display. We have three fragmentary documents from Henry, bearing dates April 18, April 24, and August 22, 1832, in which he noted the angle of the auroral arch above the horizon and the behavior of the magnetic needle (Henry Papers, Smithsonian Archives).

[2] Alexander, like Henry, was seeking correlations between the aurora borealis and terrestrial magnetism. A year before, during the auroral display of April 1831, Alexander had helped Henry measure variations in the earth's magnetism. See Henry's reference to Alexander's aid in his "On a Disturbance of the Earth's Magnetism, in Connexion with the Appearance of an Aurora Borealis, as Observed at Albany, April 19th, 1831," *Silliman's Journal*, 1832, 22:143–155. In their search for

magnetic disturbances, Henry and Alexander were attempting to verify the geophysical theories of Prof. Hansteen of Oslo. (See above, Henry to L. C. Beck, September 21, 1827, footnote 11.)

[3] The top half of the opposite page has been torn off (possibly by Henry), but Alexander could be referring to a diagram which perhaps existed there. The letter is hastily and carelessly written on a scrap of paper, which has brief notes on the verso unrelated to the aurora or to Henry. Alexander was obviously only jotting down for Henry some on-the-spot impressions of the aurora.

[4] The aurora was still a scientific mystery, but atmospheric variations, such as the darkening sky and the changing winds which Alexander notes, were thought somehow to be involved. In general, scientists of the day sus-

P.S. To Mr. Ḣ. If you have not taken too much supper don't look at the aurora any more but go to bed. Mrs H says "that's good advice."

S. A.

---

pected an interworking of the aurora, meteorological effects, and terrestrial magnetism, all of which Henry and Alexander assiduously observed and measured.

FROM EDWARD HITCHCOCK
Henry Papers, Smithsonian Archives

Amherst April 23ᵈ 1832

Dear Sir,

I feel much indebted to you for your very minute reply to my queries about the construction of the electro-magnet.[1] I have prepared one which with the armature weighs 80 pounds & have all the materials ready for fitting it up. But I find a little difficulty in regard to one or two points & venture to ask you again to reply to a few enquiries.

My principal difficulty lies in the construction of the galvanic apparatus to be attached to the magnet. Although I have frequently constructed apparatus of this kind yet I have never made any where the copper & zinc were in coils and have none of that kind of apparatus in my laboratory. I suppose in this case coils are preferable.

The battery which you describe[2] Am. Journal Science vol. 20 p 202 is the one which I wish to construct. Are the copper & zinc coils made complete cylinders by soldering together   their edges or are they left open —Suppose these circles to be an   end view of these cylinders. Are they entire[ly] like *b* or open like *a*?

How many of these cylinders do you employ in the battery already referred to? Or what is the interval between the cylinders?

Do you interpose bits of wood between the cylinders? How are the wires from the magnet connected with the poles of the battery? Suppose the adjoining figure to be an end view of the battery, & the cylinders 1, 3 & 5 to be copper & 2 & 4 zinc. Let a & b be the rods to which the wires are soldered, a being intended to connect the zinc pole with the magnet & b the copper pole. Will it answer to solder these rods, *a* to all the zinc plates & *b* to all the copper plates, as is done in the calorimotor,[3] cutting away the rods

---

[1] See Henry's letter of January 27, 1832, above.

[2] "An Account of a Large Electro-Magnet,

Made for the Laboratory of Yale College."

[3] A battery invented by Robert Hare. See his "A New Theory of Galvanism, Supported

where they pass over the edges of the plates of a different name from those to which they are soldered, or else cutting away a portion of these plates? If such an arrangement of the rods will answer is it desirable to extend

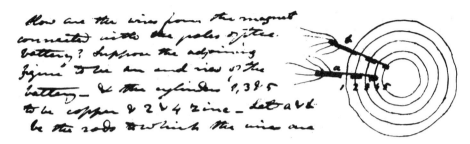

them across the whole end of the battery or only to the center as in the drawing? And will it be necessary to connect the plates in any other way?

In estimating the size of your battery already referred to do you reckon *both* sides of *both* the plates, that is of the copper & the zinc?

Is the second battery of which you speak of any use except to reverse the poles of the magnet: and would such an experiment be of much interest before a class? In case the second battery is added might it not be attached by rods like the one described above?

Will not a lead tube answer for the rod connecting the wires with the battery?

I am endeavoring to suspend my magnet upon a pivot on the inside of a ring passing around it. I mean to do the same also with the weight attached to the armature, that is suspend it upon a pivot resting exactly upon the center of the upper surface of the armature. Will there be any objection to such an arrangement? It has struck me that in this way there would be more chance of seeing the equipollency of the machine.

In coiling the zinc on the magnet so as to make several thicknesses of the same strand I understand it that it should be always wound in the same direction around the magnet whether the coil advance forward or backward. If not so I should like to be set right.

As my chemical course of lectures closes [in] two weeks I am anxious to fit up the m[agnet] as soon as possible so as to exhibit it [this term] and if you can answer these enquiries immediately it will lay [me] under additional obligations.

Your friend & servant
Edward Hitchcock

---

by Some Experiments and Observations Made by Means of the Calorimotor," *Silliman's Journal*, 1818, 1:413–423.

FROM BENJAMIN SILLIMAN, SR.

Henry Papers, Smithsonian Archives

New Haven April 26, 1832

Dear Sir

Before yours of Mar 31[1] arrived your piece was *all* printed but I have made the statements you request, on a blank page. The Journal has been detained by the printing of a large geological map but every thing is now done & nothing remains but to dispatch the Journal which will I trust be with you next week. I shall be glad to receive any continuation of your auroral & magnetic observations & will give any credit you may desire to your Institute, Regents &c. I am pleased that you are going to cultivate the chemics-physique & physics-chemique[2] which I agree with you are too much neglected here & on this as well as every department of your ingenious observations the Journal is open to you as above. I shall feel interested also to know the result of your large magnet should you persevere in its construction. I did not attempt the reversal of the poles. I did not succeed in giving the rotary motion by the iron cylinders,[3] or, it went so tardily that I did not think it worth while to exhibit it but contented myself with describing that part of the apparatus & illustrating the fact by a small apparatus such as was in use some years ago. At your leisure if you would put down those more particular directions as to reversing the poles &c. to which you allude I should be pleased to receive them & I thank you for the directions as to management which are given in your late letter.[4] Should you prosecute your suggestions as to the separation of iron by electro-magnetism I should like to know the result. I have never seen the apparatus "now in use" to which you allude as being described in the Journal about a year'

---

[1] Although the outgoing copy of Henry's letter has not survived, we have found among Henry's papers a partial draft of the letter, dated March 28 and printed above. In his letter Silliman refers to a number of matters which were not discussed in Henry's retained draft.

[2] In his retained draft, Henry does not mention his interest in these subjects. Without Henry's specific reference, it is difficult to know what Silliman meant by the terms "chemics-physique" and "physics-chemique." In this period, the boundary between physics and chemistry was obscure. For instance, electromagnetic experiments, which involved electrochemistry, could be regarded as both

chemistry and physics. Henry may have alluded to experiments with his electromagnet or he may have referred to the chemical lectures he and L. C. Beck delivered at the Albany Academy in early 1832. We know of no other activities of Henry's at this period conceivably falling under Silliman's rubrics.

[3] The Marsh-Ampère revolving apparatus. See above, Henry to Silliman, December 28, 1830. Silliman's reference to iron cylinders is puzzling, since the revolving apparatus, a modified battery, required cylinders made of two different metals, usually copper and zinc.

[4] The directions were not included in Henry's draft.

since. You do not refer I suppose to your reciprocating apparatus & I do not remember any other.[5]

We are I conceive entirely ignorant of the intrinsic nature of the *imponderables* as they are called & are not sure that we have yet a single fundamental fact as to their real essence—whether one cause produces all these effects—luminous, calorific, colorific, magnetic, electrical &c. It would best comport with the general simplicity of natural causes that these should be but one in this case.[6]

> I remain dear Sir with much regard
> Yours very truly
> B Silliman

[5] The separation apparatus already in use employed permanent magnets. See above, Penfield and Taft to Henry, May 30, 1831, footnote 1. In his retained draft, Henry did allude to the apparatus but not to any description in *Silliman's Journal.* Silliman was correct in replying that no such article appeared in the earlier numbers of his *Journal.*

[6] Unfortunately, Henry's draft does not raise the question about the imponderables.

In this period, the various forces of nature were associated with the action of weightless, invisible fluids. Henry and Silliman, like most scientists of their day, suspected that the various forces of nature were all manifestations of a single force. See Henry's later article "On the Theory of the So-Called Imponderables," *Proceedings of the American Association for the Advancement of Science,* 1851, 6:84–91.

TO JAMES COCHRAN

*General Manuscripts, Rare Book Collection,
University of Pennsylvania Library*

Albany May 7th 1832

Dear Sir

A few days since I received from Surveyor General De Witt your letter[1] stating the ammount due you for advice relative to lot in Hannibal and for inspecting the same. At the time of the receipt of your letter it was not quite convenient to transmit the money. I now enclose 8 dollars, the smaller sum you mentioned, not however because I object to the other, to the 10 dollars, but because I am acting for others in the affair.[2] We have sold the Lot agreeably to your advice[3] but are much disappointed in the ammount. It falls short of the complement more than 150 acres.

> I am Sir Respectfully
> Yours &c
> Joseph Henry

[1] Not found.

[2] Meaning Harriet Henry and Stephen Alexander.

[3] See Cochran's letter of November 9, 1831, to Henry, above.

TO PARKER CLEAVELAND[1]

Manuscript Collection, Burndy Library, Norwalk, Connecticut

Albany May 8th 1832

Dear Sir

After a delay which I fear has nearly exhausted your patience I have at length sent off your magnet according to the directions given in your letter of the 8th of Dec.[2] I can get nothing made in Albany in the philosophical line except I stand continually over the workman during the operation or unless, which is most often the case, I do the work intirely myself, and for two months past my time not devoted to my duties in the academy has been so much occupied by an engagement which required my particular attention that I could find no leisure until lately to make the necessary experiments relative to the proper size of the battery. I hope however the article will be received in time for exhibition to your present class[3] and that you and they will not be disappointed in its magnetic power. It was shipped from here on the 4th inst. The following is a particular description of the magnet its construction method of experimenting with it etc.

The horseshoe[4] was formed of a bar of American iron which according to the mechanic who did the filing was unusually hard. It was by no means selected on this account but was taken because it happened to be the only piece of the proper size to be procured in Albany at the time. After bending it into the required form the edges were first rounded with the hammer and afterwards with a file and in order to prevent the slipping off of the wires to be coiled around it a deep groove was filed into each leg about ½

[1] Although we have other correspondence of Henry's on the subject of electromagnets, their construction, and their intensity, this is clearly the most extensive. In writing to Cleaveland, Henry prepared a preliminary draft which he subsequently expanded into the letter below. It is in the Henry Papers at the Smithsonian Archives. A comparison of the retained draft and Henry's outgoing letter reveals some important differences. The draft is written in general terms with less attention to details and few explanatory sketches. It is uncommonly neat in appearance, shows signs of careful preparation, and is noticeably lacking in canceled matter and marginal insertions. In sum, it has all the characteristics of an outgoing letter, but bears the following note: "Draft of Letter to Prof Cleaveland Describing Magnet, May 8th 1832," and is, therefore, without address or postmark. Where significant differences in content occur, the text of the draft is given in footnotes. Stylistic differences and minor changes have been silently passed over.

[2] See above, December 8, 1831.

[3] Unfortunately, the magnet did not arrive until June 1, too late to be exhibited by Cleaveland to his chemistry students. See Cleaveland's letter of June 2, 1832, to Henry, below.

[4] The core of the Cleaveland magnet here described is now in the collections of the Smithsonian Institution's National Museum of History and Technology, Washington, D.C.

an inch from the end. The horseshoe when it came from the hands of the "Finisher" weighed 60 lbs and the armature about 20 lbs: these are almost precisely the same weights of the armature and magnet of Yale College. The winding on of the wires was done with great care under my constant inspection and according to a method which I think much preferable to any before adopted. Instead of covering the wires with cotton or silk thread as in former experiments I gave them several coatings of a varnish made of shellack and mastic and in order to render the insulation still more perfect a thickness of silk was woven as it were between every spire or turn of each wire and the several layers of wires were separated from each other by an intervening thickness of silk and varnish. The operation was as follows: the iron horseshoe was in the first place covered with a coating of varnish and while this was yet soft the whole was wound with strips or ribbons of silk. A coating of varnish was then given to the silk and suffered to become dry before the winding of the wire was commenced. In coiling on the wire one *spire* was passed around the horseshoe with the end of a broad flap of silk between it and the iron. The silk flap was then turned back and the second *spire* coiled under it, the third *spire* passed over the silk and the fourth again under it and so on until the whole surface was thus covered with one <*coating*> thickness of wire. The whole was again varnished and covered with ribbons of silk. A second thickness of wire was then coiled on in the same manner as the first and so on until the operation was finished, care being taken to have the varnish well dried before winding on the several layers of wires. This process was a very tedious one and occupied myself and two other persons every evening for two weeks. It is one however which will insure success if other circumstances are favourable. The iron is intirely covered in the above manner with four thicknesses of wire and near the ends with five. There are in all 30 strands each 35 feet long so that exclusive of the projecting ends there are about 1000 feet of wire actually coiled around the magnet. In the construction of a large magnet of this kind much caution is required in arranging the several wires so that the galvanic current shall pass through none in an adverse direction and also that two projecting ends belonging to different poles of the battery do not project from the magnet from the same point for in this case the galvanic current will have a strong tendency to pass directly from one wire to the other without making the intire circuit of the wire around the magnet and these conditions you will observe it is somewhat difficult to fulfil when as in the present case there are 60 projecting ends. By not attending to these particulars in one instance a magnet which was partially wound for me by a mechanic entirely failed. You will probably think me unnecessarily minute in my descriptions but

I have thought it best to err on the safe side even at the hazard on your time with much that is perfectly obvious to you.[5]

The construction of the battery will be evident from inspection and therefore requires but little description. It may perhaps be necessary to mention that it is intended to have the zinc separated from the copper by wooden wedges driven in at the *top* and not at the *bottom* and these should not be more than two inches long; with this construction the battery can be nearly all immersed without wetting the wood with the acid which causes a slight galvanic action to be continued after the acid is withdrawn and which in some experiments is very inconvenient. The zinc cylenders of the battery are formed of thin plates of sheet zinc soldered together as to form two thicknesses. You can have these replaced in proper time by cylenders of cast zinc but I do not think from my own experience that the galvanic action continues as long from a piece of cast as from a plate of rolled zinc. All the wires[6] as you will see from the magnet are connected together into two poles by means of two slips of copper; on one of these I have scratched a *C* and on the other a *Z* indicating to which pole of the battery the copper slip is to be soldered. It is necessary to be particular in attaching these in their proper order as from the circumstance of the hardness of the iron it has acquired a perminent magnetism the polarity of which corresponds to that induced by the action of the galvanic current when the battery is attached as I directed. You will also notice two thimbles soldered one to each pole of the battery. These are intended to be filled with mercury after being amalgamated with a solution of the nitrate of the same metal and to receive the poles of a second battery which is necessary in the experiment of changing the polarity of the magnet. For immercing the battery into the acid I use a common earthen ware jar or *crock* which should be of sufficient depth to allow the cylender to be intirely submerged; it may for convenience be suspended by pullies and counter weights. For a plan of a frame for suspending the magnet with a scale and steelyard attached I must refer you to my paper in the 19th vol of the Jour. of Science.[7] The method of exhibiting the power of the magnet is very simple except in the case where it is required to show the absolute *maximum* of magnetic intensity which the iron is capable of receiving; in this case particular attention must be paid to every circumstance which will in the least affect the result. 1st the Acid should be of such a strength and

---

[5] In the manuscript, this sentence appears in the left margin of the second page.

[6] i.e., "30 strands," forming as many parallel circuits.

[7] "On the Application of the Principle of the Galvanic Multiplier to Electro-Magnetic Apparatus, and Also to the Development of Great Magnetic Power in Soft Iron, with a Small Galvanic Element," *Silliman's Journal,* 1831, *19*:400–408.

quality as to act powerfully and suddenly on the zinc. Mr. Sturgeon[8] rec-
commends nitric acid with six or eight times its weight of water only.
2nd the battery should be new although not covered with the oxide attached
to the surface of sheet zinc as it is found in commerce. 3rd it should not be
immersed into the acid 24 hours previous to the experiment or I mean to
say that the experiment should not be tried until after the battery has reposed that length of time. 4th care must be taken that the face of the armature and the extremities of the magnet are perfectly clean and free from
rust. 5th the stirrup which passes over the armature should rest on the middle of the ridge of the armature and so placed as not to touch the sides
when the weight comes to bear upon it. 6th the scale beneath the magnet
must be loaded with nearly as much weight as you suppose [the] magnet
will carry.[9] A sliding weight of about 30 lbs[10] must then be placed on the
lever which can be quickly moved from one end of the bar to the other. To
estimate the power more minutely a second sliding weight can be used of
about 10 lbs or less. 7th when everything is thus arranged the whole weight
should be raised by two men lifting at the longer end of the lever, a third
person attending [to] place and hold the armature in its proper position
and a fourth to raise the jar of acid. At the given word the battery must be
suddenly and entirely immersed, the weight quickly although gently lowered so as to bear on the stirrup. The sliding weight must then be quickly
placed on the lever close to the magnet and afterwards moved successively
towards the farther end until the pressure becomes too great for the power
of the magnet and the whole falls. The last position of the sliding weight
by allowing for the leverage, with the weight on the scale, gives the *maximum* of magnetic power. It must be reccollected that the greatest effect is
produced at the first moment of immersion and consequently the experiment should only occupy if possible a few seconds of time.[11] In observing
all the precaution above enumerated I succeeded in making your magnet
sustain for a few seconds and with the smaller battery first used 1700 lbs.
By employing the larger battery which I send attached to the magnet its
power is increased at least 500 lbs. I have determined this not by actual experiment with weights as in the former case but by means of a *magnetom-*

[8] William Sturgeon (1783–1850), lecturer at the Adelaide Gallery in 1832, electrician, inventor, and author whose publications, electromagnetic experiments, and soft-iron electromagnet interested and influenced Henry. In his own writings, Henry sometimes referred to Sturgeon's work, and the Henry Library contains a complete set of Sturgeon's *Annals of Electricity, Magnetism, & Chemistry; and Guardian of Experimental Science,* the first English journal specializing in electrical subjects. Sturgeon will appear in subsequent volumes of the Henry Papers. *DNB.*

[9] In his draft, Henry wrote "¾ or more of the weight calculated to be lifted."

[10] Henry suggested a sliding weight of "about 20 lbs" in his draft.

[11] The draft reads "½ a minute or even less than this if possible."

eter[12] which I have lately applied to such investigations. I was much disappointed in its not producing a greater effect in the first instance as the insulation of the wires was more perfect than in any other I have constructed and the wires [?more numerous] but the effect is explained by the hardness of the iron which requires a larg[er] quantity of Galvanism to develope in it the same intensity of magnetism than a softer piece of iron. This magnet from the same cause retains the magnetism more powerfully and longer after the acid has been withdrawn than any I have before constructed. In one case the armature could scarcely be removed by the hand after it had adhered more than a month from the time of the excitation and it will continue to support several hundred pounds for some time after the acid is first withdrawn from the battery.[13] I have noted in this magnet a very singular circumstance which arises in part from the hardness of the iron. It is this: the magnet possesses a permanent polarity which has probably been communicated to it by constantly exciting it with galvanic currents from the same battery in the same direction; now when I have changed the polarity by using a small battery containing about ½ foot of zinc this change is not perminent but on withdrawing the battery the magnet spontaneously resumes its former polarity as if this second polarity was only superimposed upon the first.

To exhibit the lifting power of the magnet to a class I find the following method the most convenient. The scale is first loaded with about 12 or 15 hundred pounds or the amount of weight the magnet will redily sustain without any very particular precautions. This is raised by means of the lever and the battery entirely immersed and kept immersed until all have seen that the magnet fairly supports the weight. The acid is then slowly withdrawn and the whole weight suffered to fall. Pieces of plank or timber should be placed on the floor so that the fall may not be more than 5 or 6 inches. If a greater effect be required and the action to be continued for some time it will be necessary to employ a larger battery and to immerse this but partially at first and gradually let it into the acid so that while the power decreases in the part [first] immersed a fresh portion will continually come in contact with the acid, but I presume your class will be sufficiently gratified in seeing it support 15 hundred.

To show the experiment of the instantaneous change of polarity a second battery containing about a foot or more of zinc must be attached by means of the thimbles of mercury in such a manner that the galvanic cur-

---

[12] An instrument for measuring magnetic intensity, especially of the earth's magnetic field.

[13] The last two sentences in this paragraph were added by Henry in the left margin of his letter.

rent from it may circulate in an oposite direction to that from the battery permanently attached to the magnet. Let the armature be loaded with two or three hundred pounds and the magnet excited by the second battery while the weight is supported. Let an assistant quickly raise the jar containing the acid so as to immerse suddenly the first battery at the same instance you withdraw the poles or wires of the 2nd battery from the amalgamated thimble. When this is properly managed the weight will continue to adhere although there is a moment of time when the horseshoe is devoid of magnetism. To render the fact of the actual change of polarity evident to a large class I place two magnetic needles one on each side of the legs of the magnet and these at the instant of the change of polarity turn half way round and present their oposite poles to the magnet. I find it most convenient to make these needles of pieces of watch spring tied together (but first magnetized separately) with a small brass cap between them. They are supported on a stand with a fine sewing needle as the

pivot and a piece of thin card is attached to each pole with *N* on one and *S* on the other. Thus: These needles are about 10 or 12 inches long and are very convenient in many experiments on magnetism and electro-magnetism. In the box containing the battery you will find two pieces of round iron. These are for showing the power of the magnet in inducting magnetism in soft iron. The[y] must be placed upright on the face of the armature at such a distance from each other that their axis may be on the centre of the faces of the legs of the magnet thus. While in this position immerse the battery and the two pieces of iron will adhere to the magnet and the armature to them so as to make the whole nearly as sollid as one piece.[14] If you use the magnet for touching bars of steel they should be placed in contact <and removed> before the battery is immersed and withdrawn before the battery leaves the acid. In this way I have magnetized to saturation in almost an instant a bar nearly ½ an inch thick [. . .] broad and 16 inches long.

The following is the cost of materials and making not including anything of course for my own labour or superintendence.

Messrs Townsends[15] bill for forming magnet:

---

[14] The text of Henry's draft ends at this point, although he did append an abbreviated statement showing the total cost of the magnet.

[15] Isaiah and John Townsend, proprietors of a local iron manufacturing firm. See Penfield and Taft to Henry, May 30, 1831, footnote 2, above.

80 lbs at 12 cts	$9.60
Finishing do	6.00
2 pieces round iron	
12 inches	1.53
Filing do	.50
Mechanics labor winding	
varnishing etc.	12.00
Copper wire	8.00
	37.63[16]
battery double zinc plates	6.00
Silk and varnish	1.50
Boxes, packing & cartage	1.00
	46.13

The above is the actual ammount of my expenditures in the construction of the apparatus. The bill of iron and finishing was somewhat greater than I anticipated. With regard to my own labour I consider myself sufficiently paid in the additional knowledge and experience I have acquired in the construction [and] use of the instrument.

You can inclose the amount for the magnet say $45 in bills of the United States bank. I presume they will come safe to hand.[17]

> I am with much Respect
> your &c
> Joseph Henry

[P.S.] In the experiment of the change of polarity I have produced the effect of transmitting a current through a long ribbon of copper from the further end of the lecture room. Please write me if you receive the magnet safely and what success you have in experimenting with it.[18]

---

[16] In the original, Henry's invoice and explanation of the charges are crowded into two columns, the first ending with the subtotal of $37.63. At the start of the second column, Henry repeated the subtotal ("Amount brought up 37.63") and added the charges below to arrive at his final figure.

[17] Having exhausted the space available to him on both sides of the sheet, Henry turned to the first page of his letter and penned this sentence and the one preceding it in the left margin.

[18] Found on the reverse side of the final page of the letter, this postscript appears as two sentences in block form, separated by the date, above Professor Cleaveland's file notation.

May 8, 1832

FROM STEPHEN VAN RENSSELAER RYAN[1]
Mary Henry Copy, Henry Papers, Smithsonian Archives

Little Rock May 8, 1832

I received your letter[2] January last. At that time I was on the roads in charge of a party of emigrating Indians.[3] I am glad to hear that you and your lady are well. I also have to congratulate you on the accession that you have received to your family and worldly cares, no doubt a pleasing one.[4] The mathematical world and the voteries of natural science ought to watch the rise of the new luminary with great care and anxiety. His name may possibly cast those of Leibnitz, Euler, Newton, Laplace, Volta, Lavoisier &c. in the shade of oblivion. On him American Science may have to rest its hopes and that in all probability with reasonable grounds of having them gratified.

The Indians' removal takes the most of my time. Last year we emigrated over 4,000 Choctaws. About 10,000 Choctaws will be emigrated this Fall. The Creeks are about coming over, 500 Cherokees passed up the river a few days since on board of a steam boat. I think in three years all the Indians who are now east of the Mississippi River will then be west of it. The Indians are tolerably well pleased with their change. The new country is fertile and at present contains a sufficiency of game to answer all demands. It is to be hoped when that becomes scarce the Indians will have become agricultural in their habits.[5]

[1] For whom see Ryan's letter of May 24, 1827, footnote 1, above.

[2] Not found.

[3] At this point Mary Henry's transcribers indicate an omission.

[4] This may be a reference to the birth of Henry's son, William Alexander Henry (1832–1862).

[5] Indian removal became established as a national policy with the election as President of its most powerful exponent, Andrew Jackson. Grant Foreman, *Indian Removal: The Emigration of the Five Civilized Tribes of Indians,* new ed. (Norman, Oklahoma, 1953), discusses removal in terms of its injustice and concludes that much suffering would have been prevented by considerate and skillful preparation. On the other hand, F. Paul Prucha, "Andrew Jackson's Indian Policy: A Reassessment," *Journal of American History,* 1969, 56:527–539, raises some questions about the "devil theory" of American Indian policy and finds removal more reasonable than any alternative program.

"JOSEPH HENRY'S DEPOSITION"[1]

No. 28 of *Documents Accompanying the Report of the Select Committee*[2] *to Which Was Referred the Memorial of Jacob Trumpbour*[3] *and Holmes Hutchinson,*[4] *June 27, 1832* (Albany, 1832), pages 130–132. New York State Assembly Document No. 335

In Committee, May 19, *1832*
Present, Mr. M'Donald[5]
Mr. Hogeboom,[6]
Mr. Hammond,[7] *Chairman*

Joseph Henry, a witness produced, sworn and examined on the part and in behalf of Holmes Hutchinson:[8]

1Q. Are you professor of mathematics in the Albany academy, and how long have you been so?

A. I am, and have been so nearly six years.

[1] This is the earliest example we have of Henry participating in public affairs. In this instance he was an expert witness before a committee of the State Legislature. Being an expert witness was a role Henry would have on many subsequent occasions in his career. On the state level this appearance before a legislative committee was part of his preparatory experience for his role as a public figure on the national level, not only as an expert witness but as an exemplar and advocate of the roles the professional scientist should assume in the national life.

[2] *Report of a Select Committee to which was Referred the Memorial of Jacob Trumpbour and Holmes Hutchinson, in Assembly June 27, 1832,* (Albany, 1832), New York State Assembly Document No. 334. This concerns a dispute between Trumpbour and Hutchinson about a contract of the Canal Commissioners to survey state lands adjacent to the canals. Squatters had occupied unused state lands and were using property leased to the state by others. At issue were the agreements between the two surveyors and between them and the State of New York. The matter was referred to a Select Committee of the Assembly for adjudication. In the course of the hearing each contestant attempted to discredit the other's survey plans. Henry was called as a witness on behalf of Holmes Hutchinson.

[3] A surveyor on the 1825 Road Survey. See above, Description of Henry's Books of Levels, July 19–December [15], 1825, especially footnote 9.

[4] Holmes Hutchinson (1795–1865) was one of the engineers who worked on the Erie Canal. He was an active land surveyor and later built and headed the Syracuse and Oswego Railroad. F. B. Hough, *American Biographical Notes* (Albany, 1875), p. 220.

[5] John McDonald of Hebron, Washington County, served in the Assembly during 1827, 1829, and 1832. E. A. Werner, *Civil List and Constitutional History of the Colony and State of New York* (Albany, 1889), pp. 434–435, 437.

[6] Tobias L. Hogeboom, an Assemblyman from Columbia County. This was his only term in the Assembly. Hogeboom was active in local politics. *Columbia County at the End of the Century,* 2 vols. (Hudson, 1900), *1*:60, 121, 129, 167.

[7] Judah Hammond, a one-term member of the Assembly from New York County. An attorney and jurist, Hammond was active in the conservative opposition to Martin Van Buren in 1837–1838. Dixon Ryan Fox, *The Decline of Aristocracy in the Politics of New York* (New York, 1919), pp. 399–400.

[8] Questions 1–14 are by Hutchinson.

2Q. Have you paid particular attention to the science of magnetism?

A. I have.

3Q. Are not the relative positions or directions of lines obtained by the circumferenter[9] by means of the magnetic meridian, as pointed out by the magnetic needle?

A. They are determined by means of the magnetic meridian.

4Q. Does the magnetic meridian coincide with the true or astronomical meridian, and how great may be the variation within the limits of the State of New York, and in which direction, to the east or west?

A. The two meridians do not coincide in all parts of the earth's surface; the variation is different in different places; the variation at Albany is now about 6¾ degrees west of the true meridian. Near the western extremity of this State, the needle points nearly true north; the difference is 6¾ degrees nearly.

5Q. Is the variation in the same direction at different places upon the earth's surface?

A. It is not. In the States west of New-York, the variation is to the east, while at Albany it is west.

6Q. Does the variation continue uniformly the same in the same place?

A. It does not, according to the observation I have made in connection with the Surveyor-General;[10] within seven years, the variation has increased in Albany about three-fourths of a degree to the west.

Adjourned 4 P.M.

Present, the committee.[11]

7Q. Is the increase or decrease in the variation uniform, or is it variable, and is it not sometimes retrograde?

A. According to all recorded observations, and my own, it is variable. From the earliest observations in this State, the variation was westward constantly, and decreasing until 1805, when it commenced increasing, and has since continued to increase. In England, for many years, the needle continually increased in its variation to the west, until about 1824, when its movement became retrograde, and is now decreasing.

8Q. Does the variation at the same place continue the same at different hours of the day, and if not, how great is the difference?

---

9 i.e., the surveyor's compass.

10 Simeon DeWitt. DeWitt's paper, "Table of Variations of the Magnetic Needle . . . ," *Transactions*, Albany Institute, 1830, *1*:4–7, mentions (p. 5) Henry resurveying a farm in Coeymans, New York, in 1825 and finding a one-degree variation since 1798.

11 As the adjournment occurred on a Saturday, we presume the Committee reconvened on May 21, 22, or 23, the last being the date given (see below) for the conclusion of Henry's testimony.

A. I am not aware that any observations in reference to that point have been made in this country;[12] according to observations made in other countries, there is what is called a daily variation, which, according to some observations made in England, about the year 1820, amounted to a mean daily variation of about five or six minutes of a degree.[13]

9Q. How many feet would an angle of five minutes of a degree subtend at the distance of one mile?

A. About seven feet and a half.

10Q. Is the magnetic needle subject to be drawn from its true position in the magnetic meridian by local attraction, and of what nature is this attraction?

A. It is. The principal of the disturbing causes is iron ore, under or at the surface of the earth.

11Q. It is subject likewise, to similar deviations from causes of an electrical character, existing within the body of the instrument?

A. It sometimes happens that by rubbing against the clothes of the surveyor, the glass of the instrument becomes electrified and attracts the point of the needle to the glass, and keeps it stationary.—An experienced surveyor will however take care to guard against this occurrence.

12Q. What are the common defects in the construction of the circumferenter; do they not consist principally in the friction at the point of support of the needle, the shape and adjustment of the needle, and the accuracy of the centerings, and divisions?

[12] Henry is in error on this point. At least one earlier example of data for U.S. diurnal variation exists: Nathaniel Bowditch, "On the Variation of the Magnetic Needle," *Memoirs, American Academy of Arts and Sciences*, 1815, *3* (pt. 2): 337–343. Bowditch does not mention DeWitt by name, but he clearly is referring to him. Bowditch criticizes the findings of the "public surveyors" in New York because they neglected to take into account the diurnal variation which he then proceeds to determine. Henry probably was aware of Bowditch's work. See the Institute Minutes of April 15, 1829, above, especially footnote 9.

[13] Probably a reference to the work of Mark Beaufoy (1764?–1827), *DNB* and *Poggendorff*. The *Edinburgh Journal of Science* (probably David Brewster), 1819, *1*:208, credits Beaufoy's design of a compass for the study of diurnal variation (1813) as the start of the work on that topic. As the variation was found to be considerable, observations made previously which did not take it into account were called into question. Beaufoy himself contributed periodic reports on the variation of the needle. For a table giving his results for 1817–1820, see ibid., 1821, *4*:188–191.

Henry read the *Edinburgh Journal of Science*, many volumes being still in his library. He also had some connection with the Beaufoys. Mark Beaufoy was an astronomer and physicist who wanted to derive scientific laws for shipbuilding from precision experiments. He was a wealthy Quaker brewer. After his death his son Henry (1786–1851) published privately a sumptuous volume of a never-completed three-volume edition of his father's work, *Nautical and Hydraulic Experiments* (London, 1834), and sent a copy to Henry at Princeton (in Henry's Library). Henry Beaufoy's name appears in the address book Joseph Henry prepared for his 1837 trip to Europe (Henry Papers, Smithsonian Archives).

A. They do. There is however a case in which an error may arise from the magnetic axis not coinciding with the axis of the needle.

13Q. Supposing that in a circumferenter of ordinary construction, the needle were to settle precisely in the direction of the meridian, with what degree of certainty could the quantity of the angle measured be determined; or otherwise, how small a fraction of a degree can be measured with certainty, by means of a circumferenter of ordinary construction, under the most favorable circumstances?

A. Certainly within the twelfth part of a degree, and perhaps within a fifteenth; this is from my own observation.

14Q. How great is the variation which may exist between the bearings of the same line at different times, and with different circumferenters, in the hands of different surveyors?

A. I cannot tell. But if the line had been run seven years ago, at Albany, it could not differ less than three quarters of a degree, so far as the variation is concerned.

Cross-examined on the part of Judge Trumpbour.[14]

15Q. What has been for seven years past the mean annual variation?

A. Between six and seven minutes of a degree.

16Q. You say in your direct examination that the two meridians do not coincide in all parts of the earth's surface, but the variation is different in different places, and that the variation does not continue uniformly the same in the same place; if so, would not the magnetic meridian, ascertained in one particular place, be very uncertain to calculate from, to ascertain the variation of the magnetic needle, upon any given course of a different place?

A. It would be uncertain. Direct observation in the present state of magnetic science can alone determine the magnetic variation at any particular place.

17Q. Would it not be more safe in the location of property in different places of the earth, where permanent objects are given, to ascertain the variation of the magnetic needle by those permanent objects, than to be dependent upon the true meridian in all re-surveys to be made in the neighborhood of such permanent objects.

A. It is best to depend as little as possible upon the magnetic needle, and to be governed by permanent objects noted in the preceding survey.

18Q. (By the committee.) Could the true astronomical meridian be de-

---

[14] We cannot tell from the printed text if this occurred on the same day as questions 7–14.

termined without the aid of celestial observations of some body having a determinate place in the heavens?

A. No.

19Q. Suppose you were to run a new line, how would you do it, by the magnetic needle or the true meridian?

A. If I were to run a line with a common circumferenter, I would run it from point to point, as the needle directed, and mark such permanent objects as might be found in its course; if none existed on the line, I would take an angle and distance from each extremity to such permanent objects as were near, as surveyors generally do, so that it might be retraced without regard to the magnetic variation at any future time. By this means, the line would be rendered independent of the variations of the needle.[15]

JOSEPH HENRY.

Taken and sworn in committee, ⎫
    May 23, 1832.   ⎬
        J. HAMMOND, *Chairman.*   ⎭

---

[15] In its *Report* (see footnote 2) the Committee summarized Henry's testimony and concluded (pp. 19–21) that "neither the astronomic meridian nor consequently any line upon the earth's surface, can be so well determined, so accurately and easily designated, as by reference to objects having known and determined places. . . ."

It is not clear just what Hutchinson proposed doing. Trumpbour did a straightforward cadastral survey. The Committee, basing its judgment on nontechnical matters, found in his favor. Apparently Hutchinson wanted to do a survey of a higher order of precision, perhaps involving astronomic determinations of the true meridian. Henry's testimony, then, was to discredit a survey solely based on magnetic observations subject to appreciable variations in time. If that was the intention, Henry's evidence produced the opposite effect as he agreed with the practicability of doing a survey from known point to point or, as the Committee stated, "to objects having known and determined places." What was not mentioned (since contractual agreements were the principal issue) was the degree of accuracy with which places were known and determined. F. R. Hassler and, later, Henry's friend, Alexander Dallas Bache, had troubles making this point clear in their promotion of the Coast Survey.

FROM PARKER CLEAVELAND
Henry Papers, Smithsonian Archives

Brunswick (Me) June 2, 1832.

My dear Sir,

Owing to the prevalence of Northerly winds & other accidents, the Magnet did not reach College until yesterday; and I have not found leisure even to open the boxes. They however seem to have come safely.

As my course on Chemistry is closed, and I commence the next week my courses on Mineralogy & Nat. Philos. lecturing twice a day, I do not much expect to find leisure to put up the Magnet before Autumn.

Inclosed are $48. On receipt, please send me a Newspaper or pamphlet, as a token.*

I shall be much gratified by hearing from you on subjects of Science at all times.

With much esteem
Yours
P. Cleaveland

Our College feels much indebted for your kind attention to the business of our Magnet.

*I sent a copy of Regents Report. J. H.

FROM JOHN MACLEAN[1]

"Joseph Henry I" file box, Princeton University Archives[2]

Strictly confidential,

College of New Jersey[3]
Princeton, June 18th, 1832

My dear Sir.

It is probable, that in the course of three or four months the chair of

[1] John Maclean, Jr. (1800–1886), a Princeton graduate (i.e., the College of New Jersey), class of 1816. His father, John Maclean, Sr. (1771–1816), had served as Professor of Chemistry and Natural History at Princeton from 1795 to 1812. The younger Maclean entered the Princeton faculty in 1818 as a Tutor, remaining there until 1868. From 1822 to 1829, Maclean was Professor of Mathematics. After that his posts involved languages, particularly Latin and Greek. Maclean was Vice President of the College from 1829 to 1854. In that year he became President, serving until his resignation in 1868. Maclean clearly was the faculty member most actively engaged in the general administration of the College. One suspects he was responsible in large measure for both the policies and the tone of the institution. Maclean was a colleague and friend of Joseph Henry's who will appear many times in subsequent volumes of the Henry Papers. *Princeton Catalogue*, pp. 29–31 and *DAB*.

[2] This and subsequent letters appearing below are from a notebook in which John Maclean, ca. 1878, copied the correspondence concerning Joseph Henry's appointment at the College of New Jersey in 1832. The originals were not found.

Why Maclean copied these letters is unclear. Perhaps he was moved by Henry's death and was gathering up material for a necrology; perhaps he was copying these letters from his personal correspondence (now in the Rutgers University Library) to insure that the College archives had the proper documentation on so distinguished a faculty member and trustee. Still another possibility is that he simply made the copies for record purposes when he sent a set to Mary Henry for her projected biography. Copies of these letters are in the Henry Papers, Smithsonian Archives. They do not differ in any way from the Princeton copies used in this edition.

[3] The old name for Princeton. For a general account, see Thomas Jefferson Wertenbaker, *Princeton, 1746–1896* (Princeton, 1946).

Natural Philosophy in this institution will become vacant by the resignation of Professor Vethake,[4] who, to our great regret, expects to remove to New York; and my object in writing is to ascertain, whether it would suit your views to accept that chair in case it should be offered to you.

The salary will not be less than one thousand dollars and a house; and after one or two years will probably be twelve hundred dollars. Professor Dod[5] of the Mathematical Department has received the first mentioned sum for two years past, and next fall his salary will probably be increased to twelve hundred.

I am not authorized to make this communication. Still I am inclined to believe that if a favorable answer should be given to it, our Trustees, upon a proper representation being made to them, would be disposed to offer you the chair of Natural Philosophy.

> With great respect,
> Yours,
> John Maclean[6]

[4] For Vethake, see the entry for March 8, 1815, above, especially footnote 11.

[5] Albert Baldwin Dod (1805–1845), a Presbyterian clergyman who was Professor of Mathematics at Princeton from 1830 to 1845. Dod was a Princeton graduate (1822) who attended the Princeton Theological Seminary from 1827 to 1829. He received honorary D.D. degrees from New York University and the University of North Carolina. He was regarded as a superb teacher and a sparkling conversationalist. His writings are principally on theology and related topics. Dod will reappear many times in subsequent volumes of this work. *DAB.* Princeton Theological Seminary, *Biographical Catalogue, 1815–1932* (Princeton, 1933), p. 44.

[6] To this text Maclean appended the following note:

Note. This letter was written to Professor Henry with the consent of Dr. Carnahan and of Professor Dod: and at the earnest prompting of Professor Torrey, upon the writer's asking him, if he knew Henry of Albany: and it was marked confidential; there being, *at the time it was written,* important reasons for not letting it be known.

In my letter given above, I said to Professor Henry that I was *not authorized* to write to him: and in saying this, I had references to the Trustees of the College, who <*alone could*> elect the Professors.

James Carnahan (1775–1859) was President of Princeton from 1823 to 1854. *DAB.* Maclean was being very careful, in retrospect, to show that his actions were most proper in respect both of the other faculty members and of the Trustees. Torrey's role is not generally appreciated. At this date the particular reasons for confidentiality are unknown. Presumably, these were the uncertainty concerning Vethake and the need for discretion prior to approval by the Trustees.

TO JOHN MACLEAN[1]

"Joseph Henry I" file box, Princeton University Archives

Albany, June 28th, 1832

Dear Sir,

Your kind letter[2] informing me of an expected vacancy in your College was received on the 18th[3] instant. I would have answered it sooner, had I not been engaged in a series of experiments which I wished to announce in the next no. of the American Journal[4] and which has occupied almost every moment of my time, not required in the duties of the Academy for the last two weeks.

To your inquiry, whether it would suit my views to accept the chair of Natural Philosophy in your institution if it were offered to me, I answer that my only views at present are to secure a comfortable support for my family and next to establish and to deserve for myself the reputation of a man of science. I have determined to confine my attention principally to a course of study and investigation intermediate to pure Mathematics on the one hand and the more detailed parts of Chemistry on the other.[5] Any honourable situation in which it would be a part of my duty to teach those branches and which would afford me superior advantages to those I now possess for prosecuting them will be acceptable.

I would not however readily exchange my present situation for many that might offer as it is in some respects an eligible one. The Institution is very flourishing and well established. My salary is 1000 Dollars per annum with a prospect of its being increased. As Librarian of the Albany Institute I have access to a valuable collection of scientific works and most of the European periodical publications. In connection with Dr. T. R. Beck I have the principal direction of the Meteorological observations made by the different academies of the State of N.Y. to the Regents of the University. In this work I am considerably interested and have hoped at some fu-

---

[1] Also printed in Nathan Reingold, ed., *Science in Nineteenth-Century America* (New York, 1964), pp. 71–72, with some slight deviations from this text.

[2] Of June 18, 1832, above.

[3] If we accept Maclean's dating of his letter to Henry, obviously the missive could not have been received on the same date. Since no originals exist, we are assuming the date of the first letter is correctly given but are retaining this date in this text, even though it may be a transcribing error in 1878.

[4] Joseph Henry, "On the Production of Currents and Sparks of Electricity from Magnetism," *Silliman's Journal*, 1832, 22:403–408.

[5] An apt definition of physics, a term Henry would not have used as "natural philosophy" was more commonly invoked.

ture time to deduce many facts from it of importance to the science of meteorology.

On the other hand my duties in the Academy are not well suited to my taste. I am engaged on an average seven hours in a day, one half of the time in teaching the higher classes in Mathematics, and the other half in the drudgery of instructing a class of sixty boys in the elements of Arithmetic.

If I am not mistaken in the charactor of your college and in the nature of the duties which will be required of me, I think I would be more pleasantly situated in Princeton than I am at present in Albany, and shall therefore accept the chair should your trustees see fit to offer it. I could not however consistently with my feelings on this subject make much effort to obtain the appointment, but if you will be so kind as to inform me what representations are necessary to be made before the Trustees will act in the affair, I will attend to them. I can refer them to Professor Silliman and to Professor Renwick for my scientific character; particularly the first named gentleman and to the Hon. Stephen Van Rensselaer and Mr Simeon DeWitt Surveyor General of the State of N.Y., for my private character and history. I was once a private tutor in the family of Mr Van Rensselaer, and have enjoyed the confidence and friendship of Mr. DeWitt for several years. I may also refer them to your acquaintance Prof. Green of Philadelphia. If letters should be addressed to any of the above mentioned gentlemen will you have the goodness to request that they be confidential, as I am somewhat peculiarly situated, and do not wish it known at present that I have any desire to change my situation.

Are you aware of the fact that I am not a graduate of any college and that I am principally self educated? Perhaps objections may be raised on this account. I have it is true an honorary degree from Union College[6] and have lately been elected a corresponding member of the Royal Physical Society of Edinburgh;[7] but such honours you know are often cheaply purchased and will probably have but little weight with your trustees.

I understand of course that the whole affair is as yet only in anticipation and that even the vacancy may not take place and shall therefore make no calculation upon it until I hear something more. I have lately succeeded in a most interesting experiment that of drawing sparks of electricity from a

---

[6] A.M., 1829.

[7] Apparently the first formal European recognition of Henry. Unfortunately, we know no more than this reference. The Royal Physical Society of Edinburgh was founded in 1771 as the Physico-Chirurgical Society, changed its name shortly afterward, and received a royal charter in 1778. Its printed *Proceedings* started in 1854. The surviving records of the Society in the Library of Edinburgh University do not include any minutes or correspondence for this period.

magnet.[8] I have some hopes of fusing platina wire by means of the same principle.

> I am Sir with much respect
> Yours etc.
> Joseph Henry.[9]

[8] See footnote 4, above.

[9] Maclean in 1878 then notes that he wrote to Silliman, Renwick, and Green, as well as Torrey. Carnahan presented their replies (see below) to the Trustees who elected Henry to replace Vethake. Maclean goes on to note: "I did not write to General Van Rensselaer and Mr. DeWitt as no further testimony to his private character was needed beyond that given by the other gentlemen here named."

FROM BENJAMIN SILLIMAN, SR.

Henry Papers, Smithsonian Archives

N Haven June 30, 1832

My dear Sir

Send forward your observations as soon as may be & they *shall* appear.[1] Have you seen the May N° of the Phil. Mag & Ann. of Phil.

James D. Forbes,[2] Edinburgh, announces, date April 18, that he has obtained a spark from a *natural* magnet,[3] but gives no particulars, except that

[1] Henry apparently notified Silliman of his observations in an earlier letter which no longer survives. Henry's observations, concerning his independent discovery of electromagnetic induction, were published in the Appendix to the July 1832 number of *Silliman's Journal*: "On the Production of Currents and Sparks of Electricity from Magnetism," 22:403–408. According to this article, he conducted his successful experiments in the last two weeks of June. Among the surviving Henry Papers, this is the first explicit reference we have found to his discovery of electromagnetic induction.

[2] James David Forbes (1809–1868), Scottish scientist, one of the founders of the British Association, and, from 1833, Professor of Natural Philosophy at the University of Edinburgh. A scientist of wide-ranging interests, Forbes is best known for his study of glacial phenomena. *DNB*. At Princeton, Henry corresponded with Forbes on the subject of terrestrial magnetism. See above, John Turnbull to Henry, August 16, 1831, footnote 1.

[3] Forbes' brief announcement, which Silliman here repeats to Henry, appeared in the *London and Edinburgh Philosophical Magazine, or Annals of Chemistry, Mathematics, Astronomy, Natural History, and General Science*, n.s., May 1832, *11*:359–360, and was entitled "On the Obtaining of an Electric Spark from a Natural Magnet." Forbes published a full account of the experiment in the July 1832 issue of the same journal, 3d ser., *1*:49–53, and, as indicated later in Silliman's letter, in the *Transactions of the Royal Society of Edinburgh*, 1834, *12*:197–205. According to the full account in the July *Philosophical Magazine*, Forbes embarked upon his spark experiments when Michael Faraday informed him of his discovery of electromagnetic induction (see footnote 7 below). Around a soft iron bar, Forbes wound a helix of copper wire, the ends of which were dipped in a cup of mercury to form a closed circuit. He then temporarily magnetized the iron bar by touching its ends to the poles of a natural magnet (i.e., lodestone). The momentary electric current generated in the helix produced a spark when the closed circuit was simulta-

the first spark was obtained March 30; that the experiment was not however completely under his command until April 13 & that since that he has shown it repeatedly to Sir John Leslie[4] & Prof^r Hope[5] & others all of whom have expressed themselves completely satisfied with the experiment. There is no other fact named except that he had heard a report of the success of Prof^r Nobili[6] of Reggio in the same exper[imen]t, but that notice was only a vague one in the public prints & no clew given to his mode of procedure. He considers every thing of this kind as resting upon Mr Faradays discoveries[7] & promises a full account of his experiments in the Trans. of the Roy. Soc^y of Edinburgh[8] to whom it was read April 16.

---

neously interrupted at the cup of mercury. Although Faraday had already elicited a spark with an electromagnet, Forbes was the first to achieve the effect with a lodestone. See Faraday's footnote on p. 405 to "On the Electro-motive Force of Magnetism. By Signori Nobili and Antinori; (from the Antologia, No. 131): with notes by Michael Faraday," *Philosophical Magazine*, n.s., 1832, *11*.

[4] Sir John Leslie (1766–1832), Scottish mathematician and natural philosopher, appointed Professor of Natural Philosophy at Edinburgh in 1819. Upon Leslie's death, Forbes was appointed to his Professorship at Edinburgh. *DNB*.

[5] Thomas Charles Hope (1766–1844), Professor of Chemistry at Edinburgh, 1799–1843. *DNB*. Forbes noted that the magnet he used in his spark experiments was presented to the University by Dr. Hope. *Philosophical Magazine*, 3d ser., 1832, *1*:49.

[6] Leopoldo Nobili (1784–1835), Italian physicist, born in Reggio nell'Emilia, served as Captain in the Italian army, and, from 1831, was Professor of Physics at the Ducal Museum in Florence. *World Who's Who in Science*. Nobili actually conducted his spark experiments in collaboration with Vincenzio Antinori (1792–1865; *Dizionario Biographico degli Italiani*). After reading a brief report of Faraday's researches on electromagnetic induction, Nobili and Antinori, attempting to repeat and extend Faraday's results, were able to induce sparks using a permanent steel magnet. Their methods were similar to those of Forbes, who used a lodestone. In the spring of 1832, they published their results in the *Antologia di Firenze*, which was backdated November 1831. Although the Italians fully acknowledged their debt to Faraday, the backdating led many to believe they had anticipated Faraday. In a commentary to the English translation of the Nobili-Antinori article, published in the *Philosophical Magazine*, n.s., 1832, *11*:401–413, Faraday clarified the priorities. See L. Pearce Williams, *Michael Faraday, a Biography* (New York, 1965), p. 201.

Already immersed in his own spark experiments, Forbes saw only the short notice of the Italian researches in the March 24 issue of *The Literary Gazette; and Journal of Belles Lettres, Arts, Sciences, etc. for the year 1832*, p. 185. See postscript by Forbes to his July 1832 article in the *Philosophical Magazine*, cited above, footnote 3.

[7] On November 24, 1831, Faraday read his paper on electromagnetic induction to the Royal Institution. See his "First Series" of experimental researches in *Experimental Researches in Electricity*, 3 vols. in 2 (New York, 1965), *1*:1–41. While short accounts of his experiments were published soon after, the complete paper was not published until later in the *Philosophical Transactions of the Royal Society of London* for 1832, pp. 125–162. For Faraday's discovery of electromagnetic induction, see L. Pearce Williams, *Michael Faraday, a Biography* (New York, 1965), chapter 4, passim.

When Forbes conducted his spark experiments, Faraday's article was not yet published. In early March 1832, Faraday informed him of the gist of his induction experiments, including the production of a spark using an electromagnet. Having extended Faraday's results by obtaining sparks from a current generated by a natural magnet, Forbes wrote that "Finally, as far as is yet known, no one except Signori Nobili and Antinori and myself have yet obtained the spark from the natural or permanent magnet." *Philosophical Magazine*, 3d ser., 1832, *1*:52–53.

[8] See above, footnote 3.

These are *all* the facts, but do not keep back your account. I presume your spark is from your own great magnet & it is very possible they have not anticipated you then.[9]

In haste yours very truly
B Silliman

[9] Henry did indeed generate the spark from his own electromagnet. Since Forbes, Nobili, and Antinori obtained sparks from permanent magnets, they had not completely anticipated Henry. Scientists of this period suspected but could not yet prove that electricities generated by different means were ultimately the same. A current induced by a permanent magnet was not necessarily identical with that induced by an electromagnet. That both currents could be shown to produce a spark, however, provided evidence of their identity. In a note to page 405 of the Nobili-Antinori paper ("On the Electro-motive Force of Magnetism," *Philosophical Magazine*, n.s., 1832, *11*), Michael Faraday listed the different methods of producing sparks employed by Nobili, Antinori, Forbes, and himself. As L. P. Williams has pointed out, "The production of a spark had given some trouble to Faraday. In his first paper, the spark had been described as coming from the presence of an electro-magnet in the circuit." *Michael Faraday, a Biography* (New York, 1965), p. 215. In his article on induction published in *Silliman's Journal*, 1832, 22:408, Henry acknowledged the brief announcement of Forbes's experiments in the May *Philosophical Magazine* (he had not yet seen the full account), but noted that his methods were undoubtedly different. There is no mention of Nobili and Antinori.

Henry, of course, had been forestalled—at least publicly—by Faraday, who had already obtained a spark from an electromagnet (see above, footnote 7). We know from Henry's article in *Silliman's Journal*, p. 404, that he had only seen a short account of Faraday's researches in the April 1832 number of the *Philosophical Magazine*, p. 386, which did not indicate that Faraday had produced a spark. Moreover, in the same article (pp. 403 and 408), Henry stressed that he had commenced his experiments independently of Faraday and Forbes, only learning generally of their work after his own experiments were well under way.

The observations which Henry published in *Silliman's Journal* included much more than the production of sparks from his electromagnet. They dealt broadly with his independent discovery of electromagnetic induction. Henry also dealt briefly with a related effect, the self-induction of an electric circuit.

FROM JOHN MACLEAN
Henry Papers, Smithsonian Archives

Princeton July 10. 1832.

My dear Sir

I thank you for your letter:[1] it was every thing I could desire in regard to the subject of my correspondence; and my reason for not writing to you immediately upon the receipt of your letter was, that I entertained the hope of being able to give you some more definite information in regard to the expected vacancy. As yet, however, I cannot speak with absolute cer-

[1] Of June 28, above.

tainty; though it is more than probable that the vacancy will occur: in a few days, I shall probably be able to inform you of Mr Vethake's determination, and I am almost confident, that he will make up his mind to leave us in the fall. I do not deem it necessary to make any inquiries of the gentlemen referred to you, in your letter; your character as a man [of] science is sufficiently well known & appreciated among us to render such reference unnecessary; at least so far as our Faculty are concerned, and if I should find it requisite in order to satisfy our Trustees, I will write in a confidential manner to one or more of the gentlemen you named. Prof. Green's[2] Opinion I know already, though he has no knowledge of the expected vacancy. It was an expression of his opinion that more particularly directed my attention to you. His brother[3] is one of our Trustees, & his opinion will be of service in effecting my purposes.

Nothing shall be wanting on my part to secure for you the appointment, & I shall have the co-operation of my colleagues. If your engagements should permit you to make us a visit this summer, I shall be much pleased to see you. Please to excuse my haste.

With sincere esteem
Yours
John Maclean.

P.S. I was much gratified to learn from you the result of your interesting experiments.

---

[2] Jacob Green. In 1878, Maclean remembered Torrey as the chief instigator of the Henry appointment (see footnote 6 of June 18, 1832). Here Green's opinion is given primacy. Henry himself, undoubtedly because of this letter, credited Green's influence for the appointment.

[3] James Sproat Green (1792–1862), an attorney and son of Ashbel Green (1762–1848), President of the College of New Jersey, 1812–1822. The son was Treasurer of the Board of Trustees of Princeton Theological Seminary (and its predecessor), 1819–1862, and served in a similar capacity in Princeton in 1828. James Sproat Green was a Trustee of the College from 1828 to 1862. From 1830 to 1834 he was in the New Jersey Senate and was U.S. Attorney for the District of New Jersey, 1837–1849. Green was a graduate of Dickinson College (1811) and was Professor of Jurisprudence at Princeton, 1847–1855. He published reports of cases in the New Jersey Supreme Court of Judicature for the years 1831–1836. *Princeton Catalogue,* pp. 31, 409. Princeton Theological Seminary, *Biographical Catalogue* (Princeton, 1933), pp. viii, xvi.

July 13, 1832

EXCERPT,[1] MINUTES, ACADEMY TRUSTEES
Trustees' Minutes, 2:56, Albany Academy Archives

July 13. 1832

In consequence of the prevalence of Cholera,[2] & the absences of students, (more than one half) reported by the Principal,[3] the following resolutions were adopted.

Resolved that the vacations for the present Year commence on the 1st of August & continue during that month.

Resolved that the Annual Examination & public exercises be postponed until the further order of the Board.

Resolved that in case there be any deficiency in the monies for the payment of the salaries of the Teachers, the Treasurer be authorized to borrow what may be required for 60 to 90 days.   Adjourned.

---

[1] Routine opening matters have been omitted.

[2] Charles E. Rosenberg, *The Cholera Years: The United States in 1832, 1849, and 1866* (Chicago, 1962), p. 91, indicates that Albany spent over $19,000 in public funds in fighting the cholera epidemic of 1832.

[3] T. R. Beck.

FROM JOHN MACLEAN
Henry Papers, Smithsonian Archives

Princeton, Aug. 2. 1832

My dear Sir

It is definitely settled that Prof. Vethake is to leave us in the fall; and I sincerely hope that we shall be so much favoured as to have you for his successor.

On an average, you will not be occupied more than from one to two hours of the day.

The intercourse between the several members of the Faculty is of the most social & friendly character.

I would repeat my invitation, that you should visit us this summer. At present, most of the students have gone home, for fear of the cholera. I hope however, that we shall have over full complement at the beginning of the next session, i.e. about the 10th of Nov.

With sincere esteem
Yours
John Maclean

P.S. The appointment will be made in Sept. next.

441

FROM AMOS EATON

Henry Papers, Smithsonian Archives

Albany, Aug. 16. 1832.

My dear friend,

The bearer, M⸢r⸣ Storrs,[1] is an adjunct professor. He will probably be useful as a teacher in the Northern part of the Union, being a native of New Hampshire. He is desirous to see the collections and library of the Institute, and still more desirous to see your improvements in the apparatus illustrative of electro-magnetism; which has (as Pope says) "damned you to everlasting fame," in the remotest parts of the Earth, wherever the word, *Science,* has been told.[2]

Any favor theron bearing and to M⸢r⸣ Hall,[3] will be thankfully rec⸢d⸣

by your friend,
Amos Eaton

[1] Abel Storrs (1807–?) received his A.B. from Rensselaer Polytechnic Institute in 1831 and served the following year as an assistant to Eaton. He returned to New Hampshire and farming. *Nason,* p. 197, reports him as still living in 1887.

[2] The use of such extravagant language, we can speculate, must have placed Henry in an ambiguous position. On the one hand, he wanted fame from science and knew the worth of his findings. On the other hand, he was well aware of competing claims of other scientists and of the need to be fair to them. For a general discussion of this problem, see Robert K. Merton, "Priorities in Scientific Discovery, A Chapter in the Sociology of Science," *American Sociological Review,* 1957, 22:635–659.

The quotation is from Alexander Pope's *An Essay on Man,* epistle 4, line 281. As the original reference by the Tory, Pope, is to the regicide, Oliver Cromwell, the original meaning is not quite what Eaton apparently intends to convey.

[3] In the James Hall Papers at the New York State Library is a copy of this letter. James Hall (1811–1898) was a notable geologist and paleontologist of the last century. He will appear subsequently on many occasions in these volumes.

This letter, seemingly routine, relates to one of the major controversies of Henry's career, the dispute with Morse about the invention of the telegraph. When Henry decided to present his side of the affair, Hall was asked to testify to what he had seen in 1832 when visiting Henry. In Hall's letter of January 19, 1856, he writes "In August, 1832 I visited Albany with a friend, having a letter of introduction to you from Professor Eaton," which is, strictly speaking, not true. Storrs is not named. Hall goes on to state that Henry demonstrated the use of currents of electricity to ring bells at a distance and quotes Henry as remarking that this method was adaptable for conveying signals over distances of many miles. Smithsonian Institution, *Annual Report, 1857,* p. 96.

FROM JOHN MACLEAN

Henry Papers, Smithsonian Archives

Princeton, Aug. 24, 1832.

My dear Sir

I thank you for your letter of the 17ᵗʰ instant,[1] & for the report of the Regents of the University of New York. Your communication on the Aurora Borealis appended to the Report I had read with great pleasure in the Journal of Science.[2] It is in my opinion a document of great merit.

I appreciate your motives for not visiting us at this time, & esteem you the more on account of them though I should have been gratified to have had a visit from you; chiefly, that you might see my colleagues, & have a better opportunity to judge for yourself of the expediency of your removing to this place, in case of your appointment which I hope will take place in four or five weeks.

I am of the opinion, that it would be proper for you to mention to Dr Beck that you have a prospect of an appointment here; it might be made in confidence.

I hope that you have recovered your health.

With sincere esteem
Yours
John Maclean

---

[1] Not found.

[2] Joseph Henry's article, "On a Disturbance of the Earth's Magnetism, in Connexion with the Appearance of an Aurora, as Observed at Albany on the 19ᵗʰ of April, 1831," *Silliman's* *Journal*, 1832, 22:143–155, was presented to the Albany Institute on January 26, 1832, and was also published in *Board of Regents of the University of the State of New York, Annual Report, 1831* (Albany, 1832), pp. 107–119.

TO STEPHEN ALEXANDER

Family Correspondence, Henry Papers, Smithsonian Archives

Galway Uncle John's[1]
Monday Afternoon Augst.
27ᵗʰ 1832

Dear Stephen

After a variety of adventures which will be best communicated by the tongue of Mr. Hawley, we arrived safely at this place on friday evening.

---

[1] John Alexander (1760–1841). Unpublished Alexander Family Genealogy by Robert Gaylord Lester in the Henry Papers files.

Mother was somewhat indisposed on our passage from Schenectady but found herself much better on Saturday Morning. Our jaunt thus far has apparently been of much service to the whole party. The pure air of the country has had an almost magical effect in restoring our prostrated strength. All our friends have received us with harty welcomes and we want nothing more to make us almost entirely hapy but the assurances that those we have left amidst the pestiferous atmosphere of Albany are still preserved from the effects of the disease. I had written thus far when the boy was announced from the corners with two News papers[2] and your letter[3] to Harriet. This interruption you may easily immagine was a very pleasant one and every occupation was at a stand except that of examining the papers and reading the letter.

We have as yet made no visits but have remained at Uncle Johns since our arrival. We however have some idea of going to Uncle Thomas's[4] this afternoon. We saw nearly all our friends at church at the corners yesterday and have promised more visits than I fear we will be able to pay unless indeed the trustees of the academy, in their wisdom should see fit to postpond the assembling of the Academy for a week or two longer.

On thursday evening our party separated in Schenectady, Mother stoped at Judge Ryley's,[5] Harriet & Margaret Bullions[6] at Prof. Proudfits[7] and I took lodgings at the north college with *Prof.* Jackson[8] from which place I saw and made a note of the aurora you mentioned. I regretted that I had not brought a vibrating needle for the meteor appeared brillant and in continual motion. It was also seen at Galway and has probably been noticed over the whole state. I have glanced over your calculation and although the data which rest on the equality of the breadth of the beam is hypotheical, it is very plausible and serves to establish the fact of the great height of the aurora. The supposition however that the beam is throughout of eaqual altitude is inconsistant with the observations on the position of

---

[2] Probably the *Albany Evening Journal* and the *Albany Daily Argus.*

[3] Not found.

[4] Thomas Alexander (1775–1842), Henry's half uncle. Unpublished Alexander Family Genealogy compiled by Robert Gaylord Lester in the Henry Papers files.

[5] James Van Slyck Ryley (1761–1848), a native of Schenectady. Ryley left New York for the Midwest where he became an Indian trader and a government interpreter; he was apparently influential in the signing of the Saginaw Treaty with the Chippewa Tribe. Returning to Schenectady, Ryley held various posts in the local government, ultimately be-coming a judge in Schenectady County. It is probable that Henry became acquainted with the Ryleys through the Alexander family. Later contacts between Henry and the Ryley family will appear in subsequent volumes of the Henry Papers. Information supplied by Larry Hart, Schenectady City/County Historian.

[6] Probably the daughter of Reverend Peter Bullions. See Henry's letter of August 29, 1832, below, to Stephen Alexander.

[7] Robert Proudfit, D.D., Professor of Greek and Latin Languages, 1819–1849, at Union College. *Union Catalog,* p. xii.

the *corona* which renders it evident that the beams are all parallel to the dip. But if we consider the long beam a column which you describe as composed of a number of short columns of eaqual altitude parallel to the dipping needle and over laping each other as to form a continual beam of light your supposition will then apply and without further reflection I see no objection to it.

The mail comes to Galway but three times a week. If you have any communications which it is necessary should be forwarded in the shortest time please direct them to the care of Harvey Davis, Inn Keeper, Schenectady and he will send them by the stage which leaves his house every afternoon at 2 o'clock for Galway and Galway every morning at 7 o'clock for Schenectady. If you will take the trouble of requesting the editors of the Daily to direct my papers to Galway care Harvey Davis Schenectady I will receive them every evening.

P.S. Ask Mr Bullions[9] if there be any rumor of the Academy remaining closed longer than next monday.

Dear Brother,[10]

Hubby has left a small space for me to write. You don't know how much I was disappointed when I heard here that there were only three mails a week. At Schenectady we understood there would be one every day. Do write so that we may receive a letter in each mail for anxiety respecting you is the only thing that mars our happiness. I have wished for you and Aunt[11] almost every hour. The air here is so pure and sweet it seems loaded with perfume. Before we reached Schenectady we had concluded to remain there untill Monday. But when we arrived we found Mrs Ryley sick & Mr R. quite unwell & thinking it might be burdensome to Jane we left Mother[12] there & we went up the hill.

The next morning we met at Mr Ryley's and held a council upon our further proceedings. We were all gloomy & were near concluding to return but finally resolved to proceed as soon as a conveyance could be procured.

We took a Hack & started in a shower but rode very comfortably & part of the way very pleasantly untill we reached Charlton[13] where we stopped for a short time. When we were about leaving again to proceed we found

---

[8] Isaac W. Jackson, Professor of Mathematics and Natural Philosophy at Union College. See Henry's letter of December 5, 1829, to Stephen Alexander, footnote 9, above.

[9] Reverend Peter Bullions, for whom see Minutes, Academy Trustees, April 14, 1826, footnote 7.

[10] The remarks that follow are those of Har-

riet Alexander Henry printed below in the same location in which they appear in the original document.

[11] Harriet's maternal aunt, Nancy Connor.

[12] Maria Alexander.

[13] A small town located six and one-half miles south of Galway.

the axle tree was broken & so had to get into the stage in which we reached there without further accident except [for] leaving one trunk—yes Joseph's leather trunk! But we picked it up again. We have all improved in health very much since we came here. Please give my love to all friends. Take good care of yourselves & *do not fail to take medicine if you feel at all unwell*. Please remember me to the Mead's. I am sorry Louise is sick. Tell them I have not found such beaux for them yet as I should like. I should lik[e] to write a great deal more but Hub has wasted so much of the paper I can't. And that we may all in mercy be favored to meet again in health [. . .]¹⁴ of yours dear dear brother as ever   H

[P.S.] We shall expect a letter in every mail.

N.B. On reading the communication of Mrs. H. I find she has not told all. We lost the silk umbrella. It was left in the railway car and before we missed it the car had returned to Albany. The porters denighed all knowledge of it.   J. H.¹⁵

[P.P.S.] Tell Mr Bullions that Margaret is in fine spirits and is quite at home at Uncle John's. She does not wish to visit any other place and is becoming a favorite with the old gentleman and his two daughters.¹⁶

---

¹⁴ Four illegible words.

¹⁵ This note is printed here in the order in which it was probably written. In the original document, however, it appears at the end of Henry's remarks, where one would expect to find his signature.

¹⁶ Probably Ann (1796–?) and Ruth Alexander (1798–?). Unpublished Alexander Family Genealogy by Robert Gaylord Lester in the Henry Papers files.

TO JAMES HENRY¹

Family Correspondence, Henry Papers, Smithsonian Archives

Galway Wednesday Evening
Aug 29 1832 at Uncle John's

Dear James

I wrote to Stephen on tuesday² informing him of our safe arrival in this place and that we were all recovering health and strength from the fine air and good living of the country. All our friends are well and received us

---

¹ This letter bears the following address: "James Henry Esqʳ, Care Mr. A. Goold, Law Book Store, Albany." Anthony Gould (1801 or 1802–1858) came to Albany in 1821, and after several years as a clerk in the law bookstore of his uncle William Gould, became a partner in the business. Munsell, *Ann. Alb.,* 10:417.

² See Henry's letter of August 27, 1832, to Stephen Alexander, above, which Henry probably finished on Tuesday.

with a hardy wellcome. We were somewhat affraid that they might be apprehensive of contagion from us comming as we did from the infected city but they appeared to have no feelings of this kind.

We are happy to learn from Stephen's letter[3] that you are all in tolerable health and that the cholera is somewhat subsiding in Albany as well as in New York and Philadelphia.

I have received so much benefit from this short residence in the country that if the Academy should not be opened on Monday next we will remain a few days longer than the last of this week. The mail comes to Galway 3 times per week and I have left orders to have the *"daily"*[4] forwarded to me so that we have the news tolerably regular. We have taken up our principal quarters at Uncle John's when we make our visiting excursions daily in sucession to the whole clan of relatives. Uncle John has been very anxious concerning mother and will probably visit her as soon as he conceives it safe for him to do so.

I see by the papers that old Mr Humphrey[5] has died of the cholera. From this it appears that the disease still continues on the hill around and oposite Harrises. If it should come into your street you had better shut the house and take mother and Nancy[6] into the country or down to our house as was talked of before we left.

Write me on the Receipt of this and give me all the news—direct to Galway, write immediatly on the Receipt of this as we will leave for Albany on Saturday if an advertisement in the "daily" should announce that the Academy will open on monday next. If you wish to send to me in the quickest manner possible direct your letter to Harvy Davis, Inn Keeper, Schenectady and he will forward it by the stage which leaves every afternoon for Galway.

We visited Uncle Thomas and Eliza Hanford[7] on Monday and tuesday and Lydia[8] this afternoon. Tomorrow Harriet and her Mother visit Abbey,[9] and Uncle Thomas and myself will probably take a jaunt to the springs. Hugh Alexander[10] and I made an excursion yesterday to the Fishhouse, the residence of Mother's old acquaintance John Fay.[11] We met a

---

[3] Not found.

[4] *The Albany Daily Argus.*

[5] John Humphrey (1751–1832) who died on August 26. *Proceedings of the Common Council and the Various Religious Organizations of the City of Albany Relative to the State Street Burial Grounds* (Albany, 1867), p. 43.

[6] Henry's sister.

[7] Henry's half cousin Eliza Alexander (1802–?), who married George Hanford in 1824. Unpublished Alexander Family Genealogy by

Robert Gaylord Lester in the Henry Papers files.

[8] Probably Henry's cousin Lydia Alexander Hays (1802–?), daughter of John Alexander (1760–1841) of Galway. Ibid.

[9] Abigail Alexander (1790–?), a daughter of John Alexander, and Henry's cousin. Ibid.

[10] Henry and Hugh Alexander (1793–1842), son of John Alexander, were cousins. Ibid.

[11] John Fay (1773–1855) was born in Hardwick, Massachusetts. He moved with his par-

young Lawyer by the name of Grennolds who resides at the Fish-House and trades at your store.

He has married a relative of John Fay and is said to be doing a tolerable good business.

There are several persons from Albany at the Corners and at Stimpsons Viz—Mr James Clark's family,[12] Jonas Conkling and wife,[13] Mr Herrings family,[14] two of Willard Walkes sons, Bloodgood's step son Morris, William Lush[15] (Gen. Trotters soninlaw)[16] and family.

Hugh has repaird the old store on the corner and has a fine assortment of dry goods. He is in partnership with his brotherinlaw Dr Candy and appears to be doing considerable business. He is also, as you perhaps know, a Justice of the Peace and as such receives more than an equal share of the business of the office. All our relatives in Galway have been very particular in their inquiries about Mother, Nancy, and yourself.

Your Brother
Joseph

PS. Do not for get to write and you may if it be convenient mail occasionally for me a copy of the Evening Journal.[17]   J. H.

---

ents to New York at an early age, settling first in Montgomery County, and later in Galway. In 1804 he moved to Northampton, in Fulton County, where he held various local offices and was Postmaster for several years. He was a member of the State Assembly in 1808, 1809, and 1812; elected as a Democrat to the Sixteenth Congress (1819–1821); served as Sheriff of Jefferson County from 1828 to 1831; and was a presidential elector on the Democratic ticket of James K. Polk and George Mifflin Dallas in 1844. *Biographical Directory of the American Congress.*

[12] Possibly James Clark (died October 5, 1847, aged 74), an Albany dry goods merchant whose store was located on the corner of Broadway and State Streets. Munsell, *Ann. Alb.*, *1*:160.

[13] Both of whom are unknown to us as well as other persons in this letter mentioned only briefly.

[14] This may be the family of Thomas Herring who entered Albany Academy in 1821, two years after Henry. *The Celebration of the Centennial Anniversary of the Founding of the Albany Academy, May 24, 1913* (Albany, 1914), p. 113.

[15] William Lush (?–1846) is practically unknown to us. Munsell, *Ann. Alb.*, *10*:371, notes his passing ("William Lush died.") on July 2, 1846, but fails to mention his age at the time.

[16] Matthew Trotter (?–1830), an officer in the American Revolution who participated in the siege of Fort Stanwix and afterward was an aide to Lord Stirling. Trotter engaged in trade in Albany after the war and held several municipal offices. He died in his home on the corner of Market and Patroon Streets. Franklin B. Hough, *American Biographical Notes* (Albany, 1875), p. 398.

[17] The *Albany Evening Journal*, edited by Thurlow Weed. *Howell and Tenney*, p. 377.

TO STEPHEN ALEXANDER

Family Correspondence, Henry Papers, Smithsonian Archives

Galway Aug 29th 1832 or
Wed. Eve. At Uncle John's

Dear Stephen

Your letters[1] were received this day at 11 oclock. They both came to hand at the same time acompanied with the 'Daily' of Monday & Tuesday. It appears from your letter to Harriet that you have had no intelligence from us since our departure.[2] We intended to write from Schenectady but it was defered until the stage came to the door and instead of a letter we sent a message by David Proudfit[3] who promised to call in the evening of the same day we left Schenectady, at our house and inform you of our departure for Galway.

The weather in Galway as in Albany on Saturday last was very cold and the wind very high the whole day from the N.W. Since then the temperature has been quite agreable and the sky clear except a shower last evening with some rain in the night and this morning.

Hugh Alexander and myself yesterday took a jaunt to the Fish house a place on the south branch of the Hudson about 12 miles North of Galway corners. We found it a very pleasant little village surrounded with mountains and apparently on the verge of the inhabitable part of this portion of the state. To the north beyond as far as the eye could reach only mountains piled on mountains met the view.

This place is the residence of John Fay formerly a member of Congress from the county of Montgomery an intimate acquaintance of your Father[4] and a warm friend of the Alexander family. In passing from Galway to the Fish house I was surprised to see a little beyond Colo. [. . .][5] residence a ridge of primative rock of the Gneis kind. I was not aware of the fact that the primitive formation existed in this town which is generally covered with limestone and slaty Greywacke. In the location above mentioned the primative appears to be abruptly pushed up through the other strata and is thus found in a position where it might be the least expected. The an-

---

[1] Not found.

[2] Henry had written Alexander on August 27, 1832, above, but his letter and Stephen's must have crossed in the mail.

[3] Unidentified.

[4] Alexander Alexander (1764 or 1765–1809). Father of both Stephen and Harriet, Alex-ander was a Schenectady merchant and grist mill operator. See Robert Gaylord Lester's unpublished Alexander genealogy and information supplied by Larry Hart, Schenectady City/County Historian.

[5] One illegible word which might possibly be Gear's, or Gran's.

nexed sketch will give you an idea of the position of the rocks as they appear to me to be superimposed in Galway at the place mentioned. While at Uncle Thomas's I was struck with the circumstance of seeing a very large primative boulder or rounded stone lying on the surface of the ground in the barn yard. This you probably reccollect as it is a very prominent object and must weigh many tons. It is also composed gneis and in all probability was thrown to its present situation from the ridge of Gneis which I have described or conveyed from the same place by the agency of a mighty flood. Immense blocks of the same stone are scattered for several miles around the primative ridge. I observed one in particular about ½ a mile East of Uncle Thomas's nearly as large as a small one story house and at a distance of at least a mile and a half from its primitive position. As I have nothing of the scientific kind to occupy my attention but observations of a Geological or minerological kind (I have forgotten anything I ever knew of botany) I have thought it would be some what amusing to me if I had a copy of Eatons last work on Geology.[6] I should like to compare his account of the rocky formation of the county of Saratoga with the rocks as they are actually exhibited to the eye. If you learn that my presence will not be required in Albany on monday next and can find an oportunity of sending me a copy of Eatons last publication on the Geology of the State of New York published within a few Months you will much oblige me by procuring a copy at Websters.[7] Let it be charged to my account. Send it to Schenectady to the care of Harvey Davis Inn Keeper.

I see by an advertisement in the Daily that the Female Accademy[8] does not open on the first monday of September on account of the cholera. I hope the trustees of our academy will have the same views as we will find it impossible to finish all our engagements and be in Albany the latter part of the week.[9] We learn by the papers that Mr Humphry and Mr. Frasser[10]

---

[6] Probably Amos Eaton's *Geological Text-Book* (Albany, 1832).

[7] Websters & Skinners, a prominent printing house in Albany. See Minutes of the Albany Academy Trustees, June 11, 1816, footnote 1, above.

[8] Albany Female Academy, called Union School until 1821, was founded in 1814. Initially, its students learned basic skills, some arithmetic, geography, history, and sewing. By 1836, however, the institution was divided into six departments, had a thirteen-member Board of Trustees, and offered a curriculum that included chemistry, algebra, geology, mineralogy, botany, physiology, and astronomy. See Theodore R. Sizer, ed., *The Age of the Academies* (New York, 1964), pp. 168–174.

[9] Despite Henry's wishes to the contrary, Albany Academy resumed classes on Monday, September 3, according to schedule. See Henry's letter of September 4, 1832, to Harriet, below.

[10] Hugh Fraser (1793–1832), who died on August 26. *Proceedings of the Common Council and the Various Religious Organizations of the City of Albany Relative to the State Street Burial Grounds* (Albany, 1867), p. 59.

the superintendant of the coaches at the east end of the rail way have died of the cholera. The latter person was the last acquaintance I parted with in Albany and the unexpected news of his death affected me more unpleasantly than any death which has occurred by the cholera. We wrote to you on Monday and sent the letter by Mr Lush. You have probably received it as it must have reached Albany on tuesday evening. We are much pleased to hear that all belonging to us are well in Albany and that Dr Wing[11] is recovering.   J. H.

[P.S.] Give my respects to Mr Bullions & the Meads family   J. H.[12]

My Dear Brother & Aunt,[13]

Thus far we have been mercifully preserved in health. Indeed I think we have been improving every day especially Mother and Joseph. The baby[14] has had a little of the diarhea but is better I think to day. We were very glad to receive your letter Brother—how kind you are to write so regularly! —but am sorry you did not hear from us sooner as we expected you would as David Proudfit promised to call & tell you we were well & wither we were bound. Since we have been here we have done little else than visit. On Monday we went to Uncle Thomas' & staid there till yesterday afternoon, when we came down to the corners & staid with Eliza Hanford untill evening. This afternoon we have spent with Lydia Hayes. Tomorrow if we live we are to go to Cousin Abbey's & the day following to Rachels.[15] I have had two rides on Horseback while here and Margaret has ridden everyday this week. She is delighted with it. Tell Mr Bullions when you see him that she is well & appears to enjoy herself very much.

I don't doubt you are very lonely with out the baby. He is all life & has been very good, appears to enjoy riding and visiting very much. I felt rather gloomy this evening riding home. I thought of you at home & wished that you were with us or we with you. I wish very much that we could hear from you every day. Joseph would like much to remain another week if the Academy does not open on Monday. Please give my love to all, do take care of yourselves, & please to write as often as possible. I want so much to hear from you every day. I wish you were here. I am dear Brother as ever

Harriet

---

[11] For Dr. Joel A. Wing (1788–1852), see Minutes of the Albany Academy Trustees, December 6, 1819, especially footnote 4, above.

[12] Henry wrote this postscript on the first page of his letter, in the left margin.

[13] At this point, the handwriting becomes that of Harriet Henry, who penned the remarks that follow.

[14] William Alexander Henry (1832–1862).

[15] Rachel Alexander (1804–?), Henry's cousin. Robert Gaylord Lester's unpublished Genealogy of the Alexander Family, Henry Papers files.

TO HARRIET HENRY

Family Correspondence, Henry Papers, Smithsonian Archives

Albany Monday [September 3, 1832]
morning 10 o clock & 15 minutes
At the Academy

My Dear Harriet

Margaret[1] and myself arrived about a half an hour since after a very pleasant ride.[2] I called at Mr Ryleys,[3] saw Jane and her Father both tolerably well. Jane wishes she could go into the country. Her Father is not very well but no worse than when you were in Schenectady. Mrs Ryley continued to improve until yesterday morning when she was again attacked with diarrhea after eating some ginger bread. She is better this morning although very weak. I did not see her. Aunt received me very cordially but was some what disappointed when the stage door opened not to see the boy.[4] Stephen I have not yet seen as he has gone today as a *soldier;*[5] He was warned last week and thought himself obliged to appear. Aunt says he has been well. I have not yet been at Mothers but Mr McArthur[6] says mother is about the same. Nancy[7] has been quite unwell but is better. Dr Selkirk[8] is sick.

You will see by the paper of today that the board of health have discontinued their report. The boys of the Academy inform me that there were a number of deaths yesterday. Some say 12; this is probably exaggerated. There were however 4 funerals at least. Before closing my letter I have found time to visit mother's. Nancy appears very feeble. She has been unwell during the time of our absence although not confined to her bed. She called Dr Mc Naughton[9] who gave her an emitic. She has been gaining

[1] Margaret Bullions, daughter of Reverend Peter Bullions.

[2] Along the left margin, Henry wrote: "I arrived just in time[. . .] as my class was about dispersing."

[3] For whom see above, Henry to Stephen Alexander, August 27, 1832, footnote 5.

[4] William Alexander Henry, his son.

[5] In the State Militia.

[6] Reverend Samuel McArthur, for whom see above, Minutes, Academy Trustees, January 27, 1832, footnote 7.

[7] Nancy Henry.

[8] Probably Joseph Selkirk, brother of Dr. Francis N. Selkirk (1806–1850), who died of consumption on January 15, 1833, at the age of 31. *Albany Daily Advertiser*, January 16,

1833, p. 2. Although Henry refers to Joseph Selkirk as "one of the most amiable members of the Family" in a later letter to James Henry (December 8, 1832, Family Correspondence, Smithsonian Archives), we have no information on the relationship of Joseph and Francis Selkirk to Henry's grand aunt, Elizabeth Selkirk.

[9] Dr. James McNaughton (1787 or 1796–1874), Albany physician. McNaughton was born in Scotland, graduated from the medical department of the University of Edinburgh, and settled in Albany in 1817, where he opened his medical office. James and his brother Peter became prominent Albany citizens, in civic, business, and medical affairs. In 1828, James was admitted to the Albany County

since. Mother has been unusually well since our absence. [She was] ill this morning when she was some what troubled with the cough. Mr. Kenedy[10] has had another very severe attack. His life has been despaired of but he is now apparently recovering.

Just as we were coming into the city we met Dr Mc Naughton with the rest of the medical staff who have gone today on a jaunt to the Springs. They will probably return this evening.

Uncle James[11] was at mother's one saturday. He is not well and appeared quit feeble.

Mr Bullions[12] sends you many thanks for the care you have [taken] of Margaret & is much obliged to Uncle John[13] for the lessons in riding which the young lady has received under his kind direction.

The stage starts in a few minutes and have time to collect nothing more in the way of news. Kiss the boy for me and give love to all

Your *Husband*

To My Dear little Wife
Stage Office 11½ o' c[l]ock

I met Mary Ann Lagrange. She says that Mrs Shankland has returned, is quit[e] fleshy but regretted yesterday that she had not remained longer in the country.[14]

Medical Society, later serving as its President. During the cholera epidemic of 1832, he became President of the Board of Health. From 1840 until his death, he was a professor at the Albany Medical College. McNaughton was a Resident Member of the Second Department of the Albany Institute. *Howell and Tenney*, pp. 210, 214, 532, 534. Franklin B. Hough, *American Biographical Notes* (Albany, 1875), p. 272. Munsell, *Coll. Alb.*, 2:214, 223–224. Munsell, *Ann. Alb.*, 6:126. *Transac-*

tions, Albany Institute, 1830, *1*, part 2: Appendix, p. 73.
   [10] Not identified.
   [11] James Henry (1767–?), the half uncle of Joseph and Harriet. Unpublished Alexander Family Genealogy by Robert Gaylord Lester in the Henry Papers files.
   [12] Reverend Peter Bullions.
   [13] John Alexander (1760–1841).
   [14] This note appears on the cover sheet.

TO HARRIET HENRY

Family Correspondence, Henry Papers, Smithsonian Archives

Albany Tuesday morning
25 minutes past 8 Sept 4th 1832

My Dear Harriet

I have slept so late this morning that I have only a few minutes left to devote to you. This morning is cold rainy gloomy. The house appears lonely. I shall however soon be in the Academy and amidst my pupils will regain my usual state of feelings. Stephen came home from his training[1] at 12 o'clock or a little before; the company was dismissed at that time for the day. He did not complain of fatigue and as the duty did not last long it is probable it will do him some good in the way of exercise. Miss La Grange spent the afternoon with Aunt and visited the Misses Meads. She was much pleased with the family and said we were favoured in having agreable neighbors. I have little more to communicat in the way of news than what I wrote yesterday except it be that James[2] took Dr. Selkirk into the country yesterday. Aunt was at Mothers with Mary Ann La Grange yesterday afternoon for a short time. They advised Nancy and Mother both to go into the country for a few days. The little girl has left Nancy[3] and she is now obliged to attend to the family herself. Fortunatly none of the boarder's have yet returned except Mr McArthur. I shall see them to day and make arrangements for their going out of the city if they will consent.

The Academy was dismissed yesterday afternoon at about 4 o'clock and as I had considerable head-ache after my ride I came home and laid down until called to tea. After this I felt much better but all things appeared gloomy after enjoying myself so much in the country. I wandered involuntary from room to room as if in expectation of meeting you and the *boy*.[4] In the front room up stairs the cradle with its top counterpain neatly arranged, I suppose by Aunt, probably reminded me of its little owner. The clock strikes nine so I must away. 10 o'clock, I have found a few moments leisure in the Academy to finish my letter. Livingston Ludlow[5] informs me that his mother is much better and that his aunt Anna is very well for her. I delivered to Aunt the message about the plumbs. They are ripe and will be attended to as mother directed.

I have not seen Aunt Betsys people or Mr Johnson's but I will visit them probably to day and deliver the messages with which I have been charged from Galway.

The Academy in my department is very slim. I have this morning only 12 boys so that my duties at present are not very arduous. There are about 100 in all the rooms.

Stephen would have written this morning but I have taken the only sheet of paper. Aunt is much affraid that you will stay so long in the country with the boy that he will forget her before you return. She has made

---

[1] Apparently a reference to Alexander's service with the State Militia.
[2] James Henry.
[3] Nancy Henry.

[4] Henry's first child, William Alexander Henry.
[5] Not identified.

many inquiries concerning him how he behaves in visiting wether he has had a looseness etc.

Stay in Galway as long as possible. Give my love to all friends Mother Uncle John in particular. Kiss the boy for me & be assured that I would be much more happy were you in Albany or I in Galway.

Your Husband

JAMES RENWICK, SR., TO JOHN MACLEAN
"Joseph Henry I" file box, Princeton University Archives

Col. College, New York
18th of September, 1832

Dear Sir,

I have only this instant returned from an absence of some weeks. This will account for your not having received a reply to your confidential communication of the 7th instant.[1]

In respect to Mr. Joseph Henry of the Albany Academy, I have had the pleasure of his acquaintance, and frequent communications with him on subjects of mutual interest. These however have been confined to the purely physical branches of Natural Philosophy. In these I can with confidence recommend Mr. Henry as possessed of knowledge probably unequaled in this country. In relation to the branches of Mechanical Philosophy and Astronomy my opportunities of forming a judgment of his proficiency have been small. In consequence I cannot speak decidedly of his ability to teach those departments.[2] Still such is my opinion of his general knowledge, and of his talent and industry, that I would not hesitate to recommend him as capable of filling the chair of which you speak in a manner that would be most advantageous to the institution with which you are connected.

I am Dear sir
Your Obedient Servant,
James Renwick

[1] Not found.

[2] Renwick is saying that while Henry is good in experimental physics, that he (Renwick) cannot vouch for Henry's knowledge of the mathematical parts of natural philosophy.

BENJAMIN SILLIMAN, SR., TO JOHN MACLEAN
"Joseph Henry I" file box, Princeton University Archives

New Haven, Sept 23, 1832

Dear Sir,

In passing through Albany a few days since I saw Mr. Joseph Henry who informed me that his name had been mentioned in connection with the vacant professorship of Natural Philosophy in your Institution; that reference had been to me for an opinion as to Mr. Henry's merits.

To yourself at least I trust that it will not be considered intrusive, if I say that I think Mr. Henry a young man of very uncommon talents and acquirements in the departments of knowledge to which he had devoted himself. He has a very Superior mind, active, inquisitive, inventive and ardent: he is I understand a fine Mathematician and I need nothing more than the evidence which I have myself seen and most of which is before the public in the American Journal of Science to convince me, that as a physical philosopher he has no superior in our country: certainly not among the young men. He has the important advantage of being an excellent practical mechanic and if placed in favorable circumstances I doubt not that he will add to the Science of physics and bring forward other discoveries besides the brillant ones which have already made him extensively and advantageously known to the Scientific world.

I believe he has not cultivated classical literature but his style of communication both in conversation and writing is pleasing, perspicuous & correct. I have no interest in promoting his success other than what is very honourable to him namely a warm interest in his advancement springing from a high opinion of his intellectual power, his scientific attainments and his moral excellence.

I remain My dear sir with very
kind regard, Yours very truly
B Silliman[1]

---

[1] MacLean added the following note to the text: "Dr. Silliman probably wrote the above letter immediately upon his return to New Haven; and before reading the letter I had written to him."

JACOB GREEN TO JOHN MACLEAN
"Joseph Henry I" file box, Princeton University Archives

Philadelphia, Sept:24ʰ 1832

My dear Sir,

I am rejoiced that my conversation with you, sometime since, should have directed your attention to Professor Henry of the Albany Academy, as a fit person to fill one of the scientific chairs of your college. Of his qualifications to teach well the branches of Nat. Phil. & Mechanics usually taught, no one acquainted with these subjects and with Professor Henry can doubt. His own communications to our scientific Journals will be his best recommendation. In the latest Volˢ of Silliman's periodical you will find a number of his papers.

Believing that he will prove a valuable acquisition to your college, I hope he will be appointed.

Yours truly
Jacob Green[1]

[1] To this letter Maclean notes that the original conversation with Green did not relate to Princeton as no vacancy then existed:

But in the course of one of our conversations during a visit he made to Princeton, Prof. G. mentioned to me that he had a friend in Albany, by the name of Joseph Henry, whom he was desirous to see connected with one of our colleges, and of whom he spoke in the highest terms. It was the recalling to mind of Professor Green's high and earnest commendation of Professor Henry that first directed my attention to Prof. H. as being very probably a suitable person to succeed Professor Vethake. . . .

JOHN TORREY TO JOHN MACLEAN
"Joseph Henry I" file box, Princeton University Archives

New York, September 24ʰ, 1832

My dear Sir,

I cheerfully comply with your request respecting the scientific character of Professor Henry of Albany. I have known this gentleman for several years, and have marked with great satisfaction his course, since he commenced his career as a cultivator of physical science. He gave promise from the first that he would be one of the foremost in pursuits of this kind: and he has already, though so young, gained a reputation that would do honour to grey hairs. I have no doubt, should his health be spared for a few years, but he will stand among the first philosophers of the country.

He would be a great acquisition to your College, and I should be rejoiced to see him appointed to the situation recently vacated by the resignation of Professor Vethake.

Yours truly
John Torrey

EXCERPT,[1] MINUTES, TRUSTEES, COLLEGE OF NEW JERSEY[2]
Trustees' Minutes, 3:219–224, Princeton University Archives

Sept. 26. 1832 ½ past 8 O'clock A.M.

. . . The Board proceeded to the election of a Professor of Natural Philosophy, when Mr. Joseph Henry was duly elected.

Resolved. That the Salary of the Professor of Natural Philosophy be $1000. per annum together with the use of the house & lot lately occupied by Professor Vethake.

Resolved. That the committee of Repairs be authorized to put the above named house in tenantable order. . . .

[1] Omitted from these minutes are the preceding and subsequent portions of the session relating to various routine actions of the Trustees. These few lines occur roughly in the middle of the proceedings; the Henry appointment was also a routine action of the Trustees.

[2] The formal title of the College will be used in designating administrative sources such as the Minutes of the Trustees. "Princeton" will usually be used in reference to the College of New Jersey, as was often done during this period. The present name was adopted in 1896 when the College formally assumed university status. See Thomas Jefferson Wertenbaker, *Princeton, 1746–1896* (Princeton, 1946), p. 373.

FROM JOHN MACLEAN
Henry Papers, Smithsonian Archives

Princeton, Sept. 26. 1832

My dear Sir

I have the pleasure to inform you, that you have been unanimously appointed Professor of Nat. Philosophy, on the terms mentioned in my former letters.

The particulars tomorrow.

In great haste
Yours
J. Maclean

FROM JOHN MACLEAN

Mary Henry Copy, Henry Papers, Smithsonian Archives

Princeton Sep. 27th 1832

My dear Sir

So perfectly satisfactory were the testimonials in regard to yourself from Professors Silliman, Renwick, Green, & Torrey, that our Trustees did not hesitate for a moment.

Your salary for the coming year is fixed at a thousand dollars, and a house; this may also be the salary for the second year but probably more, and in third year $1200 and a house. I am not authorized to make this statement, but I have no doubt of its accuracy unless something altogether unforseen should occur. The house will be repaired forthwith, if you are disposed to move your family this fall.

Our next session commences on the 11th of next month. As it may be altogether inconvenient for you to leave Albany by that time, please to let me know what time will suit you, and we will make our arrangements accordingly.

The Trustees have placed at your disposal $100, for the purchase of a new electrical machine &c.

With much esteem
Yours
J. Maclean

MINUTES, ACADEMY TRUSTEES

Trustees' Minutes, 2:62, Albany Academy Archives

Albany. Septr 29. 1832

A Special meeting of the Board was held this day, at the Academy, at the request of several Trustees

October 11, 1832

Present

A Conkling	J Stevenson
O. Kane	Revd Mr Ferris,
A. Campbell	T R Beck

On Motion

Resolved that Messrs Conkling & Stevenson be a Committee on the improvement of the Park Grounds, with power [to] confer with the Corporation & to procure trees for the same.

The Principal communicated to the Trustees, the resignation by Professor Henry of the Offices he holds in this institution.[1]

Adjourned.

[1] There is no evidence in the manuscripts examined as to who requested the meeting of the Trustees or, indeed, if the call for a meeting was because of Henry's resignation, or the concern for improving the park grounds, or both. Presumably, Beck had known before this date of the strong possibility of Henry's departure.

FROM BENJAMIN SILLIMAN, SR.
Henry Papers, Smithsonian Archives

New Haven Octob^r 11, 1832

My dear Sir

I congratulate you very cordially on your appointment. I wrote on your behalf of my return & found a letter from Prof. Maclean[1] & another was returned from Angelica,[2] both on your subject. I gave you my most decided support & I do not doubt you had that of other warm friends.

I have taken it upon me since I heard of your election to write another letter to Mr Maclean strongly recommending to the trustees to aid you in making researches & experiments, both by bearing the expense of them & by allowing you time & I have told them that in my opinion it would well repay the college. I have stated that you were ignorant of my taking such a step & not improbably your modesty would disapprove of it. But I trust that whether they aid you in the way proposed or not—such an opinion expressed regarding your power & disposition to advance science will do

[1] Confirming Maclean's memory as given in his note on Silliman's letter of September 23, 1832, above.

[2] Apparently another letter soliciting Silliman's aid was sent to Angelica, New York, where Silliman was visiting his daughter and son-in-law, and forwarded from there to New Haven. As we have found no such letter, the sender is unknown. Suspicion centers on John Torrey.

you no harm.[3] I am this morning writing to Dr Hare[4] & will mention you so that when you are in Phil^a you may call on him & just give your name which will be all that will be necessary for an introduction. I will do the same with Dr Morton,[5] an eminent naturalist & you can call on him in the same way—both are frank open-hearted men. When you are settled in your new place, I should be very glad if you would keep watch of the whole subject of electro dynamics electro-magnetism etc. & favor me with notices of its progress—not only in your own researches but in those abroad so as to keep up a regular (so far as may see) chain of information on the subject. I see in my recent Journals some long Italian researches[6] but have had no time to attempt an analysis of them.

If you are willing I should be glad to have you take charge of this department & I will pay for the communications.[7]

Mrs Silliman unites with me in the kindest remembrances to Mrs Henry.

I remain my dear sir with very sincere regard truly

Your friend

B Silliman

We are now in the miscellaneous department[8] of the Journal for this month.

---

[3] Letter not found. For Henry's research environment at Princeton, see subsequent volumes of the Henry Papers.

[4] For Hare, see Silliman's letter to him of this date, below.

[5] The letter of this date is in the Morton Papers in the Library of the American Philosophical Society. In it Silliman writes:

You may have observed that Prof^r Joseph Henry of Albany is appointed at Princeton. I have assured him that he may call on you in Phil^a without any other introduction than to mention his name. He is you may recollect the discoverer of the wonderful galvanic magnet & is a young man of the greatest promise & worth & of most amiable manners.

Samuel George Morton (1799–1851) was a leading naturalist of the day and the principal figure in the Academy of Natural Sciences of Philadelphia. A physician, he had the M.D. from both the University of Pennsylvania (1820) and Edinburgh (1823). Morton worked in a wide number of areas, but his greatest contributions, in all probability, were in paleontology and in physical anthropology.

Morton will reappear in subsequent volumes of the Henry Papers. *DAB*.

[6] That is, Silliman is reading about Italian research in overseas periodicals. Very little of this nature appears in his *Journal* which did have reprints and translations, as well as abstracts. Two examples appearing not too long before this letter are a note on Matteucci's use of the pile to study the state of chlorides and iodides in solution (*Silliman's Journal*, 1832, 21:368–369, from vol. 1 of the *Journal of the Royal Institution*) and A. Fusinieri on the transference of ponderable matter by electricity (ibid., 22:355–357, from the *Bibliothèque universelle* of December 1831).

[7] We have not found Henry's reply but have no evidence of his accepting Silliman's offer.

[8] A feature of *Silliman's Journal* of that day containing brief notices of foreign and domestic research, necrologies, and accounts of new publications. This was filler material, and Silliman's mentioning it indicates that he was far along in the preparation of an issue. As some of the contents were significant, their frequent absence from the volume indexes constitute a hazard to the unwary.

BENJAMIN SILLIMAN, SR., TO ROBERT HARE[1]
Edgar Fahs Smith Collection, University of Pennsylvania

New Haven Octob.[r] 11, 1832

My dear friend

I find all the wood cuts except the prism & shall forward them by the first private opportunity. I ought to have returned them before. I do not recollect that the prism was ever borrowed again after the return of the box but I shall be perfectly satisfied, provided you do not find it that it should be cut again at my expence & I request that you will cause it to be done accordingly. I was thinking it was long since I had heard of you & am happy to hear of your safe return from so long a tour & after, it appears, unusual perils.[2] I shall expect the fulfilment of your promise to send me some account of your adventures. I hope that they have resulted in improved health to fit you for a new course of public duty now at hand. You may have observed that M.[r] Henry of Albany the gentleman who constructed the great galvanic magnet is appointed to the chair of Natural Philosophy in Princeton. He wishes to become personally acquainted with you & I

---

[1] Robert Hare (1781–1858), an American chemist associated for most of his professional career with the University of Pennsylvania. Hare will appear subsequently on many occasions in the Henry Papers. He was undoubtedly the leading chemist in America of that day and also had a wide range of contributions to other fields, including the study of electricity and magnetism. There is a biography of Hare by Edgar Fahs Smith, *The Life of Robert Hare, an American Chemist (1781–1858)* (Philadelphia, 1917) which is useful because of the copious extracts from Hare manuscripts but is quite uncritical and fails to set Hare in the context of his scientific era. This is a particular pity as Hare is an American original both in personality and in his work.

Perhaps the best introduction to this interesting personage are the words in his necrology in *Silliman's Journal* (1858), 2d series, 26:104. Although unsigned, internal evidence indicates that this was written by the elder Silliman, Hare's student, collaborator, and longtime friend:

> . . . No one can review the numerous letters which he has addressed to the Senior Editor of this Journal, to Berzelius, to Liebig and Faraday, and published in this Journal, without perceiving that he was no ordinary antagonist. . . .

In his family and among his friends Dr. Hare was very kind, and his feelings generous, amiable and genial, although occasionally, his manner was abrupt—from absence of mind occasioned by his habitual abstraction and absorbtion in thought; his mind was ever active, and conversation would sometimes seem to awaken him from an intellectual reverie. He had high colloquial powers, but to give them full effect, it was necessary that they should be roused by a great and interesting subject, and especially if it assumed an antagonistic form. He would then discourse with commanding ability, and his hearers were generally as willing to listen as he was to speak.

Hare's relationship to Henry's work in electromagnetism will be dealt with in subsequent volumes. Suffice it to say that he hardly appears in the surviving manuscripts of this period, although Henry was obviously aware of the leading American in this area prior to his own appearance on the scene. For a contrary opinion see L. Pearce Williams, "The Simultaneous Discovery of Electro-Magnetic Induction by Michael Faraday and Joseph Henry," *Bullétin de la Société des Amis d'André-Marie Ampère*, 1965, 20:12–21.

[2] Not referred to in Smith, op. cit. We suspect this is an allusion to a European trip.

have assured him that nothing more would be necessary than to call & mention his name. He is a most promising man of a fine tone of character & with modest & winning manners. I know you will treat him kindly & have assured him so. I also have been absent with Mrs Silliman for 5 or 6 weeks visiting our children at Angelica. Mr Church[3] is now with us with a little son but 6 weeks old a promising child. The little thing has given me a shove forward in placing me among the venerables.

Our kind regards to Mrs Hare when you write mention her health—your own & your hand how it is. The journal is near winding up for this N^o. Shall you have any thing for the next? In this I might add some short thing among the miscellanies.

Yours affec^y

B Silliman

I hear of the Revd Mr Davis[4] going tomorrow to Phil^d to preach & by him I hope to send the cuts.

---

[3] John B. Church, Silliman's son-in-law.   [4] Unidentified.

EXCERPT,[1] MINUTES, ACADEMY TRUSTEES
Trustees' Minutes, 2:60–61, Albany Academy Archives

Special Meeting.[2]

Octr 16. 1832

The Trustees met, pursuant to adjournment.

Present

Mr James	Mr Ferris	Mr Campbell
The Recorder[3]	Mr Conkling	M^r DeWitt
The Mayor[4]	Mr Webster	Mr Kane
Dr Ludlow	Mr Stevenson	Mr Beck
Dr Sprague[5]	Mr Norton[6]	

---

[1] Routine business has been omitted below the list of Trustees present. Further omissions are noted below, footnote 9.

[2] Obviously this was an important meeting as evidenced by the number of Trustees present to choose Henry's successor.

[3] James McKown (1788 or 1789–1847). See Minutes, Albany Academy Trustees, April 14, 1826, especially footnote 2, above..

[4] Francis Bloodgood (1775–1867), a lawyer, banker, and businessman who graduated from Yale College in 1787. Bloodgood was Clerk of the New York State Supreme Court, Director and President of the New York State Bank, and President of the Albany Insurance Company. He was Mayor of Albany from 1831 to 1834. See *Howell and Tenney*, p. 664; and *Catalogue of the Officers and Graduates of Yale University in New Haven, Connecticut, 1701–1904* (New Haven, 1905), p. 345.

Phillips' Mineralogy,[7] the text book on that subject being out of print, it was *resolved* that the Faculty report on the propriety of Emmons' Mineralogy[8] as the text book.

The Board then proceeded to the election of a Professor of Mathematics & Natural Philosophy & on counting the ballots, it appeared that
Philip Ten Eyck MD of the City of Albany was unanimously elected. Whereupon
Resolved that Philip Ten Eyck be & he is hereby appointed Professor of Mathematics & Natural Philosophy.
Resolved that the Clerk notify him of his election.[9]

Adjourned

---

[5] William Buell Sprague (1795–1876), clergyman, biographer, collector, was born in Tolland County, Connecticut. He graduated from Yale College in 1815 and from Princeton Theological Seminary in 1819. Sprague became the minister of the Second Presbyterian Church in Albany in 1829. He was elected a resident member of the Albany Institute on November 23, 1829, and on July 9, 1830, became a Trustee of the Albany Academy. He will appear in subsequent volumes as a friend and correspondent of Henry's. See *DAB*; Minutes, Albany Institute, November 23, 1829; and *Academy Seventy-fifth Anniversary*, p. 66.

[6] John Treadwell Norton (1795–1869), an Albany businessman and banker. He was a close personal friend of Erastus Corning (probably Albany's most successful businessman) and frequently joined Corning in the iron and hardware industry. Norton was President of the Canal Bank from 1829 to 1835 and in 1846 was elected President of the Mohawk and Hudson Railroad. He was a resident member of the Albany Institute, and was a Trustee of the Albany Academy from 1829 to 1834. See Munsell, *Ann. Alb.*, *8*:113; *9*:182, 187; *10*:240, 373; *Howell and Tenney*, pp. 531, 534, 537, 539–540, 746; *Transactions*, Albany Institute, 1830, *1*, part 2: Appendix, p. 73; and especially Irene D. Neu, *Erastus Corning, Merchant and Financier, 1794–1872* (Ithaca, 1960), pp. 23, 35, 39. His son, the chemist John Pitkin Norton (1822–1852; *DAB*), will appear in later volumes of the Henry Papers.

[7] William Phillips, *An Outline of Mineralogy and Geology, Intended for the Use of Those Who May Desire to Become Acquainted with the Elements of Those Sciences; Especially of Young Persons* (New York, 1816).

[8] Ebenezer Emmons, *Manual of Mineralogy and Geology* (Albany, 1826).

[9] The few remaining lines of these minutes are concerned with the "expediency & practicability of establishing a Law School in connexion with the Academy."

EXCERPT,[1] MINUTES, ALBANY INSTITUTE
Institute Minutes, Albany Institute Archives

Oct[r] 23. 1832.

The Recording Secretary of the first Department reported that said Department had elected Rev. Peter Bullions, Librarian in the room of Professor Henry, who is about leaving the city.

---

[1] Routine matters have been omitted.

LECTURE NOTES ON MAGNETISM
AND ELECTROMAGNETISM[1]

Miscellaneous Henry Papers, Smithsonian Archives

1 The property of attraction & repulsion for iron possessed by the loadstone seems to have been known from the remotest antiquity. It is said to have derived its name from a city in Asia where it was first discovered.

2 The Load stone or natural magnet is an impure ore of iron. It is by no [means] a rare substance in nature as almost all the ores of iron possess this property in a greater or less degree.

Show Loadstone.

3 The magnetic energy does not reside equally in every part of the surface but at certain points called poles of the magnet. These points are readily discovered by rolling the magnet in iron filings.

4 Magnetism may be communicated to bars of iron & steel & as these can be formed into any shape & can be shaped to almost any degree of intensity they are allways used insted of the natural magnet.

---

[1] These lecture notes are undated, but internal evidence indicates they were written in Albany (see footnote 3), undoubtedly for the natural philosophy classes at the Albany Academy sometime between September 1826 and October 1832. We suspect this is an early lecture (i.e., pre-1830) since there are no explicit references to his large electromagnets. However, Henry does mention certain pieces of apparatus—such as the "large revolvers"—which were used in conjunction with his large magnets; our early dating must be tentative. Among Henry's papers there are many other examples of scientific lecture notes, but this is the only such document we have been able to assign definitely to the Albany period. Other lecture notes will appear in subsequent volumes.

This document is important for two reasons. First, it illustrates Henry's style of lecturing, his thoroughness, and his reliance upon experimental demonstration. More importantly, we believe it reflects Henry's current scientific ideas and interests, such as his concern for the electromagnetic theories of Ampère and his interest in terrestrial magnetism. In his dissertation, Charles Weiner, relying primarily on notes taken by Henry's students at Princeton, emphasizes the intimate relationship between Henry's teaching and his original scientific research. "Joseph Henry's Lectures on Natural Philosophy" (Case Institute of Technology, 1965).

Show Artificial Magnet show lines with chalk.

5 The power resides at or near the two extremities. A line joining the two poles is called the magnetic axis. A plane at right angles to this line through the middle is called the magnetic equator and a plane through the axis the magnetic meridian.

6 The poles of the magnet are best shown by an experiment.

Show two magnets under a paper on which iron filings are [strewed].

7 This experiment was thought at one time to exhibit the direction of the magnetic fluid. It is now known to be caused by each particle of iron becoming a little magnet having two poles. The arrangement is due to the mechanical action of these poles on each other.[2]

8 To understand this it is necessary to mention a very important fact in magnetism & that is that in two magnets there are two poles which attract and also two which repel.

9 *Show this by a suspended magnet.*

10 Another important property of the magnet is its power of inducing magnetism in soft iron or steel when in contact with them.

(Show this by suspending several iron balls from a magnet.)
(A bar of iron with a magnet at a small distance.)

11 A bar of steel cannot be rendered magnetic in this manner but may, by being rubbed in a certain manner by the magnet.

12 Various methods have been invented to touch or magnetize bars of steel. The easiest method is to place them in contact with a powerful magnet.

13 The most important property of the magnet is that of its polarity with regard to the earth.

14 If a needle be freely suspended by its centre of gravity so as to be free to move in all directions it will take a position nearly north at this place & inclined to the horizon in an angle of about 73°.

15 It was at one time supposed that the magnetic needle pointed exactly to the north in every part of the earth but this has since been found to be erroneous as there are but few places where it points exactly north.

---

[2] A similar molecular theory of magnetism was proposed by Coulomb. *DSB*. One of Henry's early notebooks (Henry Papers Control No. 6123, p. 122) contains his reading notes on the article "Coulomb," *Supplement to the Ency-* *clopaedia Britannica*, 1824, 3:414–419. Closely paraphrasing a summary of one of Coulomb's articles (p. 417), Henry wrote, "He considers every magnet as made up of minute parts, each poss[essing] a north & south pole."

16 Mention variation at Albany. *Show diagram* of variation at Albany & London.[3]

17 *Explaine the cause of the variation with a globe.*

18 *Show dipping needle.* Explain dipping needle.

19 Magnetic intensity.[4]

20 All iron bodies become magnetic by the action of the earth. *Show a piece of soft iron with a needle.*

21 Barlows correcting plate.[5]

22 Magnetism was formerly thought to be peculiar to iron and some of its compounds. But it has been shewn not long since that it is possessed in a greater or less degree by every matter.[6]

23 Theory of magnetism:

24 It has long been supposed that some connexion actually exists between electricity & magnetism. These phenomina in many instances are very similar. Lightning is often found to render iron in its passage strongly magnetic.[7]

25 Electrical induction resembles magnetism. Two needles may be formed of glass which will attract & repell like magnets when electrified.

26 On the other hand no action is observable between the glass needle

27 & a bar magnet. Indeed a needle of steel may be charged at the same time with magnetism & electricity & exhibit seperately the phenomena of each.

28 From all that was known previous to 1820 on the subject no other conclusion could be deduced than that electricity & magnetism could in no way be considered as effects of a common cause or principle

29 but that they were powers totally independent of each other although marked by characters similar in their action.

---

[3] From this, and from paragraph 14 above, we conclude that Henry delivered the lecture at Albany.

[4] For the measurement of magnetic intensity with the vibrating needle and a description of the dipping needle, see Henry's notes of April 19, 1831 and September 25, 1830, respectively.

[5] Peter Barlow's correcting plate allowed mariners to correct for errors of the compass due to the attraction of iron on shipboard. Barlow describes his method in *An Essay on Magnetic Attractions* (London, 1824), pp. 79–99, which Henry owned.

[6] Coulomb announced this discovery in 1802. See his articles "Expériences qui prouvent que tous les corps de quelque nature qu'ils soient, obéissent à l'action magnétique, et que l'on peut même mesurer l'influence de cette action sur les différentes espèces de corps," *Journal de physique*, 1802, 54:367–369; and "Recherches relatives à l'action que les barreaux aimantés exercent sur tous les corps," ibid., pp. 454–462.

[7] Henry notebook 6123, p. 71, contains a note on lightning:

Would it not be of some interest to place a piece of steele around the rod of several buildings and examine them from time to time in order to see if they are magnetic.

The steel should be hardened and formed in a small horse shoe. They would be magnetized at every discharge of lightning.

30 This was the general opinion of the Scientific world at the period when Prof. Oersted[8] of Copenhagen made a discovery which changed the whole face of the sources of magnetism.

31 He discovered that when a current of galvanic electricity is transmitted through a wire it acts powerfully on a magnetic needle. *Show a small battery with connecting wire.*

32 It was a long time befor the direction of the action could be made out. *Explain the positions of the needle. Show Exp.*

33 The enunciation of this discovery awakened the attention of philosophers in every part of the world. Several other eminent persons became engaged in the persuit.

34 It was discovered about the same time both by Sir Humphrey Davey & Biot[9] that this conjunctive wire itself was magnetic although made of any metal whatever.

35 *Show a wire magnetic by passing a stream of galvan[ism].*

36 *Another* important discovery was made by Ampere, a French philosopher. He found that the conjunctive wire not only attracted iron filings but also another conjunctive wire &c.

37 Two conjunctive wires attract when the currents pass in the same direction. Repell in different directions. *Show Experiment.*

38 On this fact Ampere formed his theory of magnetism and electromagnetism.

39 Explain the theory. This theory supposes that all magnetic bodies & the earth among their number derive their magnetism from currents of electricity.[10]

40 The theory based upon one fact and assumes one hypothesis.[11]

The facts of electro. mag. may be divided into three:

  1 The action of currents upon currents.
  2 The action of the magnet on currents.
  3 The action of the magnetism of the earth on currents.[12]

[8] The Danish physicist Hans Christian Oersted (1777–1851) made this momentous discovery in 1820.

[9] That the current-carrying wire itself became a magnet was actually demonstrated by Davy and D. F. J. Arago. *Encyclopaedia Metropolitana*, 1830 ed., s.v. "Electro-magnetism," p. 8. Henry's mention of Biot suggests he might have read of the experiments in his heavily annotated copy of John Farrar's *Elements of Electricity, Magnetism, and Electro-Magnetism* (Cambridge, Massachusetts, 1826), which comprises translated selections from Biot's *Précis élémentaire de physique*, 3d ed. (Paris, 1824). The reference to the independent experiments of Davy and Arago appears on p. 307, which bears markings by Henry.

[10] For Ampère's derivation of terrestrial magnetism from circular electric currents, see *DSB*, s.v. "Ampère."

[11] i.e., the fact and hypothesis noted in paragraphs 37–39.

[12] The action of terrestrial magnetism on electric currents was thoroughly investigated

Appendix

As the action of currents forms the basis of the Theory it is necessary to have a clear idea of it.

Show Diagram 2 currents.[13]
Find their equilibrium in the same plane
Action when one wire is in different [?plane]; other short

Experiment Revolution by currents.[14]
Action much increased by Spiral

Action of currents on magnets.
1 Explain magnetism.
2 Explain voltaic magnet.
3 Show model of magnet.
5 Show De La Rives ring.[15]
6 Show revolution by magnets. Large Revolver.[16]
7 Explain how magnetism is induced on soft iron by Galvanism.
8 Show small magnet with 5 & 6.
9 With two bars of iron.

Magnetism of Earth—Thermo-magnetism.[17]
Large magnet.[18]

---

by Ampère. See *Encyclopaedia Metropolitana,* 1830 ed., s.v. "Electro-magnetism," p. 7, for a contemporary description.

[13] This portion of the manuscript contains two minute diagrams, which we have omitted.

[14] Perhaps a reference to the rotation of a current-carrying wire around a magnetic pole, discovered by Faraday. See L. Pearce Williams, *Michael Faraday, a Biography* (New York, 1965), pp. 158ff.

[15] The manuscript lacks a number four. For De La Rive's ring, see above, Henry to Jacob Green, February 3, 1831, especially footnote 3.

[16] The Marsh-Ampère revolving apparatus is described above, Henry to Silliman, December 28, 1830, footnote 9.

[17] On the investigation of the relationship between terrestrial magnetism and the earth's temperature, see *Encyclopaedia Britannica,* 8th ed., s.v. "Magnetism," p. 11.

[18] Probably a steel magnet, not one of Henry's large electromagnets.

Under a name, "letter from" signifies a letter from that person to Henry, while "letter to" indicates a letter from Henry to that person. When Henry is neither sender nor recipient, the names of both parties are given. In the case of Henry, "letters from," followed by a list of names, indicates letters to Henry; "letters to," Henry's letters to various recipients. Subentries are so arranged that letters and documents precede the customary alphabetical listing.